Remembering Kimberley

Kirk Gardino

Remembering Kimberley

Published by Spines Publishing Platform

Isbn: 979-8-89691-051-0

Remembering Kimberley

KIRK GARDINO

Remembering Kimberley

Kim understood my sense of humor and we played off each other very well. She had a great sense of humor and had a very sharp wit and came up with some very good wise cracks once in a while.

In these two texts she is inside Walmart shopping for us. At this time, we were living out of a motel in Portsmouth Virginia which lasted for 5 weeks while we were waiting for Kim's mother Chris to wrap things up with the sale of her home in Oregon and then we all move into her home in Portsmouth.

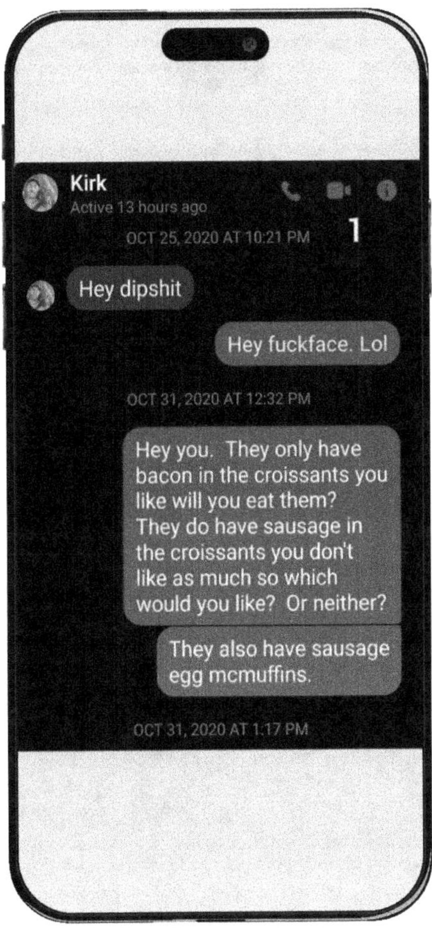

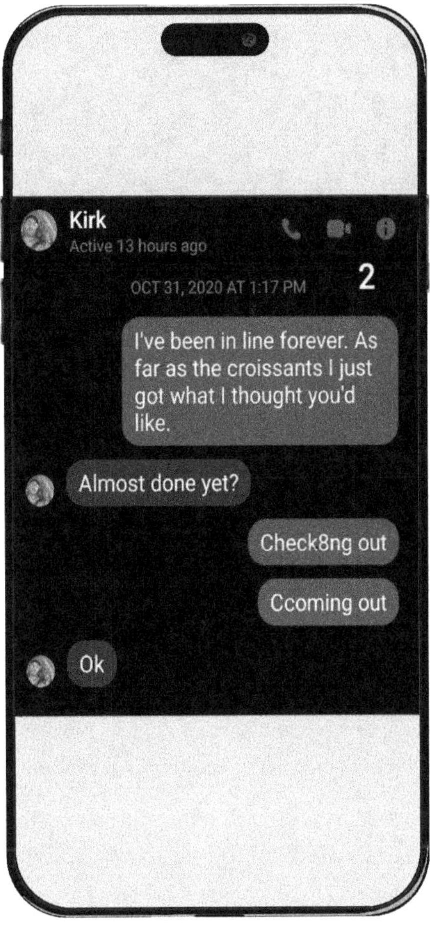

Kim was out with her mother shopping for beds when she messaged me here. She was a real trooper because she was having pain in her lower back and pelvic region. At this point we thought that Kim was cancer free and we were enjoying life.

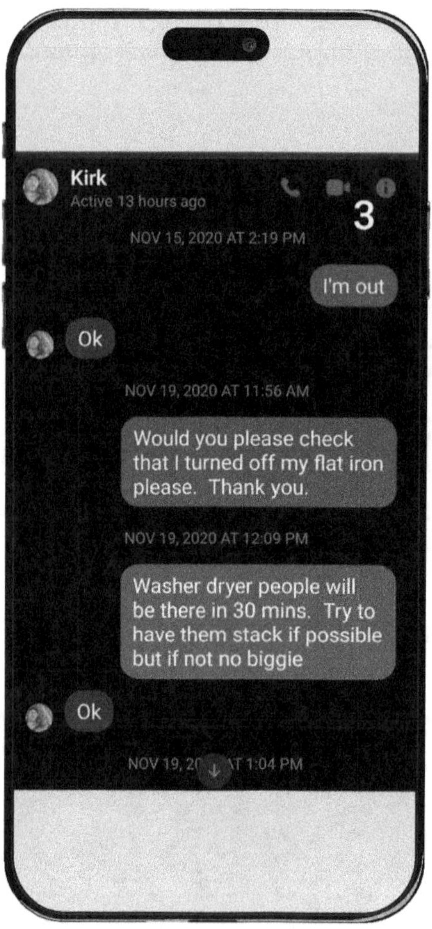

This is the day I made Kim go to the Emergency for her pain in her lower back. At this time, we are still waiting to be seen by pain management and the Oncology department at the main VA hospital in Hampton Virginia.

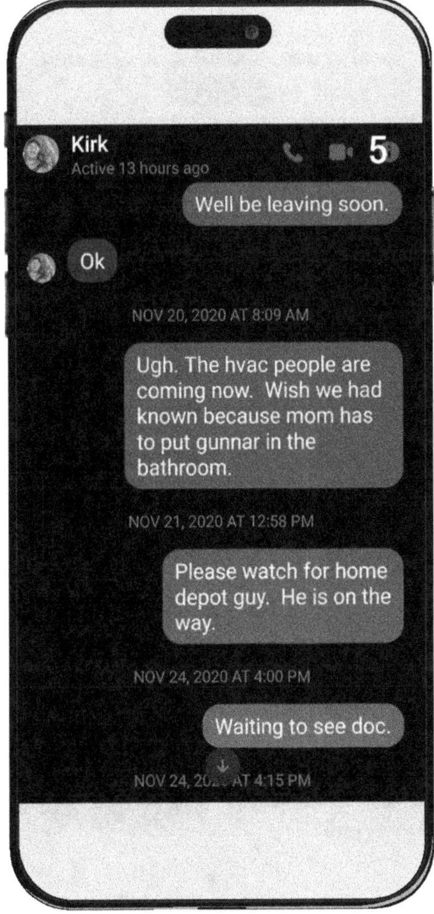
Kirk
Active 13 hours ago
5
Well be leaving soon.
Ok
NOV 20, 2020 AT 8:09 AM
Ugh. The hvac people are coming now. Wish we had known because mom has to put gunnar in the bathroom.
NOV 21, 2020 AT 12:58 PM
Please watch for home depot guy. He is on the way.
NOV 24, 2020 AT 4:00 PM
Waiting to see doc.
NOV 24, 2020 AT 4:15 PM

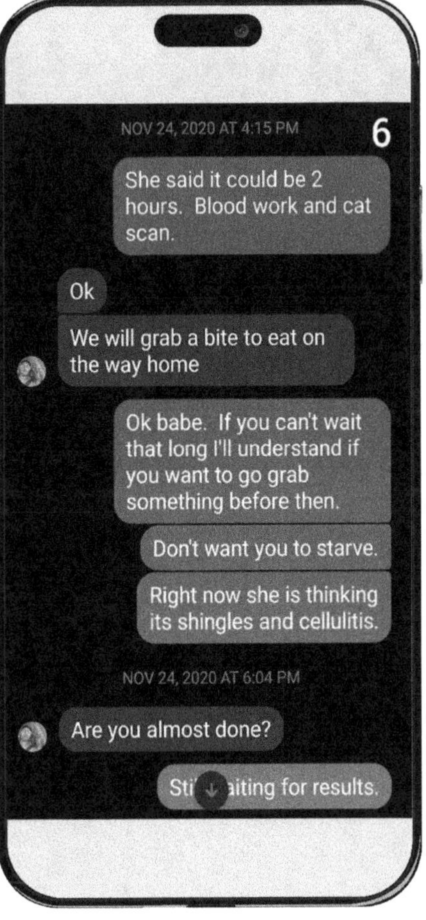
NOV 24, 2020 AT 4:15 PM
6
She said it could be 2 hours. Blood work and cat scan.
Ok
We will grab a bite to eat on the way home
Ok babe. If you can't wait that long I'll understand if you want to go grab something before then.
Don't want you to starve.
Right now she is thinking its shingles and cellulitis.
NOV 24, 2020 AT 6:04 PM
Are you almost done?
Still aiting for results.

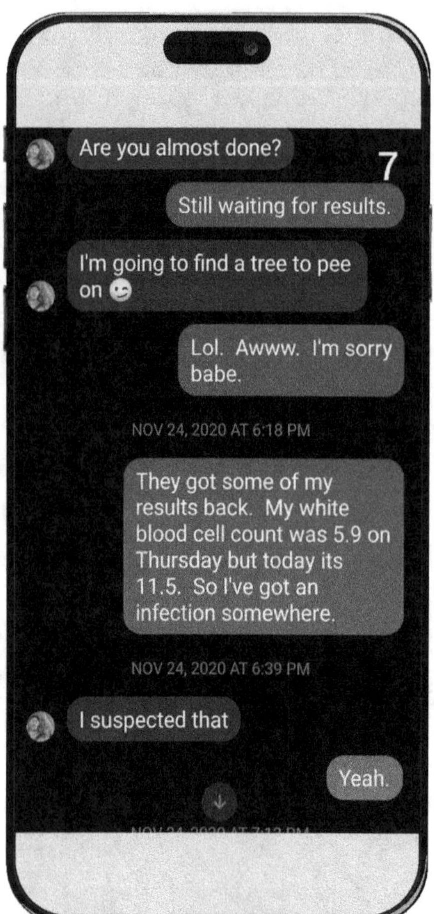

Are you almost done?
7
Still waiting for results.
I'm going to find a tree to pee on
Lol. Awww. I'm sorry babe.
NOV 24, 2020 AT 6:18 PM
They got some of my results back. My white blood cell count was 5.9 on Thursday but today its 11.5. So I've got an infection somewhere.
NOV 24, 2020 AT 6:39 PM
I suspected that
Yeah.

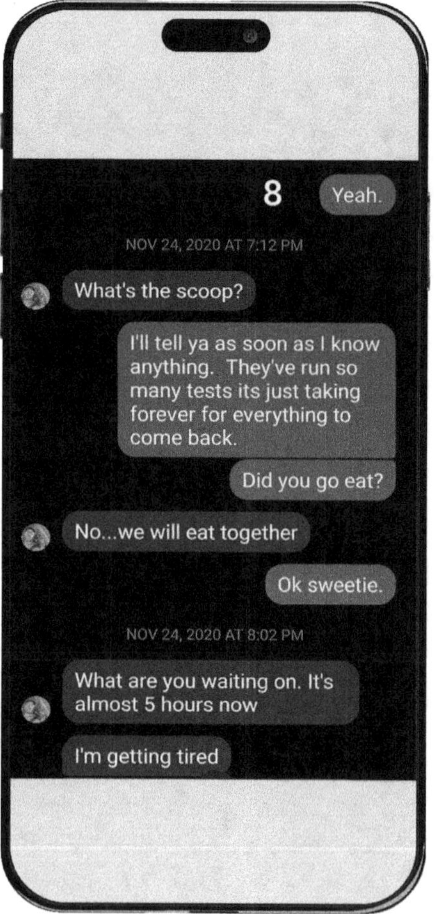

8
Yeah.
NOV 24, 2020 AT 7:12 PM
What's the scoop?
I'll tell ya as soon as I know anything. They've run so many tests its just taking forever for everything to come back.
Did you go eat?
No...we will eat together
Ok sweetie.
NOV 24, 2020 AT 8:02 PM
What are you waiting on. It's almost 5 hours now
I'm getting tired

At this point I was tired, grumpy and hungry. Kim could sense that and was trying to ease the situation. Keep in mind that I had the mindset that Kim was cancer free based on her last scan in July. I was getting upset at all the tests the VA was running that I thought were senseless but I was later going to be proven wrong.

Since this was still in the era of Covid restrictions I was forced to wait in the car while she was being treated in the ER.

I feel like a sissy now compared to the pain Kim was going through at this time and we needed to find out what was causing her pain.

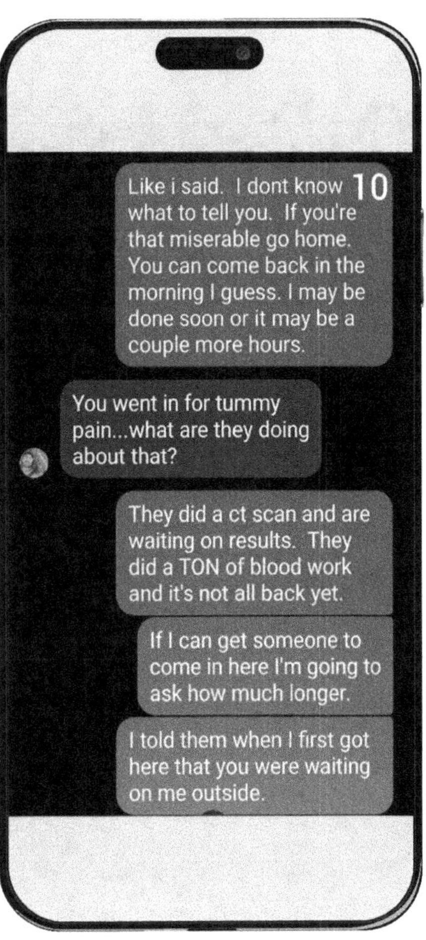

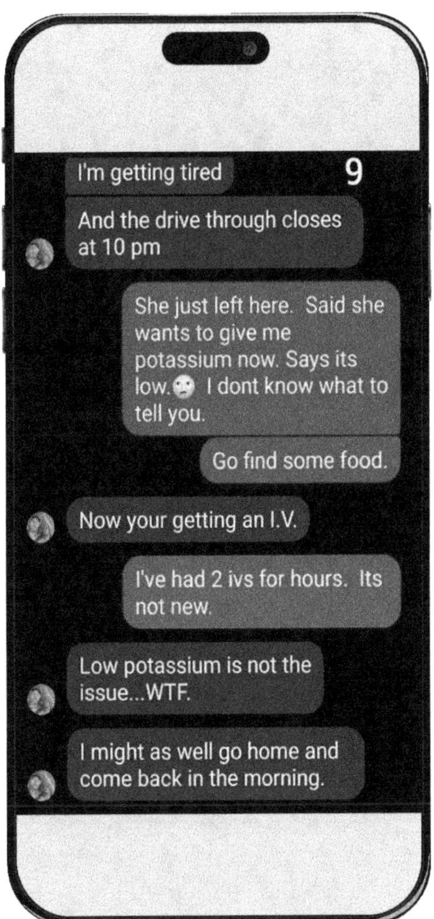

When I said "It's not like you're dying." How little did I know how I would regret ever saying those words. But my mindset was that Kim was cancer free and that this was just some generic health issue. But this is the day we found out that Kim had a large mass growing on her ovaries

I did not skip text #11.
I misnumbered the text message

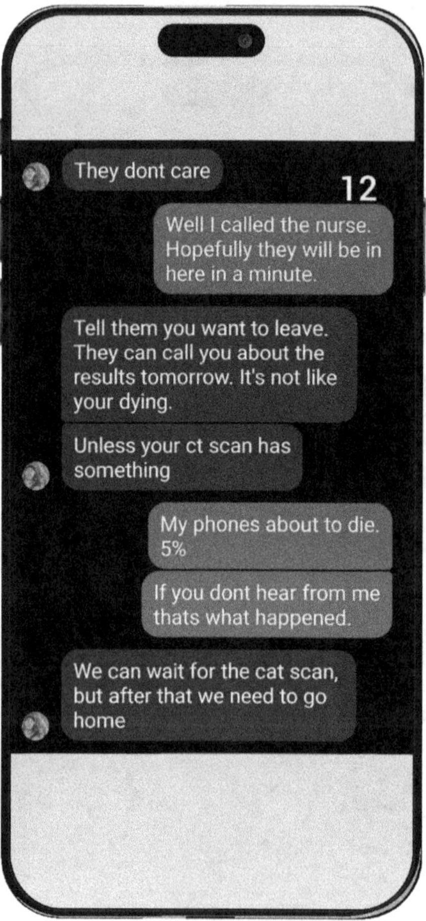

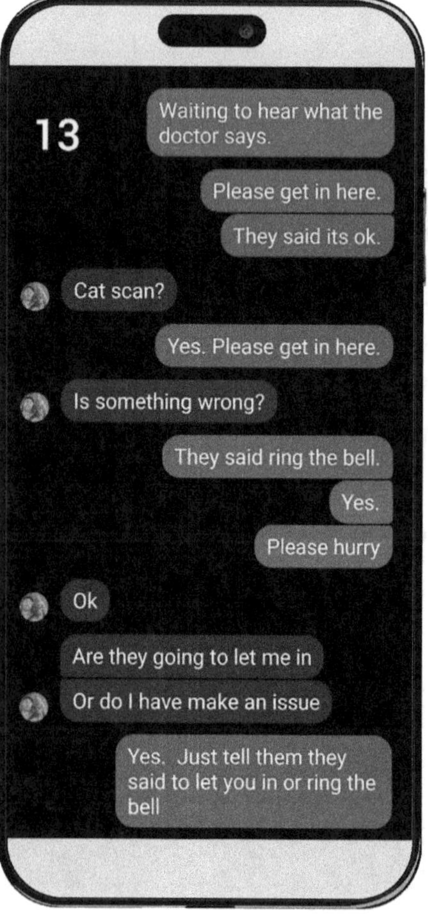

This is the day that Kim's Oncologist told her that she doesn't cure pain, she cures cancer. She also put in Kim's medical records that she is just looking for pain medication and accusing her of being addicted to opiates. She obviously didn't take the growth in Kim very seriously even though that she was already diagnosed with stage 4 colon cancer and they are treating this as if she had no history of cancer. That is why it took so long to get her into the pain clinic and that her next visit with the oncologist was 30 days out. Her primary care physician and her oncologist did not want to prescribe her pain medication and wanted her to go through pain management which could take up to 90 days. This really pissed me off because her doctors were hiding behind hospital bureaucracy and not doing the right thing.

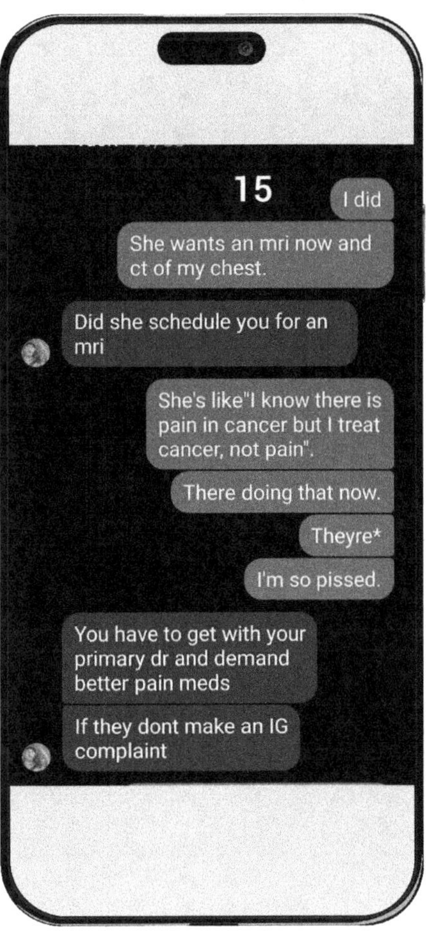

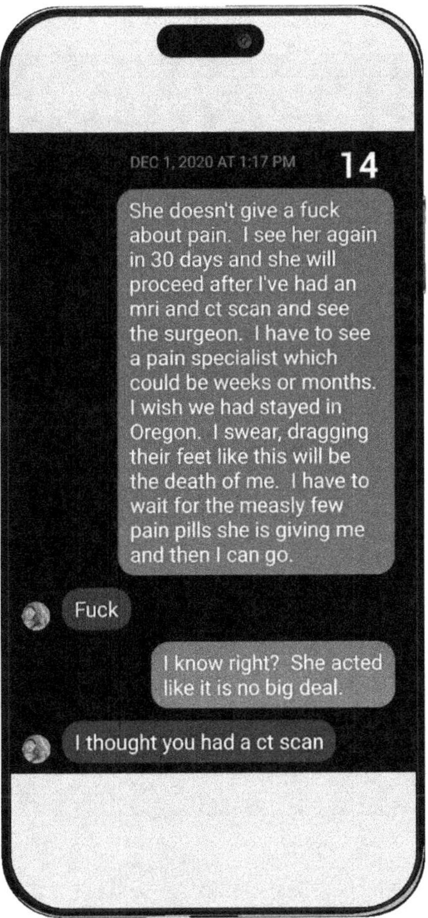

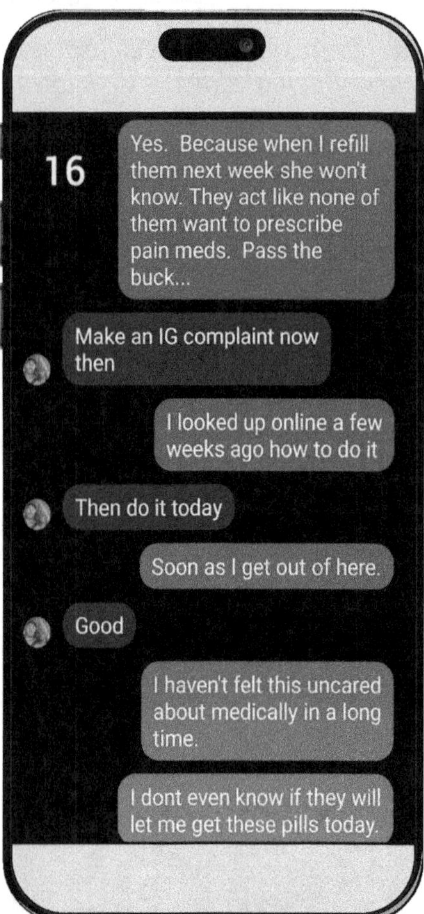
16
Yes. Because when I refill them next week she won't know. They act like none of them want to prescribe pain meds. Pass the buck...
Make an IG complaint now then
I looked up online a few weeks ago how to do it
Then do it today
Soon as I get out of here.
Good
I haven't felt this uncared about medically in a long time.
I dont even know if they will let me get these pills today.

Maybe we should go Iowa to get you treatment and stay with my friend Linda
17
DEC 1, 2020 AT 1:44 PM
She has doubled my dose but ill be out of the original prescription next Wednesday. I'm at the pharmacy now waiting for the meds.
And a no on staying with your friend. I want to g back to oregon.
Ok
I wish we were rich.
We were rich 3 years ago lol
Lol

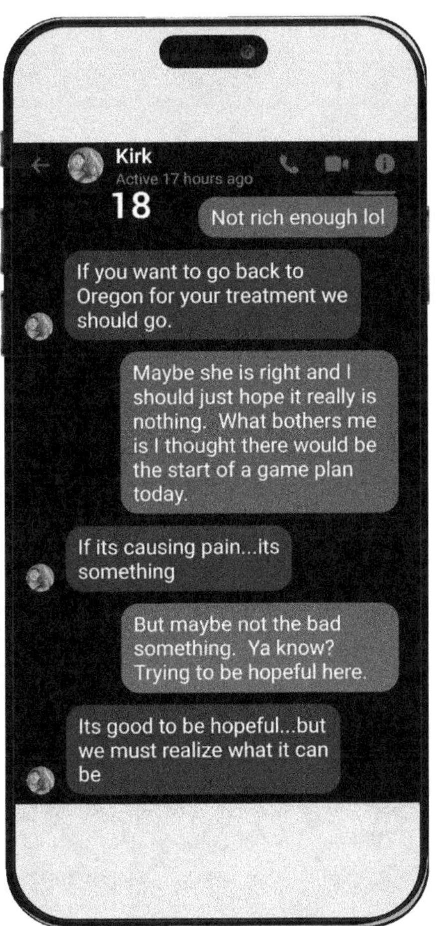
Kirk
Active 17 hours ago
18
Not rich enough lol
If you want to go back to Oregon for your treatment we should go.
Maybe she is right and I should just hope it really is nothing. What bothers me is I thought there would be the start of a game plan today.
If its causing pain...its something
But maybe not the bad something. Ya know? Trying to be hopeful here.
Its good to be hopeful...but we must realize what it can be

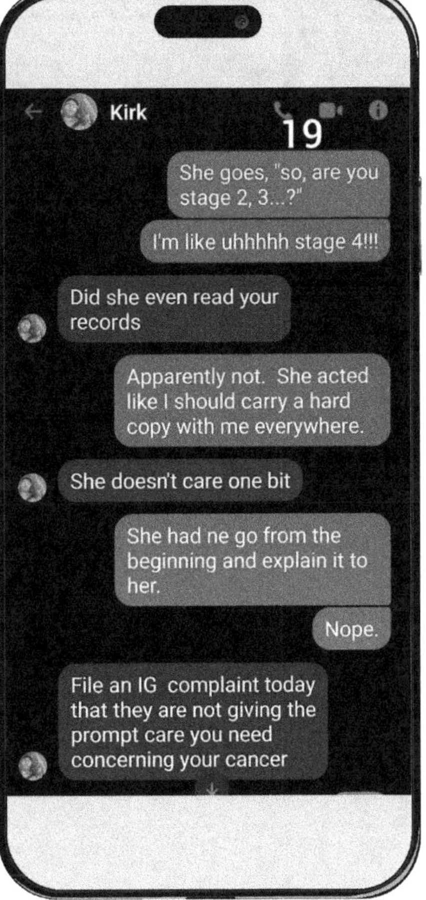
Kirk
19
She goes, "so, are you stage 2, 3...?"
I'm like uhhhhh stage 4!!!
Did she even read your records
Apparently not. She acted like I should carry a hard copy with me everywhere.
She doesn't care one bit
She had ne go from the beginning and explain it to her.
Nope.
File an IG complaint today that they are not giving the prompt care you need concerning your cancer

Kirk
20
Yep.
Let's see what the surgeon says...if he doesn't take you seriously we will pack up and go back to Oregon
We cant wait around
Yeah. This is my fucking life.
And your my wife. I dont want to lose you
I dont want to leave you either. Our marriage just got good.
Yep.
Your making me cry

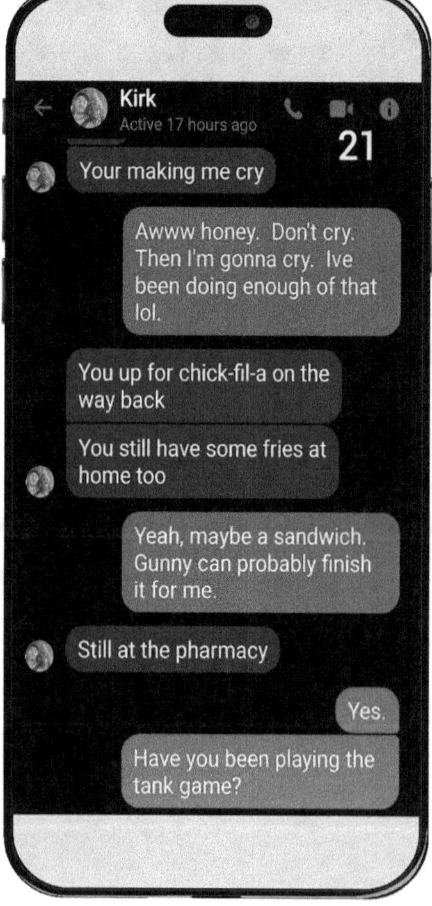
Kirk
Active 17 hours ago
21
Your making me cry
Awww honey. Don't cry. Then I'm gonna cry. Ive been doing enough of that lol.
You up for chick-fil-a on the way back
You still have some fries at home too
Yeah, maybe a sandwich. Gunny can probably finish it for me.
Still at the pharmacy
Yes.
Have you been playing the tank game?

Kirk
Active 17 hours ago
22
Nope...listening to the radio...want to make sure I dont miss your messages
Awww. Thanks babe.
DEC 1, 2020 AT 2:31 PM
Coming out.
Ok
Be there in 5min
Had to come back in for a min.
I'm waiting
Be right there
Ok

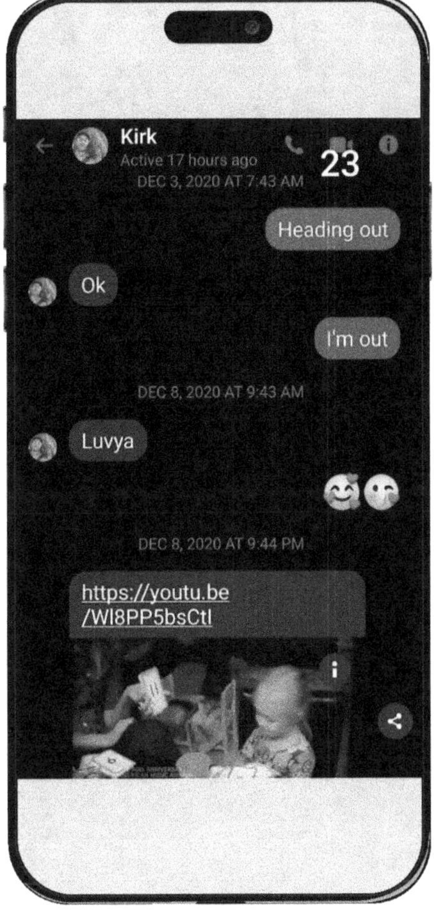
Kirk
Active 17 hours ago
23
DEC 3, 2020 AT 7:43 AM
Heading out
Ok
I'm out
DEC 8, 2020 AT 9:43 AM
Luvya
DEC 8, 2020 AT 9:44 PM
https://youtu.be
/Wl8PP5bsCtl

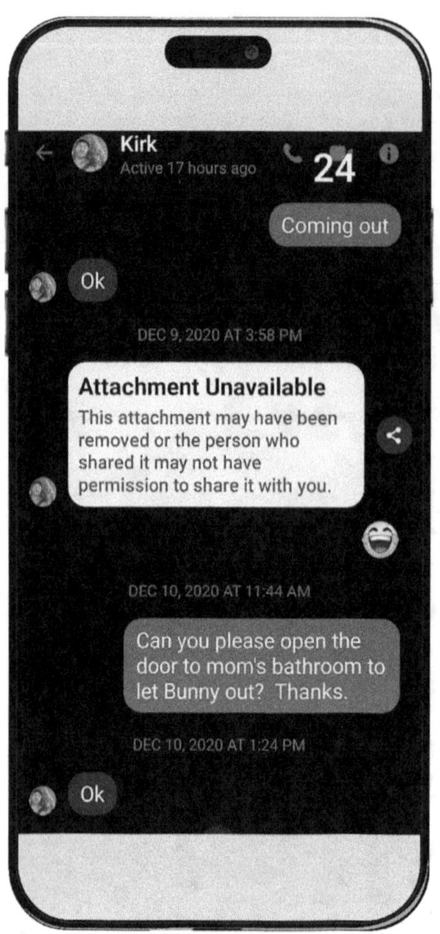

Kirk
Active 17 hours ago
24
Coming out
Ok
DEC 9, 2020 AT 3:58 PM
Attachment Unavailable
This attachment may have been removed or the person who shared it may not have permission to share it with you.
DEC 10, 2020 AT 11:44 AM
Can you please open the door to mom's bathroom to let Bunny out? Thanks.
DEC 10, 2020 AT 1:24 PM
Ok

Kirk
DEC 10, 2020 AT 1:44 PM
25
Which toothpaste is it?
DEC 10, 2020 AT 1:55 PM
Sensodyne
DEC 11, 2020 AT 4:27 PM
I love you
I love you too sweetie. Are you getting hungry? Hamburger helper tonight
I'm getting hungry...having tummy problems again
Awww.
DEC 12, 2020 AT 3:29 PM
Heading out

I did not skip a message. Message 27 was just a repeat of message 26.

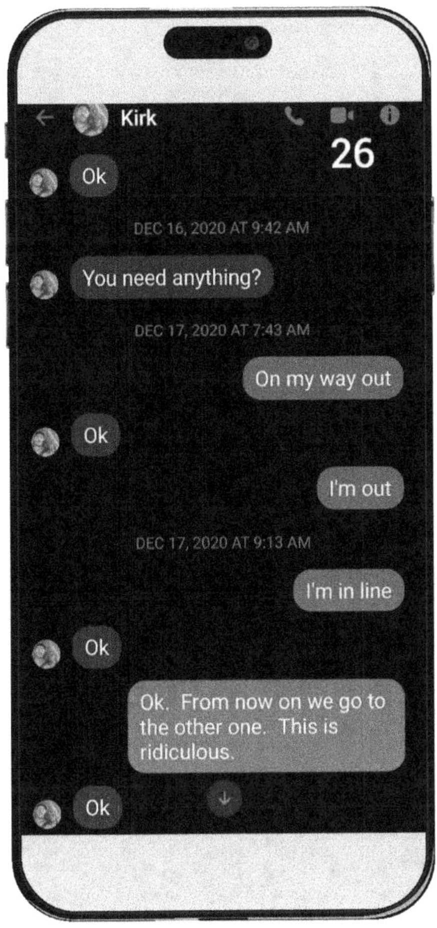

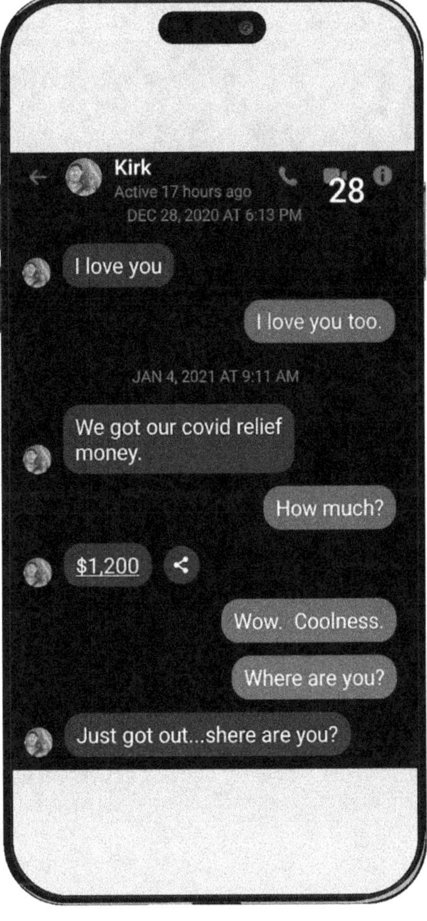

Kim had a doctor's appointment with her primary care team.

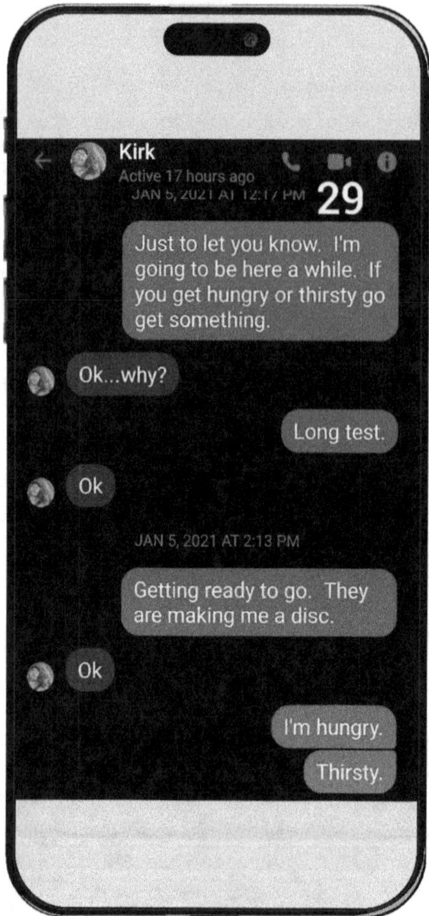

This was Kim doing our grocery shopping

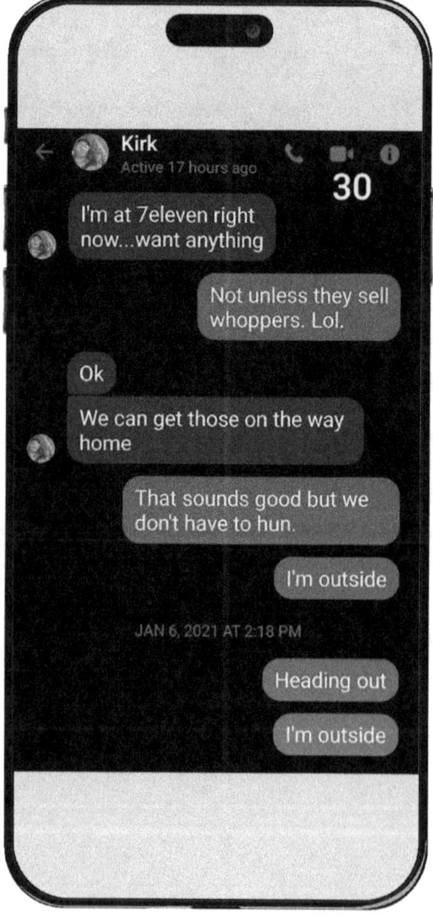

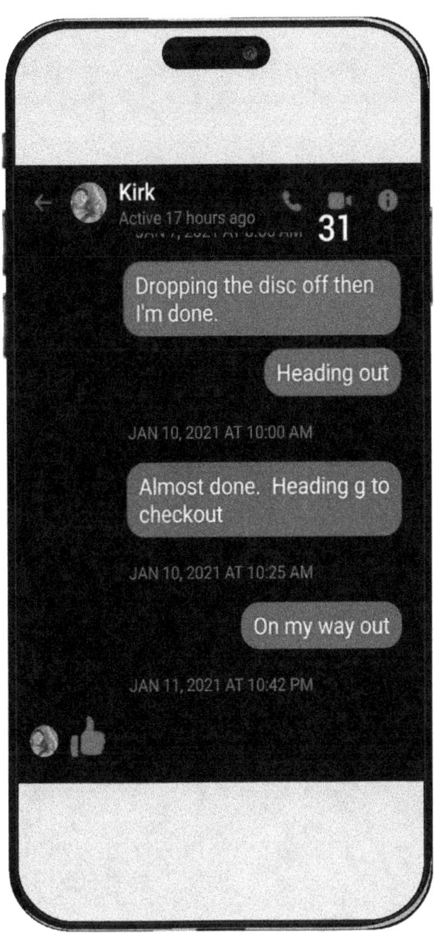

Kirk
Active 17 hours ago
31
Dropping the disc off then I'm done.
Heading out
JAN 10, 2021 AT 10:00 AM
Almost done. Heading g to checkout
JAN 10, 2021 AT 10:25 AM
On my way out
JAN 11, 2021 AT 10:42 PM

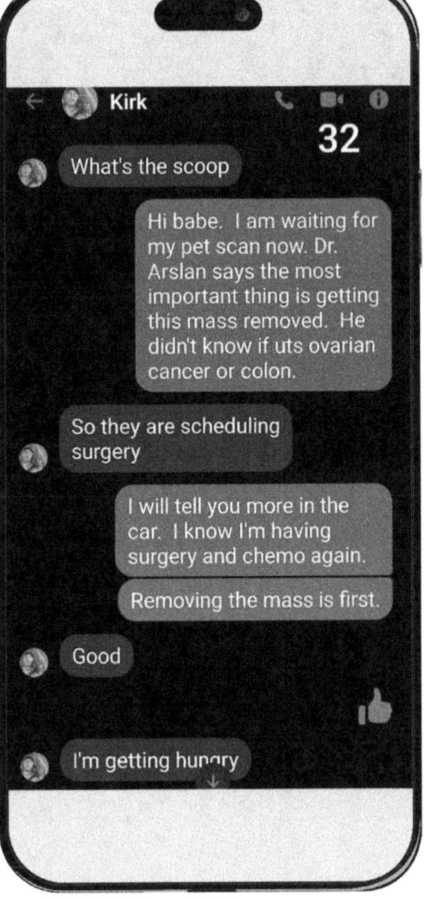

Kirk
32
What's the scoop
Hi babe. I am waiting for my pet scan now. Dr. Arslan says the most important thing is getting this mass removed. He didn't know if uts ovarian cancer or colon.
So they are scheduling surgery
I will tell you more in the car. I know I'm having surgery and chemo again.
Removing the mass is first.
Good
I'm getting hungry

Kirk
Active 17 hours ago
33
Me too. You gotta feed me as soon as I'm done. I. Freaking starving and dying of thirst
Ok
JAN 14, 2021 AT 3:16 PM
All done. I'm outside.
JAN 15, 2021 AT 1:41 PM
Babe, can you bring me your card? I forgot to ask you for it.
You called Kirk.
28 secs, Jan 15, 2021 at 1:43 PM
CALL AGAIN
JAN 15, 2021 AT 2:27 PM
I'm outside

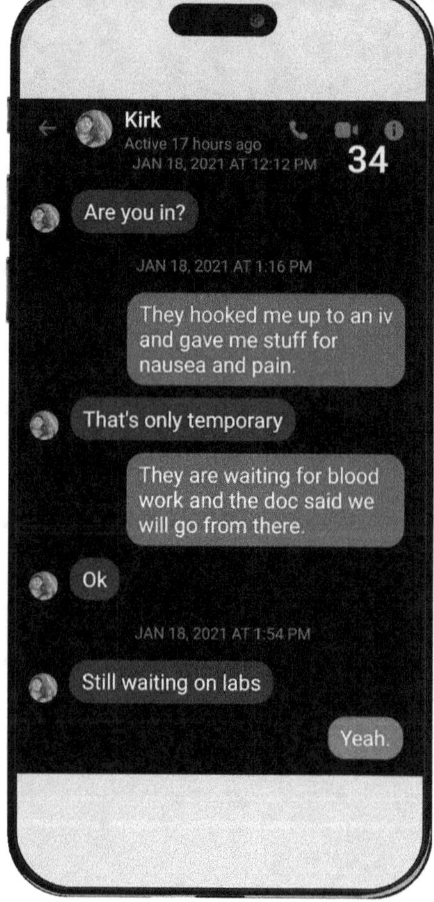

Kirk
Active 17 hours ago
JAN 18, 2021 AT 12:12 PM
34
Are you in?
JAN 18, 2021 AT 1:16 PM
They hooked me up to an iv and gave me stuff for nausea and pain.
That's only temporary
They are waiting for blood work and the doc said we will go from there.
Ok
JAN 18, 2021 AT 1:54 PM
Still waiting on labs
Yeah.

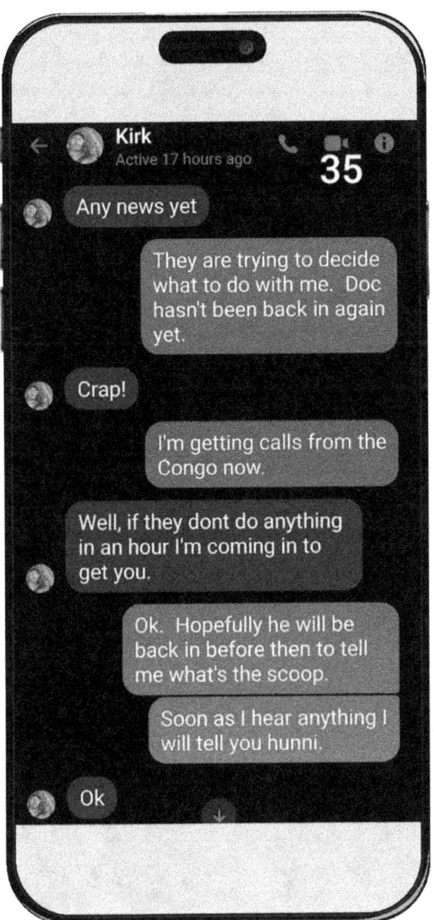
Kirk
Active 17 hours ago
35
Any news yet
They are trying to decide what to do with me. Doc hasn't been back in again yet.
Crap!
I'm getting calls from the Congo now.
Well, if they dont do anything in an hour I'm coming in to get you.
Ok. Hopefully he will be back in before then to tell me what's the scoop.
Soon as I hear anything I will tell you hunni.
Ok

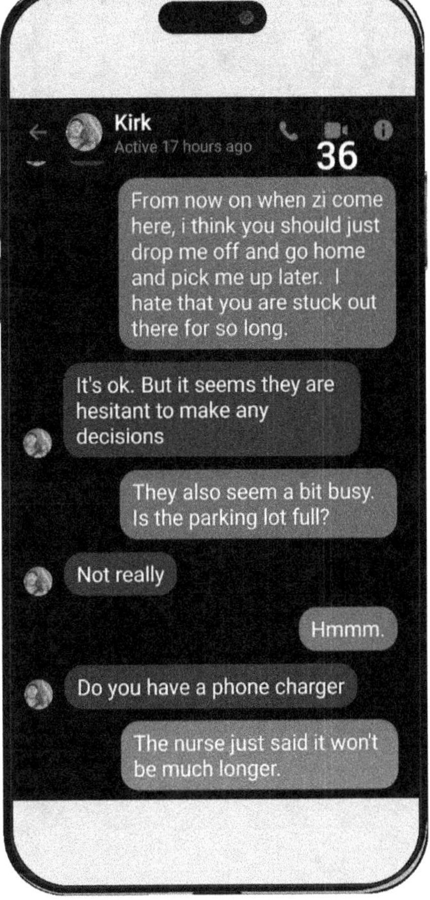
Kirk
Active 17 hours ago
36
From now on when zi come here, i think you should just drop me off and go home and pick me up later. I hate that you are stuck out there for so long.
It's ok. But it seems they are hesitant to make any decisions
They also seem a bit busy. Is the parking lot full?
Not really
Hmmm.
Do you have a phone charger
The nurse just said it won't be much longer.

Kirk
Active 17 hours ago
37
Ok...you hungry
And yes. I brought my charger
A little. Mostly thirsty.
I'll give you some jiz when you come out lol
Lol. Too salty
They giving you good pain meds
Pretty good. I wish I could have this stuff at home instead of what I got. Lol Even the nausea stuff worked better because it was through an iv.

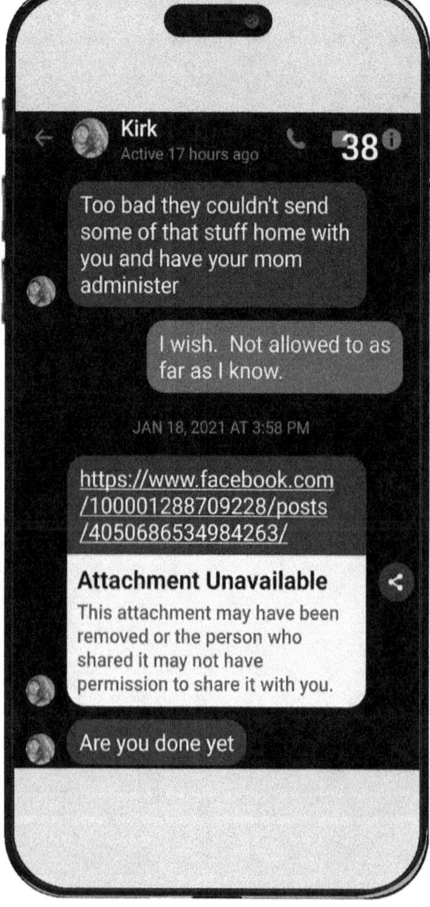

Kirk
Active 17 hours ago
38
Too bad they couldn't send some of that stuff home with you and have your mom administer
I wish. Not allowed to as far as I know.
JAN 18, 2021 AT 3:58 PM
https://www.facebook.com/100001288709228/posts/4050686534984263/
Attachment Unavailable
This attachment may have been removed or the person who shared it may not have permission to share it with you.
Are you done yet

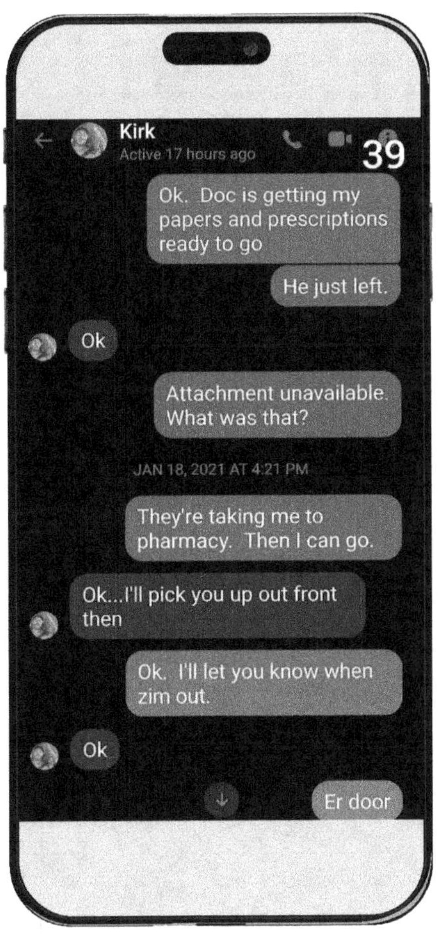

Kirk
Active 17 hours ago
39
Ok. Doc is getting my papers and prescriptions ready to go
He just left.
Ok
Attachment unavailable. What was that?
JAN 18, 2021 AT 4:21 PM
They're taking me to pharmacy. Then I can go.
Ok...I'll pick you up out front then
Ok. I'll let you know when zim out.
Ok
Er door

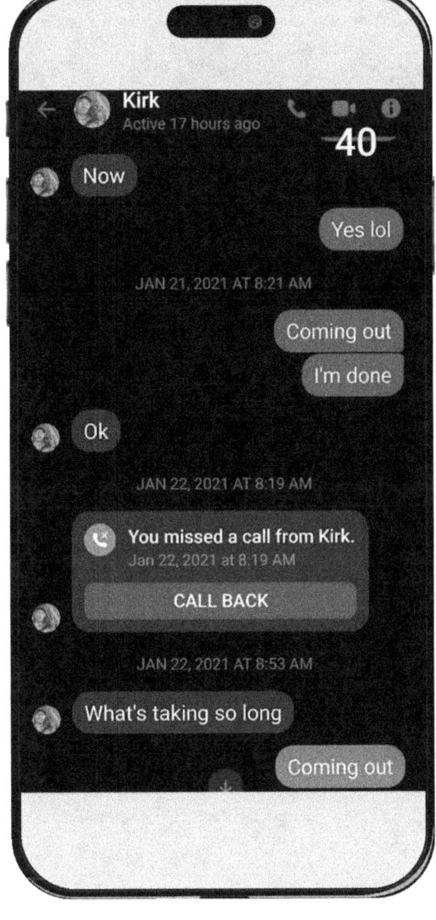

Kirk
Active 17 hours ago
40
Now
Yes lol
JAN 21, 2021 AT 8:21 AM
Coming out
I'm done
Ok
JAN 22, 2021 AT 8:19 AM
You missed a call from Kirk.
Jan 22, 2021 at 8:19 AM
CALL BACK
JAN 22, 2021 AT 8:53 AM
What's taking so long
Coming out

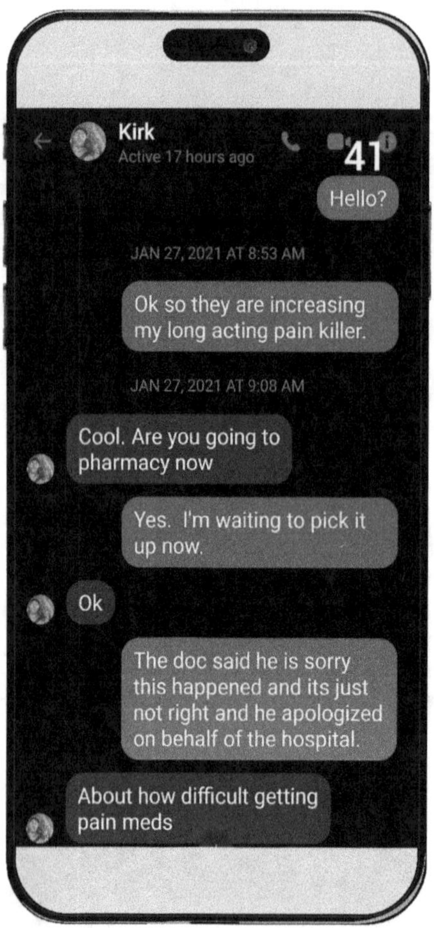

Kirk
Active 17 hours ago
41
Hello?
JAN 27, 2021 AT 8:53 AM
Ok so they are increasing my long acting pain killer.
JAN 27, 2021 AT 9:08 AM
Cool. Are you going to pharmacy now
Yes. I'm waiting to pick it up now.
Ok
The doc said he is sorry this happened and its just not right and he apologized on behalf of the hospital.
About how difficult getting pain meds

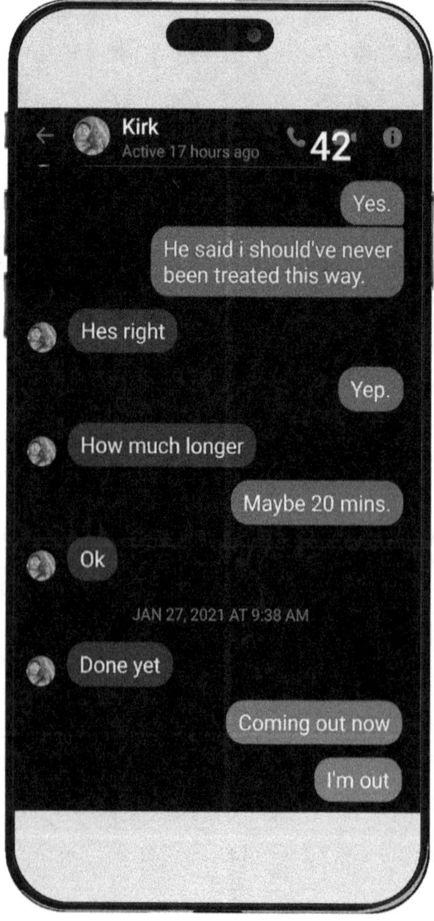

Kirk
Active 17 hours ago
42
Yes.
He said i should've never been treated this way.
Hes right
Yep.
How much longer
Maybe 20 mins.
Ok
JAN 27, 2021 AT 9:38 AM
Done yet
Coming out now
I'm out

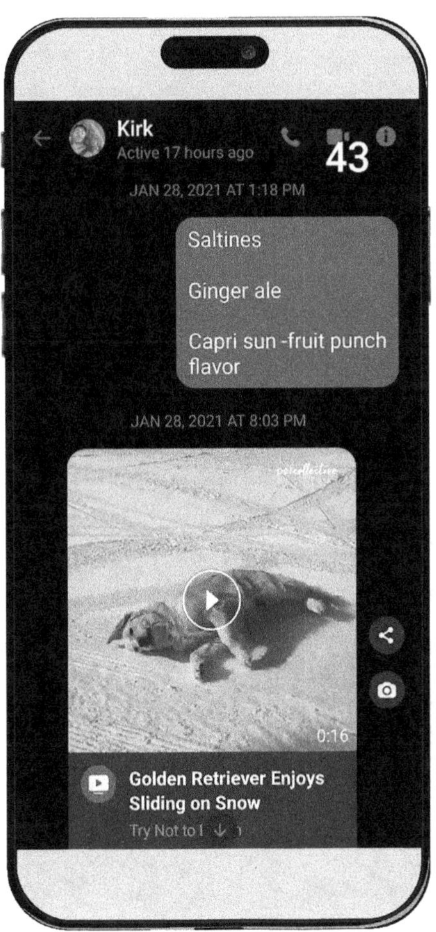

Kirk
Active 17 hours ago
43
JAN 28, 2021 AT 1:18 PM
Saltines
Ginger ale
Capri sun -fruit punch flavor
JAN 28, 2021 AT 8:03 PM
0:16
Golden Retriever Enjoys Sliding on Snow
Try Not to I

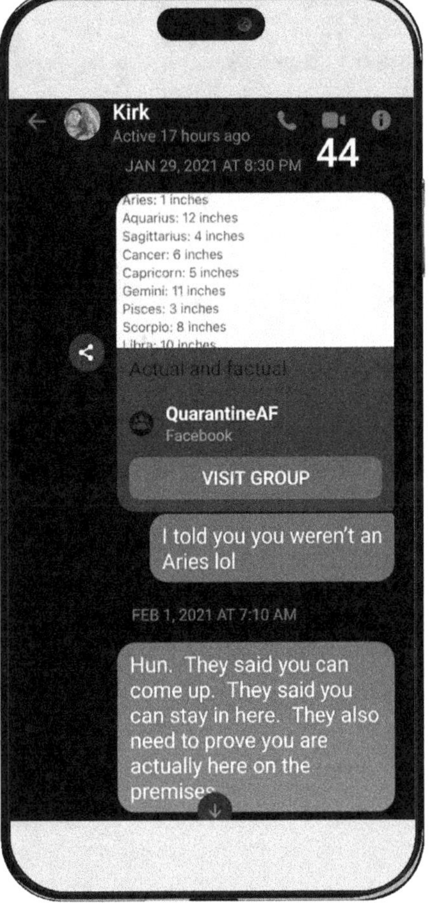

Kirk
Active 17 hours ago
44
JAN 29, 2021 AT 8:30 PM
Aries: 1 inches
Aquarius: 12 inches
Sagittarius: 4 inches
Cancer: 6 inches
Capricorn: 5 inches
Gemini: 11 inches
Pisces: 3 inches
Scorpio: 8 inches
Libra: 10 inches
Actual and factual
QuarantineAF
Facebook
VISIT GROUP
I told you you weren't an Aries lol
FEB 1, 2021 AT 7:10 AM
Hun. They said you can come up. They said you can stay in here. They also need to prove you are actually here on the premises.

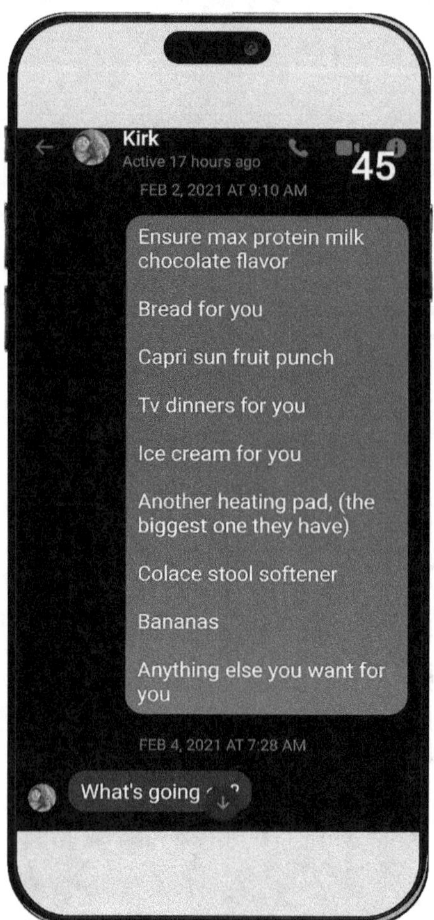

Kirk
Active 17 hours ago
45
FEB 2, 2021 AT 9:10 AM
Ensure max protein milk chocolate flavor
Bread for you
Capri sun fruit punch
Tv dinners for you
Ice cream for you
Another heating pad, (the biggest one they have)
Colace stool softener
Bananas
Anything else you want for you
FEB 4, 2021 AT 7:28 AM
What's going on?

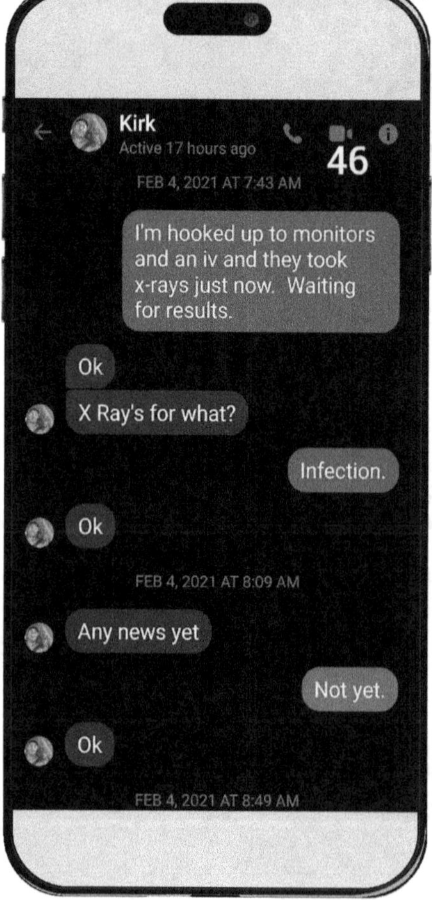

Kirk
Active 17 hours ago
46
FEB 4, 2021 AT 7:43 AM
I'm hooked up to monitors and an iv and they took x-rays just now. Waiting for results.
Ok
X Ray's for what?
Infection.
Ok
FEB 4, 2021 AT 8:09 AM
Any news yet
Not yet.
Ok
FEB 4, 2021 AT 8:49 AM

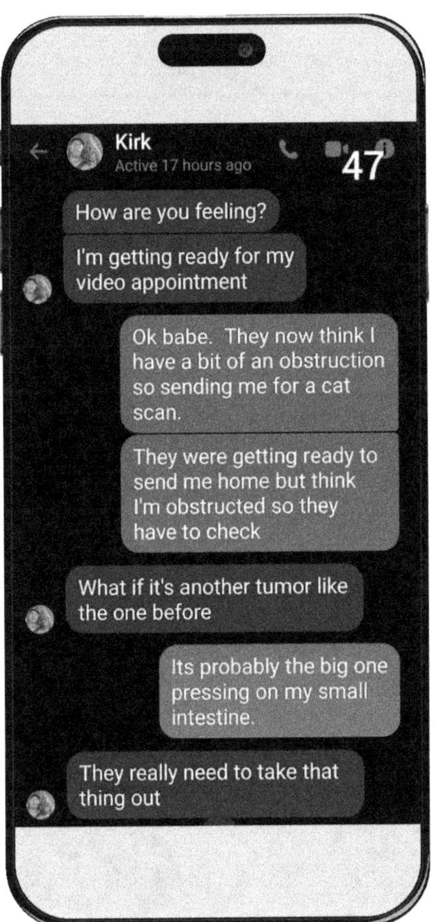
Kirk
Active 17 hours ago
47
How are you feeling?
I'm getting ready for my video appointment
Ok babe. They now think I have a bit of an obstruction so sending me for a cat scan.
They were getting ready to send me home but think I'm obstructed so they have to check
What if it's another tumor like the one before
Its probably the big one pressing on my small intestine.
They really need to take that thing out

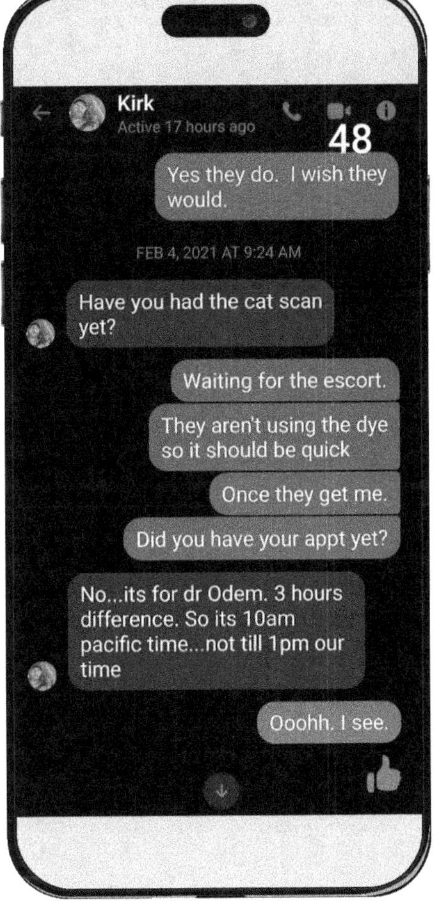
Kirk
Active 17 hours ago
48
Yes they do. I wish they would.
FEB 4, 2021 AT 9:24 AM
Have you had the cat scan yet?
Waiting for the escort.
They aren't using the dye so it should be quick
Once they get me.
Did you have your appt yet?
No...its for dr Odem. 3 hours difference. So its 10am pacific time...not till 1pm our time
Ooohh. I see.

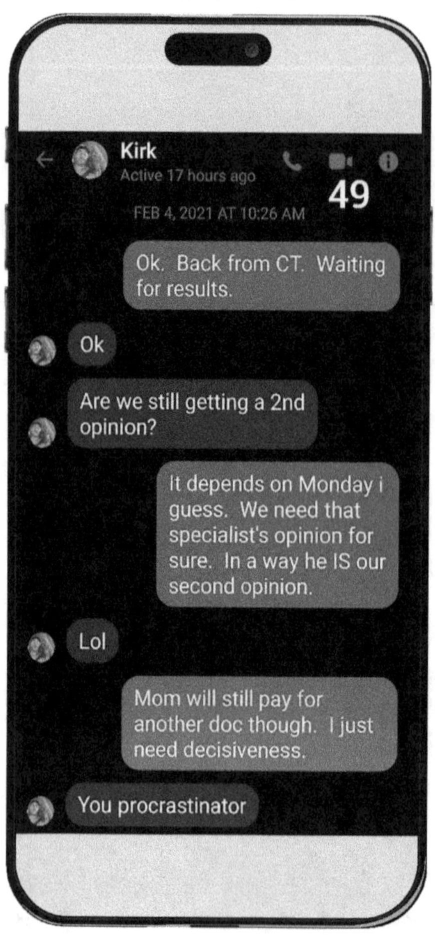

Kirk
Active 17 hours ago
49
FEB 4, 2021 AT 10:26 AM
Ok. Back from CT. Waiting for results.
Ok
Are we still getting a 2nd opinion?
It depends on Monday i guess. We need that specialist's opinion for sure. In a way he IS our second opinion.
Lol
Mom will still pay for another doc though. I just need decisiveness.
You procrastinator

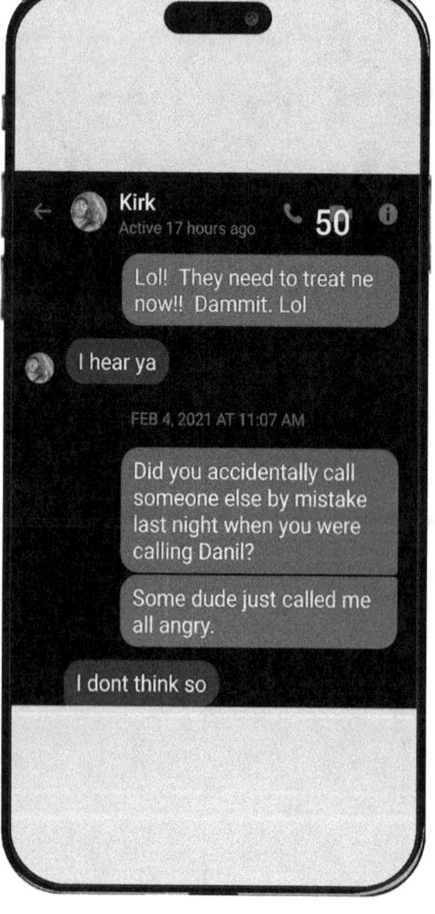

Kirk
Active 17 hours ago
50
Lol! They need to treat ne now!! Dammit. Lol
I hear ya
FEB 4, 2021 AT 11:07 AM
Did you accidentally call someone else by mistake last night when you were calling Danil?
Some dude just called me all angry.
I dont think so

Kirk
Active Now
51
0:07
Any word on your cat scan results
He demanded my name and when I just said "who were you trying to reach" he got pissy and said he didn't know someone called his phone. I said well, it wasn't me and he hung up.
Whats happening?
Dont know.
And no. Doc hasn't been in yet.
He is probably discussing with another doc. Maybe Chang. I dont know.

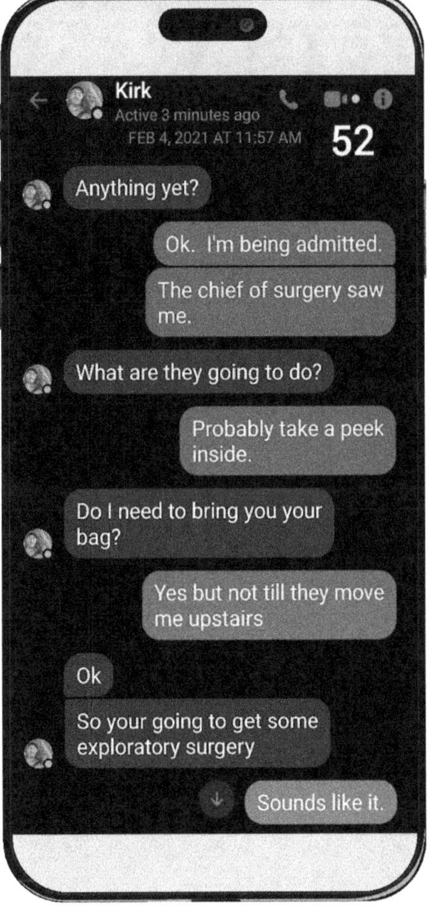

Kirk
Active 3 minutes ago
FEB 4, 2021 AT 11:57 AM
52
Anything yet?
Ok. I'm being admitted.
The chief of surgery saw me.
What are they going to do?
Probably take a peek inside.
Do I need to bring you your bag?
Yes but not till they move me upstairs
Ok
So your going to get some exploratory surgery
Sounds like it.

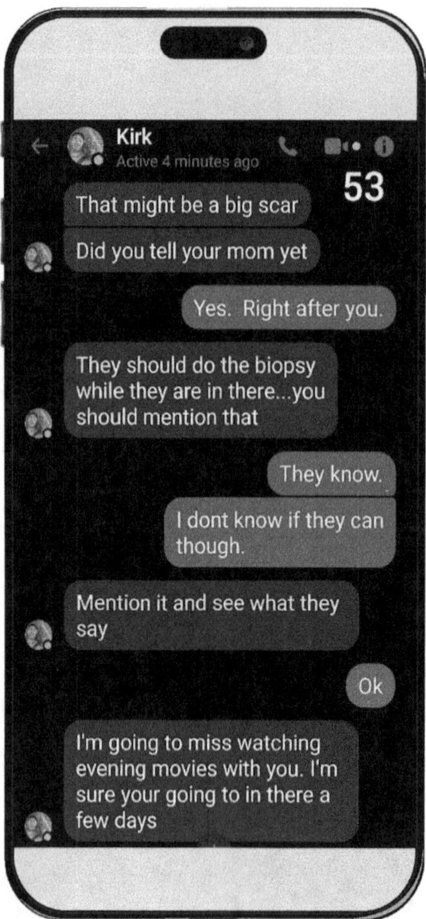

Kirk
Active 4 minutes ago
53
That might be a big scar
Did you tell your mom yet
Yes. Right after you.
They should do the biopsy while they are in there...you should mention that
They know.
I dont know if they can though.
Mention it and see what they say
Ok
I'm going to miss watching evening movies with you. I'm sure your going to in there a few days

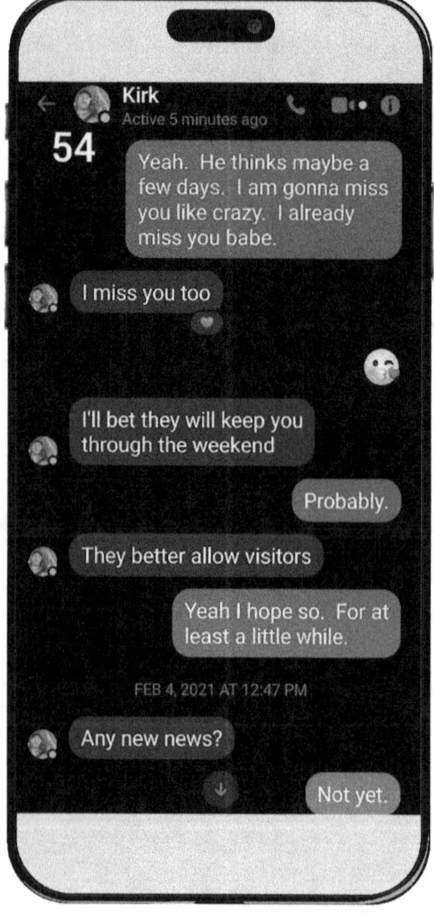

Kirk
Active 5 minutes ago
54
Yeah. He thinks maybe a few days. I am gonna miss you like crazy. I already miss you babe.
I miss you too
I'll bet they will keep you through the weekend
Probably.
They better allow visitors
Yeah I hope so. For at least a little while.
FEB 4, 2021 AT 12:47 PM
Any new news?
Not yet.

Kirk
Active 6 minutes ago
55
You still in ER?
Yes.
Crap
Have you eaten?
No...no medicine either
Go grab a bite then babe.
I will after they get you a room and I bring your things up to you
Ok sweetheart. I will tell you as soon as I hear anything.
Its so damned hot in here.
It's better than being too cold
True

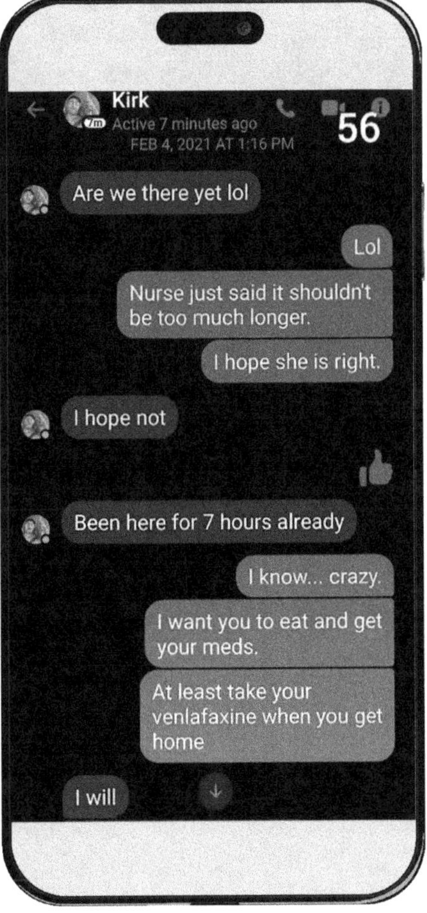
Kirk
Active 7 minutes ago
FEB 4, 2021 AT 1:16 PM
56
Are we there yet lol
Lol
Nurse just said it shouldn't be too much longer.
I hope she is right.
I hope not
Been here for 7 hours already
I know... crazy.
I want you to eat and get your meds.
At least take your venlafaxine when you get home
I will

Kim was just getting admitted to the hospital to treat her cancer since they found the new growth on November 24, 2020. That is roughly a nine-week delay in her treatment which is the main reason for the negative outcome and Kim's death five months later. She should have had the surgery within 14 days, not waiting nine weeks to biopsy the mass to see if it is cancer. Because Kim was diagnosed with stage four cancer previously, they should have assumed that it was cancer and react quickly to find out if the mass she had was cancerous. Instead, we got bureaucratic slow walking and got the impression that they didn't want to treat her and was hoping that she would pass away so they didn't have bother with her.

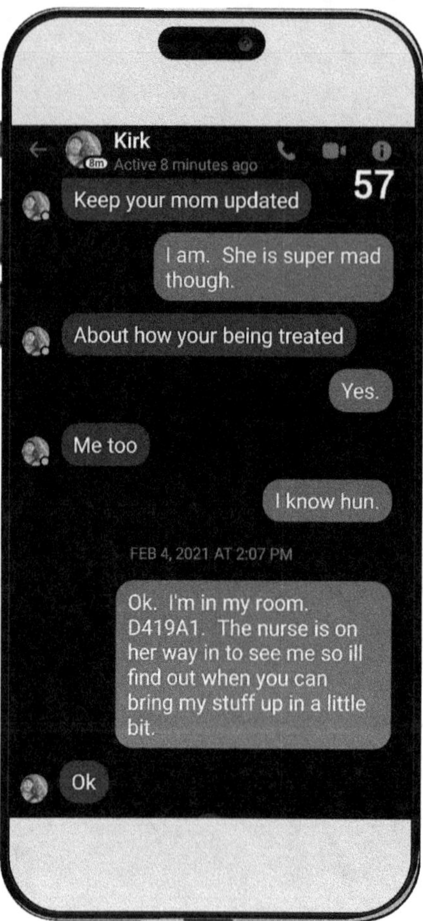

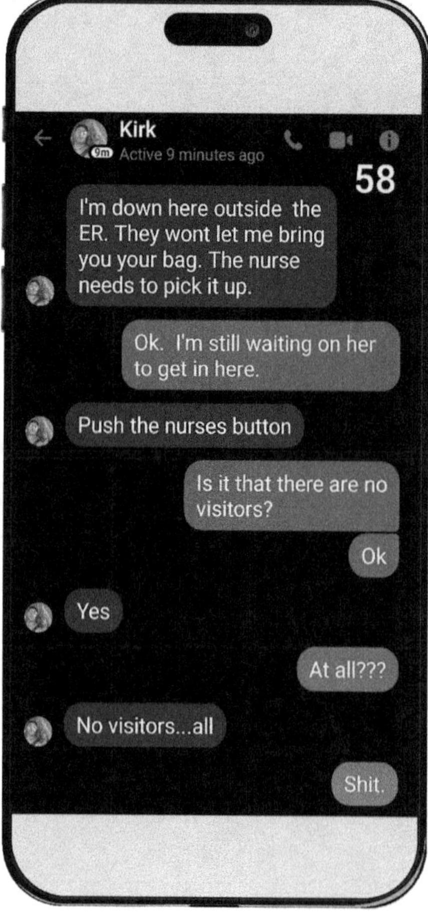

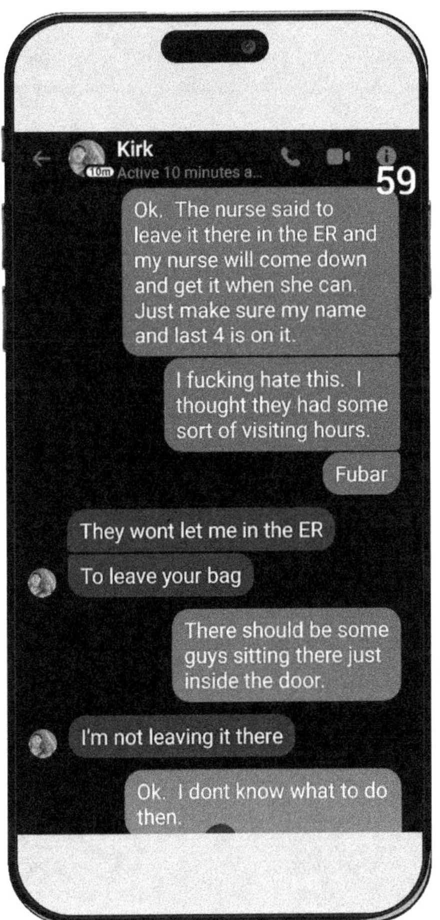
Kirk
Active 10 minutes a...
59
Ok. The nurse said to leave it there in the ER and my nurse will come down and get it when she can. Just make sure my name and last 4 is on it.
I fucking hate this. I thought they had some sort of visiting hours.
Fubar
They wont let me in the ER
To leave your bag
There should be some guys sitting there just inside the door.
I'm not leaving it there
Ok. I dont know what to do then.

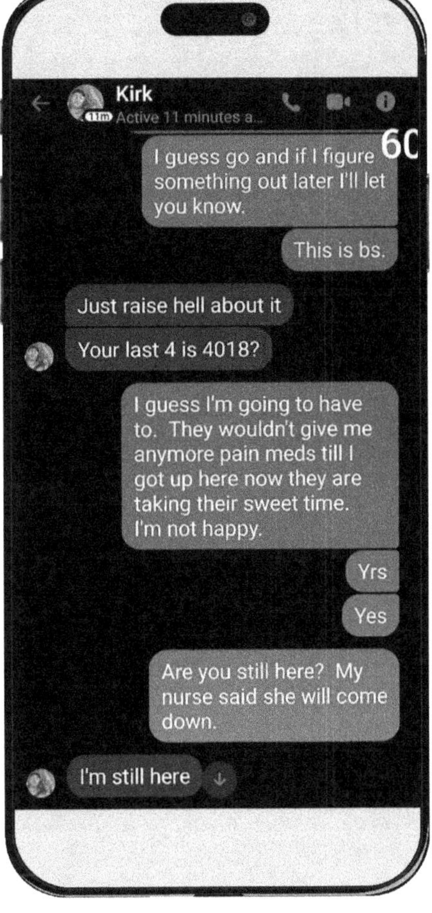
Kirk
Active 11 minutes a...
60
I guess go and if I figure something out later I'll let you know.
This is bs.
Just raise hell about it
Your last 4 is 4018?
I guess I'm going to have to. They wouldn't give me anymore pain meds till I got up here now they are taking their sweet time. I'm not happy.
Yrs
Yes
Are you still here? My nurse said she will come down.
I'm still here

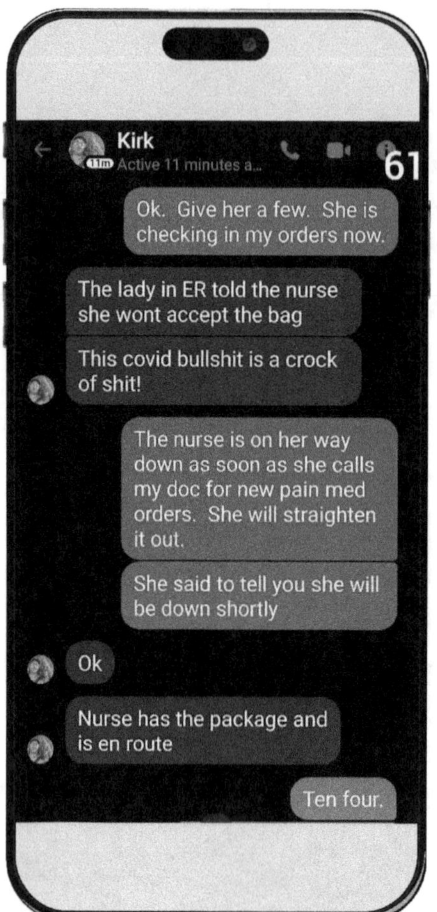
Kirk
Active 11 minutes a...
61
Ok. Give her a few. She is checking in my orders now.
The lady in ER told the nurse she wont accept the bag
This covid bullshit is a crock of shit!
The nurse is on her way down as soon as she calls my doc for new pain med orders. She will straighten it out.
She said to tell you she will be down shortly
Ok
Nurse has the package and is en route
Ten four.

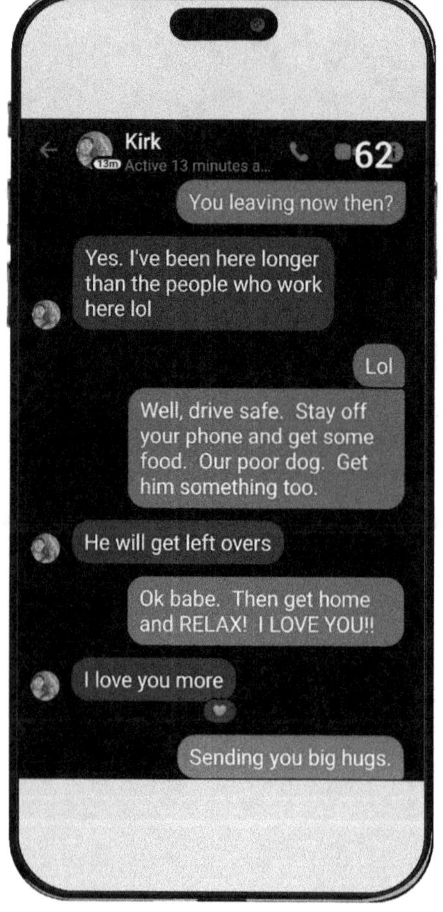
Kirk
Active 13 minutes a...
62
You leaving now then?
Yes. I've been here longer than the people who work here lol
Lol
Well, drive safe. Stay off your phone and get some food. Our poor dog. Get him something too.
He will get left overs
Ok babe. Then get home and RELAX! I LOVE YOU!!
I love you more
Sending you big hugs.

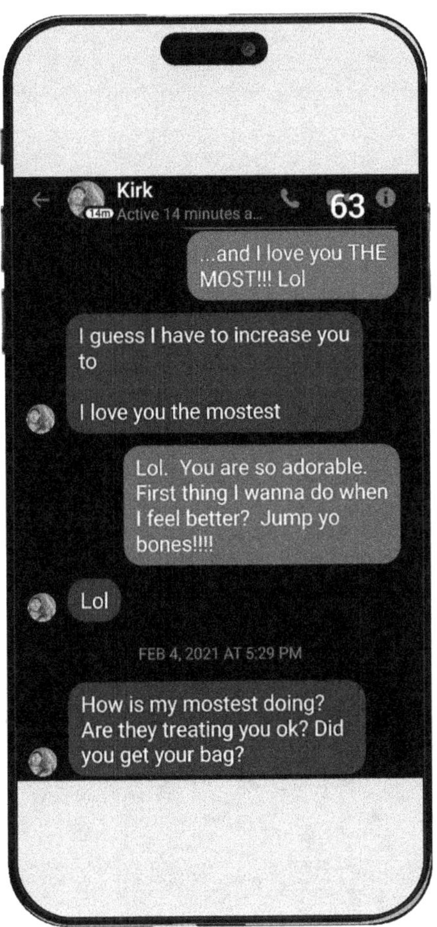
Kirk
Active 14 minutes a...
63
...and I love you THE MOST!!! Lol
I guess I have to increase you to
I love you the mostest
Lol. You are so adorable. First thing I wanna do when I feel better? Jump yo bones!!!!
Lol
FEB 4, 2021 AT 5:29 PM
How is my mostest doing? Are they treating you ok? Did you get your bag?

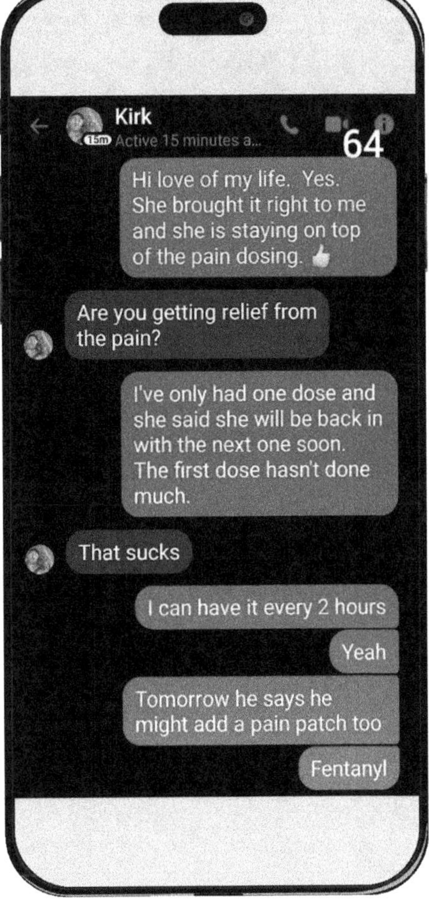
Kirk
Active 15 minutes a...
64
Hi love of my life. Yes. She brought it right to me and she is staying on top of the pain dosing. 👍
Are you getting relief from the pain?
I've only had one dose and she said she will be back in with the next one soon. The first dose hasn't done much.
That sucks
I can have it every 2 hours
Yeah
Tomorrow he says he might add a pain patch too
Fentanyl

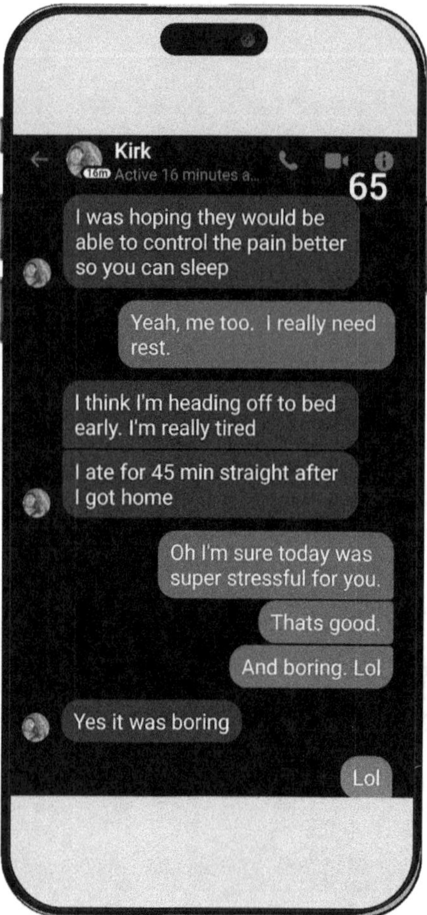
Kirk
Active 16 minutes a…
65
I was hoping they would be able to control the pain better so you can sleep
Yeah, me too. I really need rest.
I think I'm heading off to bed early. I'm really tired
I ate for 45 min straight after I got home
Oh I'm sure today was super stressful for you.
Thats good.
And boring. Lol
Yes it was boring
Lol

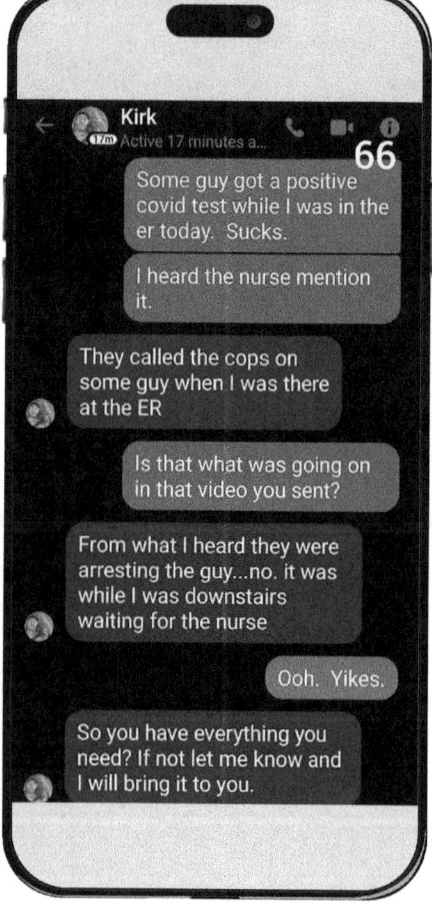
Kirk
Active 17 minutes a…
66
Some guy got a positive covid test while I was in the er today. Sucks.
I heard the nurse mention it.
They called the cops on some guy when I was there at the ER
Is that what was going on in that video you sent?
From what I heard they were arresting the guy...no. it was while I was downstairs waiting for the nurse
Ooh. Yikes.
So you have everything you need? If not let me know and I will bring it to you.

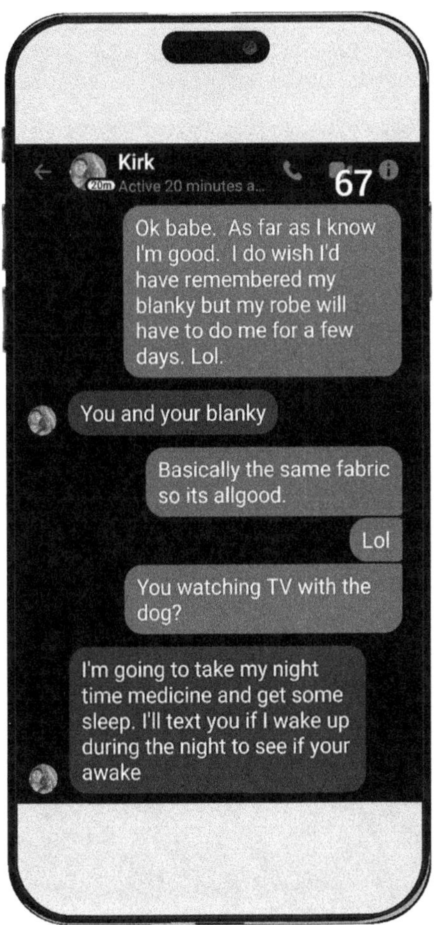
Kirk
Active 20 minutes a...
67
Ok babe. As far as I know I'm good. I do wish I'd have remembered my blanky but my robe will have to do me for a few days. Lol.
You and your blanky
Basically the same fabric so its allgood.
Lol
You watching TV with the dog?
I'm going to take my night time medicine and get some sleep. I'll text you if I wake up during the night to see if your awake

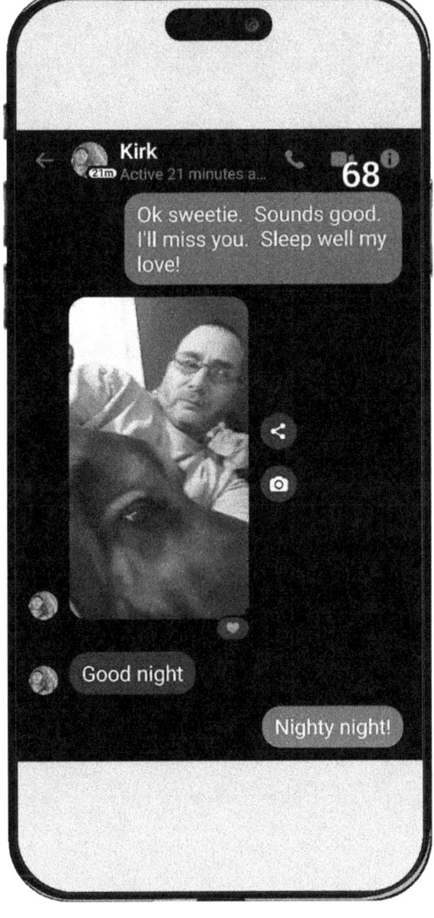
Kirk
Active 21 minutes a...
68
Ok sweetie. Sounds good. I'll miss you. Sleep well my love!
Good night
Nighty night!

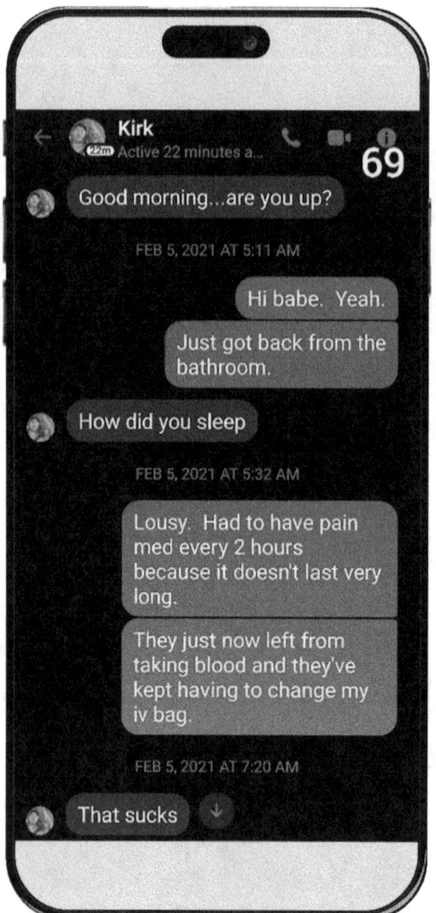
Kirk
Active 22 minutes a...
69
Good morning...are you up?
FEB 5, 2021 AT 5:11 AM
Hi babe. Yeah.
Just got back from the bathroom.
How did you sleep
FEB 5, 2021 AT 5:32 AM
Lousy. Had to have pain med every 2 hours because it doesn't last very long.
They just now left from taking blood and they've kept having to change my iv bag.
FEB 5, 2021 AT 7:20 AM
That sucks

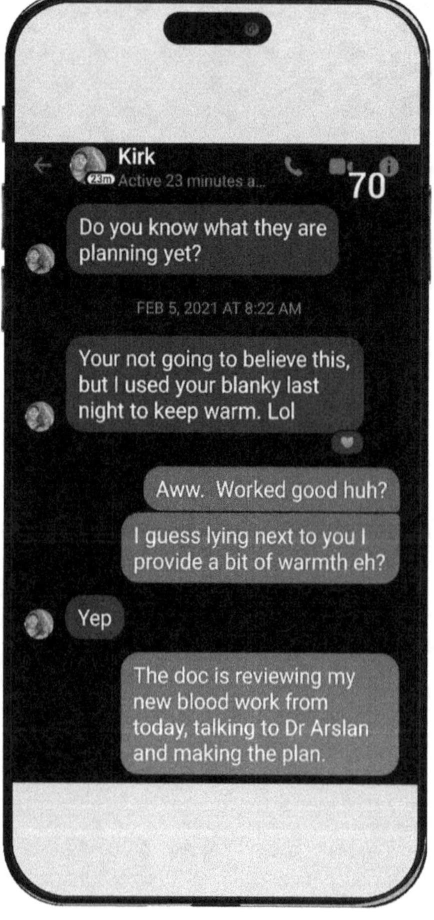
Kirk
Active 23 minutes a...
70
Do you know what they are planning yet?
FEB 5, 2021 AT 8:22 AM
Your not going to believe this, but I used your blanky last night to keep warm. Lol
Aww. Worked good huh?
I guess lying next to you I provide a bit of warmth eh?
Yep
The doc is reviewing my new blood work from today, talking to Dr Arslan and making the plan.

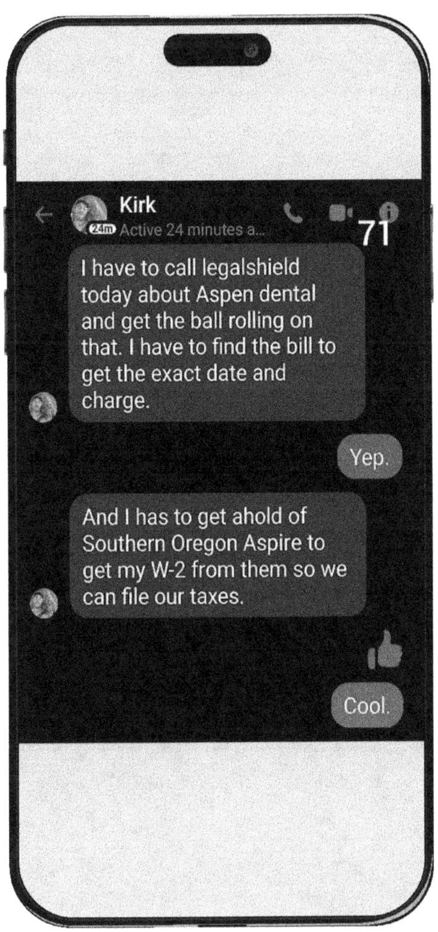

Kirk
24m Active 24 minutes a...
71
I have to call legalshield today about Aspen dental and get the ball rolling on that. I have to find the bill to get the exact date and charge.
Yep.
And I has to get ahold of Southern Oregon Aspire to get my W-2 from them so we can file our taxes.
Cool.

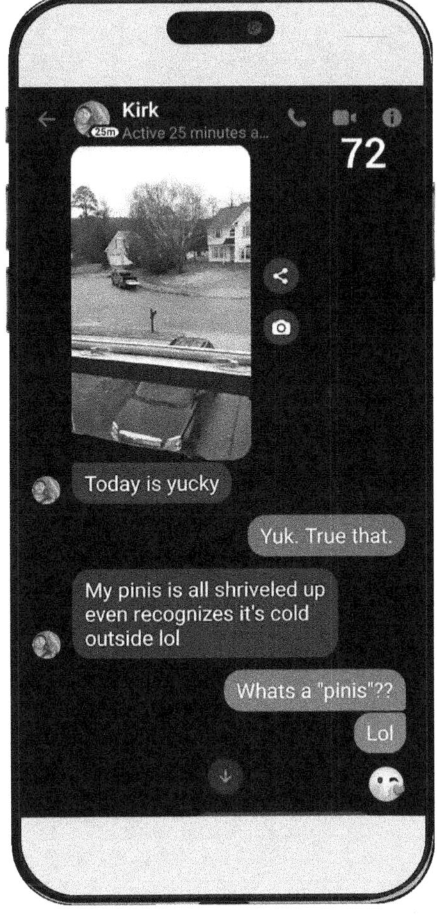

Kirk
25m Active 25 minutes a...
72
Today is yucky
Yuk. True that.
My pinis is all shriveled up even recognizes it's cold outside lol
Whats a "pinis"??
Lol

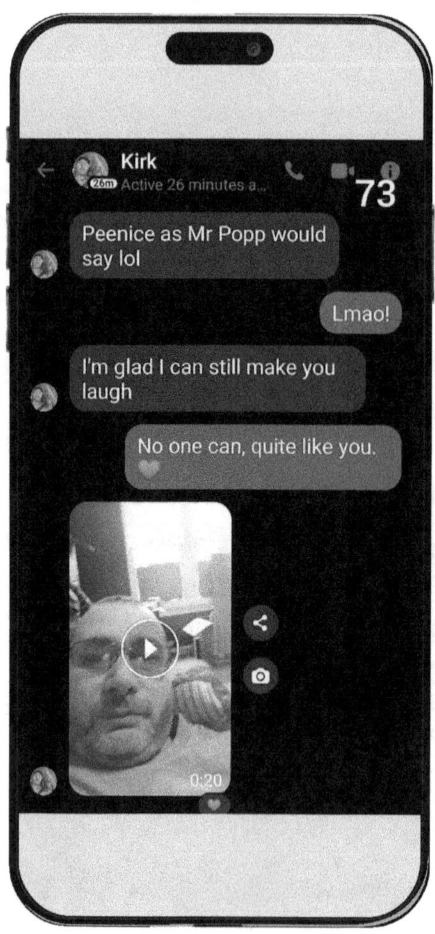
Kirk
Active 26 minutes a...
73
Peenice as Mr Popp would say lol
Lmao!
I'm glad I can still make you laugh
No one can, quite like you.
0:20

Kirk
Active 27 minutes a...
74
Hey there
Hi babe
Whatcha doing?
Any good news. I'm getting ready for my video appointment with dr Odom at 1pm
Oh cool.
Not really. Dr Arslan called me and didn't know I was an inpatient so he said he would be up later to talk to me. He hadn't talked to Dr. Wiebke yet.
Fuck
Will they let you go to your appointment on monday
Brb

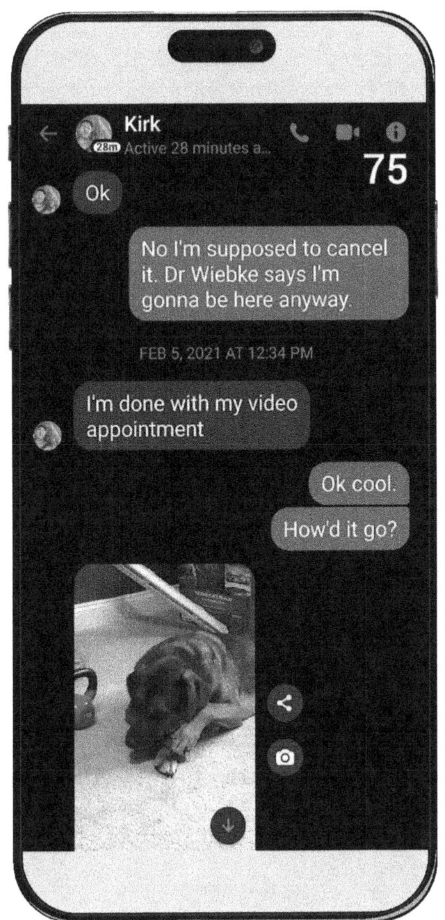

Kirk
Active 28 minutes a...
75
Ok
No I'm supposed to cancel it. Dr Wiebke says I'm gonna be here anyway.
FEB 5, 2021 AT 12:34 PM
I'm done with my video appointment
Ok cool.
How'd it go?

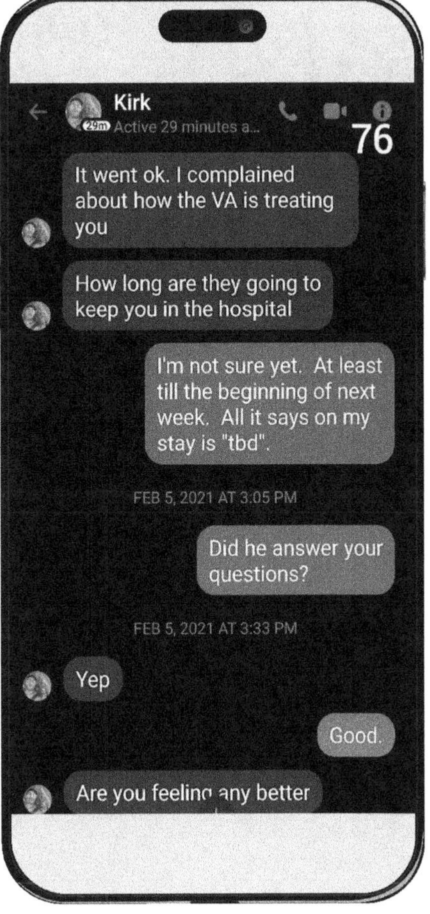

Kirk
Active 29 minutes a...
76
It went ok. I complained about how the VA is treating you
How long are they going to keep you in the hospital
I'm not sure yet. At least till the beginning of next week. All it says on my stay is "tbd".
FEB 5, 2021 AT 3:05 PM
Did he answer your questions?
FEB 5, 2021 AT 3:33 PM
Yep
Good.
Are you feeling any better

Kirk
Active 30 minutes a...
77
Waiting for pain meds. As per usual.
We will have to video chat later. I'll put on a movie and stream it to you
I haven't thrown up here at all.
Good deal
Sounds great babe. I love you.
I love you...I'll play the 3rd movie in divergent series
Coolness.
Gunny tried to climb up on the bed last night when he figured out you weren't coming home. I kicked him off.

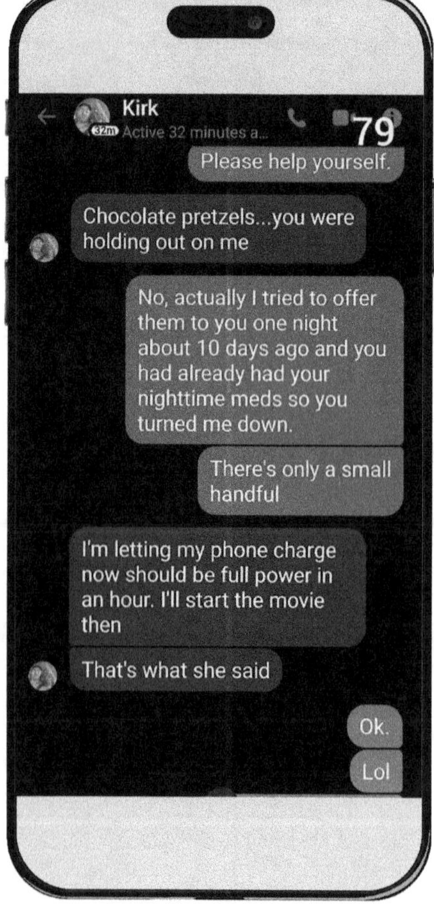
Kirk
Active 32 minutes a...
79
Please help yourself.
Chocolate pretzels...you were holding out on me
No, actually I tried to offer them to you one night about 10 days ago and you had already had your nighttime meds so you turned me down.
There's only a small handful
I'm letting my phone charge now should be full power in an hour. I'll start the movie then
That's what she said
Ok.
Lol

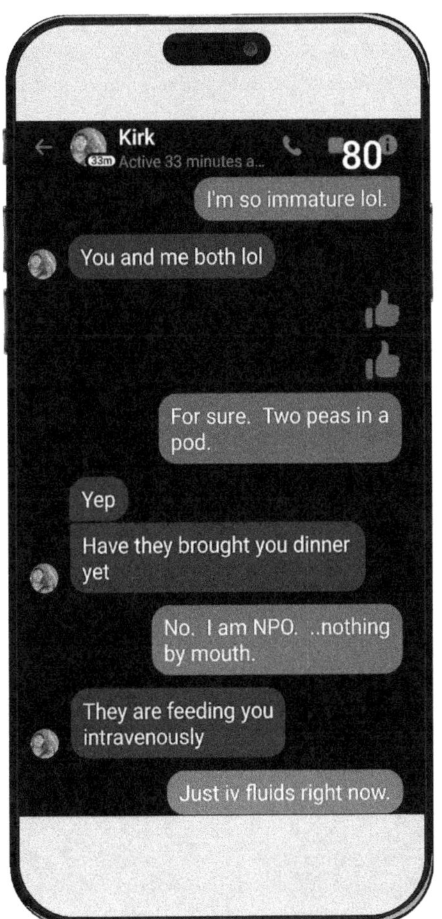
Kirk
Active 33 minutes a...
80
I'm so immature lol.
You and me both lol
For sure. Two peas in a pod.
Yep
Have they brought you dinner yet
No. I am NPO. ..nothing by mouth.
They are feeding you intravenously
Just iv fluids right now.

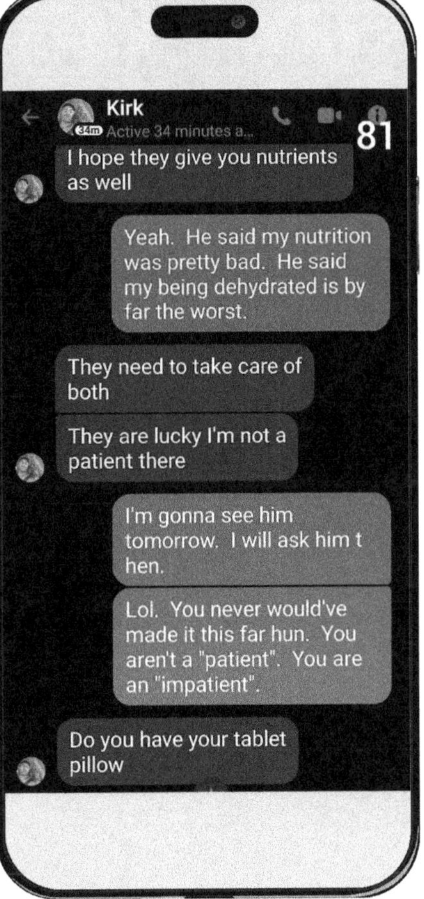
Kirk
Active 34 minutes a...
81
I hope they give you nutrients as well
Yeah. He said my nutrition was pretty bad. He said my being dehydrated is by far the worst.
They need to take care of both
They are lucky I'm not a patient there
I'm gonna see him tomorrow. I will ask him t hen.
Lol. You never would've made it this far hun. You aren't a "patient". You are an "impatient".
Do you have your tablet pillow

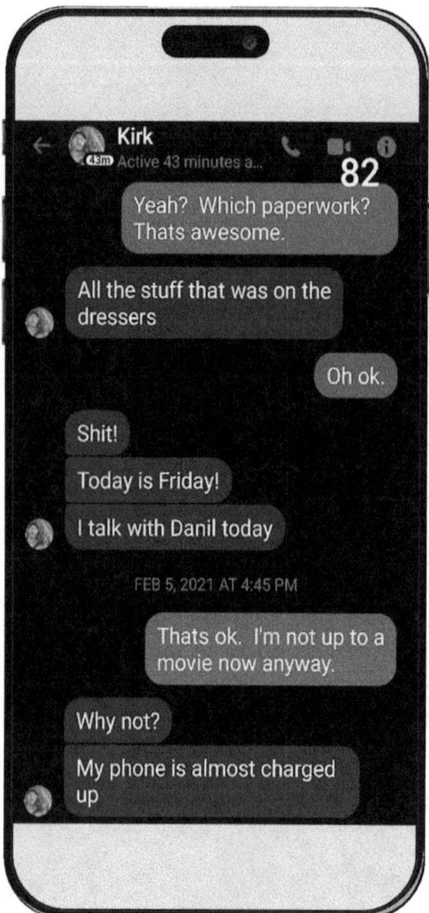

Kirk
Active 43 minutes a...
82
Yeah? Which paperwork? Thats awesome.
All the stuff that was on the dressers
Oh ok.
Shit!
Today is Friday!
I talk with Danil today
FEB 5, 2021 AT 4:45 PM
Thats ok. I'm not up to a movie now anyway.
Why not?
My phone is almost charged up

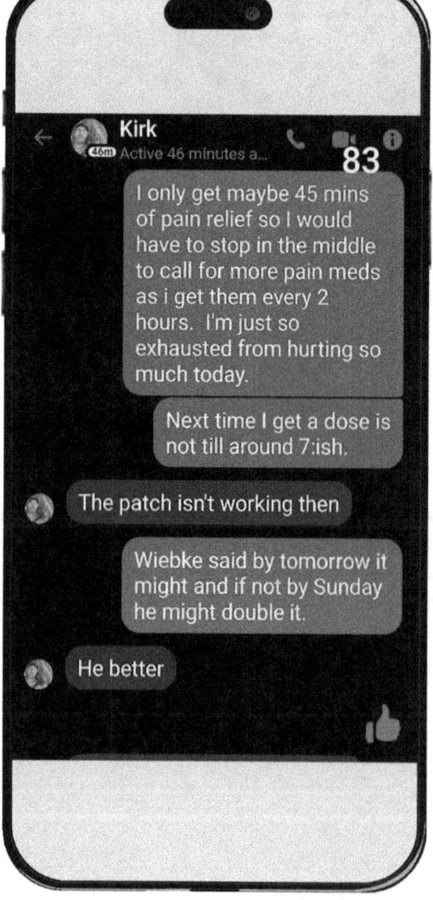

Kirk
Active 46 minutes a...
83
I only get maybe 45 mins of pain relief so I would have to stop in the middle to call for more pain meds as i get them every 2 hours. I'm just so exhausted from hurting so much today.
Next time I get a dose is not till around 7:ish.
The patch isn't working then
Wiebke said by tomorrow it might and if not by Sunday he might double it.
He better

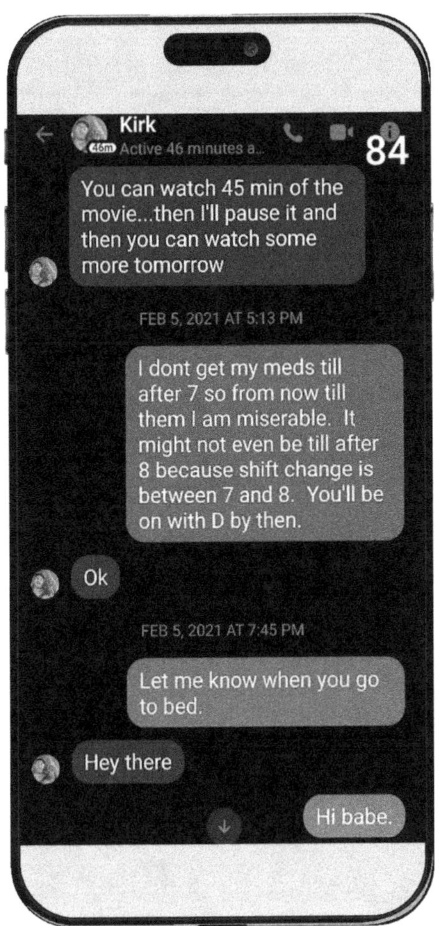
Kirk
Active 46 minutes a...
84
You can watch 45 min of the movie...then I'll pause it and then you can watch some more tomorrow
FEB 5, 2021 AT 5:13 PM
I dont get my meds till after 7 so from now till them I am miserable. It might not even be till after 8 because shift change is between 7 and 8. You'll be on with D by then.
Ok
FEB 5, 2021 AT 7:45 PM
Let me know when you go to bed.
Hey there
Hi babe.

Kirk
Active 48 minutes a...
85
Just wanted to see how your doing before OII hit the sack
Cool. Did you call D?
Yes. Just finished with him
Awesome.
You ok?
I'm waiting for my meds again. 9:15.
Not too long.
I'm exhausted
I'm sure. Today was stressful again.
How are you feeling?
Tired and stressed

Kirk
Active 49 minutes a...
86
I'm sorry.
It's not your fault
I'm just having a weak moment. I miss you so much I wish you could be here.
Me too .try and see you on Sunday
Ok. I'm hoping the pain is better controlled by then and I can enjoy it.
That would be great. Hopefully we could spend about an hour with you
That would be great.
I just wish they can take care of the pain at least

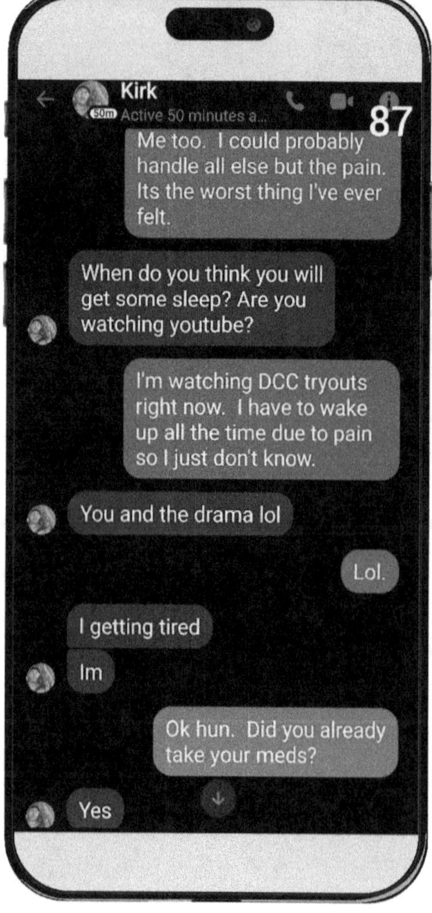

Kirk
Active 50 minutes a...
87
Me too. I could probably handle all else but the pain. Its the worst thing I've ever felt.
When do you think you will get some sleep? Are you watching youtube?
I'm watching DCC tryouts right now. I have to wake up all the time due to pain so I just don't know.
You and the drama lol
Lol.
I getting tired
Im
Ok hun. Did you already take your meds?
Yes

Kirk
Active 51 minutes a...
88
Ok sweetie. I love you. Sleep well.
I would say you too...
Lol
I know
Talk to you in the morning
Ok sweetie. Talk to ya then.
FEB 6, 2021 AT 7:24 AM
Good morning
Hi babe.
How are you?

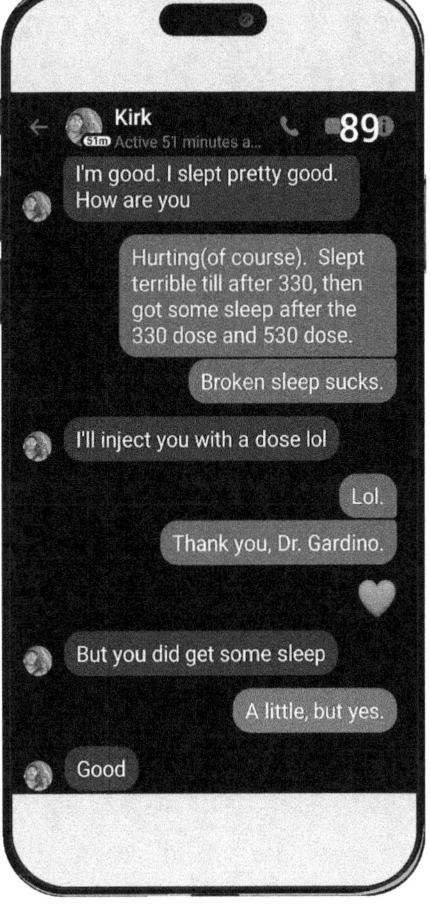

Kirk
Active 51 minutes a...
89
I'm good. I slept pretty good. How are you
Hurting(of course). Slept terrible till after 330, then got some sleep after the 330 dose and 530 dose.
Broken sleep sucks.
I'll inject you with a dose lol
Lol.
Thank you, Dr. Gardino.
But you did get some sleep
A little, but yes.
Good

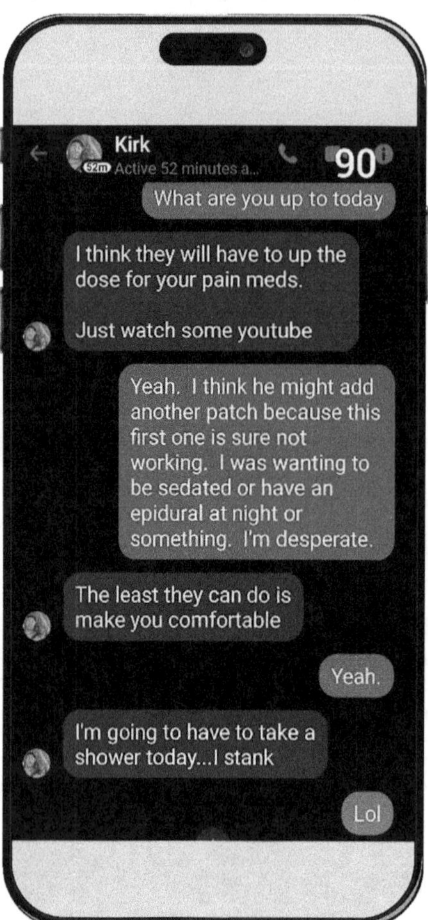

Kirk
52m Active 52 minutes a...
90
What are you up to today
I think they will have to up the dose for your pain meds.
Just watch some youtube
Yeah. I think he might add another patch because this first one is sure not working. I was wanting to be sedated or have an epidural at night or something. I'm desperate.
The least they can do is make you comfortable
Yeah.
I'm going to have to take a shower today...I stank
Lol

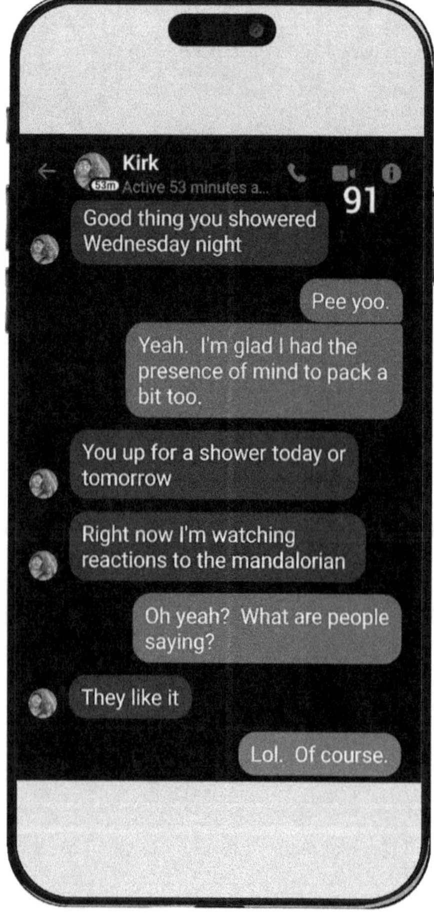

Kirk
53m Active 53 minutes a...
91
Good thing you showered Wednesday night
Pee yoo.
Yeah. I'm glad I had the presence of mind to pack a bit too.
You up for a shower today or tomorrow
Right now I'm watching reactions to the mandalorian
Oh yeah? What are people saying?
They like it
Lol. Of course.

Kirk
53m Active 53 minutes a...
92
How is his head not on fire
I know right?
I miss you
I miss you too my sweet. I want this over so I can come home and lay next to my husband at night and eat real food and hug my mom and pet the cats and yell at Gunny and everything else...

Kirk
55m Active 55 minutes a...
93
You just made me cry
Aww sweetie. Please dont cry.
I love you.
I love you too
It hasn't always been easy but you are the best man I've ever known. I'm so thankful to be your wife.
Thank you sweetie!
You getting caught up on your favorite youtube channels

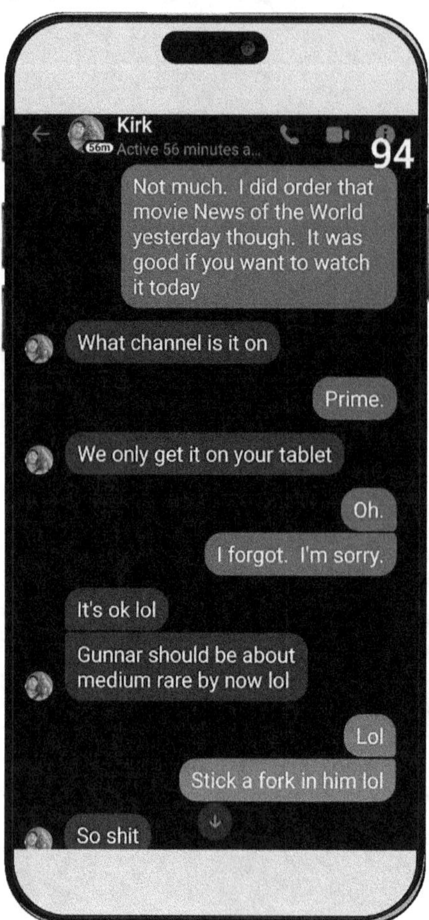
Kirk
Active 56 minutes a...
94
Not much. I did order that movie News of the World yesterday though. It was good if you want to watch it today
What channel is it on
Prime.
We only get it on your tablet
Oh.
I forgot. I'm sorry.
It's ok lol
Gunnar should be about medium rare by now lol
Lol
Stick a fork in him lol
So shit

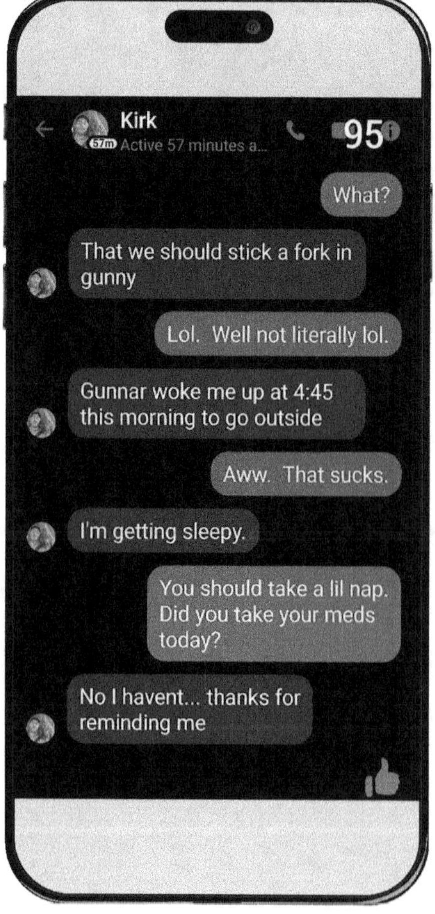
Kirk
Active 57 minutes a...
95
What?
That we should stick a fork in gunny
Lol. Well not literally lol.
Gunnar woke me up at 4:45 this morning to go outside
Aww. That sucks.
I'm getting sleepy.
You should take a lil nap. Did you take your meds today?
No I havent... thanks for reminding me

10:52
Kirk
57m Active 57 minutes a...
96
Also, I meant to tell you again, thanks for keeping Gunns off the bed. I appreciate you doing that.
He hasn't tried again
Cool.
I think I'm going to nap now. I'll text you later gater
Ok babe.
FEB 6, 2021 AT 9:25 AM

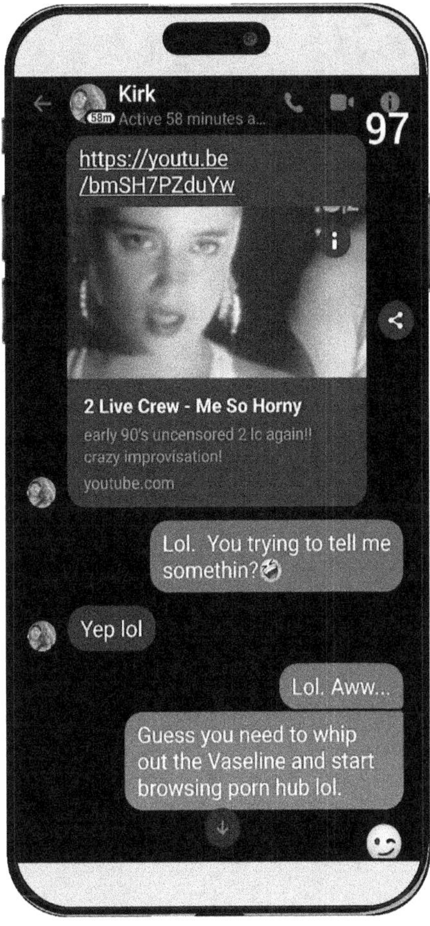
Kirk
58m Active 58 minutes a...
97
https://youtu.be /bmSH7PZduYw
2 Live Crew - Me So Horny
early 90's uncensored 2 lc again!! crazy improvisation!
youtube.com
Lol. You trying to tell me somethin?
Yep lol
Lol. Aww...
Guess you need to whip out the Vaseline and start browsing porn hub lol.

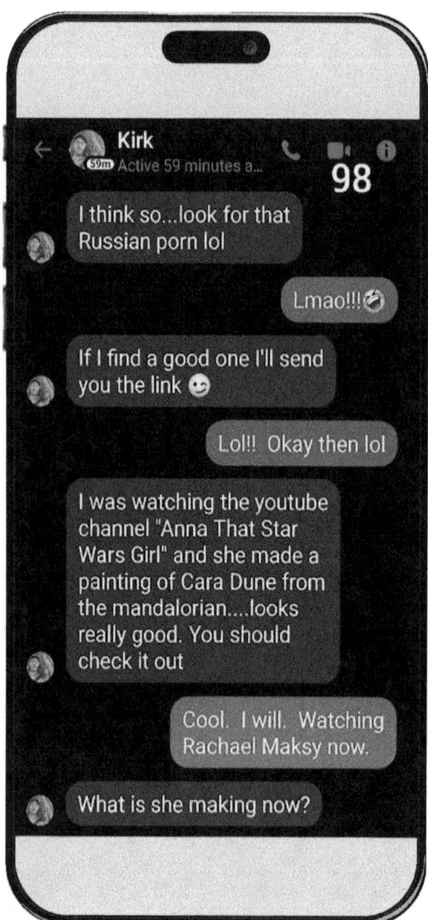
Kirk
Active 59 minutes a...
98
I think so...look for that Russian porn lol
Lmao!!!
If I find a good one I'll send you the link
Lol!! Okay then lol
I was watching the youtube channel "Anna That Star Wars Girl" and she made a painting of Cara Dune from the mandalorian....looks really good. You should check it out
Cool. I will. Watching Rachael Maksy now.
What is she making now?

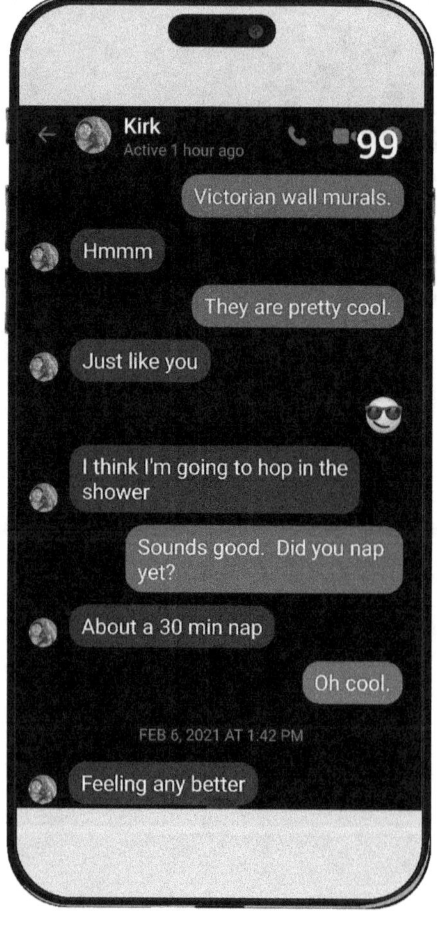
Kirk
Active 1 hour ago
99
Victorian wall murals.
Hmmm
They are pretty cool.
Just like you
I think I'm going to hop in the shower
Sounds good. Did you nap yet?
About a 30 min nap
Oh cool.
FEB 6, 2021 AT 1:42 PM
Feeling any better

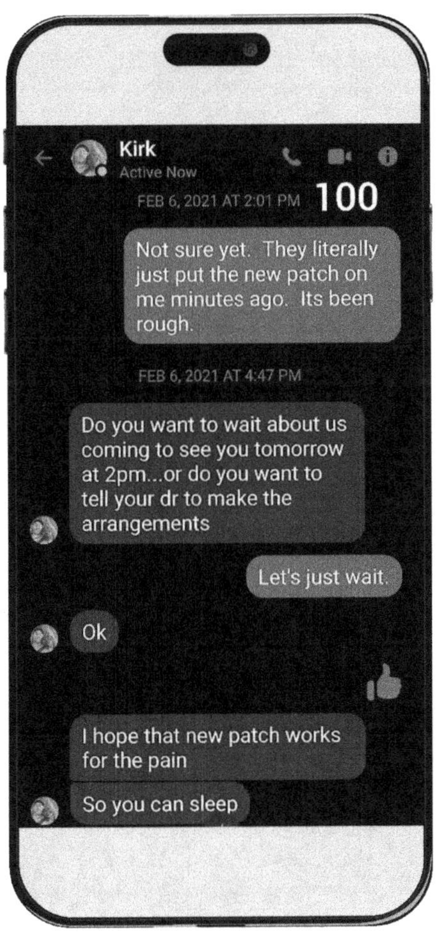
Kirk
Active Now
FEB 6, 2021 AT 2:01 PM
100
Not sure yet. They literally just put the new patch on me minutes ago. Its been rough.
FEB 6, 2021 AT 4:47 PM
Do you want to wait about us coming to see you tomorrow at 2pm...or do you want to tell your dr to make the arrangements
Let's just wait.
Ok
I hope that new patch works for the pain
So you can sleep

Kirk
Active 3 minutes ago
101
I hope so too.
I got to play the tank game with Danil today
Are you going to be up for a movie tonight
I. Dont know babe.
I'm glad you got to play with d.
Dick...I sure did lol
Lol.
Did it pay off?
Happy ending
hallelujah! Lol

Kirk
Active 4 minutes ago
102
Are you feeling hungry at all
No. I just tried to sip this nasty clear ensure. ...gross.
Ew
It was bad.
I'm going to bring you that oil I got for you when we com ed for you to use. It shrinks tumors
Ok babe. When you guys come here ill need several things.
Just let me know and I'll bring them
Thank you sweets.
Ok sweetsest

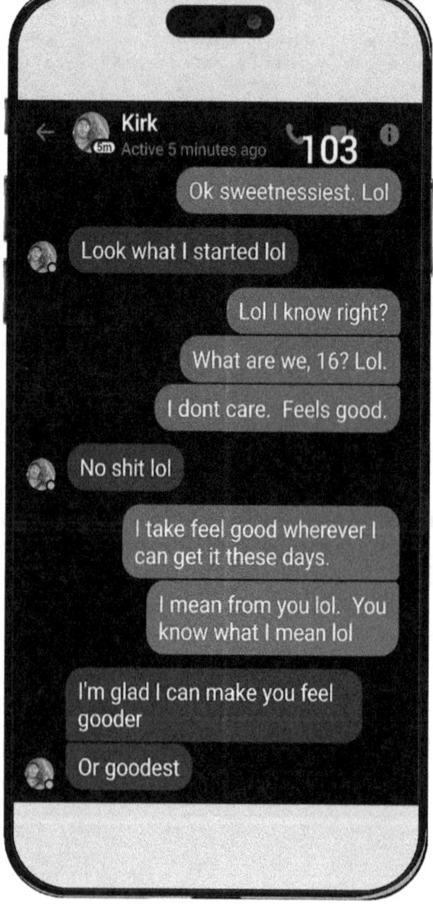

Kirk
Active 5 minutes ago
103
Ok sweetnessiest. Lol
Look what I started lol
Lol I know right?
What are we, 16? Lol.
I dont care. Feels good.
No shit lol
I take feel good wherever I can get it these days.
I mean from you lol. You know what I mean lol
I'm glad I can make you feel gooder
Or goodest

Kirk
Active 6 minutes ago
104
Aww. Youbeat me to it.
Goodlyest
Or goodmostess
Lol!
Gunnar is bugging me to take him out. I'll be back in a min
I'm back
FEB 6, 2021 AT 5:39 PM
I want a fucking epidural.
You should tell them that
Or i want propofol.

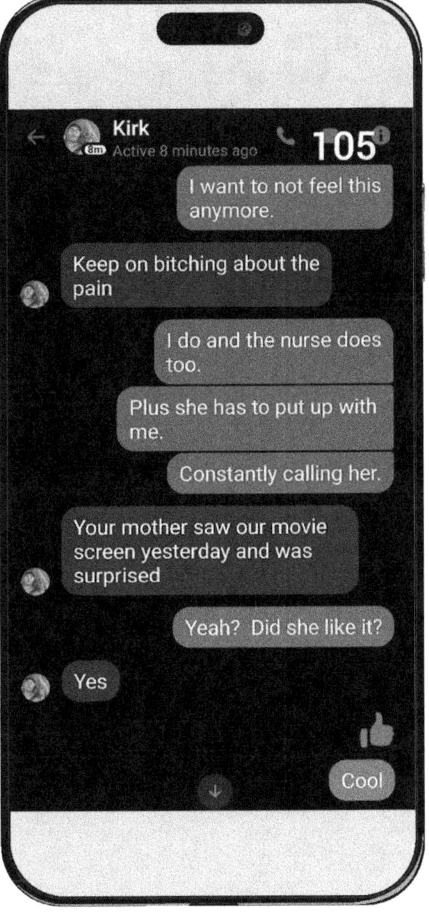
Kirk
Active 8 minutes ago
105
I want to not feel this anymore.
Keep on bitching about the pain
I do and the nurse does too.
Plus she has to put up with me.
Constantly calling her.
Your mother saw our movie screen yesterday and was surprised
Yeah? Did she like it?
Yes
Cool

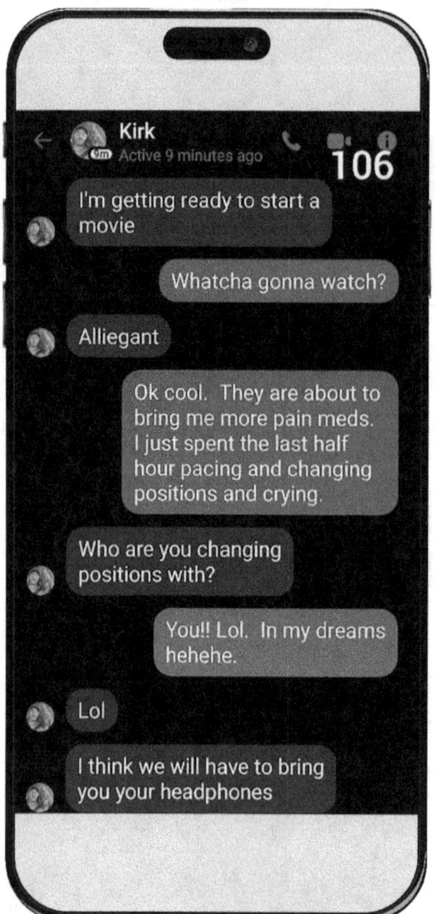
Kirk
Active 9 minutes ago
106
I'm getting ready to start a movie
Whatcha gonna watch?
Alliegant
Ok cool. They are about to bring me more pain meds. I just spent the last half hour pacing and changing positions and crying.
Who are you changing positions with?
You!! Lol. In my dreams hehehe.
Lol
I think we will have to bring you your headphones

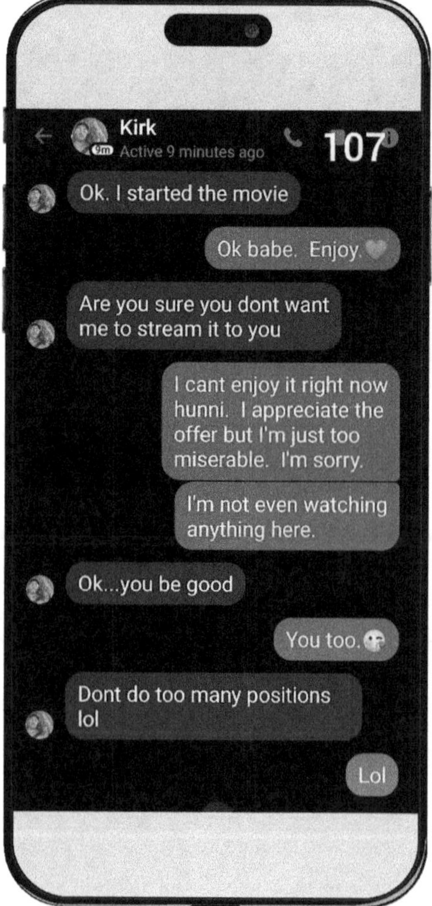
Kirk
Active 9 minutes ago
107
Ok. I started the movie
Ok babe. Enjoy.
Are you sure you dont want me to stream it to you
I cant enjoy it right now hunni. I appreciate the offer but I'm just too miserable. I'm sorry.
I'm not even watching anything here.
Ok...you be good
You too.
Dont do too many positions lol
Lol

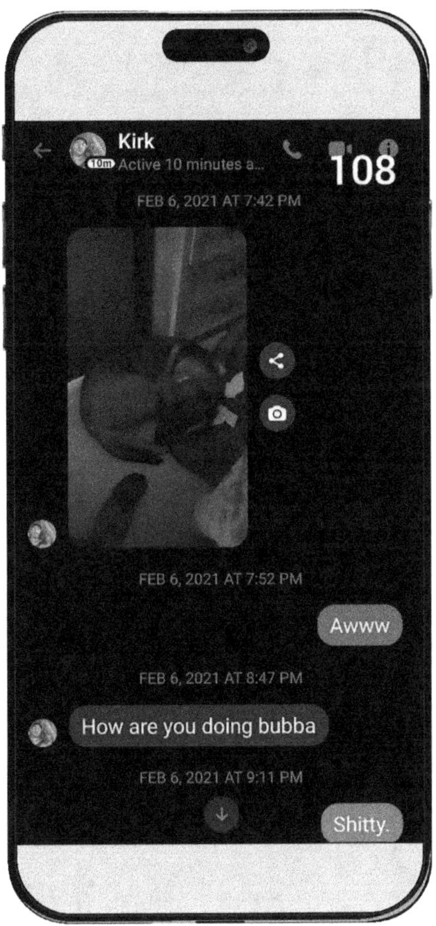
Kirk
Active 10 minutes a...
108
FEB 6, 2021 AT 7:42 PM
FEB 6, 2021 AT 7:52 PM
Awww
FEB 6, 2021 AT 8:47 PM
How are you doing bubba
FEB 6, 2021 AT 9:11 PM
Shitty.

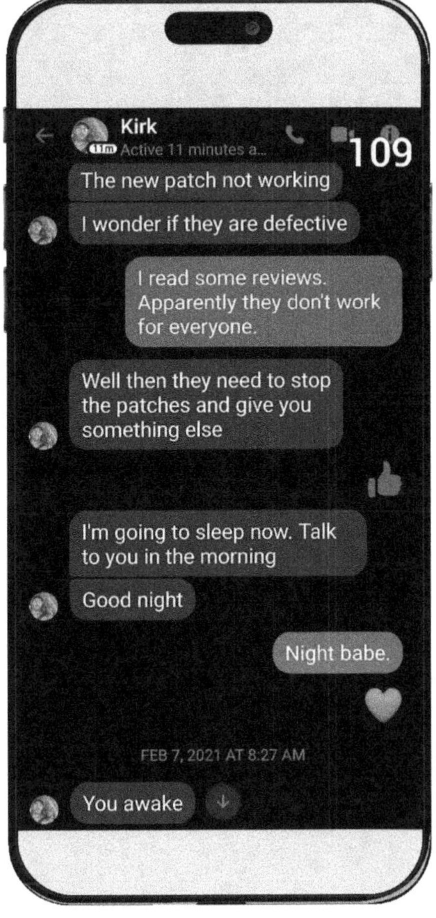
Kirk
Active 11 minutes a...
109
The new patch not working
I wonder if they are defective
I read some reviews.
Apparently they don't work
for everyone.
Well then they need to stop
the patches and give you
something else
I'm going to sleep now. Talk
to you in the morning
Good night
Night babe.
FEB 7, 2021 AT 8:27 AM
You awake

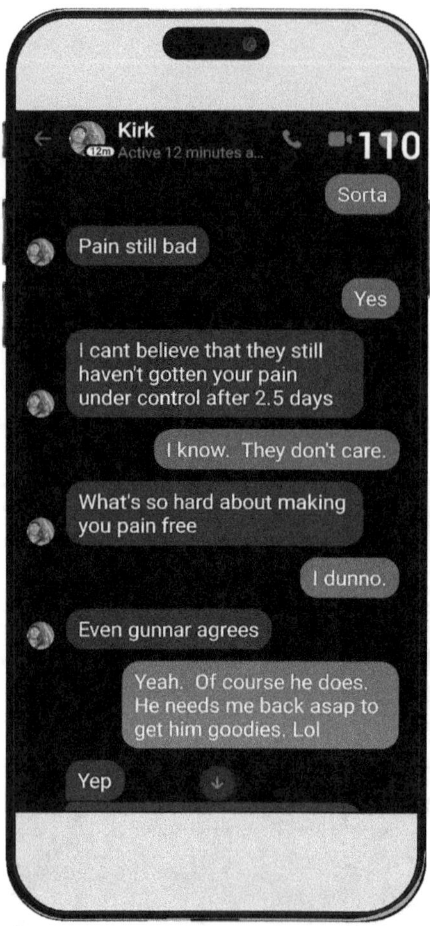
Kirk
Active 12 minutes a...
Sorta
Pain still bad
Yes
I cant believe that they still haven't gotten your pain under control after 2.5 days
I know. They don't care.
What's so hard about making you pain free
I dunno.
Even gunnar agrees
Yeah. Of course he does. He needs me back asap to get him goodies. Lol
Yep

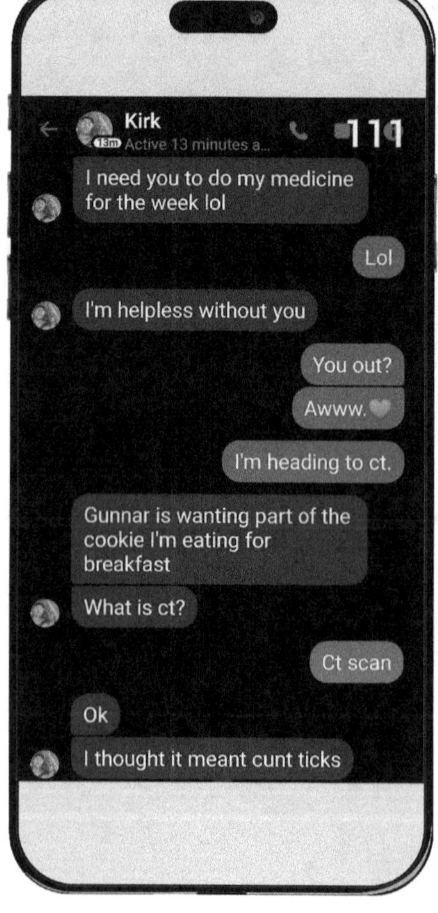
Kirk
Active 13 minutes a...
I need you to do my medicine for the week lol
Lol
I'm helpless without you
You out?
Awww.
I'm heading to ct.
Gunnar is wanting part of the cookie I'm eating for breakfast
What is ct?
Ct scan
Ok
I thought it meant cunt ticks

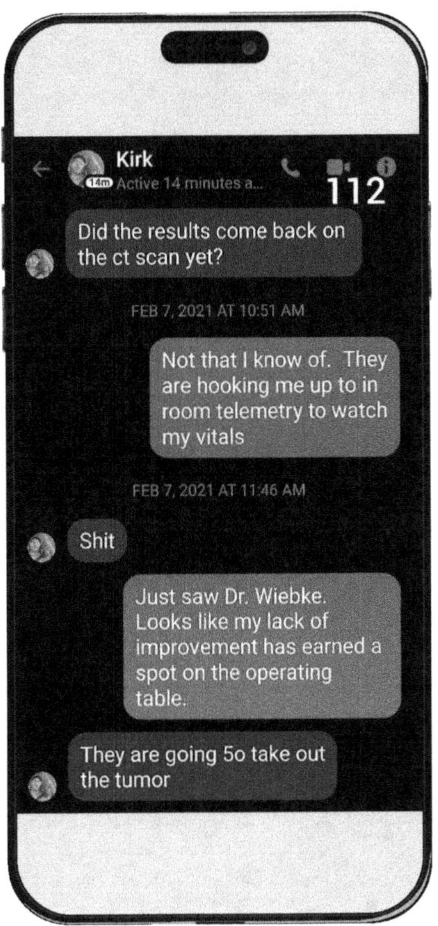
Kirk
Active 14 minutes a...
112
Did the results come back on the ct scan yet?
FEB 7, 2021 AT 10:51 AM
Not that I know of. They are hooking me up to in room telemetry to watch my vitals
FEB 7, 2021 AT 11:46 AM
Shit
Just saw Dr. Wiebke. Looks like my lack of improvement has earned a spot on the operating table.
They are going 5o take out the tumor

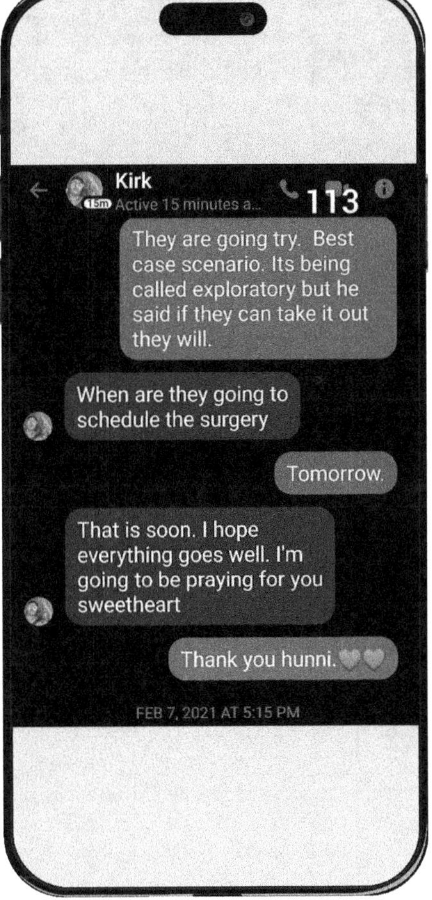
Kirk
Active 15 minutes a...
113
They are going try. Best case scenario. Its being called exploratory but he said if they can take it out they will.
When are they going to schedule the surgery
Tomorrow.
That is soon. I hope everything goes well. I'm going to be praying for you sweetheart
Thank you hunni.
FEB 7, 2021 AT 5:15 PM

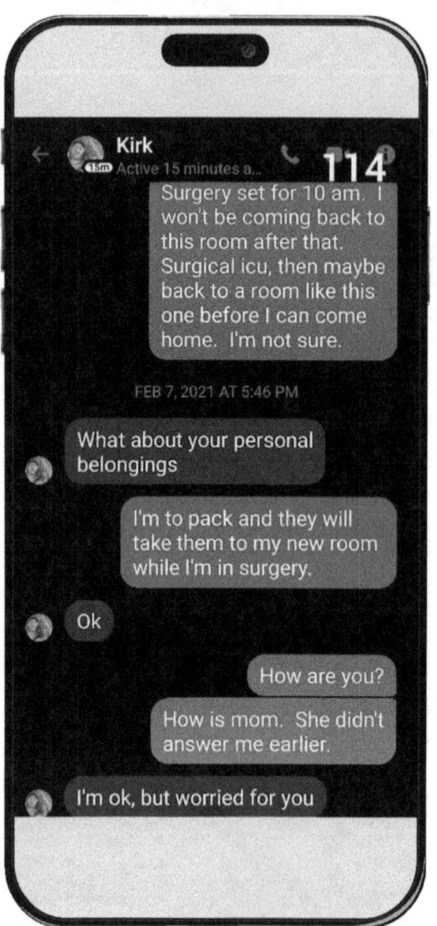
Kirk
Active 15 minutes a...
114
Surgery set for 10 am. I won't be coming back to this room after that. Surgical icu, then maybe back to a room like this one before I can come home. I'm not sure.
FEB 7, 2021 AT 5:46 PM
What about your personal belongings
I'm to pack and they will take them to my new room while I'm in surgery.
Ok
How are you?
How is mom. She didn't answer me earlier.
I'm ok, but worried for you

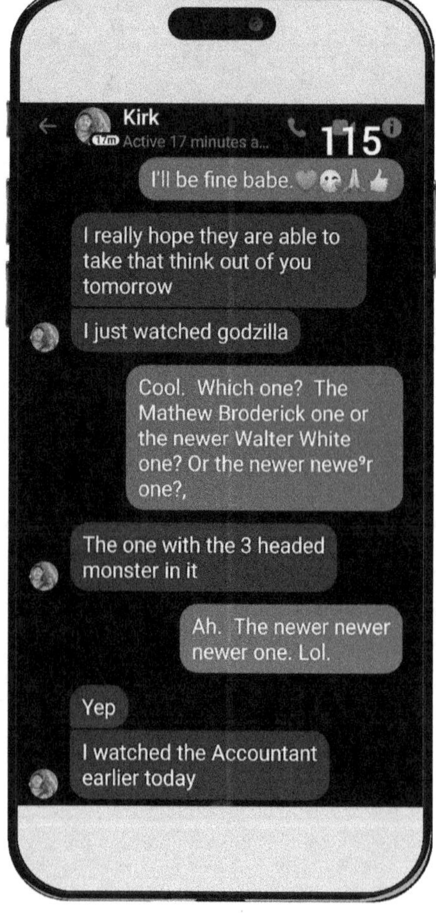
Kirk
Active 17 minutes a...
115
I'll be fine babe.
I really hope they are able to take that think out of you tomorrow
I just watched godzilla
Cool. Which one? The Mathew Broderick one or the newer Walter White one? Or the newer newe⁹r one?,
The one with the 3 headed monster in it
Ah. The newer newer newer one. Lol.
Yep
I watched the Accountant earlier today

Kirk
Active 19 minutes a...
116
I'm warning up a tv dinner now
FEB 7, 2021 AT 6:17 PM
You ok sweetheart
FEB 7, 2021 AT 6:32 PM
I'm going to listen to the X22 report now
Yeah. I'm sorry, I dozed off again.
FEB 7, 2021 AT 7:24 PM
At least you got a little sleep
Yep. I keep doing it too. Lol.
Doing it with who?
Lol

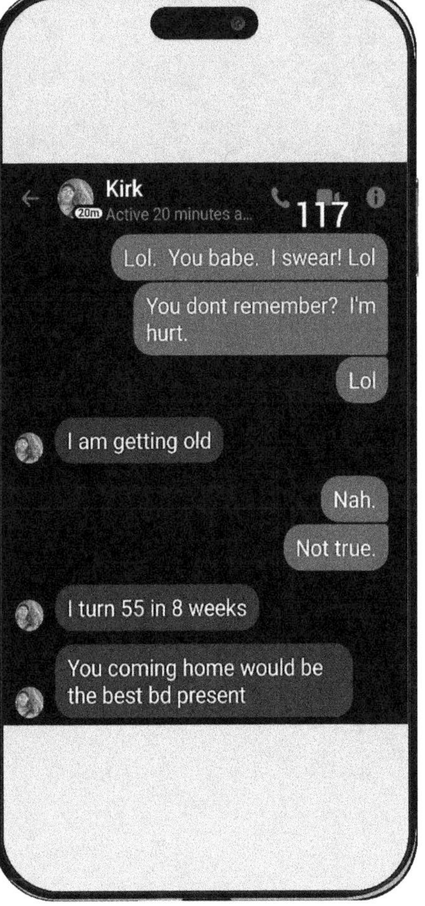
Kirk
Active 20 minutes a...
117
Lol. You babe. I swear! Lol
You dont remember? I'm hurt.
Lol
I am getting old
Nah.
Not true.
I turn 55 in 8 weeks
You coming home would be the best bd present

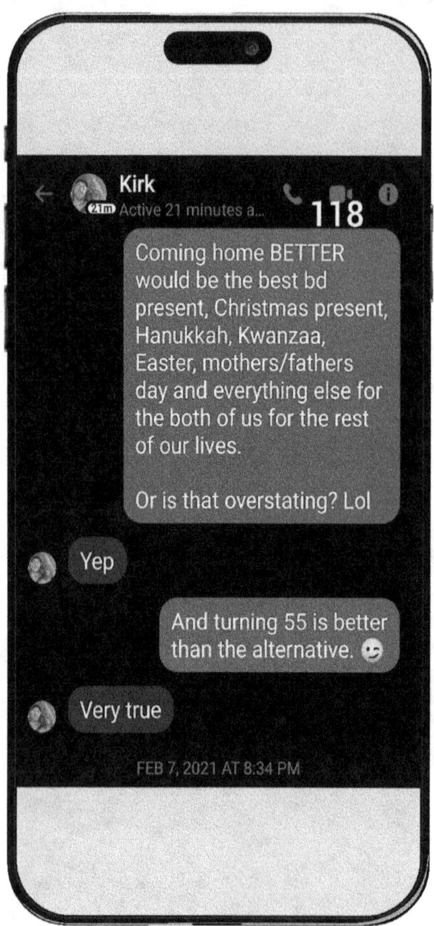
Kirk
Active 21 minutes a...
118
Coming home BETTER would be the best bd present, Christmas present, Hanukkah, Kwanzaa, Easter, mothers/fathers day and everything else for the both of us for the rest of our lives.

Or is that overstating? Lol
Yep
And turning 55 is better than the alternative.
Very true
FEB 7, 2021 AT 8:34 PM

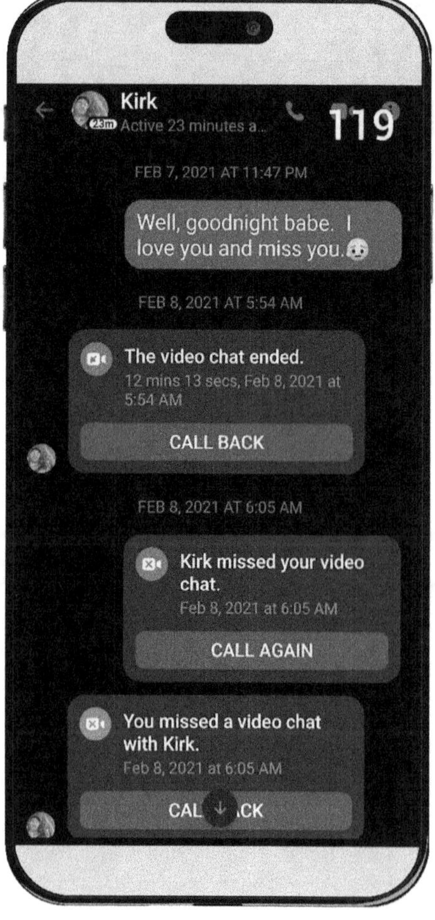
Kirk
Active 23 minutes a...
119
FEB 7, 2021 AT 11:47 PM
Well, goodnight babe. I love you and miss you.
FEB 8, 2021 AT 5:54 AM
The video chat ended.
12 mins 13 secs, Feb 8, 2021 at 5:54 AM
CALL BACK
FEB 8, 2021 AT 6:05 AM
Kirk missed your video chat.
Feb 8, 2021 at 6:05 AM
CALL AGAIN
You missed a video chat with Kirk.
Feb 8, 2021 at 6:05 AM
CALL BACK

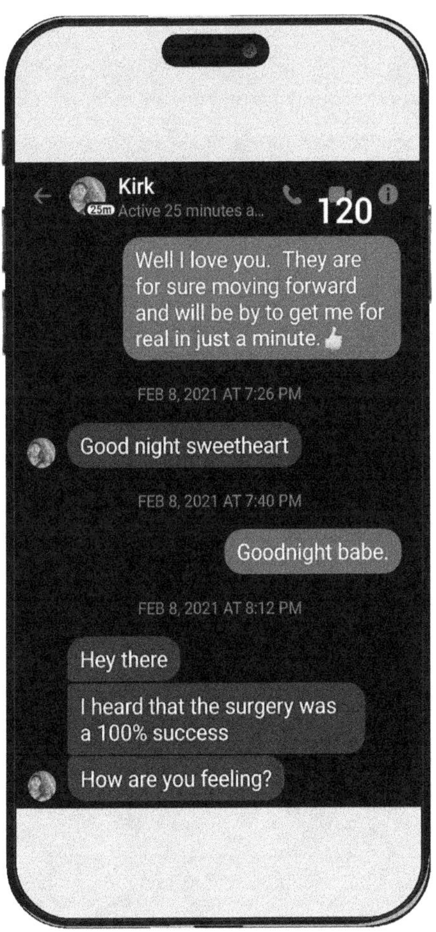
Kirk
Active 25 minutes a...
120
Well I love you. They are for sure moving forward and will be by to get me for real in just a minute. 👍
FEB 8, 2021 AT 7:26 PM
Good night sweetheart
FEB 8, 2021 AT 7:40 PM
Goodnight babe.
FEB 8, 2021 AT 8:12 PM
Hey there
I heard that the surgery was a 100% success
How are you feeling?

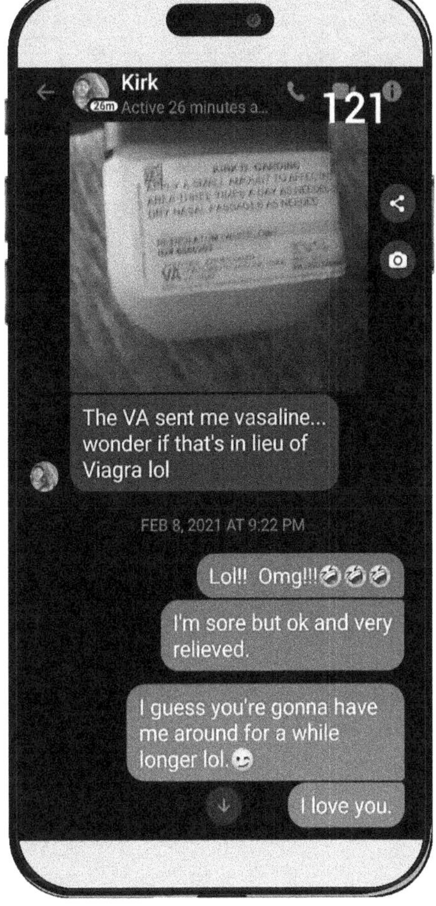
Kirk
Active 26 minutes a...
121
The VA sent me vasaline... wonder if that's in lieu of Viagra lol
FEB 8, 2021 AT 9:22 PM
Lol!! Omg!!!😂😂😂
I'm sore but ok and very relieved.
I guess you're gonna have me around for a while longer lol.😊
I love you.

Kirk
Active 1 hour ago
122
Good morning
Good morning hun.
Looks like you might be home by Friday
Doc was just in and said as long as I'm able to eat and they have my pain well controlled with pills instead of iv that I can come home. Baby steps he said but he was optimistic that it won't be long.
Your sore right now...but how is your pain
Its mostly just the pain from surgery. Hardly anything from before. Its so weird.

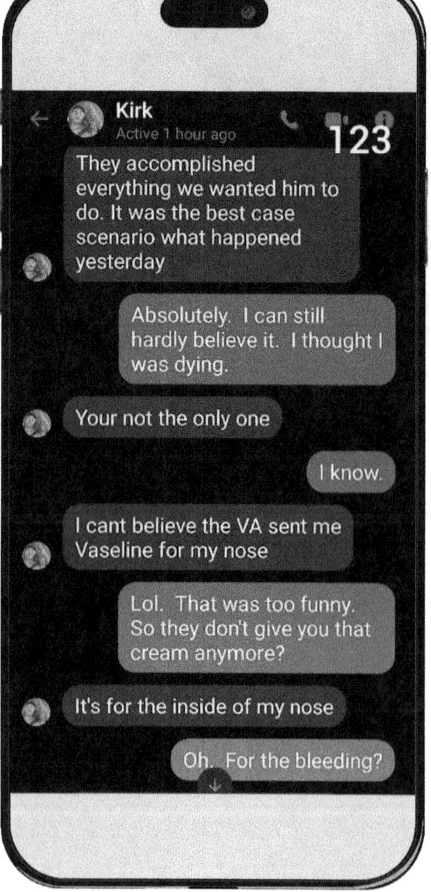
Kirk
Active 1 hour ago
123
They accomplished everything we wanted him to do. It was the best case scenario what happened yesterday
Absolutely. I can still hardly believe it. I thought I was dying.
Your not the only one
I know.
I cant believe the VA sent me Vaseline for my nose
Lol. That was too funny. So they don't give you that cream anymore?
It's for the inside of my nose
Oh. For the bleeding?

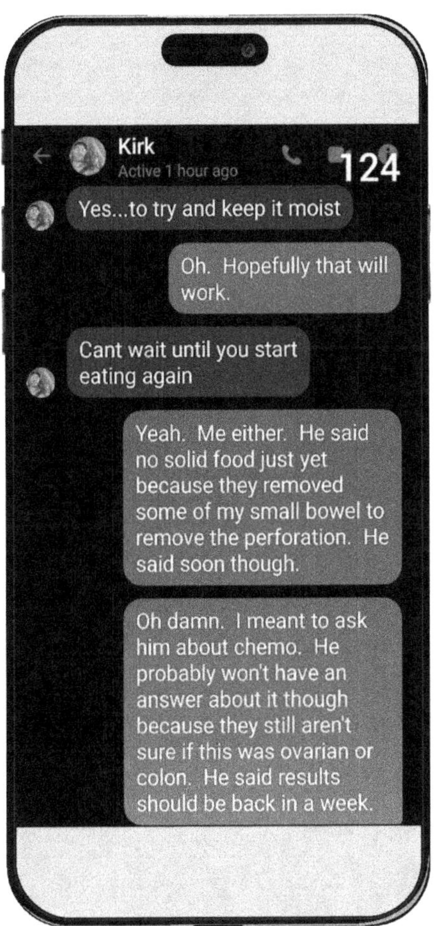

Kirk
Active 1 hour ago
124
Yes...to try and keep it moist
Oh. Hopefully that will work.
Cant wait until you start eating again
Yeah. Me either. He said no solid food just yet because they removed some of my small bowel to remove the perforation. He said soon though.
Oh damn. I meant to ask him about chemo. He probably won't have an answer about it though because they still aren't sure if this was ovarian or colon. He said results should be back in a week.

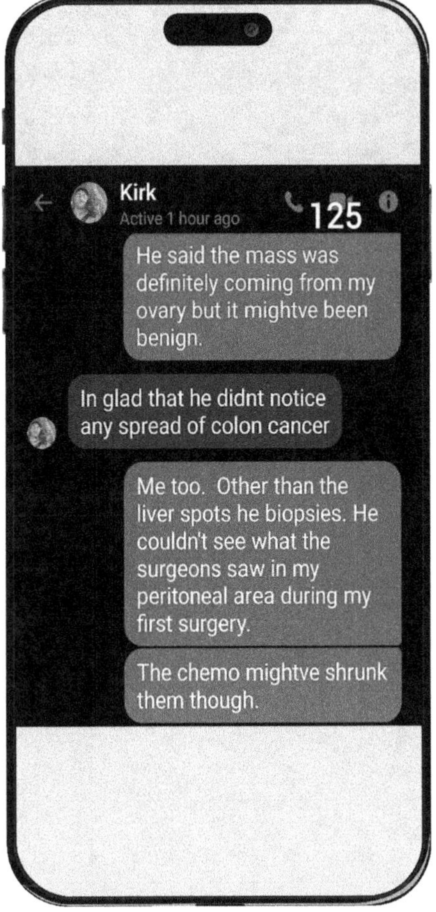

Kirk
Active 1 hour ago
125
He said the mass was definitely coming from my ovary but it mightve been benign.
In glad that he didnt notice any spread of colon cancer
Me too. Other than the liver spots he biopsies. He couldn't see what the surgeons saw in my peritoneal area during my first surgery.
The chemo mightve shrunk them though.

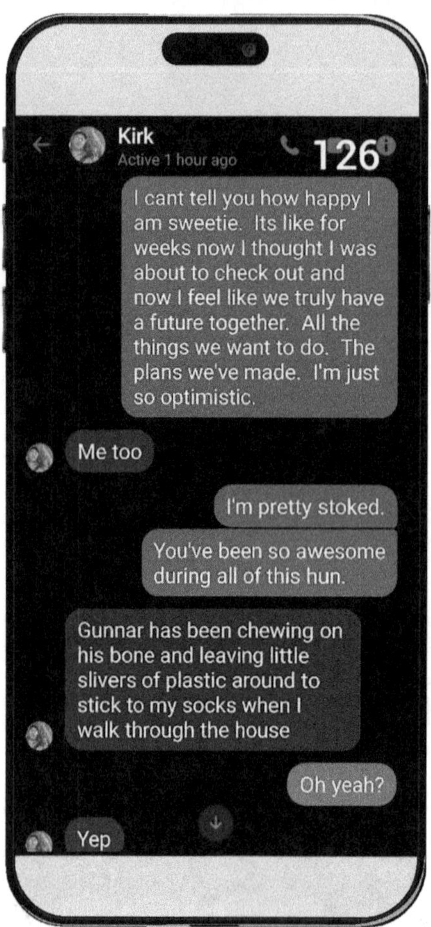

Kirk
Active 1 hour ago
126
I cant tell you how happy I am sweetie. Its like for weeks now I thought I was about to check out and now I feel like we truly have a future together. All the things we want to do. The plans we've made. I'm just so optimistic.
Me too
I'm pretty stoked.
You've been so awesome during all of this hun.
Gunnar has been chewing on his bone and leaving little slivers of plastic around to stick to my socks when I walk through the house
Oh yeah?
Yep

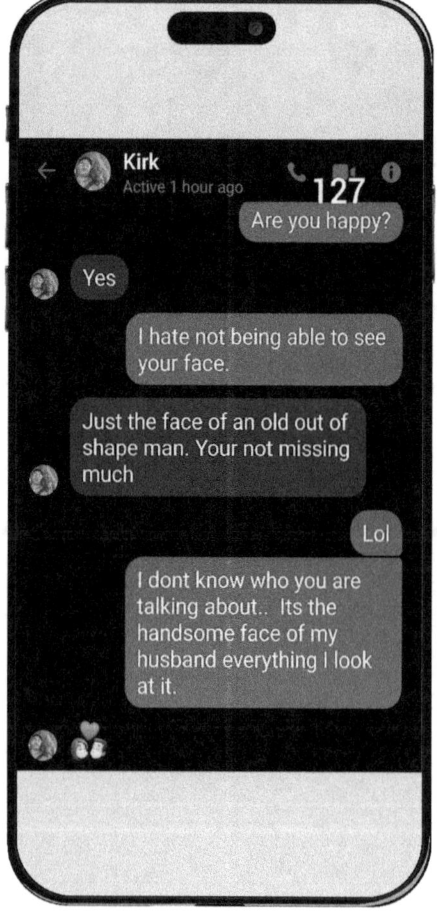

Kirk
Active 1 hour ago
127
Are you happy?
Yes
I hate not being able to see your face.
Just the face of an old out of shape man. Your not missing much
Lol
I dont know who you are talking about.. Its the handsome face of my husband everything I look at it.

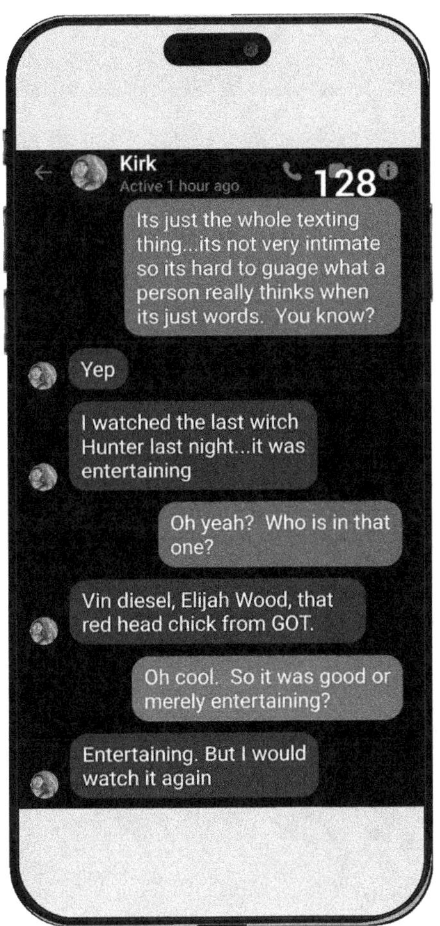

Kirk
Active 1 hour ago
128
Its just the whole texting thing...its not very intimate so its hard to guage what a person really thinks when its just words. You know?
Yep
I watched the last witch Hunter last night...it was entertaining
Oh yeah? Who is in that one?
Vin diesel, Elijah Wood, that red head chick from GOT.
Oh cool. So it was good or merely entertaining?
Entertaining. But I would watch it again

Kirk
Active 1 hour ago
129
High praise coming from you lol.
Lol
It was so embarrassing this morning. A nurse had to give me this special bath.
Did she touch your princess parts lol
Then I had to wipe my couch with these towelettes to clean it because its that time of the month. Embarrassing.
Lol
*cooch. Not couch. Lol!!
Cooch...couch

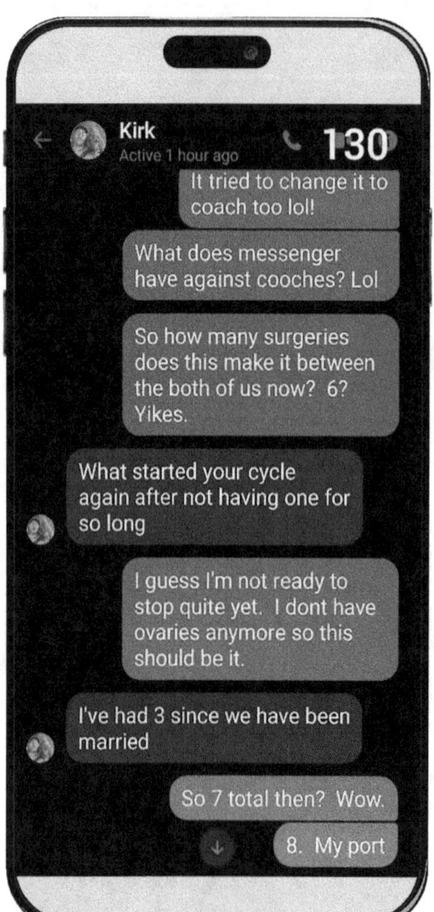

Kirk
Active 1 hour ago
130
It tried to change it to coach too lol!
What does messenger have against cooches? Lol
So how many surgeries does this make it between the both of us now? 6? Yikes.
What started your cycle again after not having one for so long
I guess I'm not ready to stop quite yet. I dont have ovaries anymore so this should be it.
I've had 3 since we have been married
So 7 total then? Wow.
8. My port

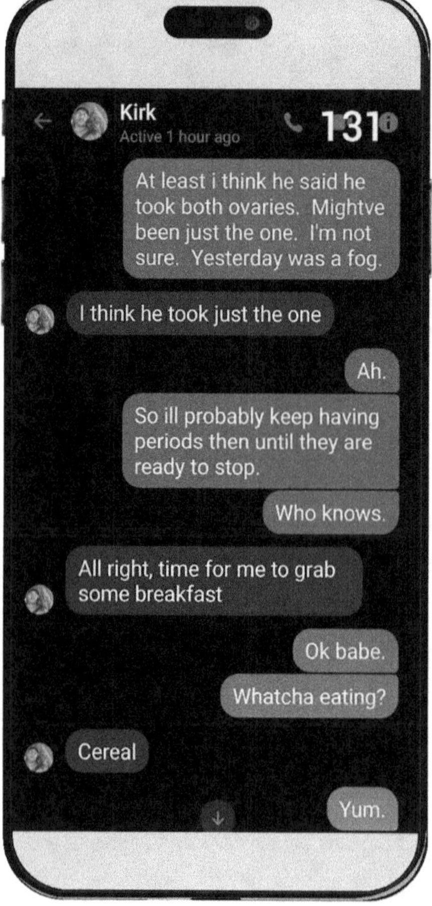

Kirk
Active 1 hour ago
131
At least i think he said he took both ovaries. Mightve been just the one. I'm not sure. Yesterday was a fog.
I think he took just the one
Ah.
So ill probably keep having periods then until they are ready to stop.
Who knows.
All right, time for me to grab some breakfast
Ok babe.
Whatcha eating?
Cereal
Yum.

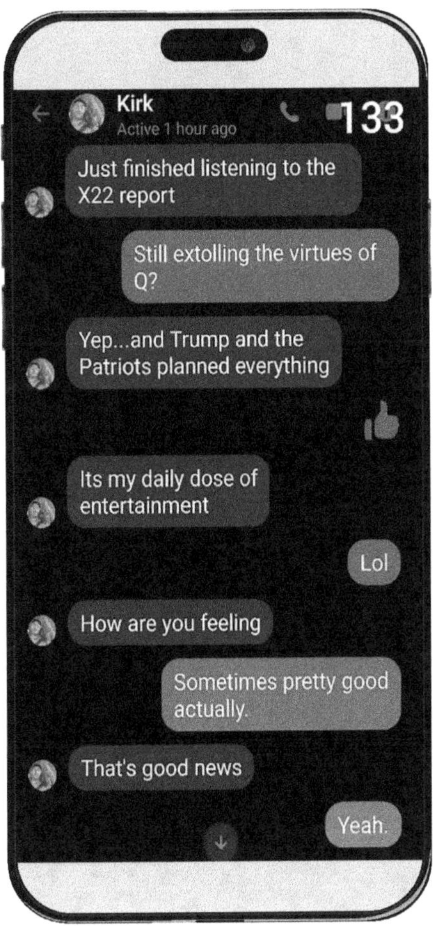

Kirk
Active 1 hour ago
133
Just finished listening to the X22 report
Still extolling the virtues of Q?
Yep...and Trump and the Patriots planned everything
Its my daily dose of entertainment
Lol
How are you feeling
Sometimes pretty good actually.
That's good news
Yeah.

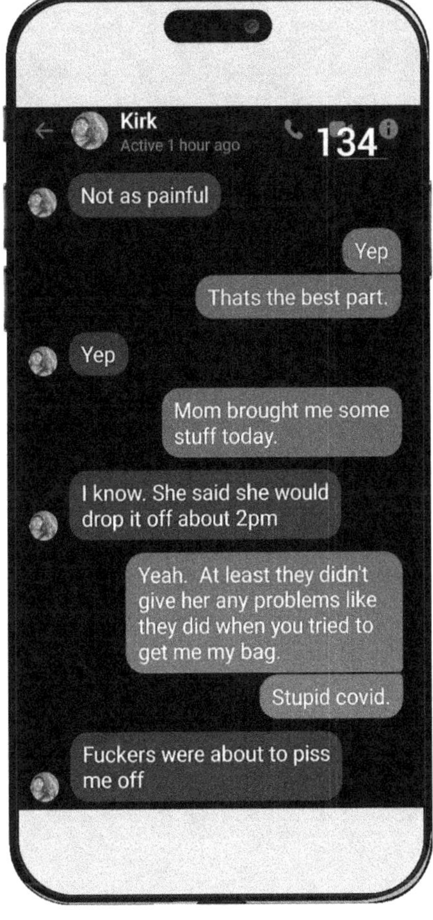

Kirk
Active 1 hour ago
134
Not as painful
Yep
Thats the best part.
Yep
Mom brought me some stuff today.
I know. She said she would drop it off about 2pm
Yeah. At least they didn't give her any problems like they did when you tried to get me my bag.
Stupid covid.
Fuckers were about to piss me off

Kirk
Active 1 hour ago
135
Yeah. I'm surprised you maintained coolness for as long as you did.
It was for you
Aww. Thank you babe.
I miss you.
Hurry up and get better
I know right? I get my catheter out tomorrow.
I'll treat you to Burger King lol
Lol.

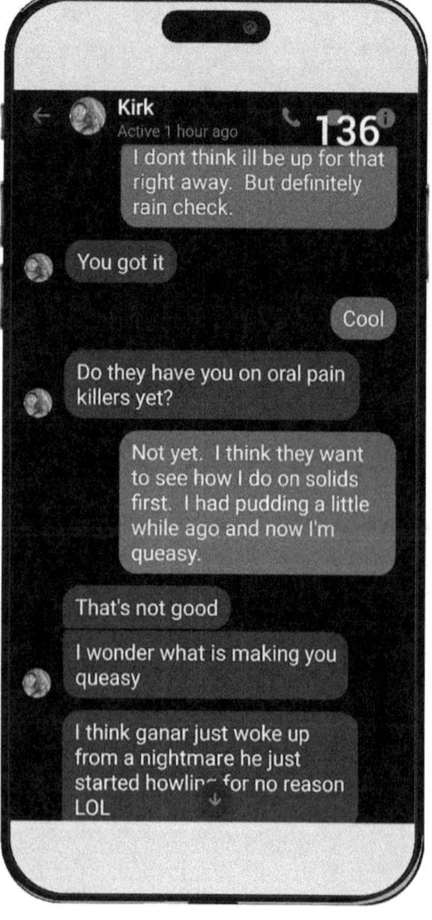
Kirk
Active 1 hour ago
136
I dont think ill be up for that right away. But definitely rain check.
You got it
Cool
Do they have you on oral pain killers yet?
Not yet. I think they want to see how I do on solids first. I had pudding a little while ago and now I'm queasy.
That's not good
I wonder what is making you queasy
I think ganar just woke up from a nightmare he just started howling for no reason LOL

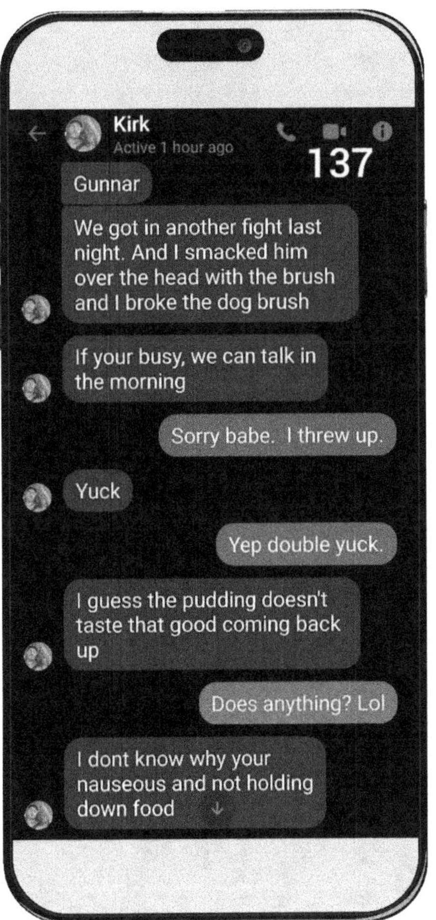
Kirk
Active 1 hour ago
137
Gunnar
We got in another fight last night. And I smacked him over the head with the brush and I broke the dog brush
If your busy, we can talk in the morning
Sorry babe. I threw up.
Yuck
Yep double yuck.
I guess the pudding doesn't taste that good coming back up
Does anything? Lol
I dont know why your nauseous and not holding down food

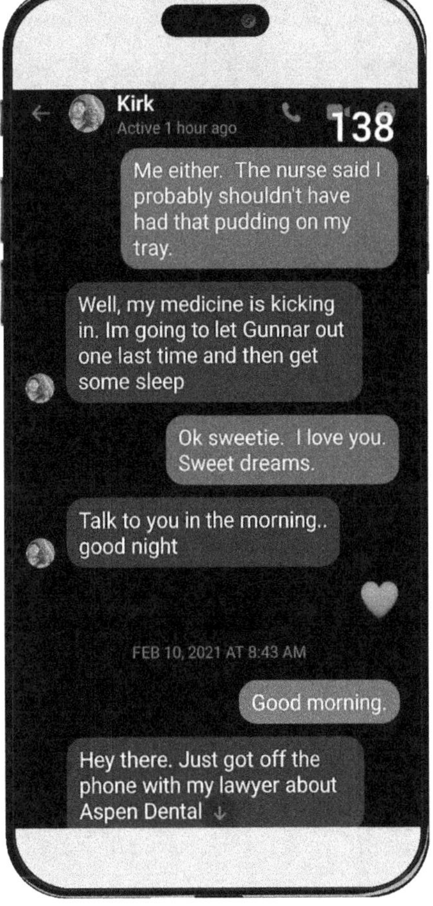
Kirk
Active 1 hour ago
138
Me either. The nurse said I probably shouldn't have had that pudding on my tray.
Well, my medicine is kicking in. Im going to let Gunnar out one last time and then get some sleep
Ok sweetie. I love you. Sweet dreams.
Talk to you in the morning.. good night
FEB 10, 2021 AT 8:43 AM
Good morning.
Hey there. Just got off the phone with my lawyer about Aspen Dental

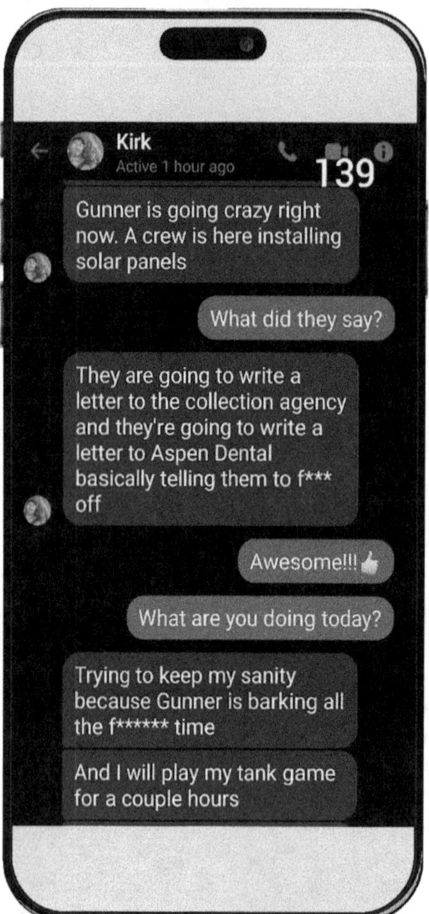

Kirk
Active 1 hour ago
139
Gunner is going crazy right now. A crew is here installing solar panels
What did they say?
They are going to write a letter to the collection agency and they're going to write a letter to Aspen Dental basically telling them to f*** off
Awesome!!!
What are you doing today?
Trying to keep my sanity because Gunner is barking all the f****** time
And I will play my tank game for a couple hours

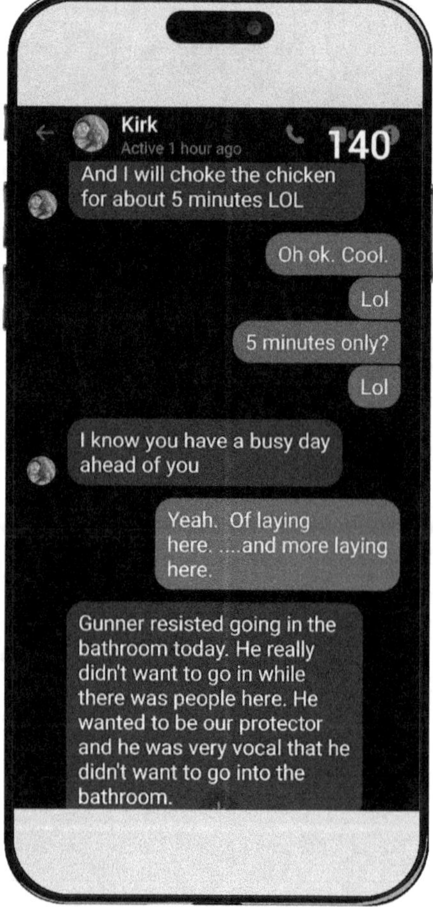

Kirk
Active 1 hour ago
140
And I will choke the chicken for about 5 minutes LOL
Oh ok. Cool.
Lol
5 minutes only?
Lol
I know you have a busy day ahead of you
Yeah. Of laying here. ....and more laying here.
Gunner resisted going in the bathroom today. He really didn't want to go in while there was people here. He wanted to be our protector and he was very vocal that he didn't want to go into the bathroom.

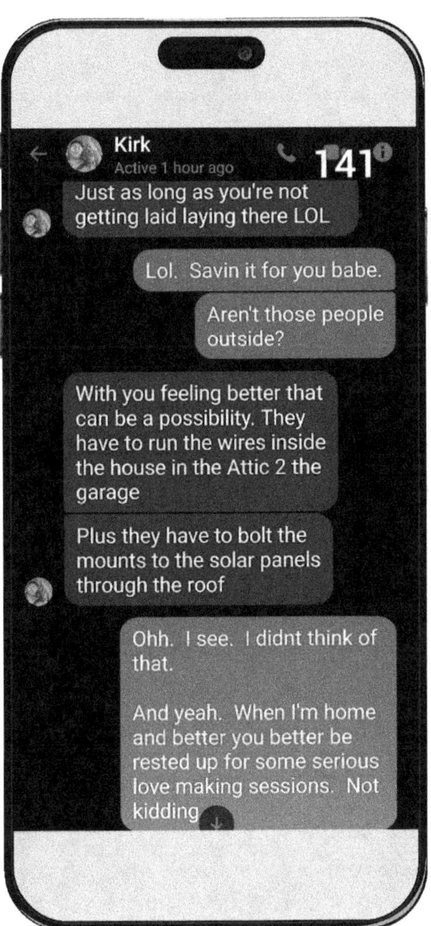

Kirk
Active 1 hour ago
141
Just as long as you're not getting laid laying there LOL
Lol. Savin it for you babe.
Aren't those people outside?
With you feeling better that can be a possibility. They have to run the wires inside the house in the Attic 2 the garage
Plus they have to bolt the mounts to the solar panels through the roof
Ohh. I see. I didnt think of that.
And yeah. When I'm home and better you better be rested up for some serious love making sessions. Not kidding

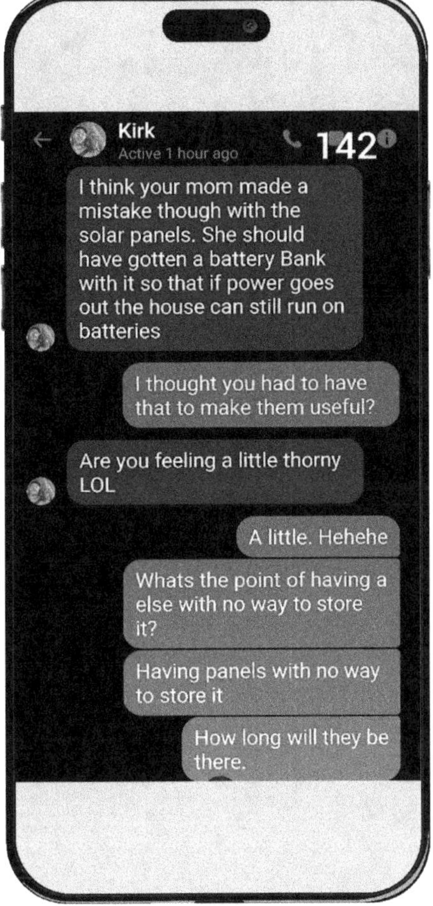

Kirk
Active 1 hour ago
142
I think your mom made a mistake though with the solar panels. She should have gotten a battery Bank with it so that if power goes out the house can still run on batteries
I thought you had to have that to make them useful?
Are you feeling a little thorny LOL
A little. Hehehe
Whats the point of having a else with no way to store it?
Having panels with no way to store it
How long will they be there.

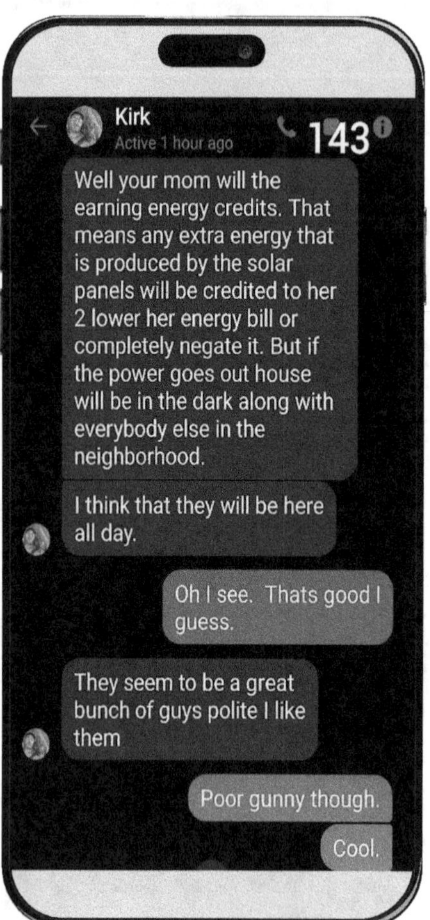

Kirk
Active 1 hour ago
143
Well your mom will the earning energy credits. That means any extra energy that is produced by the solar panels will be credited to her 2 lower her energy bill or completely negate it. But if the power goes out house will be in the dark along with everybody else in the neighborhood.
I think that they will be here all day.
Oh I see. Thats good I guess.
They seem to be a great bunch of guys polite I like them
Poor gunny though.
Cool.

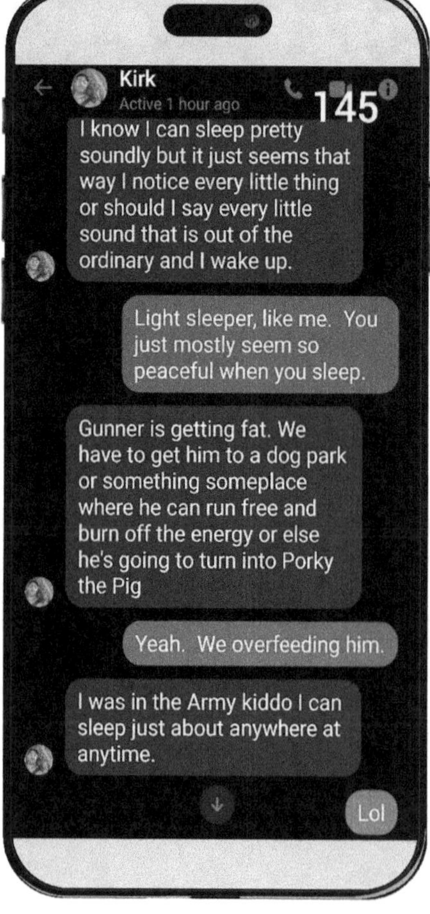

Kirk
Active 1 hour ago
145
I know I can sleep pretty soundly but it just seems that way I notice every little thing or should I say every little sound that is out of the ordinary and I wake up.
Light sleeper, like me. You just mostly seem so peaceful when you sleep.
Gunner is getting fat. We have to get him to a dog park or something someplace where he can run free and burn off the energy or else he's going to turn into Porky the Pig
Yeah. We overfeeding him.
I was in the Army kiddo I can sleep just about anywhere at anytime.
Lol

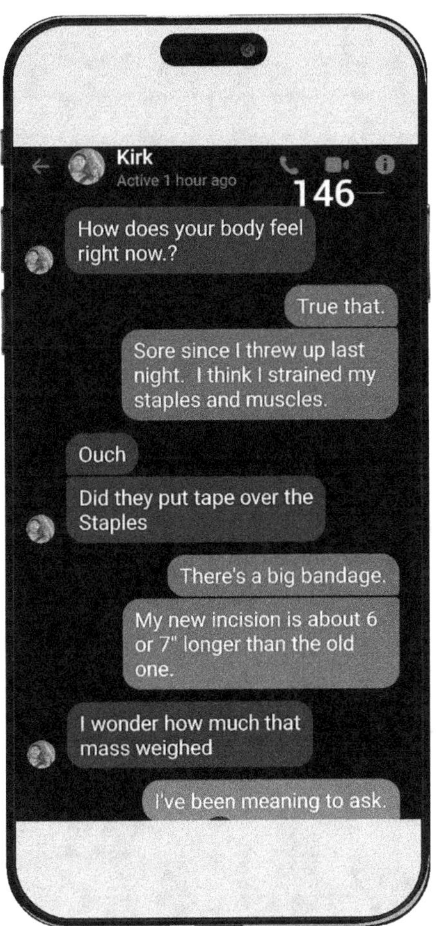

Kirk
Active 1 hour ago
146
How does your body feel right now.?
True that.
Sore since I threw up last night. I think I strained my staples and muscles.
Ouch
Did they put tape over the Staples
There's a big bandage.
My new incision is about 6 or 7" longer than the old one.
I wonder how much that mass weighed
I've been meaning to ask.

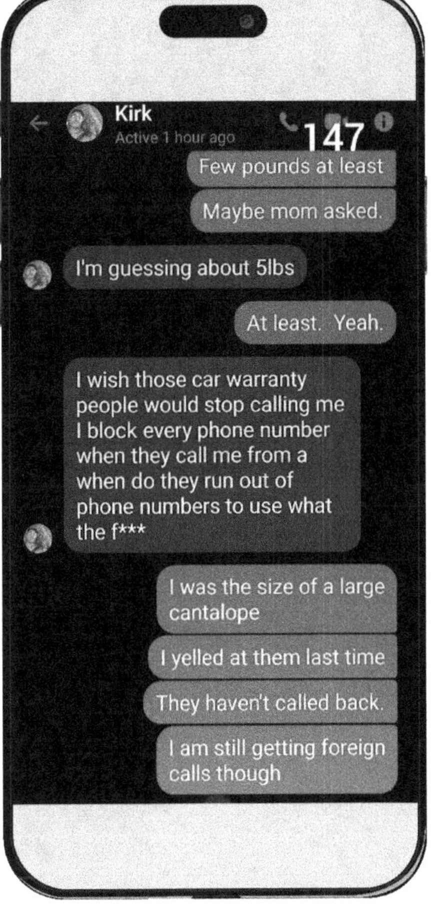

Kirk
Active 1 hour ago
147
Few pounds at least
Maybe mom asked.
I'm guessing about 5lbs
At least. Yeah.
I wish those car warranty people would stop calling me I block every phone number when they call me from a when do they run out of phone numbers to use what the f***
I was the size of a large cantalope
I yelled at them last time
They haven't called back.
I am still getting foreign calls though

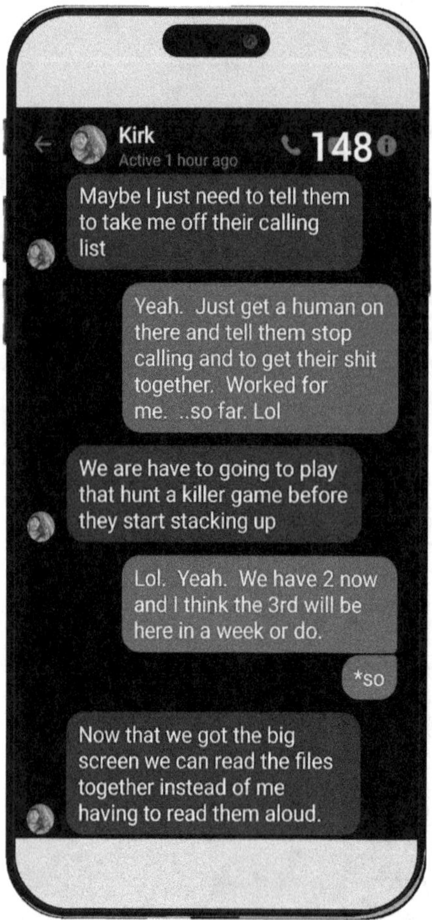

Kirk
Active 1 hour ago
148
Maybe I just need to tell them to take me off their calling list
Yeah. Just get a human on there and tell them stop calling and to get their shit together. Worked for me. ..so far. Lol
We are have to going to play that hunt a killer game before they start stacking up
Lol. Yeah. We have 2 now and I think the 3rd will be here in a week or do.
*so
Now that we got the big screen we can read the files together instead of me having to read them aloud.

Kirk
Active 1 hour ago
149
Thats true. Thatll make it funner.
Funnerest
Funnerestest
Lol
Lol
I have run out of things to say.
Lol
You know me. I don't talk very much
I gotta get a nurse in here to help me to the bathroom in a minute. Call me or text me later k babe?

Kirk
Active 1 hour ago
150
Okey dokey Stokey
Its ok. You're the quiet type.
FEB 10, 2021 AT 4:56 PM
Hey there. We now have solar panels on the house
Gunnar barked and whined for 6 hours straight
Thats awesome
Omg
He's not hoarse now?
Nope
How does he do it?

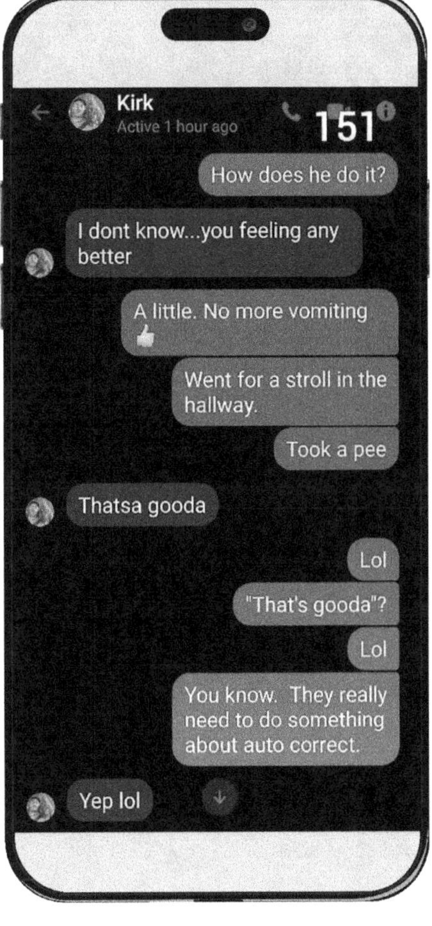
Kirk
Active 1 hour ago
151
How does he do it?
I dont know...you feeling any better
A little. No more vomiting
Went for a stroll in the hallway.
Took a pee
Thatsa gooda
Lol
"That's gooda"?
Lol
You know. They really need to do something about auto correct.
Yep lol

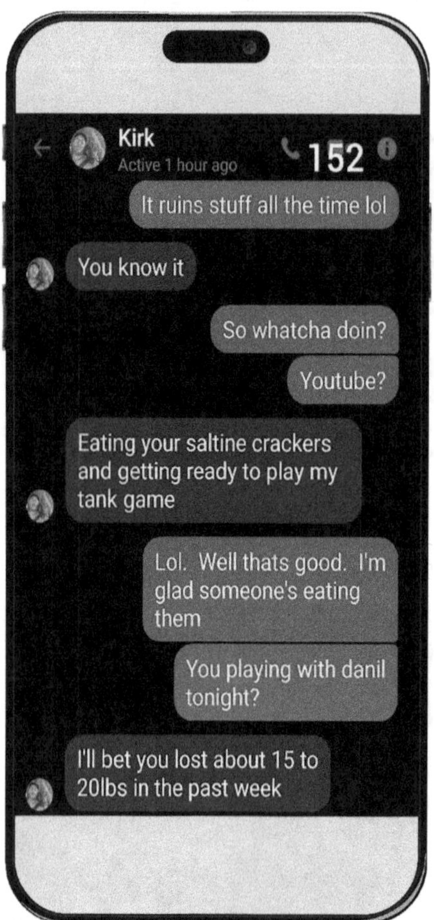
Kirk
Active 1 hour ago
152
It ruins stuff all the time lol
You know it
So whatcha doin?
Youtube?
Eating your saltine crackers and getting ready to play my tank game
Lol. Well thats good. I'm glad someone's eating them
You playing with danil tonight?
I'll bet you lost about 15 to 20lbs in the past week

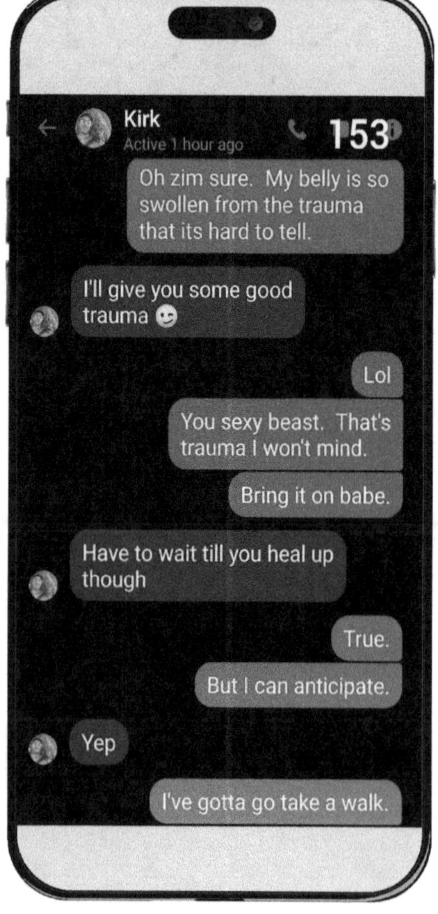
Kirk
Active 1 hour ago
153
Oh zim sure. My belly is so swollen from the trauma that its hard to tell.
I'll give you some good trauma
Lol
You sexy beast. That's trauma I won't mind.
Bring it on babe.
Have to wait till you heal up though
True.
But I can anticipate.
Yep
I've gotta go take a walk.

Her reference to sex like we had before we got married was about the nonstop sex, we had the first 6 days we were together before we got married on the 7th day and at one point gave her 23 orgasms in 90 minutes. The last time that we had had sex before she was admitted to the hospital was the second week of January which will be the last time that we ever had sex before her passing away.

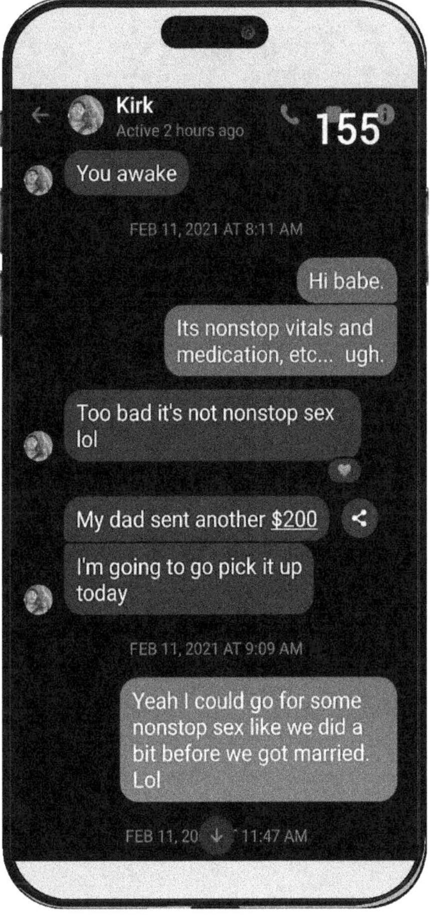

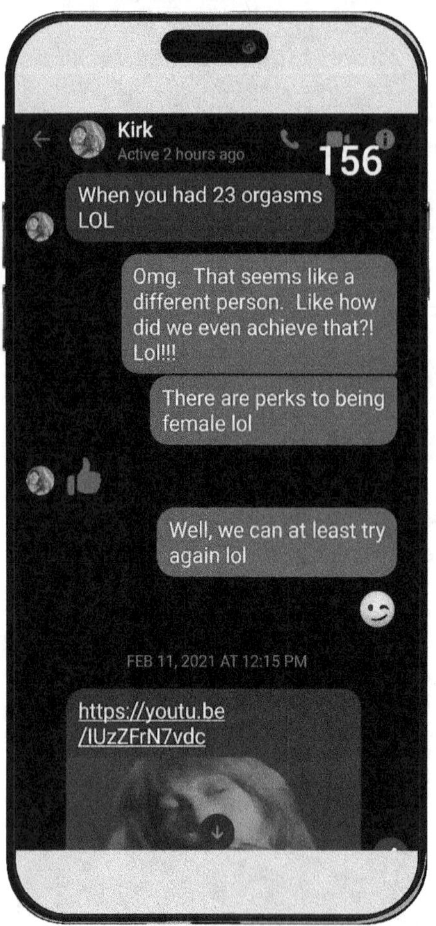
Kirk
Active 2 hours ago
156
When you had 23 orgasms LOL
Omg. That seems like a different person. Like how did we even achieve that?! Lol!!!
There are perks to being female lol
Well, we can at least try again lol
FEB 11, 2021 AT 12:15 PM
https://youtu.be/IUzZFrN7vdc

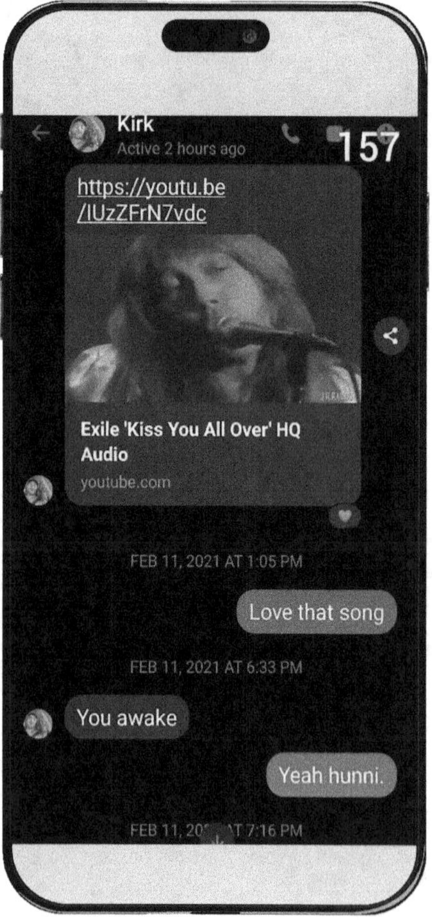
Kirk
Active 2 hours ago
157
https://youtu.be/IUzZFrN7vdc
Exile 'Kiss You All Over' HQ Audio
youtube.com
FEB 11, 2021 AT 1:05 PM
Love that song
FEB 11, 2021 AT 6:33 PM
You awake
Yeah hunni.
FEB 11, 2021 AT 7:16 PM

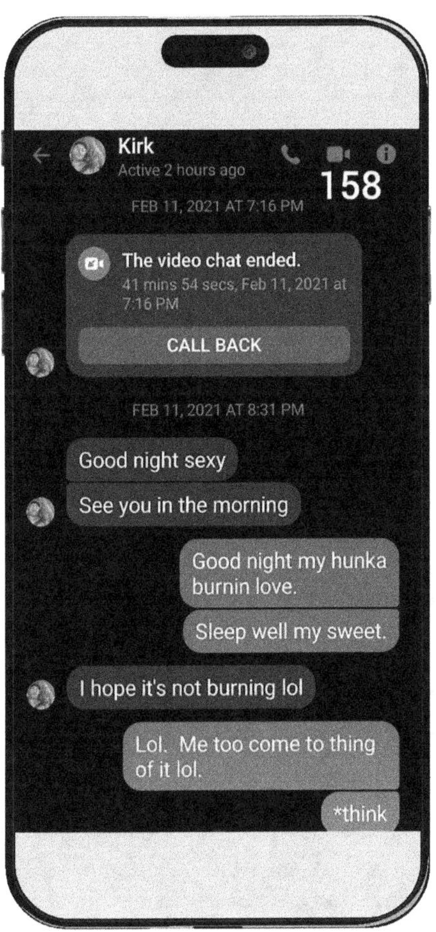
Kirk
Active 2 hours ago
158
FEB 11, 2021 AT 7:16 PM
The video chat ended.
41 mins 54 secs, Feb 11, 2021 at 7:16 PM
CALL BACK
FEB 11, 2021 AT 8:31 PM
Good night sexy
See you in the morning
Good night my hunka burnin love.
Sleep well my sweet.
I hope it's not burning lol
Lol. Me too come to thing of it lol.
*think

Kirk
Active 2 hours ago
159
See you in the morning..night night
Nighty night.
FEB 12, 2021 AT 10:41 AM
Can you send your password to your computer
FEB 12, 2021 AT 11:10 AM
Kym6k701
FEB 12, 2021 AT 11:34 AM
I'm taking care of paperwork today
Ah. Cool.
FEB 12, 2021 AT 4:48 PM
Hi there
Are you ok?

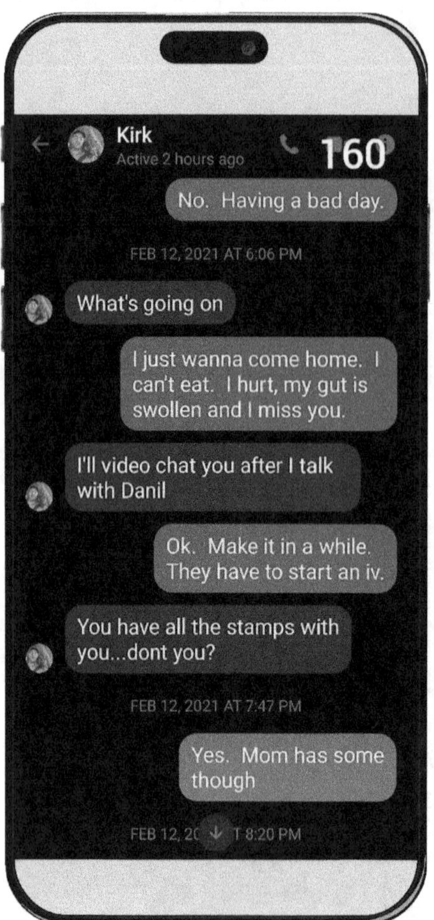

Kirk
Active 2 hours ago
160
No. Having a bad day.
FEB 12, 2021 AT 6:06 PM
What's going on
I just wanna come home. I can't eat. I hurt, my gut is swollen and I miss you.
I'll video chat you after I talk with Danil
Ok. Make it in a while. They have to start an iv.
You have all the stamps with you...dont you?
FEB 12, 2021 AT 7:47 PM
Yes. Mom has some though
FEB 12, 20   T 8:20 PM

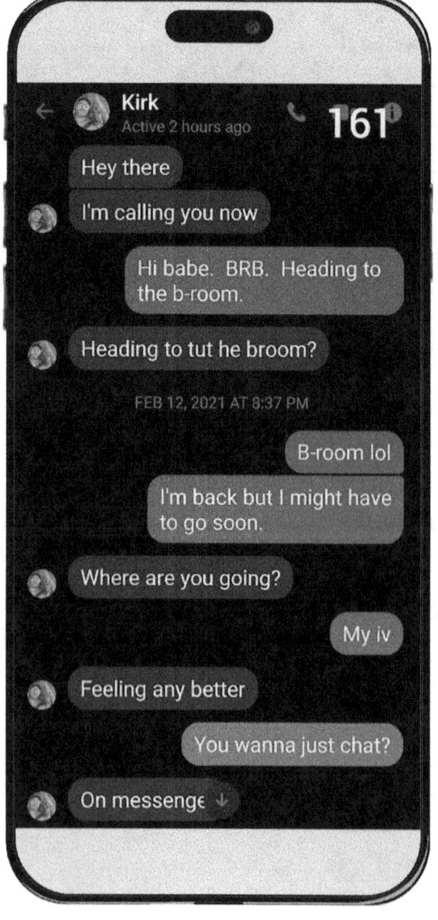

Kirk
Active 2 hours ago
161
Hey there
I'm calling you now
Hi babe. BRB. Heading to the b-room.
Heading to tut he broom?
FEB 12, 2021 AT 8:37 PM
B-room lol
I'm back but I might have to go soon.
Where are you going?
My iv
Feeling any better
You wanna just chat?
On messenge

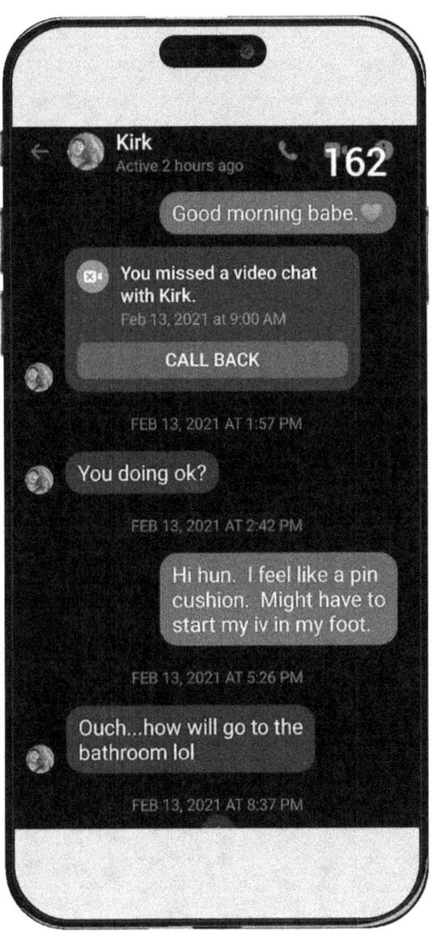
Kirk
Active 2 hours ago
162
Good morning babe.
You missed a video chat with Kirk.
Feb 13, 2021 at 9:00 AM
CALL BACK
FEB 13, 2021 AT 1:57 PM
You doing ok?
FEB 13, 2021 AT 2:42 PM
Hi hun. I feel like a pin cushion. Might have to start my iv in my foot.
FEB 13, 2021 AT 5:26 PM
Ouch...how will go to the bathroom lol
FEB 13, 2021 AT 8:37 PM

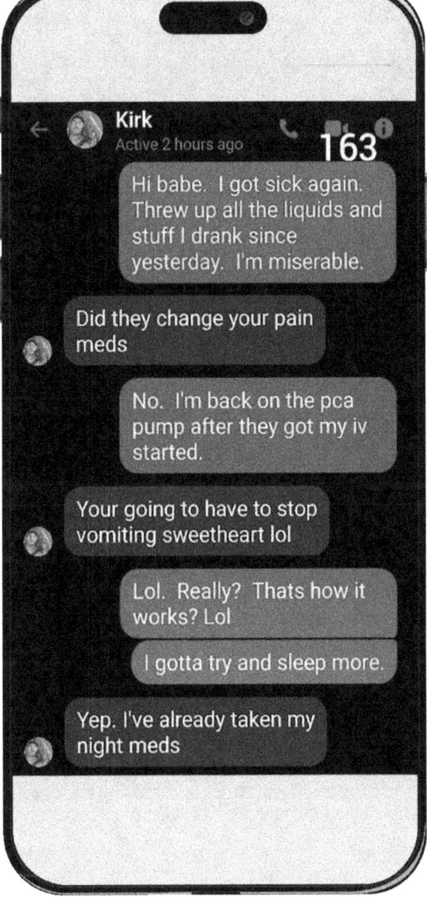
Kirk
Active 2 hours ago
163
Hi babe. I got sick again. Threw up all the liquids and stuff I drank since yesterday. I'm miserable.
Did they change your pain meds
No. I'm back on the pca pump after they got my iv started.
Your going to have to stop vomiting sweetheart lol
Lol. Really? Thats how it works? Lol
I gotta try and sleep more.
Yep. I've already taken my night meds

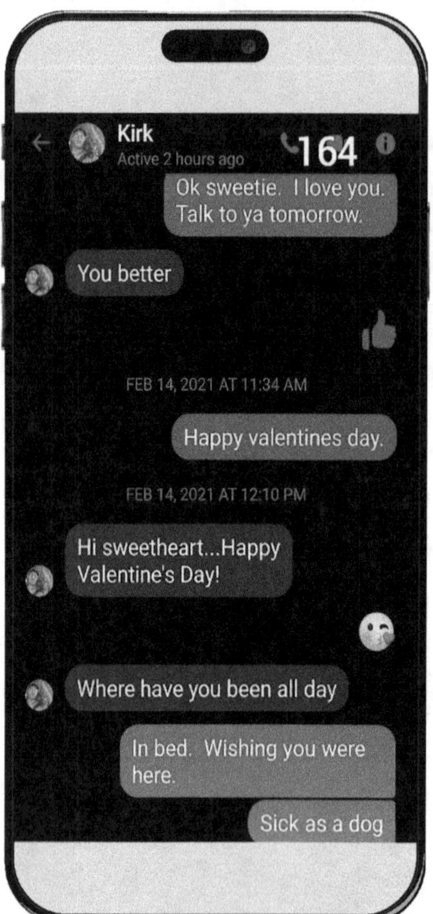

Kirk
Active 2 hours ago
164
Ok sweetie. I love you. Talk to ya tomorrow.
You better
FEB 14, 2021 AT 11:34 AM
Happy valentines day.
FEB 14, 2021 AT 12:10 PM
Hi sweetheart...Happy Valentine's Day!
Where have you been all day
In bed. Wishing you were here.
Sick as a dog

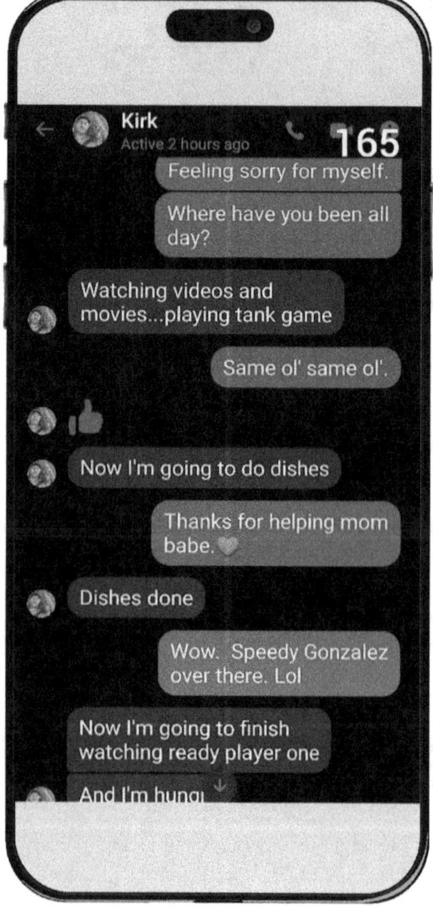

Kirk
Active 2 hours ago
165
Feeling sorry for myself.
Where have you been all day?
Watching videos and movies...playing tank game
Same ol' same ol'.
Now I'm going to do dishes
Thanks for helping mom babe.
Dishes done
Wow. Speedy Gonzalez over there. Lol
Now I'm going to finish watching ready player one
And I'm hungi

This is the start of a serious issue with Kim. Her being so nauseous and vomiting several times a day. She really couldn't hold anything down and was getting IV nutrition.

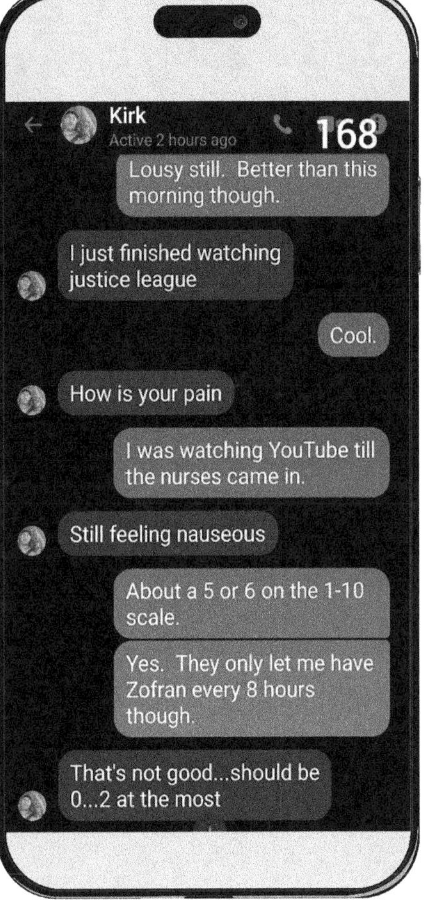

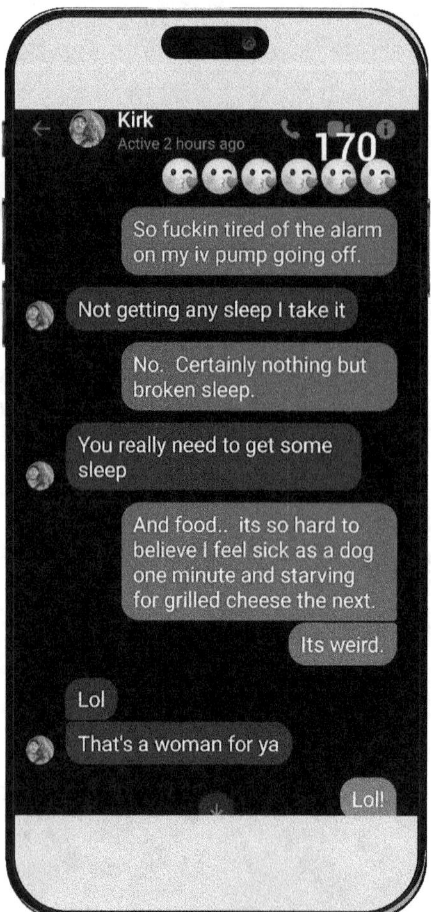

Kirk
Active 2 hours ago
170
So fuckin tired of the alarm on my iv pump going off.
Not getting any sleep I take it
No. Certainly nothing but broken sleep.
You really need to get some sleep
And food.. its so hard to believe I feel sick as a dog one minute and starving for grilled cheese the next.
Its weird.
Lol
That's a woman for ya
Lol!

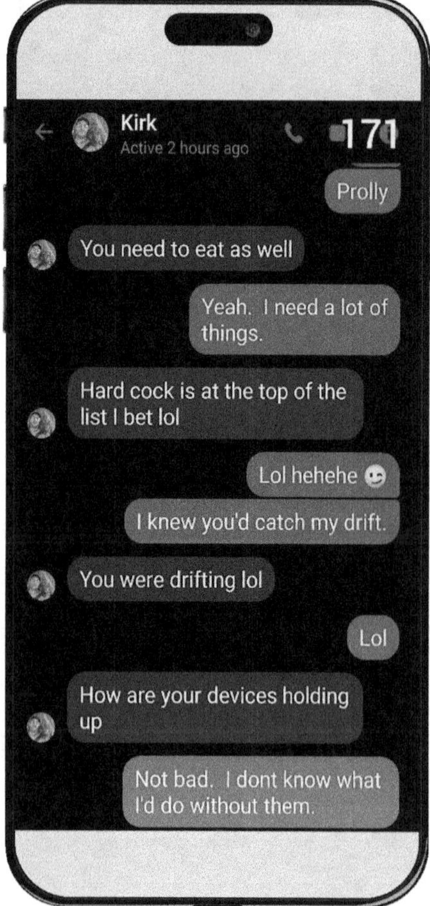

Kirk
Active 2 hours ago
171
Prolly
You need to eat as well
Yeah. I need a lot of things.
Hard cock is at the top of the list I bet lol
Lol hehehe
I knew you'd catch my drift.
You were drifting lol
Lol
How are your devices holding up
Not bad. I dont know what I'd do without them.

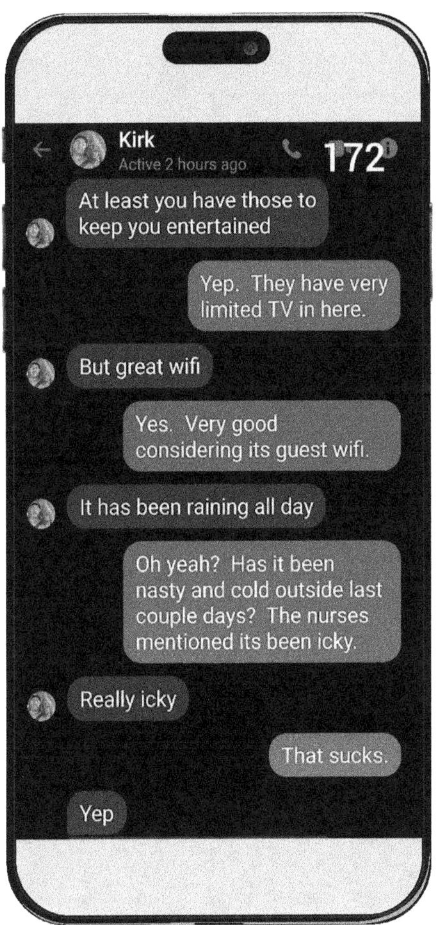
Kirk
Active 2 hours ago
172
At least you have those to keep you entertained
Yep. They have very limited TV in here.
But great wifi
Yes. Very good considering its guest wifi.
It has been raining all day
Oh yeah? Has it been nasty and cold outside last couple days? The nurses mentioned its been icky.
Really icky
That sucks.
Yep

Kirk
Active 2 hours ago
173
I'm going to take my night meds now and listen to the x22 report. I'll talk to you after to say good night
Ok babe. Talk to you later on.
FEB 14, 2021 AT 8:24 PM
You there
Yes
Just want to say good night
Ok. Goodnight sweetie.
Talk to you in the morning
Ok. Talk to ya then. Love you.
Shit...I have to let gunny out one last time

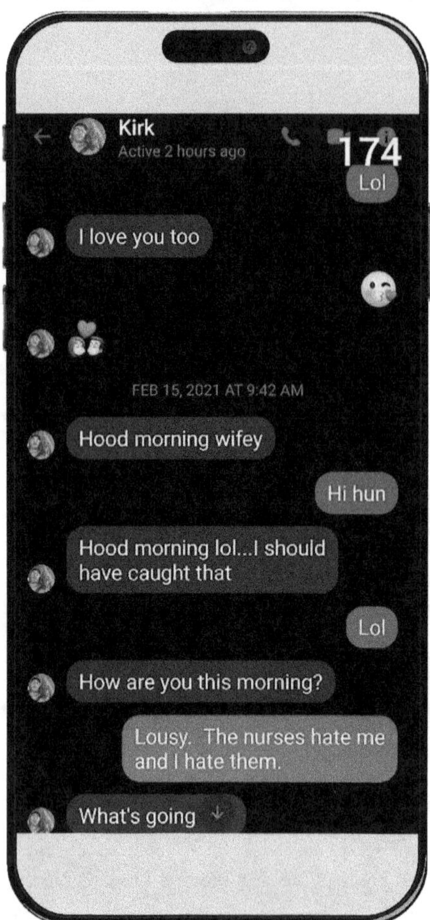

Kirk
Active 2 hours ago
174
Lol
I love you too
FEB 15, 2021 AT 9:42 AM
Hood morning wifey
Hi hun
Hood morning lol...I should have caught that
Lol
How are you this morning?
Lousy. The nurses hate me and I hate them.
What's going

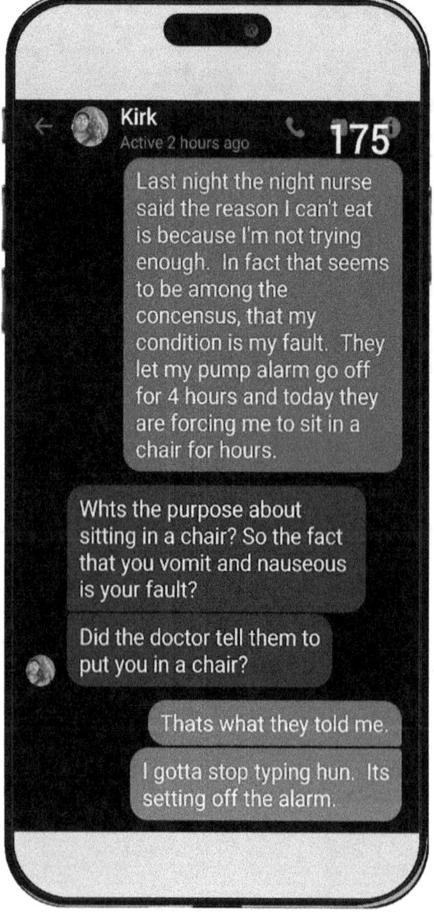

Kirk
Active 2 hours ago
175
Last night the night nurse said the reason I can't eat is because I'm not trying enough. In fact that seems to be among the concensus, that my condition is my fault. They let my pump alarm go off for 4 hours and today they are forcing me to sit in a chair for hours.
Whts the purpose about sitting in a chair? So the fact that you vomit and nauseous is your fault?
Did the doctor tell them to put you in a chair?
Thats what they told me.
I gotta stop typing hun. Its setting off the alarm.

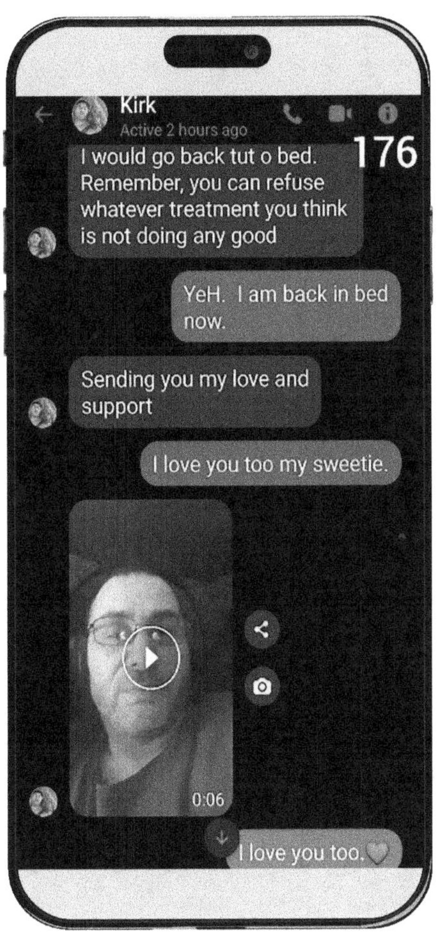

Kirk
Active 2 hours ago
176
I would go back tut o bed. Remember, you can refuse whatever treatment you think is not doing any good
YeH. I am back in bed now.
Sending you my love and support
I love you too my sweetie.
0:06
I love you too.

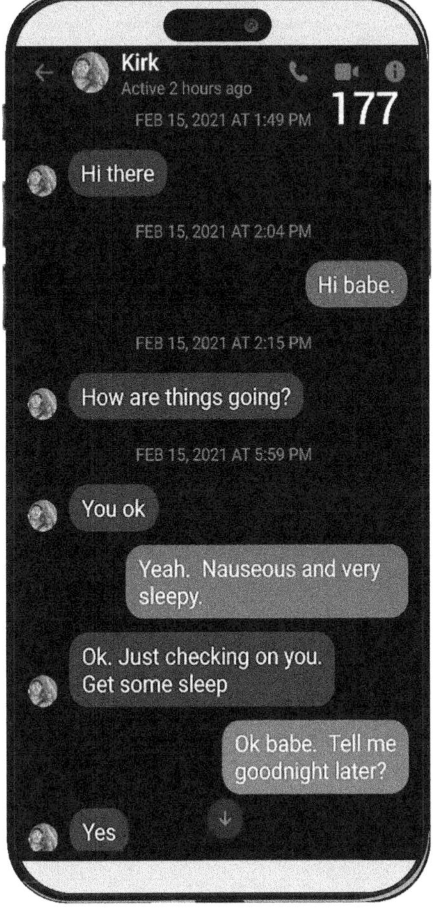

Kirk
Active 2 hours ago
177
FEB 15, 2021 AT 1:49 PM
Hi there
FEB 15, 2021 AT 2:04 PM
Hi babe.
FEB 15, 2021 AT 2:15 PM
How are things going?
FEB 15, 2021 AT 5:59 PM
You ok
Yeah. Nauseous and very sleepy.
Ok. Just checking on you. Get some sleep
Ok babe. Tell me goodnight later?
Yes

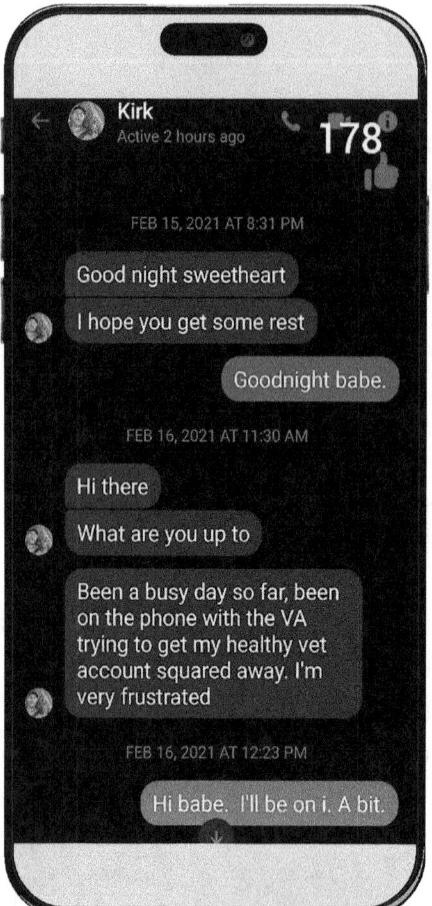
Kirk
Active 2 hours ago
178
FEB 15, 2021 AT 8:31 PM
Good night sweetheart
I hope you get some rest
Goodnight babe.
FEB 16, 2021 AT 11:30 AM
Hi there
What are you up to
Been a busy day so far, been on the phone with the VA trying to get my healthy vet account squared away. I'm very frustrated
FEB 16, 2021 AT 12:23 PM
Hi babe. I'll be on i. A bit.

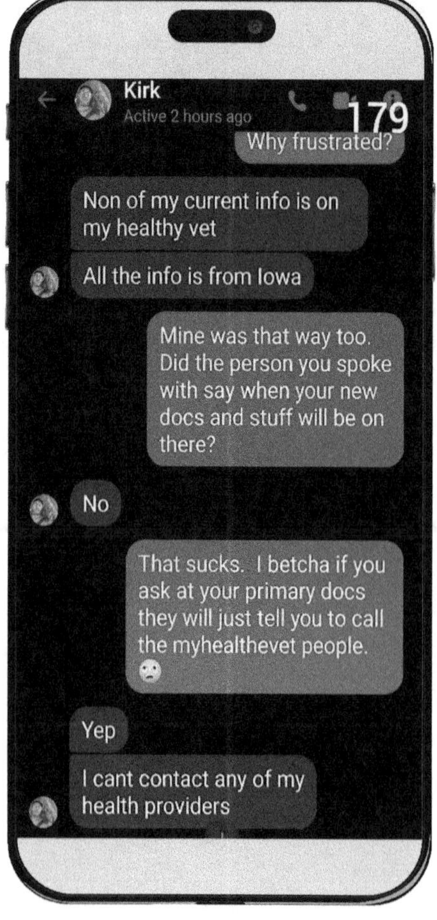
Kirk
Active 2 hours ago
179
Why frustrated?
Non of my current info is on my healthy vet
All the info is from Iowa
Mine was that way too. Did the person you spoke with say when your new docs and stuff will be on there?
No
That sucks. I betcha if you ask at your primary docs they will just tell you to call the myhealthevet people.
Yep
I cant contact any of my health providers

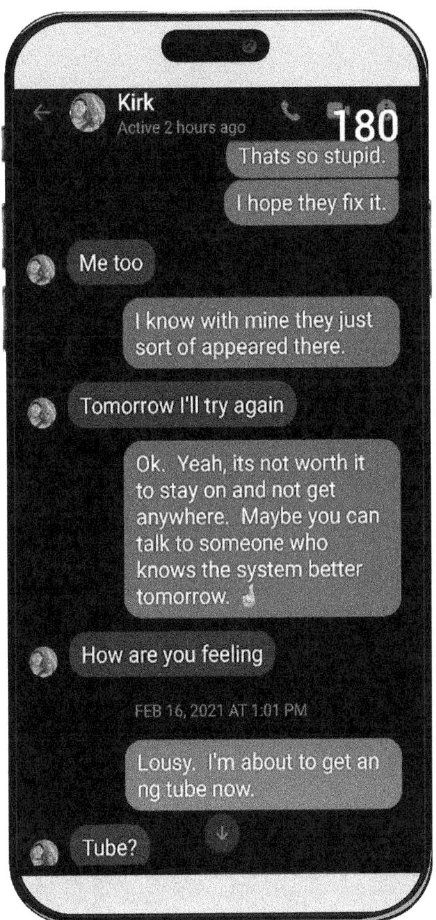

Kirk
Active 2 hours ago
180
Thats so stupid.
I hope they fix it.
Me too
I know with mine they just sort of appeared there.
Tomorrow I'll try again
Ok. Yeah, its not worth it to stay on and not get anywhere. Maybe you can talk to someone who knows the system better tomorrow.
How are you feeling
FEB 16, 2021 AT 1:01 PM
Lousy. I'm about to get an ng tube now.
Tube?

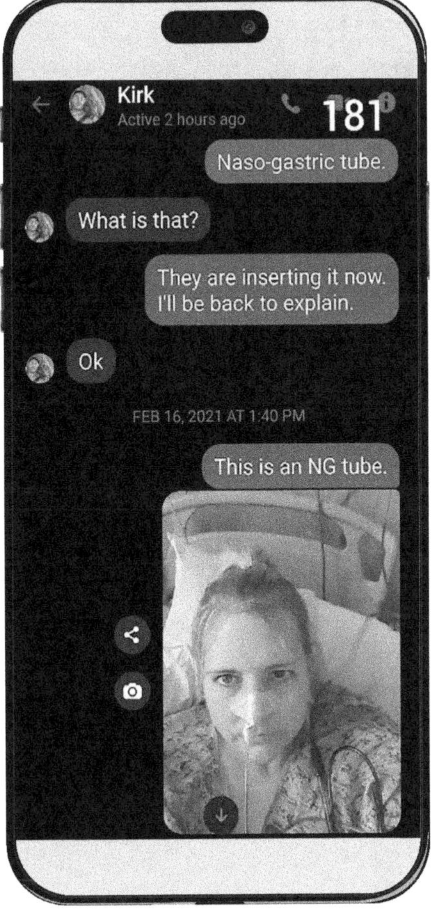

Kirk
Active 2 hours ago
181
Naso-gastric tube.
What is that?
They are inserting it now. I'll be back to explain.
Ok
FEB 16, 2021 AT 1:40 PM
This is an NG tube.

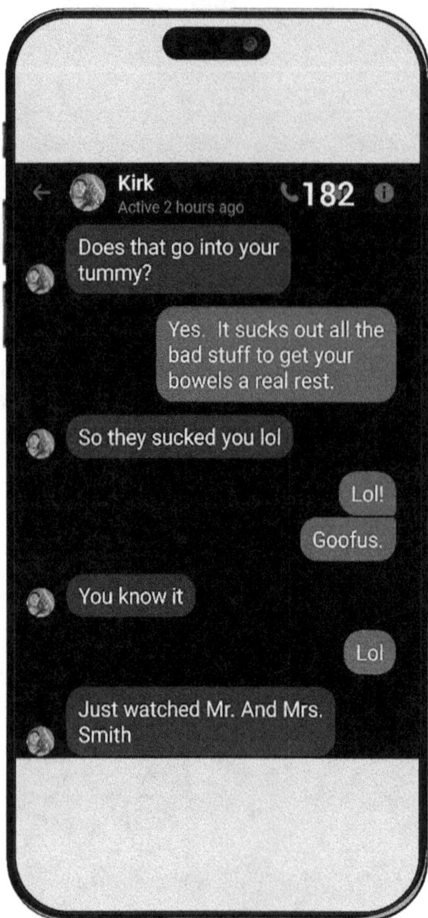

Kirk
Active 2 hours ago
182
Does that go into your tummy?
Yes. It sucks out all the bad stuff to get your bowels a real rest.
So they sucked you lol
Lol!
Goofus.
You know it
Lol
Just watched Mr. And Mrs. Smith

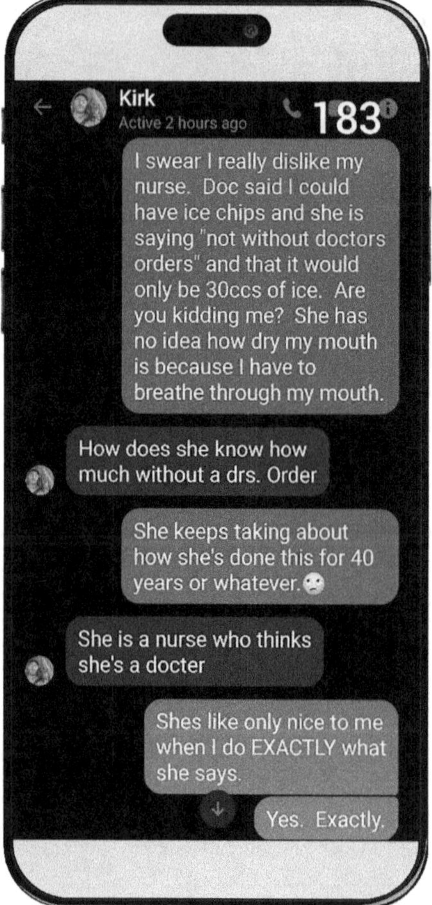

Kirk
Active 2 hours ago
183
I swear I really dislike my nurse. Doc said I could have ice chips and she is saying "not without doctors orders" and that it would only be 30ccs of ice. Are you kidding me? She has no idea how dry my mouth is because I have to breathe through my mouth.
How does she know how much without a drs. Order
She keeps taking about how she's done this for 40 years or whatever.
She is a nurse who thinks she's a docter
Shes like only nice to me when I do EXACTLY what she says.
Yes. Exactly.

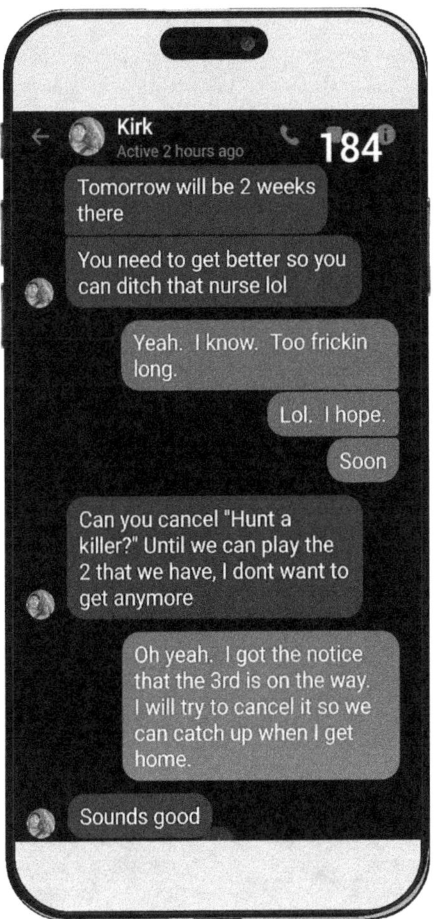

Kirk
Active 2 hours ago
184
Tomorrow will be 2 weeks there
You need to get better so you can ditch that nurse lol
Yeah. I know. Too frickin long.
Lol. I hope.
Soon
Can you cancel "Hunt a killer?" Until we can play the 2 that we have, I dont want to get anymore
Oh yeah. I got the notice that the 3rd is on the way. I will try to cancel it so we can catch up when I get home.
Sounds good

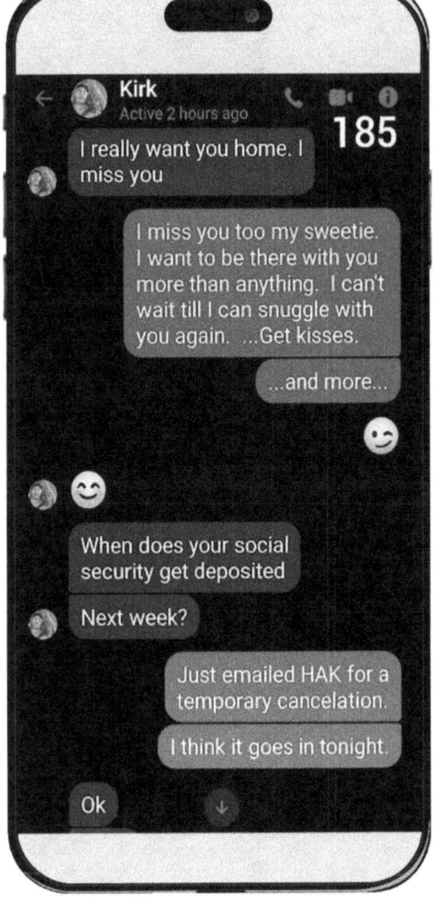

Kirk
Active 2 hours ago
185
I really want you home. I miss you
I miss you too my sweetie. I want to be there with you more than anything. I can't wait till I can snuggle with you again. ...Get kisses.
...and more...
When does your social security get deposited
Next week?
Just emailed HAK for a temporary cancelation.
I think it goes in tonight.
Ok

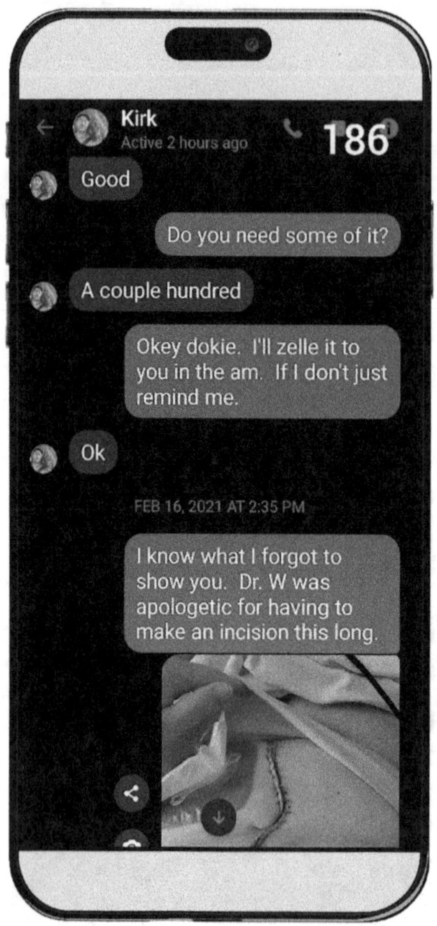

Kirk
Active 2 hours ago
186
Good
Do you need some of it?
A couple hundred
Okey dokie. I'll zelle it to you in the am. If I don't just remind me.
Ok
FEB 16, 2021 AT 2:35 PM
I know what I forgot to show you. Dr. W was apologetic for having to make an incision this long.

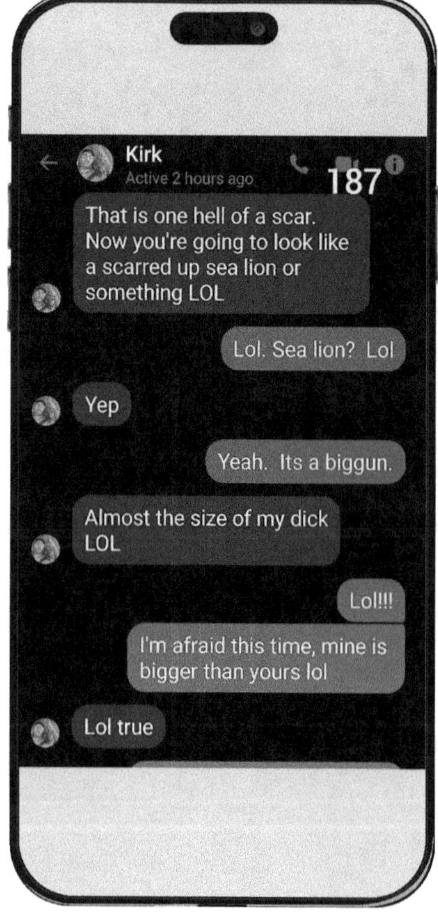

Kirk
Active 2 hours ago
187
That is one hell of a scar. Now you're going to look like a scarred up sea lion or something LOL
Lol. Sea lion? Lol
Yep
Yeah. Its a biggun.
Almost the size of my dick LOL
Lol!!!
I'm afraid this time, mine is bigger than yours lol
Lol true

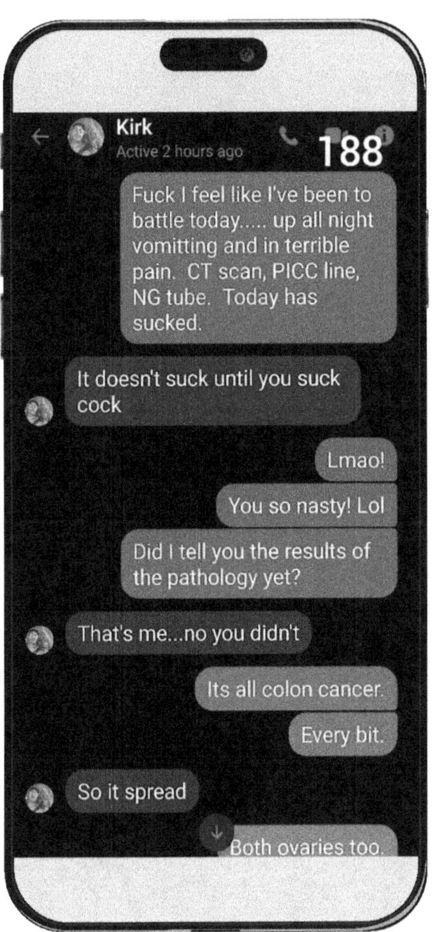

Kirk
Active 2 hours ago
188
Fuck I feel like I've been to battle today..... up all night vomitting and in terrible pain. CT scan, PICC line, NG tube. Today has sucked.
It doesn't suck until you suck cock
Lmao!
You so nasty! Lol
Did I tell you the results of the pathology yet?
That's me...no you didn't
Its all colon cancer.
Every bit.
So it spread
Both ovaries too.

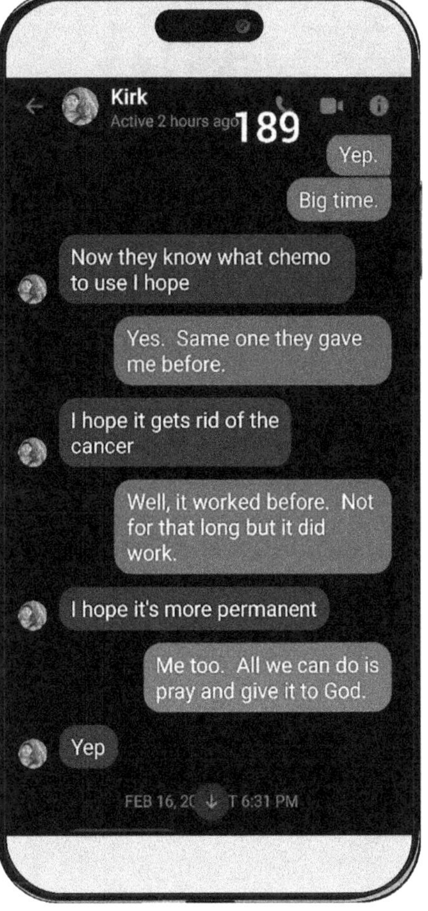

Kirk
Active 2 hours ago
189
Yep.
Big time.
Now they know what chemo to use I hope
Yes. Same one they gave me before.
I hope it gets rid of the cancer
Well, it worked before. Not for that long but it did work.
I hope it's more permanent
Me too. All we can do is pray and give it to God.
Yep
FEB 16, 20   T 6:31 PM

Kirk
Active 2 hours ago
FEB 16, 2021 AT 6:31 PM
190
You awake
FEB 16, 2021 AT 6:41 PM
Yes babe.
Are you?
Yep...warming dinner
Wow. Eating late tonight.
Heartburn is going to rage tonight
Awww.
I'll let you eat then hunni. Text me before you go to bed.
Ok.

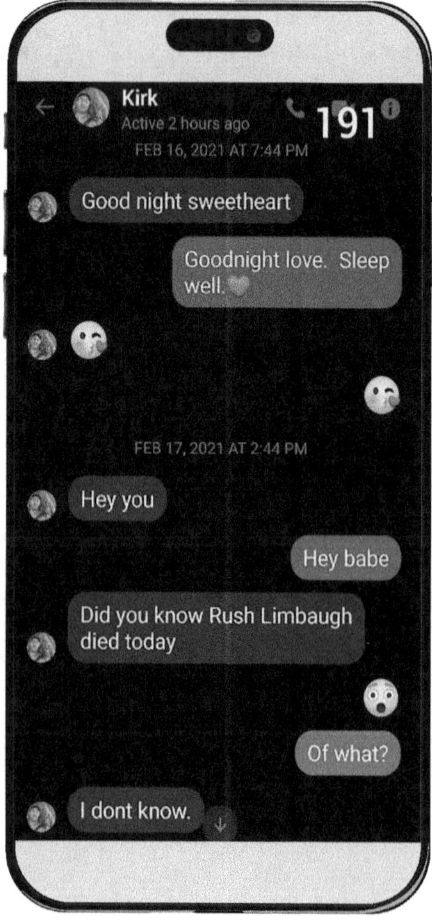
Kirk
Active 2 hours ago
FEB 16, 2021 AT 7:44 PM
191
Good night sweetheart
Goodnight love. Sleep well.
FEB 17, 2021 AT 2:44 PM
Hey you
Hey babe
Did you know Rush Limbaugh died today
Of what?
I dont know.

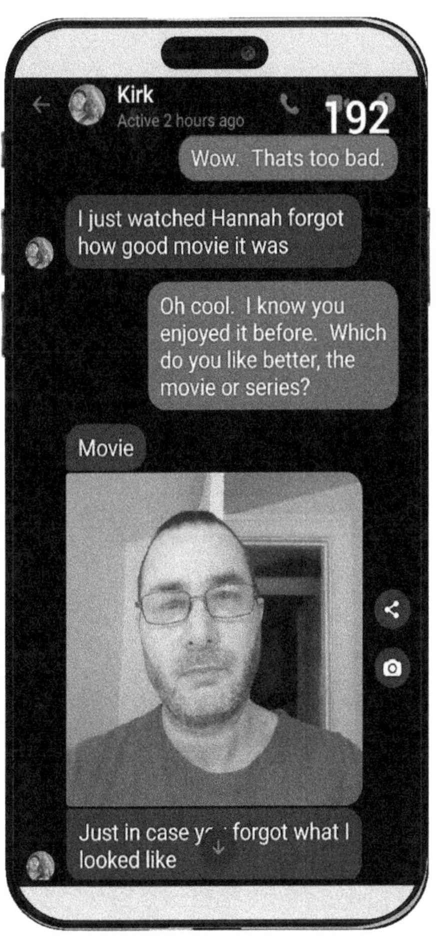

Kirk
Active 2 hours ago
192
Wow. Thats too bad.
I just watched Hannah forgot how good movie it was
Oh cool. I know you enjoyed it before. Which do you like better, the movie or series?
Movie
Just in case you forgot what I looked like

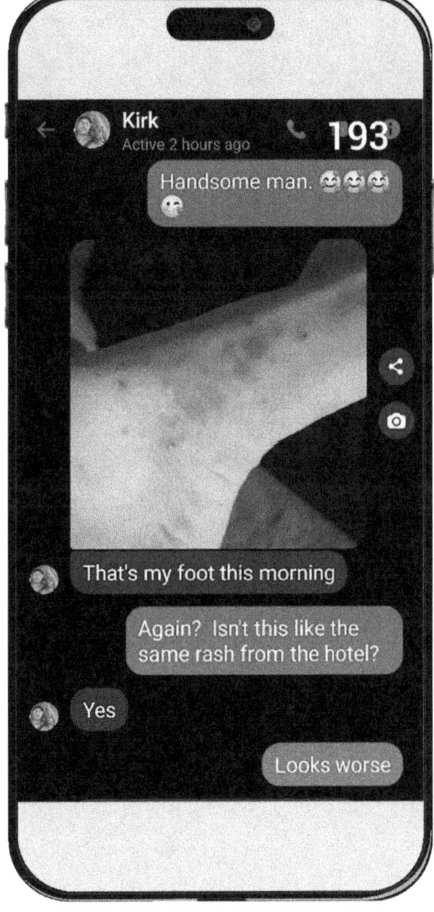

Kirk
Active 2 hours ago
193
Handsome man.
That's my foot this morning
Again? Isn't this like the same rash from the hotel?
Yes
Looks worse

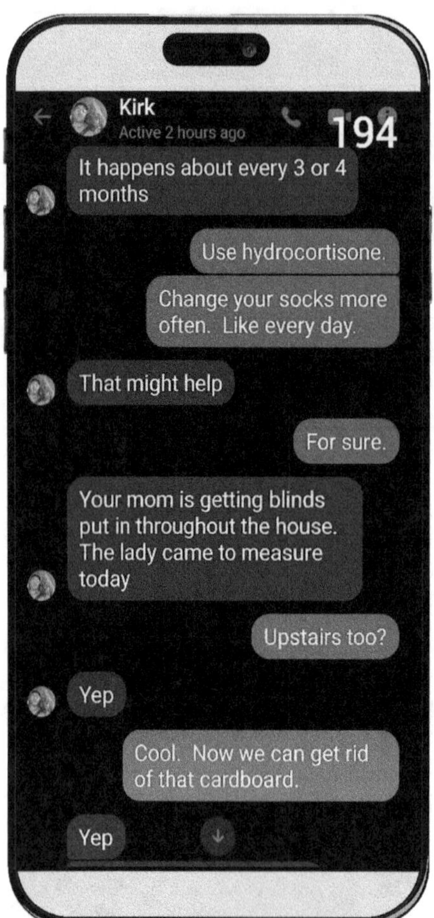
Kirk
Active 2 hours ago
194
It happens about every 3 or 4 months
Use hydrocortisone.
Change your socks more often. Like every day.
That might help
For sure.
Your mom is getting blinds put in throughout the house. The lady came to measure today
Upstairs too?
Yep
Cool. Now we can get rid of that cardboard.
Yep

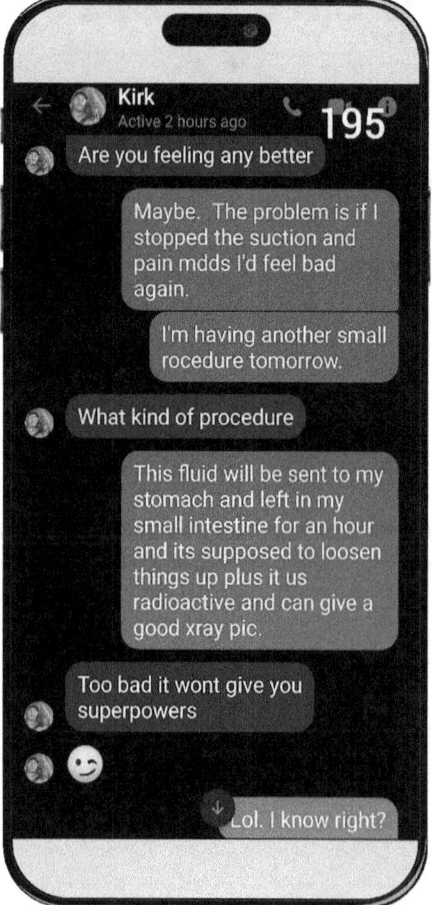
Kirk
Active 2 hours ago
195
Are you feeling any better
Maybe. The problem is if I stopped the suction and pain mdds I'd feel bad again.
I'm having another small rocedure tomorrow.
What kind of procedure
This fluid will be sent to my stomach and left in my small intestine for an hour and its supposed to loosen things up plus it us radioactive and can give a good xray pic.
Too bad it wont give you superpowers
Lol. I know right?

The reason Kim Laughed at my comment of getting hangry refers
to the time I was in the hospital to get my gall bladder removed
and I hadn't eaten in three days. I told the nurses that if they didn't get
me anything to eat, I was checking myself out of the hospital.
I complained for about two hours and realized things weren't going in
my favor. So, I had Kim order a pizza to have it delivered to the hospital.
When Kim was bringing up the pizza, the nurses asked her if she was
going to eat that in front of me? She replied that it was for me.
She then gave me the pizza and
I ate with no adverse reactions.
I ended up staying five days
in the hospital and me and Kim
no had a running joke about
how hangry I get.

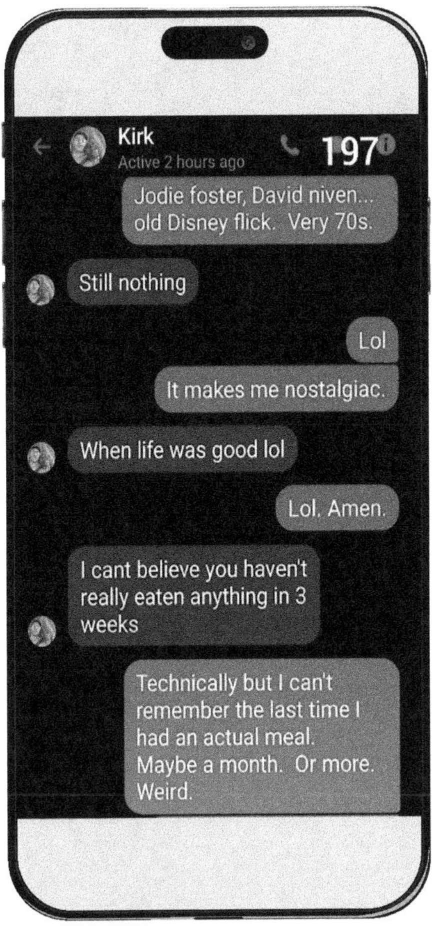

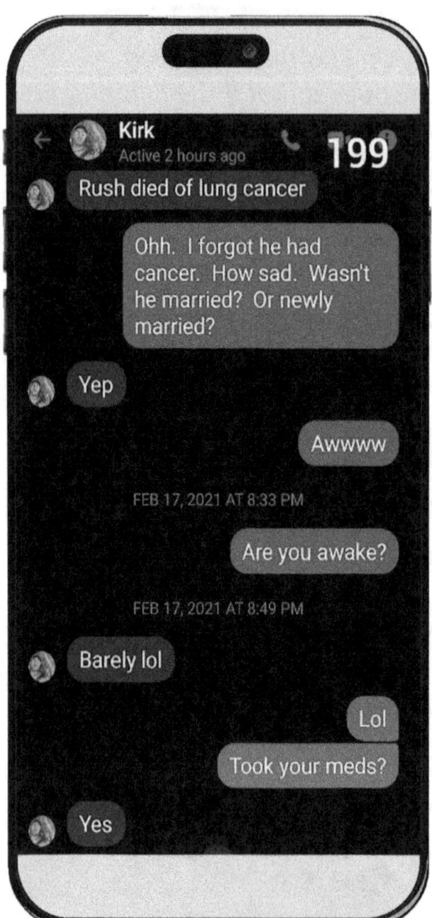

Kirk
Active 2 hours ago
199
Rush died of lung cancer
Ohh. I forgot he had cancer. How sad. Wasn't he married? Or newly married?
Yep
Awwww
FEB 17, 2021 AT 8:33 PM
Are you awake?
FEB 17, 2021 AT 8:49 PM
Barely lol
Lol
Took your meds?
Yes

Kirk
Active 2 hours ago
200
Ok sweetie. Its alright. I just wanted to say goodnight.
I love you.
I love you tooest
Lmao!
You're tooest funny. L I I
I'll talk to you tomorrow. Get some shut eye.
Good night night
FEB 18, 20   T 8:23 AM

Kirk
Active 2 hours ago
201
Have you been taking pills? Or no?
No biafra if that is what you mean
Biafra???
Lol
I don't have my glasses on LOL
Lol
Anyway. You better be ready as soon as I get home and am feeling better.
Biafra is the spanish version lol

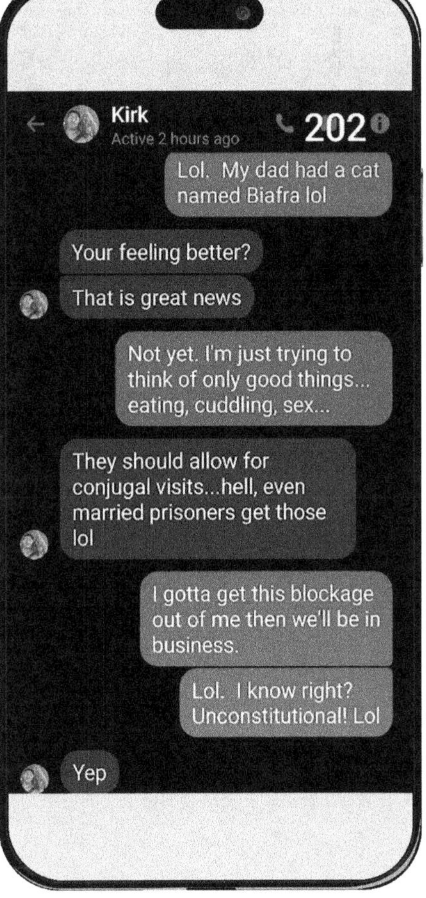
Kirk
Active 2 hours ago
202
Lol. My dad had a cat named Biafra lol
Your feeling better?
That is great news
Not yet. I'm just trying to think of only good things... eating, cuddling, sex...
They should allow for conjugal visits...hell, even married prisoners get those lol
I gotta get this blockage out of me then we'll be in business.
Lol. I know right? Unconstitutional! Lol
Yep

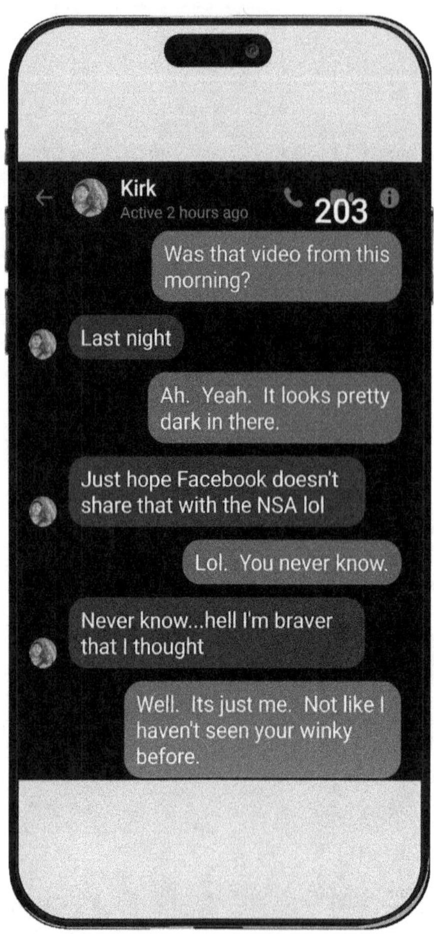
Kirk
Active 2 hours ago
203
Was that video from this morning?
Last night
Ah. Yeah. It looks pretty dark in there.
Just hope Facebook doesn't share that with the NSA lol
Lol. You never know.
Never know...hell I'm braver that I thought
Well. Its just me. Not like I haven't seen your winky before.

Kirk
Active 2 hours ago
204
Awww. Did he sleep in there?
He just stated doing that this week
Usually when I go and sit on the can

Kirk
Active 2 hours ago
205
Thats cute. I kinda can't believe he fits.
I think he does it because its cold
Cold in the shower?
On the other hand he goes and lays in front of the space heater
The floor is cold
Yeah. Theres that. I think he just wants to be close to you.
He loves me. But he has some attitude
You still doing that procedure today

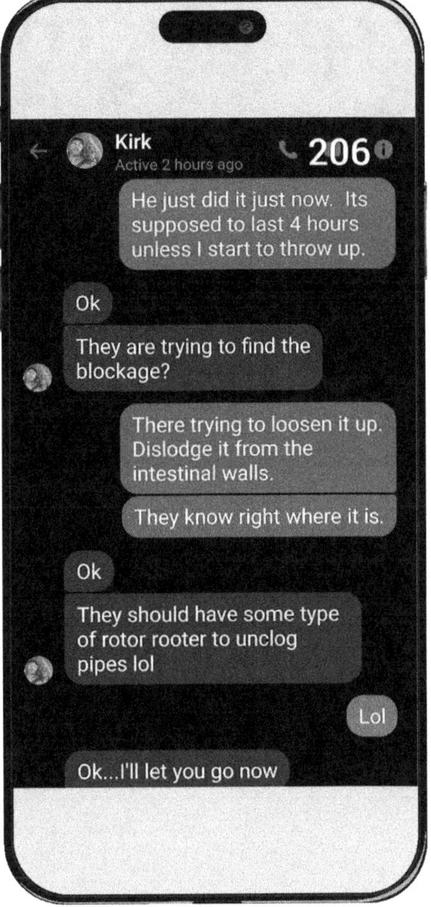

Kirk
Active 2 hours ago
206
He just did it just now. Its supposed to last 4 hours unless I start to throw up.
Ok
They are trying to find the blockage?
There trying to loosen it up. Dislodge it from the intestinal walls.
They know right where it is.
Ok
They should have some type of rotor rooter to unclog pipes lol
Lol
Ok...I'll let you go now

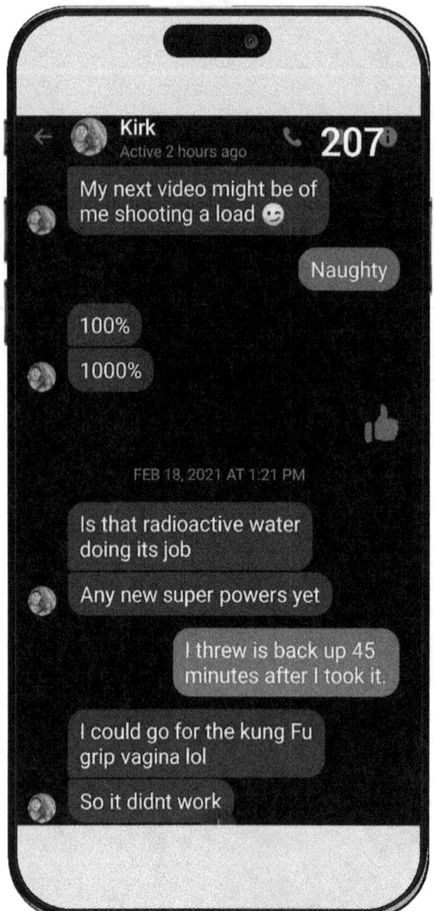
Kirk
Active 2 hours ago
207
My next video might be of me shooting a load
Naughty
100%
1000%
FEB 18, 2021 AT 1:21 PM
Is that radioactive water doing its job
Any new super powers yet
I threw is back up 45 minutes after I took it.
I could go for the kung Fu grip vagina lol
So it didnt work

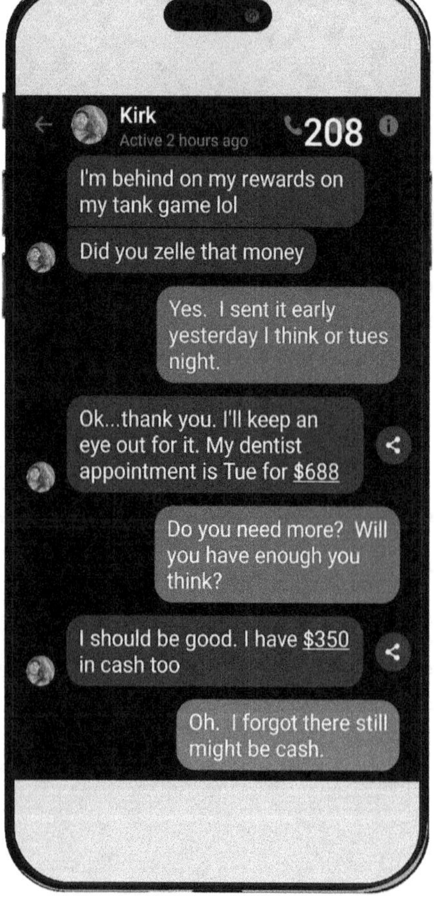
Kirk
Active 2 hours ago
208
I'm behind on my rewards on my tank game lol
Did you zelle that money
Yes. I sent it early yesterday I think or tues night.
Ok...thank you. I'll keep an eye out for it. My dentist appointment is Tue for $688
Do you need more? Will you have enough you think?
I should be good. I have $350 in cash too
Oh. I forgot there still might be cash.

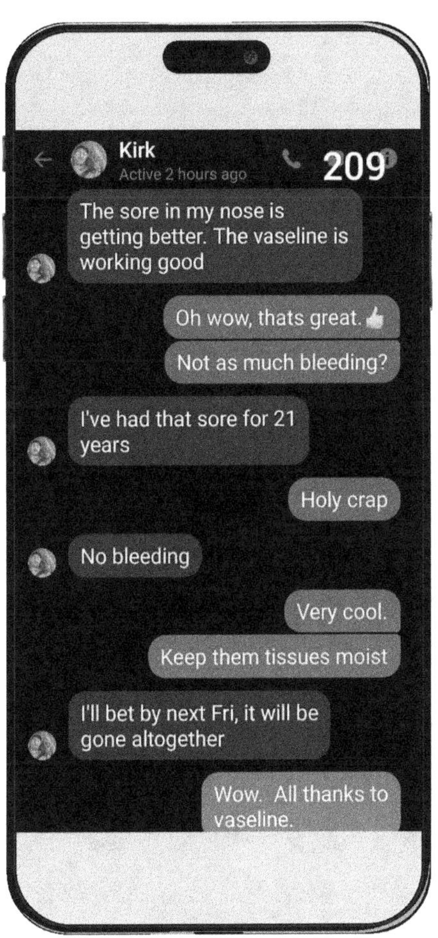
Kirk
Active 2 hours ago
209
The sore in my nose is getting better. The vaseline is working good
Oh wow, thats great. 👍
Not as much bleeding?
I've had that sore for 21 years
Holy crap
No bleeding
Very cool.
Keep them tissues moist
I'll bet by next Fri, it will be gone altogether
Wow. All thanks to vaseline.

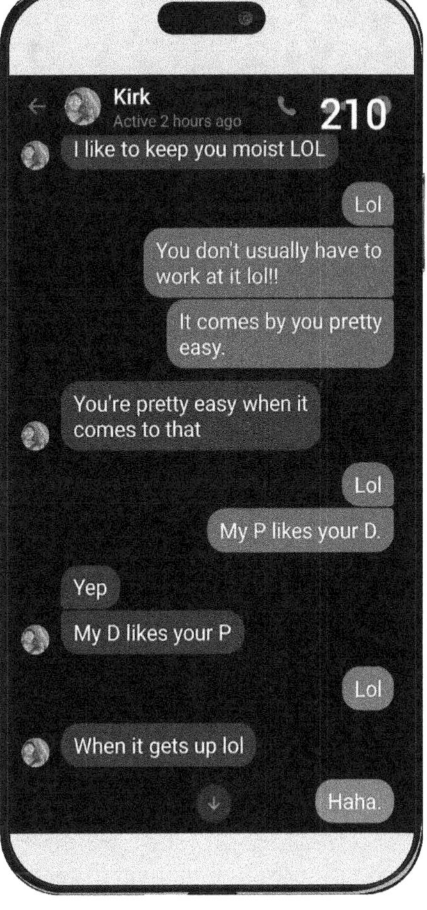
Kirk
Active 2 hours ago
210
I like to keep you moist LOL
Lol
You don't usually have to work at it lol!!
It comes by you pretty easy.
You're pretty easy when it comes to that
Lol
My P likes your D.
Yep
My D likes your P
Lol
When it gets up lol
Haha.

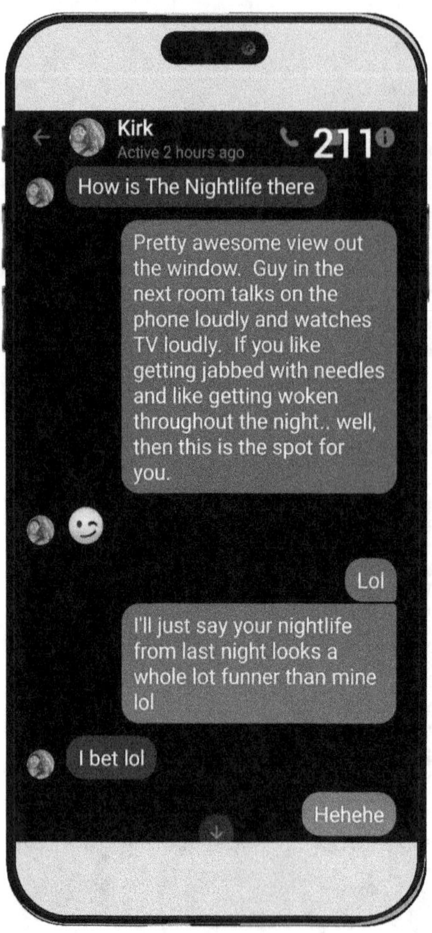
Kirk
Active 2 hours ago
211
How is The Nightlife there
Pretty awesome view out the window. Guy in the next room talks on the phone loudly and watches TV loudly. If you like getting jabbed with needles and like getting woken throughout the night.. well, then this is the spot for you.
Lol
I'll just say your nightlife from last night looks a whole lot funner than mine lol
I bet lol
Hehehe

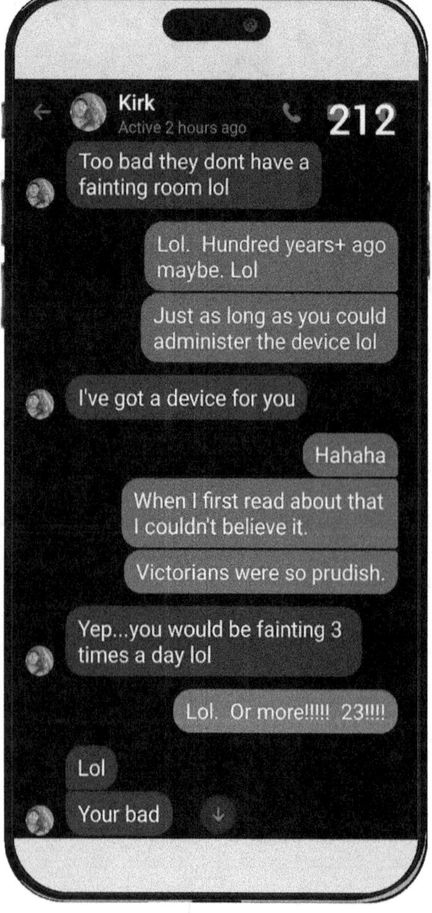
Kirk
Active 2 hours ago
212
Too bad they dont have a fainting room lol
Lol. Hundred years+ ago maybe. Lol
Just as long as you could administer the device lol
I've got a device for you
Hahaha
When I first read about that I couldn't believe it.
Victorians were so prudish.
Yep...you would be fainting 3 times a day lol
Lol. Or more!!!!! 23!!!!
Lol
Your bad

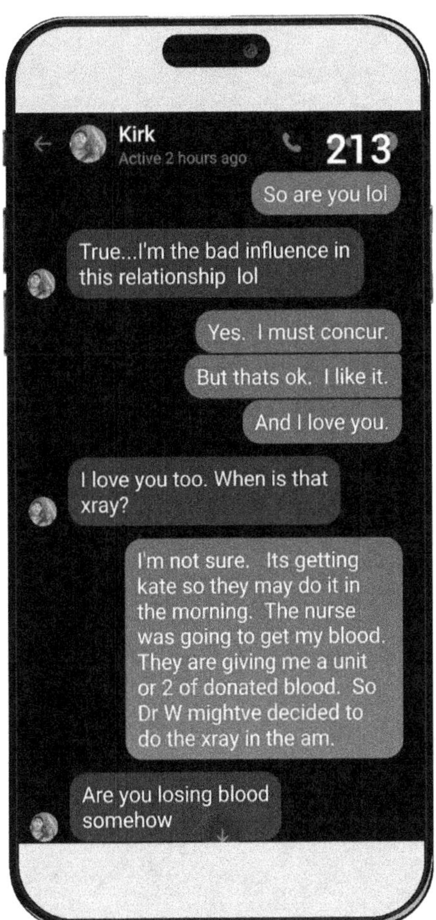

Kirk
Active 2 hours ago
213
So are you lol
True...I'm the bad influence in this relationship lol
Yes. I must concur.
But thats ok. I like it.
And I love you.
I love you too. When is that xray?
I'm not sure.   Its getting kate so they may do it in the morning. The nurse was going to get my blood. They are giving me a unit or 2 of donated blood. So Dr W mightve decided to do the xray in the am.
Are you losing blood somehow

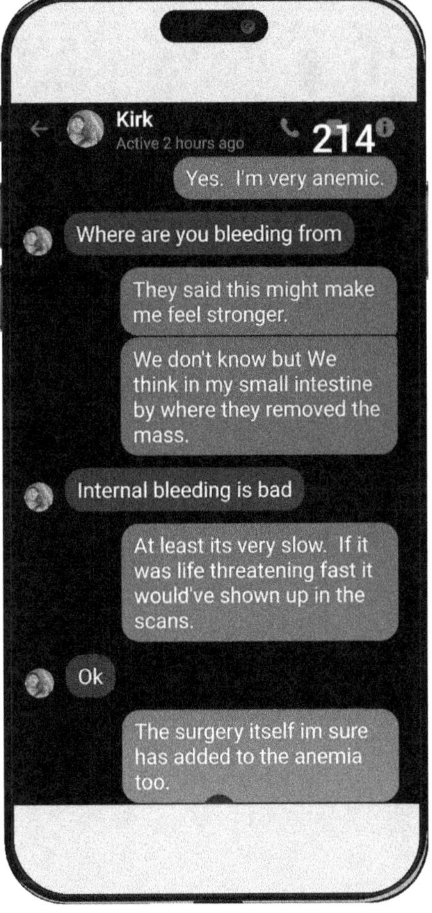

Kirk
Active 2 hours ago
214
Yes. I'm very anemic.
Where are you bleeding from
They said this might make me feel stronger.
We don't know but We think in my small intestine by where they removed the mass.
Internal bleeding is bad
At least its very slow. If it was life threatening fast it would've shown up in the scans.
Ok
The surgery itself im sure has added to the anemia too.

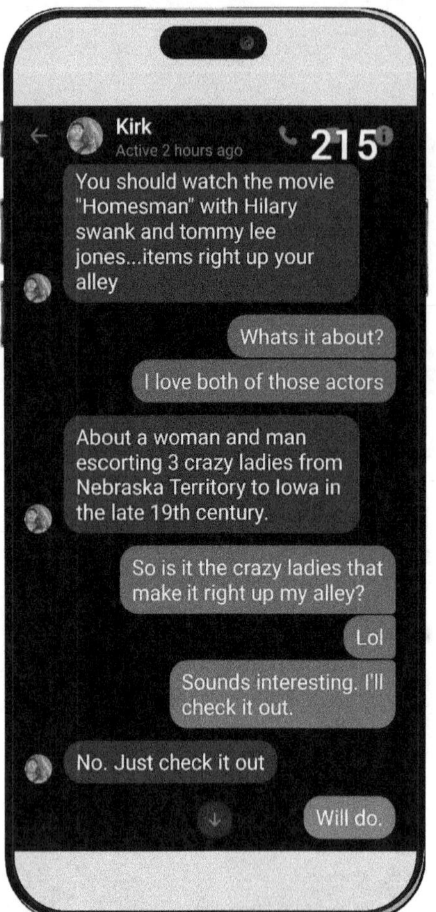
Kirk
Active 2 hours ago
215
You should watch the movie "Homesman" with Hilary swank and tommy lee jones...items right up your alley
Whats it about?
I love both of those actors
About a woman and man escorting 3 crazy ladies from Nebraska Territory to Iowa in the late 19th century.
So is it the crazy ladies that make it right up my alley?
Lol
Sounds interesting. I'll check it out.
No. Just check it out
Will do.

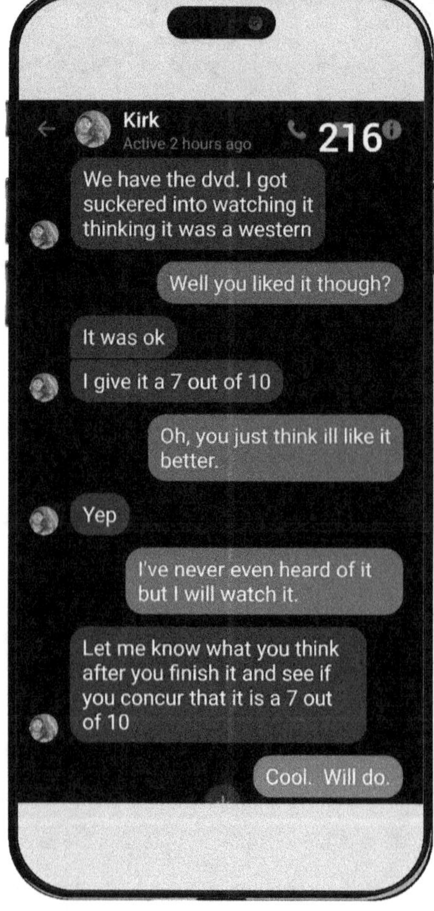
Kirk
Active 2 hours ago
216
We have the dvd. I got suckered into watching it thinking it was a western
Well you liked it though?
It was ok
I give it a 7 out of 10
Oh, you just think ill like it better.
Yep
I've never even heard of it but I will watch it.
Let me know what you think after you finish it and see if you concur that it is a 7 out of 10
Cool. Will do.

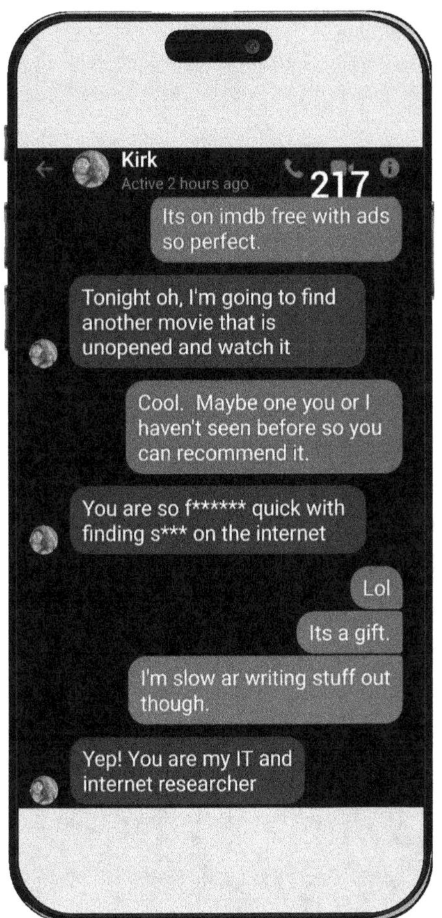
Kirk
Active 2 hours ago
217
Its on imdb free with ads so perfect.
Tonight oh, I'm going to find another movie that is unopened and watch it
Cool. Maybe one you or I haven't seen before so you can recommend it.
You are so f****** quick with finding s*** on the internet
Lol
Its a gift.
I'm slow ar writing stuff out though.
Yep! You are my IT and internet researcher

Kirk
Active 2 hours ago
218
Lol. Pretty much.
I'm going to try and get caught up I'm getting the rewards on my tank game. I'll talk to you in a couple hours.
Ok babe. Good luck on the game! Talk to ya soon.
FEB 18, 2021 AT 5:56 PM
Hey you
Hey ya
Are you going to watch that movie tonight

Kirk
Active 2 hours ago
219
I started it but kept getting interrupted. I will be finishing it up later tonight.
You already started it? How far did you get?
Where she took off to get them.
Ok. James Spader is in it too
Really?
To
Yep...he plays and asshole in it
That part in the beginning where she's begging that guy to marry her is cringey.

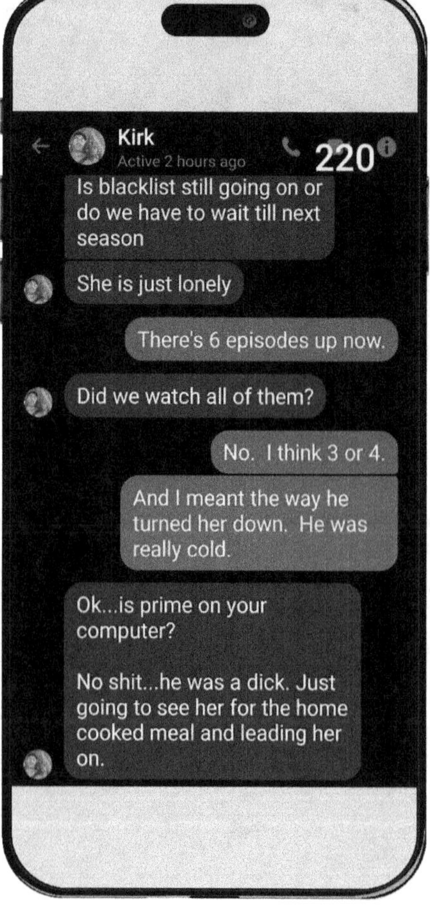
Kirk
Active 2 hours ago
220
Is blacklist still going on or do we have to wait till next season
She is just lonely
There's 6 episodes up now.
Did we watch all of them?
No. I think 3 or 4.
And I meant the way he turned her down. He was really cold.
Ok...is prime on your computer?
No shit...he was a dick. Just going to see her for the home cooked meal and leading her on.

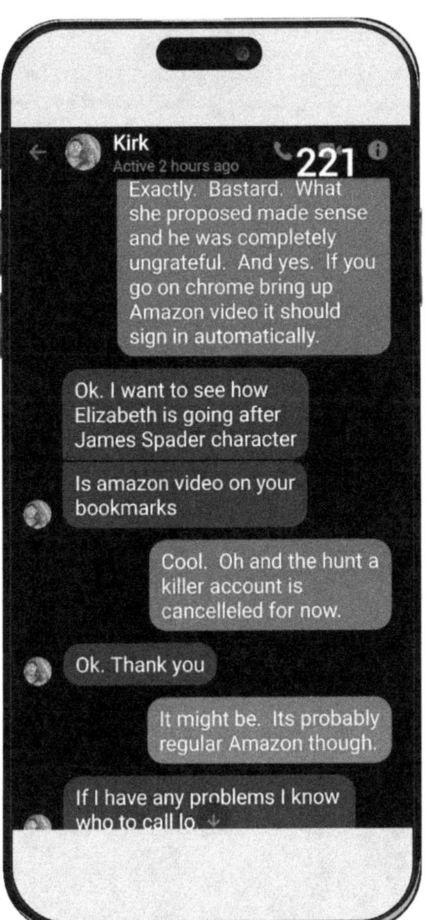
Kirk
Active 2 hours ago
221
Exactly. Bastard. What she proposed made sense and he was completely ungrateful. And yes. If you go on chrome bring up Amazon video it should sign in automatically.
Ok. I want to see how Elizabeth is going after James Spader character
Is amazon video on your bookmarks
Cool. Oh and the hunt a killer account is cancelleled for now.
Ok. Thank you
It might be. Its probably regular Amazon though.
If I have any problems I know who to call lo.

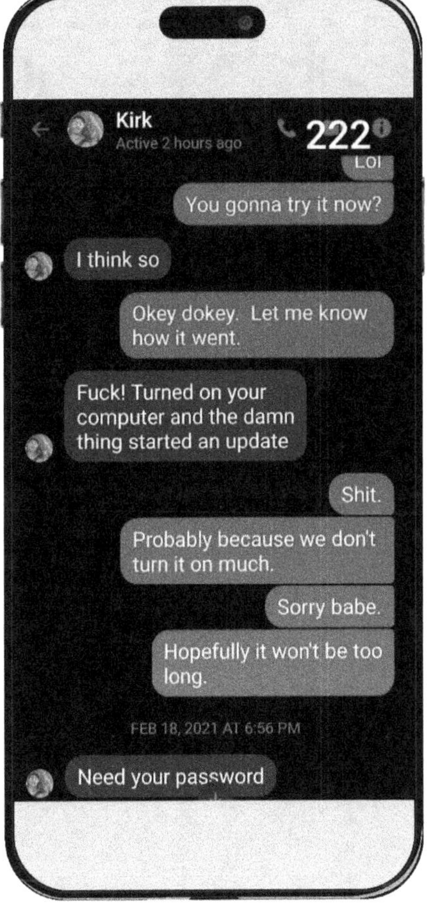
Kirk
Active 2 hours ago
222
Lol
You gonna try it now?
I think so
Okey dokey. Let me know how it went.
Fuck! Turned on your computer and the damn thing started an update
Shit.
Probably because we don't turn it on much.
Sorry babe.
Hopefully it won't be too long.
FEB 18, 2021 AT 6:56 PM
Need your password

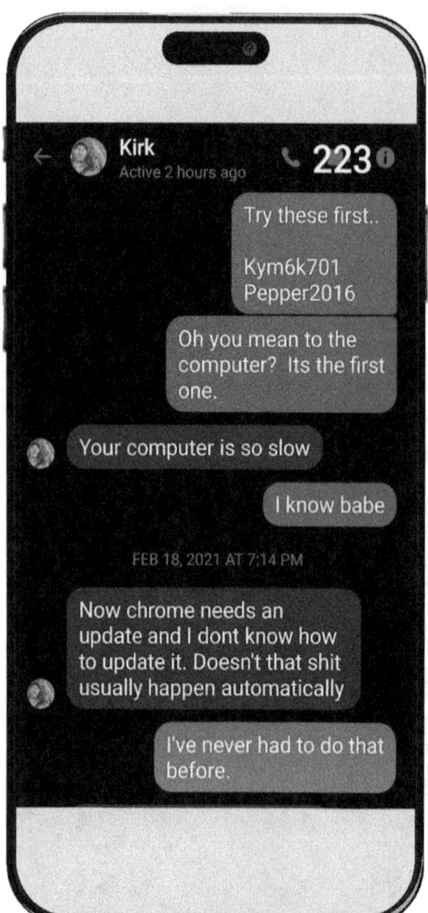
Kirk
Active 2 hours ago
223
Try these first..
Kym6k701
Pepper2016
Oh you mean to the computer? Its the first one.
Your computer is so slow
I know babe
FEB 18, 2021 AT 7:14 PM
Now chrome needs an update and I dont know how to update it. Doesn't that shit usually happen automatically
I've never had to do that before.

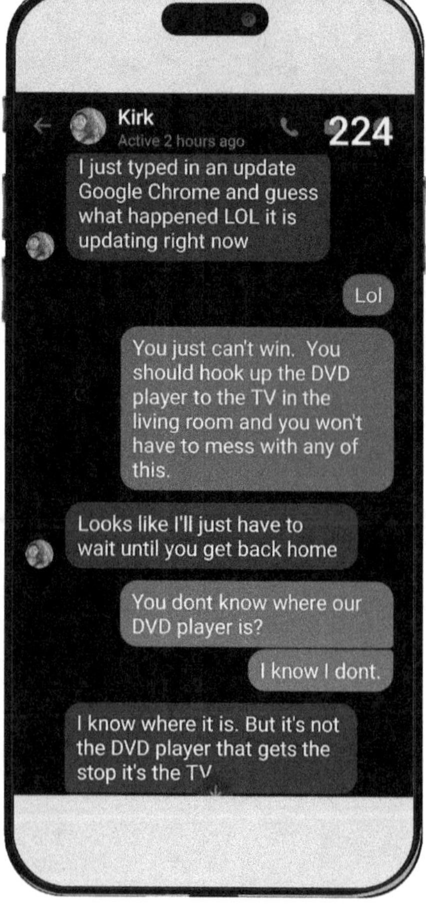
Kirk
Active 2 hours ago
224
I just typed in an update Google Chrome and guess what happened LOL it is updating right now
Lol
You just can't win. You should hook up the DVD player to the TV in the living room and you won't have to mess with any of this.
Looks like I'll just have to wait until you get back home
You dont know where our DVD player is?
I know I dont.
I know where it is. But it's not the DVD player that gets the stop it's the TV

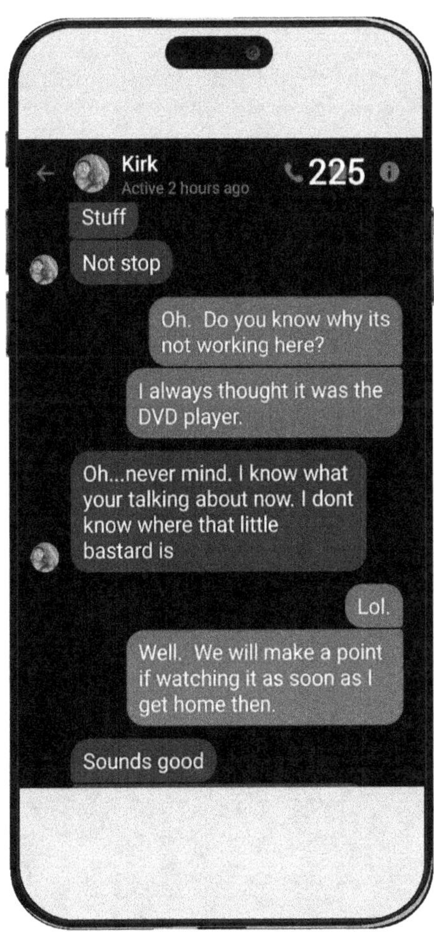

Kirk
Active 2 hours ago
225
Stuff
Not stop
Oh. Do you know why its not working here?
I always thought it was the DVD player.
Oh...never mind. I know what your talking about now. I dont know where that little bastard is
Lol.
Well. We will make a point if watching it as soon as I get home then.
Sounds good

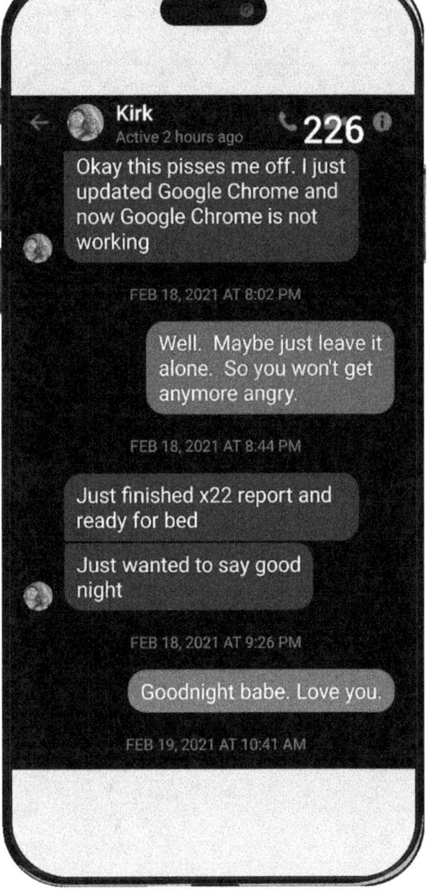

Kirk
Active 2 hours ago
226
Okay this pisses me off. I just updated Google Chrome and now Google Chrome is not working
FEB 18, 2021 AT 8:02 PM
Well. Maybe just leave it alone. So you won't get anymore angry.
FEB 18, 2021 AT 8:44 PM
Just finished x22 report and ready for bed
Just wanted to say good night
FEB 18, 2021 AT 9:26 PM
Goodnight babe. Love you.
FEB 19, 2021 AT 10:41 AM

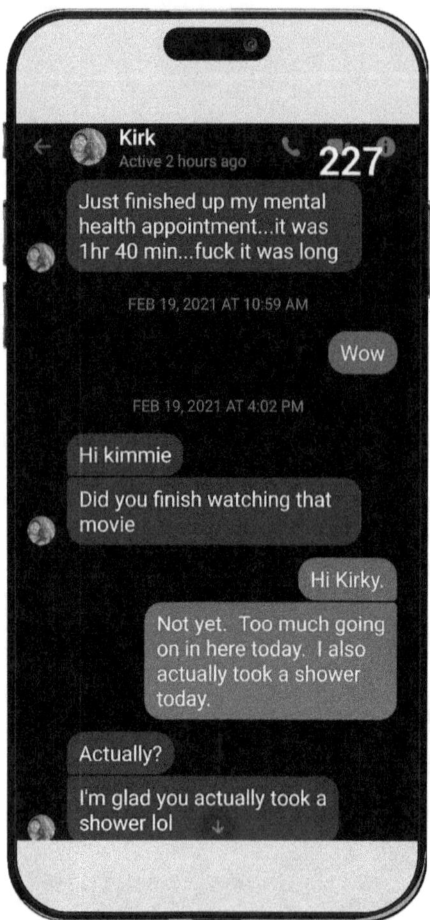
Kirk
Active 2 hours ago
227
Just finished up my mental health appointment...it was 1hr 40 min...fuck it was long
FEB 19, 2021 AT 10:59 AM
Wow
FEB 19, 2021 AT 4:02 PM
Hi kimmie
Did you finish watching that movie
Hi Kirky.
Not yet. Too much going on in here today. I also actually took a shower today.
Actually?
I'm glad you actually took a shower lol

Kirk
Active 2 hours ago
228
They've been giving me sponge baths but I actually took a real shower today.
Good. How are you feeling
What's up with that blockage
Sore, as usual. Tired, as usual.

Dr W said everything looks fine but my potassium dropped way off again.
WTF are you doing with your potassium lol
Selling it on the black market babe.
Lol
I thought so

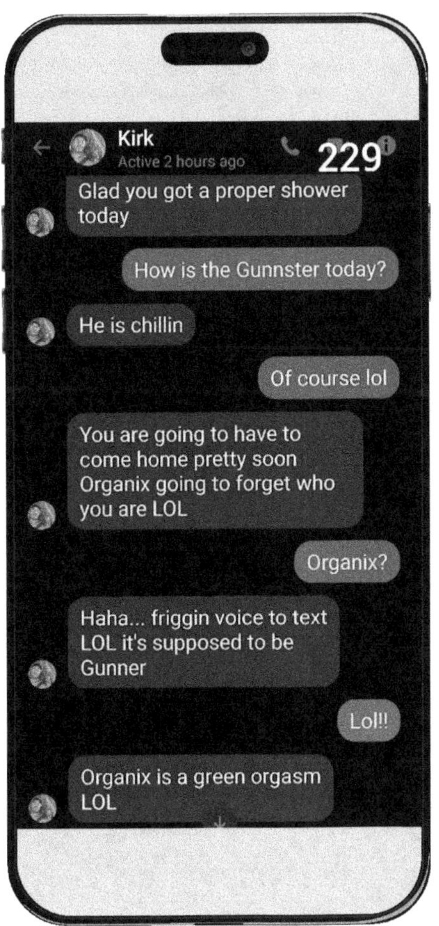
Kirk
Active 2 hours ago
229
Glad you got a proper shower today
How is the Gunnster today?
He is chillin
Of course lol
You are going to have to come home pretty soon Organix going to forget who you are LOL
Organix?
Haha... friggin voice to text LOL it's supposed to be Gunner
Lol!!
Organix is a green orgasm LOL

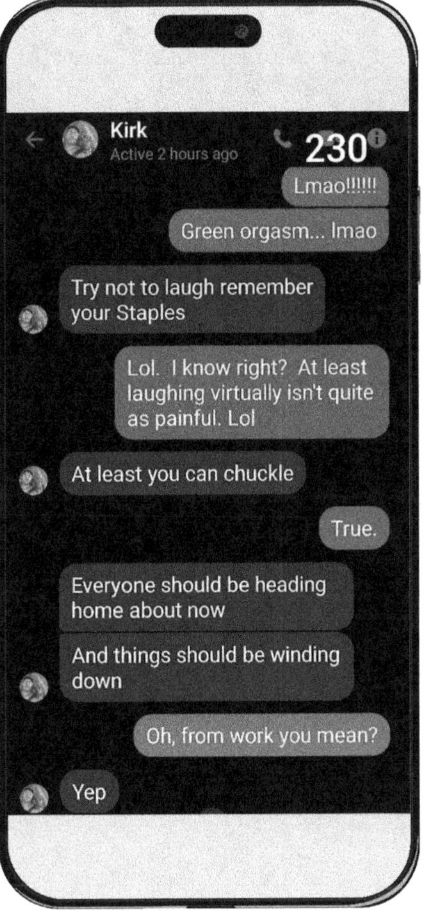
Kirk
Active 2 hours ago
230
Lmao!!!!!!
Green orgasm... lmao
Try not to laugh remember your Staples
Lol. I know right? At least laughing virtually isn't quite as painful. Lol
At least you can chuckle
True.
Everyone should be heading home about now
And things should be winding down
Oh, from work you mean?
Yep

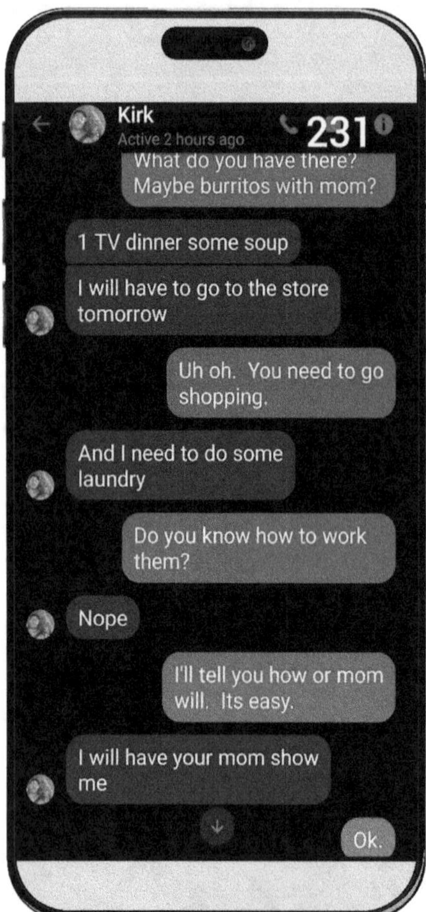

Kirk
Active 2 hours ago
231
What do you have there? Maybe burritos with mom?
1 TV dinner some soup
I will have to go to the store tomorrow
Uh oh. You need to go shopping.
And I need to do some laundry
Do you know how to work them?
Nope
I'll tell you how or mom will. Its easy.
I will have your mom show me
Ok.

Kirk
Active 2 hours ago
232
I am going to let you go we'll talk later okey dokey Stokey
FEB 19, 2021 AT 7:20 PM
Hey there! Did you watch the movie
Love you sweetheart
FEB 19, 2021 AT 8:10 PM
Love you hunni. Sorry I was sleeping.
Its ok
You getting ready for bed?
Yep
X22 report?
Yes lol

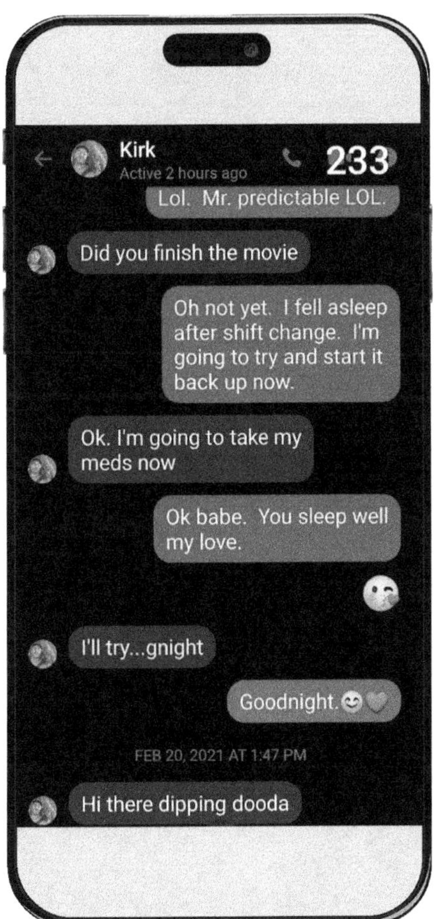
Kirk
Active 2 hours ago
233
Lol. Mr. predictable LOL.
Did you finish the movie
Oh not yet. I fell asleep after shift change. I'm going to try and start it back up now.
Ok. I'm going to take my meds now
Ok babe. You sleep well my love.
I'll try...gnight
Goodnight.
FEB 20, 2021 AT 1:47 PM
Hi there dipping dooda

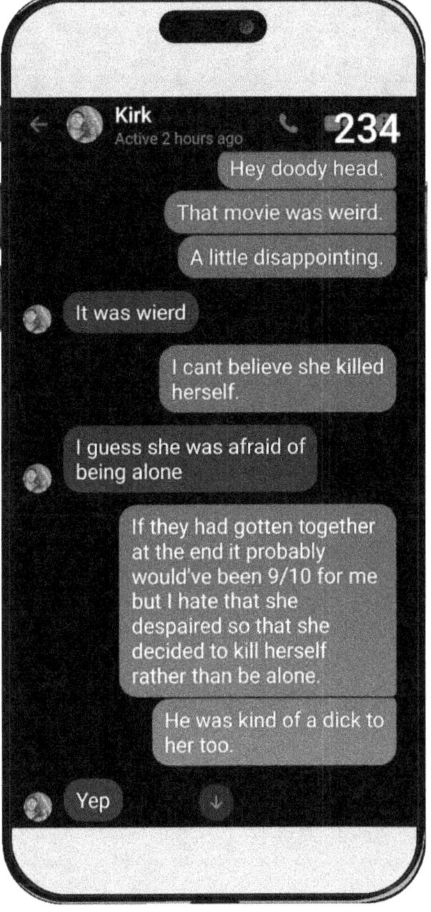
Kirk
Active 2 hours ago
234
Hey doody head.
That movie was weird.
A little disappointing.
It was wierd
I cant believe she killed herself.
I guess she was afraid of being alone
If they had gotten together at the end it probably would've been 9/10 for me but I hate that she despaired so that she decided to kill herself rather than be alone.
He was kind of a dick to her too.
Yep

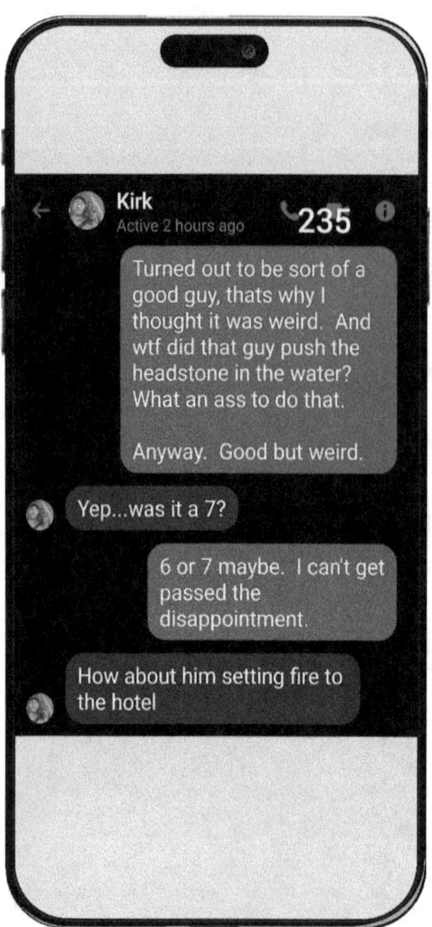
Kirk
Active 2 hours ago
235
Turned out to be sort of a good guy, thats why I thought it was weird. And wtf did that guy push the headstone in the water? What an ass to do that.
Anyway. Good but weird.
Yep...was it a 7?
6 or 7 maybe. I can't get passed the disappointment.
How about him setting fire to the hotel

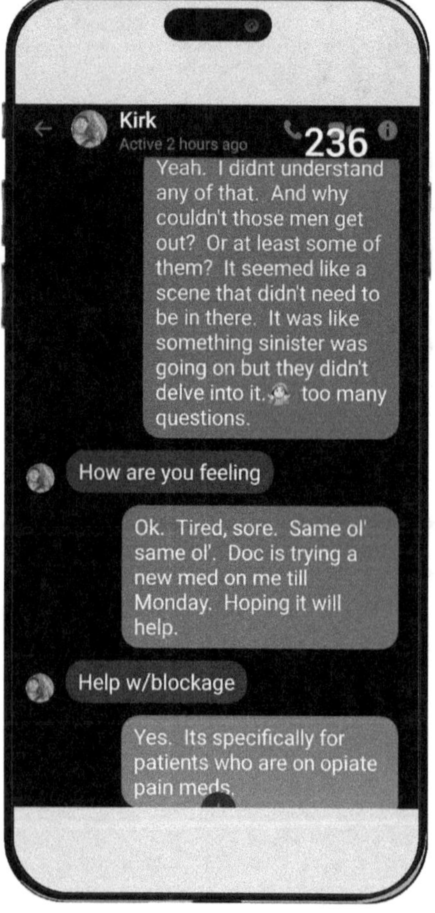
Kirk
Active 2 hours ago
236
Yeah. I didnt understand any of that. And why couldn't those men get out? Or at least some of them? It seemed like a scene that didn't need to be in there. It was like something sinister was going on but they didn't delve into it. too many questions.
How are you feeling
Ok. Tired, sore. Same ol' same ol'. Doc is trying a new med on me till Monday. Hoping it will help.
Help w/blockage
Yes. Its specifically for patients who are on opiate pain meds.

I did not skip text #237.
I misnumbered the text message

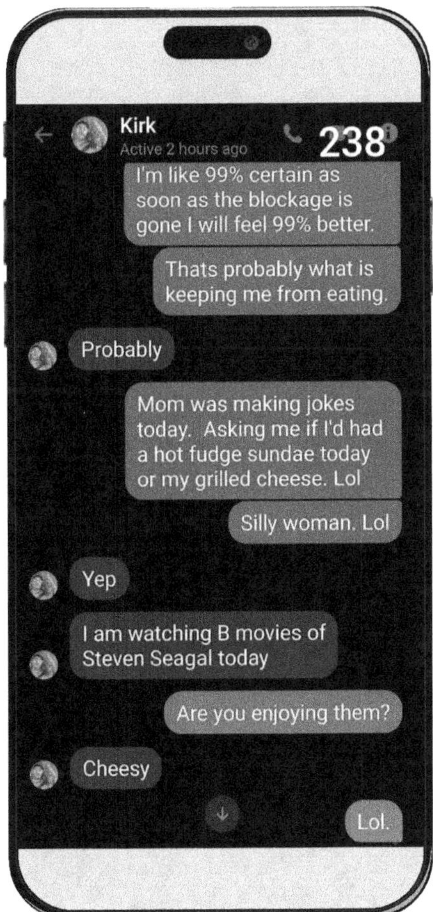

Kirk
Active 2 hours ago
238
I'm like 99% certain as soon as the blockage is gone I will feel 99% better.
Thats probably what is keeping me from eating.
Probably
Mom was making jokes today. Asking me if I'd had a hot fudge sundae today or my grilled cheese. Lol
Silly woman. Lol
Yep
I am watching B movies of Steven Seagal today
Are you enjoying them?
Cheesy
Lol.

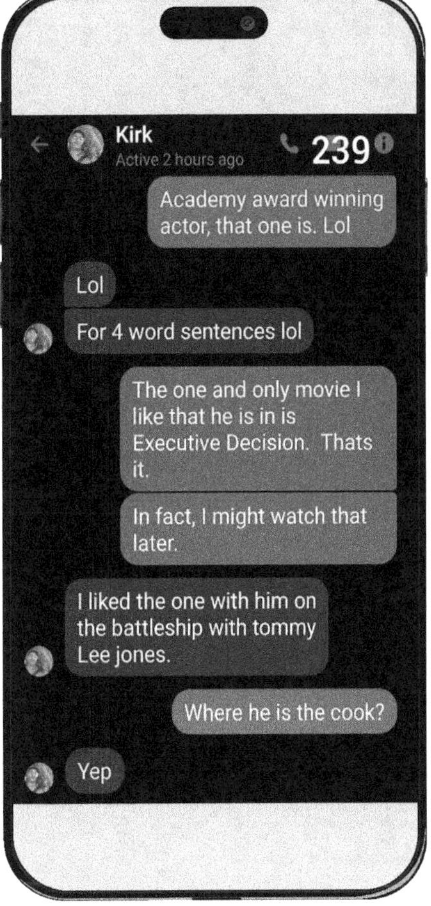

Kirk
Active 2 hours ago
239
Academy award winning actor, that one is. Lol
Lol
For 4 word sentences lol
The one and only movie I like that he is in is Executive Decision. Thats it.
In fact, I might watch that later.
I liked the one with him on the battleship with tommy Lee jones.
Where he is the cook?
Yep

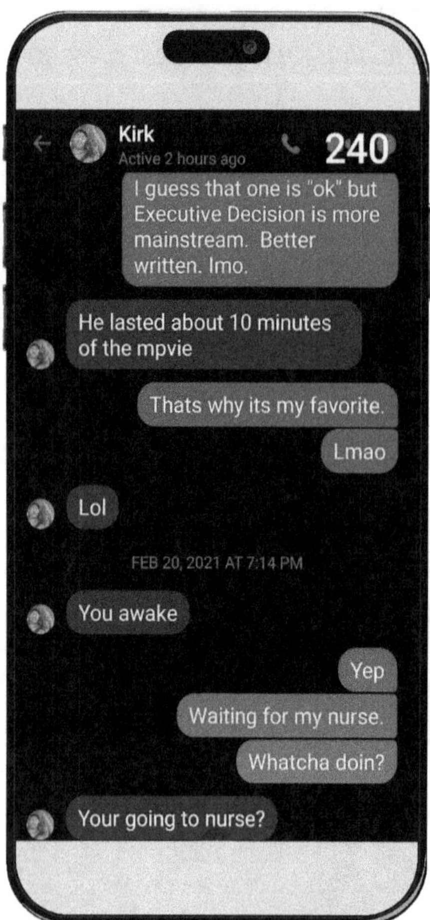
Kirk
Active 2 hours ago
240
I guess that one is "ok" but Executive Decision is more mainstream. Better written. Imo.
He lasted about 10 minutes of the mpvie
Thats why its my favorite.
Lmao
Lol
FEB 20, 2021 AT 7:14 PM
You awake
Yep
Waiting for my nurse.
Whatcha doin?
Your going to nurse?

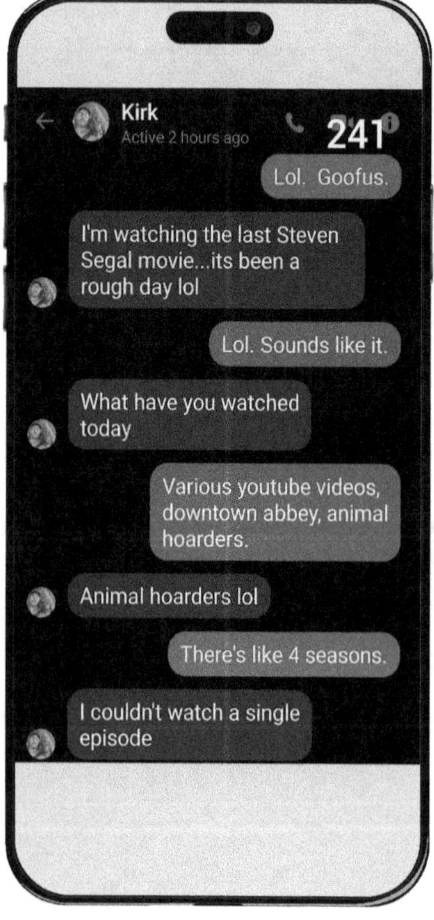
Kirk
Active 2 hours ago
241
Lol. Goofus.
I'm watching the last Steven Segal movie...its been a rough day lol
Lol. Sounds like it.
What have you watched today
Various youtube videos, downtown abbey, animal hoarders.
Animal hoarders lol
There's like 4 seasons.
I couldn't watch a single episode

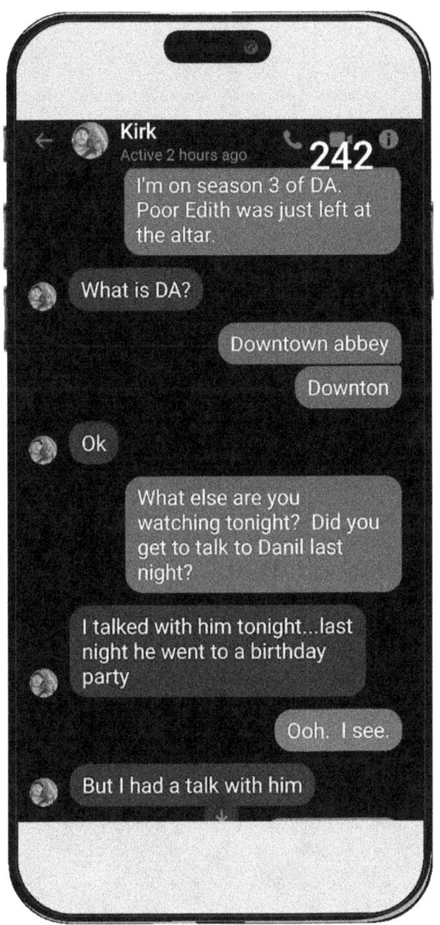
Kirk
Active 2 hours ago
242
I'm on season 3 of DA. Poor Edith was just left at the altar.
What is DA?
Downtown abbey
Downton
Ok
What else are you watching tonight? Did you get to talk to Danil last night?
I talked with him tonight...last night he went to a birthday party
Ooh. I see.
But I had a talk with him

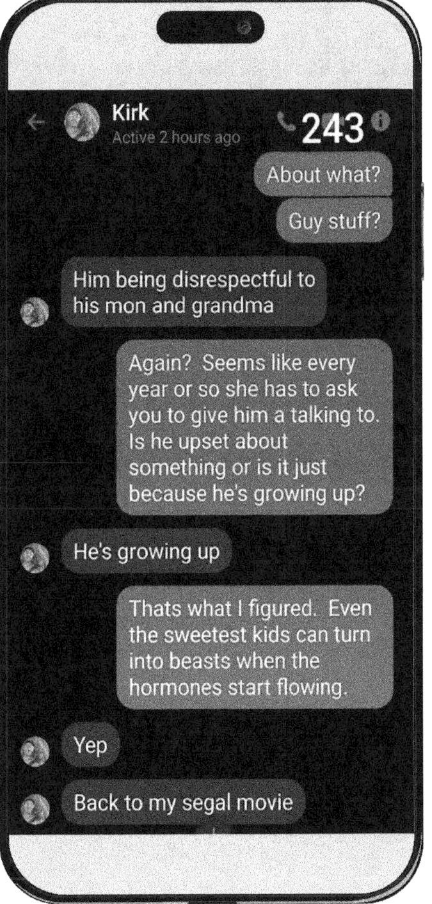
Kirk
Active 2 hours ago
243
About what?
Guy stuff?
Him being disrespectful to his mon and grandma
Again? Seems like every year or so she has to ask you to give him a talking to. Is he upset about something or is it just because he's growing up?
He's growing up
Thats what I figured. Even the sweetest kids can turn into beasts when the hormones start flowing.
Yep
Back to my segal movie

Kirk
Active 3 hours ago
244
Ok babe. Text me later.
FEB 20, 2021 AT 8:42 PM
You there
Goodnight sweetie
Sorry babe
Nurse thought it was a good idea for my sponge bath
Good night.
This late at night
Yeah. I know
Stupid

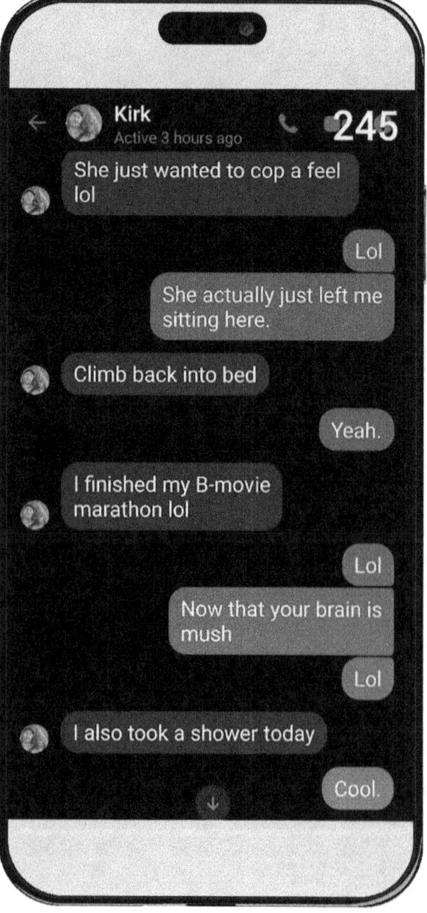
Kirk
Active 3 hours ago
245
She just wanted to cop a feel lol
Lol
She actually just left me sitting here.
Climb back into bed
Yeah.
I finished my B-movie marathon lol
Lol
Now that your brain is mush
Lol
I also took a shower today
Cool.

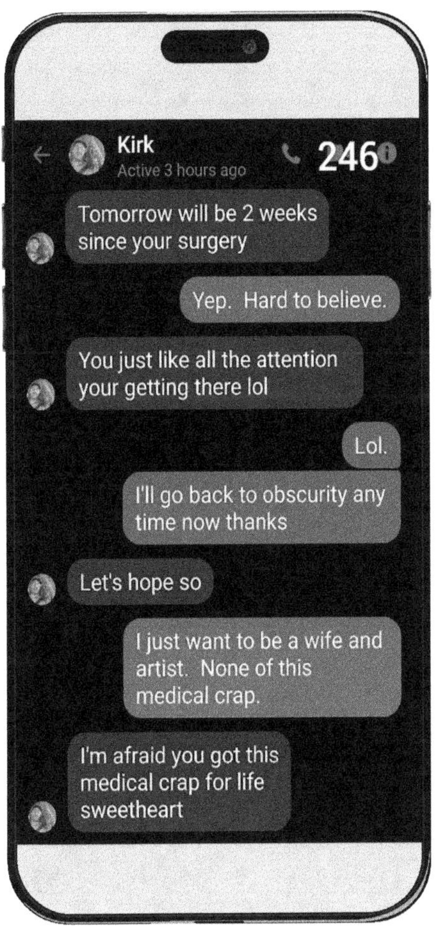

Kirk
Active 3 hours ago
246
Tomorrow will be 2 weeks since your surgery
Yep. Hard to believe.
You just like all the attention your getting there lol
Lol.
I'll go back to obscurity any time now thanks
Let's hope so
I just want to be a wife and artist. None of this medical crap.
I'm afraid you got this medical crap for life sweetheart

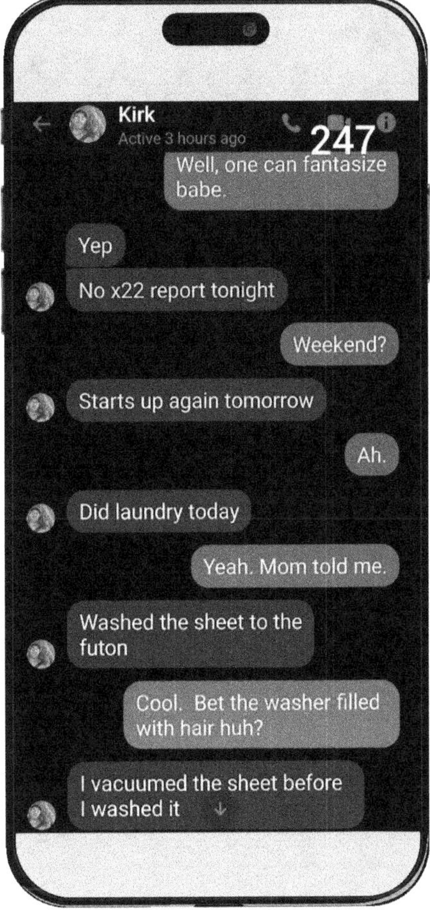

Kirk
Active 3 hours ago
247
Well, one can fantasize babe.
Yep
No x22 report tonight
Weekend?
Starts up again tomorrow
Ah.
Did laundry today
Yeah. Mom told me.
Washed the sheet to the futon
Cool. Bet the washer filled with hair huh?
I vacuumed the sheet before I washed it

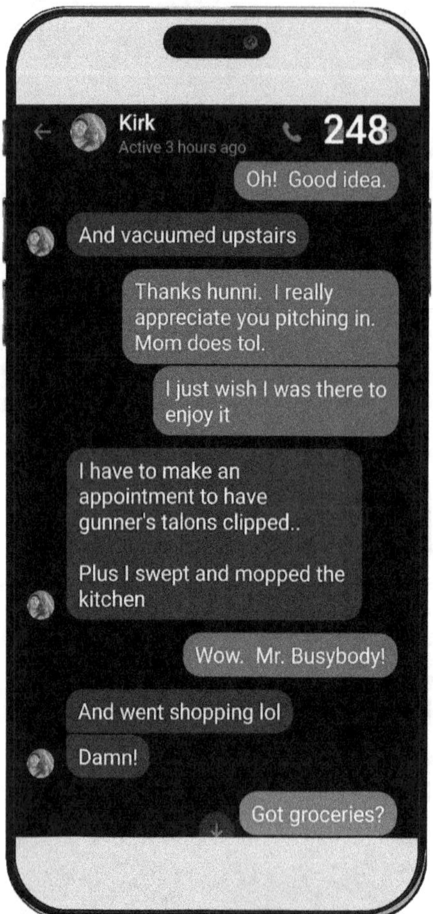
Kirk
Active 3 hours ago
248
Oh! Good idea.
And vacuumed upstairs
Thanks hunni. I really appreciate you pitching in. Mom does tol.
I just wish I was there to enjoy it
I have to make an appointment to have gunner's talons clipped..
Plus I swept and mopped the kitchen
Wow. Mr. Busybody!
And went shopping lol
Damn!
Got groceries?

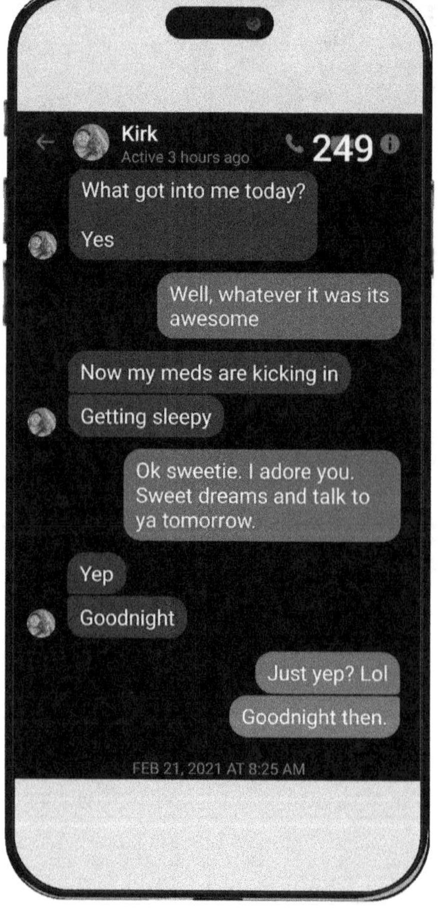
Kirk
Active 3 hours ago
249
What got into me today?
Yes
Well, whatever it was its awesome
Now my meds are kicking in
Getting sleepy
Ok sweetie. I adore you. Sweet dreams and talk to ya tomorrow.
Yep
Goodnight
Just yep? Lol
Goodnight then.
FEB 21, 2021 AT 8:25 AM

Kirk
Active 3 hours ago
250
Hey there sexyness
Hi sweetie
I miss you dip shit
I miss you too my love.
Like crazy
When you get back home you're also going to have to pay that game The Last of Us.
I haven't even taken my medicine yet and I got to take a dump LOL
Yes. For sure
Lol
Getting ready to change my bag. Goodie.
Peeew

Kirk
Active 3 hours ago
251
Lol
Love and miss you boys so much.
We miss you too

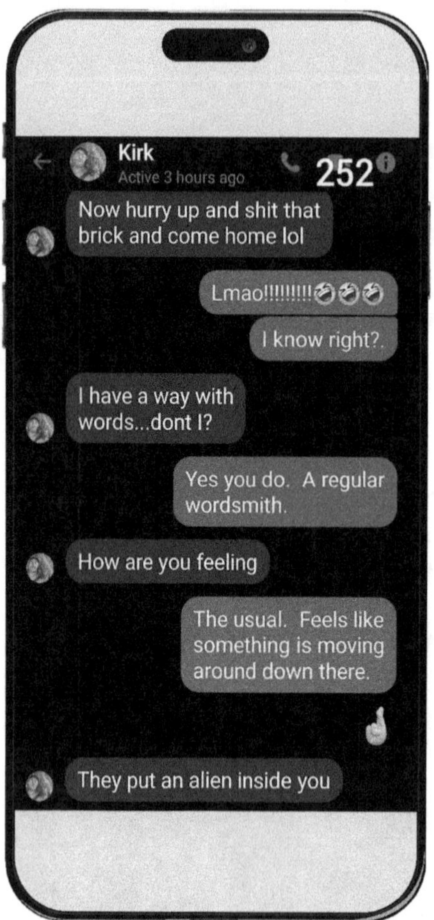

Kirk
Active 3 hours ago
252
Now hurry up and shit that brick and come home lol
Lmao!!!!!!!!!
I know right?.
I have a way with words...dont I?
Yes you do. A regular wordsmith.
How are you feeling
The usual. Feels like something is moving around down there.
They put an alien inside you

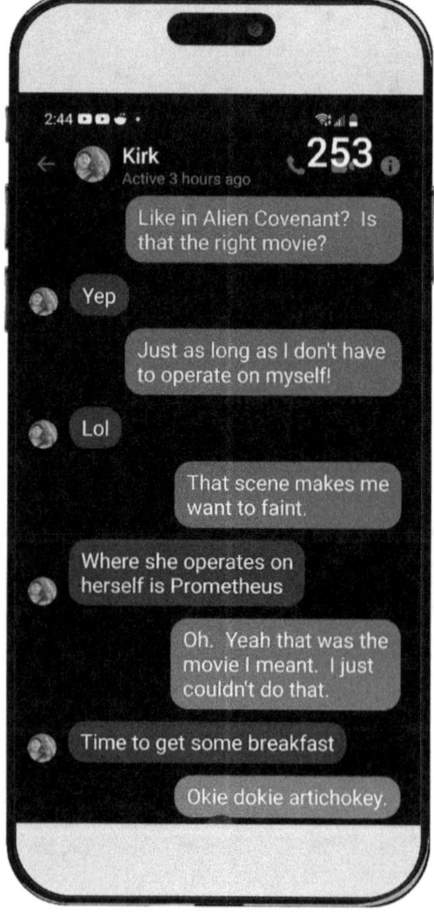

2:44
Kirk
Active 3 hours ago
253
Like in Alien Covenant? Is that the right movie?
Yep
Just as long as I don't have to operate on myself!
Lol
That scene makes me want to faint.
Where she operates on herself is Prometheus
Oh. Yeah that was the movie I meant. I just couldn't do that.
Time to get some breakfast
Okie dokie artichokey.

Kirk
Active 3 hours ago
254
Okey dokie I will poke-yee
Lol!!!
FEB 21, 2021 AT 9:15 AM
FEB 21, 2021 AT 8:22 PM
You 5here
Hi babe

Kirk
Active 3 hours ago
255
Good night sweetheart
Goodnight sweetie. Love you.
FEB 22, 2021 AT 1:10 PM
This dog is crazy
FEB 22, 2021 AT 1:43 PM
Yes he is.

Kirk
Active 3 hours ago
256
FEB 22, 2021 AT 6:35 PM
Hi sweetheart
Hi hunni
What's going on...anything new?
Unfortunately no. I was able to tough it through holding down that fluid though.
Still not producing any output
Unfortunately not.
And not eating
No. I wish.
I'm feeling hungry right now too.

Kirk
Active 3 hours ago
257
For my grilled cheese.
Lol
Lol
I'm getting ready for x22 report
Oh yeah? Getting to it early tonight eh?
I hope you get better soon. I want you home
Me too babe. My dream is to not only be home but to be able to lie next to you at night.
My dentist appointment is tomorrow morning at 8am
Same here

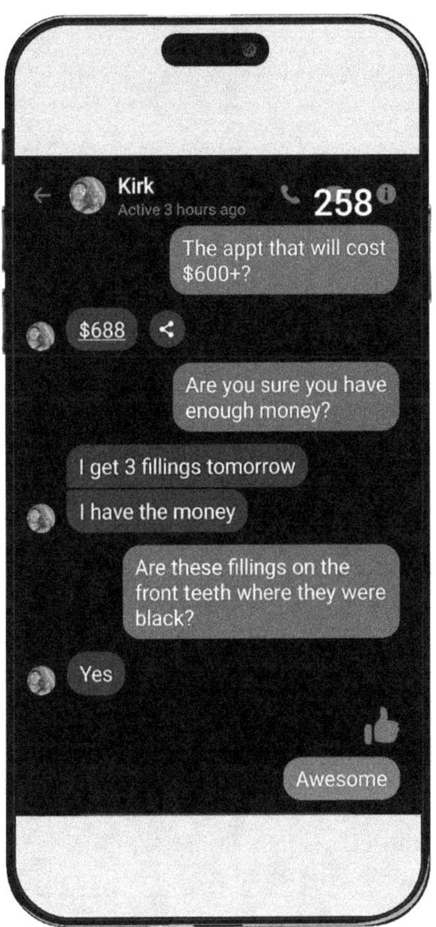
Kirk
Active 3 hours ago
258
The appt that will cost $600+?
$688
Are you sure you have enough money?
I get 3 fillings tomorrow
I have the money
Are these fillings on the front teeth where they were black?
Yes
Awesome

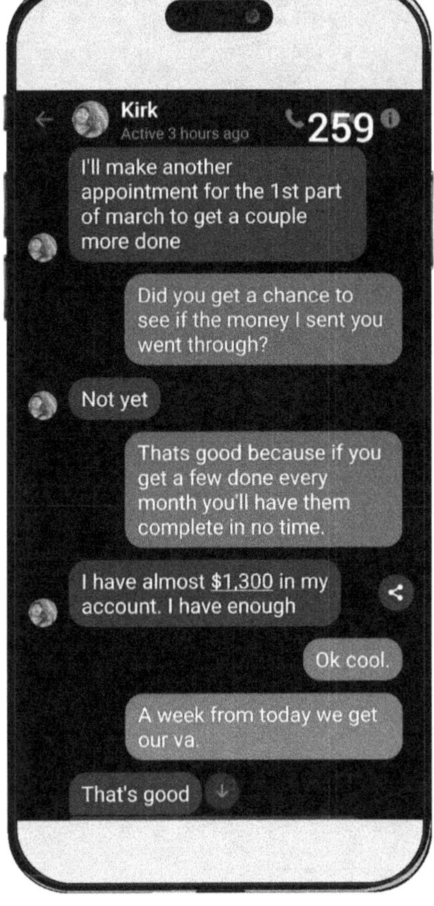
Kirk
Active 3 hours ago
259
I'll make another appointment for the 1st part of march to get a couple more done
Did you get a chance to see if the money I sent you went through?
Not yet
Thats good because if you get a few done every month you'll have them complete in no time.
I have almost $1,300 in my account. I have enough
Ok cool.
A week from today we get our va.
That's good

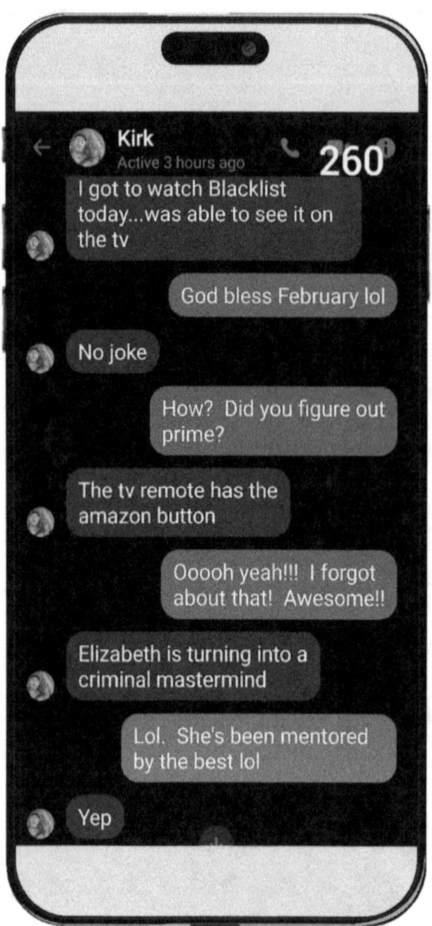
Kirk
Active 3 hours ago
260
I got to watch Blacklist today...was able to see it on the tv
God bless February lol
No joke
How? Did you figure out prime?
The tv remote has the amazon button
Ooooh yeah!!! I forgot about that! Awesome!!
Elizabeth is turning into a criminal mastermind
Lol. She's been mentored by the best lol
Yep

261
Sounds like the two of them are going to have it out. And only one will come out alive.
Its getting gooood
Glad to hear it.
Oh...they wrote that midget actor out after he died last year
Remember jellybean
They had a funeral for him on the show
Its not ringing a bell.
The guy with the funny arms

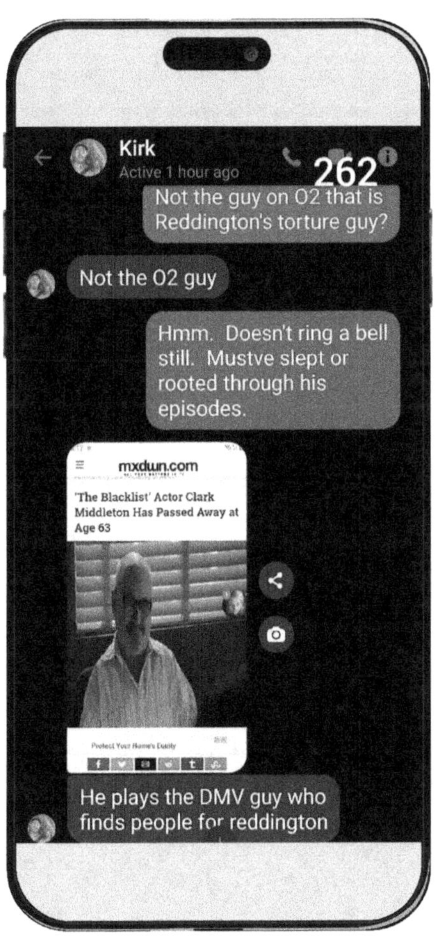

Kirk
Active 1 hour ago
262
Not the guy on O2 that is Reddington's torture guy?
Not the O2 guy
Hmm. Doesn't ring a bell still. Mustve slept or rooted through his episodes.
mxdwn.com
'The Blacklist' Actor Clark Middleton Has Passed Away at Age 63
Protect Your Home's Daddy
He plays the DMV guy who finds people for reddington

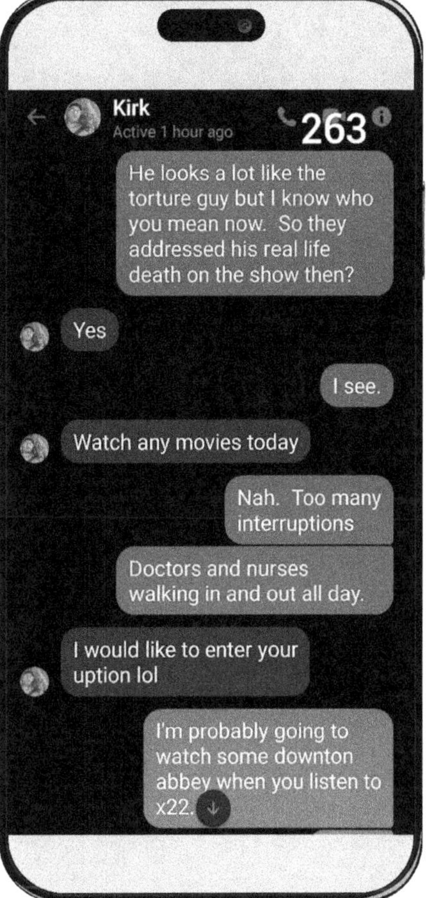

Kirk
Active 1 hour ago
263
He looks a lot like the torture guy but I know who you mean now. So they addressed his real life death on the show then?
Yes
I see.
Watch any movies today
Nah. Too many interruptions
Doctors and nurses walking in and out all day.
I would like to enter your uption lol
I'm probably going to watch some downton abbey when you listen to x22.

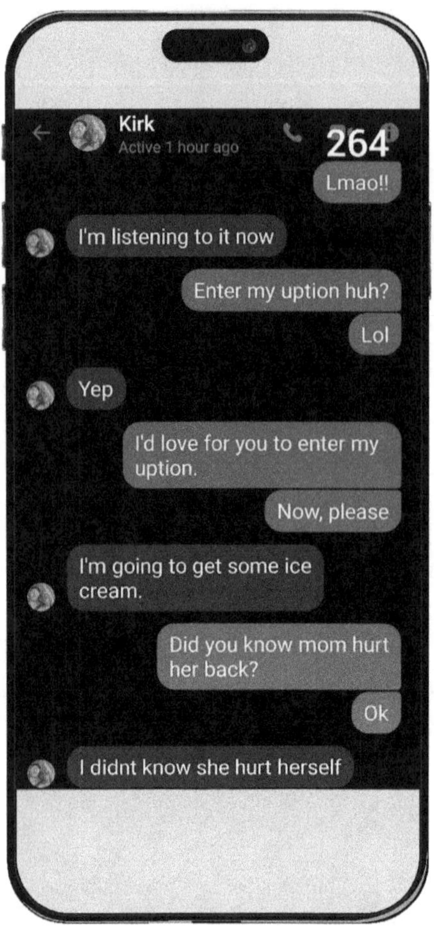
Kirk
Active 1 hour ago
264
Lmao!!
I'm listening to it now
Enter my uption huh?
Lol
Yep
I'd love for you to enter my uption.
Now, please
I'm going to get some ice cream.
Did you know mom hurt her back?
Ok
I didnt know she hurt herself

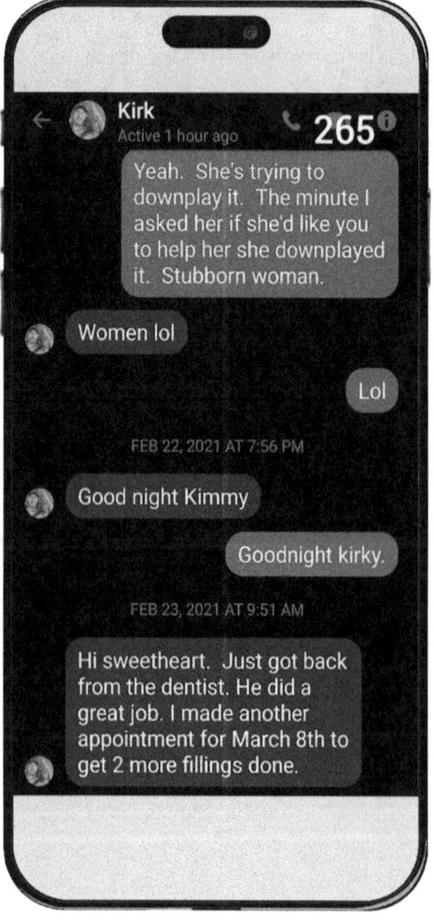
Kirk
Active 1 hour ago
265
Yeah. She's trying to downplay it. The minute I asked her if she'd like you to help her she downplayed it. Stubborn woman.
Women lol
Lol
FEB 22, 2021 AT 7:56 PM
Good night Kimmy
Goodnight kirky.
FEB 23, 2021 AT 9:51 AM
Hi sweetheart. Just got back from the dentist. He did a great job. I made another appointment for March 8th to get 2 more fillings done.

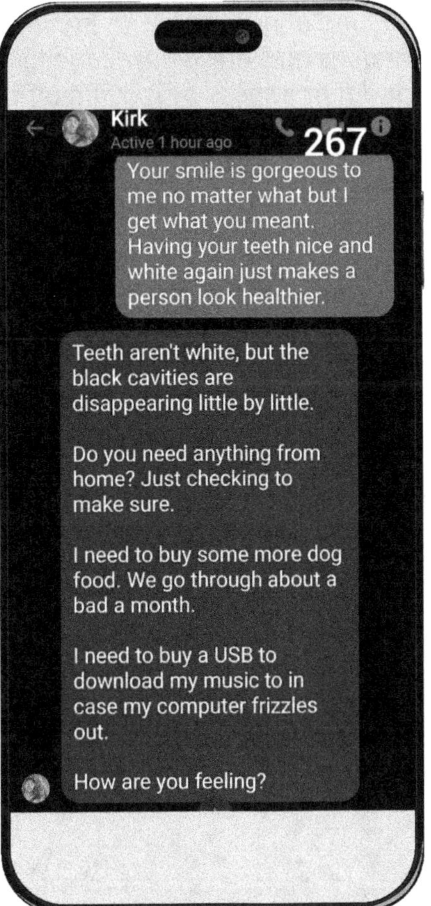

During this time, I had about 15 cavities that had turned black and lever the next 60 days cost about $2,500 to fix.

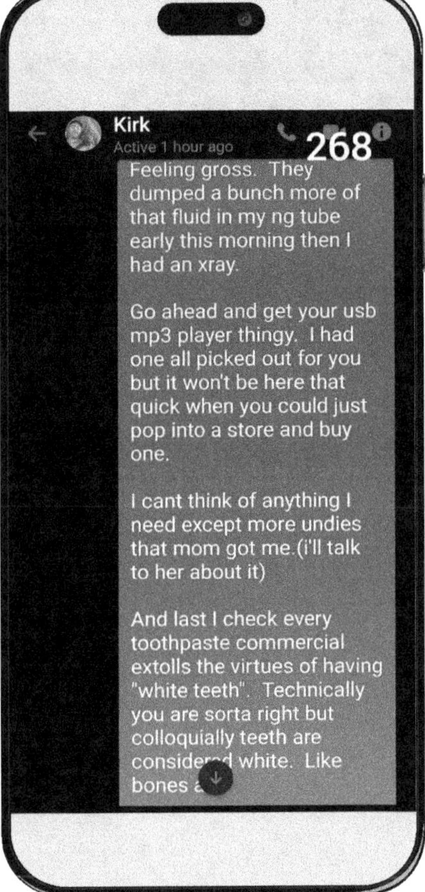

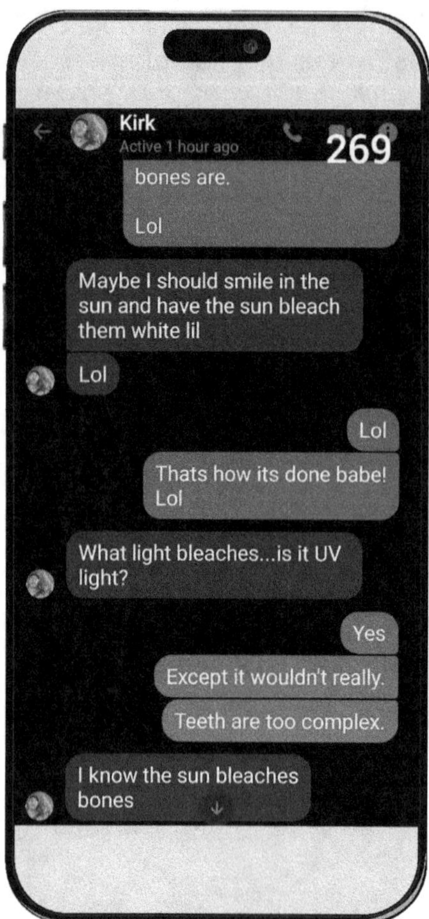

Talking about teeth with Kimmy underscores how knowledgeable and funny she is by playing off of my little joke about smiling in the sun to bleach my teeth.

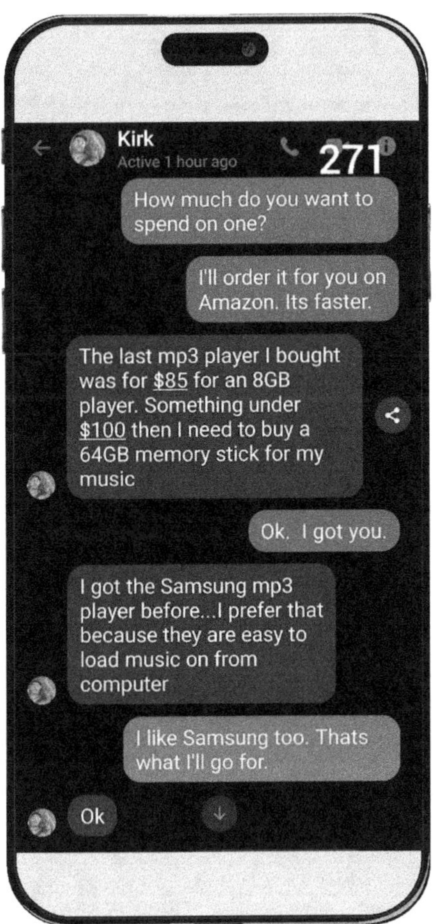

Kirk
Active 1 hour ago
271
How much do you want to spend on one?
I'll order it for you on Amazon. Its faster.
The last mp3 player I bought was for $85 for an 8GB player. Something under $100 then I need to buy a 64GB memory stick for my music
Ok. I got you.
I got the Samsung mp3 player before...I prefer that because they are easy to load music on from computer
I like Samsung too. Thats what I'll go for.
Ok

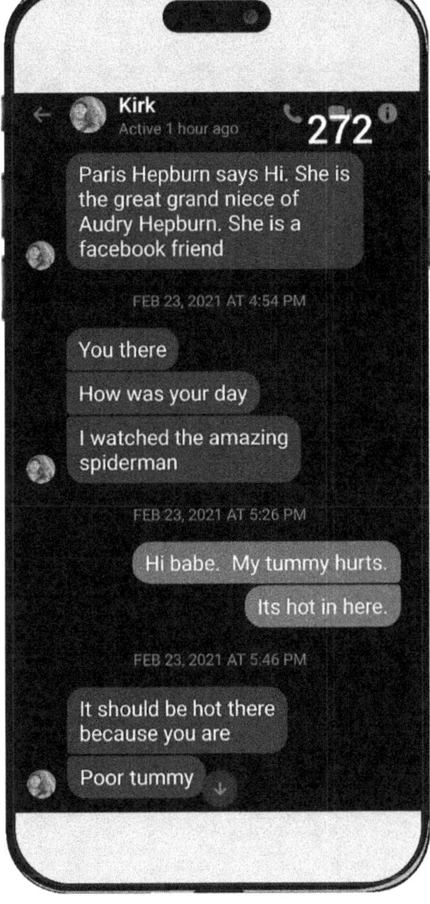

Kirk
Active 1 hour ago
272
Paris Hepburn says Hi. She is the great grand niece of Audry Hepburn. She is a facebook friend
FEB 23, 2021 AT 4:54 PM
You there
How was your day
I watched the amazing spiderman
FEB 23, 2021 AT 5:26 PM
Hi babe. My tummy hurts.
Its hot in here.
FEB 23, 2021 AT 5:46 PM
It should be hot there because you are
Poor tummy

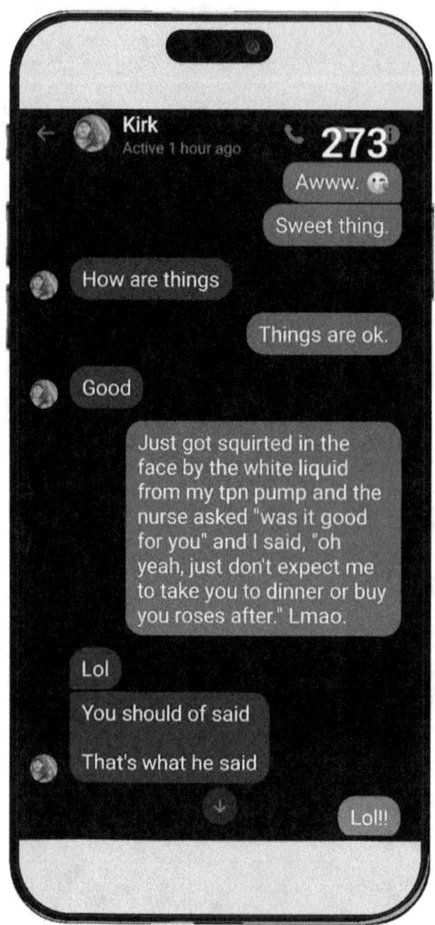

Kirk
Active 1 hour ago
273
Awww.
Sweet thing.
How are things
Things are ok.
Good
Just got squirted in the face by the white liquid from my tpn pump and the nurse asked "was it good for you" and I said, "oh yeah, just don't expect me to take you to dinner or buy you roses after." Lmao.
Lol
You should of said
That's what he said
Lol!!

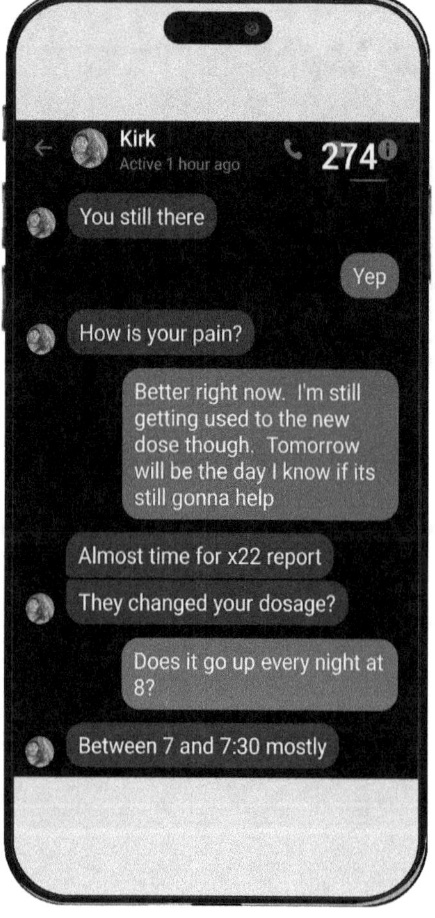

Kirk
Active 1 hour ago
274
You still there
Yep
How is your pain?
Better right now. I'm still getting used to the new dose though. Tomorrow will be the day I know if its still gonna help
Almost time for x22 report
They changed your dosage?
Does it go up every night at 8?
Between 7 and 7:30 mostly

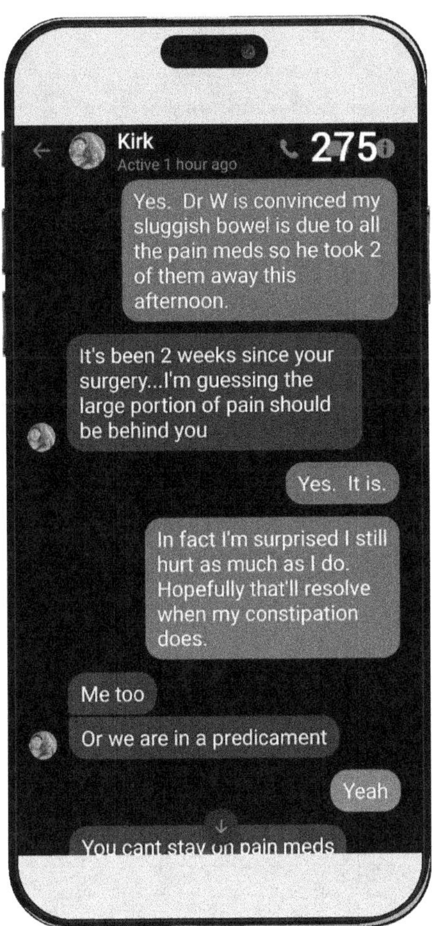

Kirk
Active 1 hour ago
275
Yes. Dr W is convinced my sluggish bowel is due to all the pain meds so he took 2 of them away this afternoon.
It's been 2 weeks since your surgery...I'm guessing the large portion of pain should be behind you
Yes. It is.
In fact I'm surprised I still hurt as much as I do. Hopefully that'll resolve when my constipation does.
Me too
Or we are in a predicament
Yeah
You cant stay on pain meds

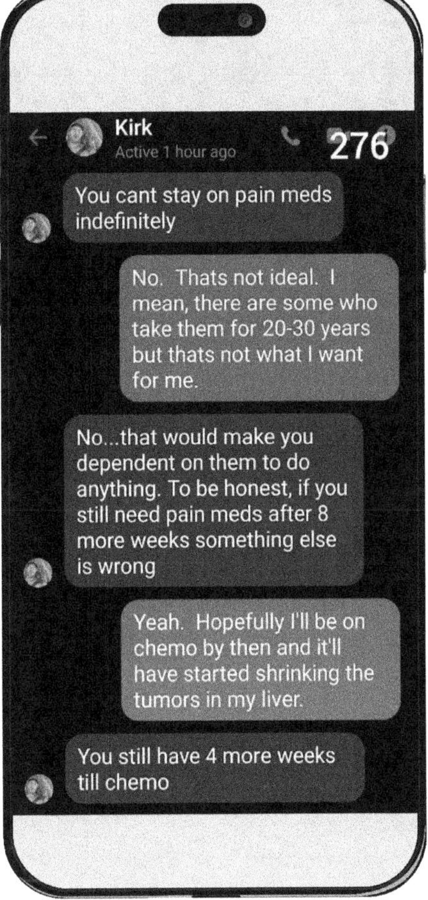

Kirk
Active 1 hour ago
276
You cant stay on pain meds indefinitely
No. Thats not ideal. I mean, there are some who take them for 20-30 years but thats not what I want for me.
No...that would make you dependent on them to do anything. To be honest, if you still need pain meds after 8 more weeks something else is wrong
Yeah. Hopefully I'll be on chemo by then and it'll have started shrinking the tumors in my liver.
You still have 4 more weeks till chemo

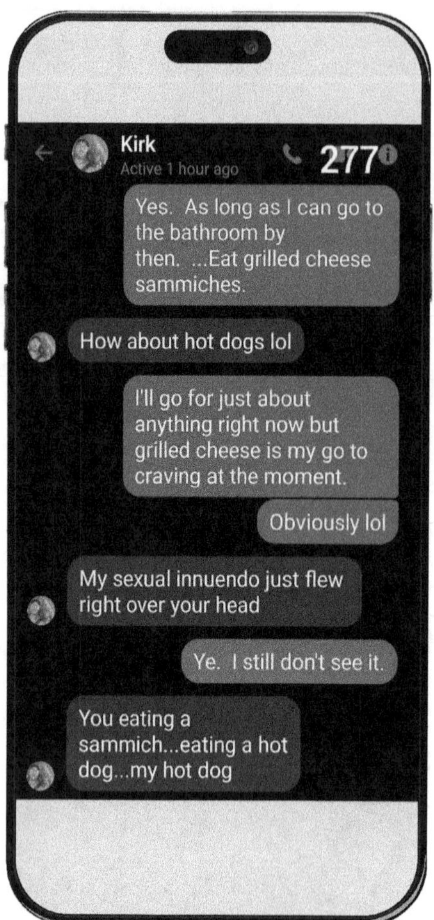

Kirk
Active 1 hour ago
277
Yes. As long as I can go to the bathroom by then. ...Eat grilled cheese sammiches.
How about hot dogs lol
I'll go for just about anything right now but grilled cheese is my go to craving at the moment.
Obviously lol
My sexual innuendo just flew right over your head
Ye. I still don't see it.
You eating a sammich...eating a hot dog...my hot dog

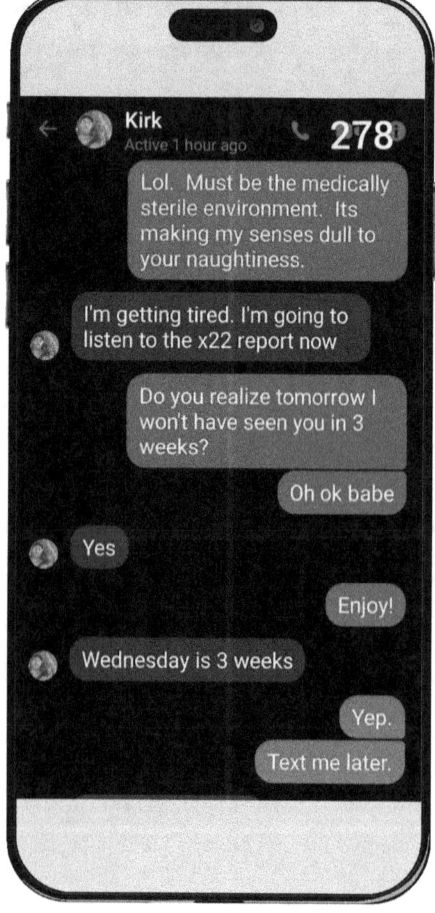

Kirk
Active 1 hour ago
278
Lol. Must be the medically sterile environment. Its making my senses dull to your naughtiness.
I'm getting tired. I'm going to listen to the x22 report now
Do you realize tomorrow I won't have seen you in 3 weeks?
Oh ok babe
Yes
Enjoy!
Wednesday is 3 weeks
Yep.
Text me later.

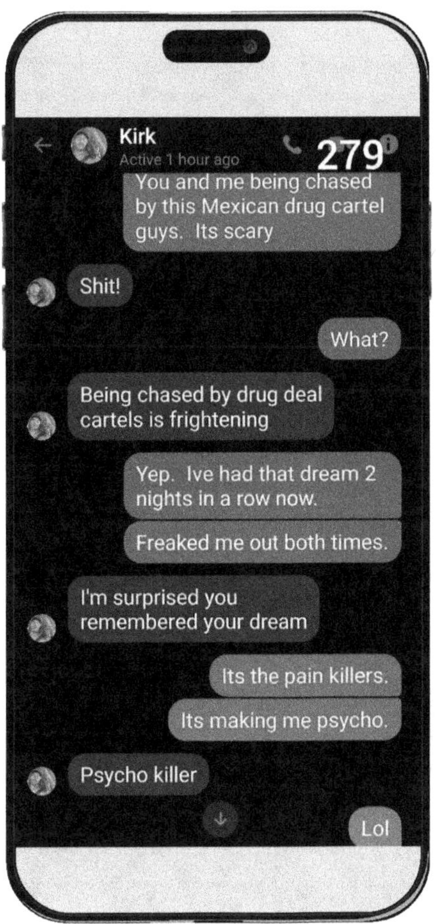
Kirk
Active 1 hour ago
279
You and me being chased by this Mexican drug cartel guys. Its scary
Shit!
What?
Being chased by drug deal cartels is frightening
Yep. Ive had that dream 2 nights in a row now.
Freaked me out both times.
I'm surprised you remembered your dream
Its the pain killers.
Its making me psycho.
Psycho killer
Lol

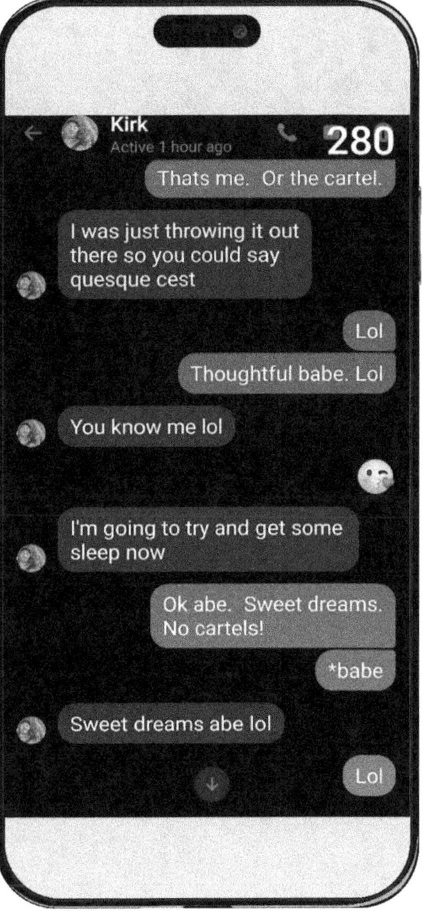
Kirk
Active 1 hour ago
280
Thats me. Or the cartel.
I was just throwing it out there so you could say quesque cest
Lol
Thoughtful babe. Lol
You know me lol
I'm going to try and get some sleep now
Ok abe. Sweet dreams. No cartels!
*babe
Sweet dreams abe lol
Lol

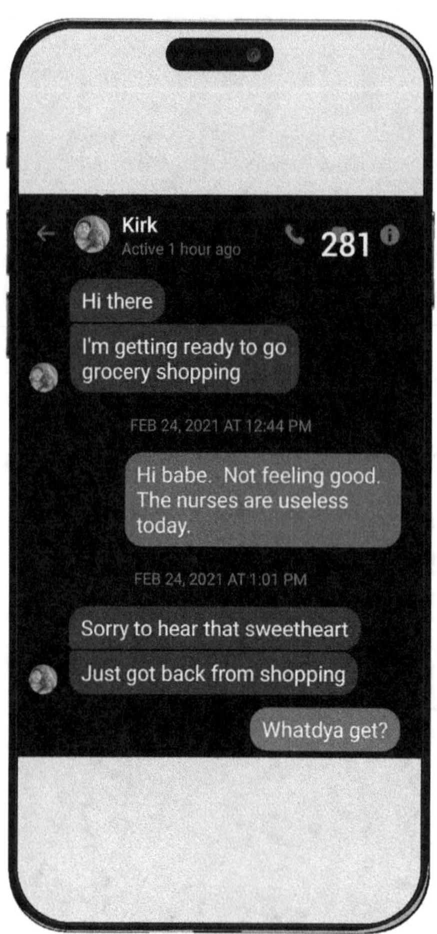

Kirk
Active 1 hour ago
281
Hi there
I'm getting ready to go grocery shopping
FEB 24, 2021 AT 12:44 PM
Hi babe. Not feeling good. The nurses are useless today.
FEB 24, 2021 AT 1:01 PM
Sorry to hear that sweetheart
Just got back from shopping
Whatdya get?

Kirk
Active 1 hour ago
282
No...that's how I found out it was warm. I was sweating outside
Ah. One of the nurses mentioned it earlier.
Do you miss snow at al?
No, but you know I like cooler temps
True.
I miss snow.
And cold winter days.

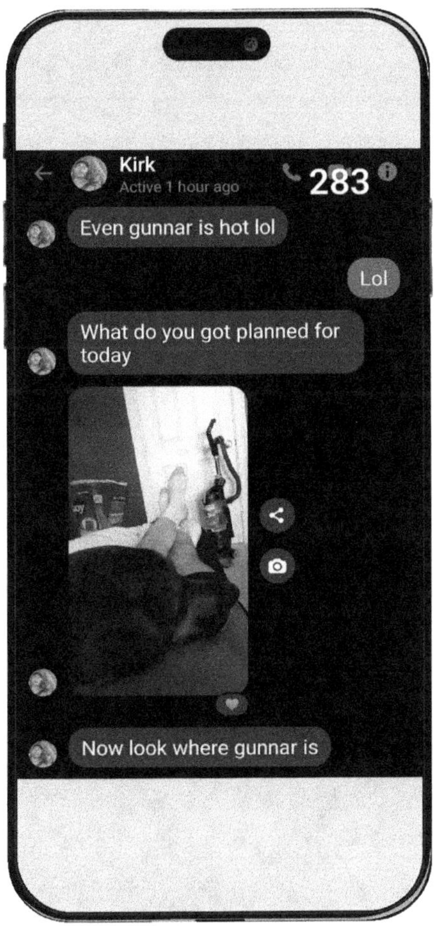

Kirk
Active 1 hour ago
283
Even gunnar is hot lol
Lol
What do you got planned for today
Now look where gunnar is

Kirk
Active 1 hour ago
285
Now he is using me as a table SMH
Lol. I think I just had some diarrhea. I know thats a weird thing to say but I think it's true!!!
Anal diarrhea?
Lol
No!
Ok

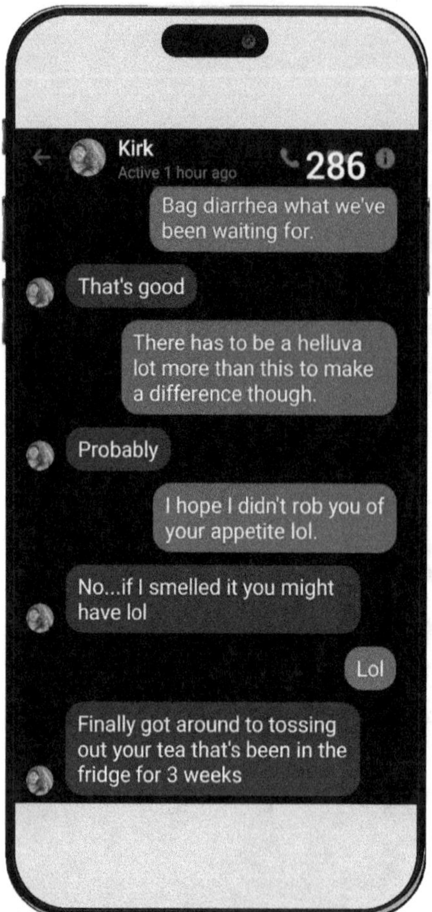

Kirk
Active 1 hour ago
286
Bag diarrhea what we've been waiting for.
That's good
There has to be a helluva lot more than this to make a difference though.
Probably
I hope I didn't rob you of your appetite lol.
No...if I smelled it you might have lol
Lol
Finally got around to tossing out your tea that's been in the fridge for 3 weeks

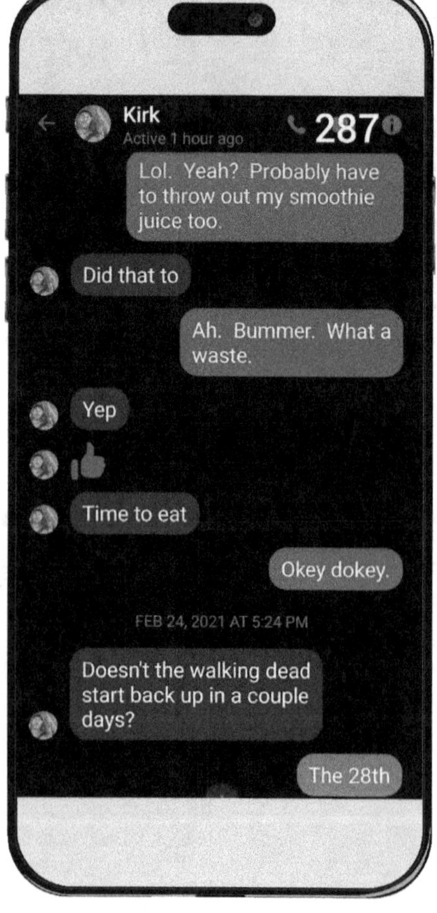

Kirk
Active 1 hour ago
287
Lol. Yeah? Probably have to throw out my smoothie juice too.
Did that to
Ah. Bummer. What a waste.
Yep
Time to eat
Okey dokey.
FEB 24, 2021 AT 5:24 PM
Doesn't the walking dead start back up in a couple days?
The 28th

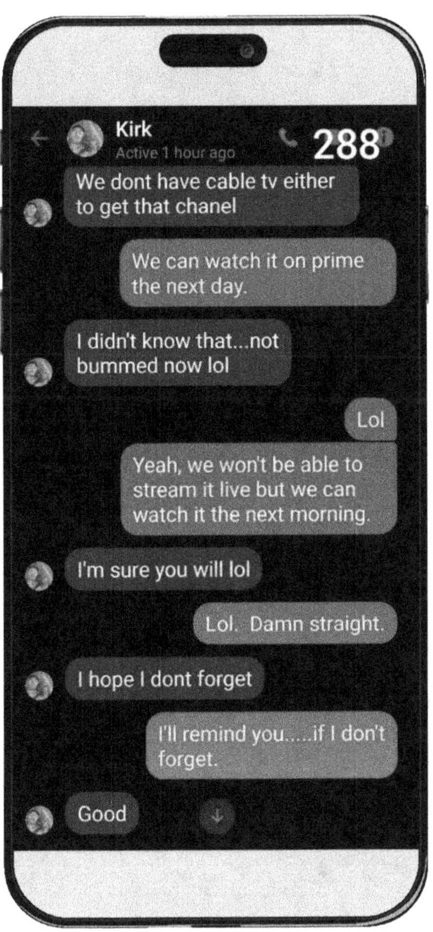

Kirk
Active 1 hour ago
288
We dont have cable tv either to get that chanel
We can watch it on prime the next day.
I didn't know that...not bummed now lol
Lol
Yeah, we won't be able to stream it live but we can watch it the next morning.
I'm sure you will lol
Lol. Damn straight.
I hope I dont forget
I'll remind you.....if I don't forget.
Good

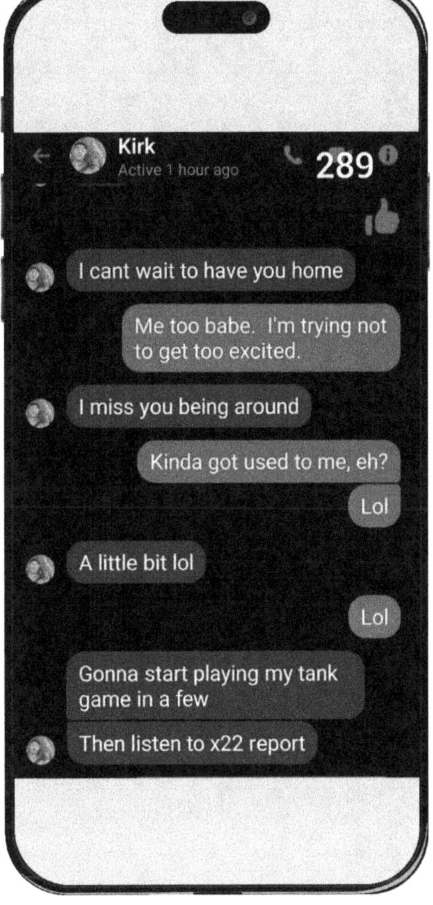

Kirk
Active 1 hour ago
289
I cant wait to have you home
Me too babe. I'm trying not to get too excited.
I miss you being around
Kinda got used to me, eh?
Lol
A little bit lol
Lol
Gonna start playing my tank game in a few
Then listen to x22 report

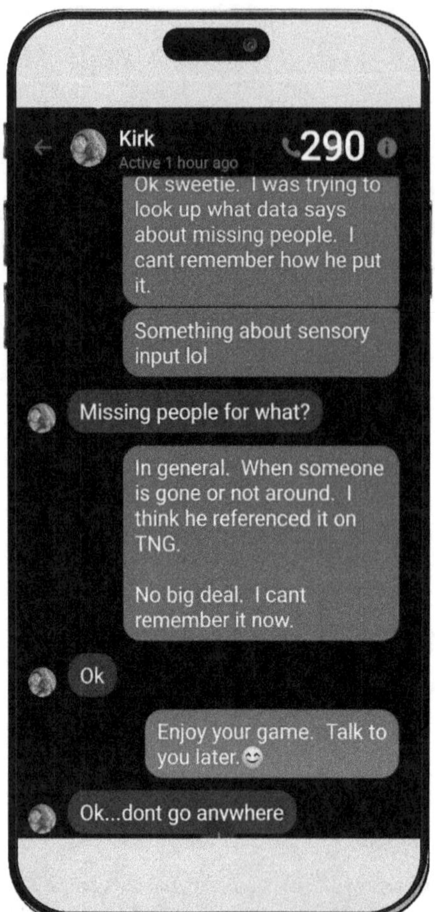

Kirk
Active 1 hour ago
290
Ok sweetie. I was trying to look up what data says about missing people. I cant remember how he put it.
Something about sensory input lol
Missing people for what?
In general. When someone is gone or not around. I think he referenced it on TNG.
No big deal. I cant remember it now.
Ok
Enjoy your game. Talk to you later.
Ok...dont go anywhere

Kirk
Active 1 hour ago
291
Lol
FEB 24, 2021 AT 8:09 PM
Good night kim
Good night sweetie.
Love you.
FEB 25, 2021 AT 12:37 PM
The package on the front porch right now is yours babe. Unless mom already brought it in.
FEB 25, 2021 AT 2:04 PM
Is it the mp3 player?
And memory stick

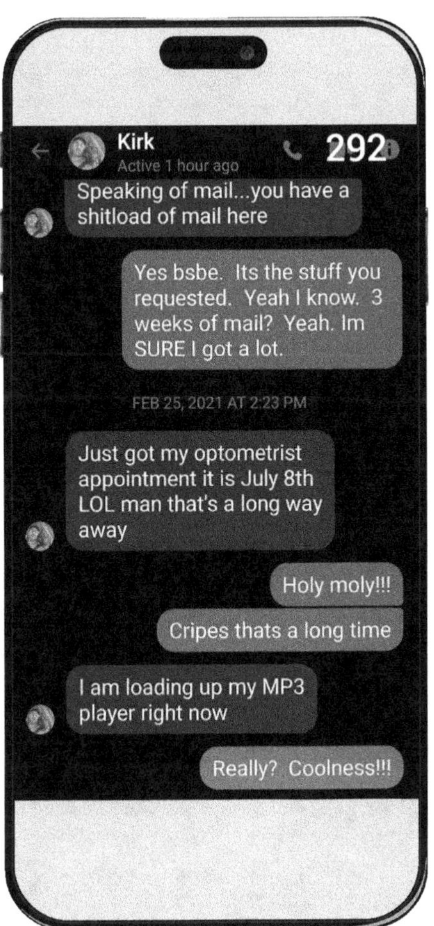

Kirk
Active 1 hour ago
292
Speaking of mail...you have a shitload of mail here
Yes bsbe. Its the stuff you requested. Yeah I know. 3 weeks of mail? Yeah. Im SURE I got a lot.
FEB 25, 2021 AT 2:23 PM
Just got my optometrist appointment it is July 8th LOL man that's a long way away
Holy moly!!!
Cripes thats a long time
I am loading up my MP3 player right now
Really? Coolness!!!

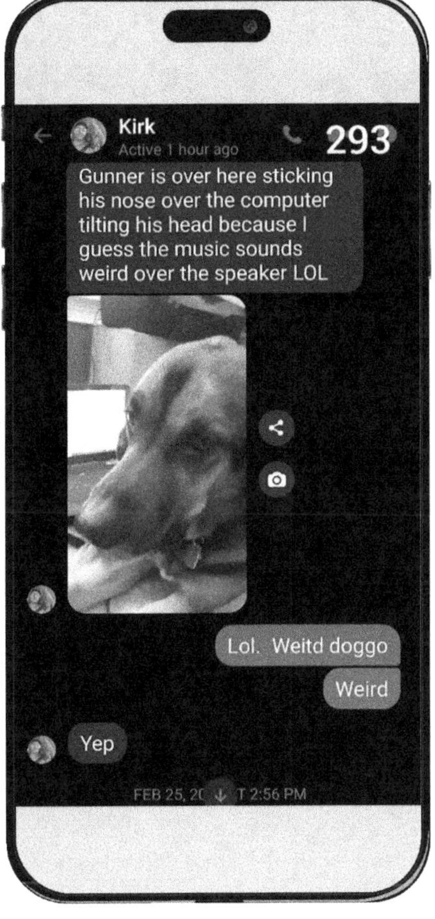

Kirk
Active 1 hour ago
293
Gunner is over here sticking his nose over the computer tilting his head because I guess the music sounds weird over the speaker LOL
Lol. Weitd doggo
Weird
Yep
FEB 25, 20 T 2:56 PM

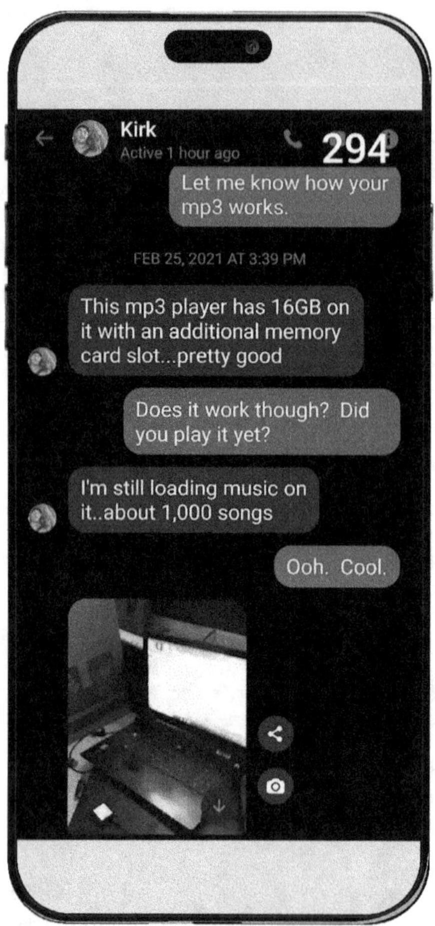

Kirk
Active 1 hour ago
294
Let me know how your mp3 works.
FEB 25, 2021 AT 3:39 PM
This mp3 player has 16GB on it with an additional memory card slot...pretty good
Does it work though? Did you play it yet?
I'm still loading music on it..about 1,000 songs
Ooh. Cool.

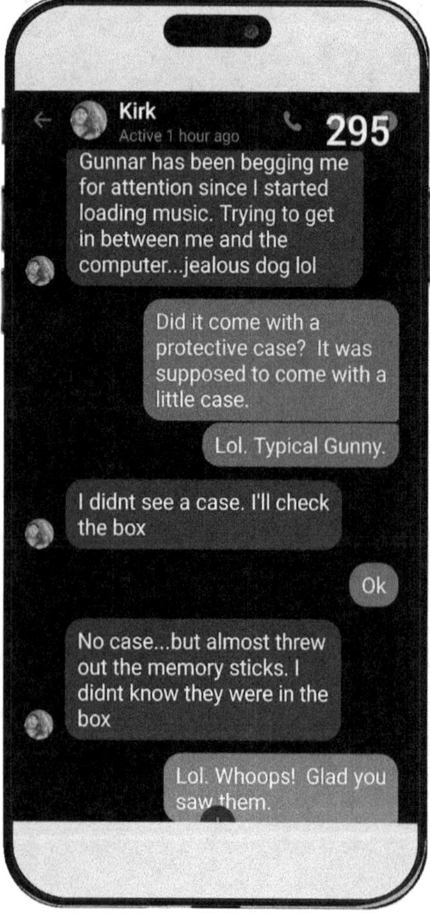

Kirk
Active 1 hour ago
295
Gunnar has been begging me for attention since I started loading music. Trying to get in between me and the computer...jealous dog lol
Did it come with a protective case? It was supposed to come with a little case.
Lol. Typical Gunny.
I didnt see a case. I'll check the box
Ok
No case...but almost threw out the memory sticks. I didnt know they were in the box
Lol. Whoops! Glad you saw them.

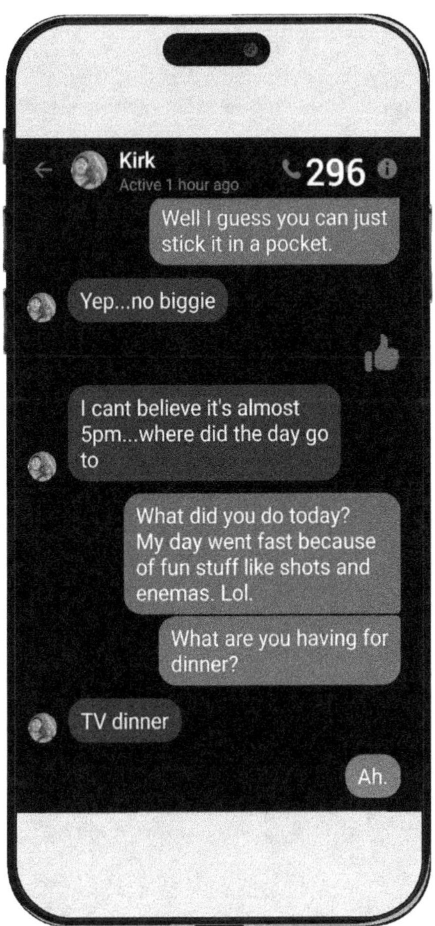
Kirk
Active 1 hour ago
296
Well I guess you can just stick it in a pocket.
Yep...no biggie
I cant believe it's almost 5pm...where did the day go to
What did you do today? My day went fast because of fun stuff like shots and enemas. Lol.
What are you having for dinner?
TV dinner
Ah.

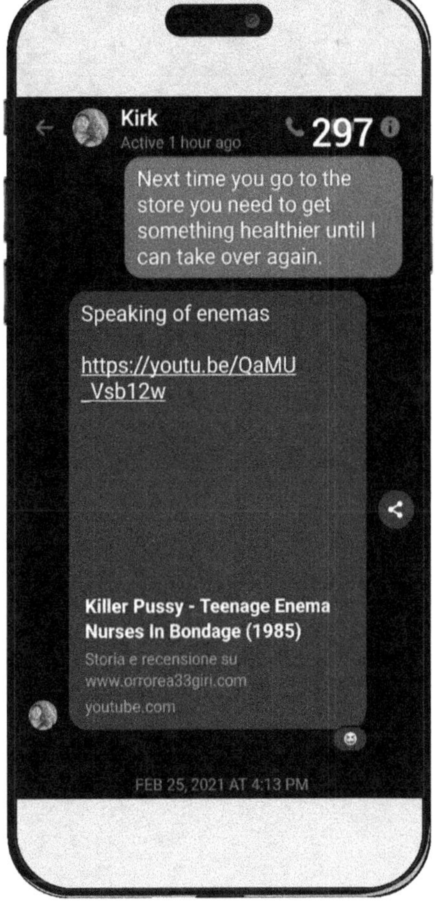
Kirk
Active 1 hour ago
297
Next time you go to the store you need to get something healthier until I can take over again.
Speaking of enemas
https://youtu.be/QaMU_Vsb12w
Killer Pussy - Teenage Enema Nurses In Bondage (1985)
Storia e recensione su www.orrorea33giri.com
youtube.com
FEB 25, 2021 AT 4:13 PM

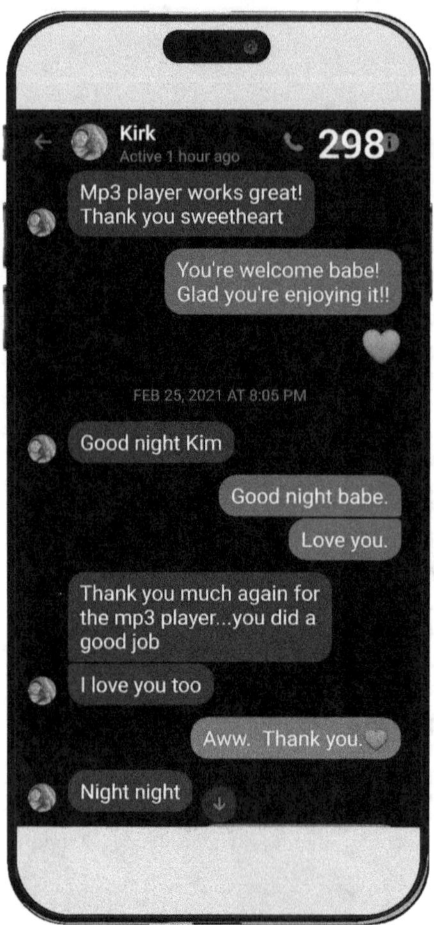

Kirk
Active 1 hour ago
298
Mp3 player works great! Thank you sweetheart
You're welcome babe! Glad you're enjoying it!!
FEB 25, 2021 AT 8:05 PM
Good night Kim
Good night babe.
Love you.
Thank you much again for the mp3 player...you did a good job
I love you too
Aww. Thank you.
Night night

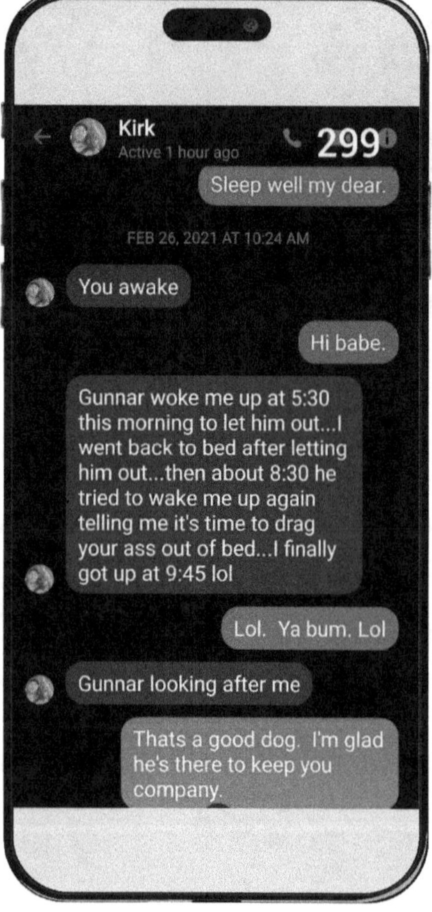

Kirk
Active 1 hour ago
299
Sleep well my dear.
FEB 26, 2021 AT 10:24 AM
You awake
Hi babe.
Gunnar woke me up at 5:30 this morning to let him out...I went back to bed after letting him out...then about 8:30 he tried to wake me up again telling me it's time to drag your ass out of bed...I finally got up at 9:45 lol
Lol. Ya bum. Lol
Gunnar looking after me
Thats a good dog. I'm glad he's there to keep you company.

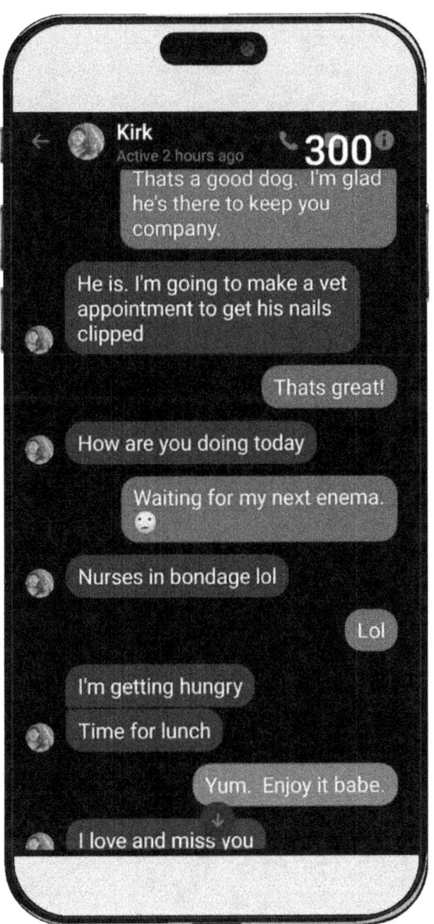

Kirk
Active 2 hours ago
300
Thats a good dog. I'm glad he's there to keep you company.
He is. I'm going to make a vet appointment to get his nails clipped
Thats great!
How are you doing today
Waiting for my next enema.
Nurses in bondage lol
Lol
I'm getting hungry
Time for lunch
Yum. Enjoy it babe.
I love and miss you

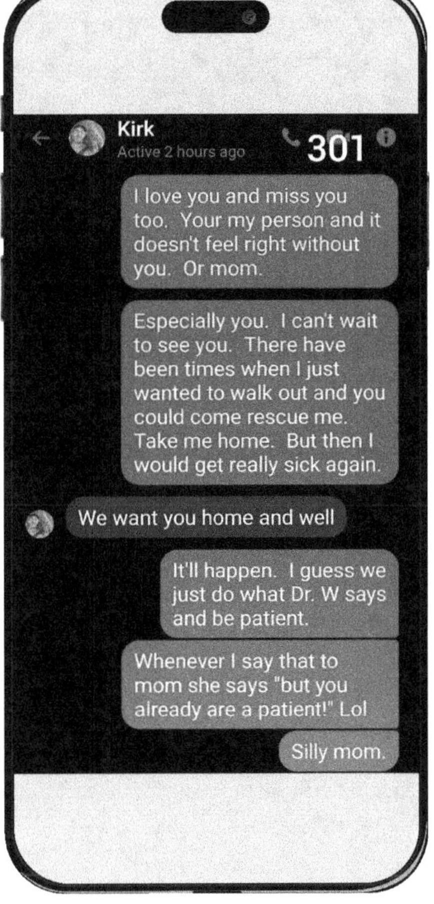

Kirk
Active 2 hours ago
301
I love you and miss you too. Your my person and it doesn't feel right without you. Or mom.
Especially you. I can't wait to see you. There have been times when I just wanted to walk out and you could come rescue me. Take me home. But then I would get really sick again.
We want you home and well
It'll happen. I guess we just do what Dr. W says and be patient.
Whenever I say that to mom she says "but you already are a patient!" Lol
Silly mom.

Kirk
Active 2 hours ago
302
Sounds like your mom for sure
Lol
SMD
SMD everytime I go to the bathroom lol
Smd?
Shaking My Dick
Lmao!!!
Goofus
Cant believe you didnt get that one
Too many drugs lol

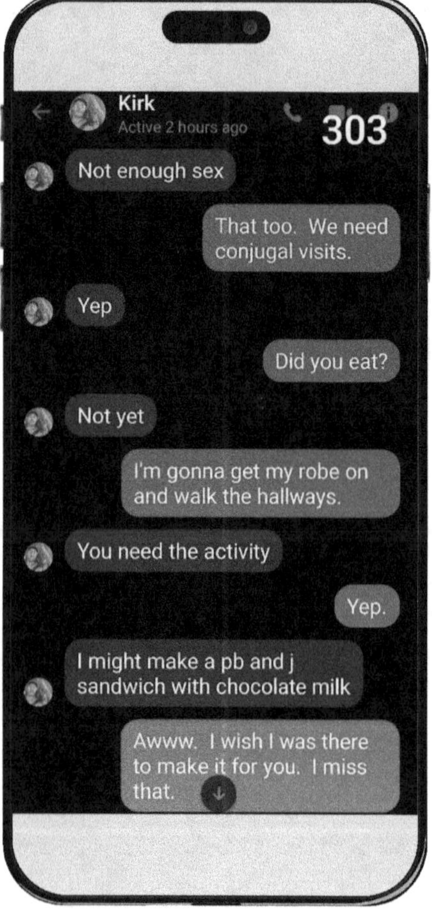

Kirk
Active 2 hours ago
303
Not enough sex
That too. We need conjugal visits.
Yep
Did you eat?
Not yet
I'm gonna get my robe on and walk the hallways.
You need the activity
Yep.
I might make a pb and j sandwich with chocolate milk
Awww. I wish I was there to make it for you. I miss that.

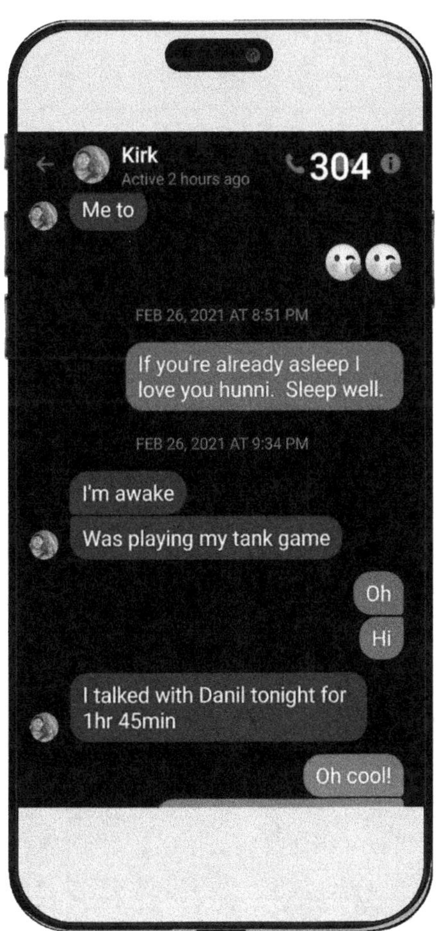
Kirk
Active 2 hours ago
304
Me to
FEB 26, 2021 AT 8:51 PM
If you're already asleep I love you hunni. Sleep well.
FEB 26, 2021 AT 9:34 PM
I'm awake
Was playing my tank game
Oh
Hi
I talked with Danil tonight for 1hr 45min
Oh cool!

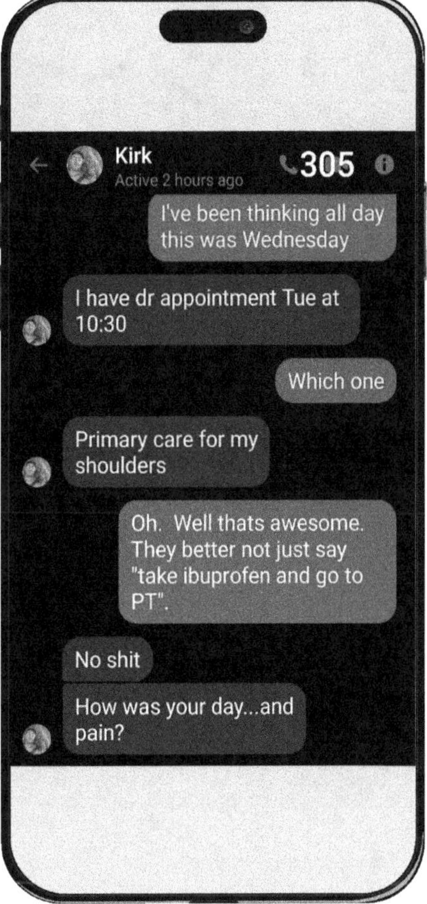
Kirk
Active 2 hours ago
305
I've been thinking all day this was Wednesday
I have dr appointment Tue at 10:30
Which one
Primary care for my shoulders
Oh. Well thats awesome. They better not just say "take ibuprofen and go to PT".
No shit
How was your day...and pain?

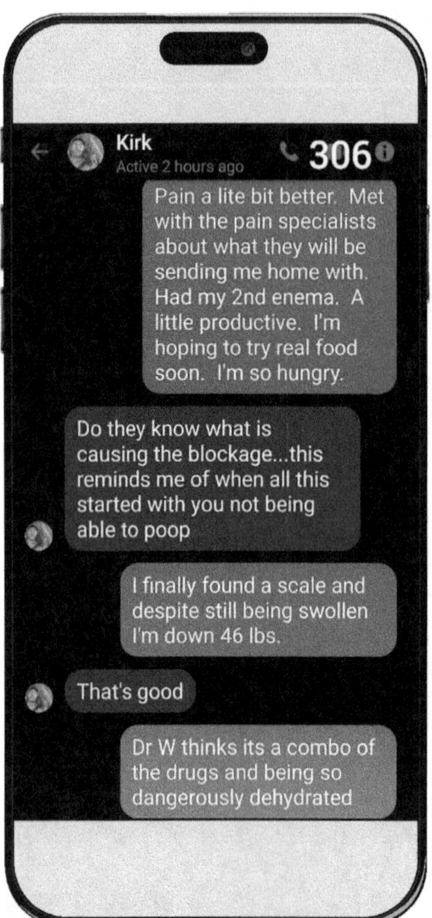
Kirk
Active 2 hours ago
306
Pain a lite bit better. Met with the pain specialists about what they will be sending me home with. Had my 2nd enema. A little productive. I'm hoping to try real food soon. I'm so hungry.
Do they know what is causing the blockage...this reminds me of when all this started with you not being able to poop
I finally found a scale and despite still being swollen I'm down 46 lbs.
That's good
Dr W thinks its a combo of the drugs and being so dangerously dehydrated

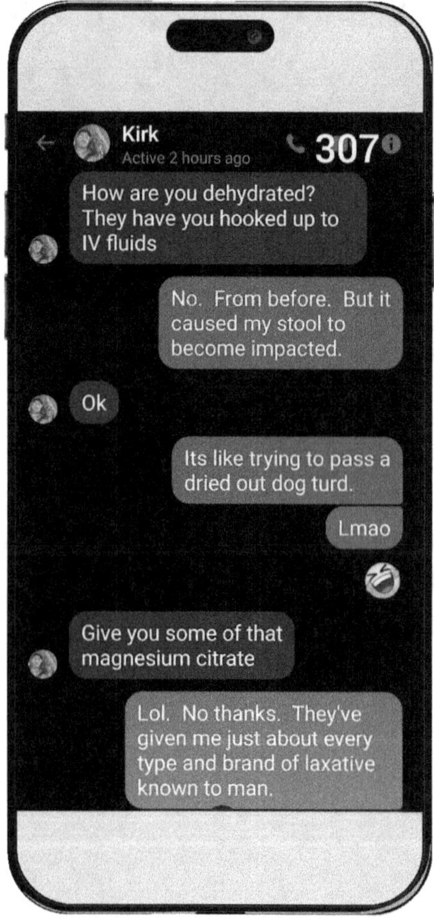
Kirk
Active 2 hours ago
307
How are you dehydrated? They have you hooked up to IV fluids
No. From before. But it caused my stool to become impacted.
Ok
Its like trying to pass a dried out dog turd.
Lmao
Give you some of that magnesium citrate
Lol. No thanks. They've given me just about every type and brand of laxative known to man.

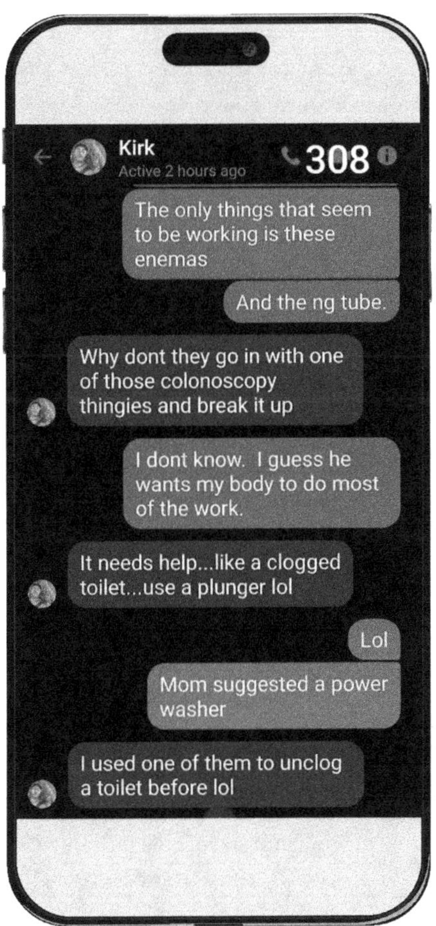

Kirk
Active 2 hours ago
308
The only things that seem to be working is these enemas
And the ng tube.
Why dont they go in with one of those colonoscopy thingies and break it up
I dont know. I guess he wants my body to do most of the work.
It needs help...like a clogged toilet...use a plunger lol
Lol
Mom suggested a power washer
I used one of them to unclog a toilet before lol

Kirk
Active 2 hours ago
309
Lol
Hehehe
Well sweetheart, I'm going to go now
Bed?
X22 report is calling
Oh. Ok love.
Talk to ya tomorrow. Love you.
Talk to you in the morning
I love you too

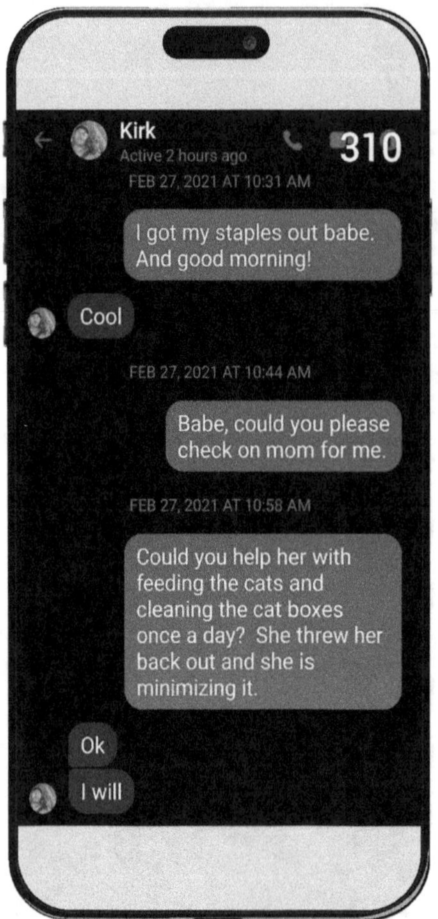
Kirk
Active 2 hours ago
310
FEB 27, 2021 AT 10:31 AM
I got my staples out babe. And good morning!
Cool
FEB 27, 2021 AT 10:44 AM
Babe, could you please check on mom for me.
FEB 27, 2021 AT 10:58 AM
Could you help her with feeding the cats and cleaning the cat boxes once a day? She threw her back out and she is minimizing it.
Ok
I will

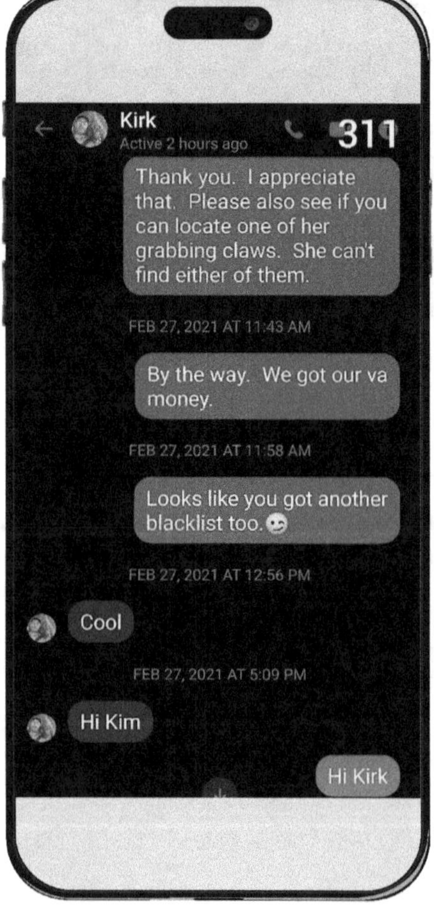
Kirk
Active 2 hours ago
311
Thank you. I appreciate that. Please also see if you can locate one of her grabbing claws. She can't find either of them.
FEB 27, 2021 AT 11:43 AM
By the way. We got our va money.
FEB 27, 2021 AT 11:58 AM
Looks like you got another blacklist too.
FEB 27, 2021 AT 12:56 PM
Cool
FEB 27, 2021 AT 5:09 PM
Hi Kim
Hi Kirk

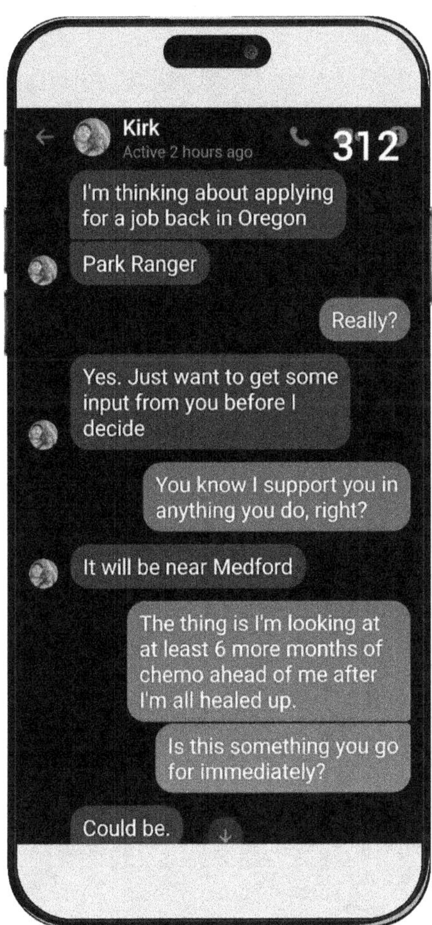
Kirk
Active 2 hours ago
312
I'm thinking about applying for a job back in Oregon
Park Ranger
Really?
Yes. Just want to get some input from you before I decide
You know I support you in anything you do, right?
It will be near Medford
The thing is I'm looking at at least 6 more months of chemo ahead of me after I'm all healed up.
Is this something you go for immediately?
Could be.

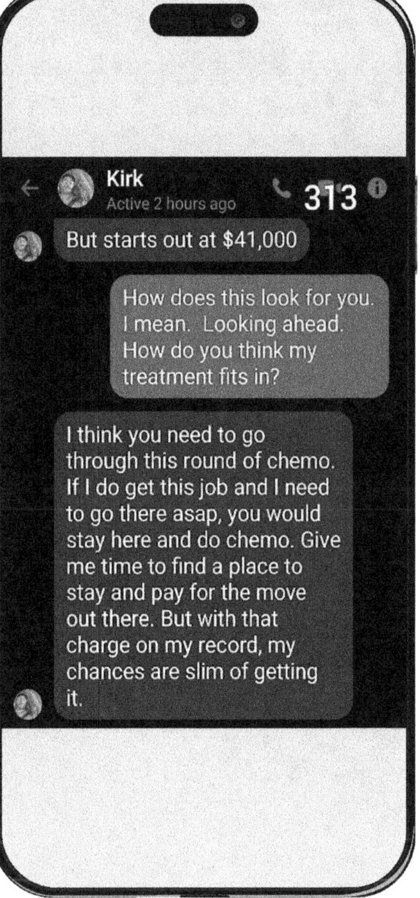
Kirk
Active 2 hours ago
313
But starts out at $41,000
How does this look for you. I mean. Looking ahead. How do you think my treatment fits in?
I think you need to go through this round of chemo. If I do get this job and I need to go there asap, you would stay here and do chemo. Give me time to find a place to stay and pay for the move out there. But with that charge on my record, my chances are slim of getting it.

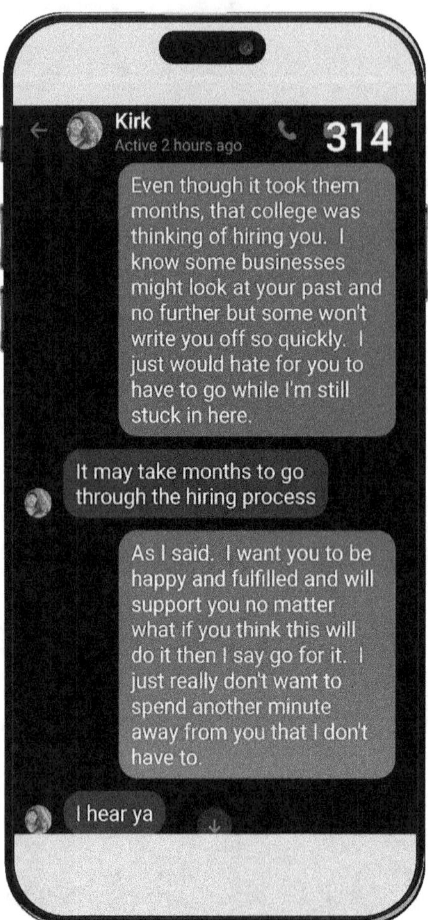
Kirk
Active 2 hours ago
314
Even though it took them months, that college was thinking of hiring you. I know some businesses might look at your past and no further but some won't write you off so quickly. I just would hate for you to have to go while I'm still stuck in here.
It may take months to go through the hiring process
As I said. I want you to be happy and fulfilled and will support you no matter what if you think this will do it then I say go for it. I just really don't want to spend another minute away from you that I don't have to.
I hear ya

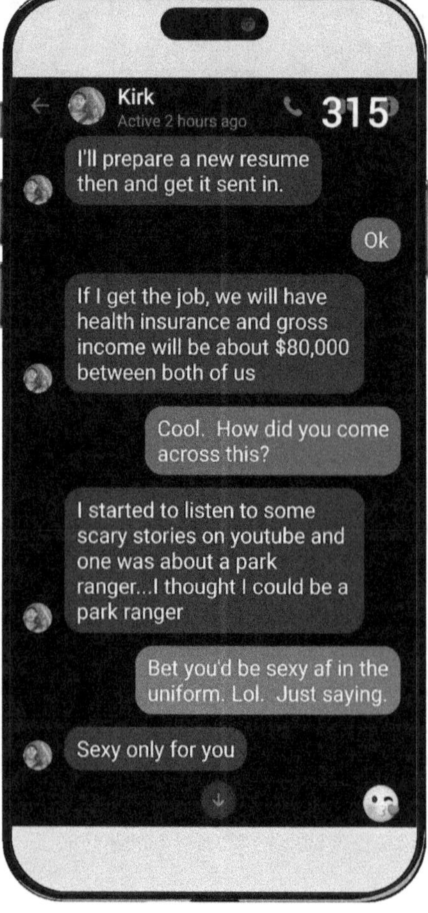
Kirk
Active 2 hours ago
315
I'll prepare a new resume then and get it sent in.
Ok
If I get the job, we will have health insurance and gross income will be about $80,000 between both of us
Cool. How did you come across this?
I started to listen to some scary stories on youtube and one was about a park ranger...I thought I could be a park ranger
Bet you'd be sexy af in the uniform. Lol. Just saying.
Sexy only for you

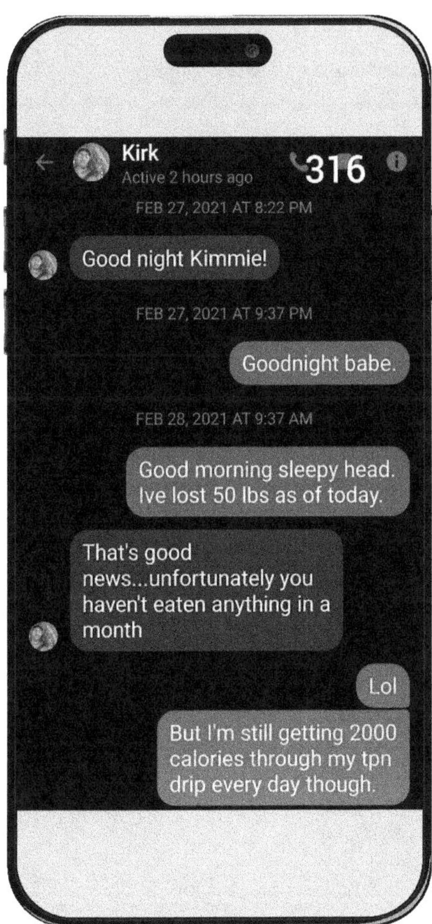
Kirk
Active 2 hours ago
316
FEB 27, 2021 AT 8:22 PM
Good night Kimmie!
FEB 27, 2021 AT 9:37 PM
Goodnight babe.
FEB 28, 2021 AT 9:37 AM
Good morning sleepy head. Ive lost 50 lbs as of today.
That's good news...unfortunately you haven't eaten anything in a month
Lol
But I'm still getting 2000 calories through my tpn drip every day though.

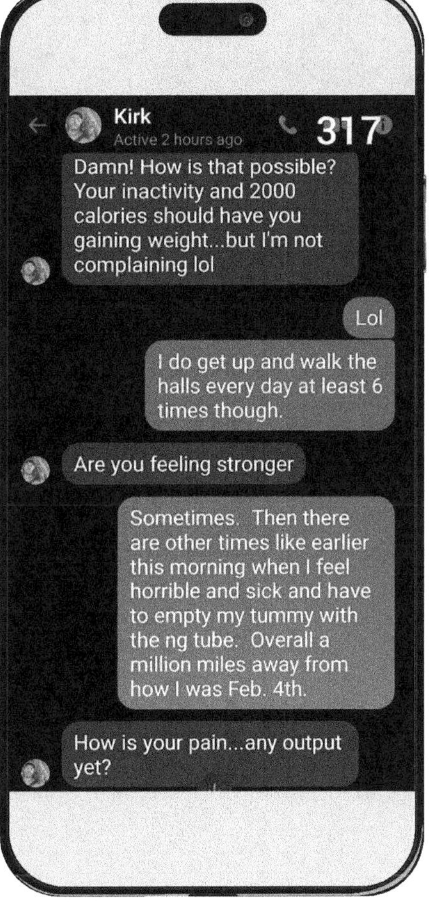
Kirk
Active 2 hours ago
317
Damn! How is that possible? Your inactivity and 2000 calories should have you gaining weight...but I'm not complaining lol
Lol
I do get up and walk the halls every day at least 6 times though.
Are you feeling stronger
Sometimes. Then there are other times like earlier this morning when I feel horrible and sick and have to empty my tummy with the ng tube. Overall a million miles away from how I was Feb. 4th.
How is your pain...any output yet?

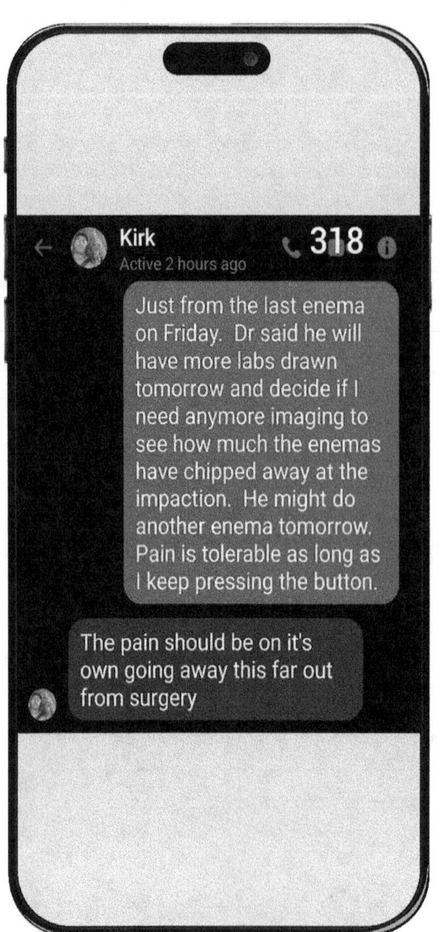

Kirk
Active 2 hours ago
318
Just from the last enema on Friday. Dr said he will have more labs drawn tomorrow and decide if I need anymore imaging to see how much the enemas have chipped away at the impaction. He might do another enema tomorrow. Pain is tolerable as long as I keep pressing the button.
The pain should be on it's own going away this far out from surgery

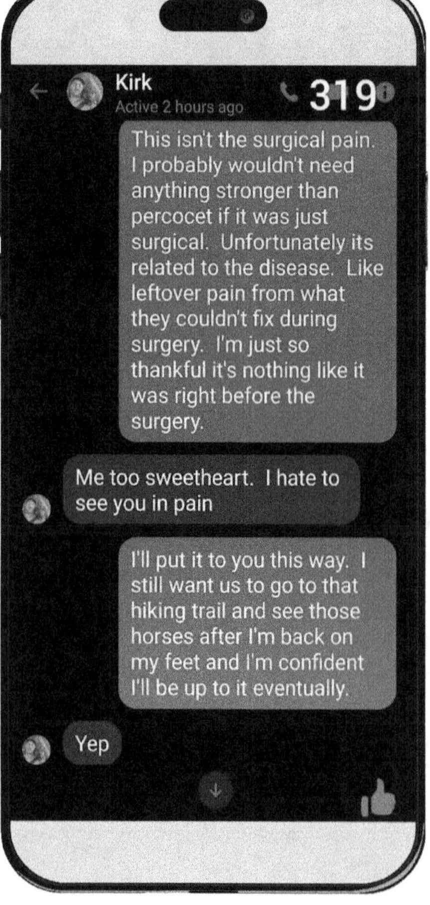

Kirk
Active 2 hours ago
319
This isn't the surgical pain. I probably wouldn't need anything stronger than percocet if it was just surgical. Unfortunately its related to the disease. Like leftover pain from what they couldn't fix during surgery. I'm just so thankful it's nothing like it was right before the surgery.
Me too sweetheart. I hate to see you in pain
I'll put it to you this way. I still want us to go to that hiking trail and see those horses after I'm back on my feet and I'm confident I'll be up to it eventually.
Yep

Kirk
Active 2 hours ago
320
Snuggling on the futon
Awww. You boys.
Hey babe, if I asked you to get me a few things would you bring them? Last time mom did it they had a volunteer pick it up and bring it up to me.
He growls when I move lol
Lol. Futon hog!!

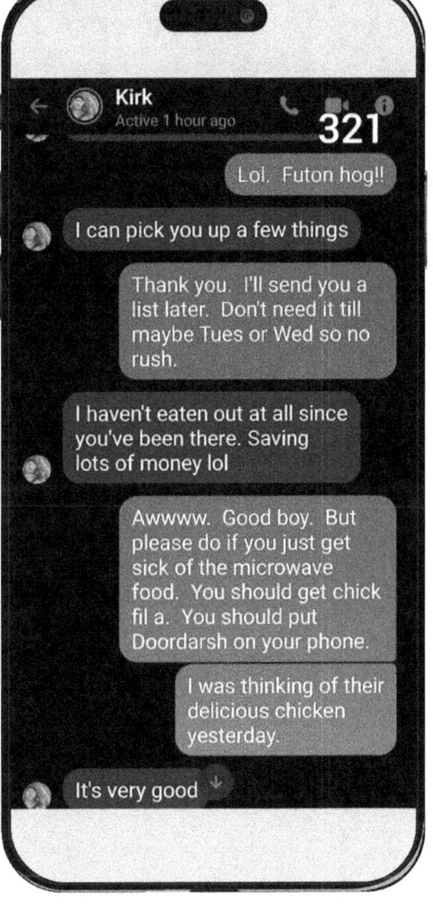
Kirk
Active 1 hour ago
321
Lol. Futon hog!!
I can pick you up a few things
Thank you. I'll send you a list later. Don't need it till maybe Tues or Wed so no rush.
I haven't eaten out at all since you've been there. Saving lots of money lol
Awwww. Good boy. But please do if you just get sick of the microwave food. You should get chick fil a. You should put Doordarsh on your phone.
I was thinking of their delicious chicken yesterday.
It's very good

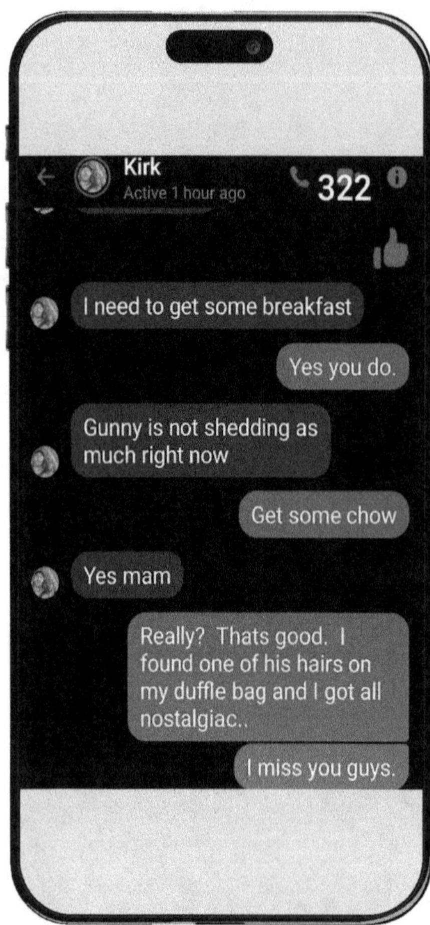
Kirk
Active 1 hour ago
322
I need to get some breakfast
Yes you do.
Gunny is not shedding as much right now
Get some chow
Yes mam
Really? Thats good. I found one of his hairs on my duffle bag and I got all nostalgiac..
I miss you guys.

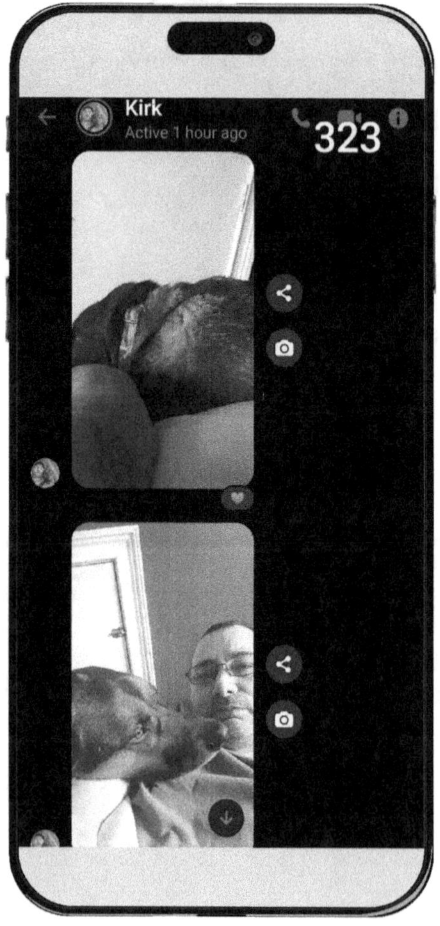
Kirk
Active 1 hour ago
323

Kirk
Active 1 hour ago
324
Love you both to pieces!!!!!
I'll bet he is going to be just as excited as me when he sees you
Oh yeah. He be like...."food lady is back!!" Lol
Breakfast sandwich...here I come
Enjoy!!
FEB 28, 2021 AT 9:15 PM
Hi babe. In case you went to sleep already I love you and goodnight.
Hey there. Just let the dog out one last time before bed
Hi hun.

Kirk
Active 1 hour ago
325
How are you? I'm tempted to stay up past midnight to see if TWD get posted on Amazon at midnight
It usually wasn't posted till the morning like 8 am.
Then I'm watching it as soon as I get up
Cool. Me too.
Well, I'm heading off to bed.
Good night
Ok sweetie. Sleep well. Love you.
MAR 1, 2021 AT 9:16 AM
You awake
Yup

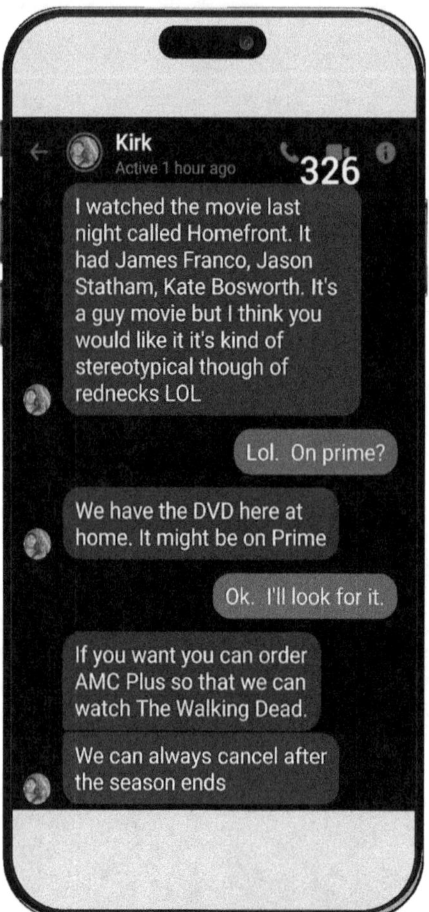
Kirk
Active 1 hour ago
326
I watched the movie last night called Homefront. It had James Franco, Jason Statham, Kate Bosworth. It's a guy movie but I think you would like it it's kind of stereotypical though of rednecks LOL
Lol. On prime?
We have the DVD here at home. It might be on Prime
Ok. I'll look for it.
If you want you can order AMC Plus so that we can watch The Walking Dead.
We can always cancel after the season ends

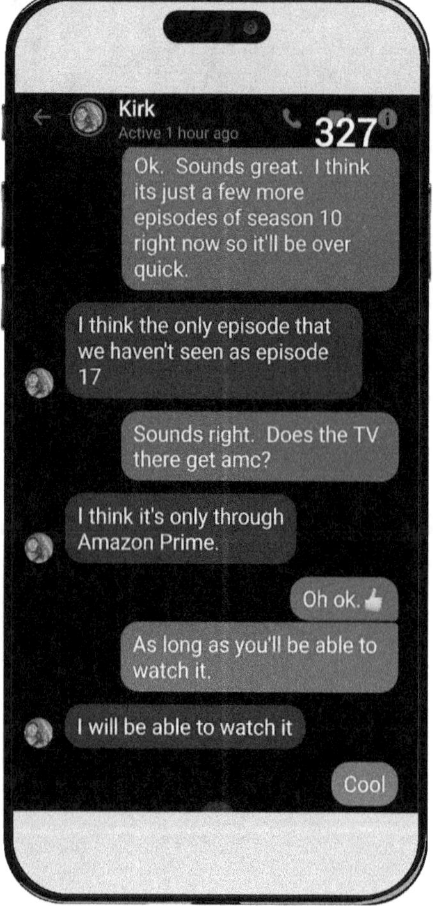
Kirk
Active 1 hour ago
327
Ok. Sounds great. I think its just a few more episodes of season 10 right now so it'll be over quick.
I think the only episode that we haven't seen as episode 17
Sounds right. Does the TV there get amc?
I think it's only through Amazon Prime.
Oh ok.
As long as you'll be able to watch it.
I will be able to watch it
Cool

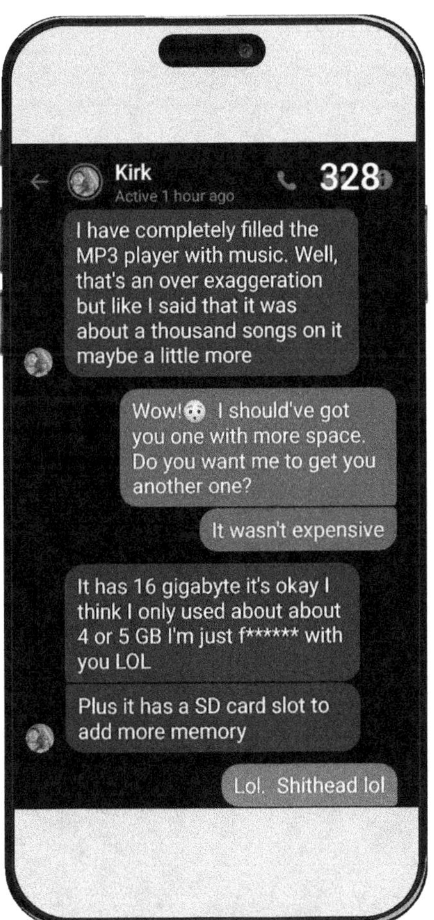
Kirk
Active 1 hour ago
328
I have completely filled the MP3 player with music. Well, that's an over exaggeration but like I said that it was about a thousand songs on it maybe a little more
Wow! I should've got you one with more space. Do you want me to get you another one?
It wasn't expensive
It has 16 gigabyte it's okay I think I only used about about 4 or 5 GB I'm just f****** with you LOL
Plus it has a SD card slot to add more memory
Lol. Shithead lol

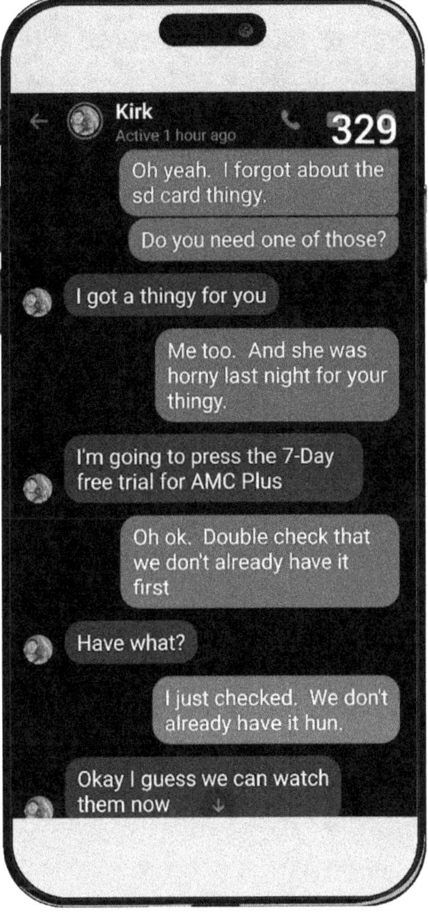
Kirk
Active 1 hour ago
329
Oh yeah. I forgot about the sd card thingy.
Do you need one of those?
I got a thingy for you
Me too. And she was horny last night for your thingy.
I'm going to press the 7-Day free trial for AMC Plus
Oh ok. Double check that we don't already have it first
Have what?
I just checked. We don't already have it hun.
Okay I guess we can watch them now

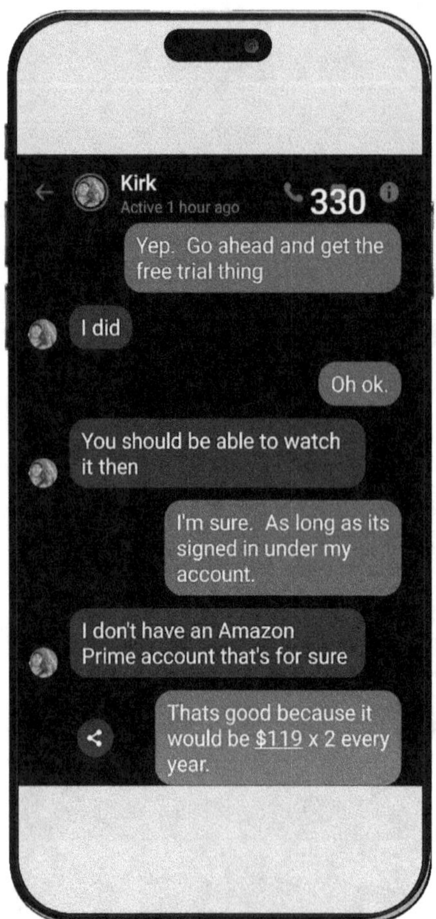

Kirk
Active 1 hour ago
330
Yep. Go ahead and get the free trial thing
I did
Oh ok.
You should be able to watch it then
I'm sure. As long as its signed in under my account.
I don't have an Amazon Prime account that's for sure
Thats good because it would be $119 x 2 every year.

Kirk
Active 1 hour ago
331
He's a big galoot.
Yep
Handsome hubby and our big galoot lol
He likes to snuggle lol
With you maybe lol
He just wants my treats

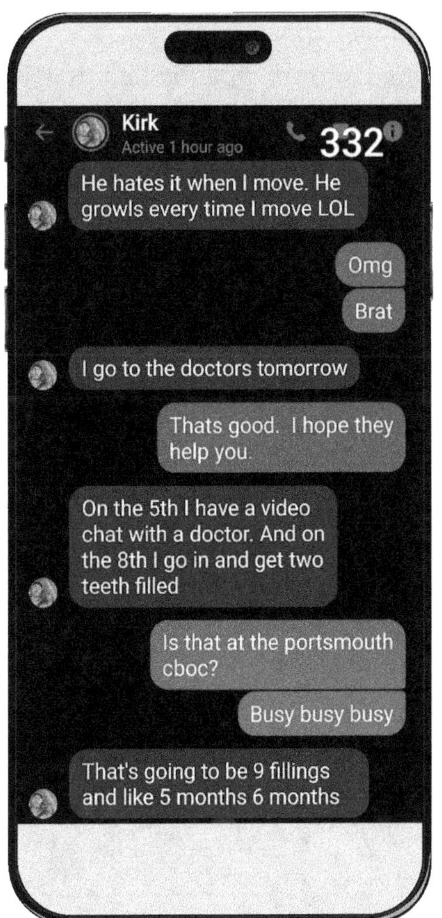

Kirk
Active 1 hour ago
332
He hates it when I move. He growls every time I move LOL
Omg
Brat
I go to the doctors tomorrow
Thats good. I hope they help you.
On the 5th I have a video chat with a doctor. And on the 8th I go in and get two teeth filled
Is that at the portsmouth cboc?
Busy busy busy
That's going to be 9 fillings and like 5 months 6 months

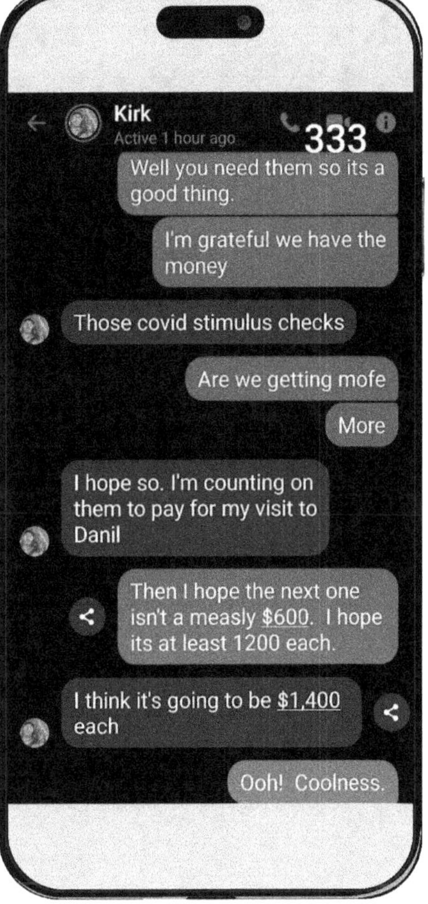

Kirk
Active 1 hour ago
333
Well you need them so its a good thing.
I'm grateful we have the money
Those covid stimulus checks
Are we getting mofe
More
I hope so. I'm counting on them to pay for my visit to Danil
Then I hope the next one isn't a measly $600. I hope its at least 1200 each.
I think it's going to be $1,400 each
Ooh! Coolness.

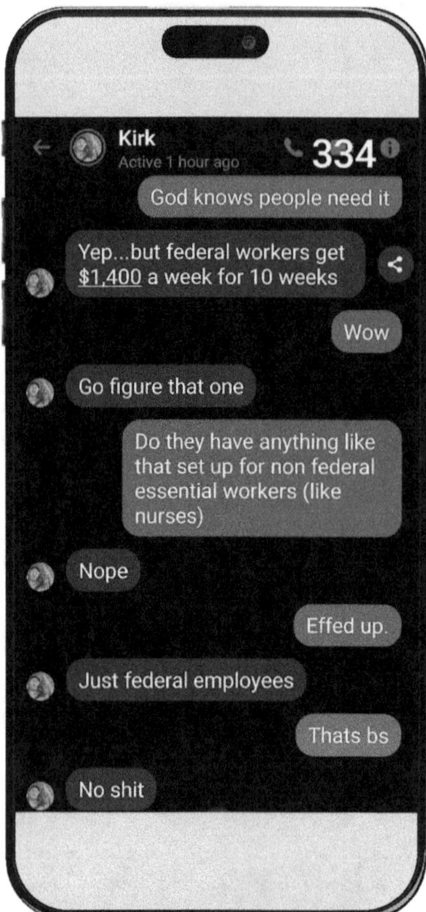

Played along with me on my take of a song by the Bare-Naked Ladies. I loved how our sense of humor matched and how we had so much in common concerning cultural references and music.

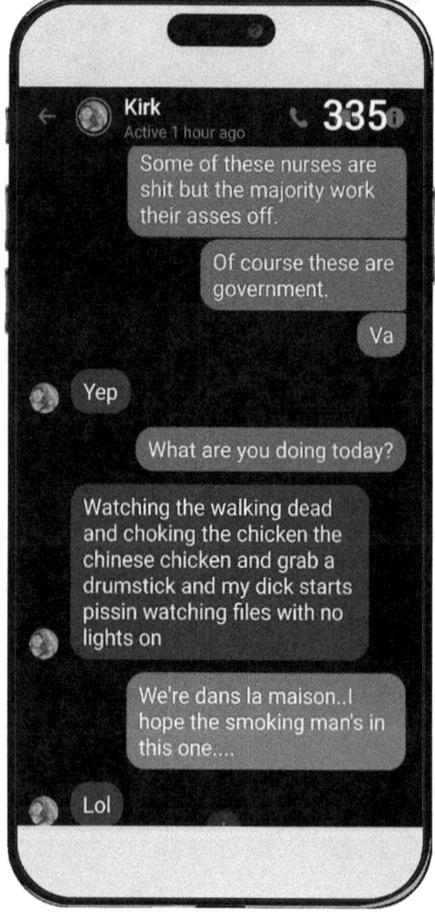

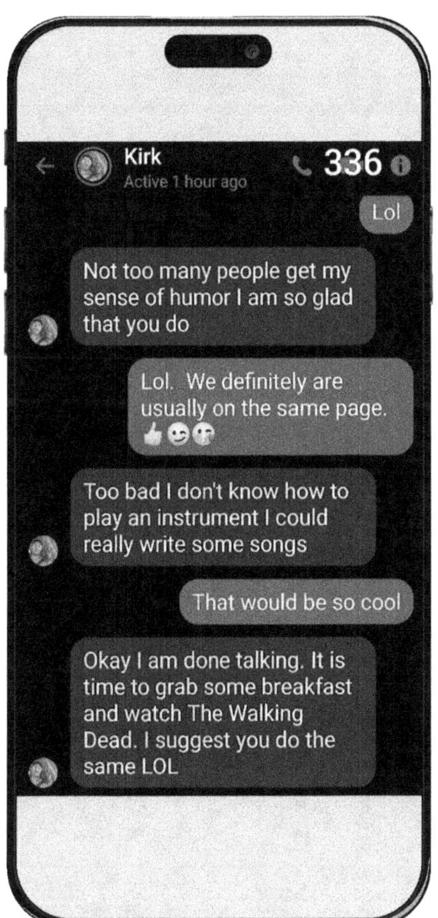

Kirk
Active 1 hour ago
336
Lol
Not too many people get my sense of humor I am so glad that you do
Lol. We definitely are usually on the same page.
Too bad I don't know how to play an instrument I could really write some songs
That would be so cool
Okay I am done talking. It is time to grab some breakfast and watch The Walking Dead. I suggest you do the same LOL

Kirk
Active 1 hour ago
337
I gotta take a quick walk first then I'm on board for sure. Talk to ya later sweetie.
I am glad that you're recovering well. And I will talk to you later gator
P.S. I've only gone through 2 rolls of tp since you've been gone
Well I'm a girl silly!!! Lol
MAR 1, 2021 AT 7:28 PM
Hi there...did you watch the walking dead today

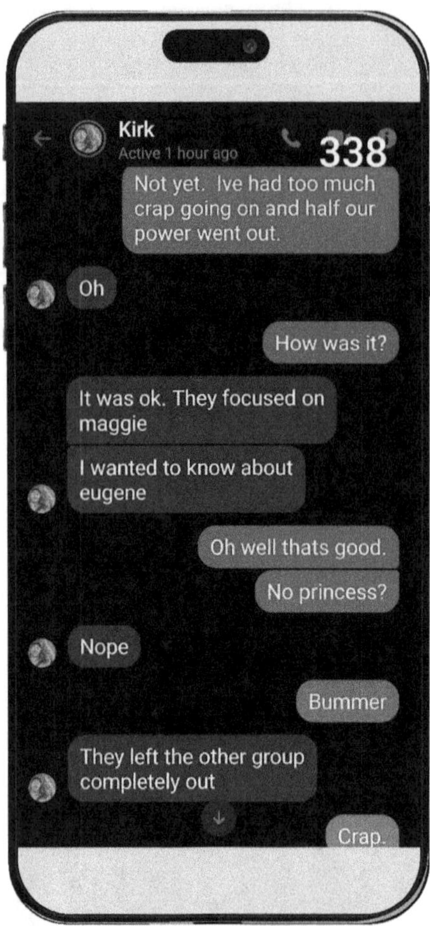
Kirk
Active 1 hour ago
338
Not yet. Ive had too much crap going on and half our power went out.
Oh
How was it?
It was ok. They focused on maggie
I wanted to know about eugene
Oh well thats good.
No princess?
Nope
Bummer
They left the other group completely out
Crap.

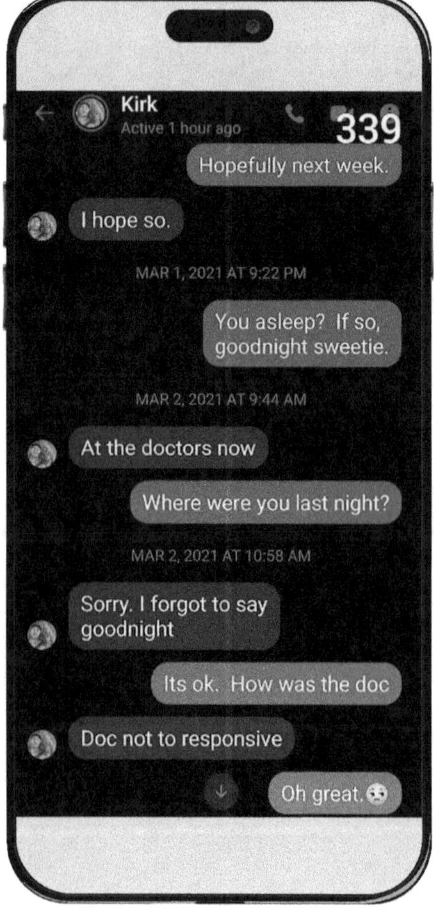
Kirk
Active 1 hour ago
339
Hopefully next week.
I hope so.
MAR 1, 2021 AT 9:22 PM
You asleep? If so, goodnight sweetie.
MAR 2, 2021 AT 9:44 AM
At the doctors now
Where were you last night?
MAR 2, 2021 AT 10:58 AM
Sorry. I forgot to say goodnight
Its ok. How was the doc
Doc not to responsive
Oh great.

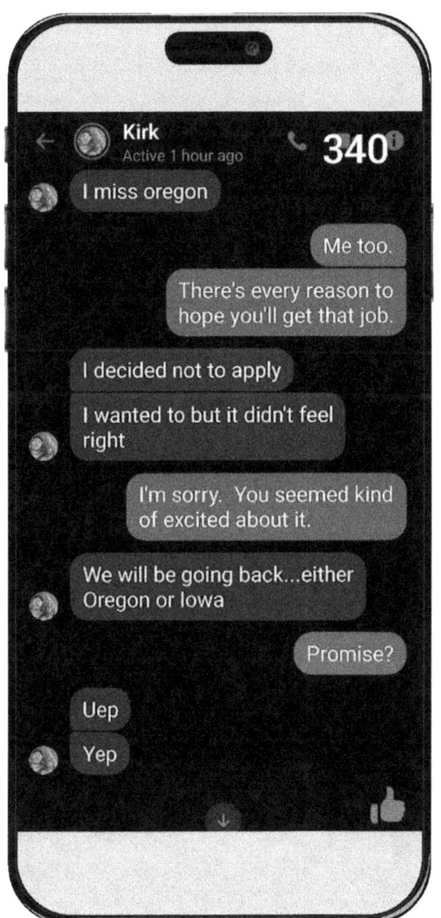

Kirk
Active 1 hour ago
340
I miss oregon
Me too.
There's every reason to hope you'll get that job.
I decided not to apply
I wanted to but it didn't feel right
I'm sorry. You seemed kind of excited about it.
We will be going back...either Oregon or Iowa
Promise?
Uep
Yep

Kirk
Active 1 hour ago
341
I really don't like it here. I love mome, therefore I love seeing her here but I just loved Oregon so much.
Mom
I think your mom finally realizes what she had in Oregon and regrets coming here
Yeah. She is very regretful.
That makes me sad though.
I dont want her to feel like that.
She wanted to be in the city close to everything. Now she has it along with higher taxes paying for sewer and water and overpriced garbage pick up

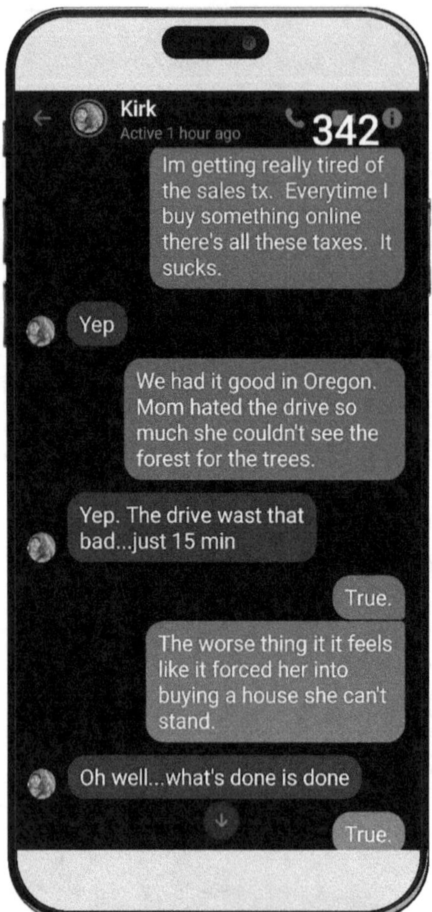
Kirk
Active 1 hour ago
342
Im getting really tired of the sales tx. Everytime I buy something online there's all these taxes. It sucks.
Yep
We had it good in Oregon. Mom hated the drive so much she couldn't see the forest for the trees.
Yep. The drive wast that bad...just 15 min
True.
The worse thing it it feels like it forced her into buying a house she can't stand.
Oh well...what's done is done
True.

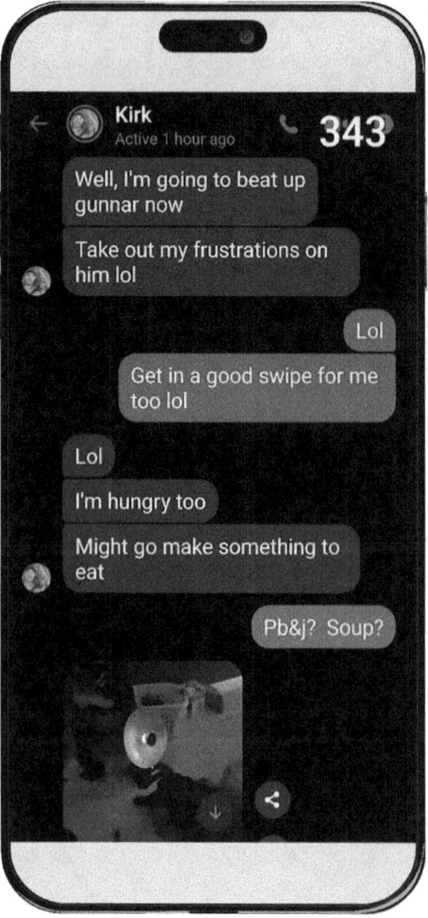
Kirk
Active 1 hour ago
343
Well, I'm going to beat up gunnar now
Take out my frustrations on him lol
Lol
Get in a good swipe for me too lol
Lol
I'm hungry too
Might go make something to eat
Pb&j? Soup?

Kirk
Active 1 hour ago
344
Awww. Is it cold enough for the heater?
Yep
Wow.
Well go eat. It'll warm you up.
Jimmy dean breakfast

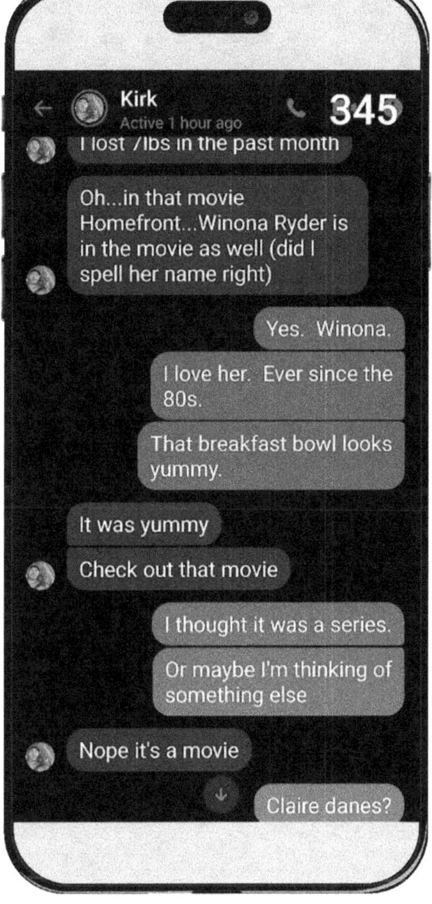

Kirk
Active 1 hour ago
345
I lost 7lbs in the past month
Oh...in that movie Homefront...Winona Ryder is in the movie as well (did I spell her name right)
Yes. Winona.
I love her. Ever since the 80s.
That breakfast bowl looks yummy.
It was yummy
Check out that movie
I thought it was a series.
Or maybe I'm thinking of something else
Nope it's a movie
Claire danes?

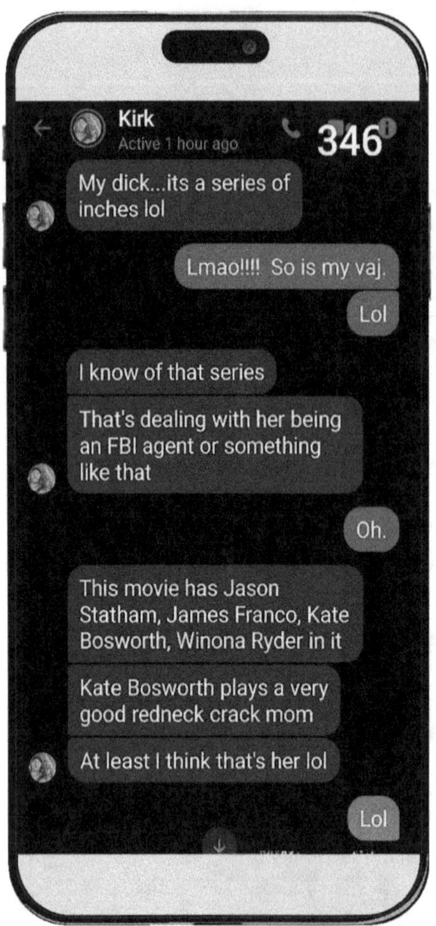

Kirk
Active 1 hour ago
346
My dick...its a series of inches lol
Lmao!!!! So is my vaj.
Lol
I know of that series
That's dealing with her being an FBI agent or something like that
Oh.
This movie has Jason Statham, James Franco, Kate Bosworth, Winona Ryder in it
Kate Bosworth plays a very good redneck crack mom
At least I think that's her lol
Lol

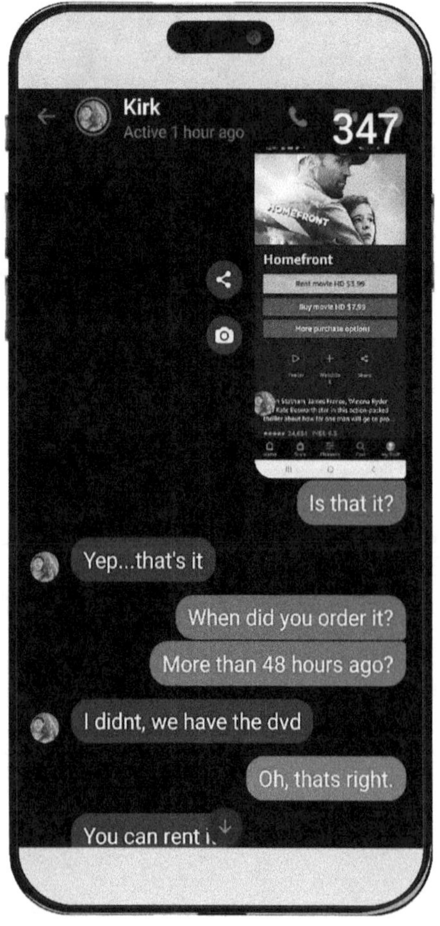

Kirk
Active 1 hour ago
347
Homefront
Rent movie HD $3.99
Buy movie HD $7.99
More purchase options
Is that it?
Yep...that's it
When did you order it?
More than 48 hours ago?
I didnt, we have the dvd
Oh, thats right.
You can rent i

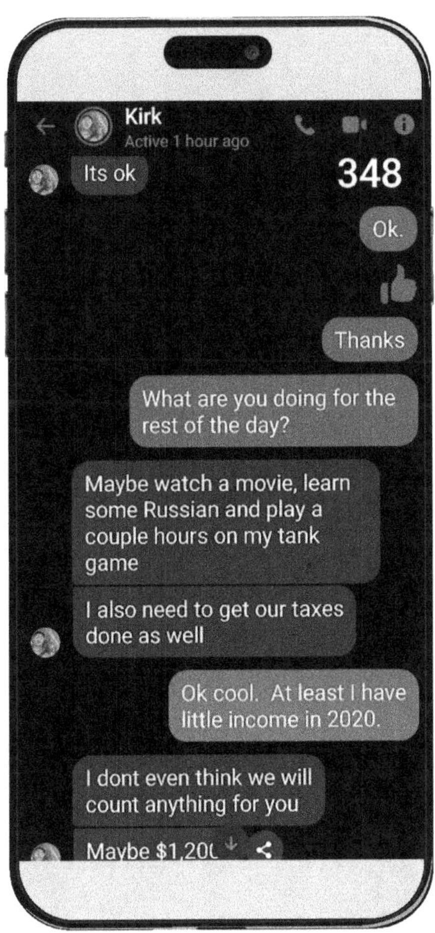

Kirk
Active 1 hour ago
348
Its ok
Ok.
Thanks
What are you doing for the rest of the day?
Maybe watch a movie, learn some Russian and play a couple hours on my tank game
I also need to get our taxes done as well
Ok cool. At least I have little income in 2020.
I dont even think we will count anything for you
Maybe $1,200

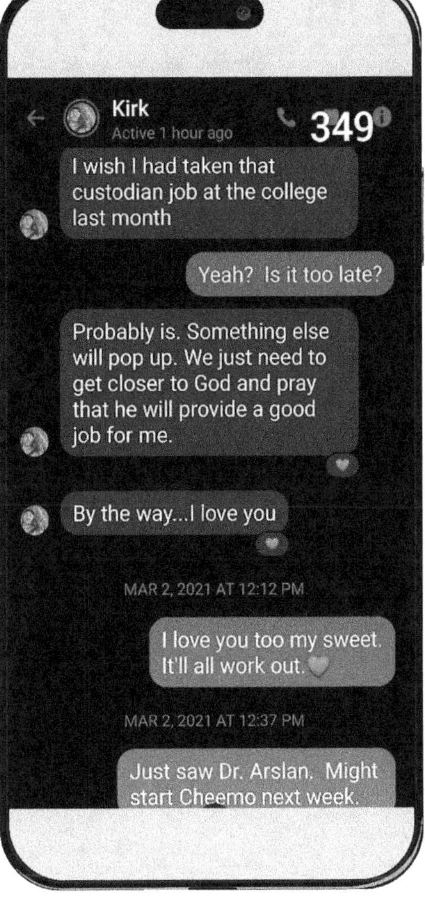

Kirk
Active 1 hour ago
349
I wish I had taken that custodian job at the college last month
Yeah? Is it too late?
Probably is. Something else will pop up. We just need to get closer to God and pray that he will provide a good job for me.
By the way...I love you
MAR 2, 2021 AT 12:12 PM
I love you too my sweet. It'll all work out.
MAR 2, 2021 AT 12:37 PM
Just saw Dr. Arslan. Might start Cheemo next week.

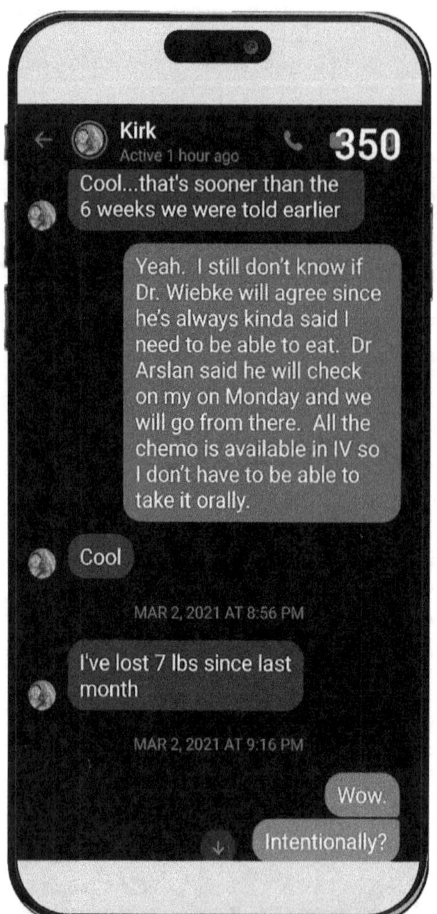
Kirk
Active 1 hour ago
350
Cool...that's sooner than the 6 weeks we were told earlier
Yeah. I still don't know if Dr. Wiebke will agree since he's always kinda said I need to be able to eat. Dr Arslan said he will check on my on Monday and we will go from there. All the chemo is available in IV so I don't have to be able to take it orally.
Cool
MAR 2, 2021 AT 8:56 PM
I've lost 7 lbs since last month
MAR 2, 2021 AT 9:16 PM
Wow.
Intentionally?

Kirk
Active 1 hour ago
351
MAR 2, 2021 AT 9:35 PM
Nope
I'm sending you a meme
Hi Joe
Oh shit!
Lol!!!
I like that one
He would be deserving of dexter lol

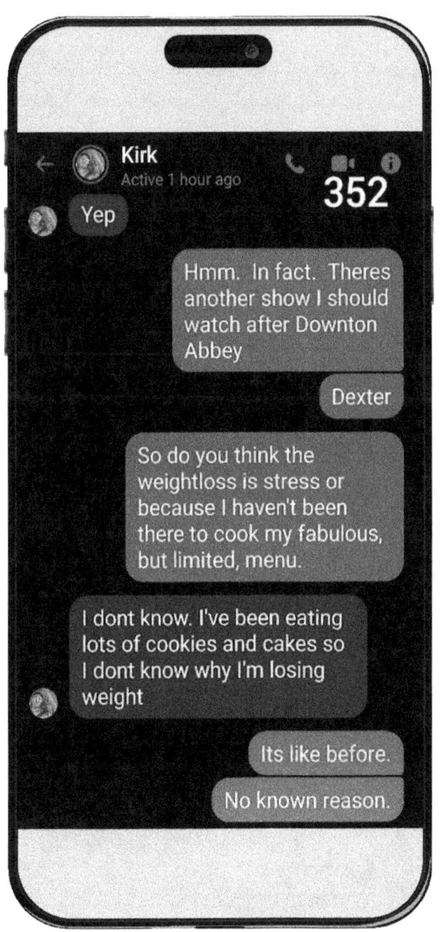
Kirk
Active 1 hour ago
352
Yep
Hmm. In fact. Theres another show I should watch after Downton Abbey
Dexter
So do you think the weightloss is stress or because I haven't been there to cook my fabulous, but limited, menu.
I dont know. I've been eating lots of cookies and cakes so I dont know why I'm losing weight
Its like before.
No known reason.

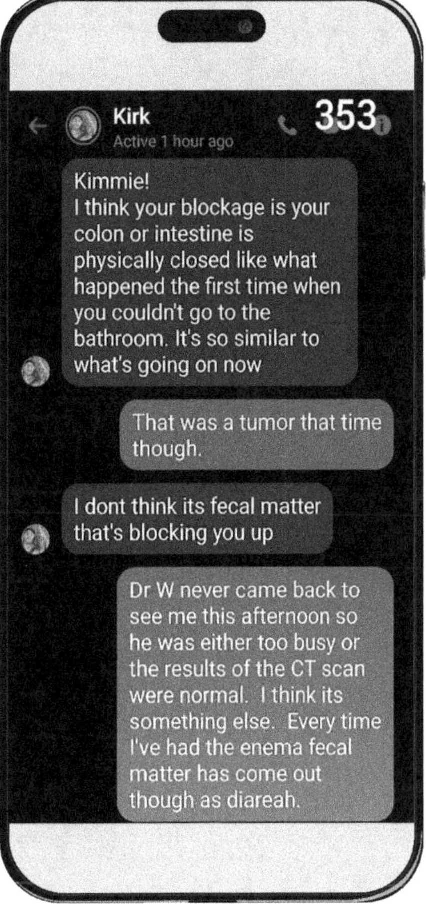
Kirk
Active 1 hour ago
353
Kimmie!
I think your blockage is your colon or intestine is physically closed like what happened the first time when you couldn't go to the bathroom. It's so similar to what's going on now
That was a tumor that time though.
I dont think its fecal matter that's blocking you up
Dr W never came back to see me this afternoon so he was either too busy or the results of the CT scan were normal. I think its something else. Every time I've had the enema fecal matter has come out though as diareah.

Kirk
Active 1 hour ago
354
It's time for bed.
I'll talk to you in the morning. I have to go get an xray of my shoulders
Ok babe. Text me when you go. Love you.
Love you too
Good night
Gunfight
Lol
Damn ac
Lol
MAR 3, 2021 AT 7:12 AM
Don't forget your appointment hunni.
MAR 3, 2021 AT 7:28 AM

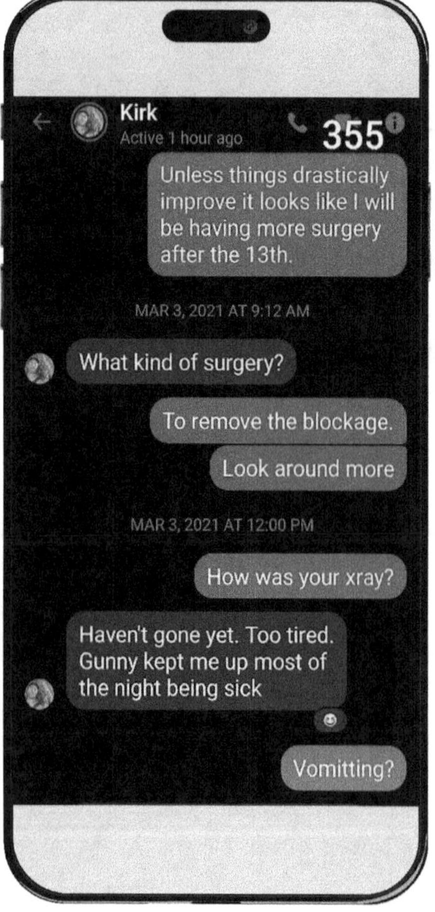
Kirk
Active 1 hour ago
355
Unless things drastically improve it looks like I will be having more surgery after the 13th.
MAR 3, 2021 AT 9:12 AM
What kind of surgery?
To remove the blockage.
Look around more
MAR 3, 2021 AT 12:00 PM
How was your xray?
Haven't gone yet. Too tired. Gunny kept me up most of the night being sick
Vomitting?

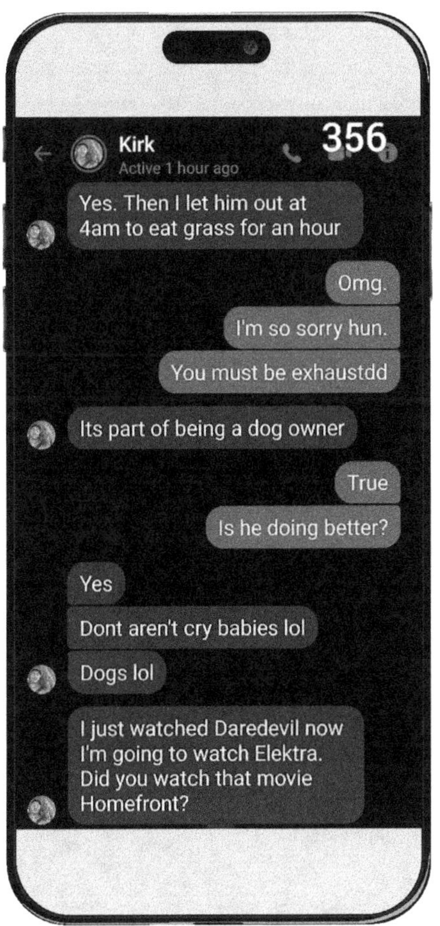
Kirk
Active 1 hour ago
356
Yes. Then I let him out at 4am to eat grass for an hour
Omg.
I'm so sorry hun.
You must be exhaustdd
Its part of being a dog owner
True
Is he doing better?
Yes
Dont aren't cry babies lol
Dogs lol
I just watched Daredevil now I'm going to watch Elektra. Did you watch that movie Homefront?

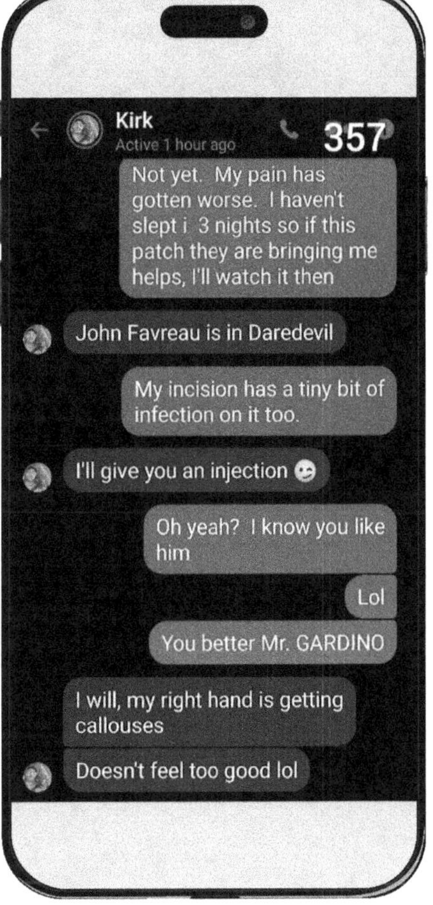
Kirk
Active 1 hour ago
357
Not yet. My pain has gotten worse. I haven't slept i 3 nights so if this patch they are bringing me helps, I'll watch it then
John Favreau is in Daredevil
My incision has a tiny bit of infection on it too.
I'll give you an injection
Oh yeah? I know you like him
Lol
You better Mr. GARDINO
I will, my right hand is getting callouses
Doesn't feel too good lol

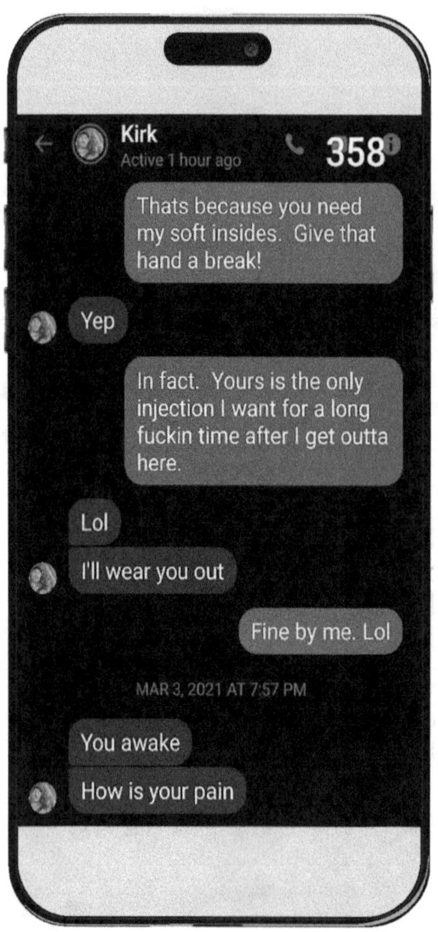

Kirk
Active 1 hour ago
358
Thats because you need my soft insides. Give that hand a break!
Yep
In fact. Yours is the only injection I want for a long fuckin time after I get outta here.
Lol
I'll wear you out
Fine by me. Lol
MAR 3, 2021 AT 7:57 PM
You awake
How is your pain

Kirk
Active 1 hour ago
359
Better. They put another fentanyl patch on me.
Its definitely taken the edge off.
Good
You getting ready for bed
Did you watch the walking dead yet?
MAR 3, 2021 AT 9:27 PM
Good night kim... talk to you in the morning
Goodnight sweetie
MAR 4, 2021 AT 10:27 AM
I'm here at the hospital getting x-rays done
Oh hi babe! Lol

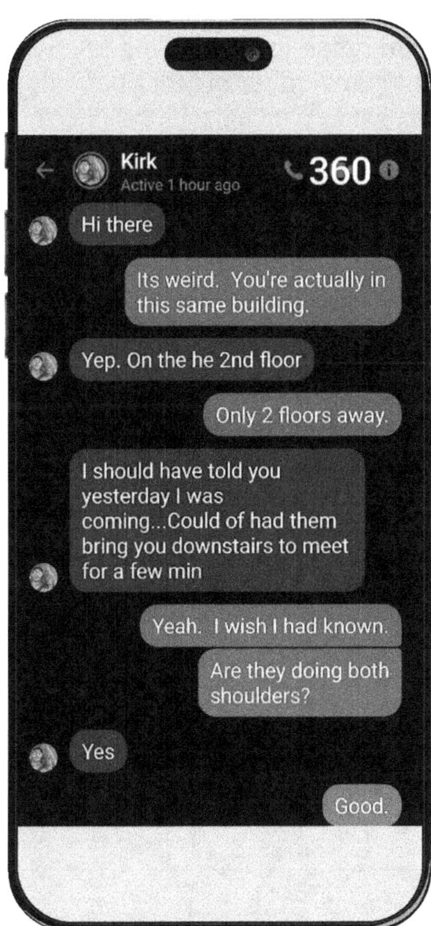

Kirk
Active 1 hour ago
360
Hi there
Its weird. You're actually in this same building.
Yep. On the he 2nd floor
Only 2 floors away.
I should have told you yesterday I was coming...Could of had them bring you downstairs to meet for a few min
Yeah. I wish I had known.
Are they doing both shoulders?
Yes
Good.

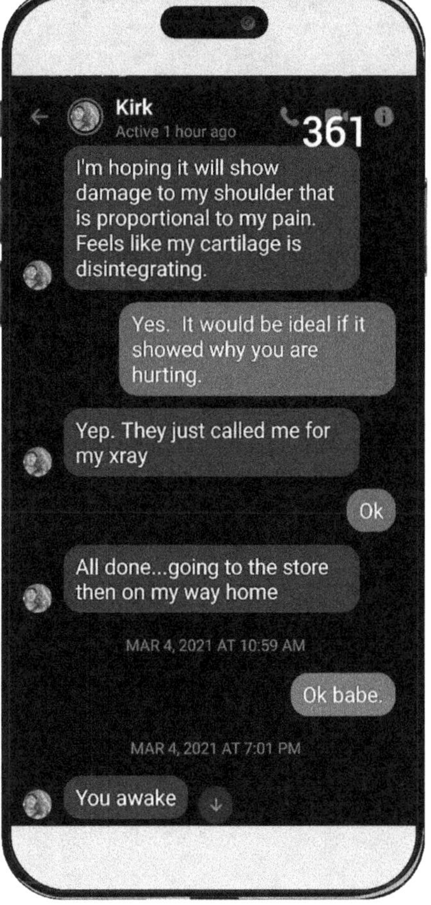

Kirk
Active 1 hour ago
361
I'm hoping it will show damage to my shoulder that is proportional to my pain. Feels like my cartilage is disintegrating.
Yes. It would be ideal if it showed why you are hurting.
Yep. They just called me for my xray
Ok
All done...going to the store then on my way home
MAR 4, 2021 AT 10:59 AM
Ok babe.
MAR 4, 2021 AT 7:01 PM
You awake

My teeth went bad when I had a full mental breakdown after the USPS falsely accused me of stealing and I quit. Kim cared for me for about a year as my depression kept me from working.
During this time, I brushed my teeth about every 2 weeks and showered once in 3 to 4 weeks. I slept between 16 and 20 hours a day.

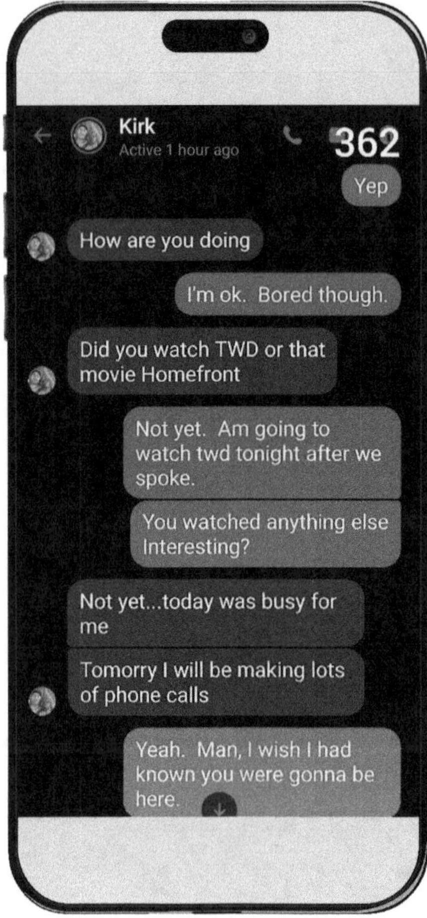

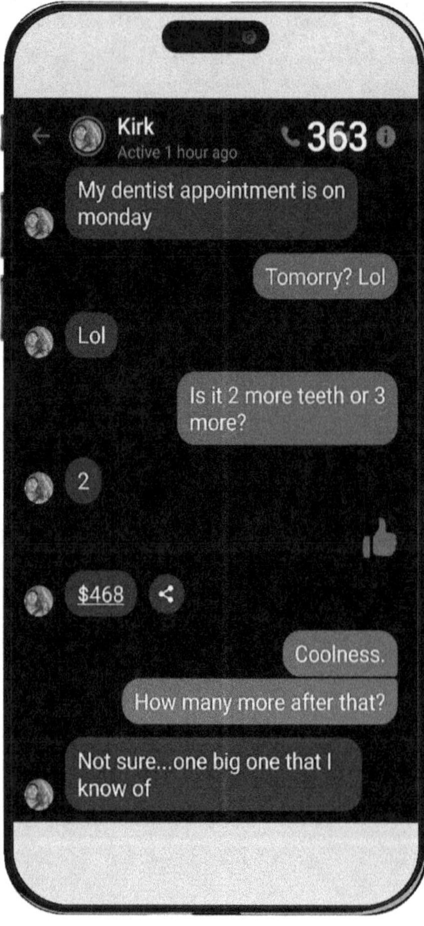

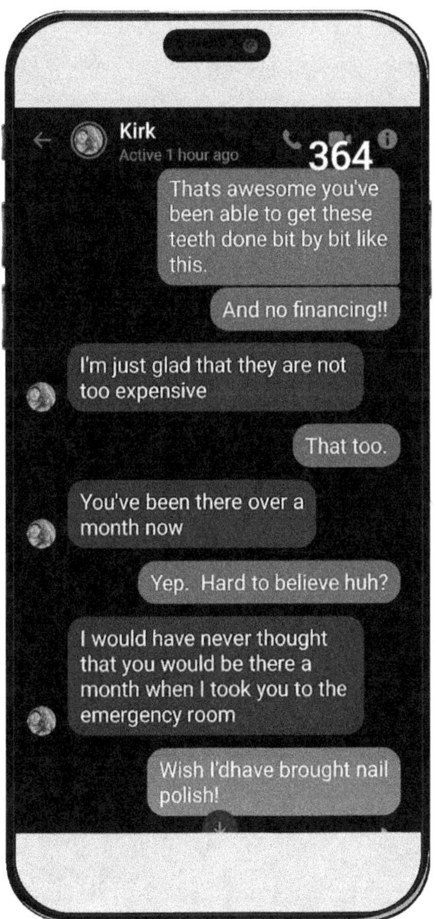

Kirk
Active 1 hour ago
364
Thats awesome you've been able to get these teeth done bit by bit like this.
And no financing!!
I'm just glad that they are not too expensive
That too.
You've been there over a month now
Yep. Hard to believe huh?
I would have never thought that you would be there a month when I took you to the emergency room
Wish I'dhave brought nail polish!

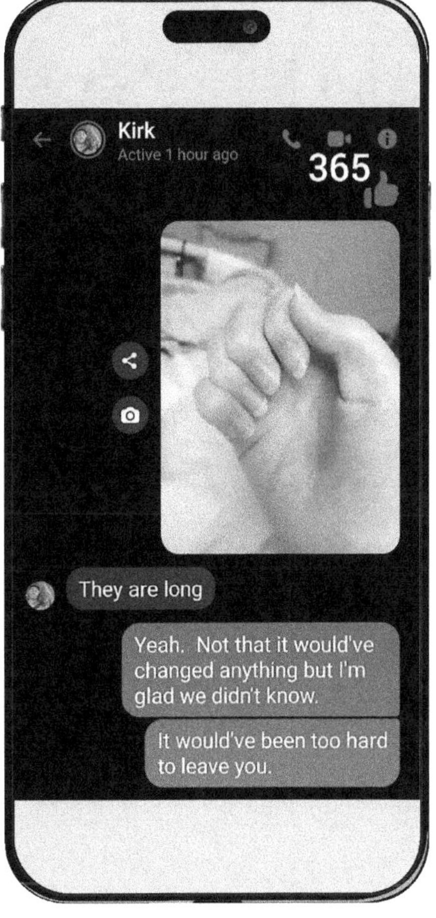

Kirk
Active 1 hour ago
365
They are long
Yeah. Not that it would've changed anything but I'm glad we didn't know.
It would've been too hard to leave you.

Kirk
Active 1 hour ago
366
You would have been fine
No I wouldn't have.
Your doing good now
Not really. You think I miss you any less than I did 3 weeks ago?
I guess not
But we do talk everyday
Do you miss me still?
Yes I miss you
Not the same. Its not like being with you in person.
I know

Kirk
Active 1 hour ago
367
A lot of times I feel bad but you say you want to go and I just let you go cause I don't want to hold you up.
Ok...I gotta go now
Just fcking with you
I know but I'm upset and want to go home.
You will be home soon
Why dont me and your mom come see you tomorrow at 2pm
Because I think we gotta get some kind of approval first. I dont know how it works.

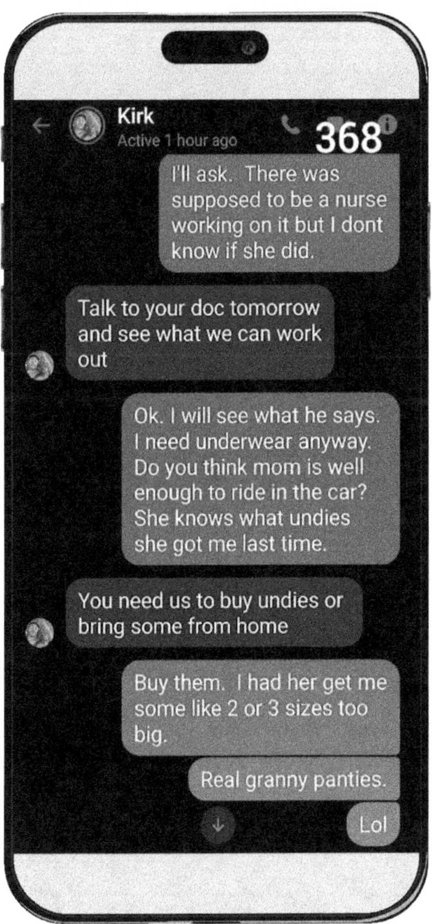

Kirk
Active 1 hour ago
368
I'll ask. There was supposed to be a nurse working on it but I dont know if she did.
Talk to your doc tomorrow and see what we can work out
Ok. I will see what he says. I need underwear anyway. Do you think mom is well enough to ride in the car? She knows what undies she got me last time.
You need us to buy undies or bring some from home
Buy them. I had her get me some like 2 or 3 sizes too big.
Real granny panties.
Lol

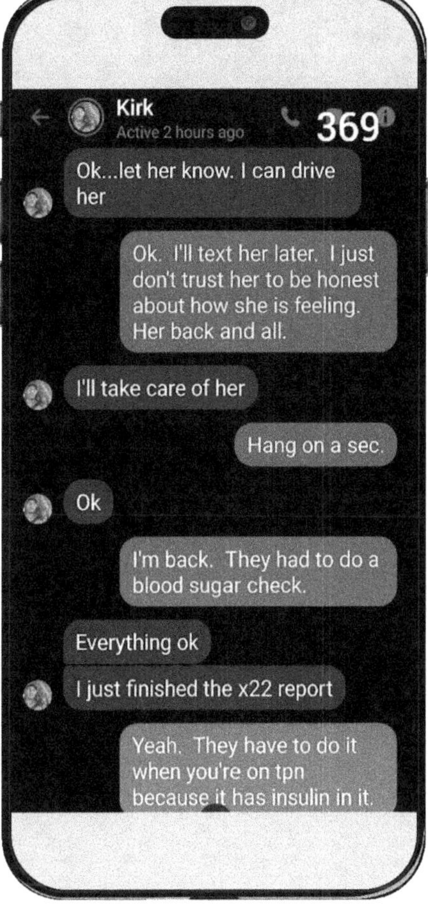

Kirk
Active 2 hours ago
369
Ok...let her know. I can drive her
Ok. I'll text her later. I just don't trust her to be honest about how she is feeling. Her back and all.
I'll take care of her
Hang on a sec.
Ok
I'm back. They had to do a blood sugar check.
Everything ok
I just finished the x22 report
Yeah. They have to do it when you're on tpn because it has insulin in it.

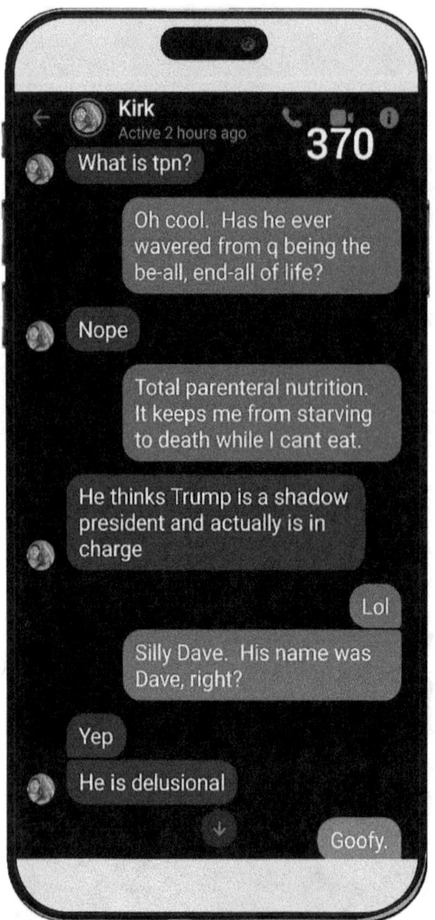

Kirk
Active 2 hours ago
370
What is tpn?
Oh cool. Has he ever wavered from q being the be-all, end-all of life?
Nope
Total parenteral nutrition. It keeps me from starving to death while I cant eat.
He thinks Trump is a shadow president and actually is in charge
Lol
Silly Dave. His name was Dave, right?
Yep
He is delusional
Goofy.

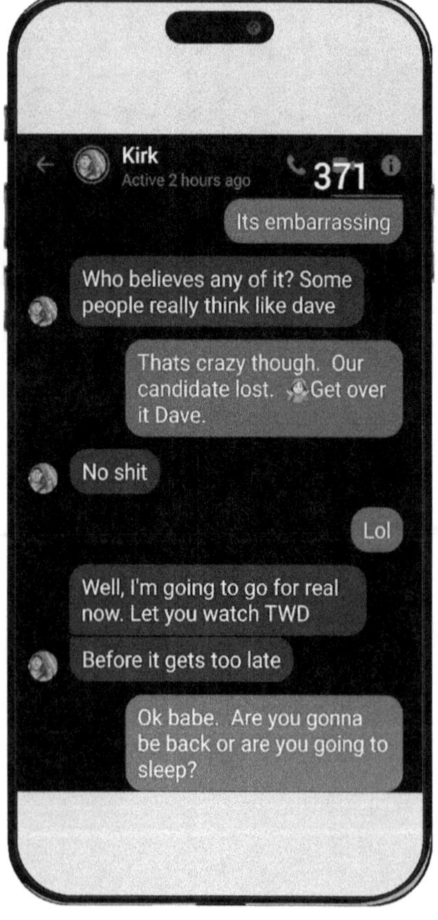

Kirk
Active 2 hours ago
371
Its embarrassing
Who believes any of it? Some people really think like dave
Thats crazy though. Our candidate lost. Get over it Dave.
No shit
Lol
Well, I'm going to go for real now. Let you watch TWD
Before it gets too late
Ok babe. Are you gonna be back or are you going to sleep?

There are two 371 messages.
I miss labeled.

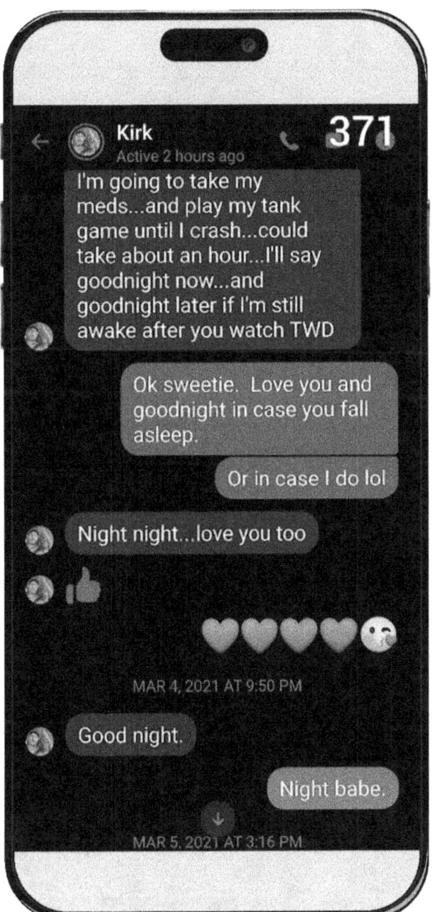
Kirk
Active 2 hours ago
371

I'm going to take my meds...and play my tank game until I crash...could take about an hour...I'll say goodnight now...and goodnight later if I'm still awake after you watch TWD

Ok sweetie. Love you and goodnight in case you fall asleep.

Or in case I do lol

Night night...love you too

MAR 4, 2021 AT 9:50 PM

Good night.

Night babe.

MAR 5, 2021 AT 3:16 PM

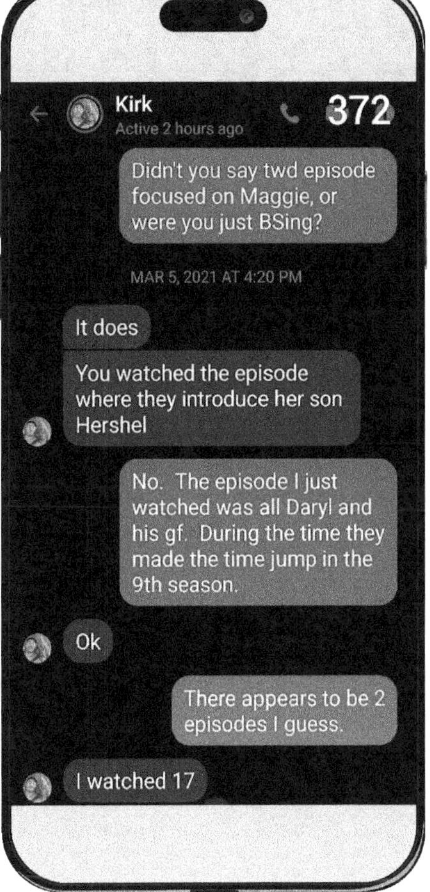
Kirk
Active 2 hours ago
372

Didn't you say twd episode focused on Maggie, or were you just BSing?

MAR 5, 2021 AT 4:20 PM

It does

You watched the episode where they introduce her son Hershel

No. The episode I just watched was all Daryl and his gf. During the time they made the time jump in the 9th season.

Ok

There appears to be 2 episodes I guess.

I watched 17

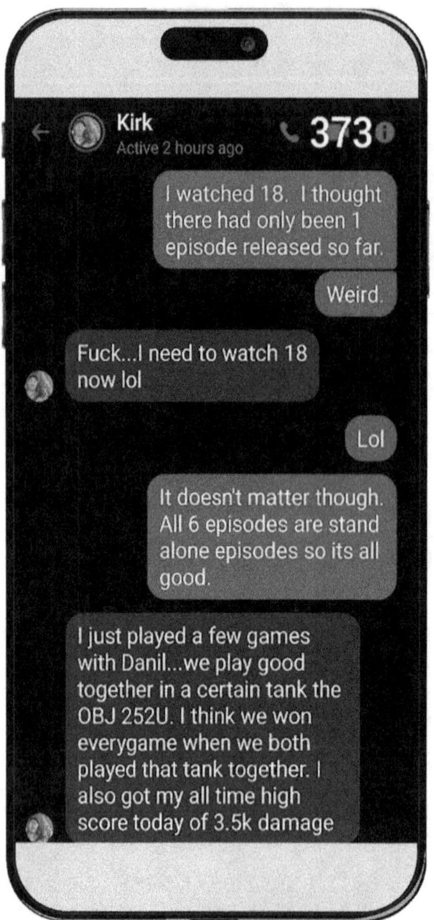
Kirk
Active 2 hours ago
373
I watched 18. I thought there had only been 1 episode released so far.
Weird.
Fuck...I need to watch 18 now lol
Lol
It doesn't matter though. All 6 episodes are stand alone episodes so its all good.
I just played a few games with Danil...we play good together in a certain tank the OBJ 252U. I think we won everygame when we both played that tank together. I also got my all time high score today of 3.5k damage

Kirk
Active 2 hours ago
375
Yay. Good job to you both hunni.
I need a snack
Ill have dinner in a couple of hours
Fill up tha belleh! Lol
Can I spend $100
For what pray tell?
The great courses is having a sale on the homesteading course. Teaches everything you need to know about chickens, goats, making cheese, candles, soap, raising bees and shit like that

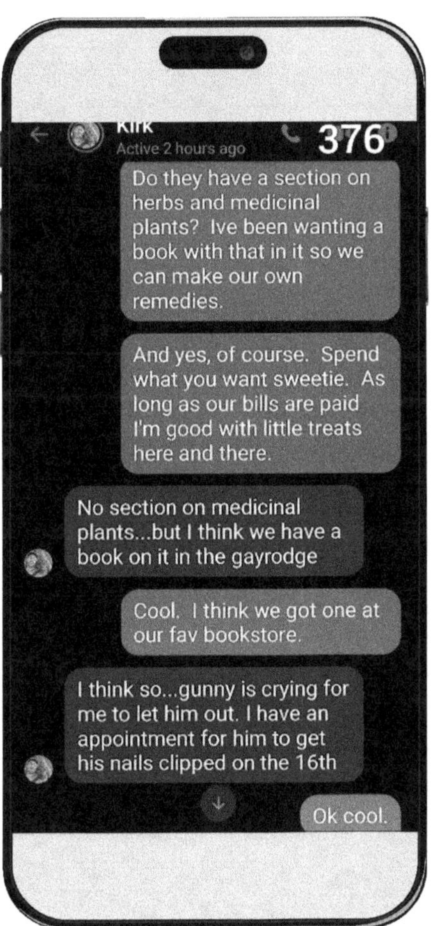
Kirk
Active 2 hours ago
376
Do they have a section on herbs and medicinal plants? Ive been wanting a book with that in it so we can make our own remedies.
And yes, of course. Spend what you want sweetie. As long as our bills are paid I'm good with little treats here and there.
No section on medicinal plants...but I think we have a book on it in the gayrodge
Cool. I think we got one at our fav bookstore.
I think so...gunny is crying for me to let him out. I have an appointment for him to get his nails clipped on the 16th
Ok cool.

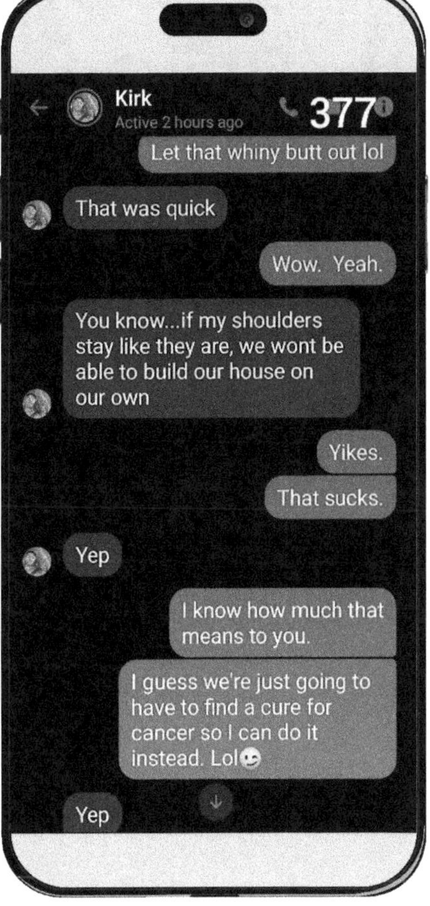
Kirk
Active 2 hours ago
377
Let that whiny butt out lol
That was quick
Wow. Yeah.
You know...if my shoulders stay like they are, we wont be able to build our house on our own
Yikes.
That sucks.
Yep
I know how much that means to you.
I guess we're just going to have to find a cure for cancer so I can do it instead. Lol
Yep

Kirk
Active 2 hours ago
378
Lol
What else are you doing tonight?
Just going to play some more with Danil later
Oh cool.
Maybe watch episode 18 of TWD after
Yeah. You should.
So should you lol
And I'm gonna watch 17 after my movie is over.
Did you watch Homefront yet?

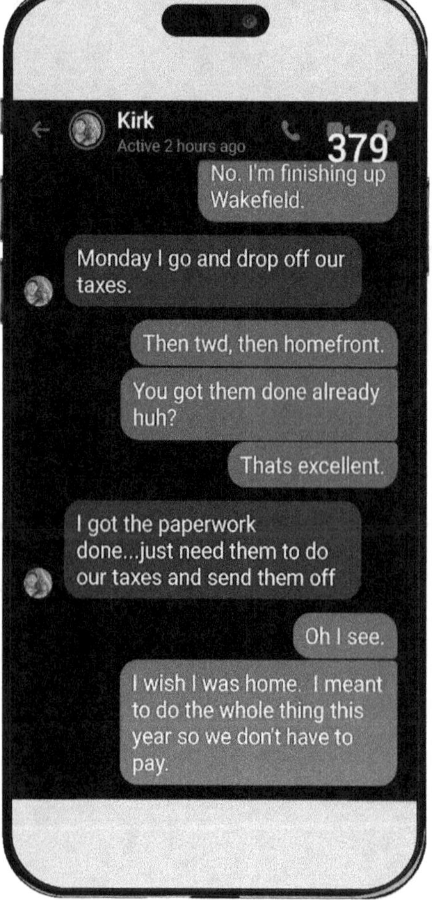

Kirk
Active 2 hours ago
379
No. I'm finishing up Wakefield.
Monday I go and drop off our taxes.
Then twd, then homefront.
You got them done already huh?
Thats excellent.
I got the paperwork done...just need them to do our taxes and send them off
Oh I see.
I wish I was home. I meant to do the whole thing this year so we don't have to pay.

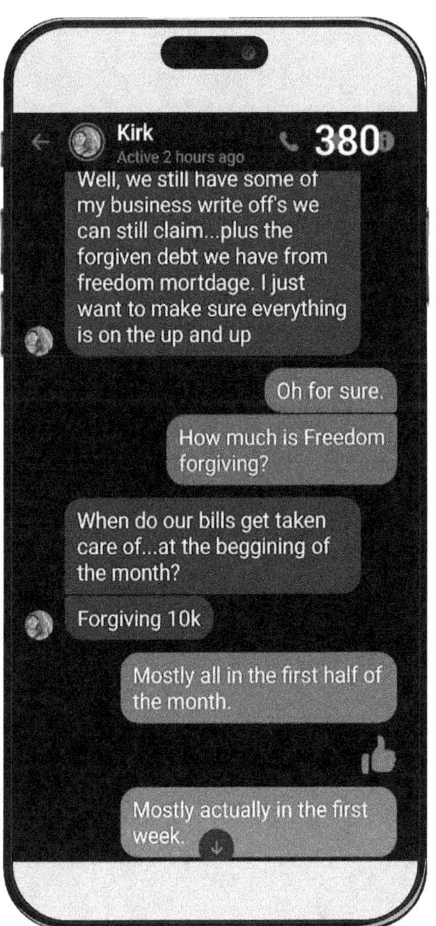
Kirk
Active 2 hours ago
380
Well, we still have some of my business write off's we can still claim...plus the forgiven debt we have from freedom mortdage. I just want to make sure everything is on the up and up
Oh for sure.
How much is Freedom forgiving?
When do our bills get taken care of...at the beggining of the month?
Forgiving 10k
Mostly all in the first half of the month.
Mostly actually in the first week.

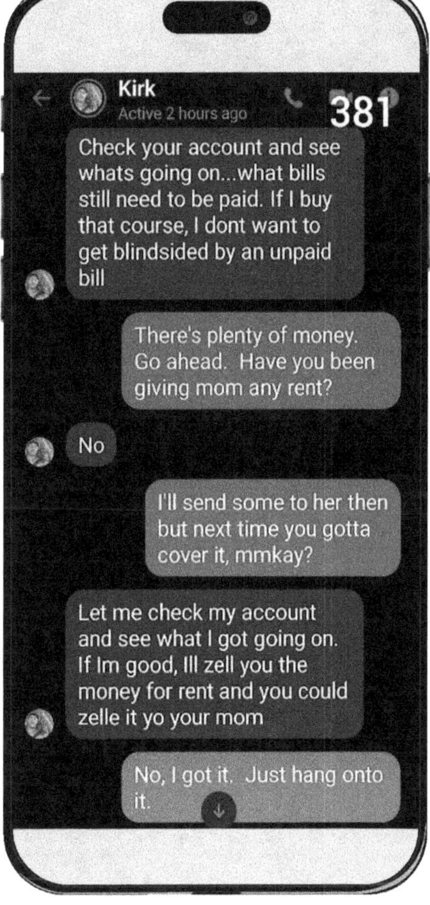
Kirk
Active 2 hours ago
381
Check your account and see whats going on...what bills still need to be paid. If I buy that course, I dont want to get blindsided by an unpaid bill
There's plenty of money. Go ahead. Have you been giving mom any rent?
No
I'll send some to her then but next time you gotta cover it, mmkay?
Let me check my account and see what I got going on. If Im good, Ill zell you the money for rent and you could zelle it yo your mom
No, I got it. Just hang onto it.

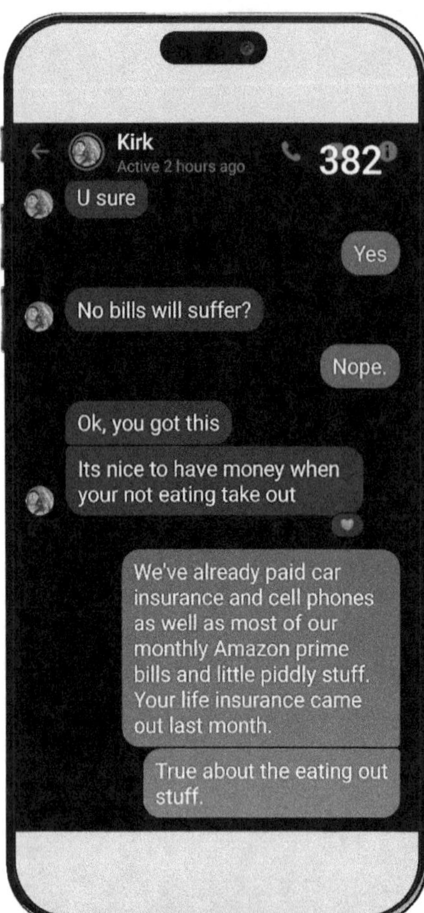

Kirk
Active 2 hours ago
382
U sure
Yes
No bills will suffer?
Nope.
Ok, you got this
Its nice to have money when your not eating take out
We've already paid car insurance and cell phones as well as most of our monthly Amazon prime bills and little piddly stuff. Your life insurance came out last month.
True about the eating out stuff.

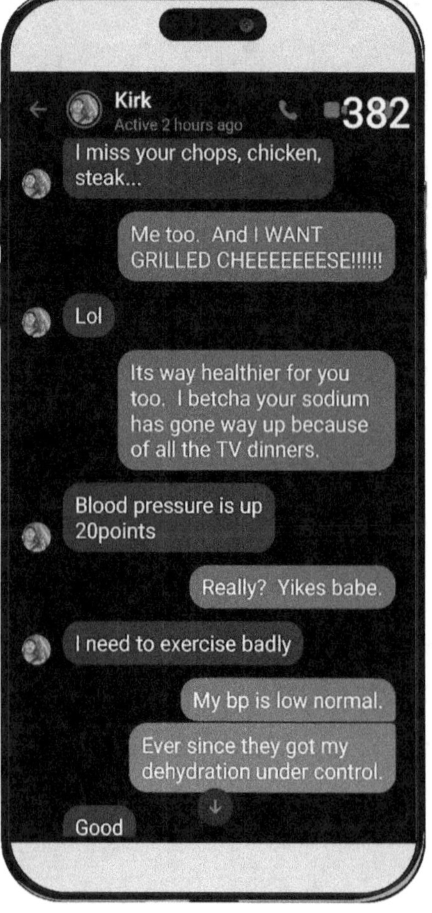

Kirk
Active 2 hours ago
382
I miss your chops, chicken, steak...
Me too. And I WANT GRILLED CHEEEEEEESE!!!!!!
Lol
Its way healthier for you too. I betcha your sodium has gone way up because of all the TV dinners.
Blood pressure is up 20points
Really? Yikes babe.
I need to exercise badly
My bp is low normal.
Ever since they got my dehydration under control.
Good

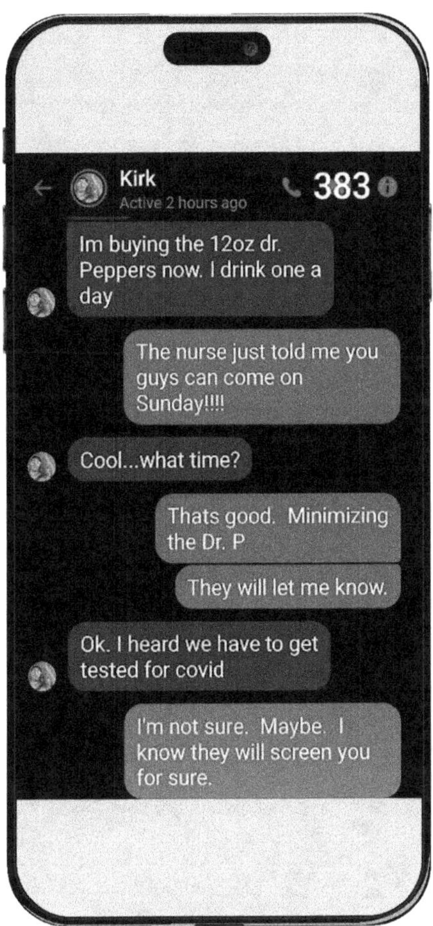

Kirk
Active 2 hours ago
383

Im buying the 12oz dr. Peppers now. I drink one a day

The nurse just told me you guys can come on Sunday!!!!

Cool...what time?

Thats good. Minimizing the Dr. P

They will let me know.

Ok. I heard we have to get tested for covid

I'm not sure. Maybe. I know they will screen you for sure.

Kirk
Active 2 hours ago
384

Nurse just said no covid test. You all just need to be approved

Ill let you finish your movie. Im going to go make a snack and watch a few youtube videos before I call Danil

No screening either.

Cool

Ok babe. Talk to ya later.

Talk to you between 8:30 and 9:30

MAR 5, 2021 AT 9:13 PM

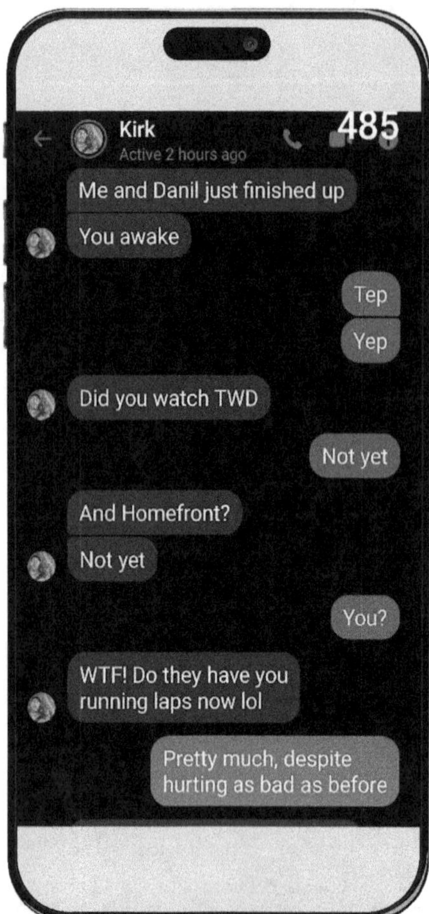
Kirk
Active 2 hours ago
485
Me and Danil just finished up
You awake
Tep
Yep
Did you watch TWD
Not yet
And Homefront?
Not yet
You?
WTF! Do they have you running laps now lol
Pretty much, despite hurting as bad as before

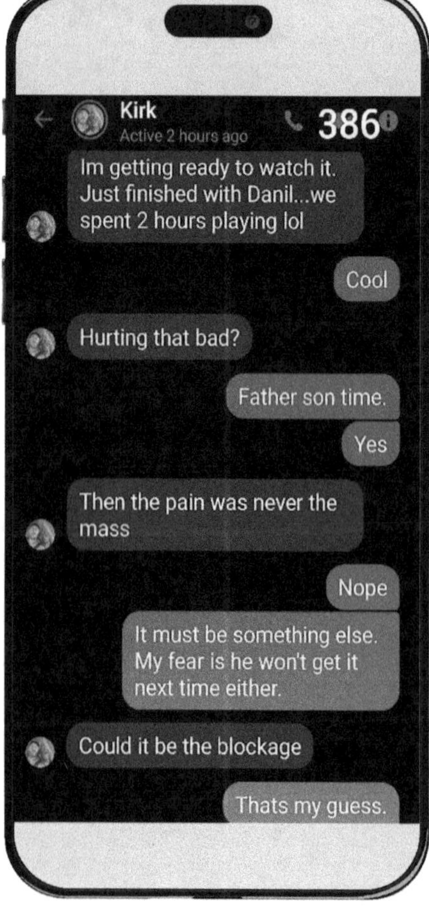
Kirk
Active 2 hours ago
386
Im getting ready to watch it. Just finished with Danil...we spent 2 hours playing lol
Cool
Hurting that bad?
Father son time.
Yes
Then the pain was never the mass
Nope
It must be something else. My fear is he won't get it next time either.
Could it be the blockage
Thats my guess.

Kirk
Active 2 hours ago
387
I swear if this nurse doesn't gtfoh Im gonna scream.
Whats going on
She stepped on my foot twice. No apology. She's kind of an idiot too. She just stands there. Staring at my iv pole.
Is she there now
No
You could stare at my pole lol
Lmao!!!!!
Thats a good thing though lol

Kirk
Active 2 hours ago
388
I might have to send you a pic...just in case you forgot what one looks like lol
Lol. I know right?
Did you zelle that money to your mom yet
No. Thanks for reminding me though.
I cant wait till Sunday when we see you
Oh me either!! I am so jazzed. I hope I dont hurt too badly but I also don't care. I just wanna see you.
Give you a hug and lots of kisses

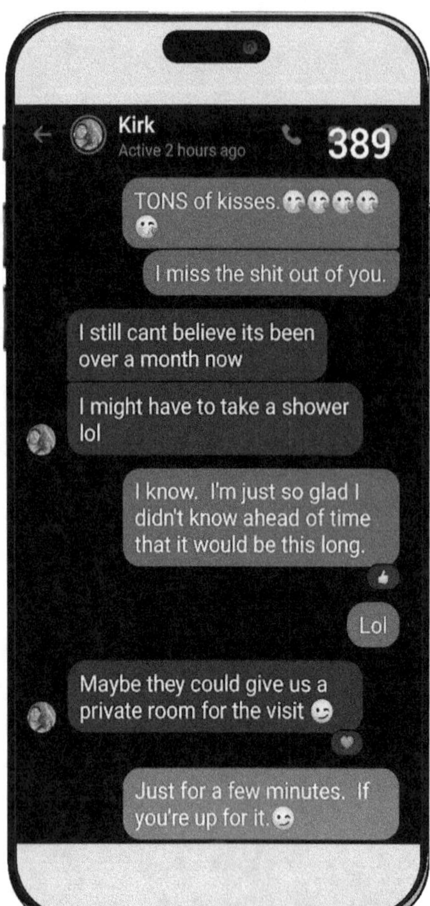
Kirk
Active 2 hours ago
389
TONS of kisses.
I miss the shit out of you.
I still cant believe its been over a month now
I might have to take a shower lol
I know. I'm just so glad I didn't know ahead of time that it would be this long.
Lol
Maybe they could give us a private room for the visit
Just for a few minutes. If you're up for it.

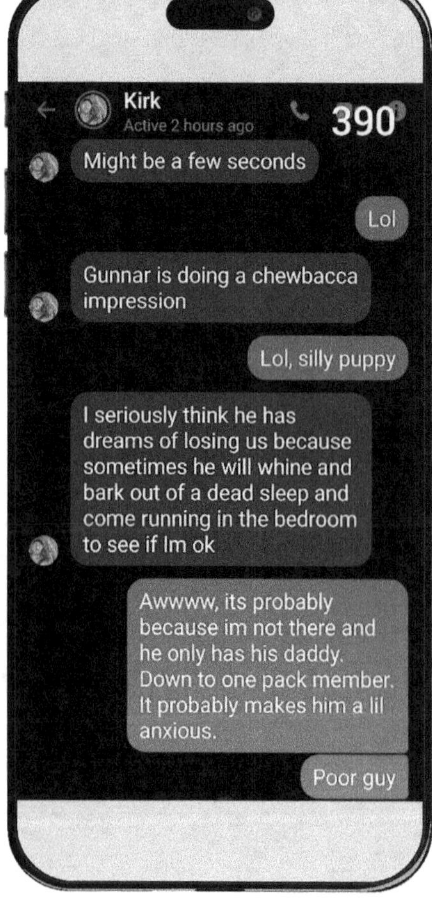
Kirk
Active 2 hours ago
390
Might be a few seconds
Lol
Gunnar is doing a chewbacca impression
Lol, silly puppy
I seriously think he has dreams of losing us because sometimes he will whine and bark out of a dead sleep and come running in the bedroom to see if Im ok
Awwww, its probably because im not there and he only has his daddy. Down to one pack member. It probably makes him a lil anxious.
Poor guy

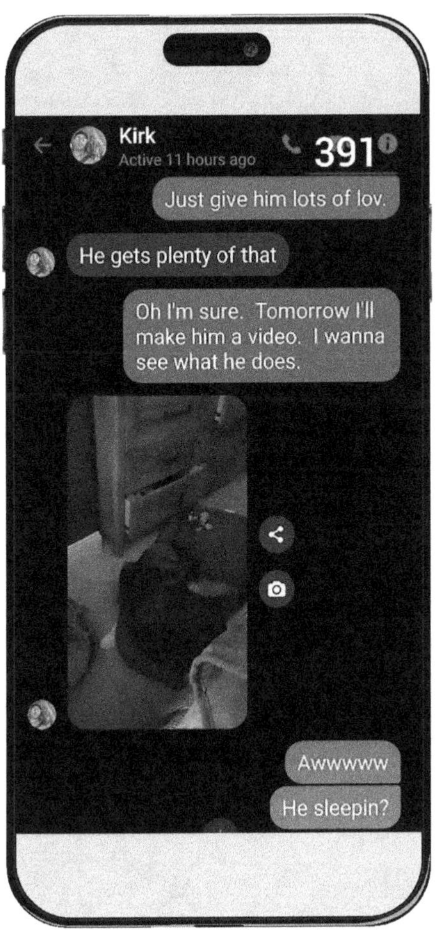

Kirk
Active 11 hours ago
391
Just give him lots of lov.
He gets plenty of that
Oh I'm sure. Tomorrow I'll make him a video. I wanna see what he does.
Awwwww
He sleepin?

Kirk
Active 11 hours ago
392
Yep.
I miss our bedspread.
Im going to take my medicine now and listen to the x22 report
I miss our bed.
Ok sweetie.
Hurry up and get better so you can sleep in it again...we might have to change your address if you stay there much longer
I know right? I was thinking about that yesterday lol
Enjoy your "fake news" babe. Lol

Kirk
Active 11 hours ago
393
I love you...talk to you in the morning
I love you too. Sleep well.
MAR 6, 2021 AT 10:30 AM
1145 tomorrow.
Cool
Dr W will be taking me downstairs himself to unlock the doors. Its at the older part of the building.
Where do we go?
Its the main entrance by the waterfront. Not the ER and the the doors you always take me to. You'll have about 30 steps to walk up

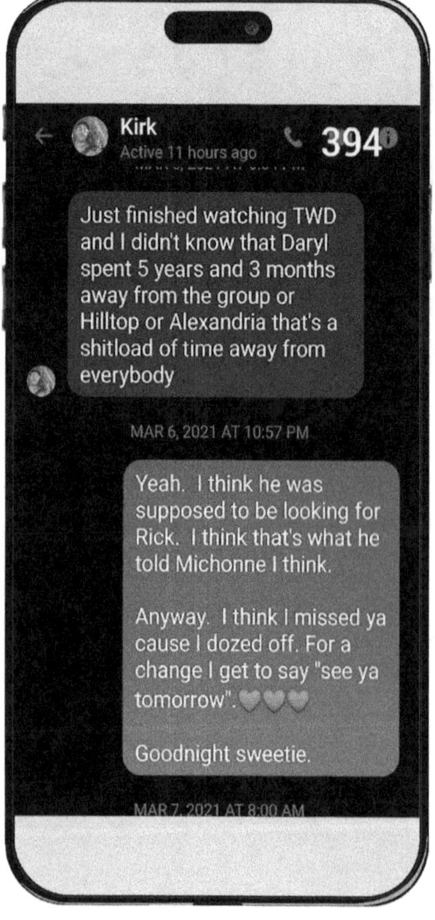
Kirk
Active 11 hours ago
394
Just finished watching TWD and I didn't know that Daryl spent 5 years and 3 months away from the group or Hilltop or Alexandria that's a shitload of time away from everybody
MAR 6, 2021 AT 10:57 PM
Yeah. I think he was supposed to be looking for Rick. I think that's what he told Michonne I think.
Anyway. I think I missed ya cause I dozed off. For a change I get to say "see ya tomorrow".
Goodnight sweetie.
MAR 7, 2021 AT 8:00 AM

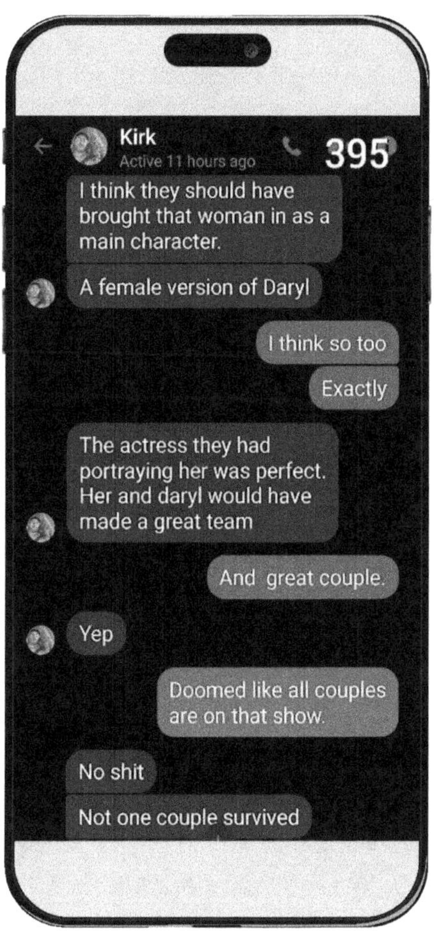
Kirk
Active 11 hours ago
395
I think they should have brought that woman in as a main character.
A female version of Daryl
I think so too
Exactly
The actress they had portraying her was perfect. Her and daryl would have made a great team
And great couple.
Yep
Doomed like all couples are on that show.
No shit
Not one couple survived

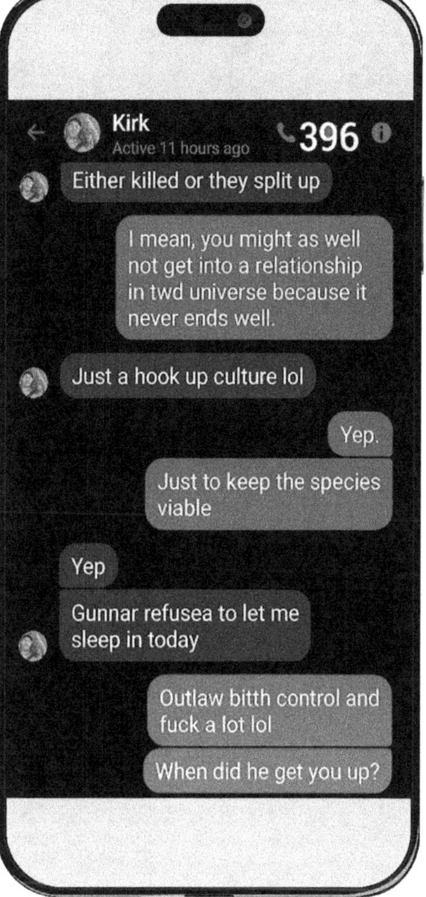
Kirk
Active 11 hours ago
396
Either killed or they split up
I mean, you might as well not get into a relationship in twd universe because it never ends well.
Just a hook up culture lol
Yep.
Just to keep the species viable
Yep
Gunnar refusea to let me sleep in today
Outlaw bitth control and fuck a lot lol
When did he get you up?

Kirk
Active 11 hours ago
397
6:30...I tried getting back to sleep but he keeps barking every 10 min
Awww. Bratty boy.
Have breakfast yet?
Yes...jimmy dean breakfast bowl
Cool.
Was good
Did you buy more?
Cause I think we only had 1 or 2
Might have a breakfast sandwich before we go

Kirk
Active 11 hours ago
398
I bought some more
You and mom should treat yourselves and eat out on the way home.
Nope
Just a suggestion
Im not goung to start eating out now
Ok
Ive probably spent $250 in groceries since you have been gone
Cool.
I've spent zero. So ha!
Lol

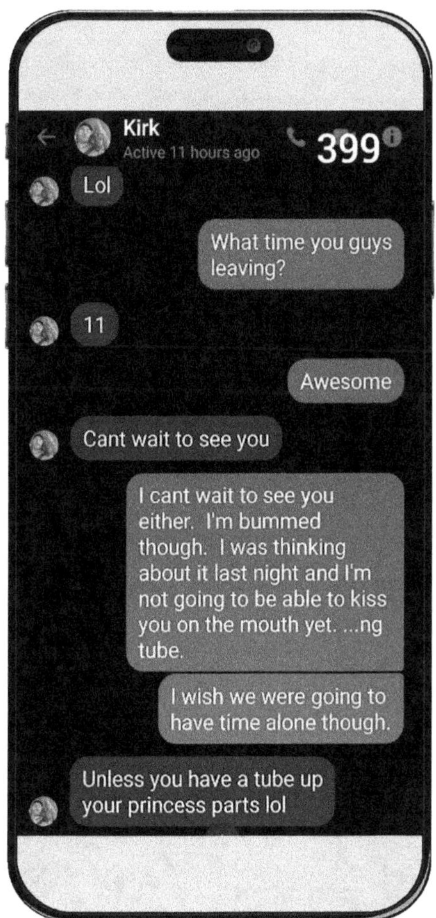
Kirk
Active 11 hours ago
399
Lol
What time you guys leaving?
11
Awesome
Cant wait to see you
I cant wait to see you either. I'm bummed though. I was thinking about it last night and I'm not going to be able to kiss you on the mouth yet. ...ng tube.
I wish we were going to have time alone though.
Unless you have a tube up your princess parts lol

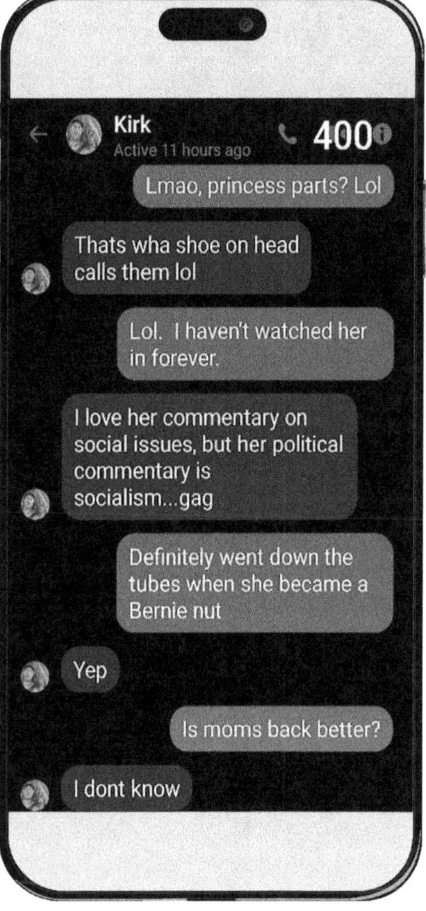
Kirk
Active 11 hours ago
400
Lmao, princess parts? Lol
Thats wha shoe on head calls them lol
Lol. I haven't watched her in forever.
I love her commentary on social issues, but her political commentary is socialism...gag
Definitely went down the tubes when she became a Bernie nut
Yep
Is moms back better?
I dont know

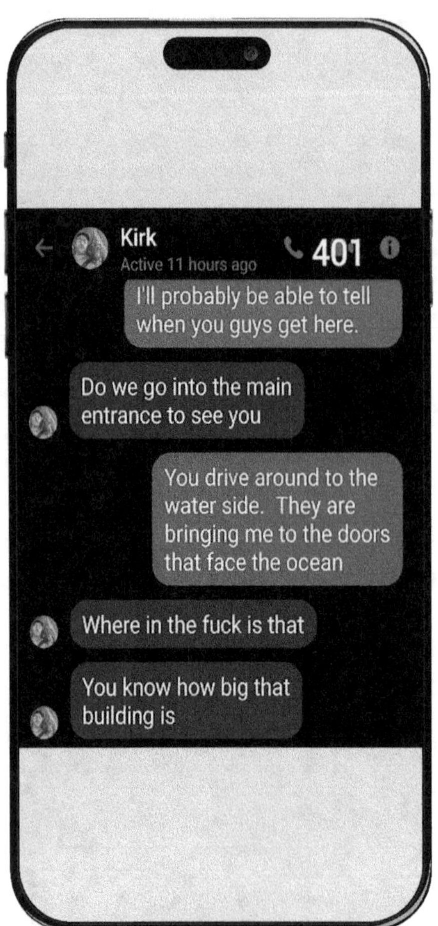

Kirk
Active 11 hours ago
401

I'll probably be able to tell when you guys get here.

Do we go into the main entrance to see you

You drive around to the water side. They are bringing me to the doors that face the ocean

Where in the fuck is that

You know how big that building is

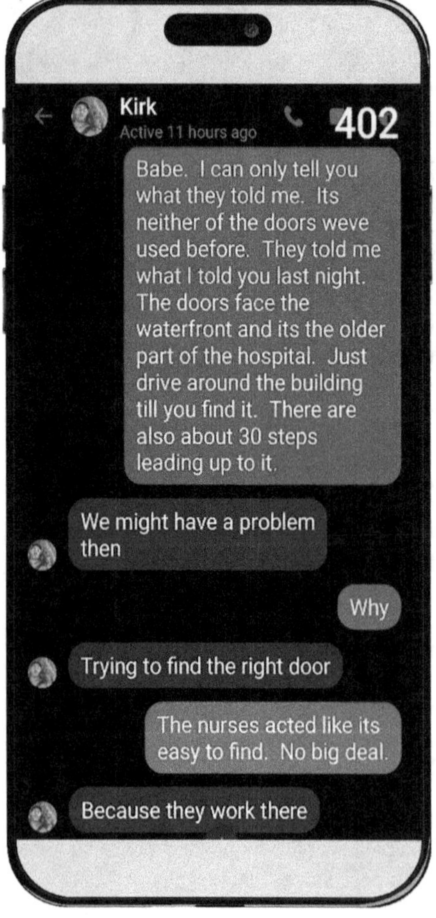

Kirk
Active 11 hours ago
402

Babe. I can only tell you what they told me. Its neither of the doors weve used before. They told me what I told you last night. The doors face the waterfront and its the older part of the hospital. Just drive around the building till you find it. There are also about 30 steps leading up to it.

We might have a problem then

Why

Trying to find the right door

The nurses acted like its easy to find. No big deal.

Because they work there

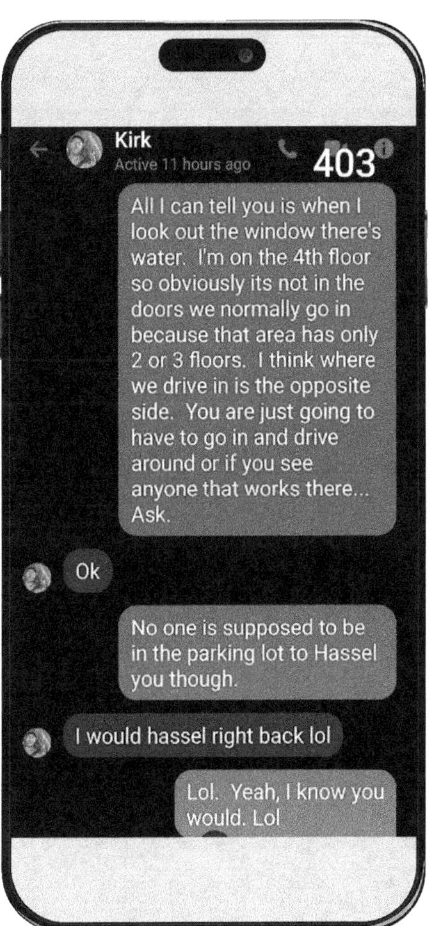
Kirk
Active 11 hours ago
403
All I can tell you is when I look out the window there's water. I'm on the 4th floor so obviously its not in the doors we normally go in because that area has only 2 or 3 floors. I think where we drive in is the opposite side. You are just going to have to go in and drive around or if you see anyone that works there... Ask.
Ok
No one is supposed to be in the parking lot to Hassel you though.
I would hassel right back lol
Lol. Yeah, I know you would. Lol

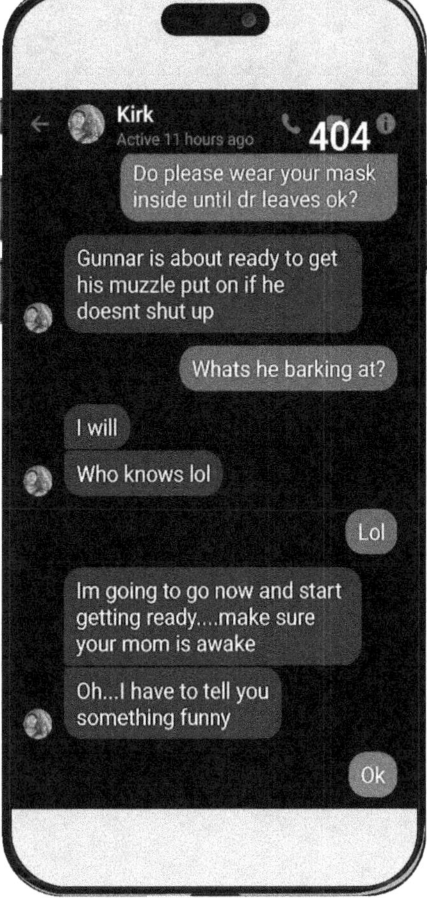
Kirk
Active 11 hours ago
404
Do please wear your mask inside until dr leaves ok?
Gunnar is about ready to get his muzzle put on if he doesnt shut up
Whats he barking at?
I will
Who knows lol
Lol
Im going to go now and start getting ready....make sure your mom is awake
Oh...I have to tell you something funny
Ok

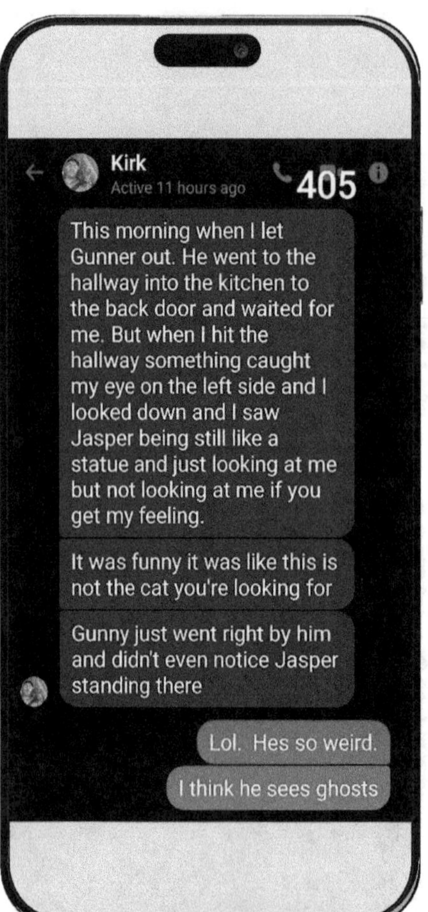
Kirk
Active 11 hours ago
405

This morning when I let Gunner out. He went to the hallway into the kitchen to the back door and waited for me. But when I hit the hallway something caught my eye on the left side and I looked down and I saw Jasper being still like a statue and just looking at me but not looking at me if you get my feeling.

It was funny it was like this is not the cat you're looking for

Gunny just went right by him and didn't even notice Jasper standing there

Lol. Hes so weird.

I think he sees ghosts

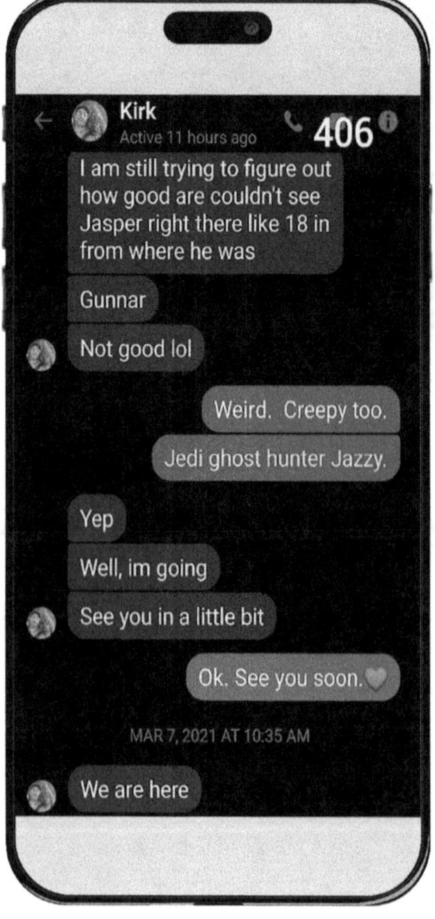
Kirk
Active 11 hours ago
406

I am still trying to figure out how good are couldn't see Jasper right there like 18 in from where he was

Gunnar

Not good lol

Weird. Creepy too.

Jedi ghost hunter Jazzy.

Yep

Well, im going

See you in a little bit

Ok. See you soon.

MAR 7, 2021 AT 10:35 AM

We are here

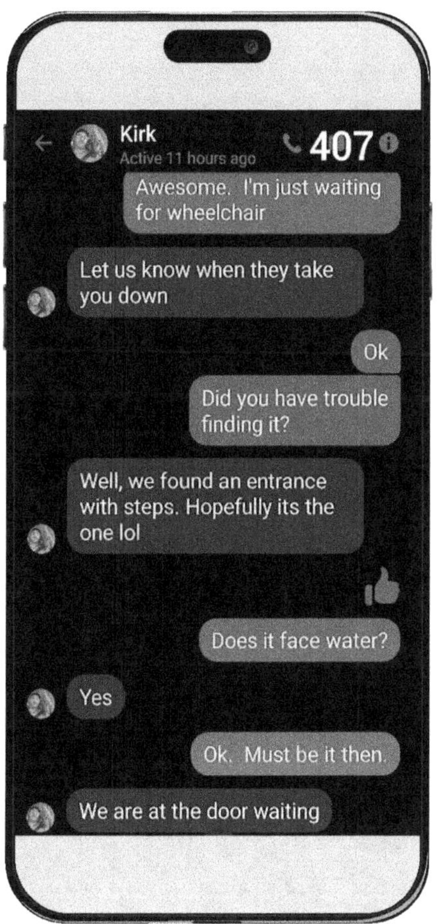

Kirk
Active 11 hours ago
407
Awesome. I'm just waiting for wheelchair
Let us know when they take you down
Ok
Did you have trouble finding it?
Well, we found an entrance with steps. Hopefully its the one lol
Does it face water?
Yes
Ok. Must be it then.
We are at the door waiting

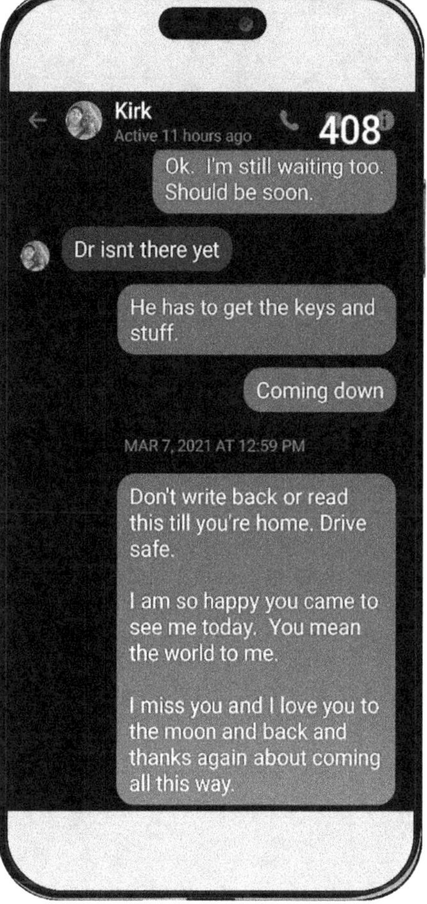

Kirk
Active 11 hours ago
408
Ok. I'm still waiting too. Should be soon.
Dr isnt there yet
He has to get the keys and stuff.
Coming down
MAR 7, 2021 AT 12:59 PM
Don't write back or read this till you're home. Drive safe.

I am so happy you came to see me today. You mean the world to me.

I miss you and I love you to the moon and back and thanks again about coming all this way.

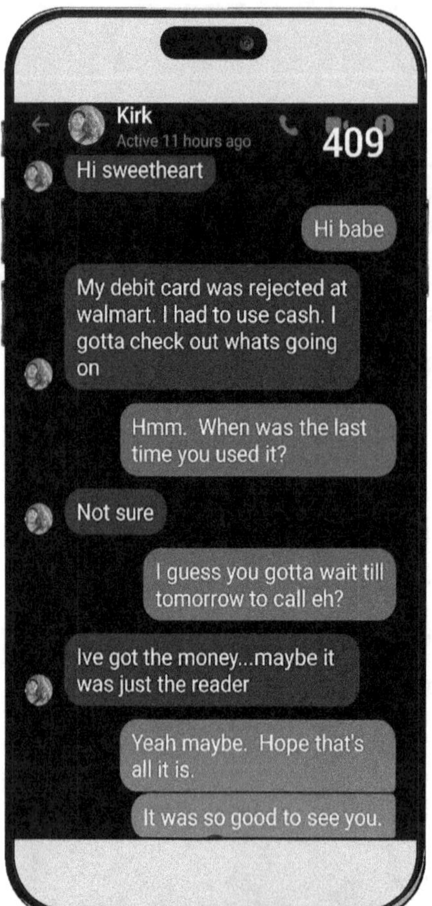

Kirk
Active 11 hours ago
409
Hi sweetheart
Hi babe
My debit card was rejected at walmart. I had to use cash. I gotta check out whats going on
Hmm. When was the last time you used it?
Not sure
I guess you gotta wait till tomorrow to call eh?
Ive got the money...maybe it was just the reader
Yeah maybe. Hope that's all it is.
It was so good to see you.

Kirk
Active 11 hours ago
410
I wish we could every day.
Time went by so fast
It sure did.
But it was good.
Yes it was
Im sharing my lunch with gunnar
Oh yeah? Thats nice. Bet he is ad you're home.
Yep...he is glad
My stomach is growling.
For a grilled cheese sammich
Yup. Grilled cheeeeez sammich.

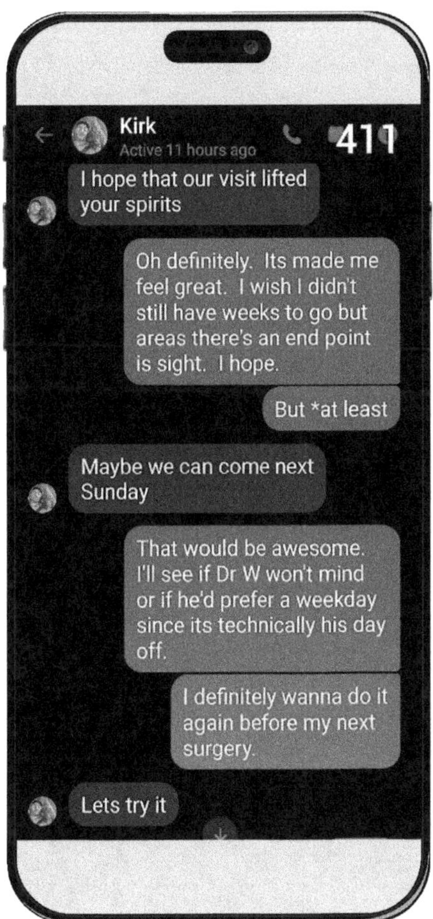
Kirk
Active 11 hours ago
411
I hope that our visit lifted your spirits
Oh definitely. Its made me feel great. I wish I didn't still have weeks to go but areas there's an end point is sight. I hope.
But *at least
Maybe we can come next Sunday
That would be awesome. I'll see if Dr W won't mind or if he'd prefer a weekday since its technically his day off.
I definitely wanna do it again before my next surgery.
Lets try it

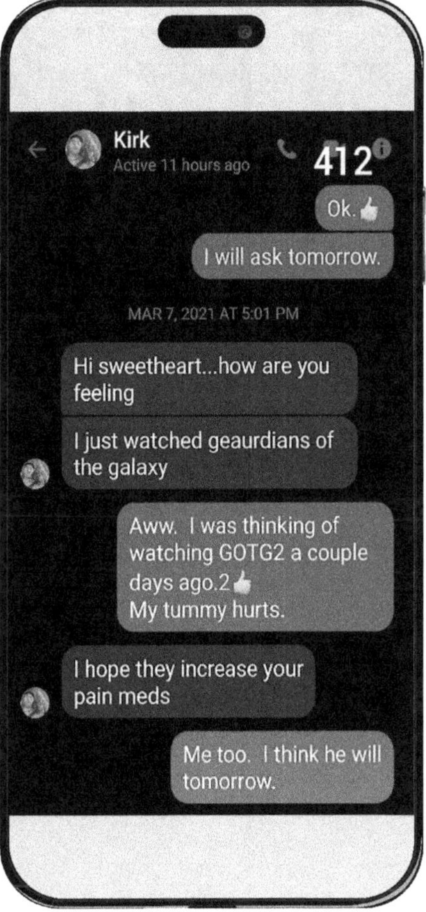
Kirk
Active 11 hours ago
412
Ok.
I will ask tomorrow.
MAR 7, 2021 AT 5:01 PM
Hi sweetheart...how are you feeling
I just watched geaurdians of the galaxy
Aww. I was thinking of watching GOTG2 a couple days ago.2
My tummy hurts.
I hope they increase your pain meds
Me too. I think he will tomorrow.

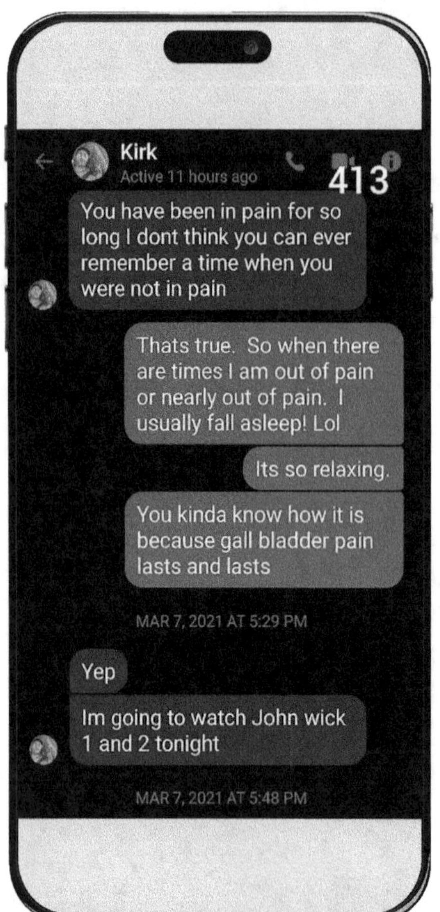

Kirk
Active 11 hours ago
413
You have been in pain for so long I dont think you can ever remember a time when you were not in pain
Thats true. So when there are times I am out of pain or nearly out of pain. I usually fall asleep! Lol
Its so relaxing.
You kinda know how it is because gall bladder pain lasts and lasts
MAR 7, 2021 AT 5:29 PM
Yep
Im going to watch John wick 1 and 2 tonight
MAR 7, 2021 AT 5:48 PM

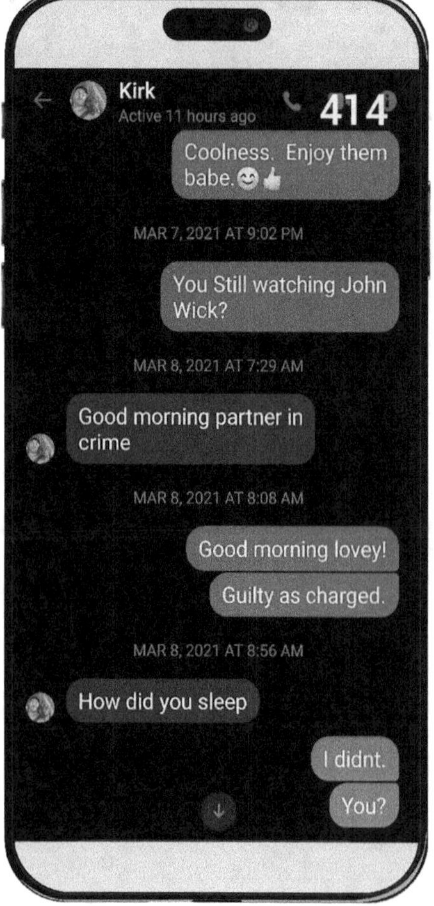

Kirk
Active 11 hours ago
414
Coolness. Enjoy them babe.😊👍
MAR 7, 2021 AT 9:02 PM
You Still watching John Wick?
MAR 8, 2021 AT 7:29 AM
Good morning partner in crime
MAR 8, 2021 AT 8:08 AM
Good morning lovey!
Guilty as charged.
MAR 8, 2021 AT 8:56 AM
How did you sleep
I didnt.
You?

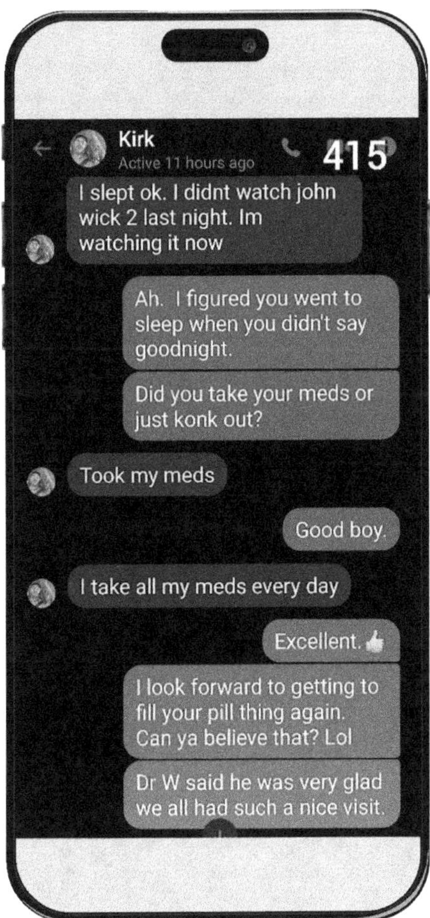
Kirk
Active 11 hours ago
415

I slept ok. I didnt watch john wick 2 last night. Im watching it now

Ah. I figured you went to sleep when you didn't say goodnight.

Did you take your meds or just konk out?

Took my meds

Good boy.

I take all my meds every day

Excellent.

I look forward to getting to fill your pill thing again. Can ya believe that? Lol

Dr W said he was very glad we all had such a nice visit.

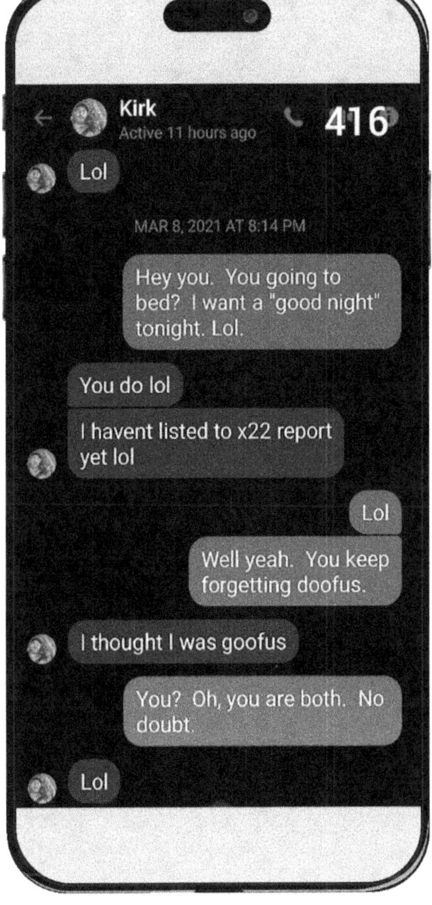
Kirk
Active 11 hours ago
416

Lol

MAR 8, 2021 AT 8:14 PM

Hey you. You going to bed? I want a "good night" tonight. Lol.

You do lol

I havent listed to x22 report yet lol

Lol

Well yeah. You keep forgetting doofus.

I thought I was goofus

You? Oh, you are both. No doubt.

Lol

Kirk
Active 11 hours ago
417
Time for the x22 report
Ok. Then talk to me or...?
MAR 8, 2021 AT 9:20 PM
Good night Kimmie
Night babe.
Love you.
MAR 9, 2021 AT 8:17 AM
Hey there...you sleep ok
Hi babe.
I slept better.
Hey, did you mean it when you said I looked good and my skin looked good the other day? The nurses keep saying it too.

Kirk
Active 11 hours ago
418
I'm bruised and my skin is dry so im just not seeing it lol.
MAR 9, 2021 AT 8:38 AM
Yes. I meant it and your mom agrees with me
Sorry for the delay...I grabbed some breakfast
Thats ok
And thank you
You know me....I tell it like it is
Truth.
Whatcha doing today?
Im glad you slept better

Kirk
Active 11 hours ago
419
Thank you, me too
I dont know yet...I think I will do some dishes. I have half of the kitchen upstairs lol
Lol
Thank you for doing that hunni.
Helping mom out..
I made baked potators last night for me and your mom
Oh yeah? Sounds yummy.
She just had butter on hers...I had all the fixins on mine
As per usual. I only like butter(margarine) on mine too.
Plain jane lol

Kirk
Active 11 hours ago
420
Unless we are having steak, then I like the drippings on mine too. Yuuuuhmeeeeee!
Shit...just sneezed and farted at the same time
Lol
Lmao!!
Some things never change
True
Have you cooked any meat since you're fending for yourself?
Im just an old fart
Lol
Nope

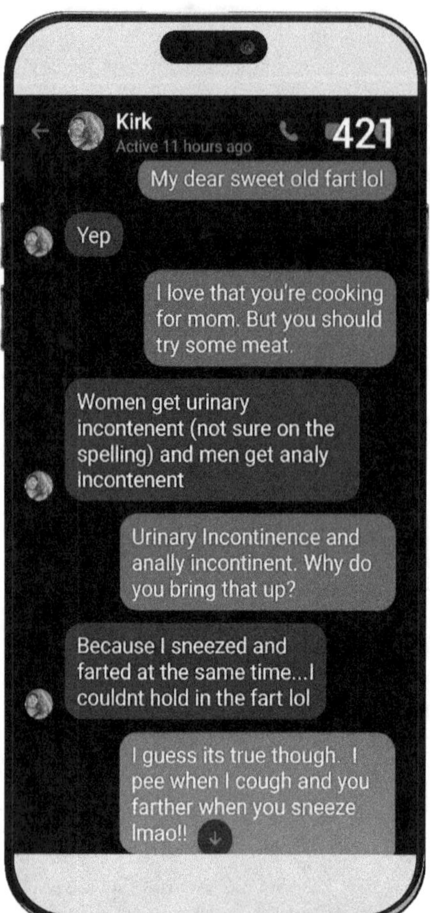

Kirk
Active 11 hours ago
421
My dear sweet old fart lol
Yep
I love that you're cooking for mom. But you should try some meat.
Women get urinary incontenent (not sure on the spelling) and men get analy incontenent
Urinary Incontinence and anally incontinent. Why do you bring that up?
Because I sneezed and farted at the same time...I couldnt hold in the fart lol
I guess its true though. I pee when I cough and you farther when you sneeze lmao!!

Kirk
Active 11 hours ago
422
Farther? Come on ac.
Women when they get older have an issue with lifting things and laughing without springing a leak
Yep. Thats me.
You know, I havent played my tank game in 3 days
What??? I thought you played it like yesterday.
Nope
How come
Just not interested I guess
Oh wow. Hey, whens your dentist appt?

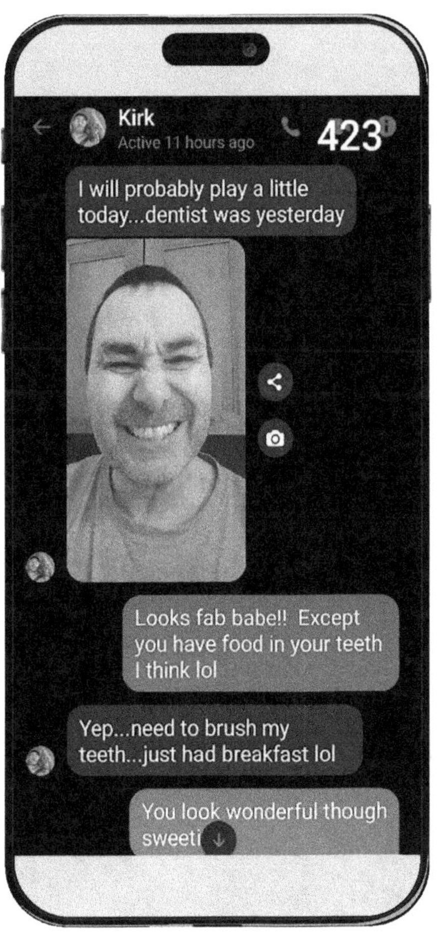

Kirk
Active 11 hours ago
423
I will probably play a little today...dentist was yesterday
Looks fab babe!! Except you have food in your teeth I think lol
Yep...need to brush my teeth...just had breakfast lol
You look wonderful though sweeti

Kirk
Active 11 hours ago
424
Handsome
Thank you sweetheart
I take it you're on the pot?
Or are you playing your game already? Lol
I guess you could do both haha.
I was on the pot
I figured lol
I think what you saw as food on my teeth might have been cavities

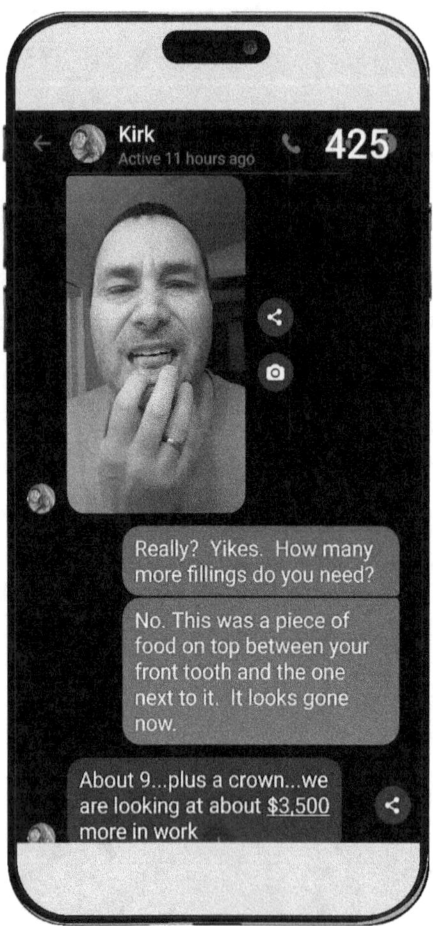
Kirk
Active 11 hours ago
425

Really? Yikes. How many more fillings do you need?

No. This was a piece of food on top between your front tooth and the one next to it. It looks gone now.

About 9...plus a crown...we are looking at about $3,500 more in work

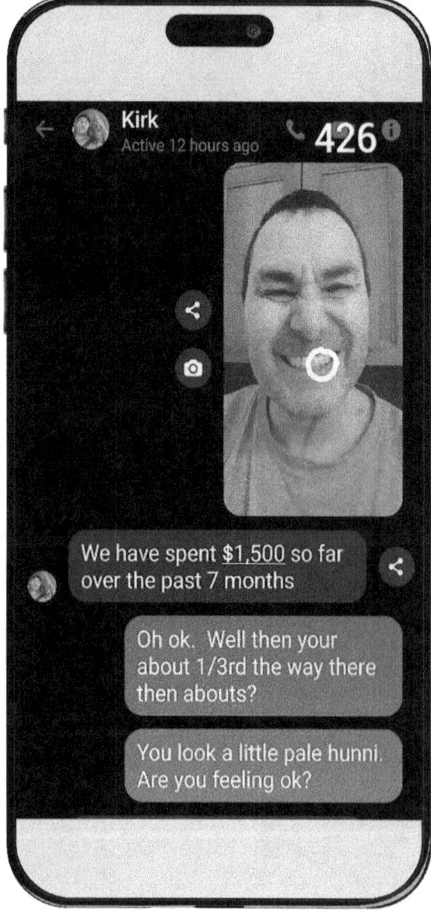
Kirk
Active 12 hours ago
426

We have spent $1,500 so far over the past 7 months

Oh ok. Well then your about 1/3rd the way there then abouts?

You look a little pale hunni. Are you feeling ok?

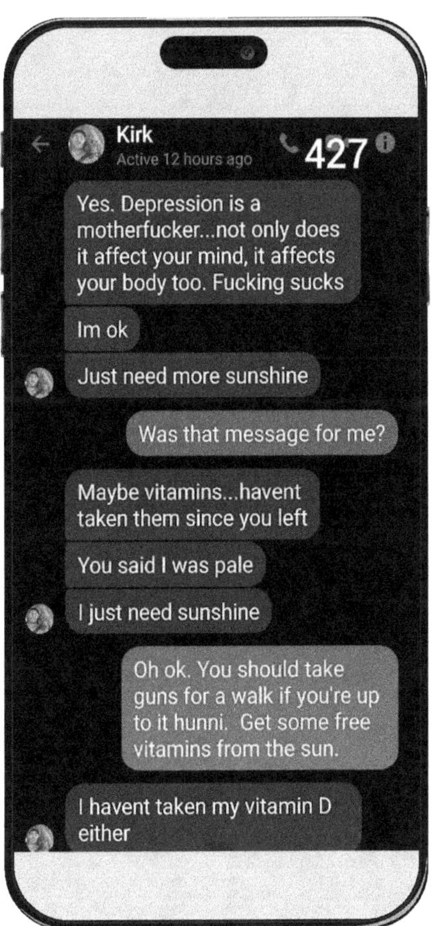
Kirk
Active 12 hours ago
427
Yes. Depression is a motherfucker...not only does it affect your mind, it affects your body too. Fucking sucks
Im ok
Just need more sunshine
Was that message for me?
Maybe vitamins...havent taken them since you left
You said I was pale
I just need sunshine
Oh ok. You should take guns for a walk if you're up to it hunni. Get some free vitamins from the sun.
I havent taken my vitamin D either

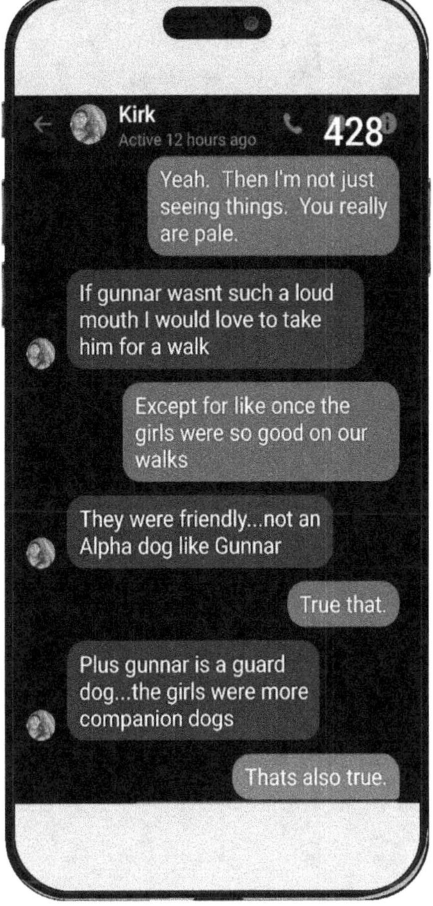
Kirk
Active 12 hours ago
428
Yeah. Then I'm not just seeing things. You really are pale.
If gunnar wasnt such a loud mouth I would love to take him for a walk
Except for like once the girls were so good on our walks
They were friendly...not an Alpha dog like Gunnar
True that.
Plus gunnar is a guard dog...the girls were more companion dogs
Thats also true.

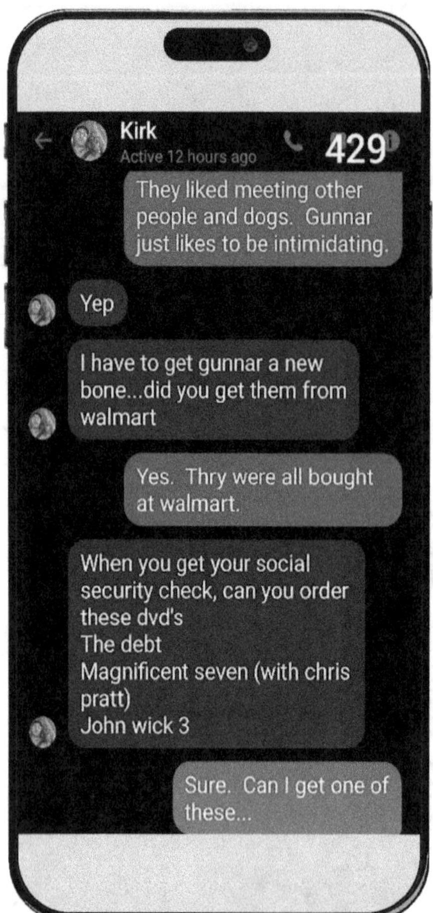

Kirk
Active 12 hours ago
429
They liked meeting other people and dogs. Gunnar just likes to be intimidating.
Yep
I have to get gunnar a new bone...did you get them from walmart
Yes. Thry were all bought at walmart.
When you get your social security check, can you order these dvd's
The debt
Magnificent seven (with chris pratt)
John wick 3
Sure. Can I get one of these...

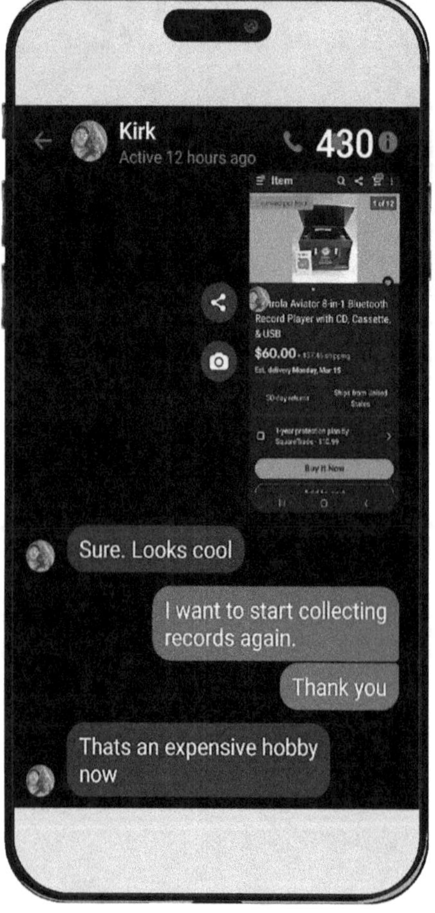

Kirk
Active 12 hours ago
430
Item
Victrola Aviator 8-in-1 Bluetooth Record Player with CD, Cassette, & USB
$60.00
Est. delivery Monday, Mar 15
Buy It Now
Sure. Looks cool
I want to start collecting records again.
Thank you
Thats an expensive hobby now

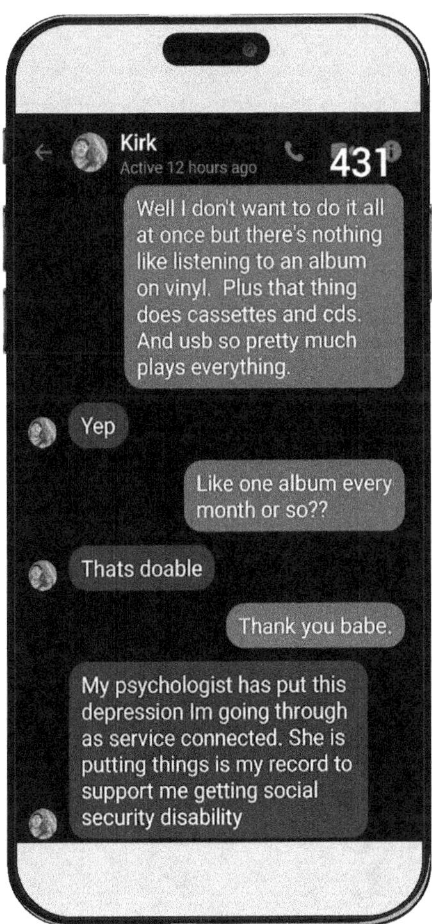

Kirk
Active 12 hours ago
431
Well I don't want to do it all at once but there's nothing like listening to an album on vinyl. Plus that thing does cassettes and cds. And usb so pretty much plays everything.
Yep
Like one album every month or so??
Thats doable
Thank you babe.
My psychologist has put this depression Im going through as service connected. She is putting things is my record to support me getting social security disability

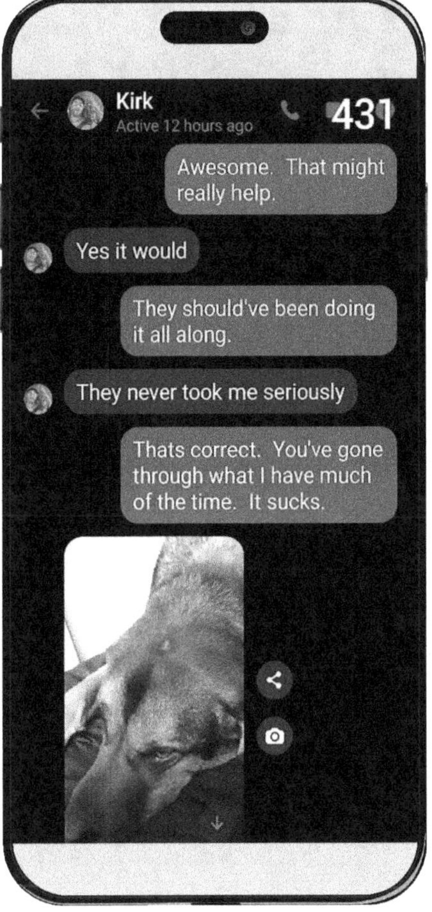

Kirk
Active 12 hours ago
431
Awesome. That might really help.
Yes it would
They should've been doing it all along.
They never took me seriously
Thats correct. You've gone through what I have much of the time. It sucks.

Kirk
Active 12 hours ago
432
That is his chew toy lol
Yikes!!
I need to change it iut before he tries to swollow that one
Lol. Or the weiner next to it lol

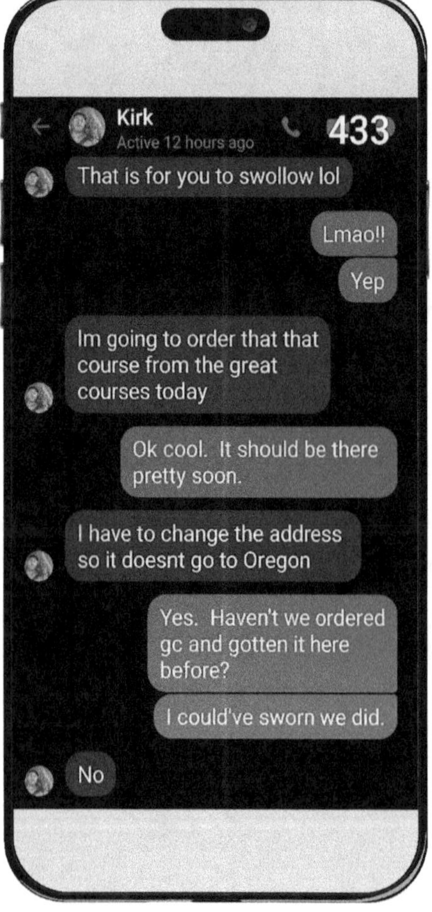

Kirk
Active 12 hours ago
433
That is for you to swollow lol
Lmao!!
Yep
Im going to order that that course from the great courses today
Ok cool. It should be there pretty soon.
I have to change the address so it doesnt go to Oregon
Yes. Haven't we ordered gc and gotten it here before?
I could've sworn we did.
No

Kirk
Active 12 hours ago
434
Maybe I'm thinking of something else
We got some in oregon
Yeah. I do remember that.
When you get home we need to start watching some of the great courses and start learning new things
There's a lot of things we need to do.
I know
I cant wait.
If I do get social security disability I want to save $1,000 a month so we can buy our property and start building our homestead

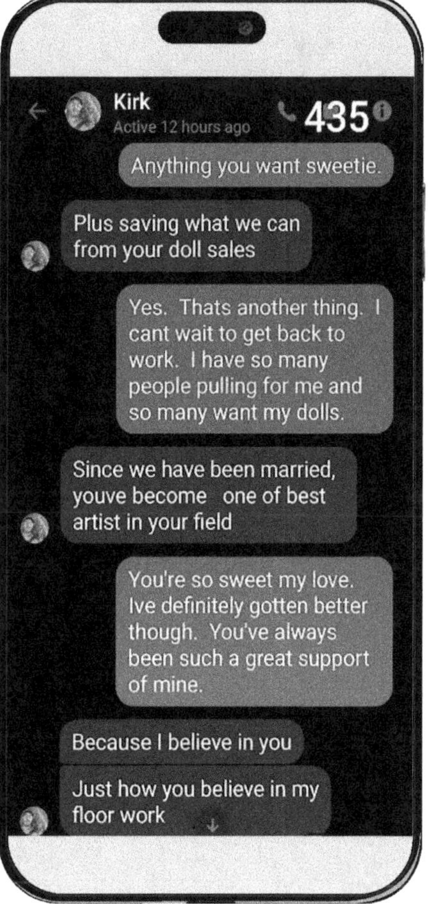
Kirk
Active 12 hours ago
435
Anything you want sweetie.
Plus saving what we can from your doll sales
Yes. Thats another thing. I cant wait to get back to work. I have so many people pulling for me and so many want my dolls.
Since we have been married, youve become   one of best artist in your field
You're so sweet my love. Ive definitely gotten better though. You've always been such a great support of mine.
Because I believe in you
Just how you believe in my floor work

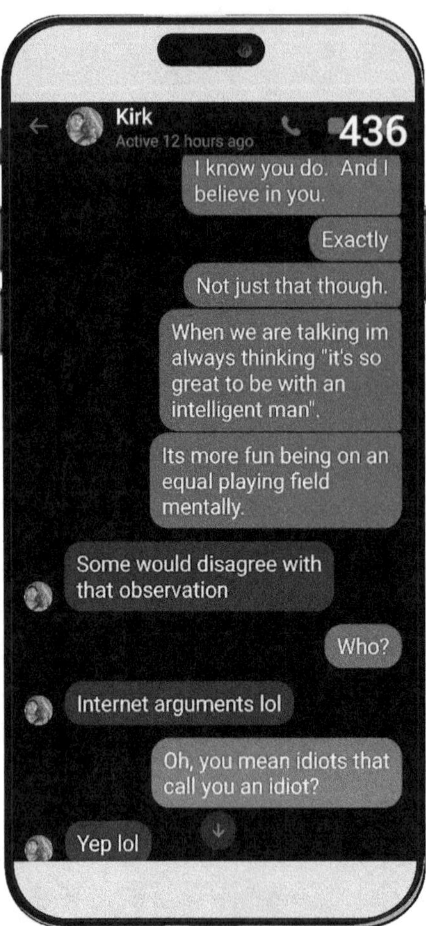

Kirk
Active 12 hours ago
436
I know you do. And I believe in you.
Exactly
Not just that though.
When we are talking im always thinking "it's so great to be with an intelligent man".
Its more fun being on an equal playing field mentally.
Some would disagree with that observation
Who?
Internet arguments lol
Oh, you mean idiots that call you an idiot?
Yep lol

Kirk
Active 12 hours ago
437
Fuck em. Seriously.
I know
Your wife knows you best
Im glad you know me
Me too.
And support me
Always.
And understand me
Forever.
I started watching a youtuber Jennifer Moleski...she is pro male anti fem...she is great. Check her out

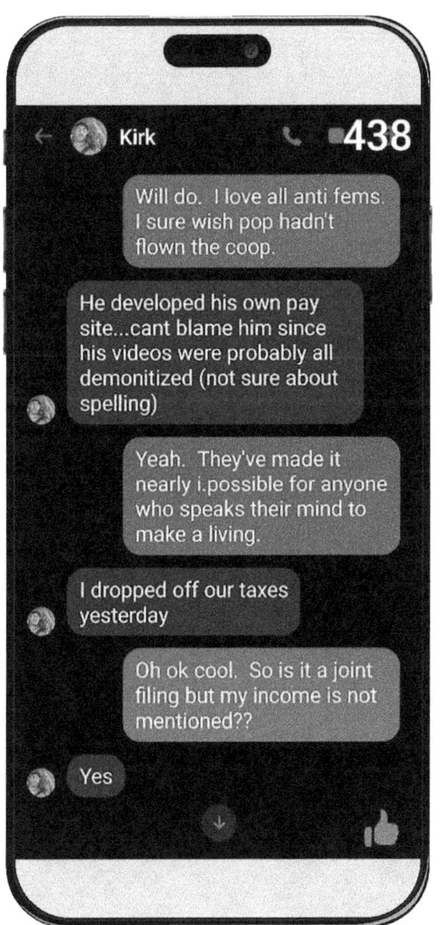
Kirk
438
Will do. I love all anti fems.
I sure wish pop hadn't
flown the coop.
He developed his own pay
site...cant blame him since
his videos were probably all
demonitized (not sure about
spelling)
Yeah. They've made it
nearly i.possible for anyone
who speaks their mind to
make a living.
I dropped off our taxes
yesterday
Oh ok cool. So is it a joint
filing but my income is not
mentioned??
Yes

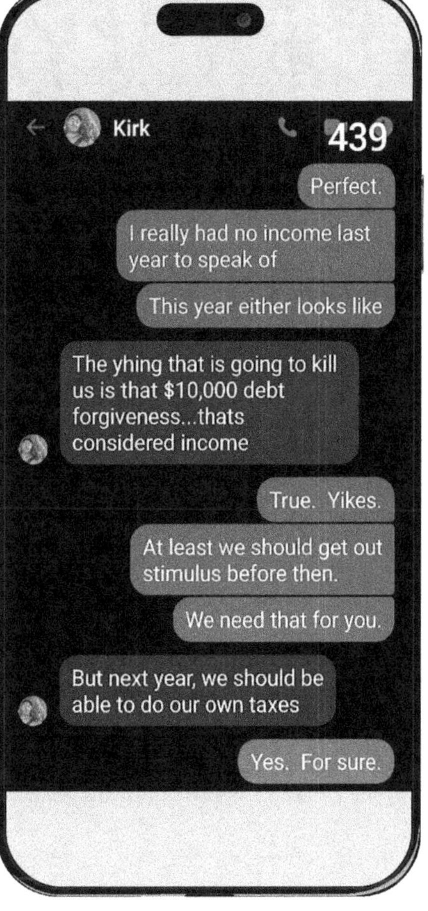
Kirk
439
Perfect.
I really had no income last
year to speak of
This year either looks like
The yhing that is going to kill
us is that $10,000 debt
forgiveness...thats
considered income
True. Yikes.
At least we should get out
stimulus before then.
We need that for you.
But next year, we should be
able to do our own taxes
Yes. For sure.

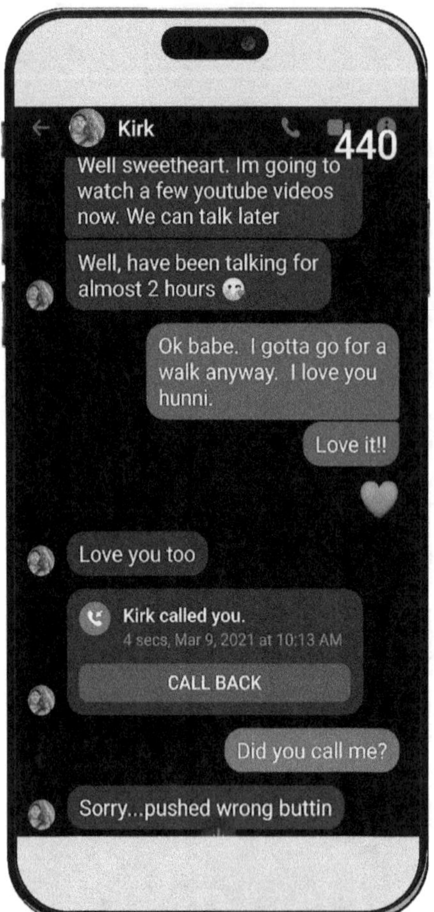
Kirk
440
Well sweetheart. Im going to watch a few youtube videos now. We can talk later
Well, have been talking for almost 2 hours
Ok babe. I gotta go for a walk anyway. I love you hunni.
Love it!!
Love you too
Kirk called you.
4 secs, Mar 9, 2021 at 10:13 AM
CALL BACK
Did you call me?
Sorry...pushed wrong buttin

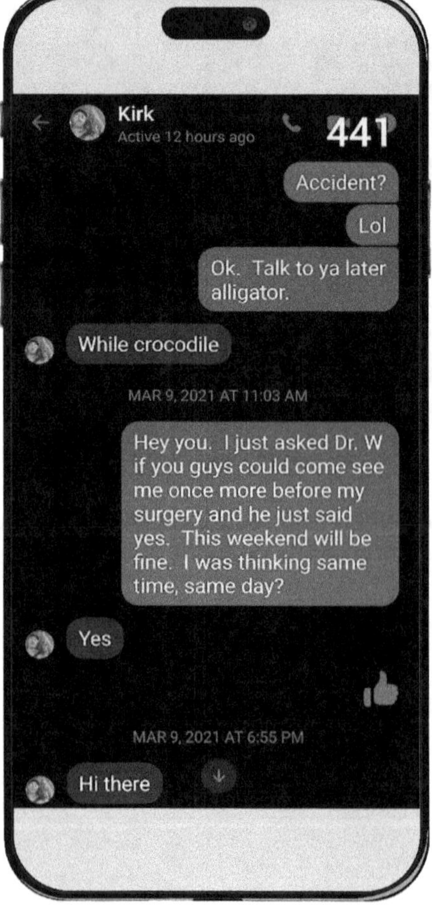
Kirk
Active 12 hours ago
441
Accident?
Lol
Ok. Talk to ya later alligator.
While crocodile
MAR 9, 2021 AT 11:03 AM
Hey you. I just asked Dr. W if you guys could come see me once more before my surgery and he just said yes. This weekend will be fine. I was thinking same time, same day?
Yes
MAR 9, 2021 AT 6:55 PM
Hi there

Kirk
Active 12 hours ago
442
Hi
Busy lol
You are?
I made a honey roasted turkey sandwhich tonight for dinner...getting ready for some ice cream
Im not busty...busy
Sounds delightful. Sounds like you are eating very well tonight.
Yep
Wish I could bring you your grilled cheese sammich
Oh I would love that so much. Ugh!!!!!!

Kirk
Active 12 hours ago
442
With some fries
Yummmmmmmmm!!!
And a milkshake
There ya go. Now you're talkin.
When you get out well make that for you
Thank you babe.
I am so looking forward to it.
TWD plays this thursday
Really?
Use to be Sundays
So no more sundays?

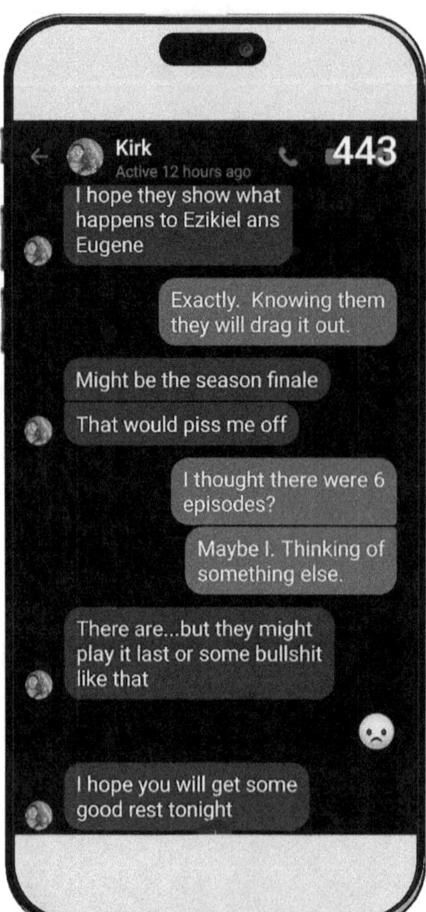
Kirk
Active 12 hours ago
443
I hope they show what happens to Ezikiel ans Eugene
Exactly. Knowing them they will drag it out.
Might be the season finale
That would piss me off
I thought there were 6 episodes?
Maybe I. Thinking of something else.
There are...but they might play it last or some bullshit like that
I hope you will get some good rest tonight

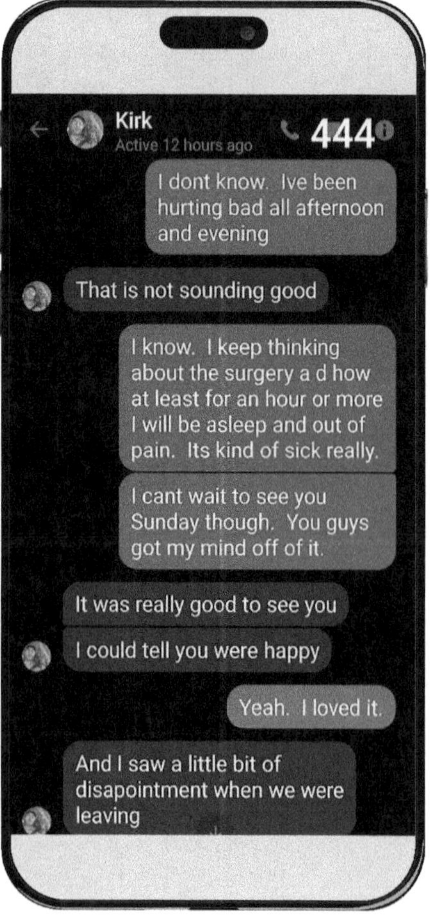
Kirk
Active 12 hours ago
444
I dont know. Ive been hurting bad all afternoon and evening
That is not sounding good
I know. I keep thinking about the surgery a d how at least for an hour or more I will be asleep and out of pain. Its kind of sick really.
I cant wait to see you Sunday though. You guys got my mind off of it.
It was really good to see you
I could tell you were happy
Yeah. I loved it.
And I saw a little bit of disapointment when we were leaving

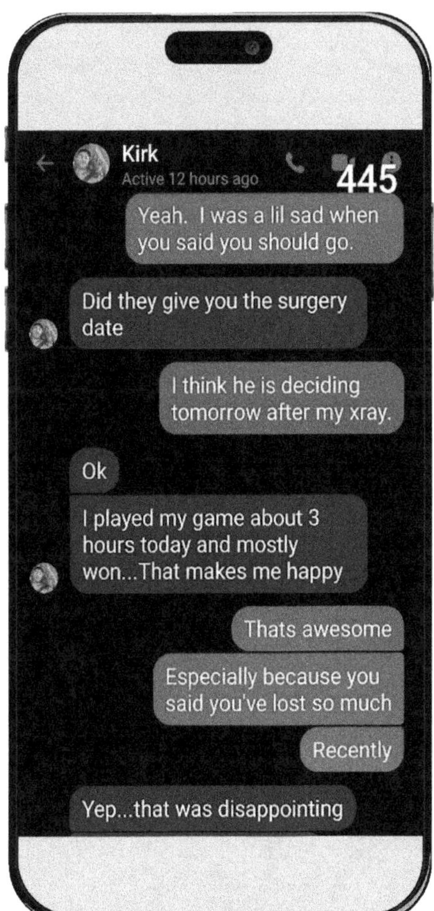
Kirk
Active 12 hours ago
445
Yeah. I was a lil sad when you said you should go.
Did they give you the surgery date
I think he is deciding tomorrow after my xray.
Ok
I played my game about 3 hours today and mostly won...That makes me happy
Thats awesome
Especially because you said you've lost so much
Recently
Yep...that was disappointing

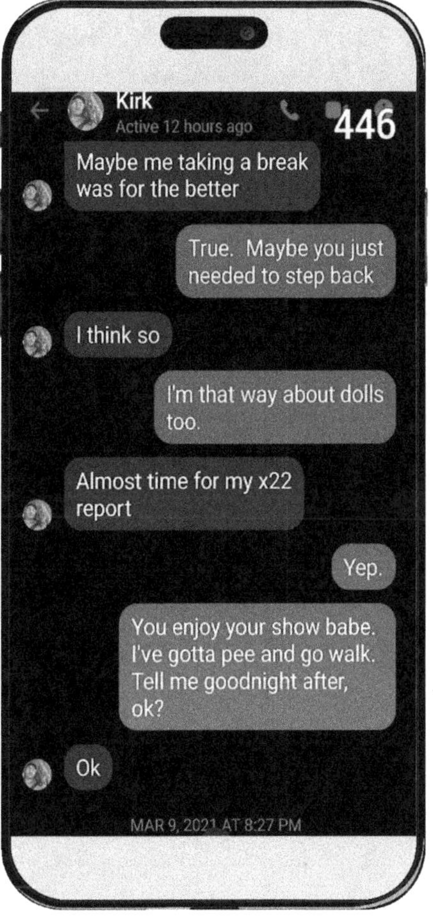
Kirk
Active 12 hours ago
446
Maybe me taking a break was for the better
True. Maybe you just needed to step back
I think so
I'm that way about dolls too.
Almost time for my x22 report
Yep.
You enjoy your show babe. I've gotta pee and go walk. Tell me goodnight after, ok?
Ok
MAR 9, 2021 AT 8:27 PM

Kirk
Active 12 hours ago
447
Goodnight kim
Night babe.
Talk to you in the morning
Ok babe. Sleep well.
MAR 10, 2021 AT 9:43 AM
Hey there
Good morning
MAR 10, 2021 AT 10:36 AM
Hi babe. Sorry. There was a first in the hosp so I had to evacuate because I was at my ct scan.
A fire

Kirk
Active 12 hours ago
448
Stop smoking that weed...how many times do I have to tell you lol
Lol
Did you sleep ok
MAR 10, 2021 AT 10:53 AM
Bo
No
Doc had to be called
Sorry to hear that
I cleaned up the kitchen and living room today...and did dishes
Thank you sweetie. You're such a good guy. I'm sure mom appreciates it too.

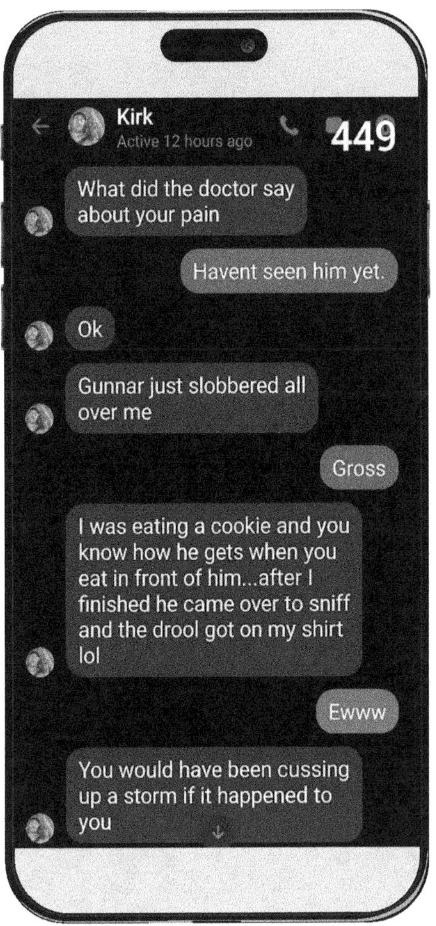

Kirk
Active 12 hours ago
449
What did the doctor say about your pain
Havent seen him yet.
Ok
Gunnar just slobbered all over me
Gross
I was eating a cookie and you know how he gets when you eat in front of him...after I finished he came over to sniff and the drool got on my shirt lol
Ewww
You would have been cussing up a storm if it happened to you

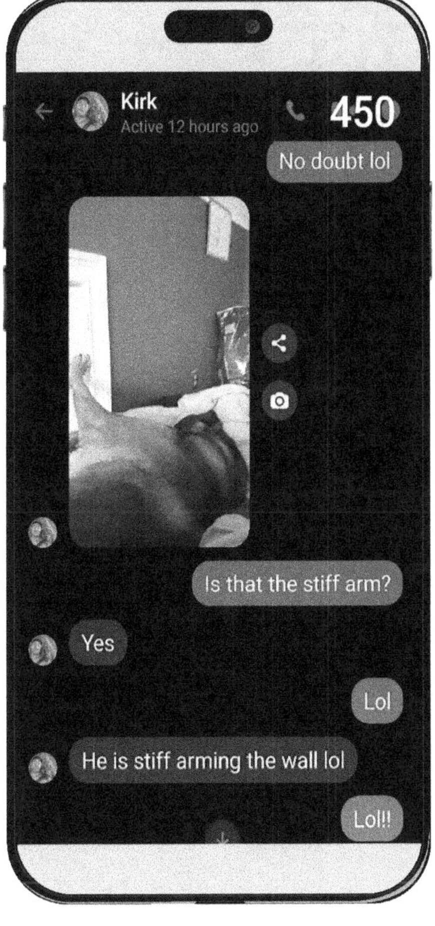

Kirk
Active 12 hours ago
450
No doubt lol
Is that the stiff arm?
Yes
Lol
He is stiff arming the wall lol
Lol!!

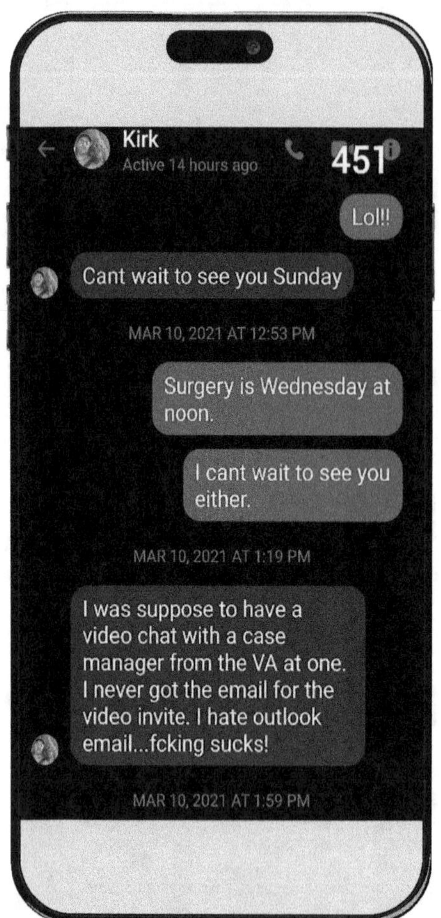
Kirk
Active 14 hours ago
451
Lol!!
Cant wait to see you Sunday
MAR 10, 2021 AT 12:53 PM
Surgery is Wednesday at noon.
I cant wait to see you either.
MAR 10, 2021 AT 1:19 PM
I was suppose to have a video chat with a case manager from the VA at one. I never got the email for the video invite. I hate outlook email...fcking sucks!
MAR 10, 2021 AT 1:59 PM

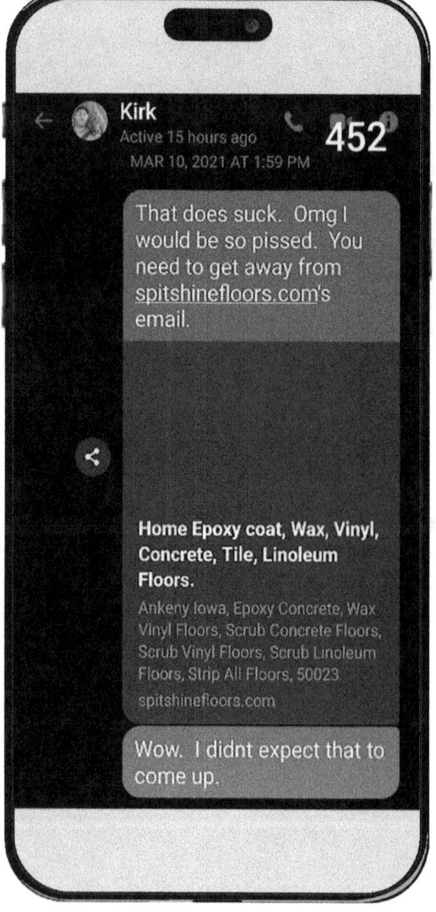
Kirk
Active 15 hours ago
452
MAR 10, 2021 AT 1:59 PM
That does suck. Omg I would be so pissed. You need to get away from spitshinefloors.com's email.
Home Epoxy coat, Wax, Vinyl, Concrete, Tile, Linoleum Floors.
Ankeny Iowa, Epoxy Concrete, Wax Vinyl Floors, Scrub Concrete Floors, Scrub Vinyl Floors, Scrub Linoleum Floors, Strip All Floors, 50023
spitshinefloors.com
Wow. I didnt expect that to come up.

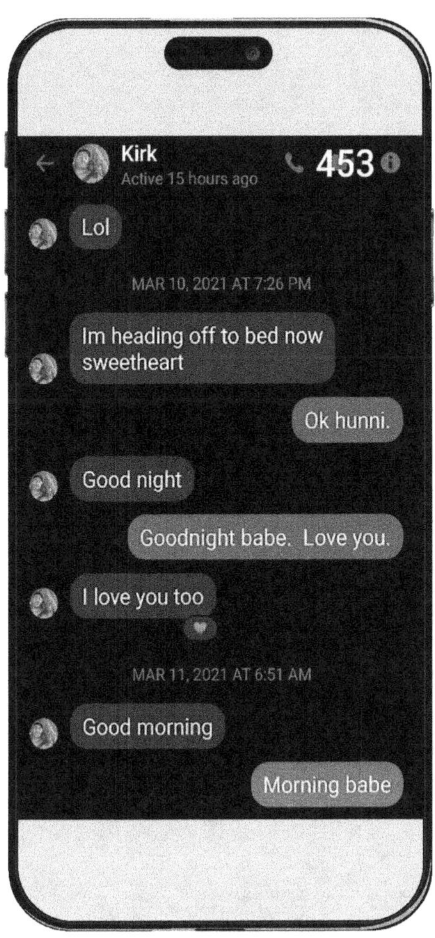

Kirk
Active 15 hours ago
453
Lol
MAR 10, 2021 AT 7:26 PM
Im heading off to bed now sweetheart
Ok hunni.
Good night
Goodnight babe. Love you.
I love you too
MAR 11, 2021 AT 6:51 AM
Good morning
Morning babe

Kirk
Active 15 hours ago
454
I got my highest damage game yesterday in my tank game 3.7k damage
Awesome!
??

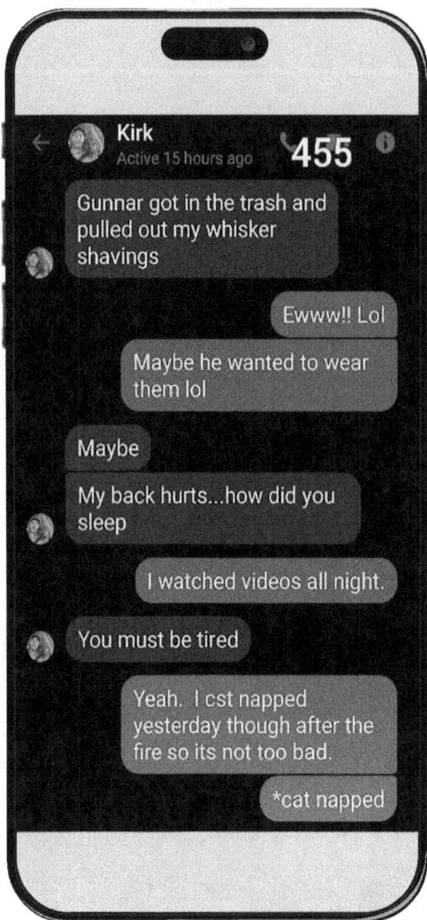
Kirk
Active 15 hours ago
455
Gunnar got in the trash and pulled out my whisker shavings
Ewww!! Lol
Maybe he wanted to wear them lol
Maybe
My back hurts...how did you sleep
I watched videos all night.
You must be tired
Yeah. I cst napped yesterday though after the fire so its not too bad.
*cat napped

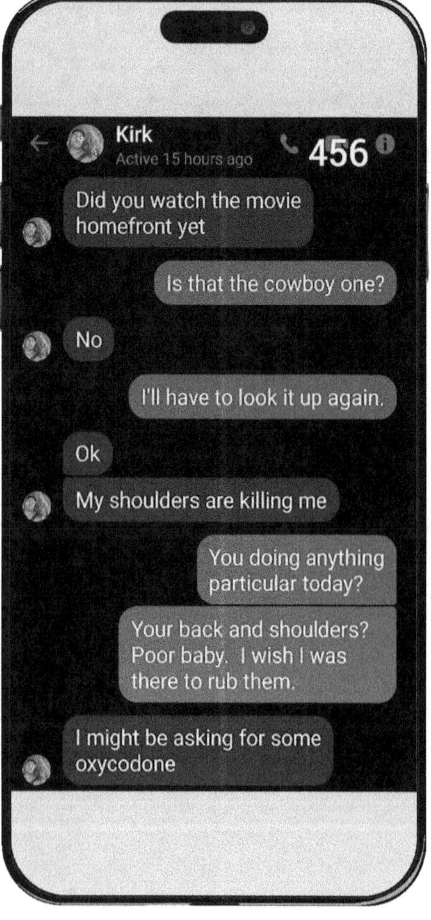
Kirk
Active 15 hours ago
456
Did you watch the movie homefront yet
Is that the cowboy one?
No
I'll have to look it up again.
Ok
My shoulders are killing me
You doing anything particular today?
Your back and shoulders? Poor baby. I wish I was there to rub them.
I might be asking for some oxycodone

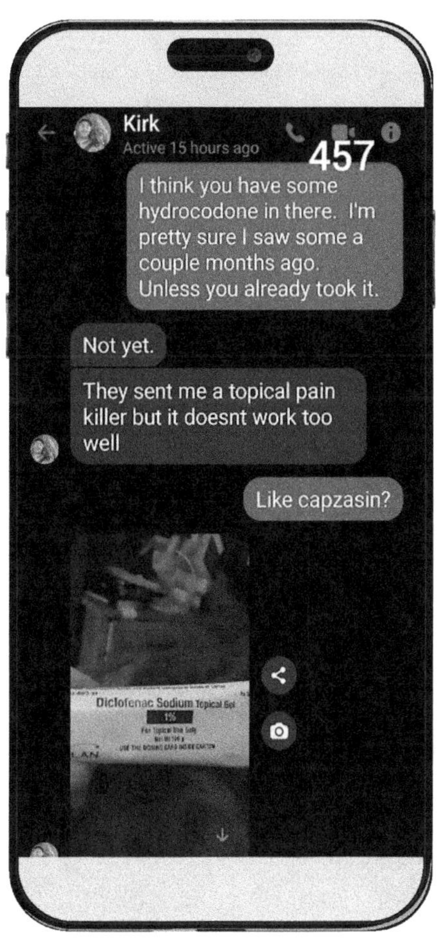

Kirk
Active 15 hours ago
457
I think you have some hydrocodone in there. I'm pretty sure I saw some a couple months ago.
Unless you already took it.
Not yet.
They sent me a topical pain killer but it doesnt work too well
Like capzasin?
Diclofenac Sodium Topical Gel

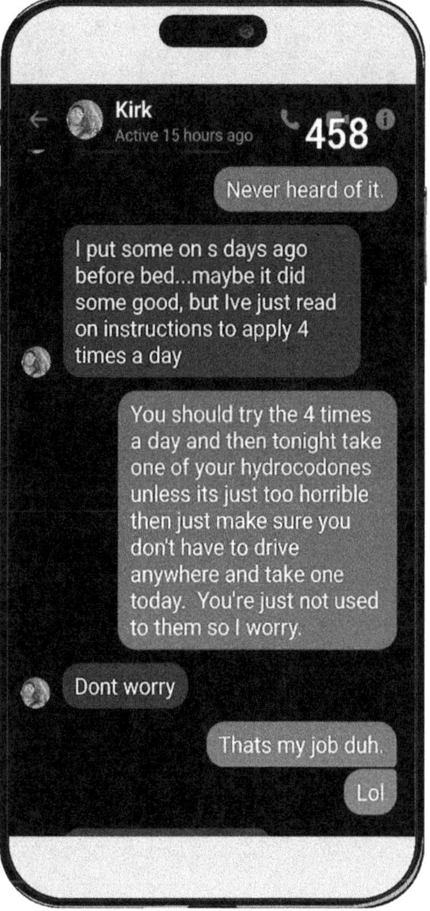

Kirk
Active 15 hours ago
458
Never heard of it.
I put some on s days ago before bed...maybe it did some good, but Ive just read on instructions to apply 4 times a day
You should try the 4 times a day and then tonight take one of your hydrocodones unless its just too horrible then just make sure you don't have to drive anywhere and take one today. You're just not used to them so I worry.
Dont worry
Thats my job duh.
Lol

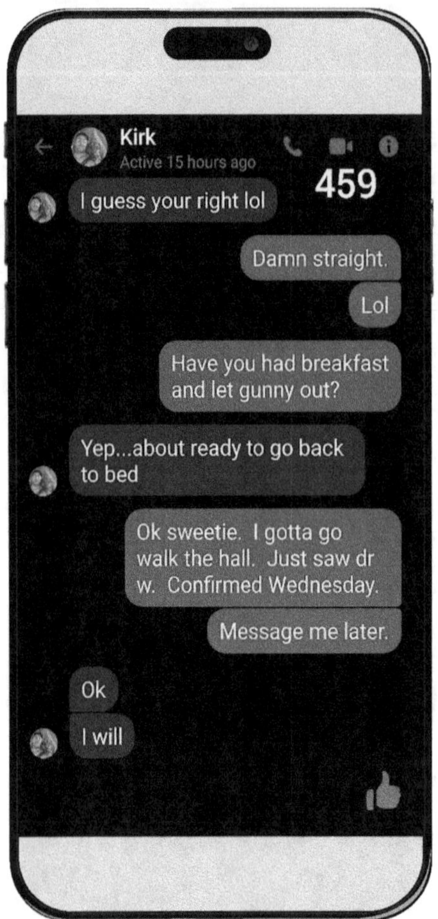
Kirk
Active 15 hours ago
459
I guess your right lol
Damn straight.
Lol
Have you had breakfast and let gunny out?
Yep...about ready to go back to bed
Ok sweetie. I gotta go walk the hall. Just saw dr w. Confirmed Wednesday.
Message me later.
Ok
I will

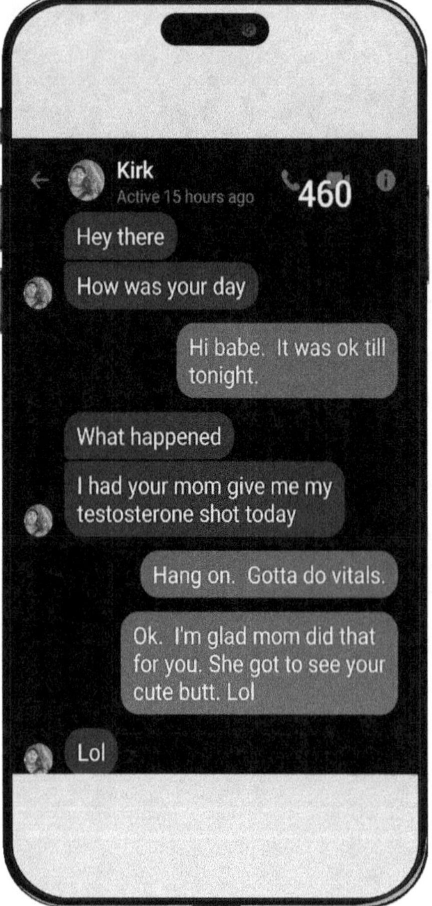
Kirk
Active 15 hours ago
460
Hey there
How was your day
Hi babe. It was ok till tonight.
What happened
I had your mom give me my testosterone shot today
Hang on. Gotta do vitals.
Ok. I'm glad mom did that for you. She got to see your cute butt. Lol
Lol

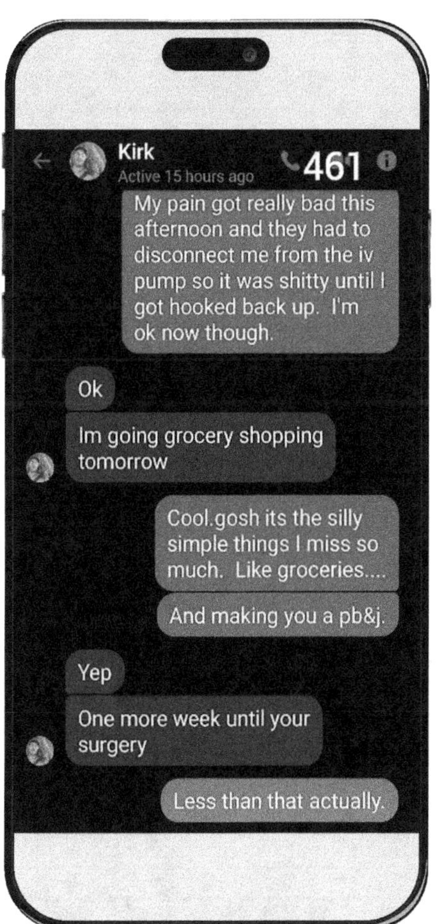
Kirk
Active 15 hours ago
461
My pain got really bad this afternoon and they had to disconnect me from the iv pump so it was shitty until I got hooked back up. I'm ok now though.
Ok
Im going grocery shopping tomorrow
Cool.gosh its the silly simple things I miss so much. Like groceries....
And making you a pb&j.
Yep
One more week until your surgery
Less than that actually.

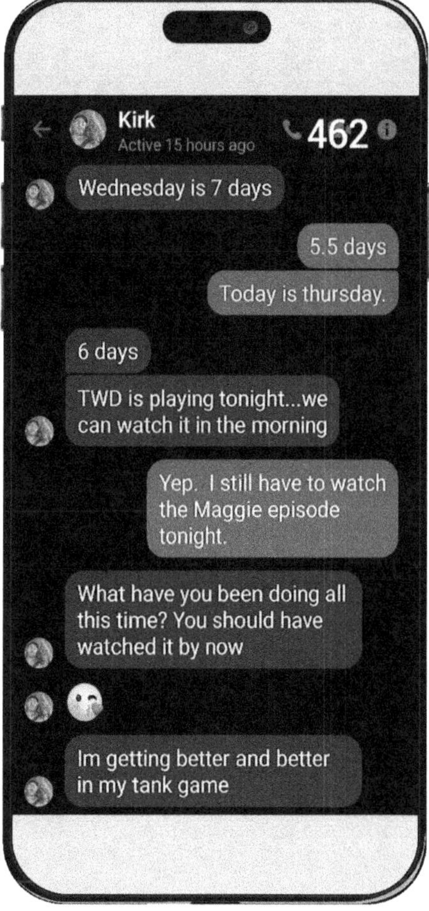
Kirk
Active 15 hours ago
462
Wednesday is 7 days
5.5 days
Today is thursday.
6 days
TWD is playing tonight...we can watch it in the morning
Yep. I still have to watch the Maggie episode tonight.
What have you been doing all this time? You should have watched it by now
Im getting better and better in my tank game

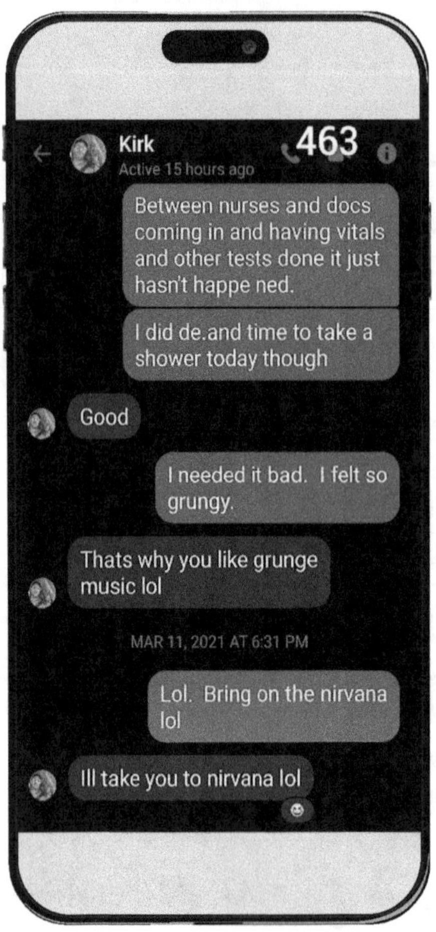

Kirk
Active 15 hours ago
463
Between nurses and docs coming in and having vitals and other tests done it just hasn't happe ned.
I did de.and time to take a shower today though
Good
I needed it bad. I felt so grungy.
Thats why you like grunge music lol
MAR 11, 2021 AT 6:31 PM
Lol. Bring on the nirvana lol
Ill take you to nirvana lol

Kirk
Active 15 hours ago
464
You have taken me there quite a few times if memory serves. Lol
Lol
MAR 11, 2021 AT 7:49 PM
Just sneezed and farted again lol
Lmao!!
MAR 11, 2021 AT 10:37 PM
Goodnight sweetie.
MAR 12, 2021 AT 8:42 AM
Good morning
Mornin
Today is Friday

Kirk
Active 15 hours ago
465
Today is Friday
Gunnar is chillin in the sun lol
And tomorrow is Saturday.
Aww.
And the Sunday...Yippie!

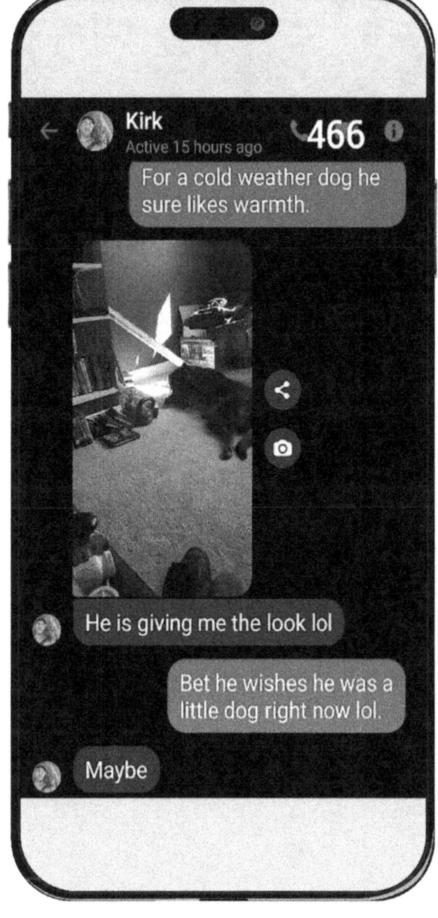
Kirk
Active 15 hours ago
466
For a cold weather dog he sure likes warmth.
He is giving me the look lol
Bet he wishes he was a little dog right now lol.
Maybe

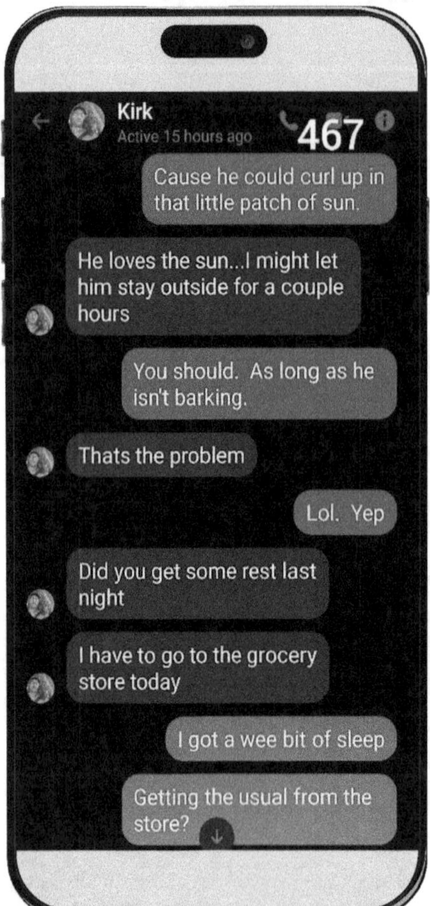
Kirk
Active 15 hours ago
467
Cause he could curl up in that little patch of sun.
He loves the sun...I might let him stay outside for a couple hours
You should. As long as he isn't barking.
Thats the problem
Lol. Yep
Did you get some rest last night
I have to go to the grocery store today
I got a wee bit of sleep
Getting the usual from the store?

Kirk
Active 15 hours ago
468
Yep
Did you watch twd yet?
Not yet...you?
Nah. Not yet.
Im watching trent and allie right now
Col. How arethey?
They are doing good.
And their house?
They are doing electrucal now
Wow. They must be ready far along then. Cool.

Kirk
Active 15 hours ago
469
They are getting there
Have you ordered more testosterone?
My shoulder hurts...not yet
I need to though
Awww.   I wish I could kiss it better. Did you try some hydrocodone at night?
There is none here. The bottle was empty
Oh. How weird. I am sure I saw some . I guess I was wrong. I worry the ones I have there are too strong for you. Have you tried the cream?
Yes

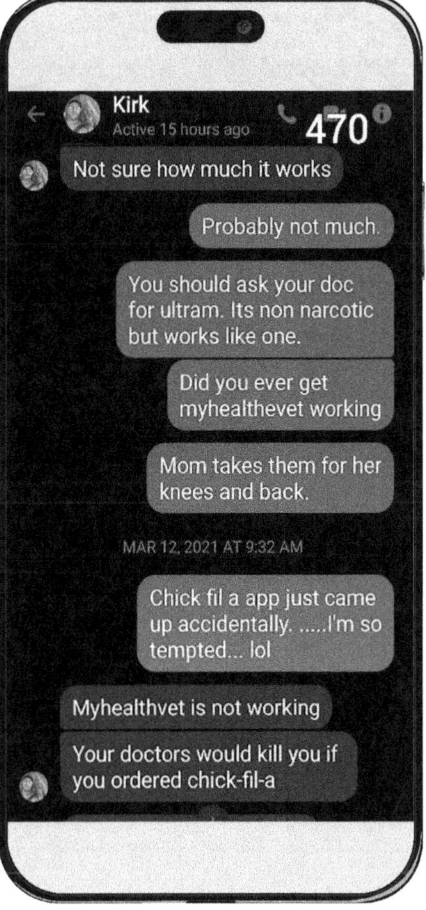

Kirk
Active 15 hours ago
470
Not sure how much it works
Probably not much.
You should ask your doc for ultram. Its non narcotic but works like one.
Did you ever get myhealthevet working
Mom takes them for her knees and back.
MAR 12, 2021 AT 9:32 AM
Chick fil a app just came up accidentally. .....I'm so tempted... lol
Myhealthvet is not working
Your doctors would kill you if you ordered chick-fil-a

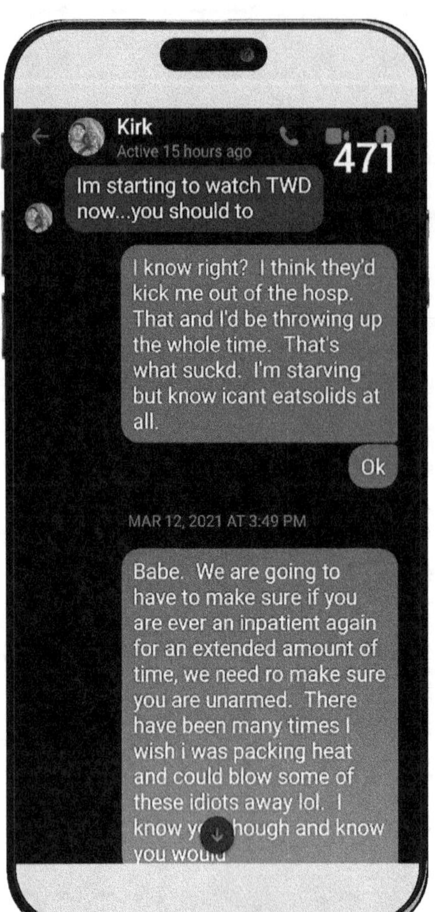
Kirk
Active 15 hours ago
471
Im starting to watch TWD now...you should to
I know right? I think they'd kick me out of the hosp. That and I'd be throwing up the whole time. That's what suckd. I'm starving but know icant eatsolids at all.
Ok
MAR 12, 2021 AT 3:49 PM
Babe. We are going to have to make sure if you are ever an inpatient again for an extended amount of time, we need ro make sure you are unarmed. There have been many times I wish i was packing heat and could blow some of these idiots away lol. I know yo hough and know you would

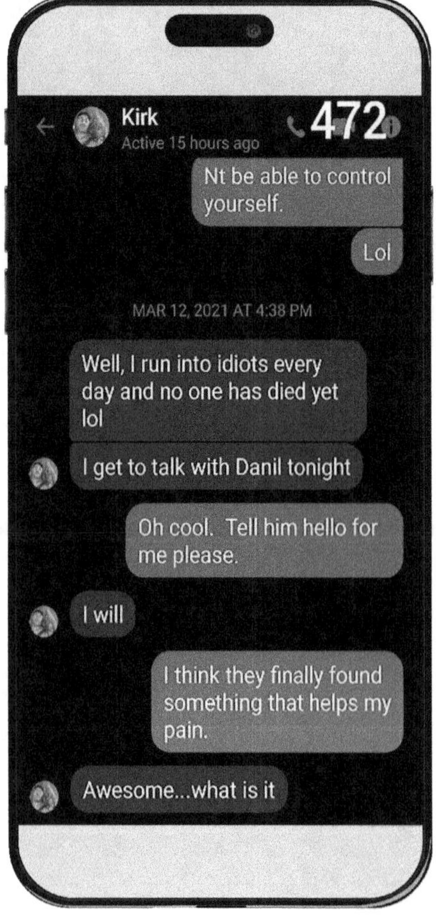
Kirk
Active 15 hours ago
472
Nt be able to control yourself.
Lol
MAR 12, 2021 AT 4:38 PM
Well, I run into idiots every day and no one has died yet lol
I get to talk with Danil tonight
Oh cool. Tell him hello for me please.
I will
I think they finally found something that helps my pain.
Awesome...what is it

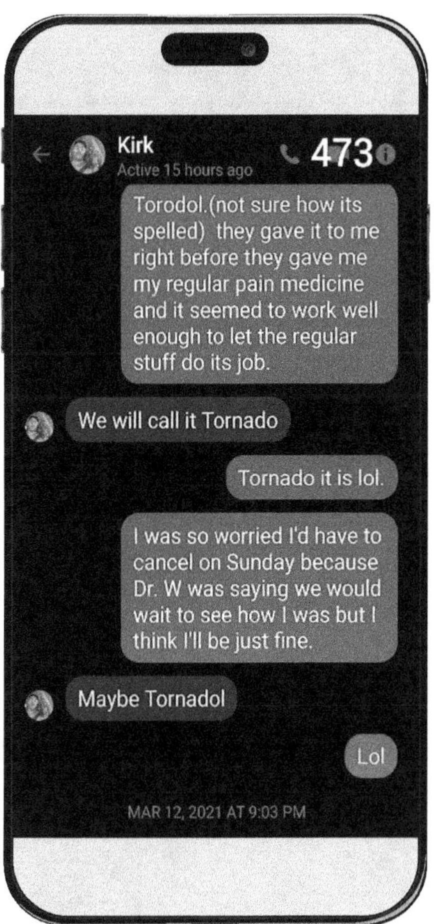
Kirk
Active 15 hours ago
473
Torodol.(not sure how its spelled) they gave it to me right before they gave me my regular pain medicine and it seemed to work well enough to let the regular stuff do its job.
We will call it Tornado
Tornado it is lol.
I was so worried I'd have to cancel on Sunday because Dr. W was saying we would wait to see how I was but I think I'll be just fine.
Maybe Tornadol
Lol
MAR 12, 2021 AT 9:03 PM

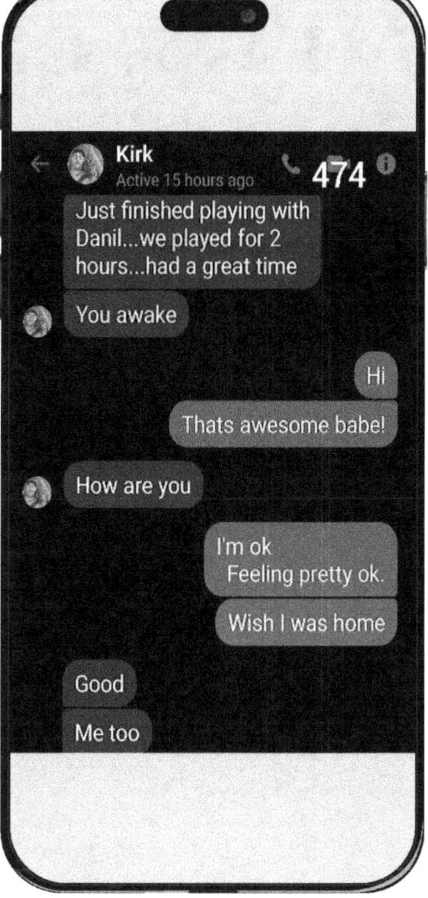
Kirk
Active 15 hours ago
474
Just finished playing with Danil...we played for 2 hours...had a great time
You awake
Hi
Thats awesome babe!
How are you
I'm ok
Feeling pretty ok.
Wish I was home
Good
Me too

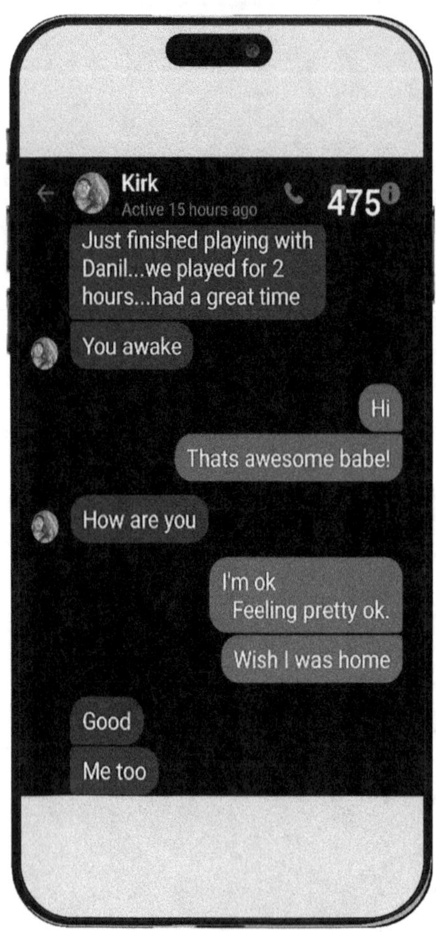

Kirk
Active 15 hours ago
475
Just finished playing with Danil...we played for 2 hours...had a great time
You awake
Hi
Thats awesome babe!
How are you
I'm ok
Feeling pretty ok.
Wish I was home
Good
Me too

Kirk
Active 15 hours ago
476
Hopefully soon. I cant wait to try and eat again. I'm so hungry
This is gunny right now
Lol
I bet you are
Lazy bone Jones

Kirk
477
Got him a new chew toy today
Im getting ready to take him outside one last time before bed
Awww.. yay! Daddy's on board buying toys! 👍
Looks like he's already tuckered out but I know he won't miss a chance to go out.
The other one has become a choking hazard
Lol. I'll bet.
That was quick
Been out and in already?
Yep...but not as good as in n out

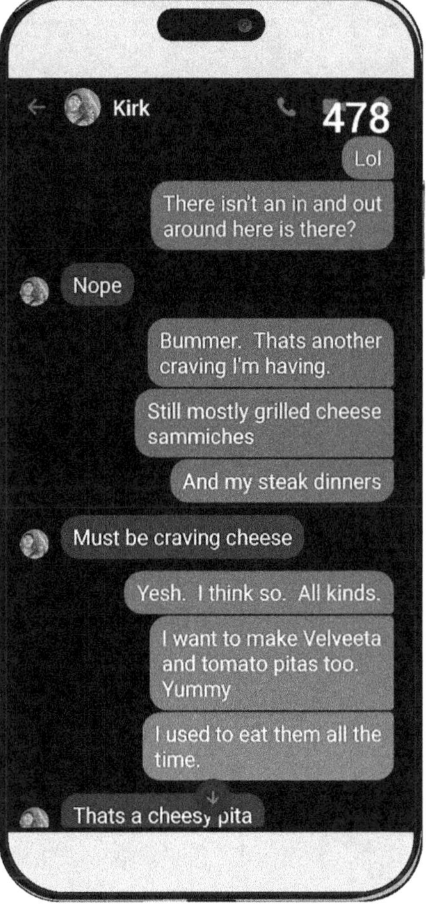
Kirk
478
Lol
There isn't an in and out around here is there?
Nope
Bummer. Thats another craving I'm having.
Still mostly grilled cheese sammiches
And my steak dinners
Must be craving cheese
Yesh. I think so. All kinds.
I want to make Velveeta and tomato pitas too. Yummy
I used to eat them all the time.
Thats a cheesy pita

Kirk
479
Yep. I shred it up and dice up a tomato and shove it in a pita. So good.
I'd probably like to add some shredded chicken too it too.
Man I'm driving myself nuts.
Thats sounds good...fajita chicken
At least your nuts arent driving you
Yeah. Kinda like a fajita. Except not stir-fried.
Guys have that problem alot lol

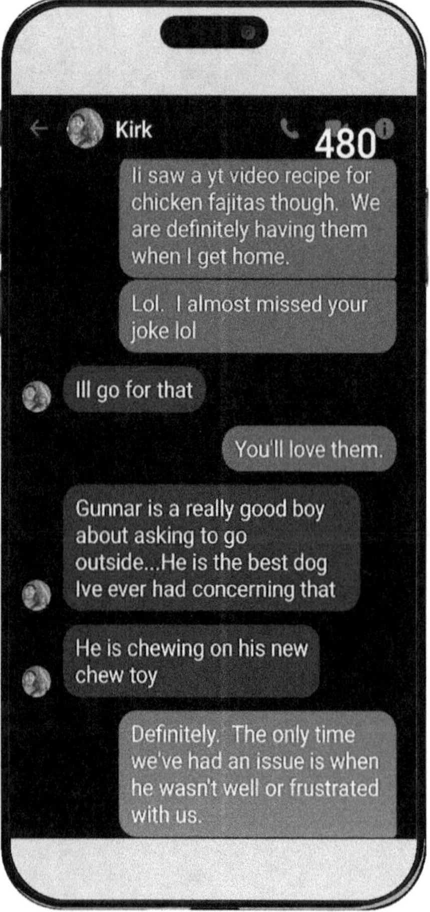
Kirk
480
Ii saw a yt video recipe for chicken fajitas though. We are definitely having them when I get home.
Lol. I almost missed your joke lol
Ill go for that
You'll love them.
Gunnar is a really good boy about asking to go outside...He is the best dog Ive ever had concerning that
He is chewing on his new chew toy
Definitely. The only time we've had an issue is when he wasn't well or frustrated with us.

Kirk
Active 15 hours ago
481

Thats good. Is it just like his other one?

I got that homesteading course in the mail yesterday

Wow! Fast!!!

Im going to start watching it tomorrow

It was fast

Thats awesome!

Just a few days

I cang believe it got their so fast.

Im going to watch how to make soap first since I like soap lol

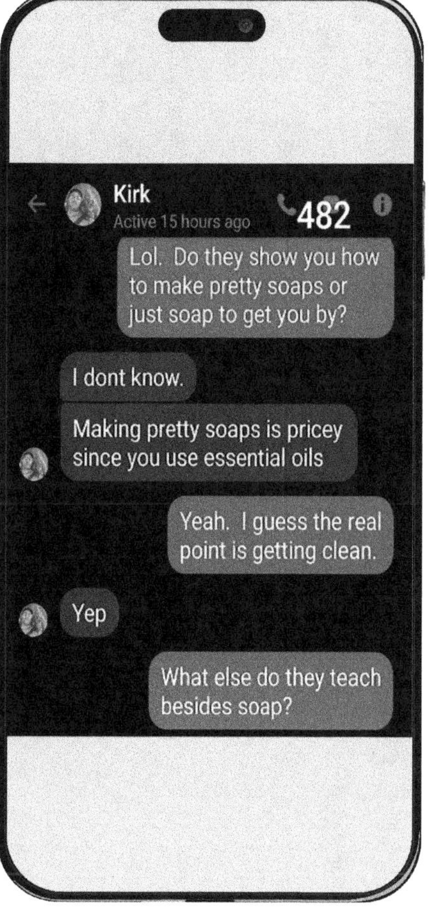

Kirk
Active 15 hours ago
482

Lol. Do they show you how to make pretty soaps or just soap to get you by?

I dont know.

Making pretty soaps is pricey since you use essential oils

Yeah. I guess the real point is getting clean.

Yep

What else do they teach besides soap?

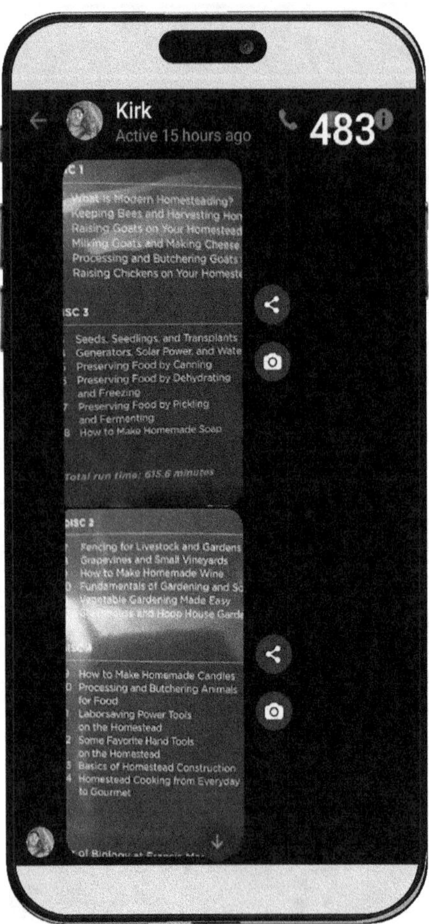

Kirk
Active 15 hours ago
483
What Is Modern Homesteading?
Keeping Bees and Harvesting Hon
Raising Goats on Your Homestead
Milking Goats and Making Cheese
Processing and Butchering Goats
Raising Chickens on Your Homeste
Seeds, Seedlings, and Transplants
Generators, Solar Power, and Wate
Preserving Food by Canning
Preserving Food by Dehydrating
and Freezing
Preserving Food by Pickling
and Fermenting
How to Make Homemade Soap
Total run time: 615.6 minutes
Fencing for Livestock and Gardens
Grapevines and Small Vineyards
How to Make Homemade Wine
Fundamentals of Gardening and So
Vegetable Gardening Made Easy
How to Make Homemade Candles
Processing and Butchering Animals
for Food
Laborsaving Power Tools
on the Homestead
Some Favorite Hand Tools
on the Homestead
Basics of Homestead Construction
Homestead Cooking from Everyday
to Gourmet

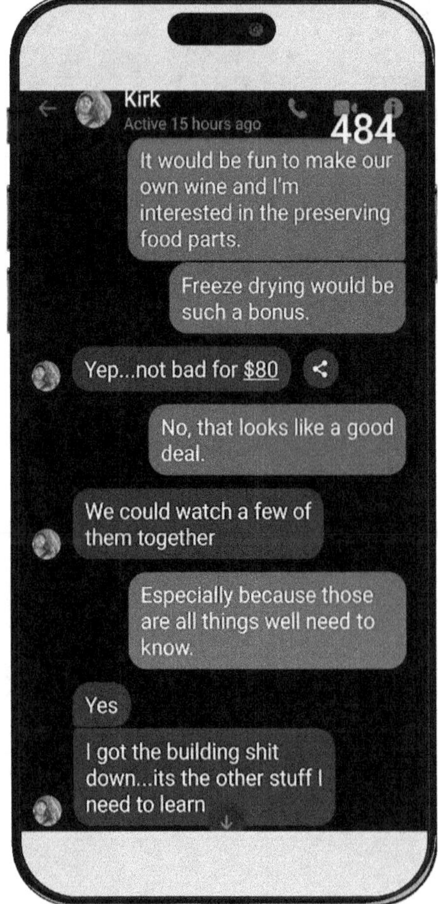

Kirk
Active 15 hours ago
484
It would be fun to make our own wine and I'm interested in the preserving food parts.
Freeze drying would be such a bonus.
Yep...not bad for $80
No, that looks like a good deal.
We could watch a few of them together
Especially because those are all things well need to know.
Yes
I got the building shit down...its the other stuff I need to learn

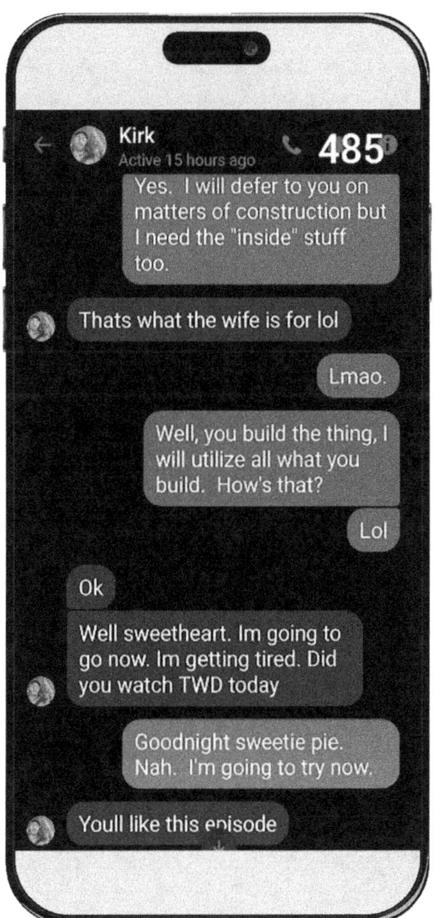
Kirk
Active 15 hours ago
485
Yes. I will defer to you on matters of construction but I need the "inside" stuff too.
Thats what the wife is for lol
Lmao.
Well, you build the thing, I will utilize all what you build. How's that?
Lol
Ok
Well sweetheart. Im going to go now. Im getting tired. Did you watch TWD today
Goodnight sweetie pie. Nah. I'm going to try now.
Youll like this episode

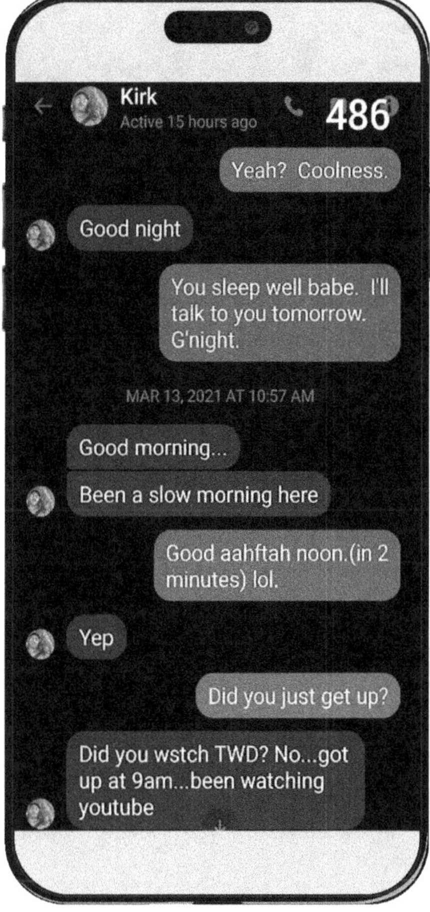
Kirk
Active 15 hours ago
486
Yeah? Coolness.
Good night
You sleep well babe. I'll talk to you tomorrow. G'night.
MAR 13, 2021 AT 10:57 AM
Good morning...
Been a slow morning here
Good aahftah noon.(in 2 minutes) lol.
Yep
Did you just get up?
Did you wstch TWD? No...got up at 9am...been watching youtube

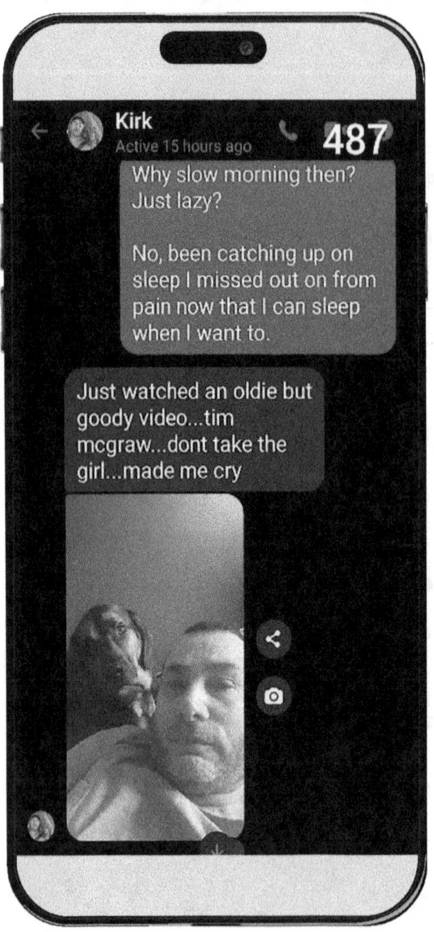

Kirk
Active 15 hours ago
487
Why slow morning then? Just lazy?
No, been catching up on sleep I missed out on from pain now that I can sleep when I want to.
Just watched an oldie but goody video...tim mcgraw...dont take the girl...made me cry

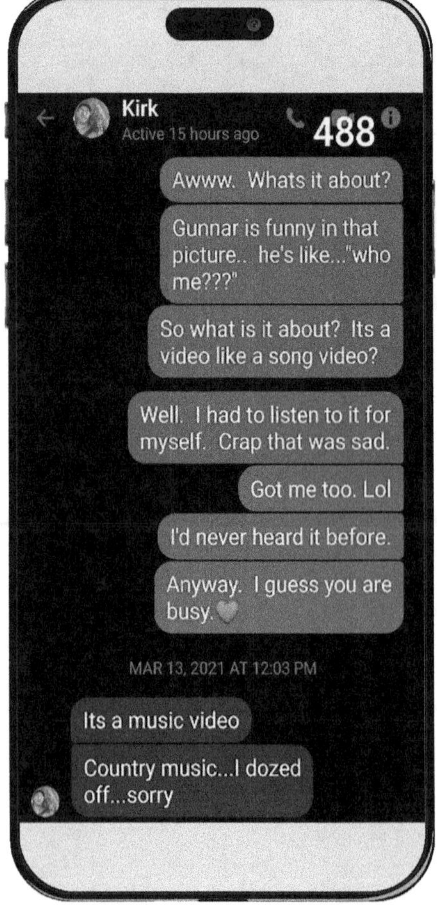

Kirk
Active 15 hours ago
488
Awww. Whats it about?
Gunnar is funny in that picture.. he's like..."who me???".
So what is it about? Its a video like a song video?
Well. I had to listen to it for myself. Crap that was sad.
Got me too. Lol
I'd never heard it before.
Anyway. I guess you are busy.
MAR 13, 2021 AT 12:03 PM
Its a music video
Country music...I dozed off...sorry

During this time, Me and Kim were planning our future together. We were confident that she would beat the cancer since she was cancer free the previous June or July of 2020. We were sure that after the surgery and chemo that she would again be cancer free and we will be able to live our lives as husband and wife until old age.

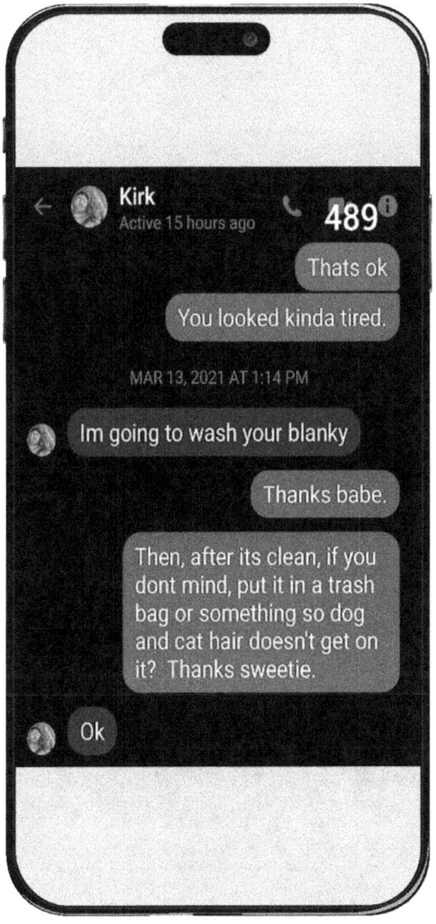

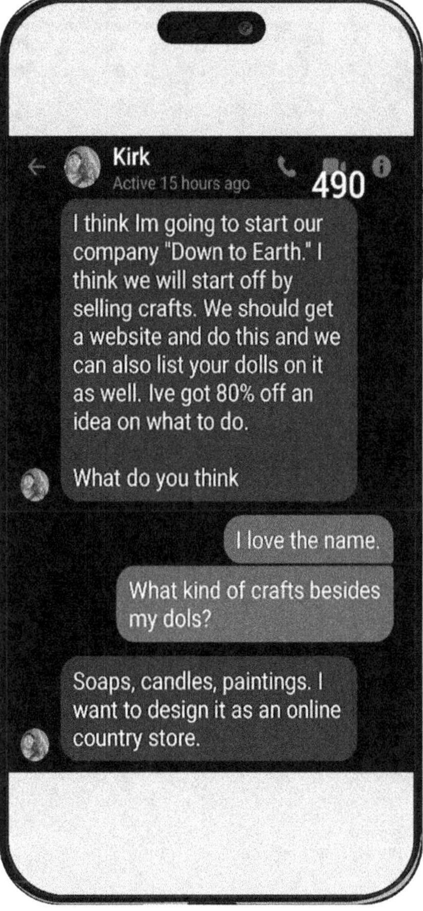

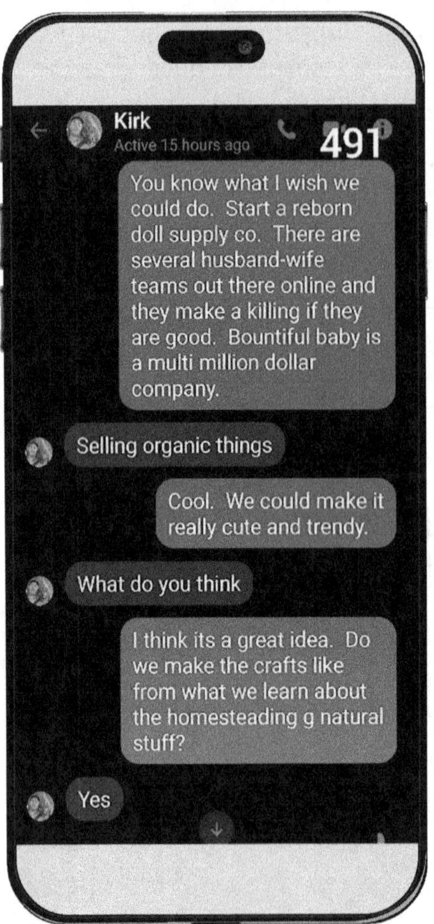

Kirk
Active 15 hours ago
491
You know what I wish we could do. Start a reborn doll supply co. There are several husband-wife teams out there online and they make a killing if they are good. Bountiful baby is a multi million dollar company.
Selling organic things
Cool. We could make it really cute and trendy.
What do you think
I think its a great idea. Do we make the crafts like from what we learn about the homesteading g natural stuff?
Yes

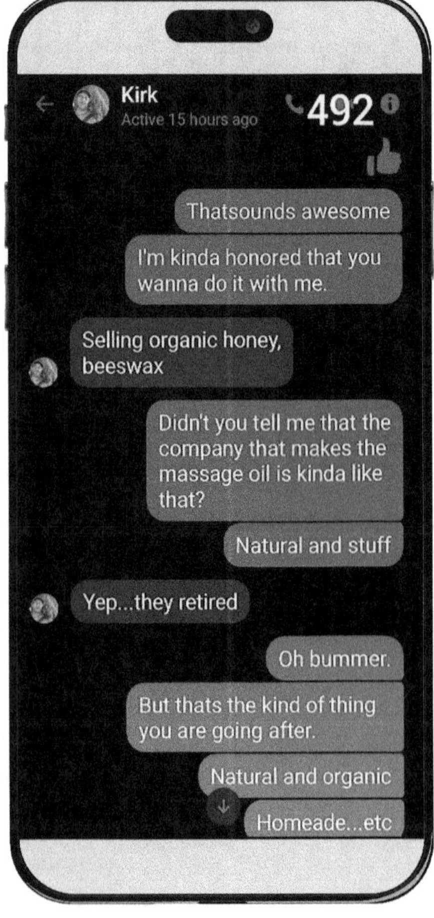

Kirk
Active 15 hours ago
492
Thatsounds awesome
I'm kinda honored that you wanna do it with me.
Selling organic honey, beeswax
Didn't you tell me that the company that makes the massage oil is kinda like that?
Natural and stuff
Yep...they retired
Oh bummer.
But thats the kind of thing you are going after.
Natural and organic
Homeade...etc

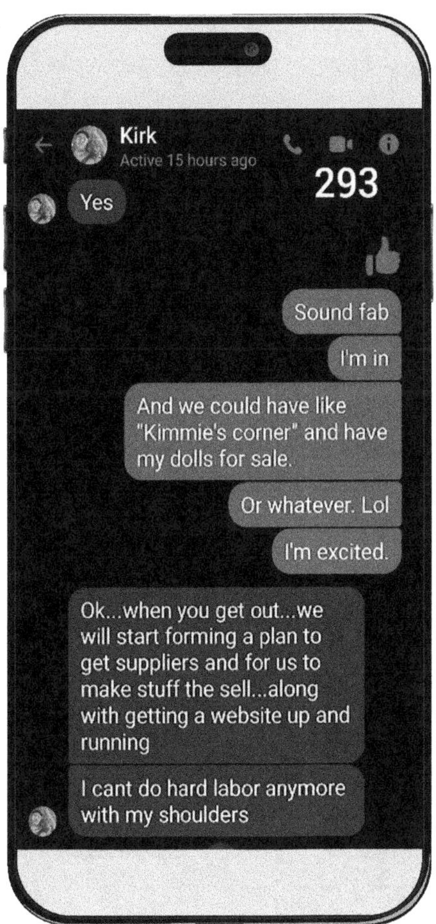

Kirk
Active 15 hours ago
293
Yes
Sound fab
I'm in
And we could have like "Kimmie's corner" and have my dolls for sale.
Or whatever. Lol
I'm excited.
Ok...when you get out...we will start forming a plan to get suppliers and for us to make stuff the sell...along with getting a website up and running
I cant do hard labor anymore with my shoulders

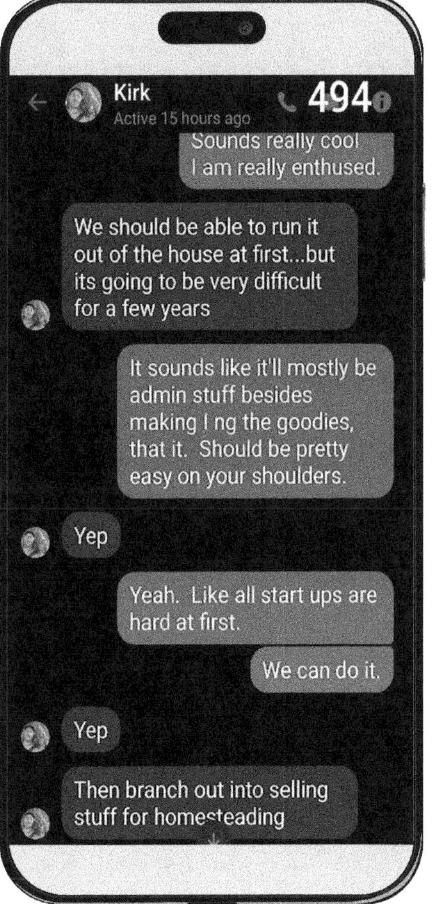

Kirk
Active 15 hours ago
494
Sounds really cool I am really enthused.
We should be able to run it out of the house at first...but its going to be very difficult for a few years
It sounds like it'll mostly be admin stuff besides making I ng the goodies, that it. Should be pretty easy on your shoulders.
Yep
Yeah. Like all start ups are hard at first.
We can do it.
Yep
Then branch out into selling stuff for homesteading

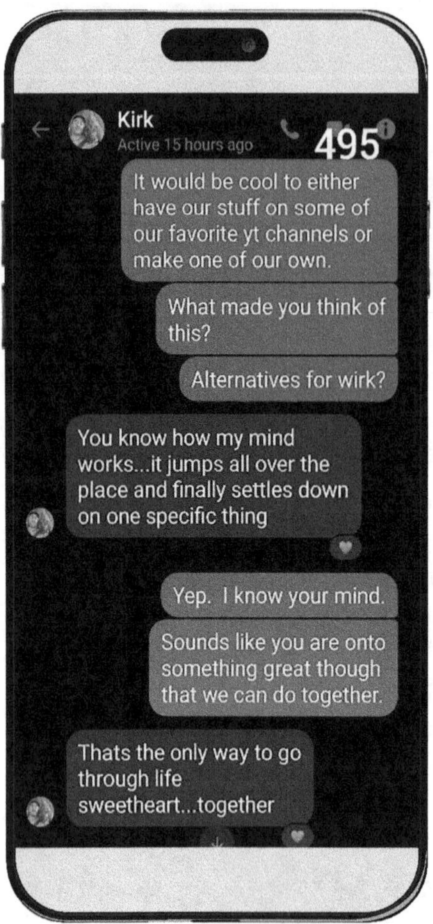

Kirk
Active 15 hours ago
495
It would be cool to either have our stuff on some of our favorite yt channels or make one of our own.
What made you think of this?
Alternatives for wirk?
You know how my mind works...it jumps all over the place and finally settles down on one specific thing
Yep. I know your mind.
Sounds like you are onto something great though that we can do together.
Thats the only way to go through life sweetheart...together

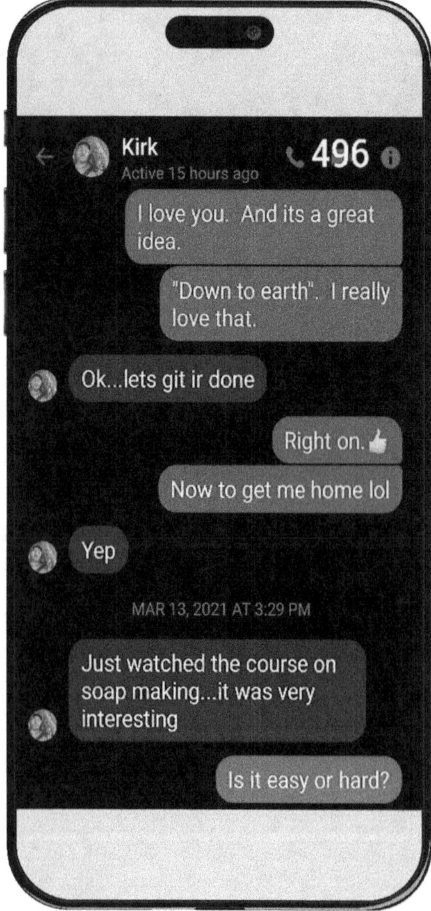

Kirk
Active 15 hours ago
496
I love you. And its a great idea.
"Down to earth". I really love that.
Ok...lets git ir done
Right on.
Now to get me home lol
Yep
MAR 13, 2021 AT 3:29 PM
Just watched the course on soap making...it was very interesting
Is it easy or hard?

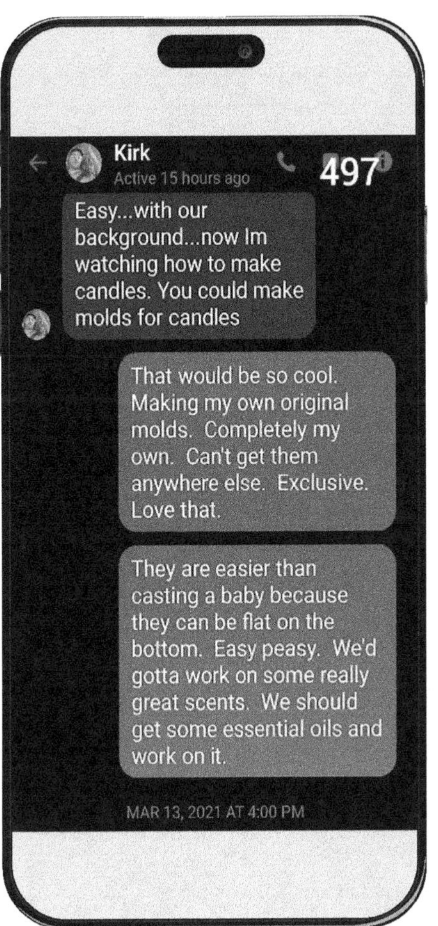
Kirk
Active 15 hours ago
497
Easy...with our background...now Im watching how to make candles. You could make molds for candles
That would be so cool. Making my own original molds. Completely my own. Can't get them anywhere else. Exclusive. Love that.
They are easier than casting a baby because they can be flat on the bottom. Easy peasy. We'd gotta work on some really great scents. We should get some essential oils and work on it.
MAR 13, 2021 AT 4:00 PM

Kirk
Active 15 hours ago
498
Yep. Sounds like tou are really excited about this
Im for sure
Im going to play my tank game now
MAR 13, 2021 AT 4:56 PM
Ok babe. Text me later.
MAR 13, 2021 AT 10:48 PM
Goodnight sweetie. See you tomorrow.
MAR 14, 2021 AT 8:53 AM
So you're not talking to me anymore? Lol
MAR 14, 2021 AT 9:05 AM
Well. At least let me know when you leave.

Kirk
Active 15 hours ago
499
I cant find your clear nail polish or your polish remover
Ok.
Don't worry about it.
Time for a shower...then we will be heading out
Ok
MAR 14, 2021 AT 10:54 AM
You guys on the way?
We are here
Ok. We may have a problem. I will be heading down in 5 minutes.
Ok
Whats the scoop

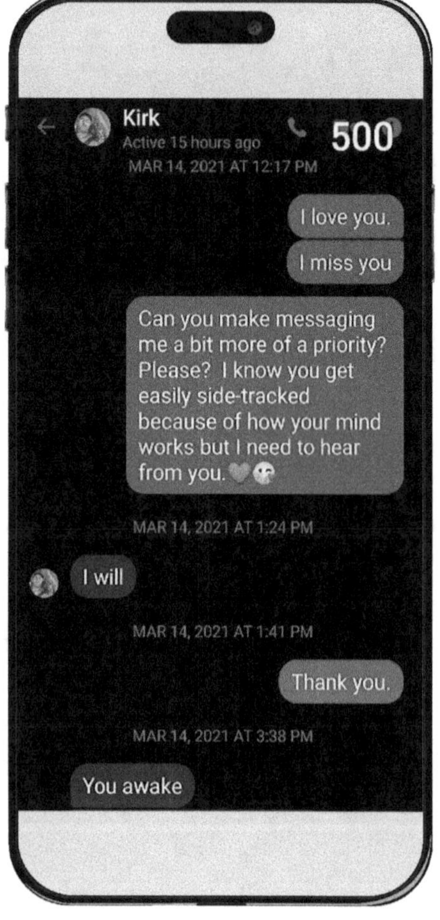

Kirk
Active 15 hours ago
500
MAR 14, 2021 AT 12:17 PM
I love you.
I miss you
Can you make messaging me a bit more of a priority? Please? I know you get easily side-tracked because of how your mind works but I need to hear from you.
MAR 14, 2021 AT 1:24 PM
I will
MAR 14, 2021 AT 1:41 PM
Thank you.
MAR 14, 2021 AT 3:38 PM
You awake

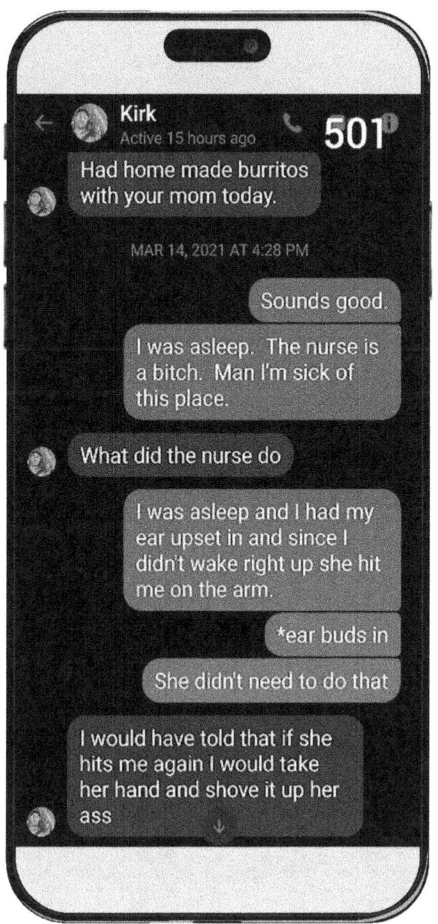
Kirk
Active 15 hours ago
501
Had home made burritos with your mom today.
MAR 14, 2021 AT 4:28 PM
Sounds good.
I was asleep. The nurse is a bitch. Man I'm sick of this place.
What did the nurse do
I was asleep and I had my ear upset in and since I didn't wake right up she hit me on the arm.
*ear buds in
She didn't need to do that
I would have told that if she hits me again I would take her hand and shove it up her ass

Kirk
Active 15 hours ago
502
Yeah. If I was you I would've said that. Lol.
It was just rude.
Yes it was
Anyway. What are you up yo?
Letting the phone charge...nothing on youtube...might watch a movie
Oh cool. I'm going to watch that movie.
What is is called? Time-something??
Finally
Homefront
Home front lol

Kirk
Active 15 hours ago
503
I wouldve been searching all night lol.
Remind me, if we ever visit China, we wont.
Ill never go yo china
Their food preparation and regulations are non existant.
To
Good
Plus they eat dog...hardly any cows in china
I dont understand how they can eat what we consider, members of the family.
Chinese people will eat anything

Kirk
Active 15 hours ago
504
Well, they are starving. Thanks to communism.
Yep
It was good to see you today
Aww. It was good to see you too. I cant wait till this is all a distant memory.
Me too
I've spent a lot of time thinking about the first thing I want to eat when I'm able but I think I'll wait till I know my body better.

Kirk
Active 15 hours ago
505
What Im eating right now
You're practically an instagrammer babe!
New episode of Blacklist is out
I saw that. You gonna watch?
Yep

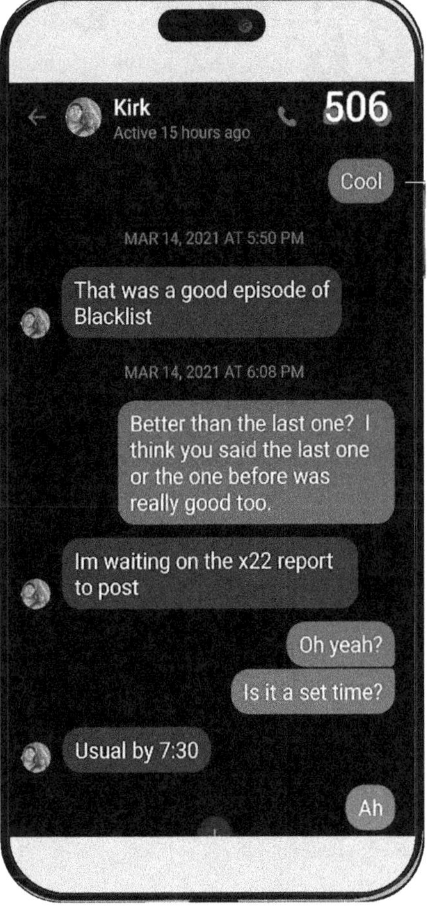
Kirk
Active 15 hours ago
506
Cool
MAR 14, 2021 AT 5:50 PM
That was a good episode of Blacklist
MAR 14, 2021 AT 6:08 PM
Better than the last one? I think you said the last one or the one before was really good too.
Im waiting on the x22 report to post
Oh yeah?
Is it a set time?
Usual by 7:30
Ah

Kirk
Active 15 hours ago
507
I'm getting ready to start the movie. Is this the one you wanted to discuss when its over?
Thats me right now
You look tired and Gunns looks asleep lol
Yep
Lol

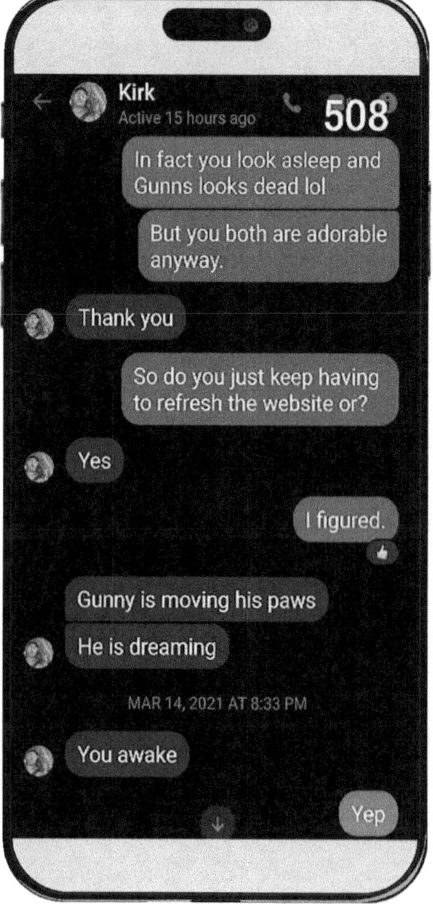

Kirk
Active 15 hours ago
508
In fact you look asleep and Gunns looks dead lol
But you both are adorable anyway.
Thank you
So do you just keep having to refresh the website or?
Yes
I figured.
Gunny is moving his paws
He is dreaming
MAR 14, 2021 AT 8:33 PM
You awake
Yep

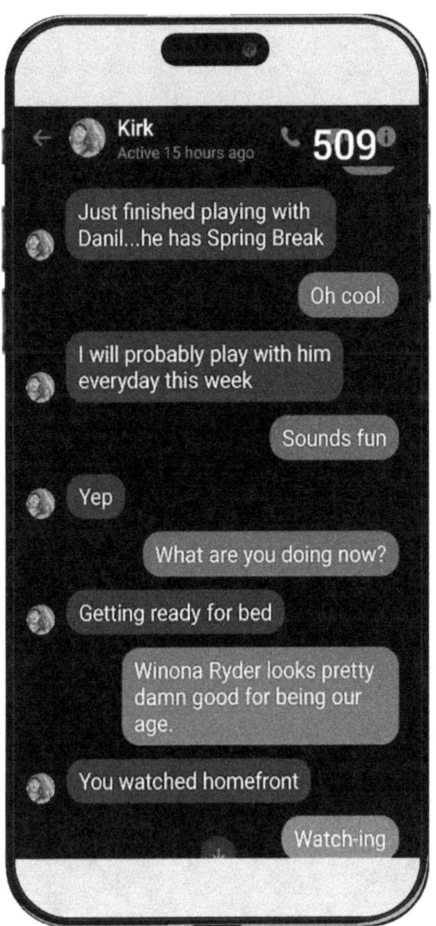

Kirk
Active 15 hours ago
509
Just finished playing with Danil...he has Spring Break
Oh cool.
I will probably play with him everyday this week
Sounds fun
Yep
What are you doing now?
Getting ready for bed
Winona Ryder looks pretty damn good for being our age.
You watched homefront
Watch-ing

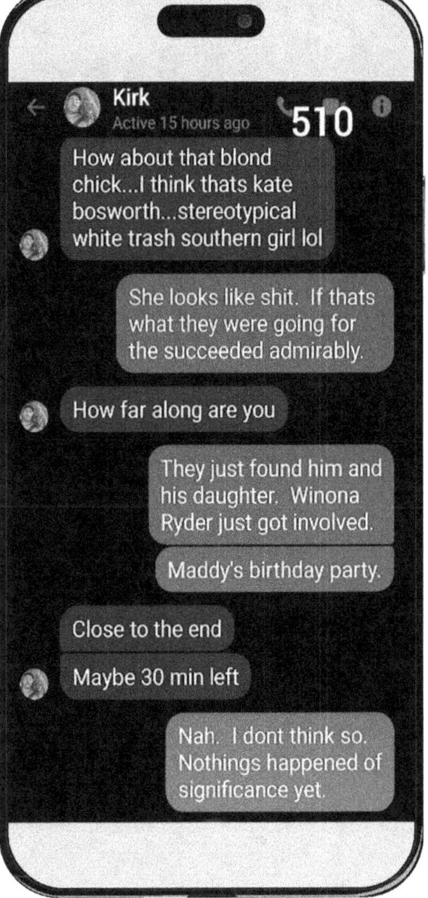

Kirk
Active 15 hours ago
510
How about that blond chick...I think thats kate bosworth...stereotypical white trash southern girl lol
She looks like shit. If thats what they were going for the succeeded admirably.
How far along are you
They just found him and his daughter. Winona Ryder just got involved.
Maddy's birthday party.
Close to the end
Maybe 30 min left
Nah. I dont think so. Nothings happened of significance yet.

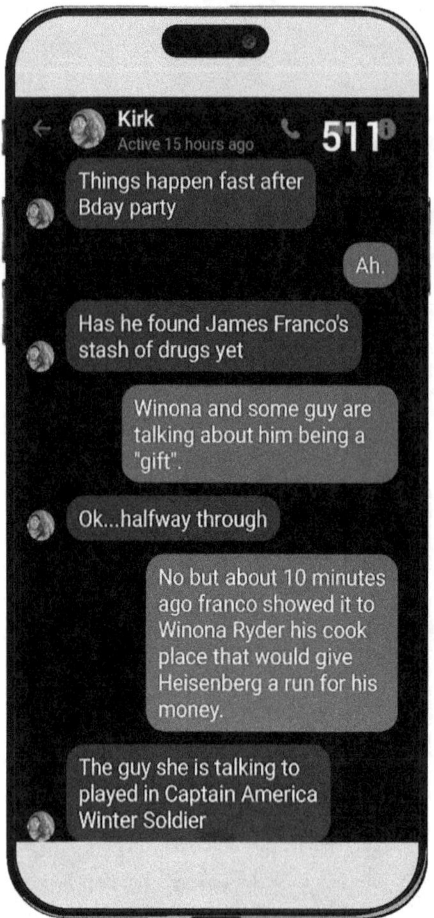
Kirk
Active 15 hours ago
511
Things happen fast after Bday party
Ah.
Has he found James Franco's stash of drugs yet
Winona and some guy are talking about him being a "gift".
Ok...halfway through
No but about 10 minutes ago franco showed it to Winona Ryder his cook place that would give Heisenberg a run for his money.
The guy she is talking to played in Captain America Winter Soldier

Kirk
Active 15 hours ago
512
Really?
Played one of the bad shield agents
Oh
Ill let you finishe the movie. Im going to take my meds now.
Ok babe. Don't forget to tell me goodnight and stuff.
Ill stuff you alright
What state are they in by the way?
Lol
Louisiana

Kirk
Active 15 hours ago
513
Oops. I think he just found the drugs.
Yep
Im going to check and see if x22 report has posted yet
Oh. I thought you watched it already.
Not yet
Then talked to D man.
He is D-man
Lol. Apparently when it comes to video games. Lol
Yep
See you in a litue bit

Kirk
Active 15 hours ago
514
Ok.
Its not playing...son a bitch
I'm sorry babe.
MAR 14, 2021 AT 9:38 PM
Got it working and finished it up...good night
Goodnight babe. Luv you.
Love you too
MAR 15, 2021 AT 9:31 AM
Hi sweetheart...you awake
Hi babe. Yes.

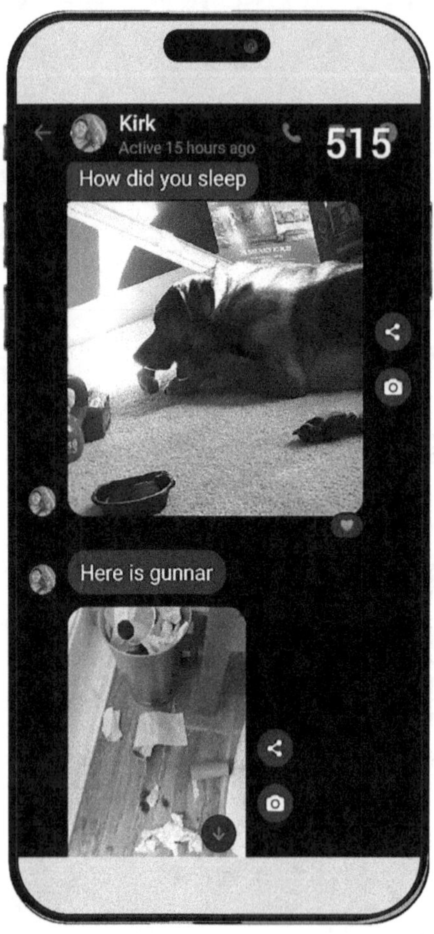

Kirk
Active 15 hours ago
515
How did you sleep
Here is gunnar

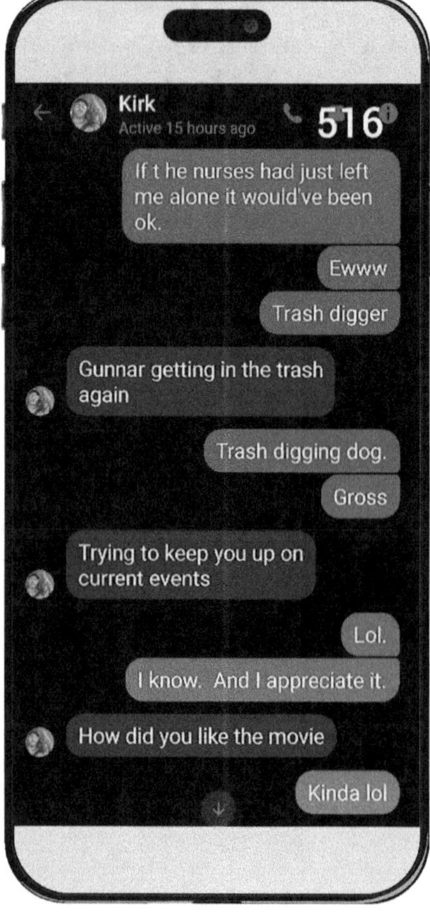

Kirk
Active 15 hours ago
516
If t he nurses had just left me alone it would've been ok.
Ewww
Trash digger
Gunnar getting in the trash again
Trash digging dog.
Gross
Trying to keep you up on current events
Lol.
I know. And I appreciate it.
How did you like the movie
Kinda lol

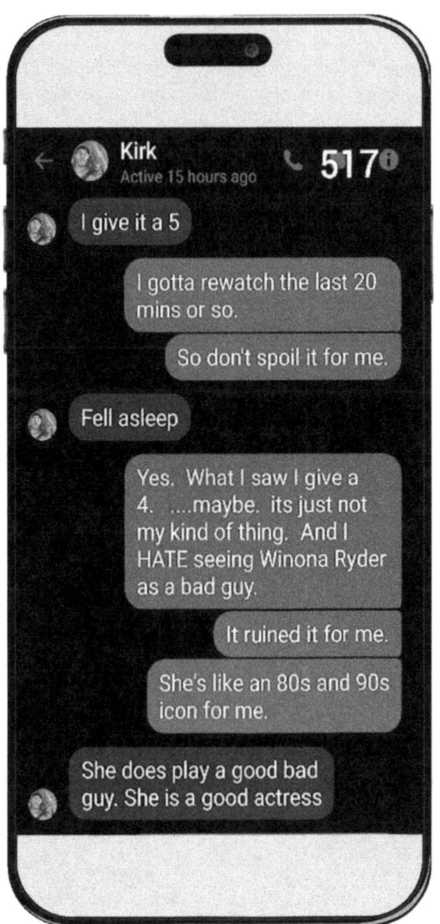
Kirk
Active 15 hours ago
517
I give it a 5
I gotta rewatch the last 20 mins or so.
So don't spoil it for me.
Fell asleep
Yes. What I saw I give a 4. ....maybe. its just not my kind of thing. And I HATE seeing Winona Ryder as a bad guy.
It ruined it for me.
She's like an 80s and 90s icon for me.
She does play a good bad guy. She is a good actress

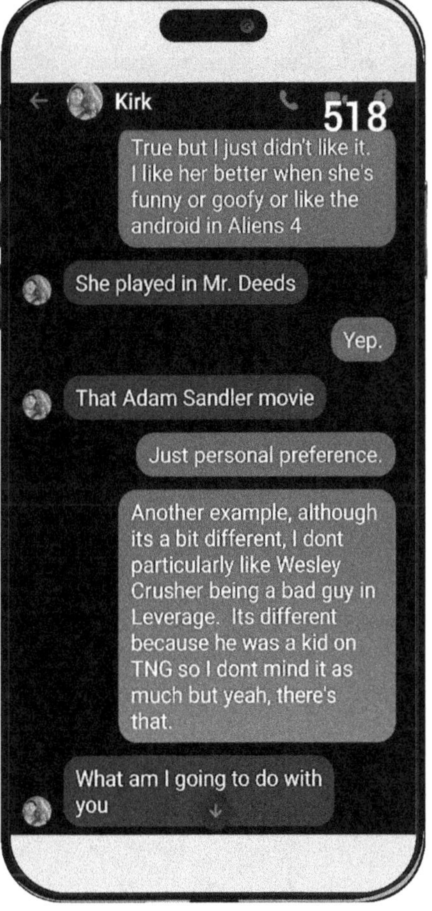
Kirk
518
True but I just didn't like it. I like her better when she's funny or goofy or like the android in Aliens 4
She played in Mr. Deeds
Yep.
That Adam Sandler movie
Just personal preference.
Another example, although its a bit different, I dont particularly like Wesley Crusher being a bad guy in Leverage. Its different because he was a kid on TNG so I dont mind it as much but yeah, there's that.
What am I going to do with you

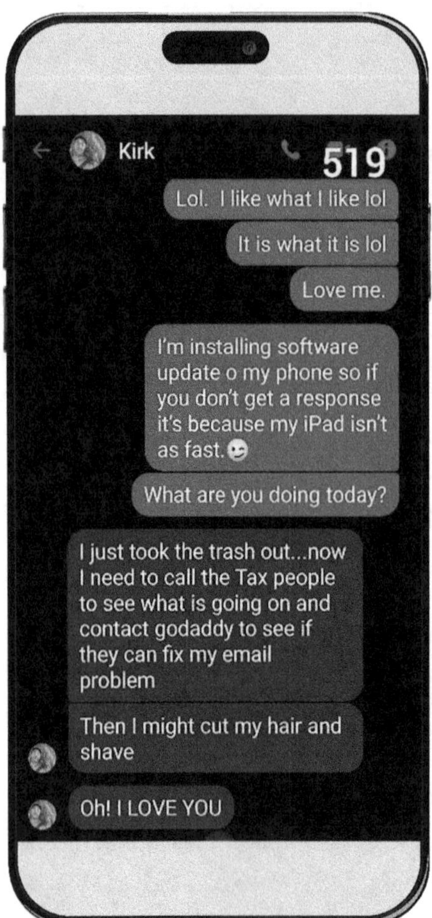
Kirk
519
Lol. I like what I like lol
It is what it is lol
Love me.
I'm installing software update o my phone so if you don't get a response it's because my iPad isn't as fast.
What are you doing today?
I just took the trash out...now I need to call the Tax people to see what is going on and contact godaddy to see if they can fix my email problem
Then I might cut my hair and shave
Oh! I LOVE YOU

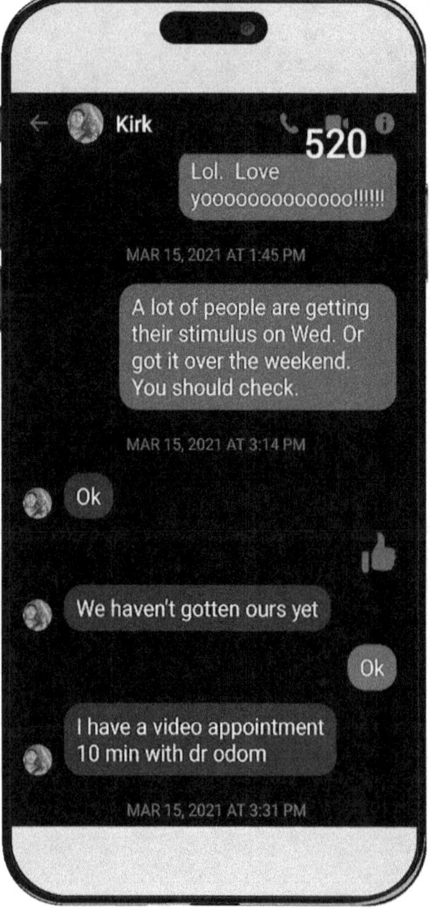
Kirk
520
Lol. Love yoooooooooooooo!!!!!!
MAR 15, 2021 AT 1:45 PM
A lot of people are getting their stimulus on Wed. Or got it over the weekend. You should check.
MAR 15, 2021 AT 3:14 PM
Ok
We haven't gotten ours yet
Ok
I have a video appointment 10 min with dr odom
MAR 15, 2021 AT 3:31 PM

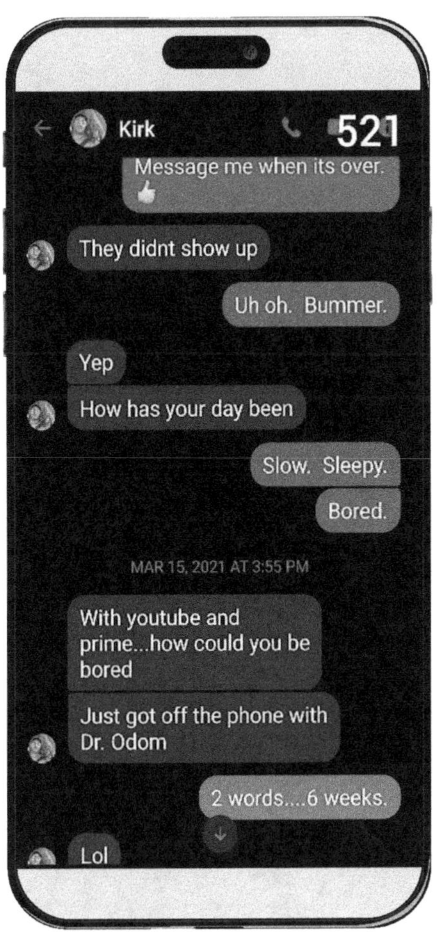
Kirk
521
Message me when its over.
👍
They didnt show up
Uh oh. Bummer.
Yep
How has your day been
Slow. Sleepy.
Bored.
MAR 15, 2021 AT 3:55 PM
With youtube and prime...how could you be bored
Just got off the phone with Dr. Odom
2 words....6 weeks.
Lol

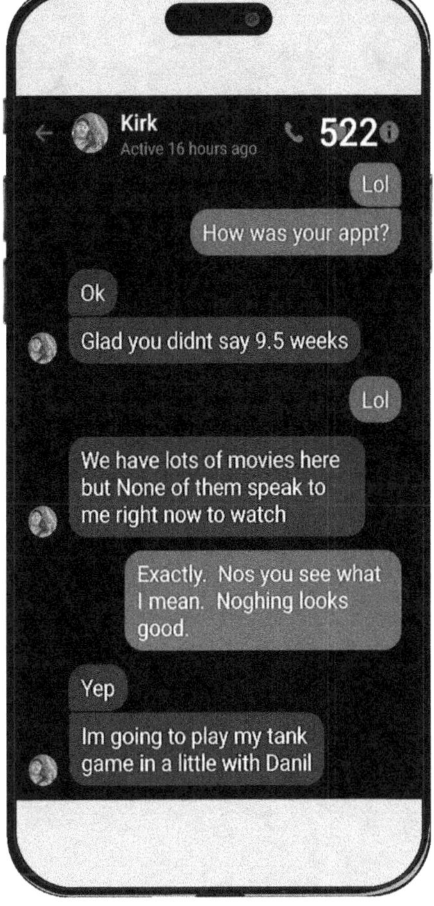
Kirk
Active 16 hours ago
522
Lol
How was your appt?
Ok
Glad you didnt say 9.5 weeks
Lol
We have lots of movies here but None of them speak to me right now to watch
Exactly. Nos you see what I mean. Noghing looks good.
Yep
Im going to play my tank game in a little with Danil

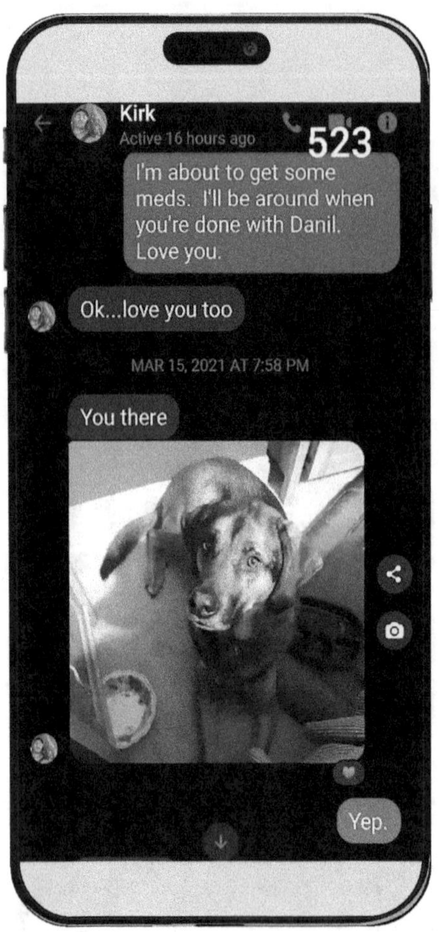
Kirk
Active 16 hours ago
523
I'm about to get some meds. I'll be around when you're done with Danil. Love you.
Ok...love you too
MAR 15, 2021 AT 7:58 PM
You there
Yep.

Kirk
Active 16 hours ago
524
Whats up
How are you feeling
Doing ok. Tired though. Sleepy. If I fall asleep now though I'll be up at 3.
I take gunnar to the vet in the morning
Doctor came by. Getting ready for Wed.

This jerk of a pain specialist came by, tried to say my pain is mostly in my head. No tf it is not!!!
Did you tell him that
Not the "tf" part.
Lol

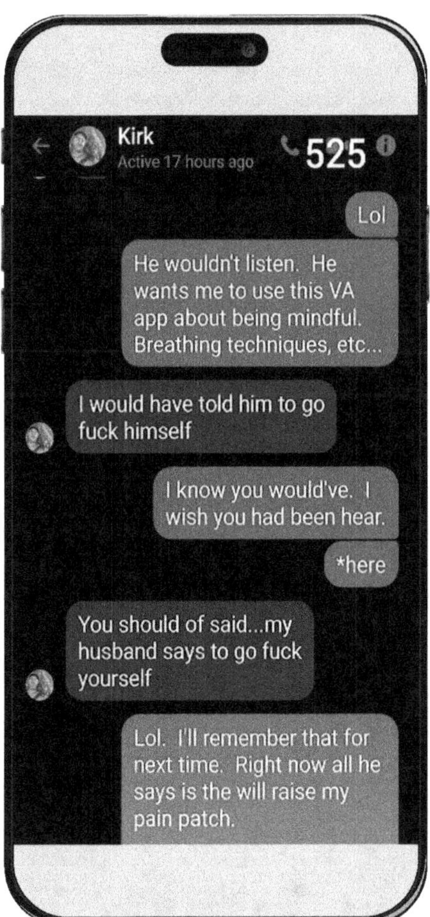
Kirk
Active 17 hours ago
525
Lol
He wouldn't listen. He wants me to use this VA app about being mindful. Breathing techniques, etc...
I would have told him to go fuck himself
I know you would've. I wish you had been hear.
*here
You should of said...my husband says to go fuck yourself
Lol. I'll remember that for next time. Right now all he says is the will raise my pain patch.

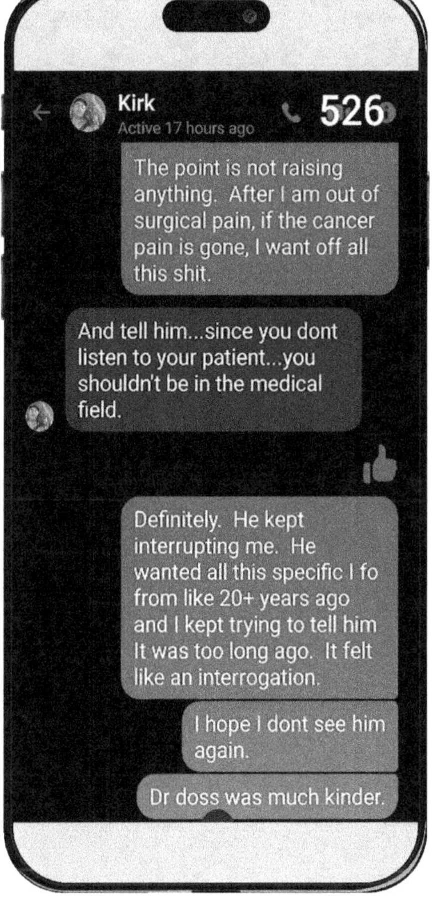
Kirk
Active 17 hours ago
526
The point is not raising anything. After I am out of surgical pain, if the cancer pain is gone, I want off all this shit.
And tell him...since you dont listen to your patient...you shouldn't be in the medical field.
Definitely. He kept interrupting me. He wanted all this specific I fo from like 20+ years ago and I kept trying to tell him It was too long ago. It felt like an interrogation.
I hope I dont see him again.
Dr doss was much kinder.

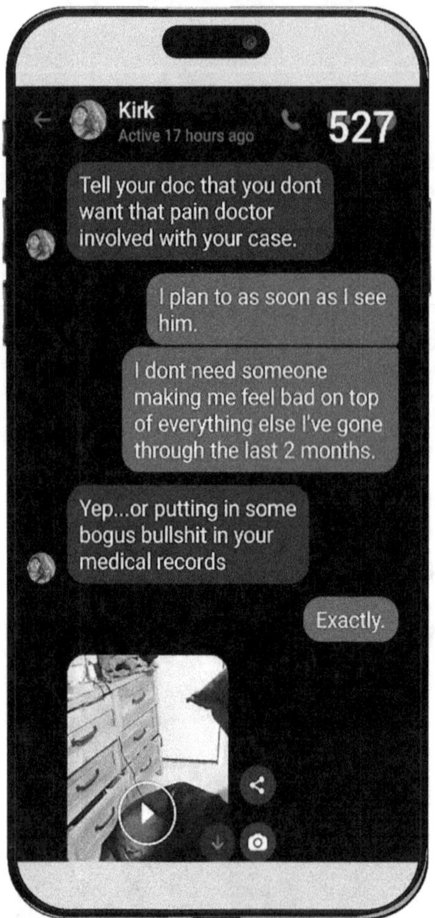
Kirk
Active 17 hours ago
527
Tell your doc that you dont want that pain doctor involved with your case.
I plan to as soon as I see him.
I dont need someone making me feel bad on top of everything else I've gone through the last 2 months.
Yep...or putting in some bogus bullshit in your medical records
Exactly.

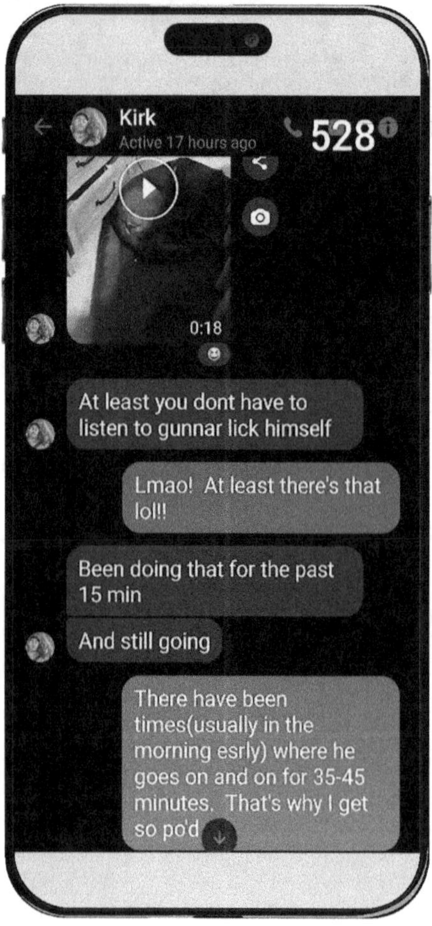
Kirk
Active 17 hours ago
528
0:18
At least you dont have to listen to gunnar lick himself
Lmao! At least there's that lol!!
Been doing that for the past 15 min
And still going
There have been times(usually in the morning esrly) where he goes on and on for 35-45 minutes. That's why I get so po'd

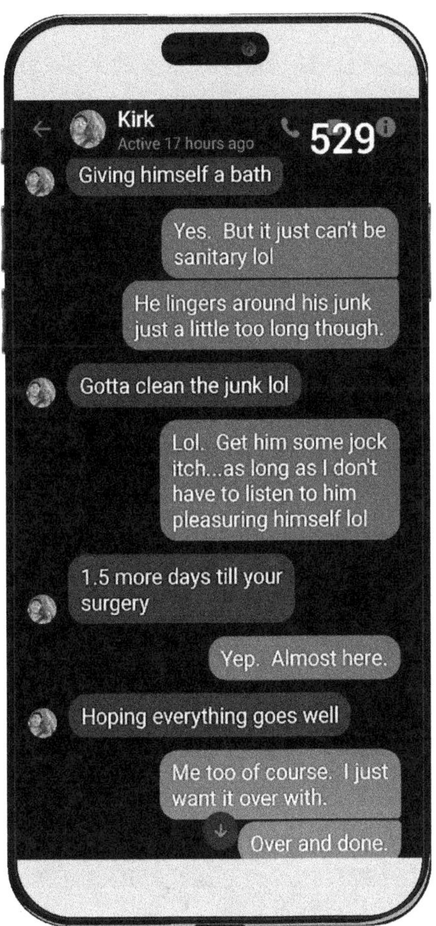

Kirk
Active 17 hours ago
529
Giving himself a bath
Yes. But it just can't be sanitary lol
He lingers around his junk just a little too long though.
Gotta clean the junk lol
Lol. Get him some jock itch...as long as I don't have to listen to him pleasuring himself lol
1.5 more days till your surgery
Yep. Almost here.
Hoping everything goes well
Me too of course. I just want it over with.
Over and done.

Kirk
Active 17 hours ago
530
Dont we all
Then I can eat and come home.
Yep
Eat, poop, love
Lol
I'm so hungry. My stomachs been growling kinda tonight.
That sucks
You gotta take me someplace fantastic when I can eat again.
Yep

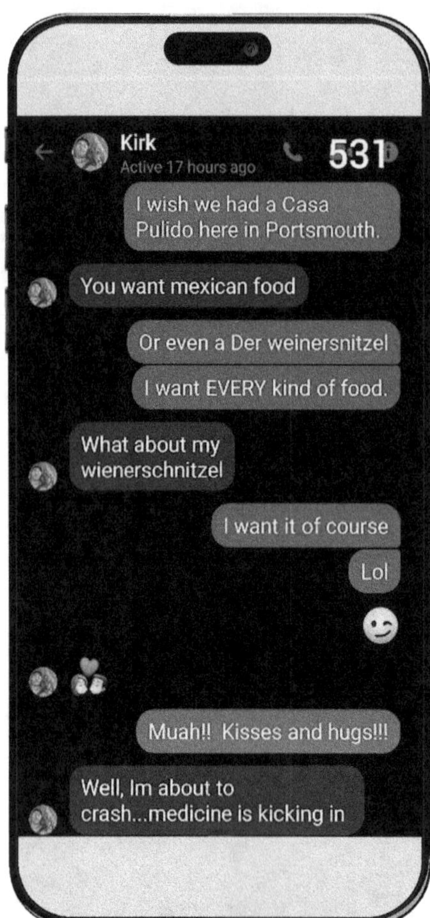

Kirk
Active 17 hours ago
531
I wish we had a Casa Pulido here in Portsmouth.
You want mexican food
Or even a Der weinersnitzel
I want EVERY kind of food.
What about my wienerschnitzel
I want it of course
Lol
Muah!! Kisses and hugs!!!
Well, Im about to crash...medicine is kicking in

Kirk
Active 17 hours ago
532
I just can't wait till we have some alone time.
Ok babe.
You have a great sleep
Love you.
Alone time...you mean lovin time
That too! Lol
G'night sweetie.
Dont stay up too late and try and get some rest
I will. Promise. I got lots of healing to do.
Gunny went to the futon
Lol
Of course

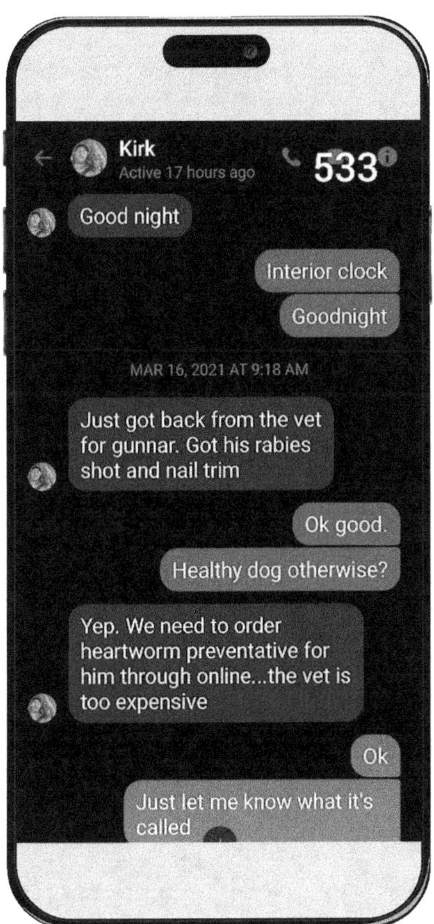
Kirk
Active 17 hours ago
533
Good night
Interior clock
Goodnight
MAR 16, 2021 AT 9:18 AM
Just got back from the vet for gunnar. Got his rabies shot and nail trim
Ok good.
Healthy dog otherwise?
Yep. We need to order heartworm preventative for him through online...the vet is too expensive
Ok
Just let me know what it's called

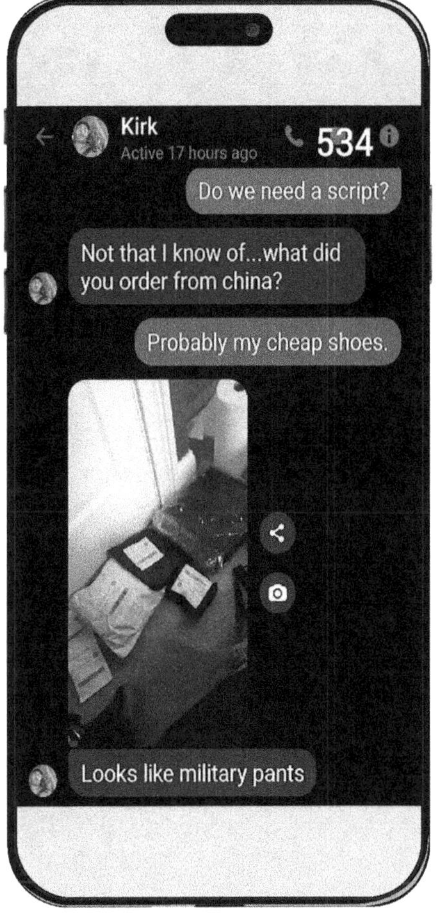
Kirk
Active 17 hours ago
534
Do we need a script?
Not that I know of...what did you order from china?
Probably my cheap shoes.
Looks like military pants

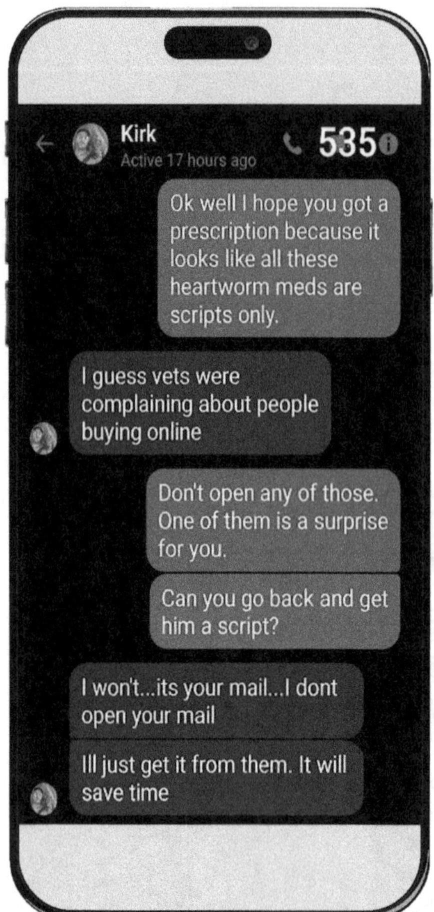

Kirk
Active 17 hours ago
535

Ok well I hope you got a prescription because it looks like all these heartworm meds are scripts only.

I guess vets were complaining about people buying online

Don't open any of those. One of them is a surprise for you.

Can you go back and get him a script?

I won't...its your mail...I dont open your mail

Ill just get it from them. It will save time

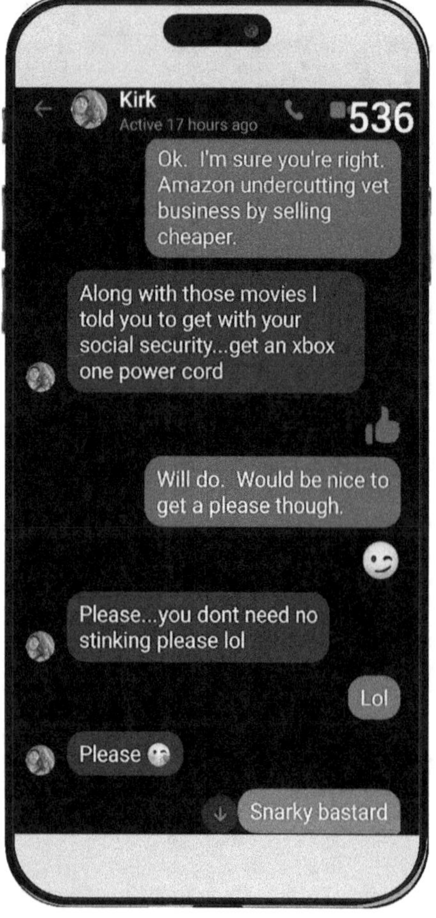

Kirk
Active 17 hours ago
536

Ok. I'm sure you're right. Amazon undercutting vet business by selling cheaper.

Along with those movies I told you to get with your social security...get an xbox one power cord

Will do. Would be nice to get a please though.

Please...you dont need no stinking please lol

Lol

Please

Snarky bastard

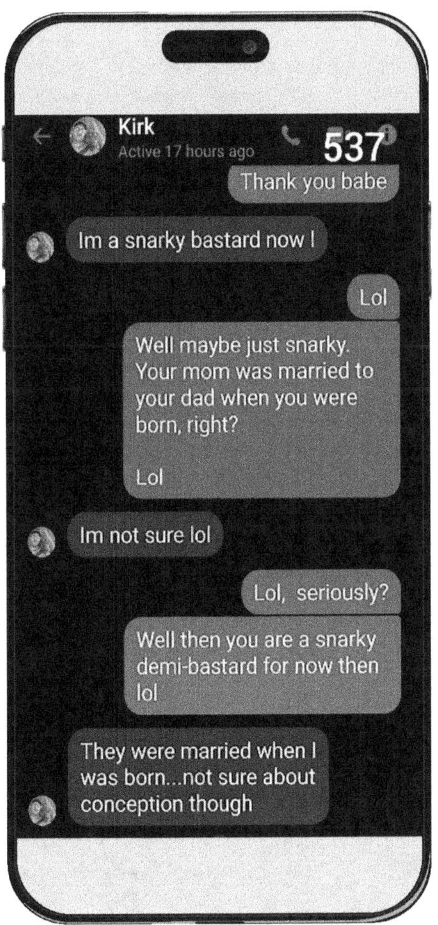
Kirk
Active 17 hours ago
537
Thank you babe
Im a snarky bastard now l
Lol
Well maybe just snarky. Your mom was married to your dad when you were born, right?
Lol
Im not sure lol
Lol, seriously?
Well then you are a snarky demi-bastard for now then lol
They were married when I was born...not sure about conception though

Kirk
Active 17 hours ago
538
I think it only matters if they were married at the time of your birth. Conception doesn't matter.
I'll love you either way.
I love you too
Tomorrow is the big day
Yep. Already saw the head honcho.
Your doc?
Yes. About him taking away my tpn tonight(liquid food) and the procedure for tomorrow.... a lot like last time.

Kirk
Active 17 hours ago
539
Did you tell him about the pain doctor
Fuck. No. I was in the middle of emptying my ng tube when he walked it. Dammit.
*in
Take care of it next time
Dont forget
I'll talk to him later. He will be back
Cool
I have papers to sign and whatnot.
So he is going to bring those bsck

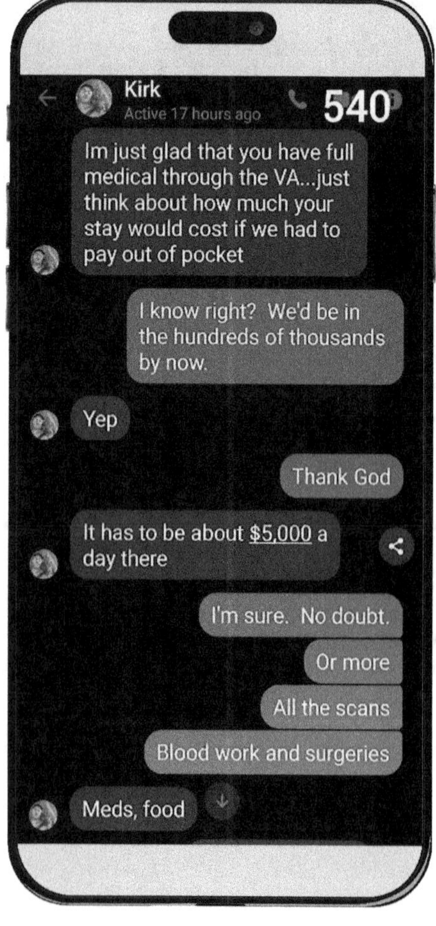
Kirk
Active 17 hours ago
540
Im just glad that you have full medical through the VA...just think about how much your stay would cost if we had to pay out of pocket
I know right? We'd be in the hundreds of thousands by now.
Yep
Thank God
It has to be about $5,000 a day there
I'm sure. No doubt.
Or more
All the scans
Blood work and surgeries
Meds, food

Kirk
Active 17 hours ago
541
Yeah.
Labor
Delivery
Lol
I wish it was just a baby. It'd be cheaper lol
True
You gonna play with danil today?
Probably
Only played with him about a half hour last night
Neat-o
I swear this place is haunted

Kirk
Active 17 hours ago
542
Right up your alley
One of the nurses told me
That its haunted
Yes doors slam. I hear my name in the middle of the night...etc..
Creepy
Yes it is. One of the doors is my bathroom door and I'm nowhere near it.
It just did it
Better you than me
Lol
Probably

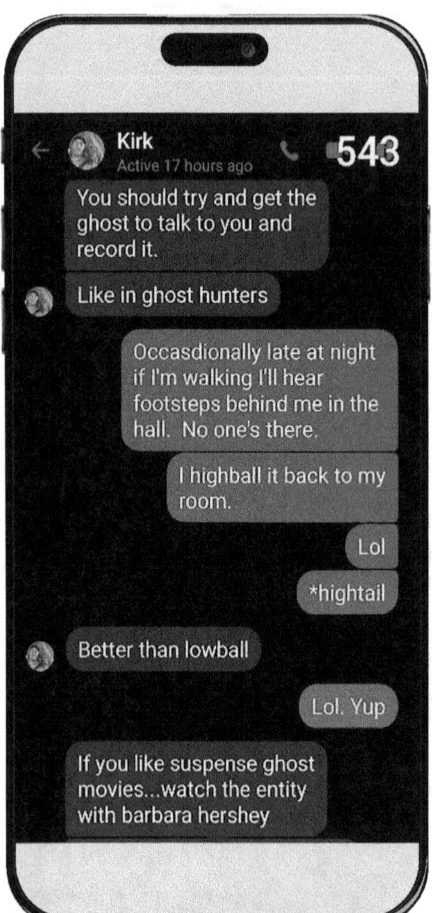

Kirk
Active 17 hours ago
543
You should try and get the ghost to talk to you and record it.
Like in ghost hunters
Occasdionally late at night if I'm walking I'll hear footsteps behind me in the hall. No one's there.
I highball it back to my room.
Lol
*hightail
Better than lowball
Lol. Yup
If you like suspense ghost movies...watch the entity with barbara hershey

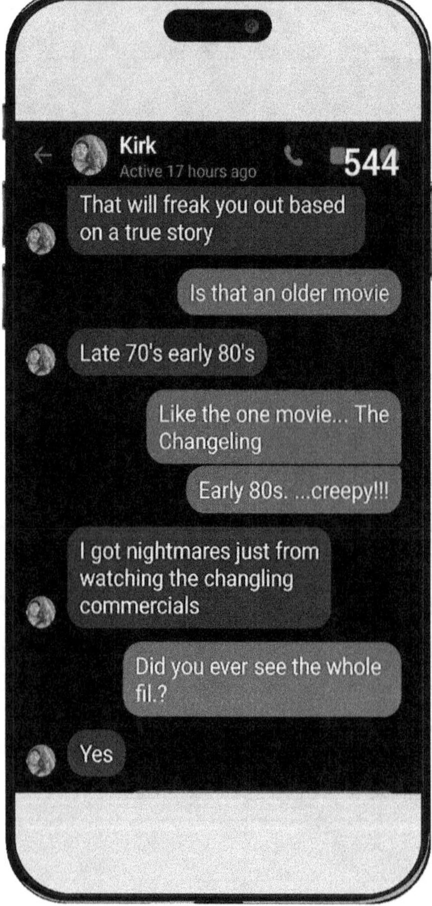

Kirk
Active 17 hours ago
544
That will freak you out based on a true story
Is that an older movie
Late 70's early 80's
Like the one movie... The Changeling
Early 80s. ...creepy!!!
I got nightmares just from watching the changling commercials
Did you ever see the whole fil.?
Yes

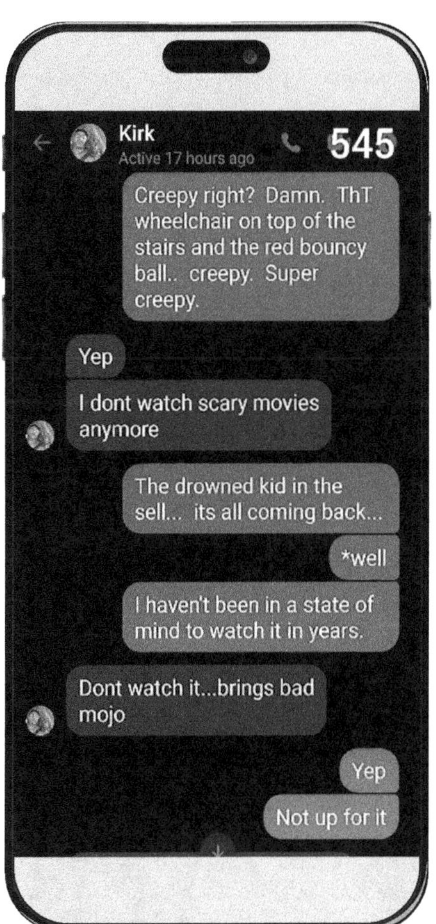
Kirk
Active 17 hours ago
545
Creepy right? Damn. ThT wheelchair on top of the stairs and the red bouncy ball.. creepy. Super creepy.
Yep
I dont watch scary movies anymore
The drowned kid in the sell... its all coming back...
*well
I haven't been in a state of mind to watch it in years.
Dont watch it...brings bad mojo
Yep
Not up for it

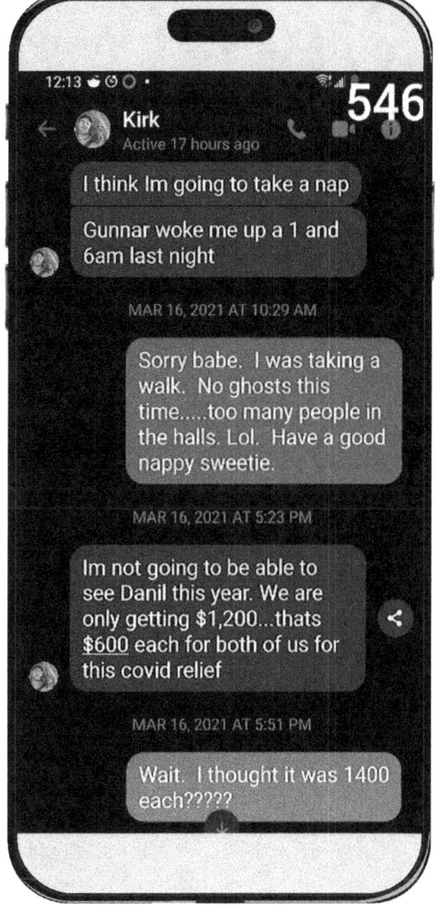
12:13
546
Kirk
Active 17 hours ago
I think Im going to take a nap
Gunnar woke me up a 1 and 6am last night
MAR 16, 2021 AT 10:29 AM
Sorry babe. I was taking a walk. No ghosts this time.....too many people in the halls. Lol. Have a good nappy sweetie.
MAR 16, 2021 AT 5:23 PM
Im not going to be able to see Danil this year. We are only getting $1,200...thats $600 each for both of us for this covid relief
MAR 16, 2021 AT 5:51 PM
Wait. I thought it was 1400 each?????

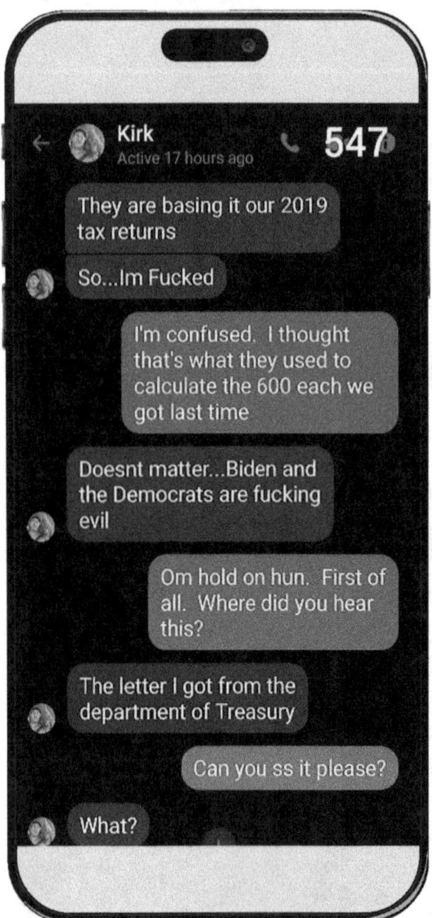

Kirk
Active 17 hours ago
547
They are basing it our 2019 tax returns
So...Im Fucked
I'm confused. I thought that's what they used to calculate the 600 each we got last time
Doesnt matter...Biden and the Democrats are fucking evil
Om hold on hun. First of all. Where did you hear this?
The letter I got from the department of Treasury
Can you ss it please?
What?

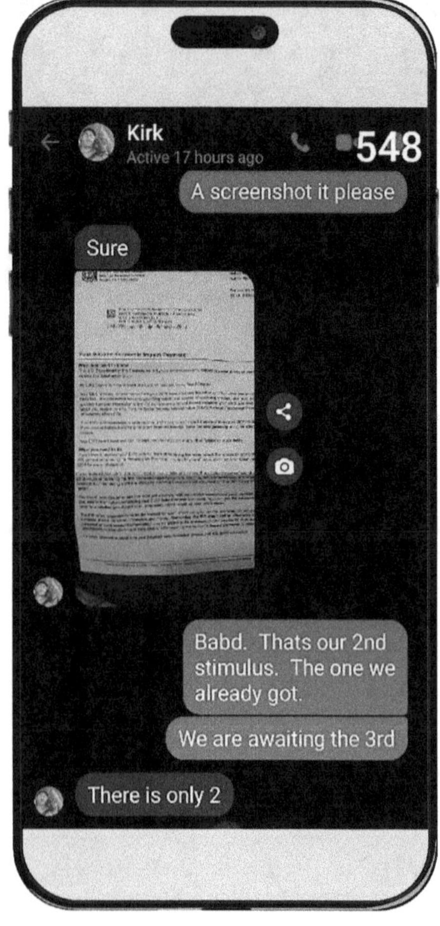

Kirk
Active 17 hours ago
548
A screenshot it please
Sure
Babd. Thats our 2nd stimulus. The one we already got.
We are awaiting the 3rd
There is only 2

Kirk
Active 17 hours ago
549
There are 3. 1200, 600 and 1400.
We didn't get the 1st
Chikd support
We never got the $600
Yes we did hunni
Did we
600 each
Yed
Fuck me
Babe. Were good. We get 1400 this time each.
You ok sweetie? Were fine. You are going to get to see danil.

Kirk
Active 17 hours ago
550
Ok
Im watching the green lantern
Jesus. I need to get home so I can calm you down faster when stuff like this happens
Yep...I agree
Cool. Thats one you haven't seen in a while
A couple years
At least
Time for dinner...tv dinner
Enjoy. I'm eating the last of my ice chips till after the surgery tomorrow. Yum.

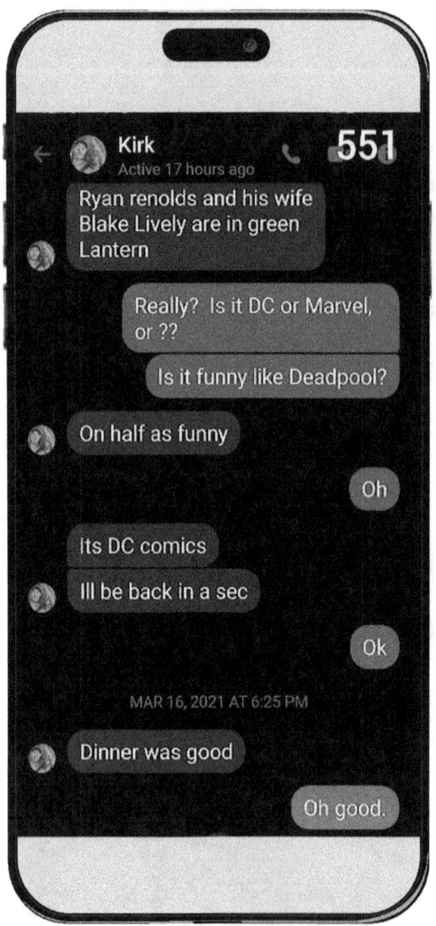

Kirk
Active 17 hours ago
551
Ryan renolds and his wife Blake Lively are in green Lantern
Really? Is it DC or Marvel, or ??
Is it funny like Deadpool?
On half as funny
Oh
Its DC comics
Ill be back in a sec
Ok
MAR 16, 2021 AT 6:25 PM
Dinner was good
Oh good.

Kirk
Active 17 hours ago
552
Awww. You guys settling in for the evening?
Yep
I let him lick the tv dinner tray
. Which one did you have tonight?
Hamburger patties
Ooh. Bet Gunn's loved that.
Yep

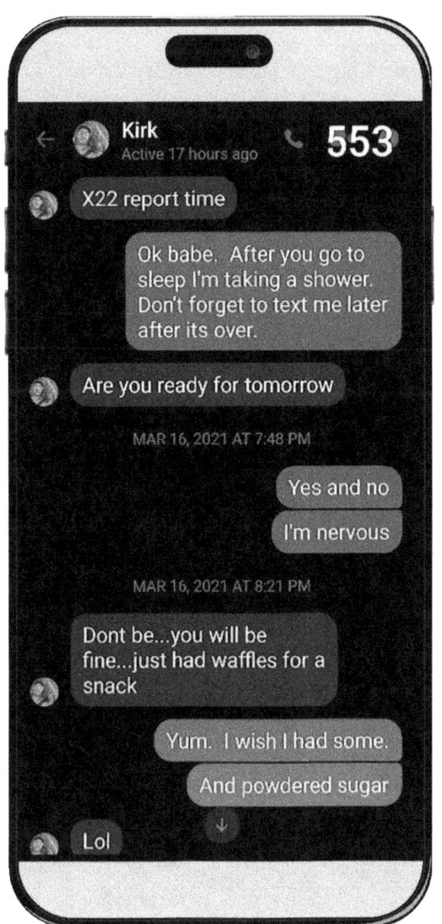
Kirk
Active 17 hours ago
553
X22 report time
Ok babe. After you go to sleep I'm taking a shower. Don't forget to text me later after its over.
Are you ready for tomorrow
MAR 16, 2021 AT 7:48 PM
Yes and no
I'm nervous
MAR 16, 2021 AT 8:21 PM
Dont be...you will be fine...just had waffles for a snack
Yum. I wish I had some.
And powdered sugar
Lol

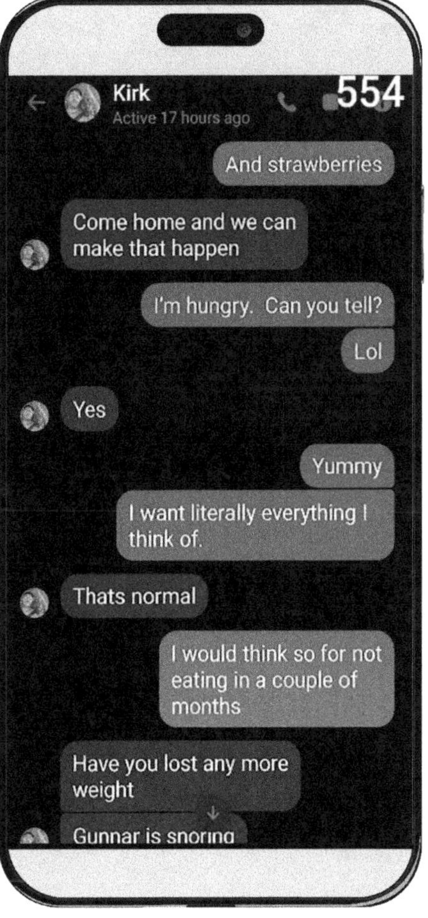
Kirk
Active 17 hours ago
554
And strawberries
Come home and we can make that happen
I'm hungry. Can you tell?
Lol
Yes
Yummy
I want literally everything I think of.
Thats normal
I would think so for not eating in a couple of months
Have you lost any more weight
Gunnar is snoring

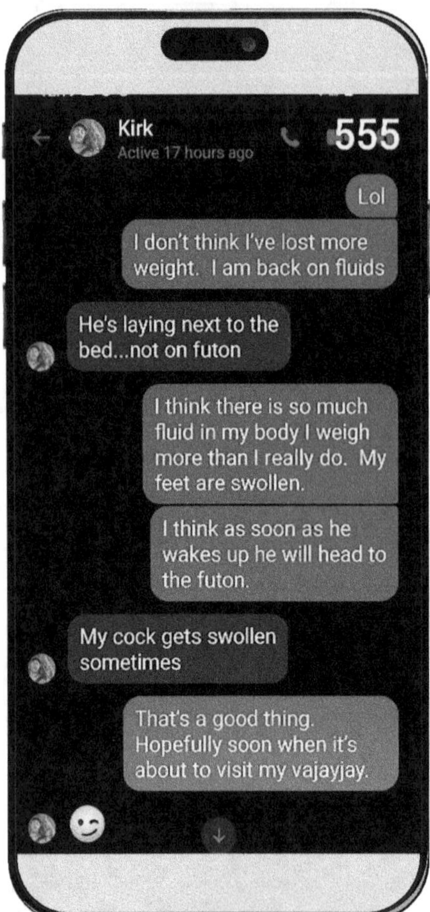
Kirk
Active 17 hours ago
555
Lol
I don't think I've lost more weight. I am back on fluids
He's laying next to the bed...not on futon
I think there is so much fluid in my body I weigh more than I really do. My feet are swollen.
I think as soon as he wakes up he will head to the futon.
My cock gets swollen sometimes
That's a good thing. Hopefully soon when it's about to visit my vajayjay.

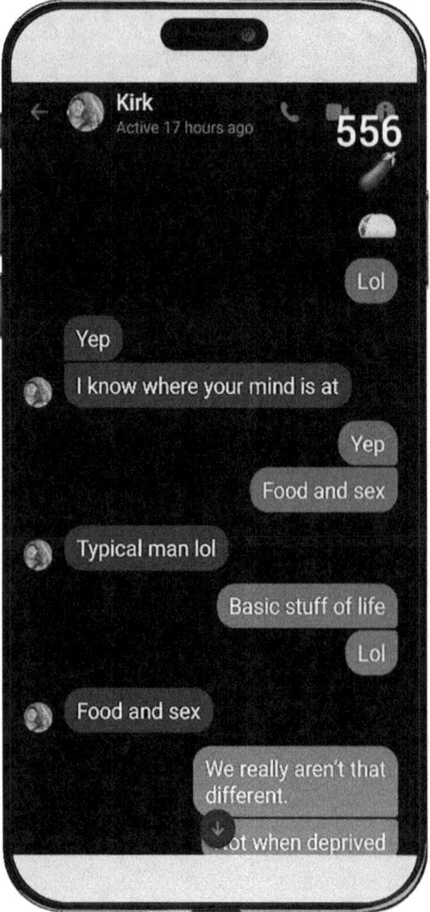
Kirk
Active 17 hours ago
556
Lol
Yep
I know where your mind is at
Yep
Food and sex
Typical man lol
Basic stuff of life
Lol
Food and sex
We really aren't that different.
ot when deprived

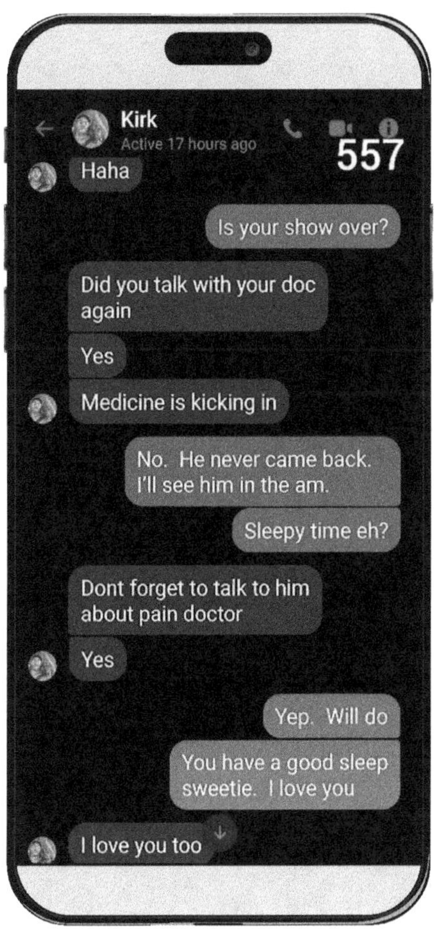
Kirk
Active 17 hours ago
557
Haha
Is your show over?
Did you talk with your doc again
Yes
Medicine is kicking in
No. He never came back. I'll see him in the am.
Sleepy time eh?
Dont forget to talk to him about pain doctor
Yes
Yep. Will do
You have a good sleep sweetie. I love you
I love you too

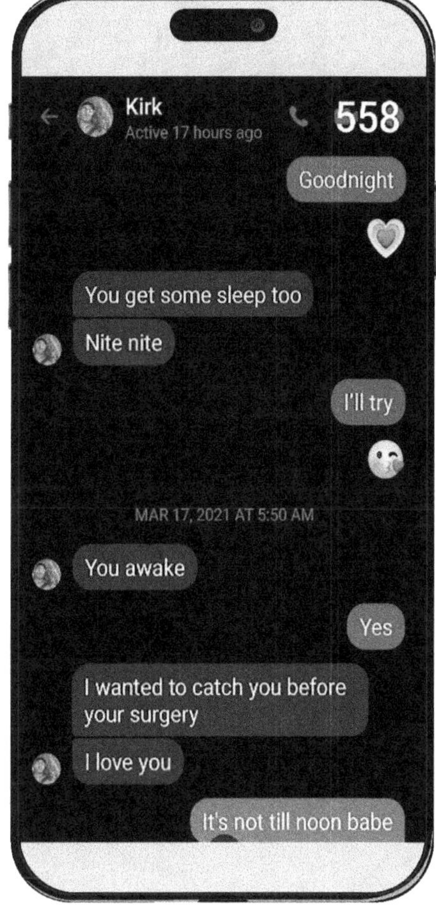
Kirk
Active 17 hours ago
558
Goodnight
You get some sleep too
Nite nite
I'll try
MAR 17, 2021 AT 5:50 AM
You awake
Yes
I wanted to catch you before your surgery
I love you
It's not till noon babe

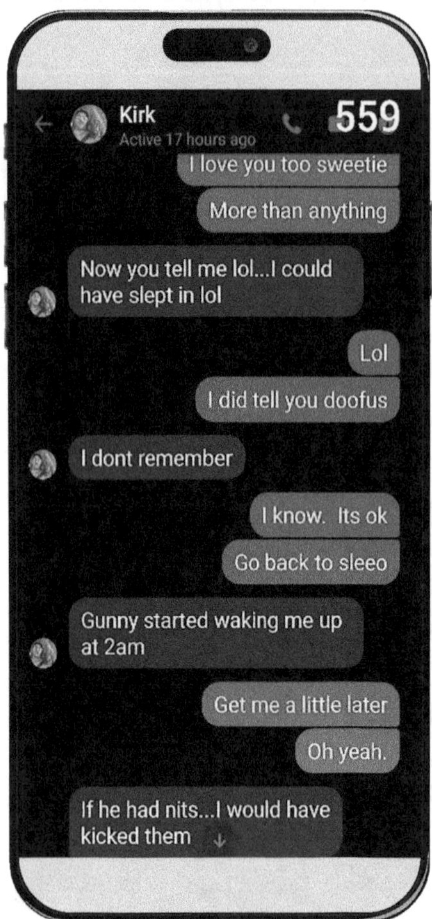
Kirk
Active 17 hours ago
559
I love you too sweetie
More than anything
Now you tell me lol...I could have slept in lol
Lol
I did tell you doofus
I dont remember
I know. Its ok
Go back to sleeo
Gunny started waking me up at 2am
Get me a little later
Oh yeah.
If he had nits...I would have kicked them

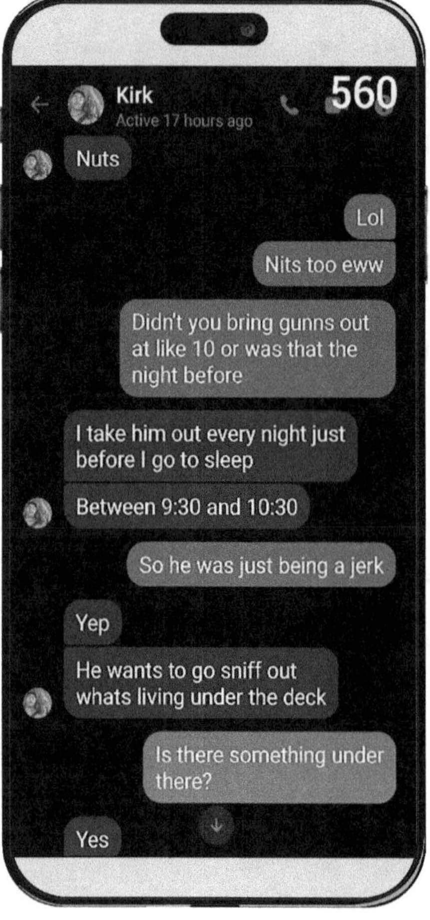
Kirk
Active 17 hours ago
560
Nuts
Lol
Nits too eww
Didn't you bring gunns out at like 10 or was that the night before
I take him out every night just before I go to sleep
Between 9:30 and 10:30
So he was just being a jerk
Yep
He wants to go sniff out whats living under the deck
Is there something under there?
Yes

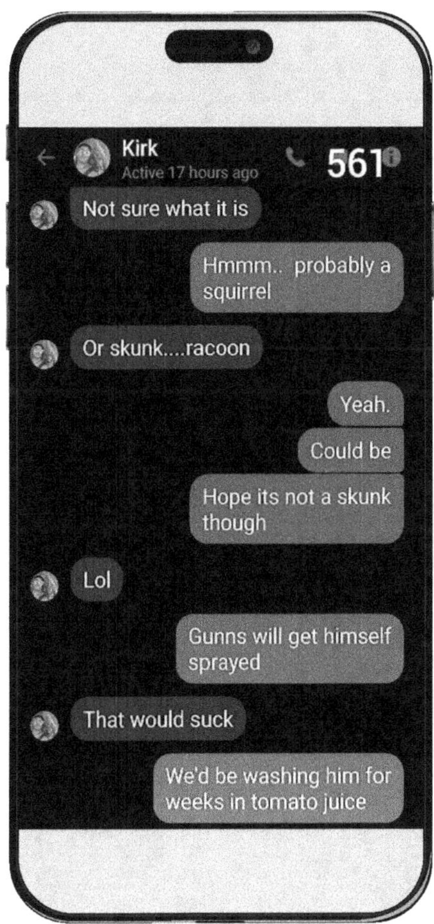

Kirk
Active 17 hours ago
561
Not sure what it is
Hmmm.. probably a squirrel
Or skunk....racoon
Yeah.
Could be
Hope its not a skunk though
Lol
Gunns will get himself sprayed
That would suck
We'd be washing him for weeks in tomato juice

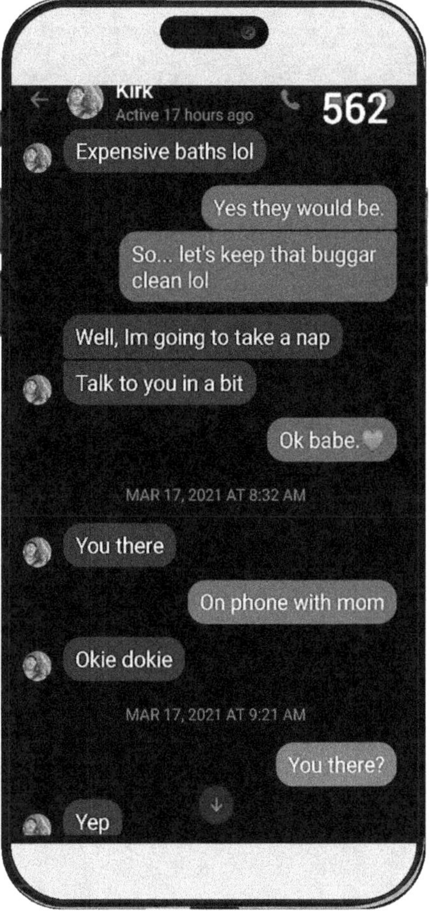

Kirk
Active 17 hours ago
562
Expensive baths lol
Yes they would be.
So... let's keep that buggar clean lol
Well, Im going to take a nap
Talk to you in a bit
Ok babe.
MAR 17, 2021 AT 8:32 AM
You there
On phone with mom
Okie dokie
MAR 17, 2021 AT 9:21 AM
You there?
Yep

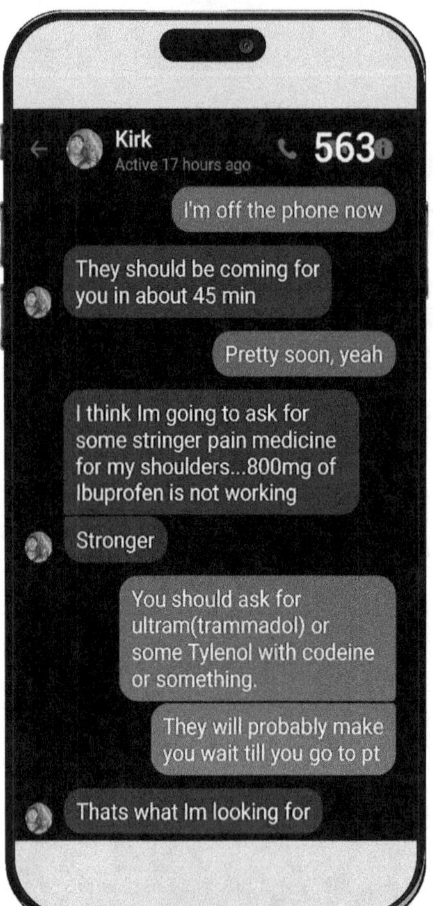

Kirk
Active 17 hours ago
563
I'm off the phone now
They should be coming for you in about 45 min
Pretty soon, yeah
I think Im going to ask for some stringer pain medicine for my shoulders...800mg of Ibuprofen is not working
Stronger
You should ask for ultram(trammadol) or some Tylenol with codeine or something.
They will probably make you wait till you go to pt
Thats what Im looking for

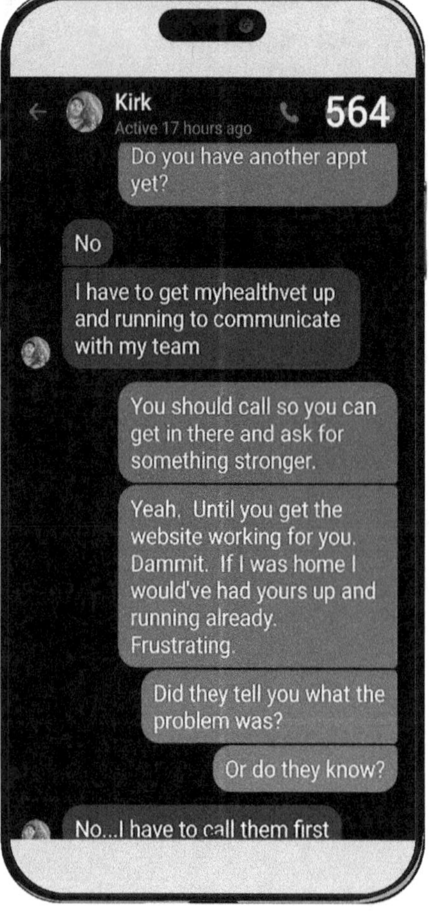

Kirk
Active 17 hours ago
564
Do you have another appt yet?
No
I have to get myhealthvet up and running to communicate with my team
You should call so you can get in there and ask for something stronger.
Yeah. Until you get the website working for you. Dammit. If I was home I would've had yours up and running already. Frustrating.
Did they tell you what the problem was?
Or do they know?
No...I have to call them first

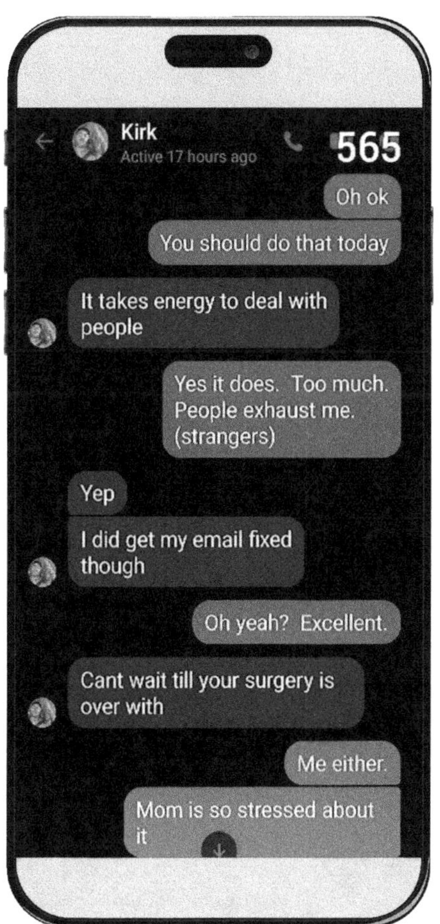

Kirk
Active 17 hours ago
565
Oh ok
You should do that today
It takes energy to deal with people
Yes it does. Too much. People exhaust me. (strangers)
Yep
I did get my email fixed though
Oh yeah? Excellent.
Cant wait till your surgery is over with
Me either.
Mom is so stressed about it

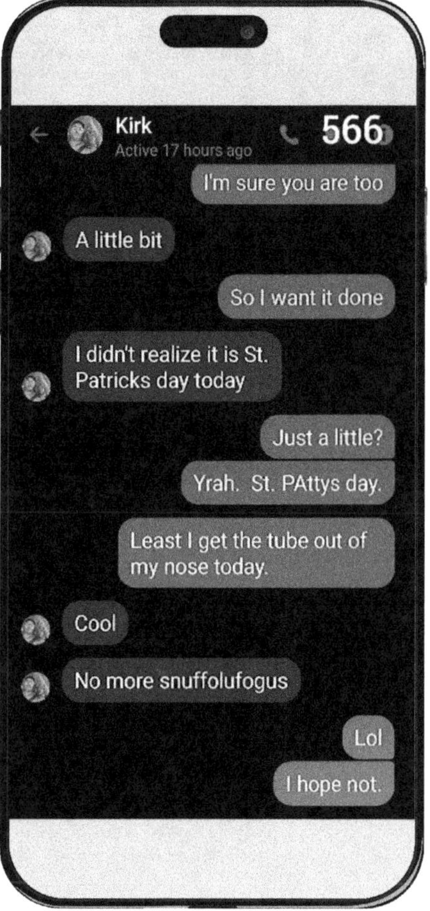

Kirk
Active 17 hours ago
566
I'm sure you are too
A little bit
So I want it done
I didn't realize it is St. Patricks day today
Just a little?
Yrah. St. PAttys day.
Least I get the tube out of my nose today.
Cool
No more snuffolufogus
Lol
I hope not.

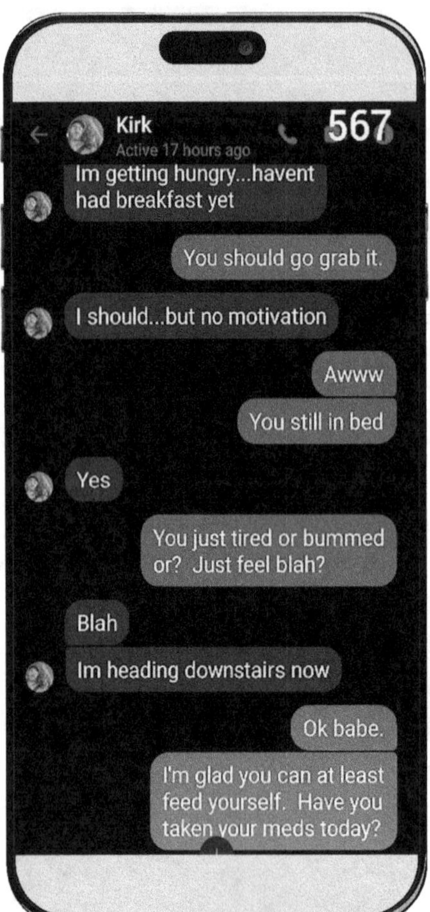
Kirk
Active 17 hours ago
567
Im getting hungry...havent had breakfast yet
You should go grab it.
I should...but no motivation
Awww
You still in bed
Yes
You just tired or bummed or? Just feel blah?
Blah
Im heading downstairs now
Ok babe.
I'm glad you can at least feed yourself. Have you taken your meds today?

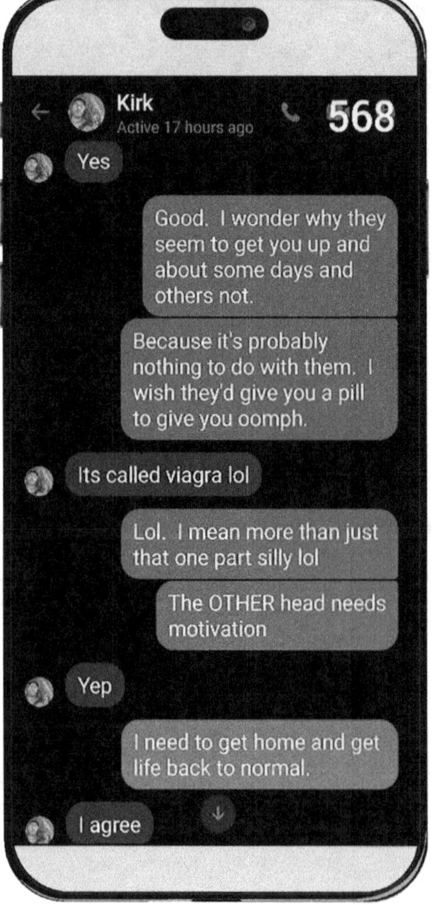
Kirk
Active 17 hours ago
568
Yes
Good. I wonder why they seem to get you up and about some days and others not.
Because it's probably nothing to do with them. I wish they'd give you a pill to give you oomph.
Its called viagra lol
Lol. I mean more than just that one part silly lol
The OTHER head needs motivation
Yep
I need to get home and get life back to normal.
I agree

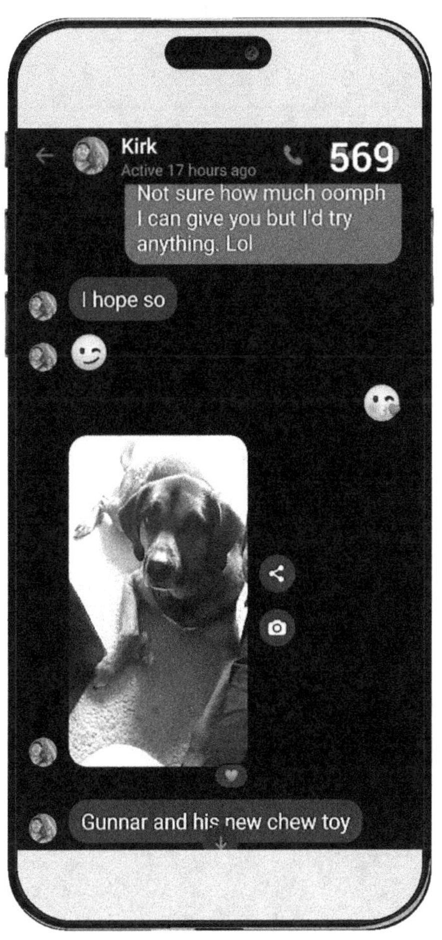
Kirk
Active 17 hours ago
569
Not sure how much oomph I can give you but I'd try anything. Lol
I hope so
Gunnar and his new chew toy

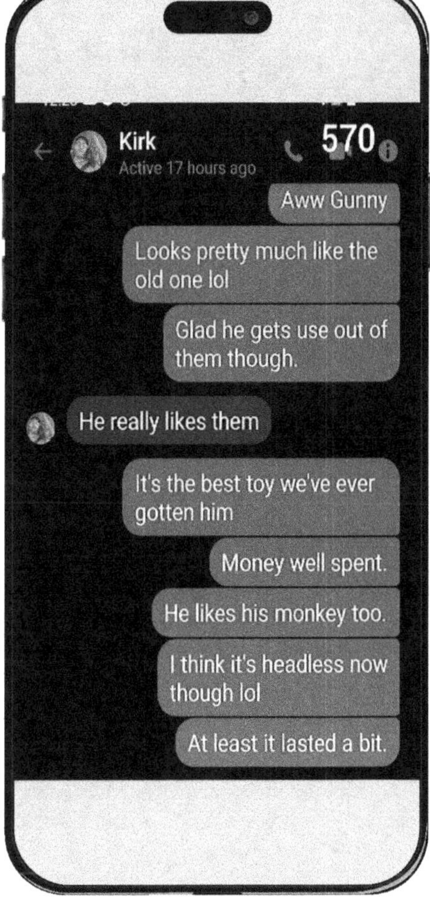
Kirk
Active 17 hours ago
570
Aww Gunny
Looks pretty much like the old one lol
Glad he gets use out of them though.
He really likes them
It's the best toy we've ever gotten him
Money well spent.
He likes his monkey too.
I think it's headless now though lol
At least it lasted a bit.

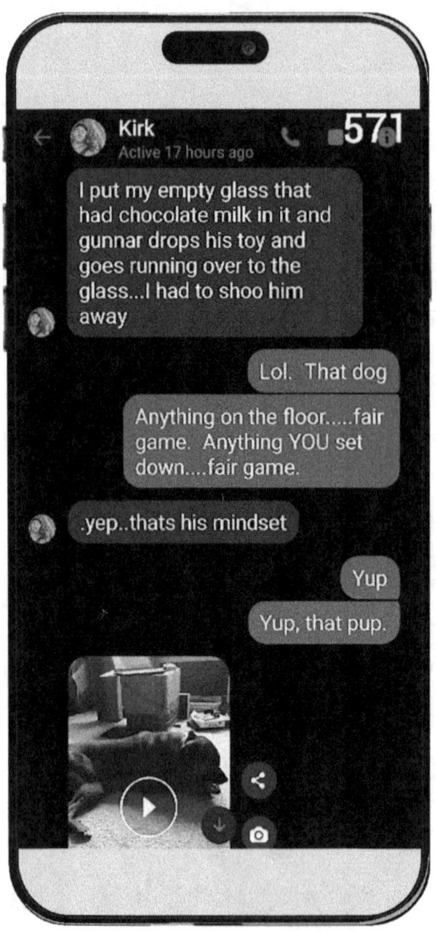

Kirk
Active 17 hours ago
571
I put my empty glass that had chocolate milk in it and gunnar drops his toy and goes running over to the glass...I had to shoo him away
Lol. That dog
Anything on the floor.....fair game. Anything YOU set down....fair game.
.yep..thats his mindset
Yup
Yup, that pup.

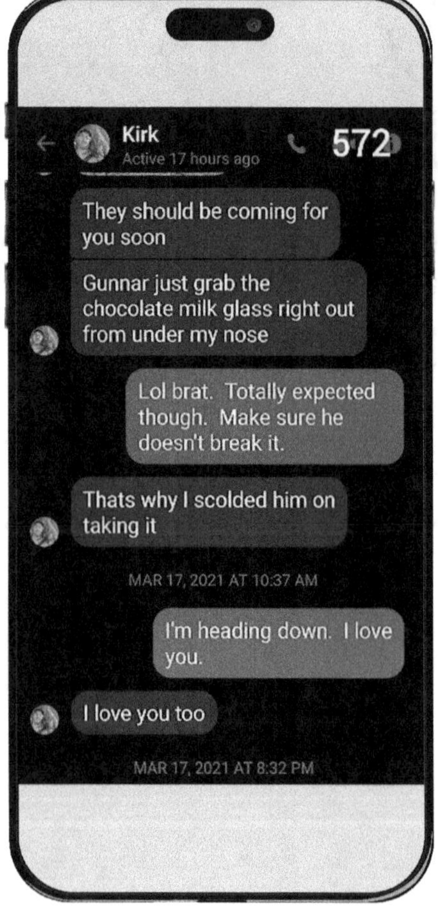

Kirk
Active 17 hours ago
572
They should be coming for you soon
Gunnar just grab the chocolate milk glass right out from under my nose
Lol brat. Totally expected though. Make sure he doesn't break it.
Thats why I scolded him on taking it
MAR 17, 2021 AT 10:37 AM
I'm heading down. I love you.
I love you too
MAR 17, 2021 AT 8:32 PM

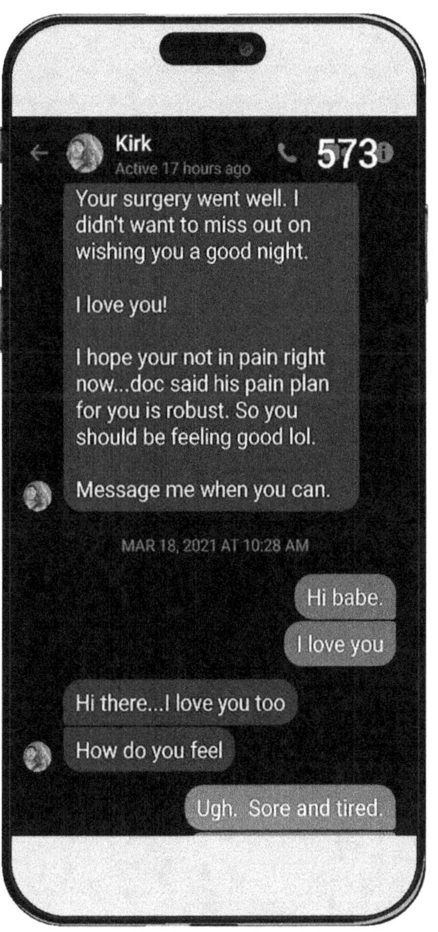
Kirk
Active 17 hours ago
573
Your surgery went well. I didn't want to miss out on wishing you a good night.

I love you!

I hope your not in pain right now...doc said his pain plan for you is robust. So you should be feeling good lol.

Message me when you can.
MAR 18, 2021 AT 10:28 AM
Hi babe.
I love you
Hi there...I love you too
How do you feel
Ugh. Sore and tired.

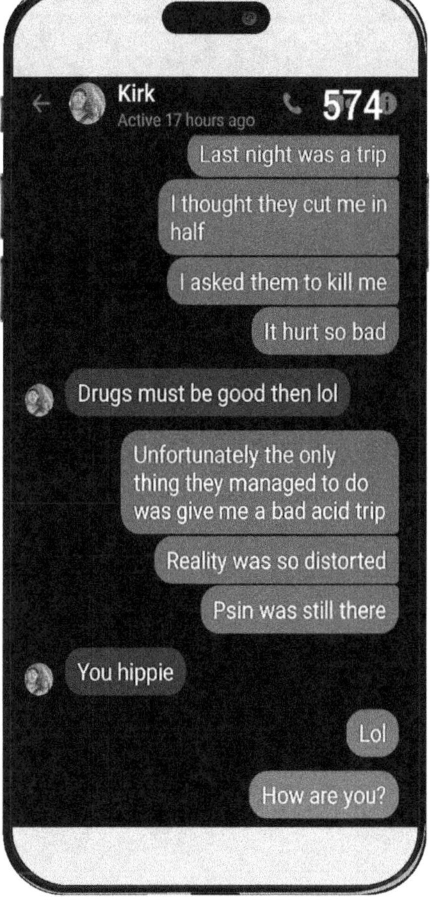
Kirk
Active 17 hours ago
574
Last night was a trip
I thought they cut me in half
I asked them to kill me
It hurt so bad
Drugs must be good then lol
Unfortunately the only thing they managed to do was give me a bad acid trip
Reality was so distorted
Psin was still there
You hippie
Lol
How are you?

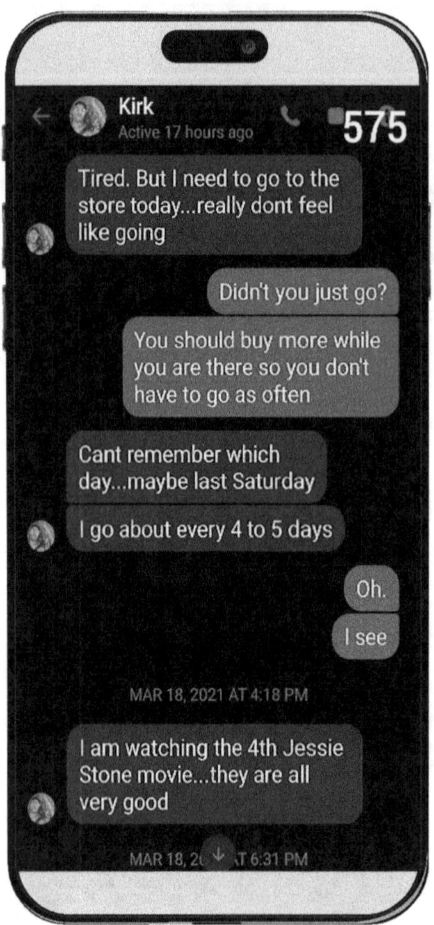

Kirk
Active 17 hours ago
575
Tired. But I need to go to the store today...really dont feel like going
Didn't you just go?
You should buy more while you are there so you don't have to go as often
Cant remember which day...maybe last Saturday
I go about every 4 to 5 days
Oh.
I see
MAR 18, 2021 AT 4:18 PM
I am watching the 4th Jessie Stone movie...they are all very good
MAR 18, 20 AT 6:31 PM

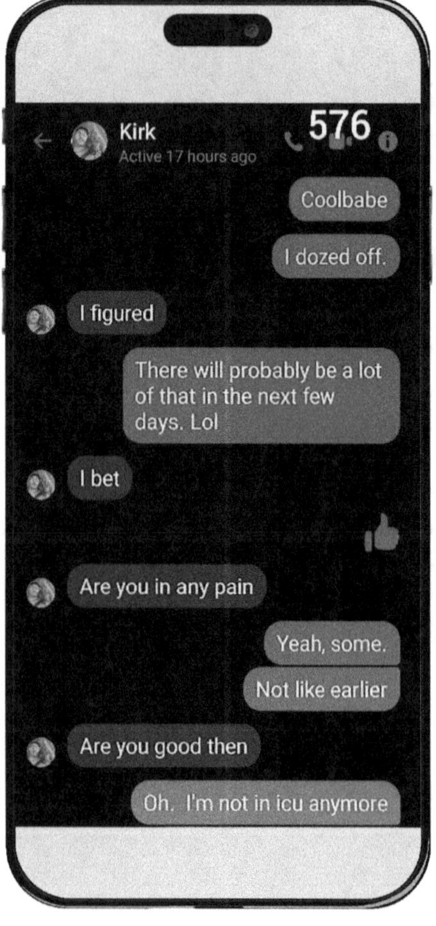

Kirk
Active 17 hours ago
57.6
Coolbabe
I dozed off.
I figured
There will probably be a lot of that in the next few days. Lol
I bet
Are you in any pain
Yeah, some.
Not like earlier
Are you good then
Oh. I'm not in icu anymore

577
Kirk
Active 17 hours ago
The moving from the icu was brutal so I hurt a lot after
Ok
Did they wheel you up or transport you on a bed
MAR 18, 2021 AT 7:00 PM
In a stretcher
I'm not up to a wheelchair quite yet
MAR 18, 2021 AT 7:45 PM
If they were going to wheel you to gey on top of me you would be up for it lol
Get...I cant see without my glasses
MAR 18, 2021 AT 9:10 PM

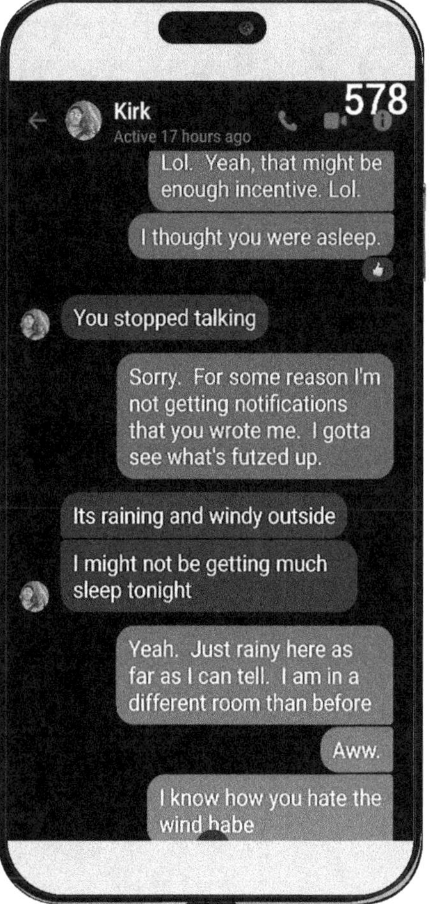
578
Kirk
Active 17 hours ago
Lol. Yeah, that might be enough incentive. Lol.
I thought you were asleep.
You stopped talking
Sorry. For some reason I'm not getting notifications that you wrote me. I gotta see what's futzed up.
Its raining and windy outside
I might not be getting much sleep tonight
Yeah. Just rainy here as far as I can tell. I am in a different room than before
Aww.
I know how you hate the wind babe

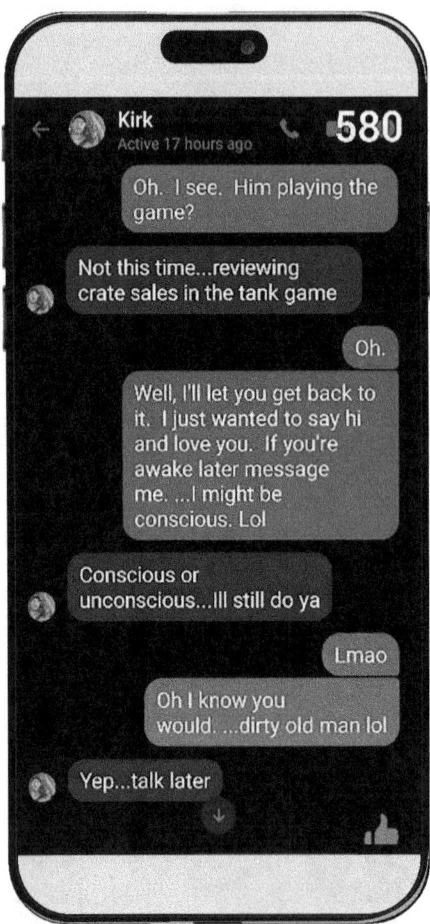

Kirk
Active 17 hours ago
580
Oh. I see. Him playing the game?
Not this time...reviewing crate sales in the tank game
Oh.
Well, I'll let you get back to it. I just wanted to say hi and love you. If you're awake later message me. ...I might be conscious. Lol
Conscious or unconscious...Ill still do ya
Lmao
Oh I know you would. ...dirty old man lol
Yep...talk later

Kirk
Yep...talk later
581
MAR 18, 2021 AT 11:32 PM
Goodnight
Night babe
MAR 19, 2021 AT 11:20 AM
You awake sweetheart
MAR 19, 2021 AT 12:13 PM
Hi babe. I am now
MAR 19, 2021 AT 1:24 PM
How are you
Ok. All things considered.

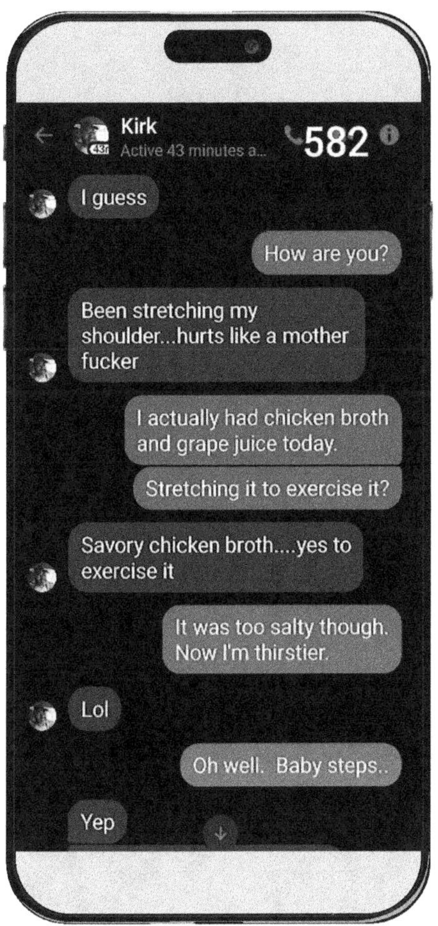

Kirk
Active 43 minutes a...
582
I guess
How are you?
Been stretching my shoulder...hurts like a mother fucker
I actually had chicken broth and grape juice today.
Stretching it to exercise it?
Savory chicken broth....yes to exercise it
It was too salty though. Now I'm thirstier.
Lol
Oh well. Baby steps..
Yep

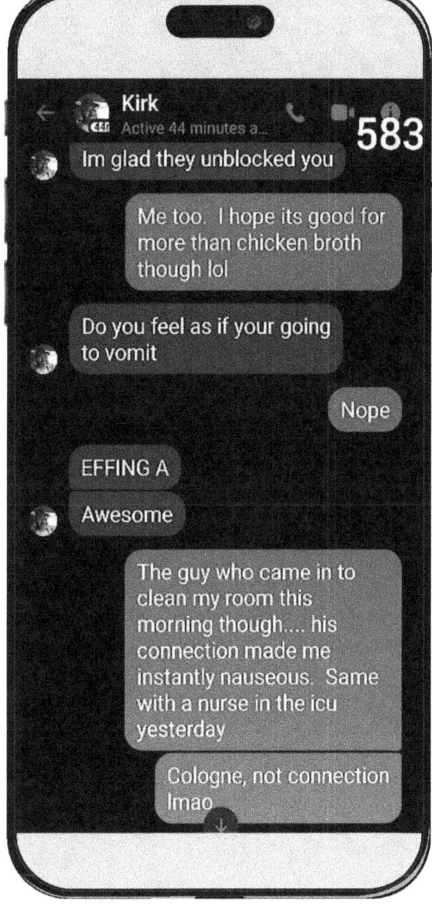

Kirk
Active 44 minutes a...
583
Im glad they unblocked you
Me too. I hope its good for more than chicken broth though lol
Do you feel as if your going to vomit
Nope
EFFING A
Awesome
The guy who came in to clean my room this morning though.... his connection made me instantly nauseous. Same with a nurse in the icu yesterday
Cologne, not connection lmao

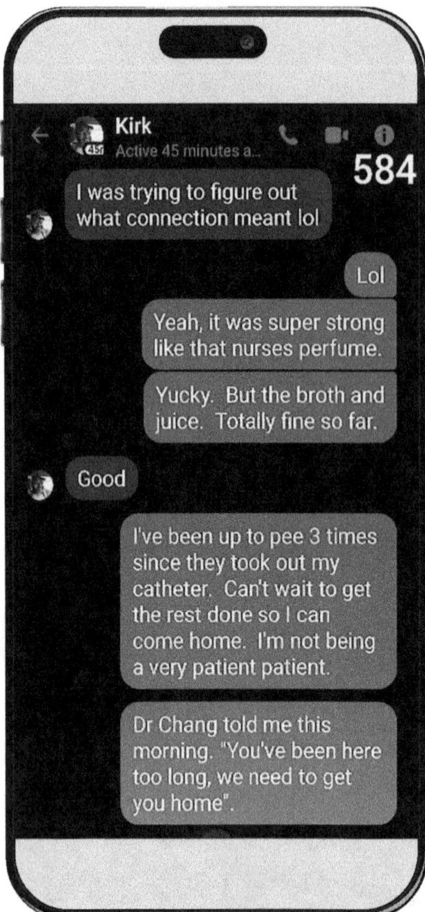

Kirk
Active 45 minutes a...
584
I was trying to figure out what connection meant lol
Lol
Yeah, it was super strong like that nurses perfume.
Yucky. But the broth and juice. Totally fine so far.
Good
I've been up to pee 3 times since they took out my catheter. Can't wait to get the rest done so I can come home. I'm not being a very patient patient.
Dr Chang told me this morning. "You've been here too long, we need to get you home".

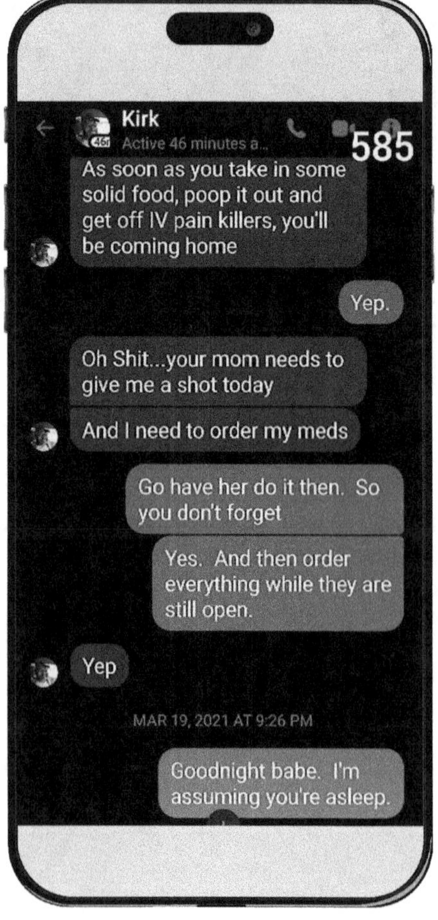

Kirk
Active 46 minutes a...
585
As soon as you take in some solid food, poop it out and get off IV pain killers, you'll be coming home
Yep.
Oh Shit...your mom needs to give me a shot today
And I need to order my meds
Go have her do it then. So you don't forget
Yes. And then order everything while they are still open.
Yep
MAR 19, 2021 AT 9:26 PM
Goodnight babe. I'm assuming you're asleep.

Kirk
Active 47 minutes a...
586
Not yet..x22 report
MAR 19, 2021 AT 10:11 PM
Oh
Well if you're still up after then say hello.
Maybe
MAR 19, 2021 AT 10:33 PM
Goodnight sweetheart
MAR 19, 2021 AT 11:41 PM
Goodnight love
MAR 20, 2021 AT 11:20 AM
You awake
Yep
Did you sleep

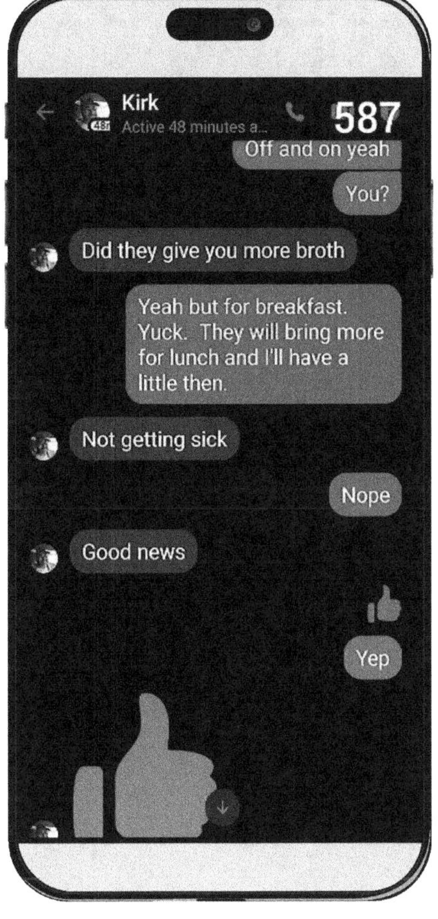
Kirk
Active 48 minutes a...
587
Off and on yeah
You?
Did they give you more broth
Yeah but for breakfast. Yuck. They will bring more for lunch and I'll have a little then.
Not getting sick
Nope
Good news
Yep

Kirk
Active 49 minutes a...
588
The doc might clamp of my g-tube tomorrow to see how I really do.
I told you I don't have that thing in my nose anymore, right?
Yes
So much more comfy
I bet it is
Things seem to be going really well
Yes. Evrryone says how good I look.
Good coloring and all
Thats good
You have been through a shitload of stuff the past 2 years

Kirk
Active 51 minutes a...
589
Yes I have. So have you.
And we are still around
Yep.
Your mom left the house. Dont know where she went
I'm glad I've had you.
Oh?
Hmm
Store probably
Im glad I've had you.
Im tired and lonely...hurry and come home

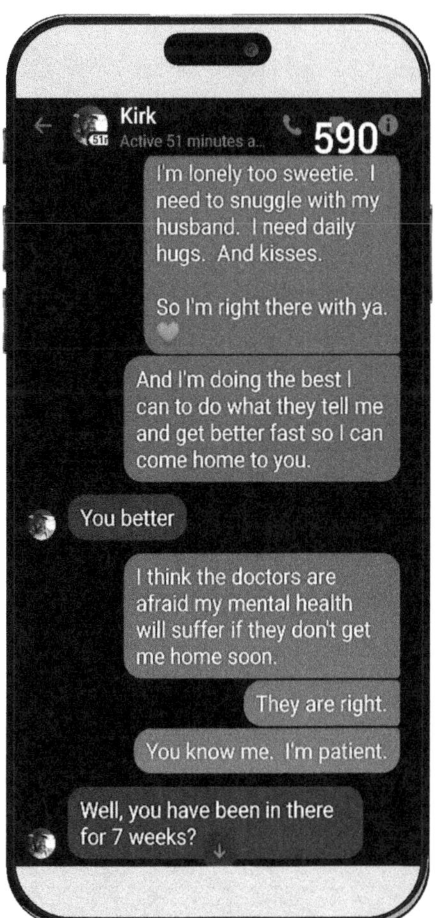

Kirk
Active 51 minutes a...
590
I'm lonely too sweetie. I need to snuggle with my husband. I need daily hugs. And kisses.
So I'm right there with ya.
And I'm doing the best I can to do what they tell me and get better fast so I can come home to you.
You better
I think the doctors are afraid my mental health will suffer if they don't get me home soon.
They are right.
You know me. I'm patient.
Well, you have been in there for 7 weeks?

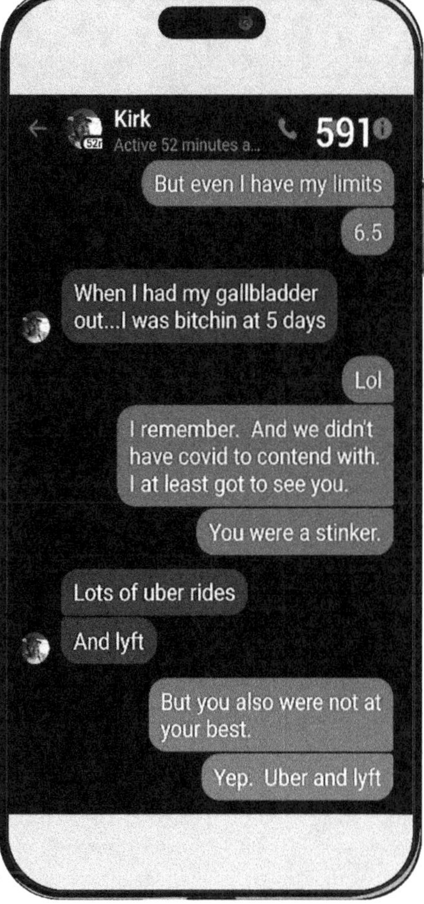

Kirk
Active 52 minutes a...
591
But even I have my limits
6.5
When I had my gallbladder out...I was bitchin at 5 days
Lol
I remember. And we didn't have covid to contend with. I at least got to see you.
You were a stinker.
Lots of uber rides
And lyft
But you also were not at your best.
Yep. Uber and lyft

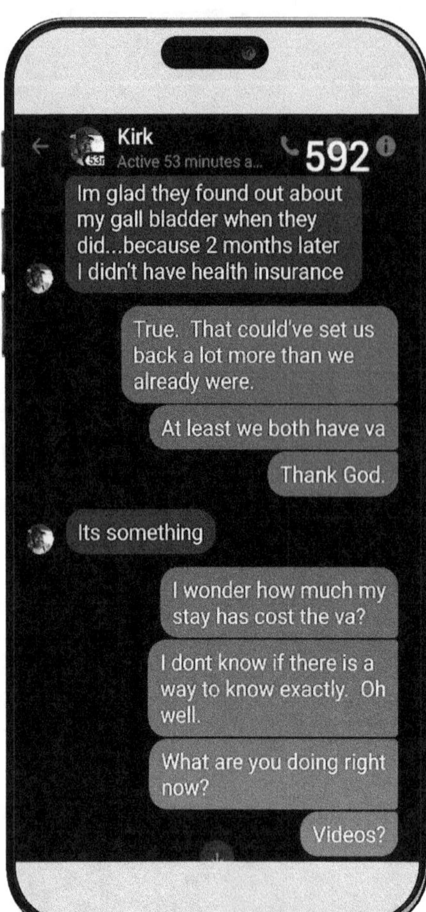
Kirk
Active 53 minutes a...
592
Im glad they found out about my gall bladder when they did...because 2 months later I didn't have health insurance
True. That could've set us back a lot more than we already were.
At least we both have va
Thank God.
Its something
I wonder how much my stay has cost the va?
I dont know if there is a way to know exactly. Oh well.
What are you doing right now?
Videos?

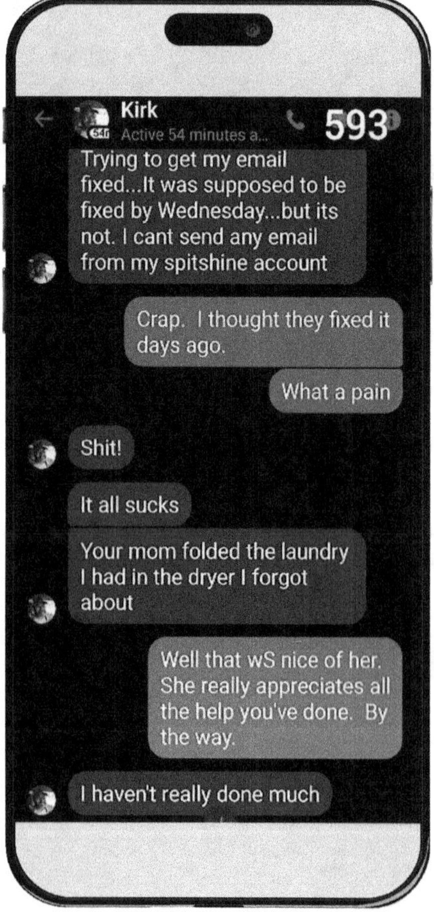
Kirk
Active 54 minutes a...
593
Trying to get my email fixed...It was supposed to be fixed by Wednesday...but its not. I cant send any email from my spitshine account
Crap. I thought they fixed it days ago.
What a pain
Shit!
It all sucks
Your mom folded the laundry I had in the dryer I forgot about
Well that wS nice of her. She really appreciates all the help you've done. By the way.
I haven't really done much

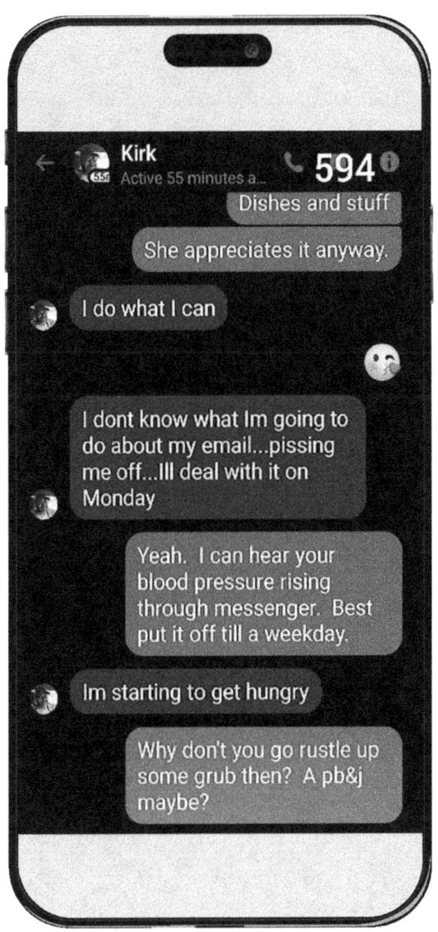

Kirk
Active 55 minutes a...
594
Dishes and stuff
She appreciates it anyway.
I do what I can
I dont know what Im going to do about my email...pissing me off...Ill deal with it on Monday
Yeah. I can hear your blood pressure rising through messenger. Best put it off till a weekday.
Im starting to get hungry
Why don't you go rustle up some grub then? A pb&j maybe?

Kirk
Active 56 minutes a...
595
Breakfast bowl
Jimmy dean
Ill be back
Okey dokie

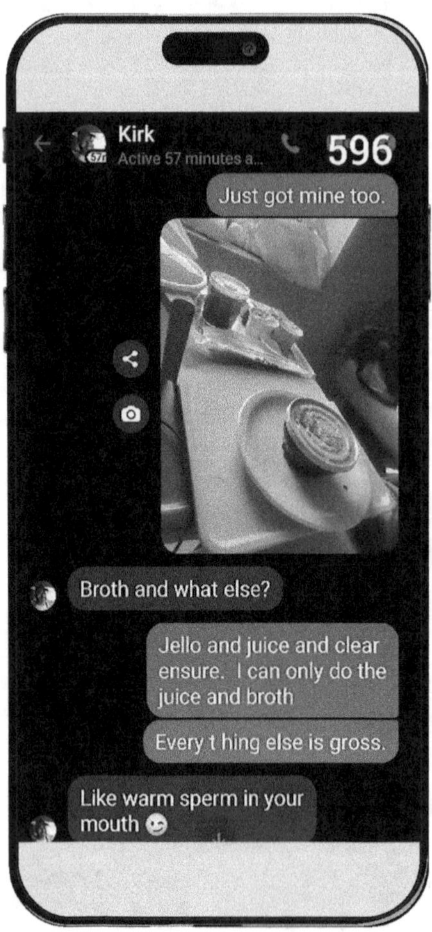
Kirk
Active 57 minutes a...
596
Just got mine too.
Broth and what else?
Jello and juice and clear ensure. I can only do the juice and broth
Every t hing else is gross.
Like warm sperm in your mouth

Kirk
Active 58 minutes a...
597
Gag. Barf. Ugh...
Thanks babe
For that visual.
Were you eating
Im sorry lol
Not yet thank God
Lol
I think Im going to play my tank game most of the day. Im trying to get an American Tier 10 tank and Im only on Tier 4
Well you better get cracking then my love.
Just for the record...I Love You

Kirk
Active 59 minutes a...
598
I'm just watching videos
I love you too. But that goes without saying.
Im letting my phone charge up now...it will be ready to go in 30 min
Cool
Danil should be online sometime today as well
Oh that's good. Did you play with him last night?
Yes...for about 1.5 hours
Oh good. That's great.
Could be 2
Not sure

Kirk
Active 1 hour ago
599
Do you have to go now while your phone charges?
No
Its been charging for about 45 min already
Oh. I thought you meant you just plugged it in. I see.
Are you eating
Trying too. The tray is jacked up
Better than jacked off
Lol
Ill leave you alone while you eat.
Focus on that

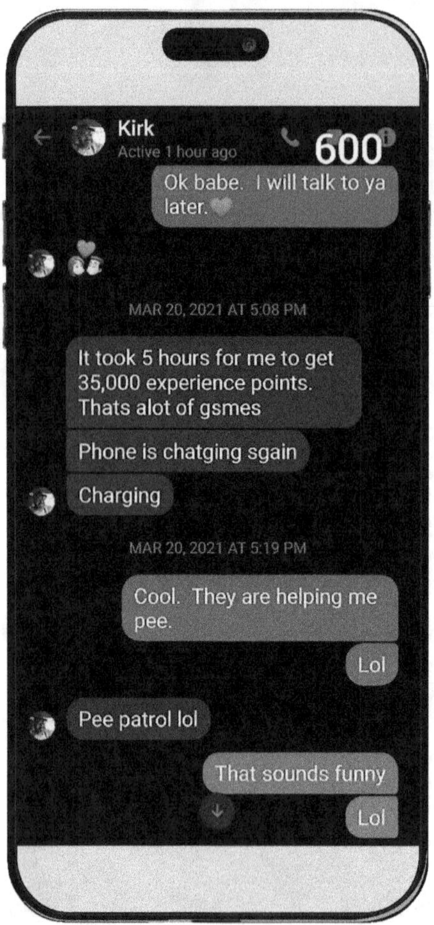
Kirk
Active 1 hour ago
600
Ok babe. I will talk to ya later. 🖤
MAR 20, 2021 AT 5:08 PM
It took 5 hours for me to get 35,000 experience points. Thats alot of gsmes
Phone is chatging sgain
Charging
MAR 20, 2021 AT 5:19 PM
Cool. They are helping me pee.
Lol
Pee patrol lol
That sounds funny
Lol

Kirk
Active 1 hour ago
601
Did I tell you a lot of people here call me Mrs G.
No
Yeah.
Your damn near part of their family you've been there so long
I know right? 😡
How.are you feeling...how was lunch
Salty
MAR 20, 2021 AT 8:56 PM
Ill give you salty lol
You awake
Yep

Kirk
Active 1 hour ago
602
Lol
Want to video chat
I'm getting ready to use the pee pot again and get my pain meds. Can we tomorrow babe?
Yep
Yay. I'm waiting for the nurse now.
I need to wsrm up my dinner
You haven't eaten?
Nope
Aww. Babe.
You need to eat

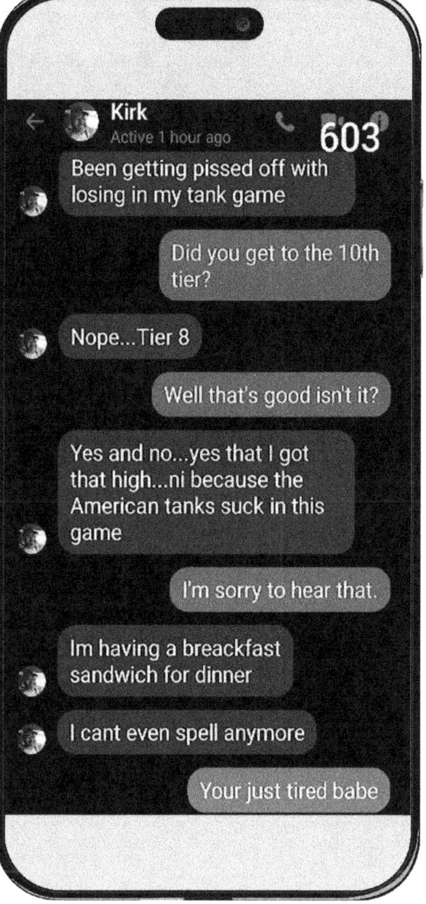
Kirk
Active 1 hour ago
603
Been getting pissed off with losing in my tank game
Did you get to the 10th tier?
Nope...Tier 8
Well that's good isn't it?
Yes and no...yes that I got that high...ni because the American tanks suck in this game
I'm sorry to hear that.
Im having a breackfast sandwich for dinner
I cant even spell anymore
Your just tired babe

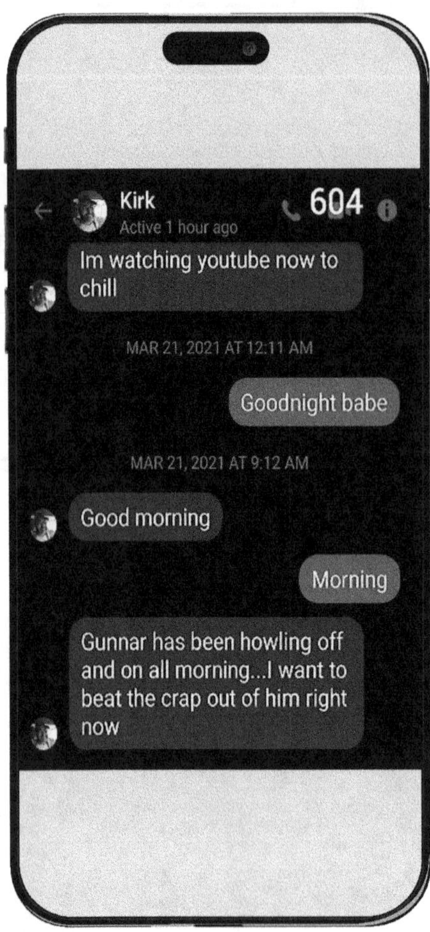

Kirk
Active 1 hour ago
604
Im watching youtube now to chill
MAR 21, 2021 AT 12:11 AM
Goodnight babe
MAR 21, 2021 AT 9:12 AM
Good morning
Morning
Gunnar has been howling off and on all morning...I want to beat the crap out of him right now

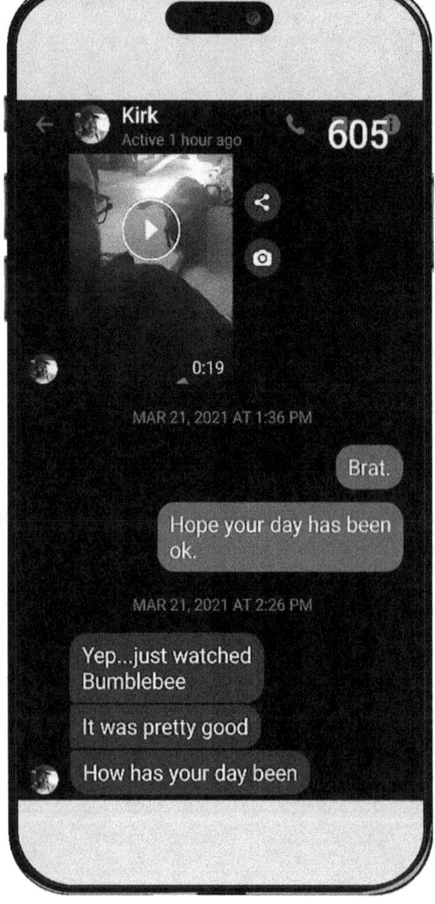

Kirk
Active 1 hour ago
605
0:19
MAR 21, 2021 AT 1:36 PM
Brat.
Hope your day has been ok.
MAR 21, 2021 AT 2:26 PM
Yep...just watched Bumblebee
It was pretty good
How has your day been

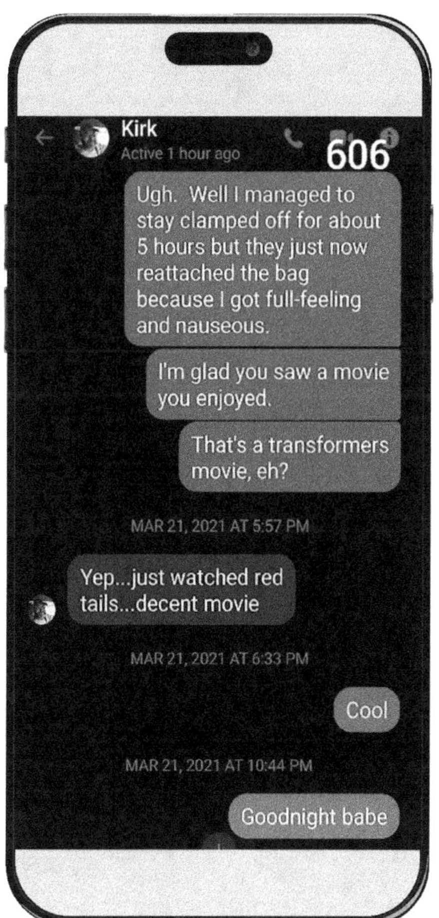
Kirk
Active 1 hour ago
606
Ugh. Well I managed to stay clamped off for about 5 hours but they just now reattached the bag because I got full-feeling and nauseous.
I'm glad you saw a movie you enjoyed.
That's a transformers movie, eh?
MAR 21, 2021 AT 5:57 PM
Yep...just watched red tails...decent movie
MAR 21, 2021 AT 6:33 PM
Cool
MAR 21, 2021 AT 10:44 PM
Goodnight babe

Kirk
Active 1 hour ago
607
Good morning
Err, I guess afternoon now.
Starting to feel kind of abandoned dude.
Just finished my appointment with my psychiatrist
How did it go?
It went ok
Dont feel abandoned
Your not forgotten
How come you don't say good morning to me anymore or goodnight?
I didnt wake up today until 10am...and my appointment was at 10:30.

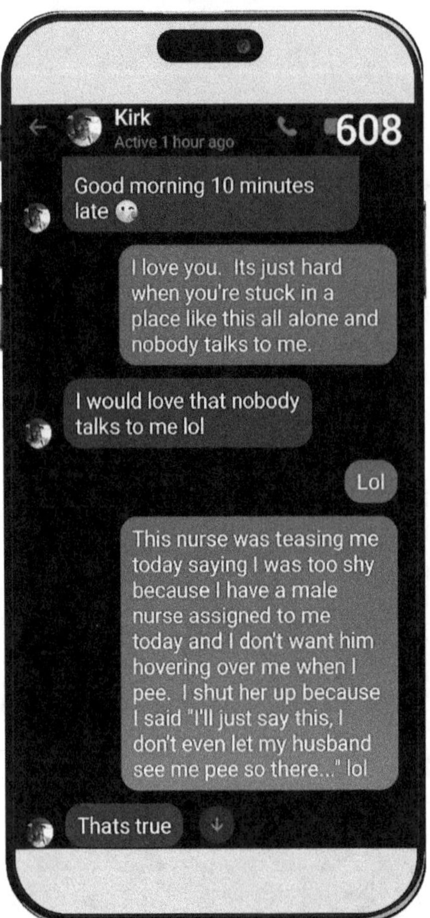
Kirk
Active 1 hour ago
608
Good morning 10 minutes late
I love you. Its just hard when you're stuck in a place like this all alone and nobody talks to me.
I would love that nobody talks to me lol
Lol
This nurse was teasing me today saying I was too shy because I have a male nurse assigned to me today and I don't want him hovering over me when I pee. I shut her up because I said "I'll just say this, I don't even let my husband see me pee so there..." lol
Thats true

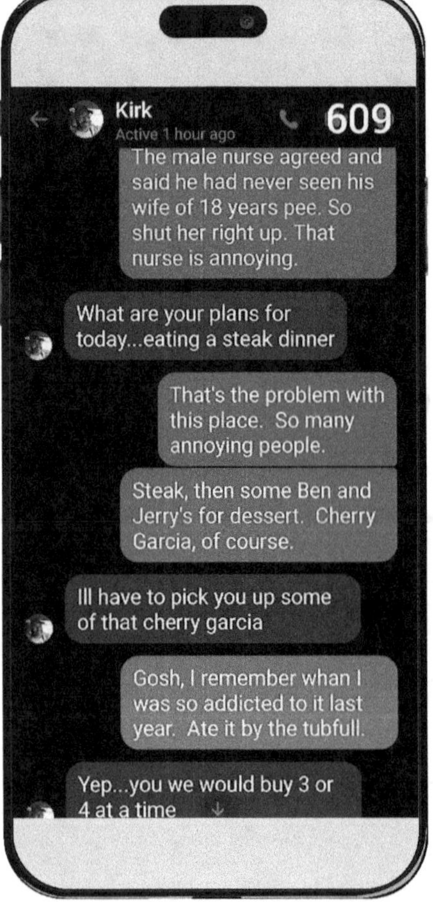
Kirk
Active 1 hour ago
609
The male nurse agreed and said he had never seen his wife of 18 years pee. So shut her right up. That nurse is annoying.
What are your plans for today...eating a steak dinner
That's the problem with this place. So many annoying people.
Steak, then some Ben and Jerry's for dessert. Cherry Garcia, of course.
Ill have to pick you up some of that cherry garcia
Gosh, I remember whan I was so addicted to it last year. Ate it by the tubfull.
Yep...you we would buy 3 or 4 at a time

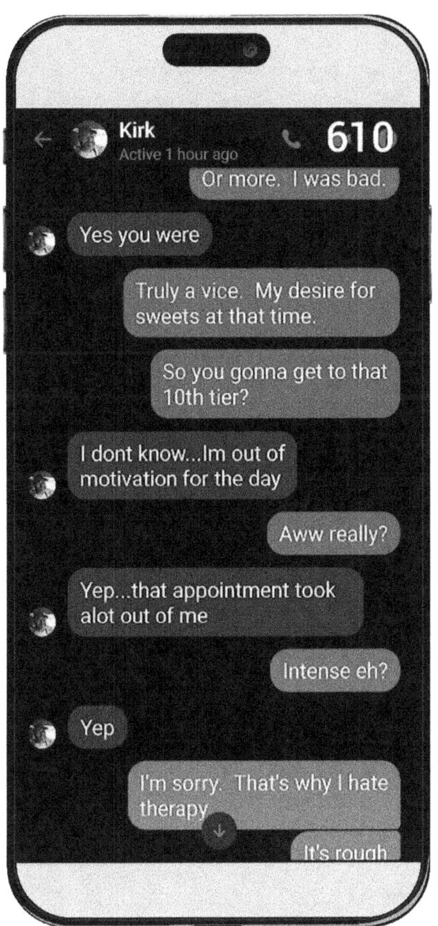
Kirk
Active 1 hour ago
610
Or more. I was bad.
Yes you were
Truly a vice. My desire for sweets at that time.
So you gonna get to that 10th tier?
I dont know...Im out of motivation for the day
Aww really?
Yep...that appointment took alot out of me
Intense eh?
Yep
I'm sorry. That's why I hate therapy
It's rough

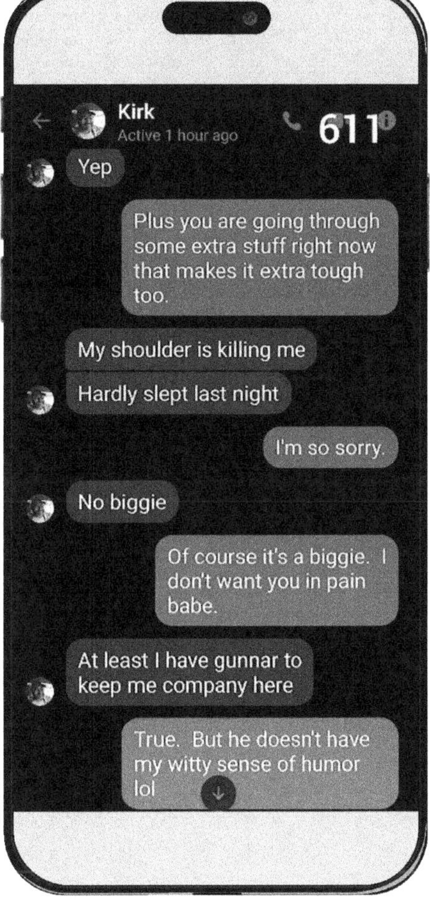
Kirk
Active 1 hour ago
611
Yep
Plus you are going through some extra stuff right now that makes it extra tough too.
My shoulder is killing me
Hardly slept last night
I'm so sorry.
No biggie
Of course it's a biggie. I don't want you in pain babe.
At least I have gunnar to keep me company here
True. But he doesn't have my witty sense of humor lol

Kirk
Active 1 hour ago
612

Lol

You wanna chill and watch TV for a while and talk later?

Since you're kinda drained?

Its ok. We can talk

Ok cool.

I finally have a bit of time where no one will bug me. At least for a few minutes lol

Then we could have sex...just takes a few seconds lol

Lol. It probably would be seconds now. Hehe I don't even have any undies on so I'm sorta dressed for it lol.

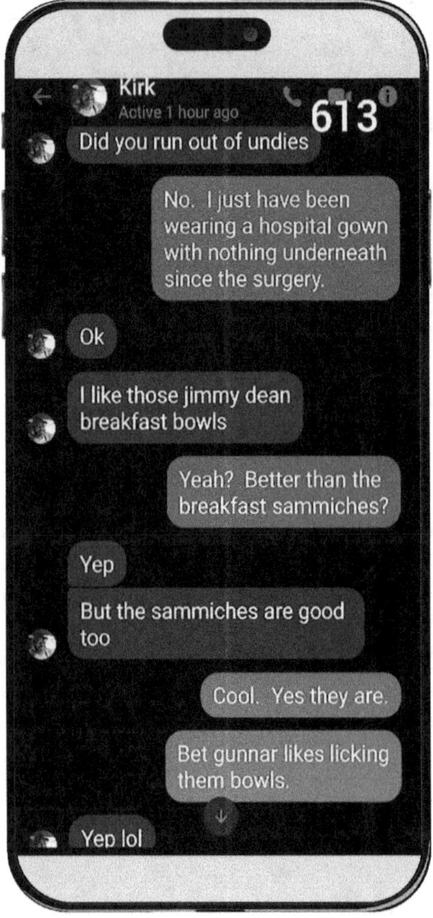

Kirk
Active 1 hour ago
613

Did you run out of undies

No. I just have been wearing a hospital gown with nothing underneath since the surgery.

Ok

I like those jimmy dean breakfast bowls

Yeah? Better than the breakfast sammiches?

Yep

But the sammiches are good too

Cool. Yes they are.

Bet gunnar likes licking them bowls.

Yep lol

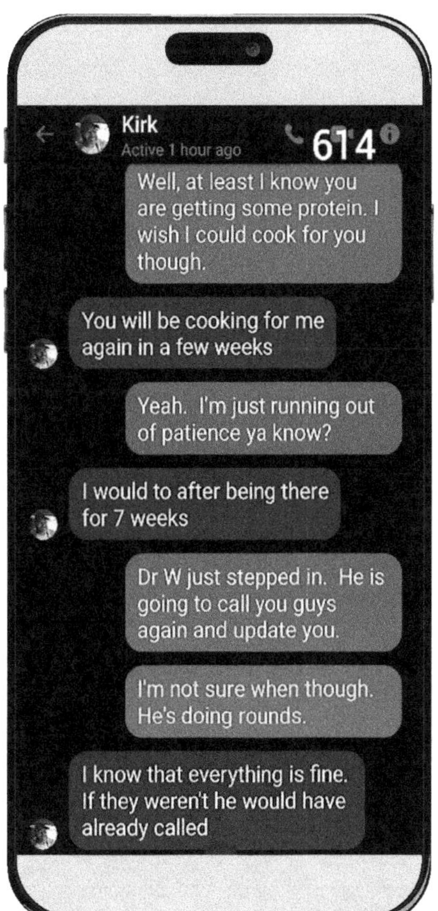

Kirk
Active 1 hour ago
614
Well, at least I know you are getting some protein. I wish I could cook for you though.
You will be cooking for me again in a few weeks
Yeah. I'm just running out of patience ya know?
I would to after being there for 7 weeks
Dr W just stepped in. He is going to call you guys again and update you.
I'm not sure when though. He's doing rounds.
I know that everything is fine. If they weren't he would have already called

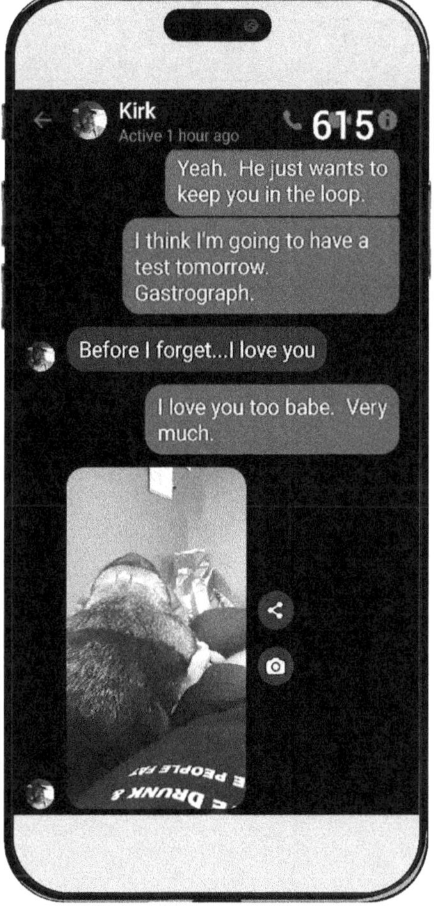

Kirk
Active 1 hour ago
615
Yeah. He just wants to keep you in the loop.
I think I'm going to have a test tomorrow. Gastrograph.
Before I forget...I love you
I love you too babe. Very much.

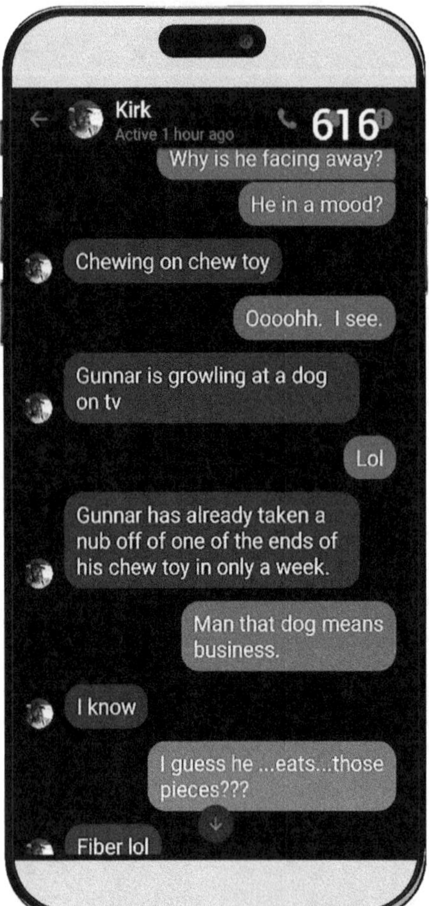

Kirk
Active 1 hour ago
616
Why is he facing away?
He in a mood?
Chewing on chew toy
Oooohh. I see.
Gunnar is growling at a dog on tv
Lol
Gunnar has already taken a nub off of one of the ends of his chew toy in only a week.
Man that dog means business.
I know
I guess he ...eats...those pieces???
Fiber lol

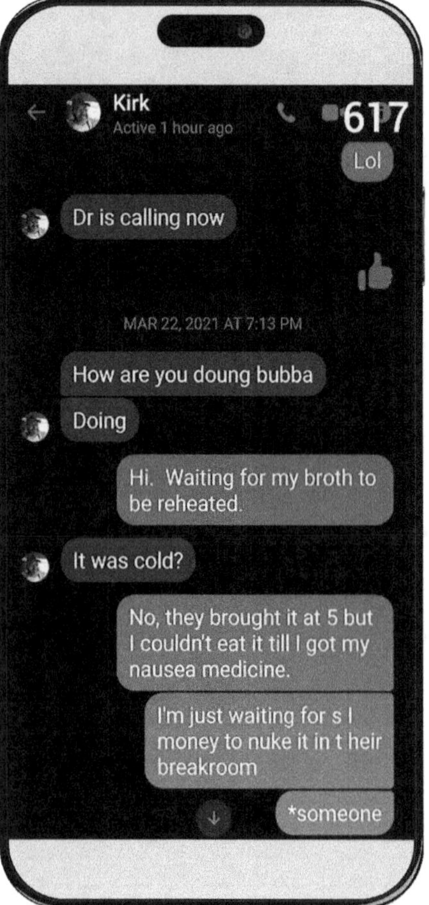

Kirk
Active 1 hour ago
617
Lol
Dr is calling now
MAR 22, 2021 AT 7:13 PM
How are you doung bubba
Doing
Hi. Waiting for my broth to be reheated.
It was cold?
No, they brought it at 5 but I couldn't eat it till I got my nausea medicine.
I'm just waiting for s I money to nuke it in t heir breakroom
*someone

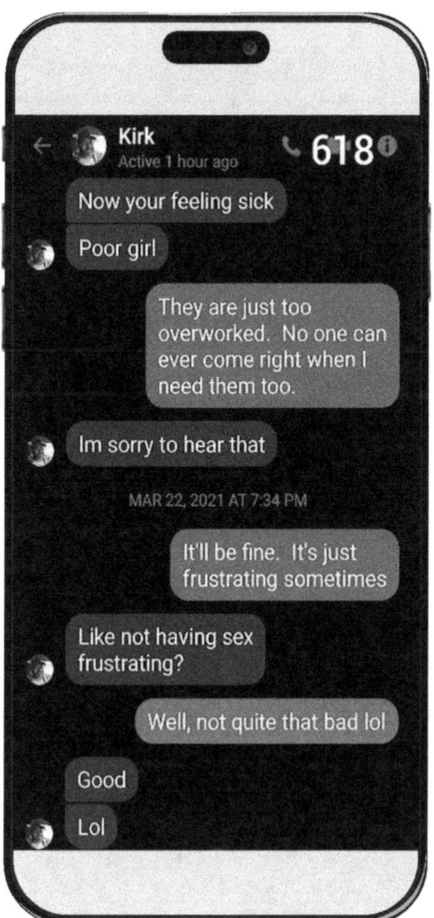
Kirk
Active 1 hour ago
618
Now your feeling sick
Poor girl
They are just too overworked. No one can ever come right when I need them too.
Im sorry to hear that
MAR 22, 2021 AT 7:34 PM
It'll be fine. It's just frustrating sometimes
Like not having sex frustrating?
Well, not quite that bad lol
Good
Lol

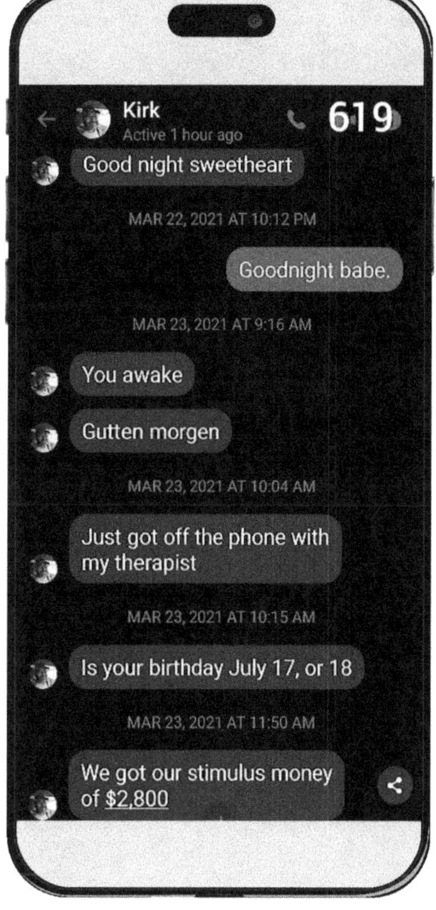
Kirk
Active 1 hour ago
619
Good night sweetheart
MAR 22, 2021 AT 10:12 PM
Goodnight babe.
MAR 23, 2021 AT 9:16 AM
You awake
Gutten morgen
MAR 23, 2021 AT 10:04 AM
Just got off the phone with my therapist
MAR 23, 2021 AT 10:15 AM
Is your birthday July 17, or 18
MAR 23, 2021 AT 11:50 AM
We got our stimulus money of $2,800

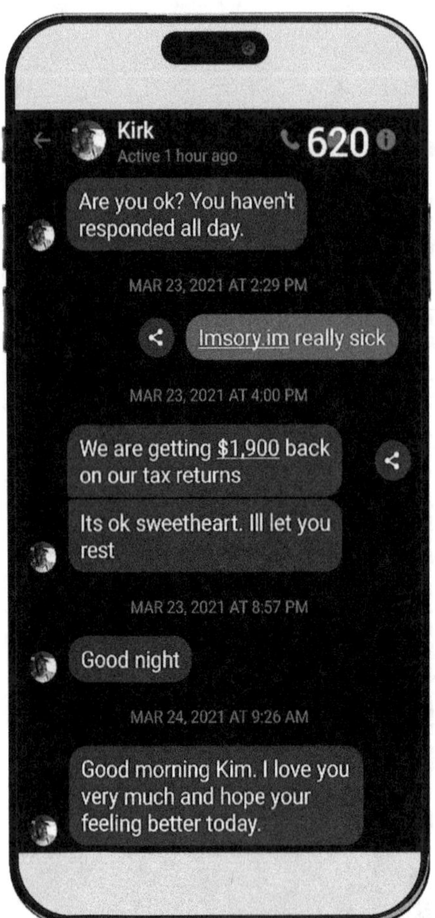
Kirk
Active 1 hour ago
620
Are you ok? You haven't responded all day.
MAR 23, 2021 AT 2:29 PM
Imsory.im really sick
MAR 23, 2021 AT 4:00 PM
We are getting $1,900 back on our tax returns
Its ok sweetheart. Ill let you rest
MAR 23, 2021 AT 8:57 PM
Good night
MAR 24, 2021 AT 9:26 AM
Good morning Kim. I love you very much and hope your feeling better today.

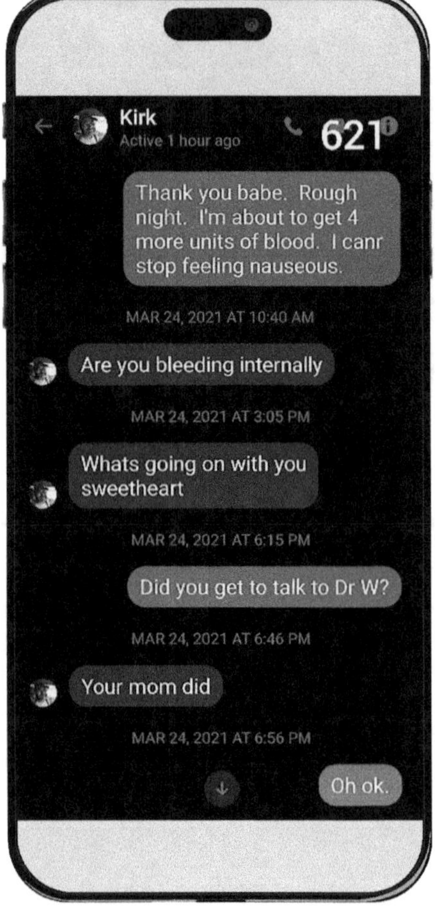
Kirk
Active 1 hour ago
621
Thank you babe. Rough night. I'm about to get 4 more units of blood. I canr stop feeling nauseous.
MAR 24, 2021 AT 10:40 AM
Are you bleeding internally
MAR 24, 2021 AT 3:05 PM
Whats going on with you sweetheart
MAR 24, 2021 AT 6:15 PM
Did you get to talk to Dr W?
MAR 24, 2021 AT 6:46 PM
Your mom did
MAR 24, 2021 AT 6:56 PM
Oh ok.

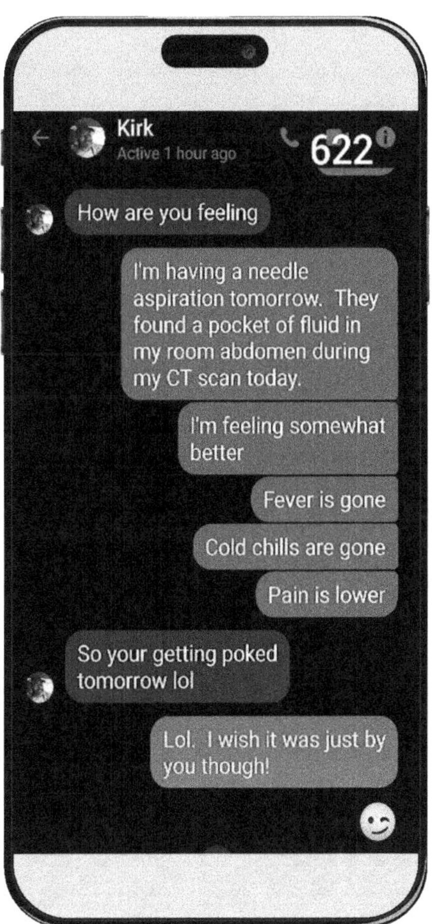

Kirk
Active 1 hour ago
622
How are you feeling
I'm having a needle aspiration tomorrow. They found a pocket of fluid in my room abdomen during my CT scan today.
I'm feeling somewhat better
Fever is gone
Cold chills are gone
Pain is lower
So your getting poked tomorrow lol
Lol. I wish it was just by you though!

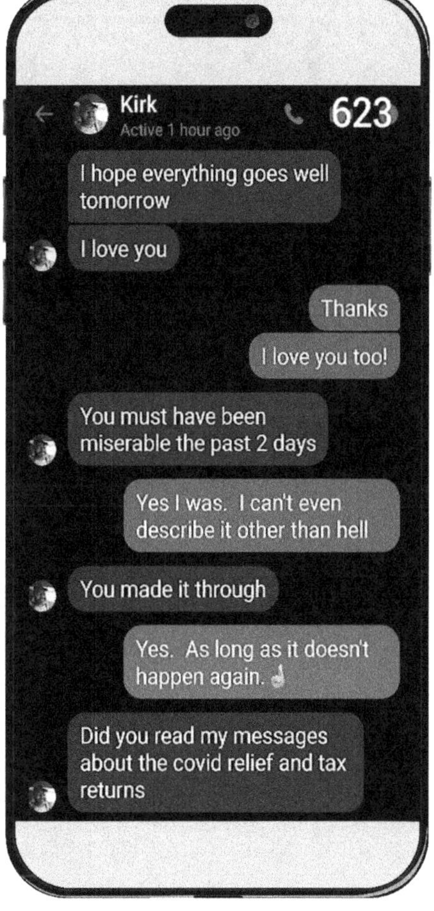

Kirk
Active 1 hour ago
623
I hope everything goes well tomorrow
I love you
Thanks
I love you too!
You must have been miserable the past 2 days
Yes I was. I can't even describe it other than hell
You made it through
Yes. As long as it doesn't happen again.
Did you read my messages about the covid relief and tax returns

Kirk
Active 1 hour ago
624
Yes I did. That's fantastic. Now you have plenty of money for seeing danil. Yay
Maybe
Maybe???
If you want me to fly there and rent a car its not enough
We will talk about it as soon as you have your dates.
Ok
I have to go to the store tomorrow
Ok cool.
Get some good food.

Kirk
Active 1 hour ago
625
Chips, m&m's, ice cream
Dr pepper
Lol. Brat
You need to get better...every time the doctors fix something...something else breaks lol
I have some chips and avocado salsa
Almost too spicey for me
Now Im farting...as usual lol
Lol
Old fart
Yes I am
But I love ya anyway.

Kirk
Active 1 hour ago
626
Thats why I love you
You put up with me
Yes I do.
I'm patient.
Lol
Have you talked to your mom much today...she is going nuts over you
Yes, I talked to her earlier after she talked to Dr w.
Good
Did they ever let you pee in private?
MAR 24, 2021 AT 8:08 PM
They sometimes step out but usually no lol.

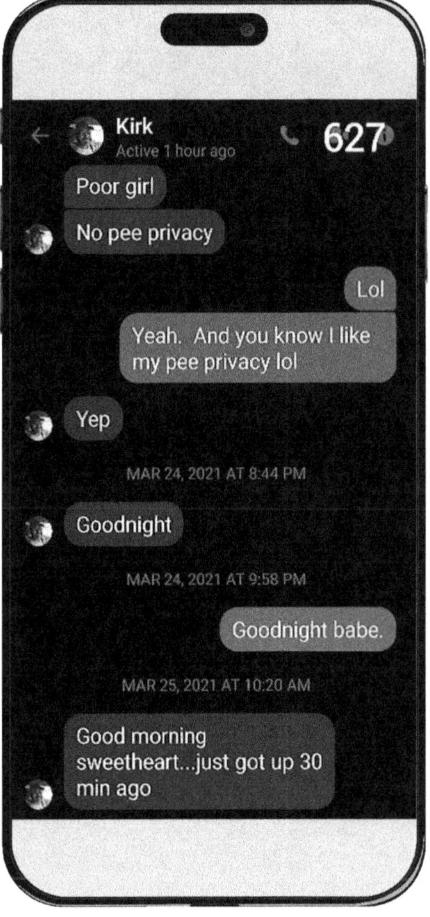
Kirk
Active 1 hour ago
627
Poor girl
No pee privacy
Lol
Yeah. And you know I like my pee privacy lol
Yep
MAR 24, 2021 AT 8:44 PM
Goodnight
MAR 24, 2021 AT 9:58 PM
Goodnight babe.
MAR 25, 2021 AT 10:20 AM
Good morning sweetheart...just got up 30 min ago

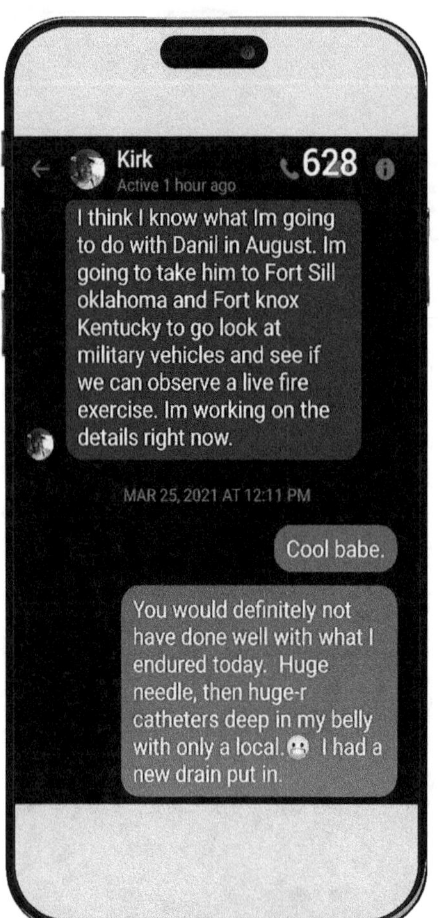

Kirk
Active 1 hour ago
628
I think I know what Im going to do with Danil in August. Im going to take him to Fort Sill oklahoma and Fort knox Kentucky to go look at military vehicles and see if we can observe a live fire exercise. Im working on the details right now.
MAR 25, 2021 AT 12:11 PM
Cool babe.
You would definitely not have done well with what I endured today. Huge needle, then huge-r catheters deep in my belly with only a local. I had a new drain put in.

Kirk
Active 1 hour ago
629
How are you feeling...heard you have an infection
Yes. I sure do.
I wish I could bare the burdon for you
I know sweetie. You would never sit still for this stuff though. I know you.
Finally ate takeout today. Went to walmart and then to Wendys...bought Gunnar a cheeseburger as well
Oh good. You've been very very good for almost 2 months.
Yep. But today I thought...What the Hell lol

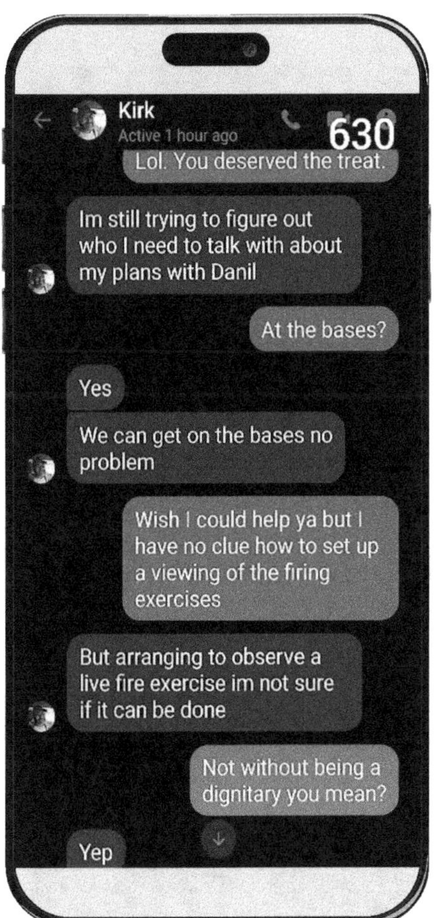

Kirk
Active 1 hour ago
630
Lol. You deserved the treat.
Im still trying to figure out who I need to talk with about my plans with Danil
At the bases?
Yes
We can get on the bases no problem
Wish I could help ya but I have no clue how to set up a viewing of the firing exercises
But arranging to observe a live fire exercise im not sure if it can be done
Not without being a dignitary you mean?
Yep

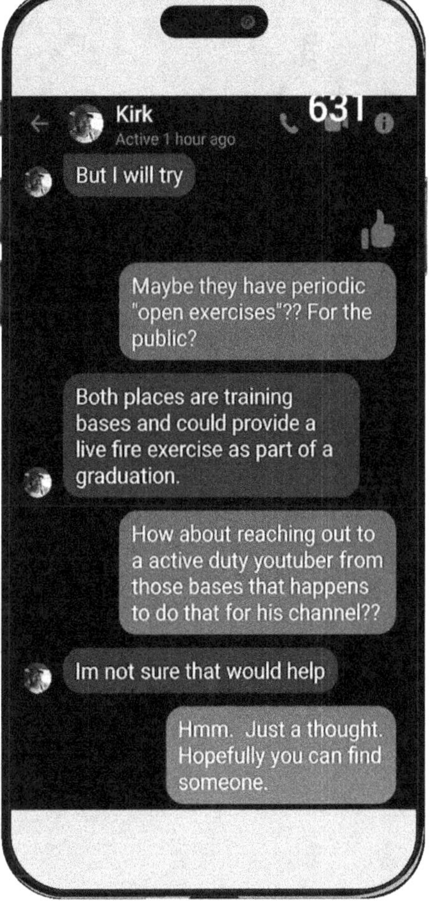

Kirk
Active 1 hour ago
631
But I will try
Maybe they have periodic "open exercises"?? For the public?
Both places are training bases and could provide a live fire exercise as part of a graduation.
How about reaching out to a active duty youtuber from those bases that happens to do that for his channel??
Im not sure that would help
Hmm. Just a thought. Hopefully you can find someone.

Kirk
Active 1 hour ago
632

My guess is that it would have to be approved by the post Commander

Yeah, unless its already a sanctioned thing for the public, then I'm sure you are right.

You need to hurry up and get better so you can Help me

I know right. I feel so stuck here.

Your good at internet stuff...I really admire that about you

Aww, thank you babe. I do seem to have the knack and patience to find stuff.

Yes you do

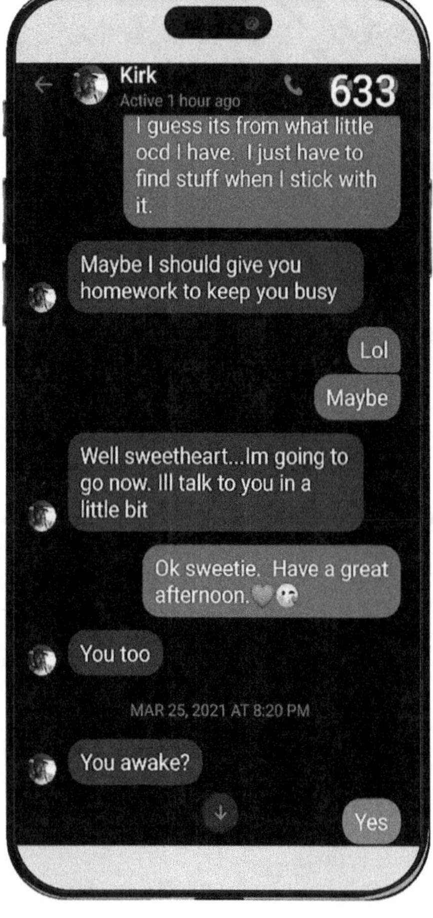

Kirk
Active 1 hour ago
633

I guess its from what little ocd I have. I just have to find stuff when I stick with it.

Maybe I should give you homework to keep you busy

Lol

Maybe

Well sweetheart...Im going to go now. Ill talk to you in a little bit

Ok sweetie. Have a great afternoon.

You too

MAR 25, 2021 AT 8:20 PM

You awake?

Yes

Kirk
Active 1 hour ago
634
Hi sweetheart
Hi hunni
How are you feeling
How was you afternoon?
I'm doing ok. Took some naps
I made some progress on my August plans
Oh? Cool
If I can make those plans, I think you should come with us if you can
I think you would like it too
If I am up to it. I'd love to.

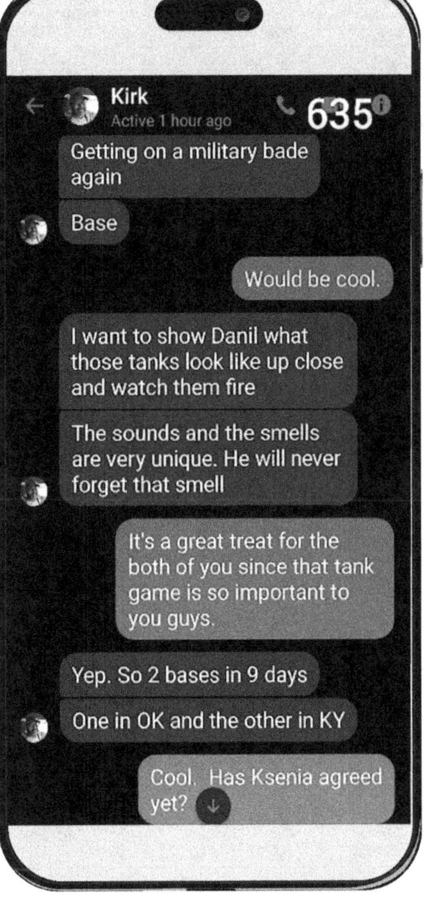

Kirk
Active 1 hour ago
635
Getting on a military bade again
Base
Would be cool.
I want to show Danil what those tanks look like up close and watch them fire
The sounds and the smells are very unique. He will never forget that smell
It's a great treat for the both of you since that tank game is so important to you guys.
Yep. So 2 bases in 9 days
One in OK and the other in KY
Cool. Has Ksenia agreed yet?

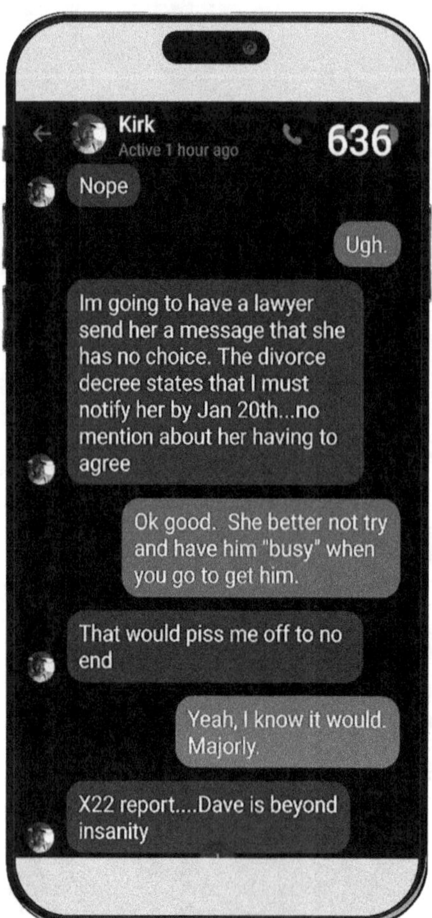

Kirk
Active 1 hour ago
636
Nope
Ugh.
Im going to have a lawyer send her a message that she has no choice. The divorce decree states that I must notify her by Jan 20th...no mention about her having to agree
Ok good. She better not try and have him "busy" when you go to get him.
That would piss me off to no end
Yeah, I know it would. Majorly.
X22 report....Dave is beyond insanity

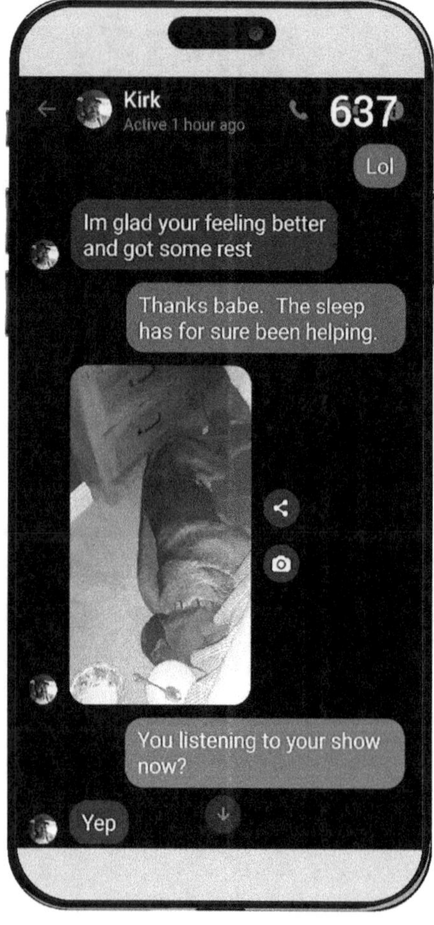

Kirk
Active 1 hour ago
637
Lol
Im glad your feeling better and got some rest
Thanks babe. The sleep has for sure been helping.
You listening to your show now?
Yep

Kirk
Active 1 hour ago
638
Looks like you both had a dish of ice cream lol
Tired pooch.
Its hot in here
Dont know how Im going to sleep
Really? I was hot earlier too.
Fan?
Fan is on
Maybe crack a window?
Maybe...its still warm outside
MAR 25, 2021 AT 9:11 PM
Good night kimmie

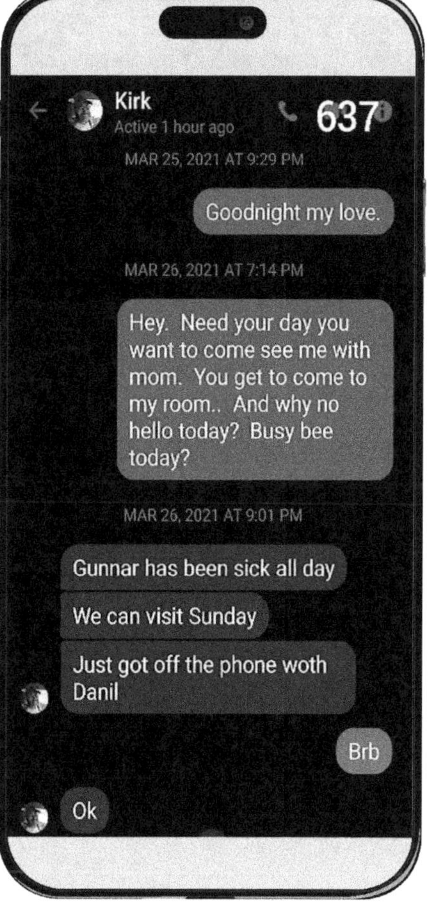

Kirk
Active 1 hour ago
637
MAR 25, 2021 AT 9:29 PM
Goodnight my love.
MAR 26, 2021 AT 7:14 PM
Hey. Need your day you want to come see me with mom. You get to come to my room.. And why no hello today? Busy bee today?
MAR 26, 2021 AT 9:01 PM
Gunnar has been sick all day
We can visit Sunday
Just got off the phone woth Danil
Brb
Ok

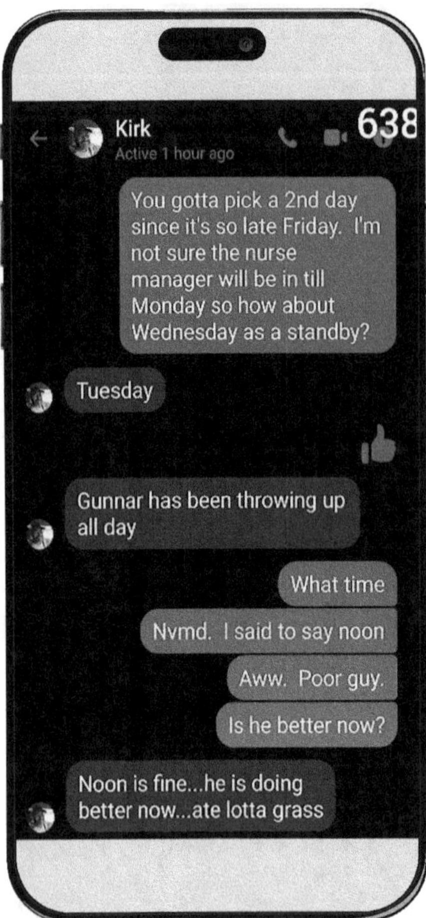
Kirk
Active 1 hour ago
638
You gotta pick a 2nd day since it's so late Friday. I'm not sure the nurse manager will be in till Monday so how about Wednesday as a standby?
Tuesday
Gunnar has been throwing up all day
What time
Nvmd. I said to say noon
Aww. Poor guy.
Is he better now?
Noon is fine...he is doing better now...ate lotta grass

Kirk
Active 1 hour ago
639
Awww. Good about the date and time. My nurse said she will get the email first thing Monday so Tuesday at noon should be no problem. She isn't in till monday.
Ok
Cant wait to see you
Me either babe.
Its soo hot upstairs
I'm sorry hun. It's too cold here.
You got your blankie
And leggings
True.
And a furry coochie lol

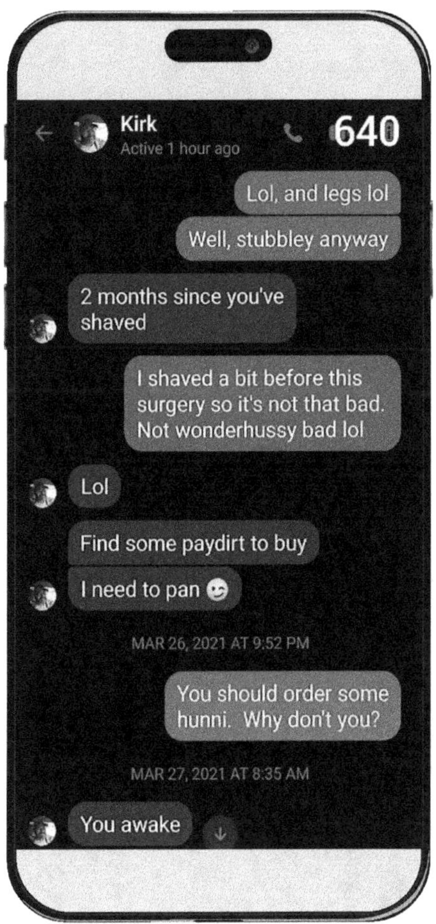
Kirk
Active 1 hour ago
640
Lol, and legs lol
Well, stubbley anyway
2 months since you've shaved
I shaved a bit before this surgery so it's not that bad. Not wonderhussy bad lol
Lol
Find some paydirt to buy
I need to pan 😉
MAR 26, 2021 AT 9:52 PM
You should order some hunni. Why don't you?
MAR 27, 2021 AT 8:35 AM
You awake

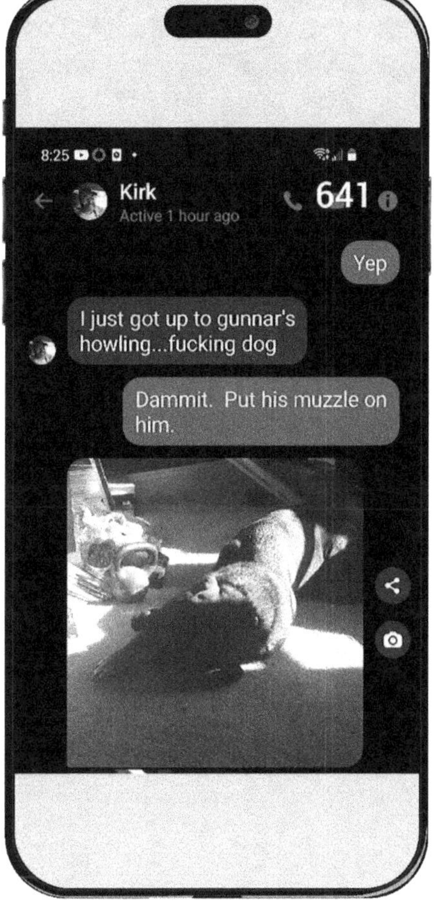
8:25
Kirk
Active 1 hour ago
641
Yep
I just got up to gunnar's howling...fucking dog
Dammit. Put his muzzle on him.

Kirk
Active 1 hour ago
642
Little pisser.
He looks made in the 2nd photo
*mad
Like he wants to kick my butt lol
Yep lol

Kirk
Active 1 hour ago
643
Ill get the paydirt...you order those movies I requested plus the xbox one cable
Power cable
Ok. Can you repeat those movie titles so I don't have to go hunting back through our texts?
The Debt
John wick 3
Magnificent seven (with Chris Pratt)
Gotcha
Will get those ordered right away.

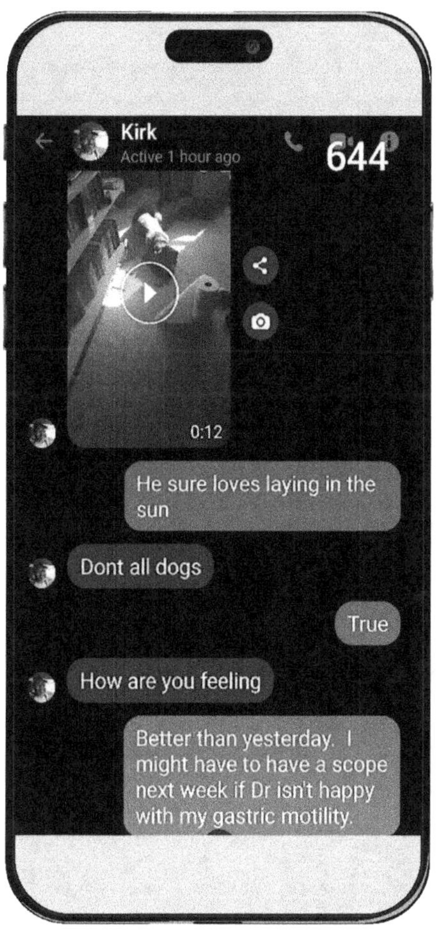
Kirk
Active 1 hour ago
644
0:12
He sure loves laying in the sun
Dont all dogs
True
How are you feeling
Better than yesterday. I might have to have a scope next week if Dr isn't happy with my gastric motility.

Kirk
Active 1 hour ago
645
Ill scope your vaginal cavity
Lol
I know you will haha
The movie the debt. Who is in it?
Helen mirren
If you want take $50 and buy yourself a gift
Ok. Maybe I will.
Thanks
You deserve it with everything your going through
Awww.

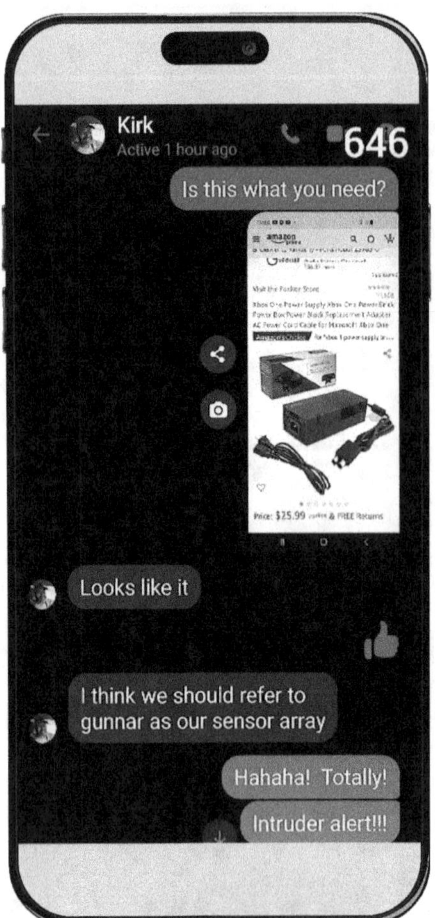
Kirk
Active 1 hour ago
646
Is this what you need?
Looks like it
I think we should refer to gunnar as our sensor array
Hahaha! Totally!
Intruder alert!!!

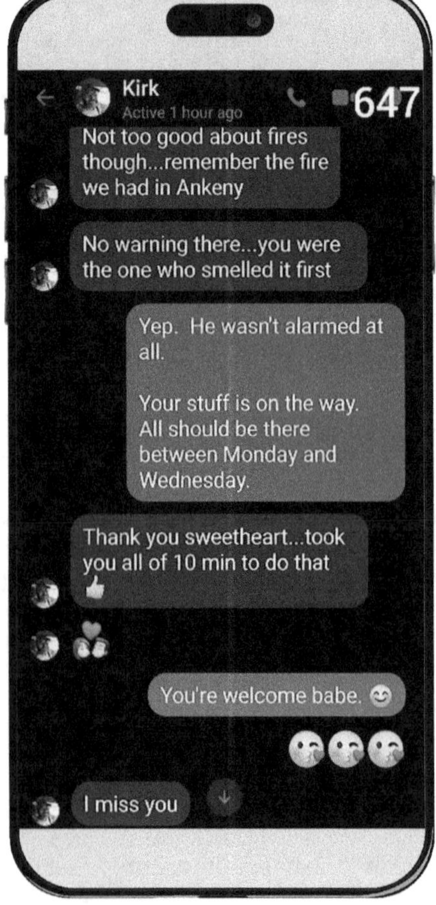
Kirk
Active 1 hour ago
647
Not too good about fires though...remember the fire we had in Ankeny
No warning there...you were the one who smelled it first
Yep. He wasn't alarmed at all.
Your stuff is on the way. All should be there between Monday and Wednesday.
Thank you sweetheart...took you all of 10 min to do that
You're welcome babe.
I miss you

Kirk
Active 1 hour ago
648
I miss you too. More than I can even say.
0:00
Did you try and send me audio
Is there any sound?
No

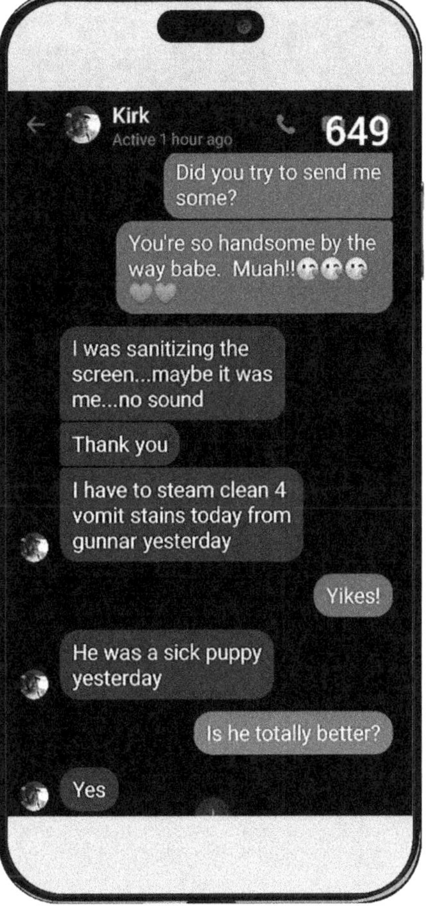
Kirk
Active 1 hour ago
649
Did you try to send me some?
You're so handsome by the way babe. Muah!!
I was sanitizing the screen...maybe it was me...no sound
Thank you
I have to steam clean 4 vomit stains today from gunnar yesterday
Yikes!
He was a sick puppy yesterday
Is he totally better?
Yes

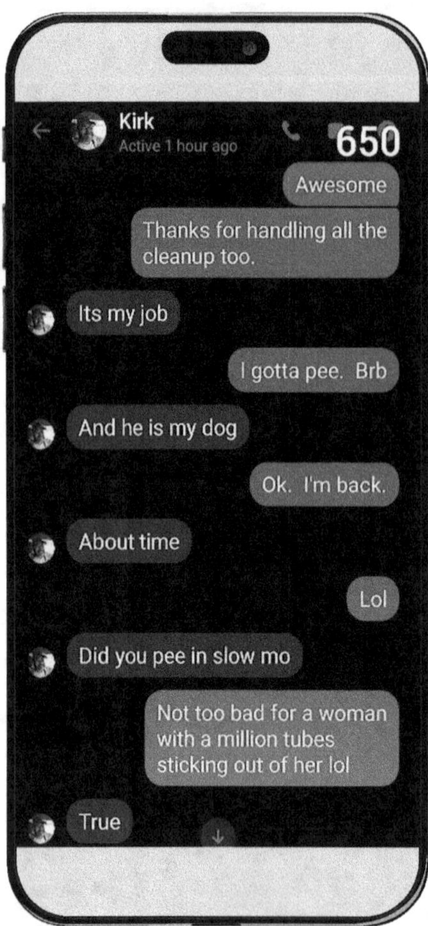

Kirk
Active 1 hour ago
650
Awesome
Thanks for handling all the cleanup too.
Its my job
I gotta pee. Brb
And he is my dog
Ok. I'm back.
About time
Lol
Did you pee in slow mo
Not too bad for a woman with a million tubes sticking out of her lol
True

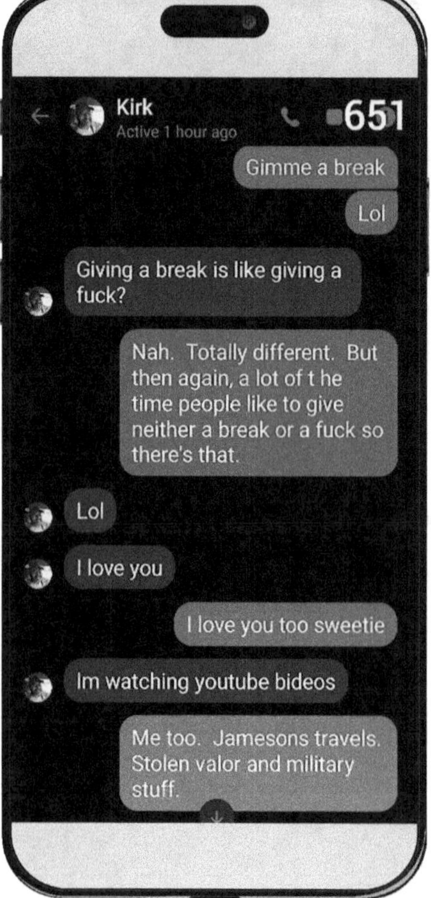

Kirk
Active 1 hour ago
651
Gimme a break
Lol
Giving a break is like giving a fuck?
Nah. Totally different. But then again, a lot of t he time people like to give neither a break or a fuck so there's that.
Lol
I love you
I love you too sweetie
Im watching youtube bideos
Me too. Jamesons travels. Stolen valor and military stuff.

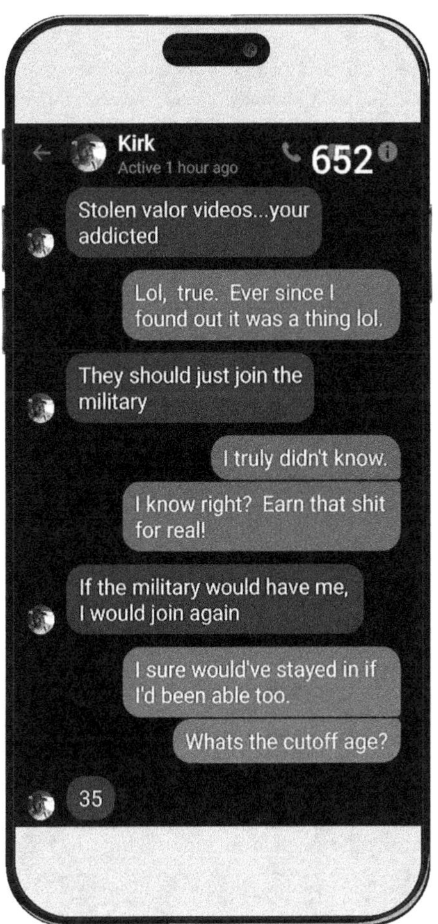

Kirk
Active 1 hour ago
652
Stolen valor videos...your addicted
Lol, true. Ever since I found out it was a thing lol.
They should just join the military
I truly didn't know.
I know right? Earn that shit for real!
If the military would have me, I would join again
I sure would've stayed in if I'd been able too.
Whats the cutoff age?
35

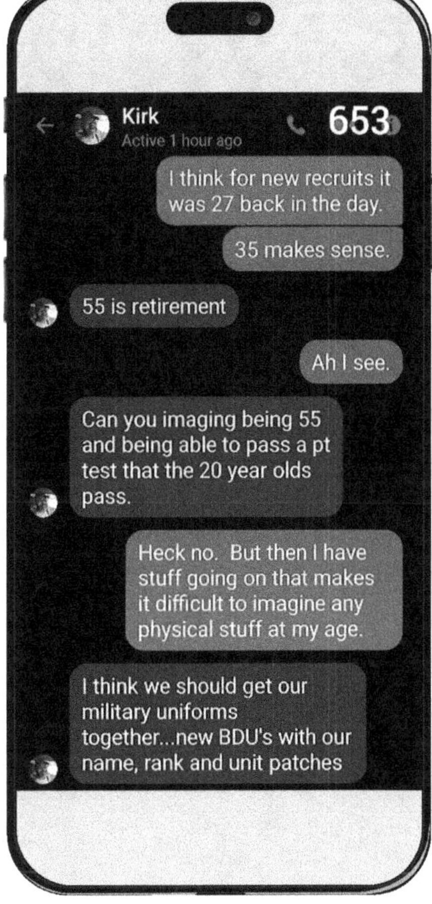

Kirk
Active 1 hour ago
653
I think for new recruits it was 27 back in the day.
35 makes sense.
55 is retirement
Ah I see.
Can you imaging being 55 and being able to pass a pt test that the 20 year olds pass.
Heck no. But then I have stuff going on that makes it difficult to imagine any physical stuff at my age.
I think we should get our military uniforms together...new BDU's with our name, rank and unit patches

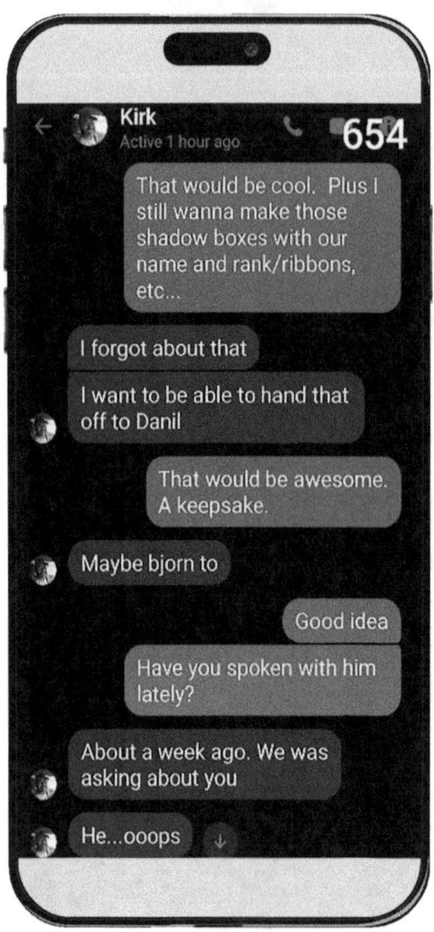
Kirk
Active 1 hour ago
654
That would be cool. Plus I still wanna make those shadow boxes with our name and rank/ribbons, etc...
I forgot about that
I want to be able to hand that off to Danil
That would be awesome. A keepsake.
Maybe bjorn to
Good idea
Have you spoken with him lately?
About a week ago. We was asking about you
He...ooops

Kirk
Active 1 hour ago
655
Aww. Tell him I said hello next time you speak.
I will
Did you hear about the devil shoes?
No
Nike has made a limited edition shoe(666 prs made) of these black and red shoes that have human blood in them. Its sick.
Satanic
Yep. Intentionally.

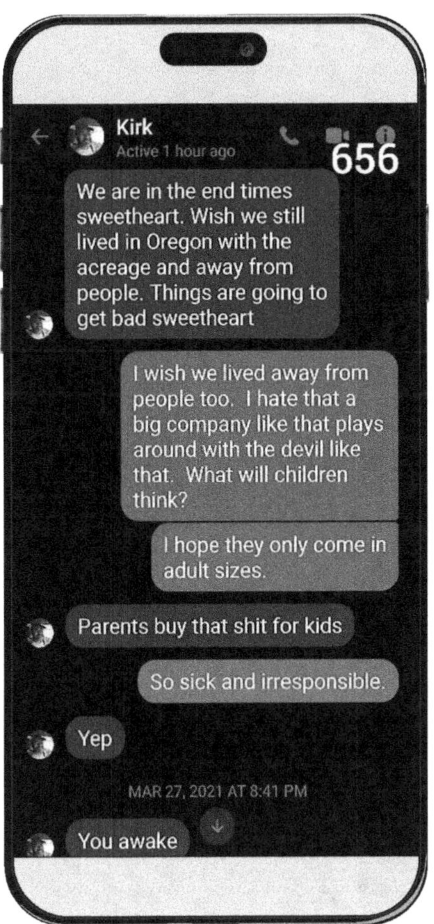
Kirk
Active 1 hour ago
656
We are in the end times sweetheart. Wish we still lived in Oregon with the acreage and away from people. Things are going to get bad sweetheart
I wish we lived away from people too. I hate that a big company like that plays around with the devil like that. What will children think?
I hope they only come in adult sizes.
Parents buy that shit for kids
So sick and irresponsible.
Yep
MAR 27, 2021 AT 8:41 PM
You awake

Kirk
Active 1 hour ago
657
Yep. Just having my dressing changed
Ranch or French?
Lol italian!!
I got some italian dressing for you
Lol. Gross
I know eww
You getting ready for bed?
Yep...took my medicine
Good boy
You listening to x22 or not because of the weekend?

Kirk
Active 1 hour ago
658
Its on tomorrow
Ah
How was your day sweetheart
It was a day.
Lol
Poor girl
Nah, it was ok
I've had worse.
I know
Im laying here in my underware onder the fan on the bed
Awww. Another very hot night?

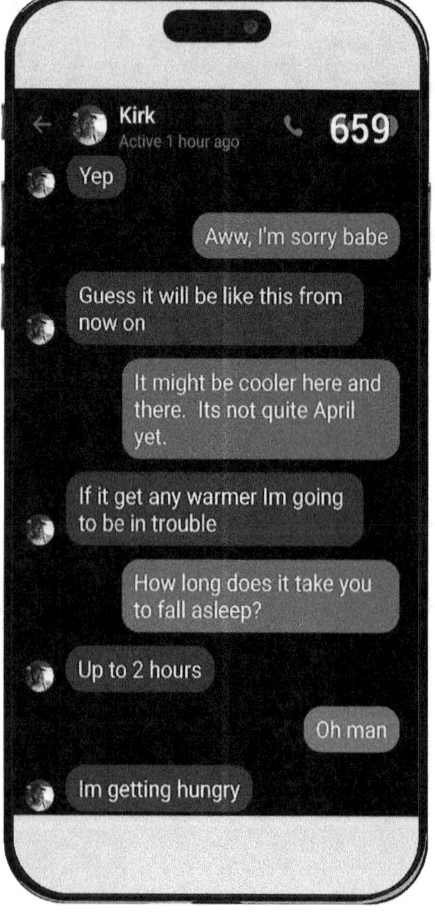

Kirk
Active 1 hour ago
659
Yep
Aww, I'm sorry babe
Guess it will be like this from now on
It might be cooler here and there. Its not quite April yet.
If it get any warmer Im going to be in trouble
How long does it take you to fall asleep?
Up to 2 hours
Oh man
Im getting hungry

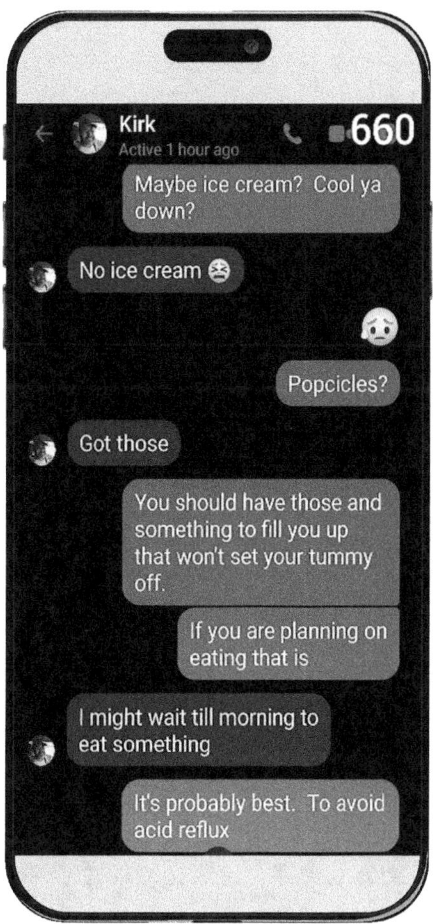
Kirk
Active 1 hour ago
660
Maybe ice cream? Cool ya down?
No ice cream 😣
Popcicles?
Got those
You should have those and something to fill you up that won't set your tummy off.
If you are planning on eating that is
I might wait till morning to eat something
It's probably best. To avoid acid reflux

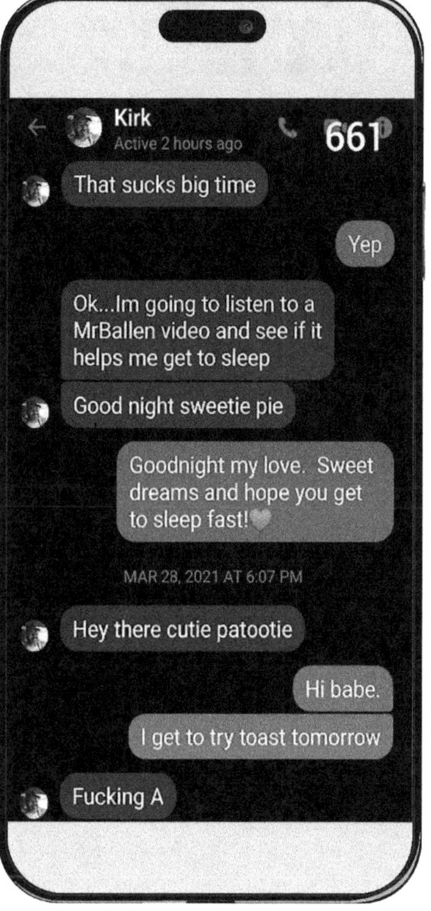
Kirk
Active 2 hours ago
661
That sucks big time
Yep
Ok...Im going to listen to a MrBallen video and see if it helps me get to sleep
Good night sweetie pie
Goodnight my love. Sweet dreams and hope you get to sleep fast!🤍
MAR 28, 2021 AT 6:07 PM
Hey there cutie patootie
Hi babe.
I get to try toast tomorrow
Fucking A

Kirk
Active 1 hour ago
662
Awesome huh? I'm excited. I'm so hungry. I was craving bacon and eggs this morning so Dr w said I could take my stomach for a spin.
I hope your tummy takes you for a Sunday drive
Me too.
Geez I'm hungry
I was telling mom, if I start eating well they allow family to bring in food from outside. Like whatever we want as long as we are able to eat it.
Thats a good sign
Grilled cheese lol
With bacon

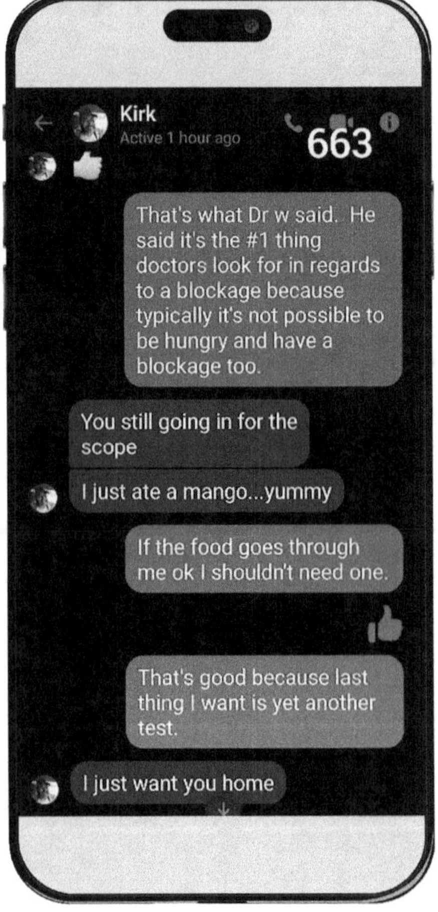
Kirk
Active 1 hour ago
663
That's what Dr w said. He said it's the #1 thing doctors look for in regards to a blockage because typically it's not possible to be hungry and have a blockage too.
You still going in for the scope
I just ate a mango...yummy
If the food goes through me ok I shouldn't need one.
That's good because last thing I want is yet another test.
I just want you home

Kirk
Active 1 hour ago
664
Me too my love.
I want my life with you back.
I found some paydirt for $110 gauranteed 1.5g
Oh cool did you buy it?
No...was going to ask you first
Oh go for it babe
Is it a monthly subscription?
No
Ok. I say get it hunni.
Ok...thank you

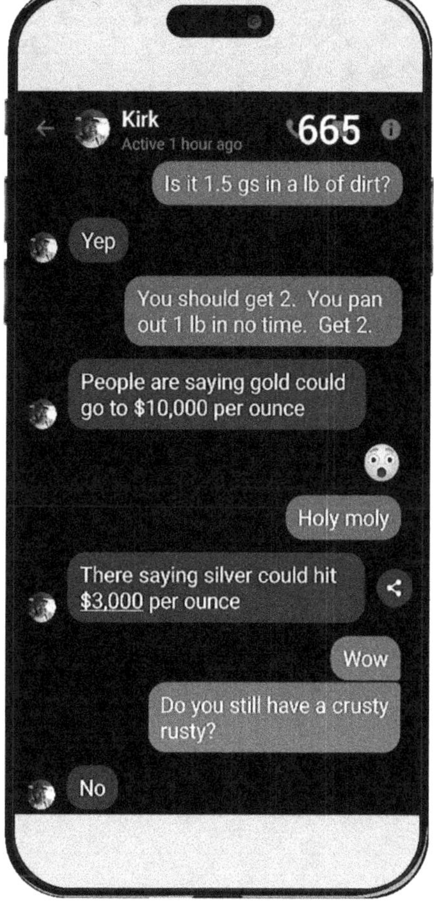
Kirk
Active 1 hour ago
665
Is it 1.5 gs in a lb of dirt?
Yep
You should get 2. You pan out 1 lb in no time. Get 2.
People are saying gold could go to $10,000 per ounce
Holy moly
There saying silver could hit $3,000 per ounce
Wow
Do you still have a crusty rusty?
No

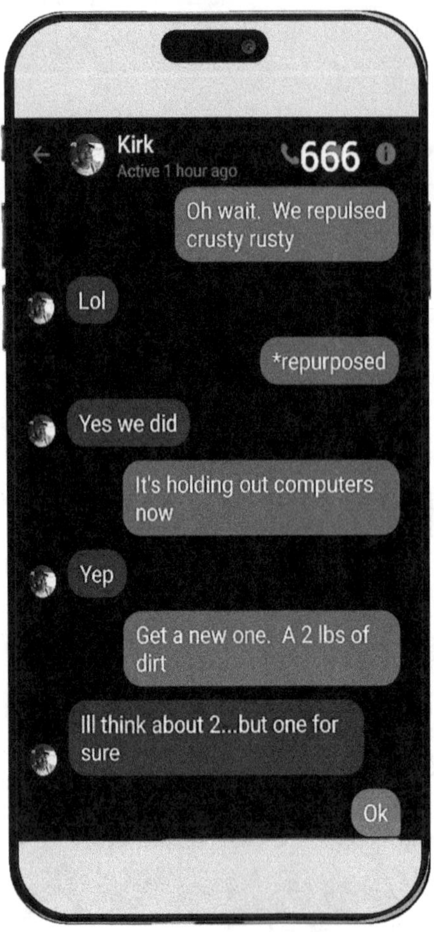

Kirk
Active 1 hour ago
666
Oh wait. We repulsed crusty rusty
Lol
*repurposed
Yes we did
It's holding out computers now
Yep
Get a new one. A 2 lbs of dirt
Ill think about 2...but one for sure
Ok

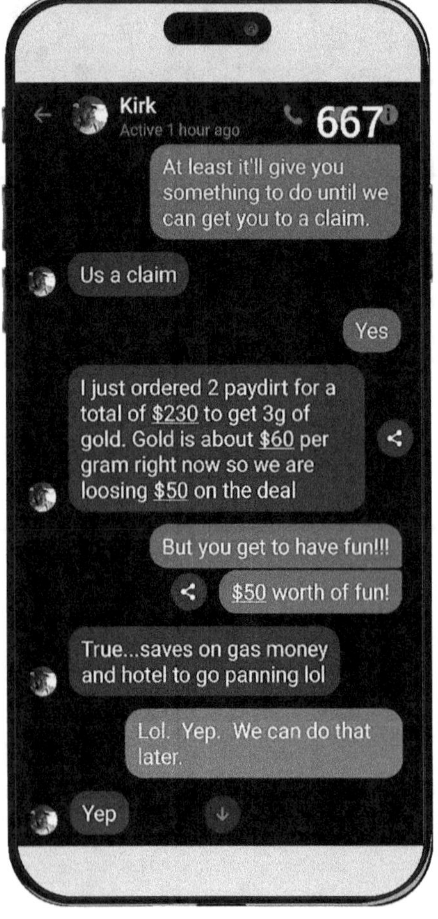

Kirk
Active 1 hour ago
667
At least it'll give you something to do until we can get you to a claim.
Us a claim
Yes
I just ordered 2 paydirt for a total of $230 to get 3g of gold. Gold is about $60 per gram right now so we are loosing $50 on the deal
But you get to have fun!!!
$50 worth of fun!
True...saves on gas money and hotel to go panning lol
Lol. Yep. We can do that later.
Yep

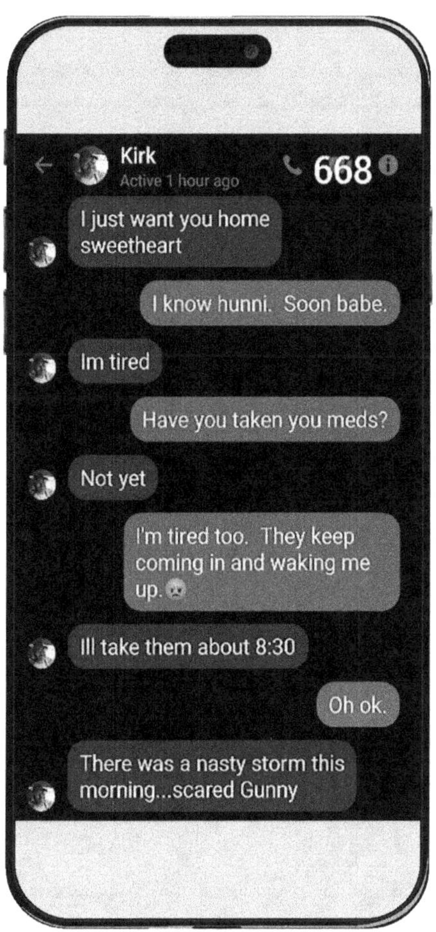

Kirk
Active 1 hour ago
668
I just want you home sweetheart
I know hunni. Soon babe.
Im tired
Have you taken you meds?
Not yet
I'm tired too. They keep coming in and waking me up.
Ill take them about 8:30
Oh ok.
There was a nasty storm this morning...scared Gunny

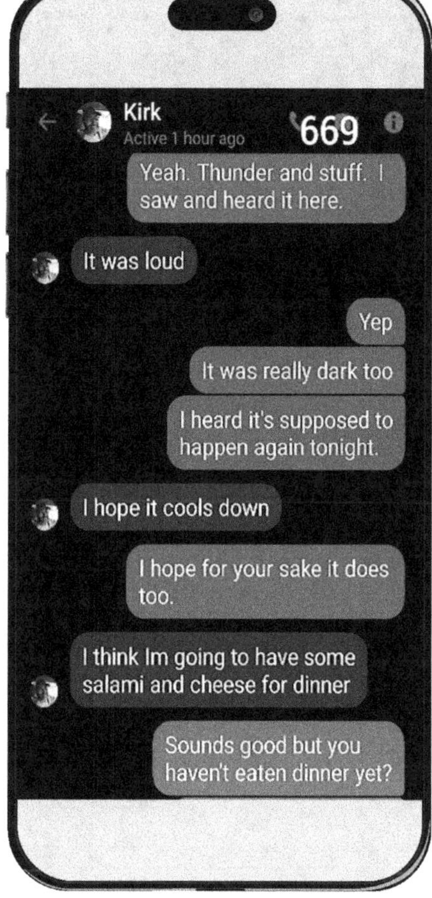

Kirk
Active 1 hour ago
669
Yeah. Thunder and stuff. I saw and heard it here.
It was loud
Yep
It was really dark too
I heard it's supposed to happen again tonight.
I hope it cools down
I hope for your sake it does too.
I think Im going to have some salami and cheese for dinner
Sounds good but you haven't eaten dinner yet?

Kirk
Active 1 hour ago
670
I need to get home and take care of my hubby. You need to eat by 6.
Yep
MAR 29, 2021 AT 1:09 AM
You awake
MAR 29, 2021 AT 1:50 AM
Yes
I had output from my bag tonight.
I love you
I love you too. Why up so late?
Im having trouble sleeping....you had output? Awesome!

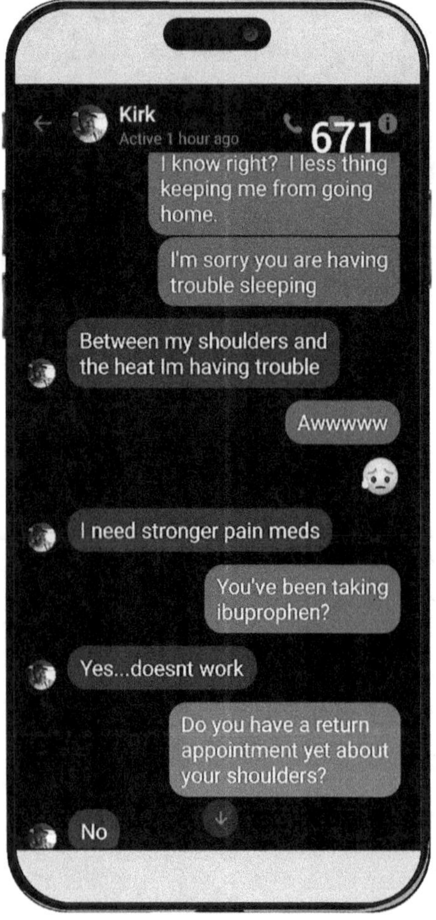
Kirk
Active 1 hour ago
671
I know right? I less thing keeping me from going home.
I'm sorry you are having trouble sleeping
Between my shoulders and the heat Im having trouble
Awwww
I need stronger pain meds
You've been taking ibuprophen?
Yes...doesnt work
Do you have a return appointment yet about your shoulders?
No

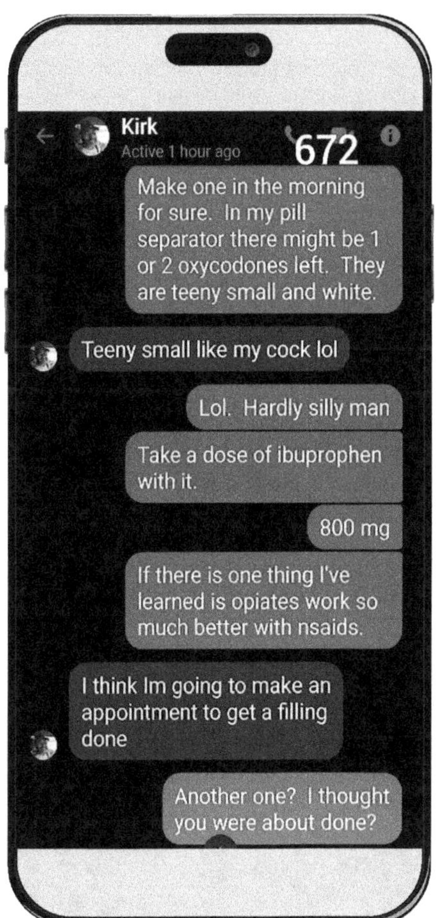
Kirk
Active 1 hour ago
672
Make one in the morning for sure. In my pill separator there might be 1 or 2 oxycodones left. They are teeny small and white.
Teeny small like my cock lol
Lol. Hardly silly man
Take a dose of ibuprophen with it.
800 mg
If there is one thing I've learned is opiates work so much better with nsaids.
I think Im going to make an appointment to get a filling done
Another one? I thought you were about done?

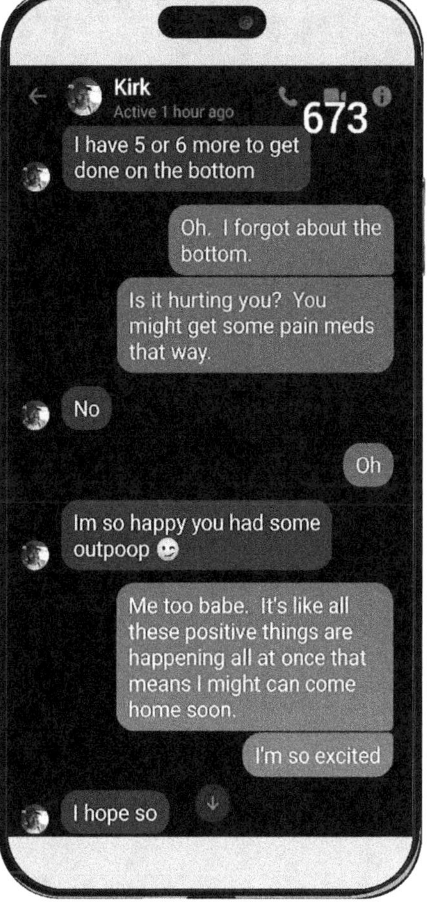
Kirk
Active 1 hour ago
673
I have 5 or 6 more to get done on the bottom
Oh. I forgot about the bottom.
Is it hurting you? You might get some pain meds that way.
No
Oh
Im so happy you had some outpoop
Me too babe. It's like all these positive things are happening all at once that means I might can come home soon.
I'm so excited
I hope so

Kirk
Active 1 hour ago
674
When I wrote you back what were you doing? Youtube?
You got a few packages from china
Cool.
Yep
Always love cheap shit from China lol
I had just gotten up to pee when I saw your message.
I got up a few minutes before I sent that
Are you in bed or the den?
Bed...under the fan
Ah. Makes sense.

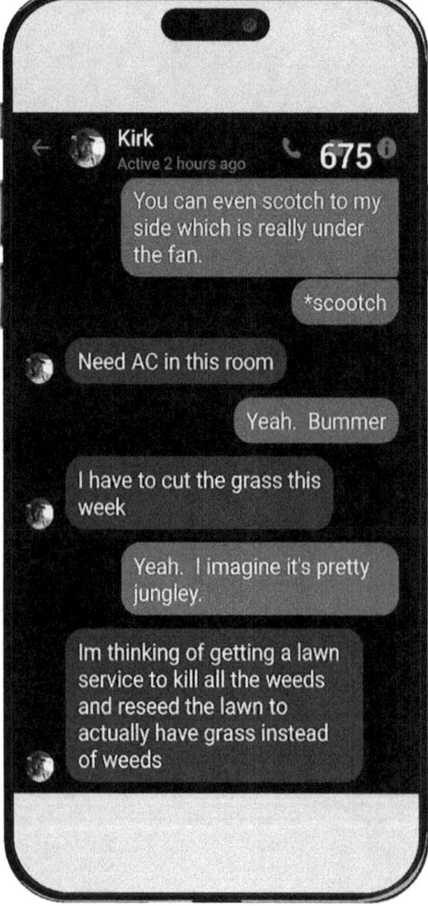
Kirk
Active 2 hours ago
675
You can even scotch to my side which is really under the fan.
*scootch
Need AC in this room
Yeah. Bummer
I have to cut the grass this week
Yeah. I imagine it's pretty jungley.
Im thinking of getting a lawn service to kill all the weeds and reseed the lawn to actually have grass instead of weeds

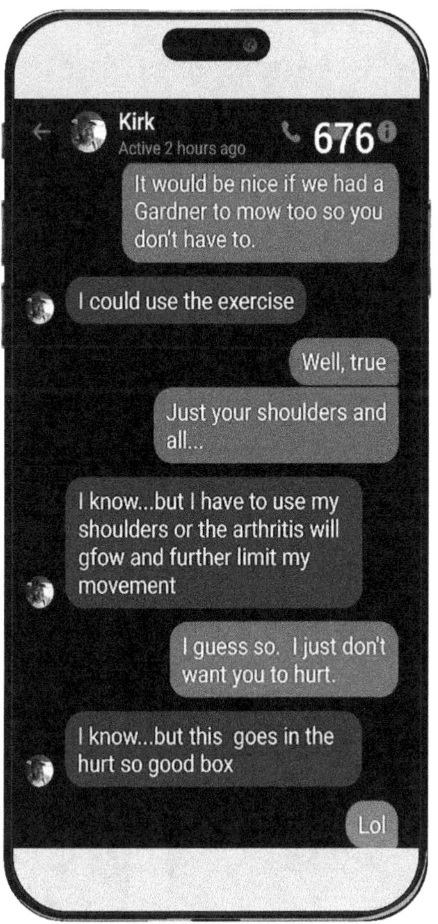

Kirk
Active 2 hours ago
676
It would be nice if we had a Gardner to mow too so you don't have to.
I could use the exercise
Well, true
Just your shoulders and all...
I know...but I have to use my shoulders or the arthritis will gfow and further limit my movement
I guess so. I just don't want you to hurt.
I know...but this goes in the hurt so good box
Lol

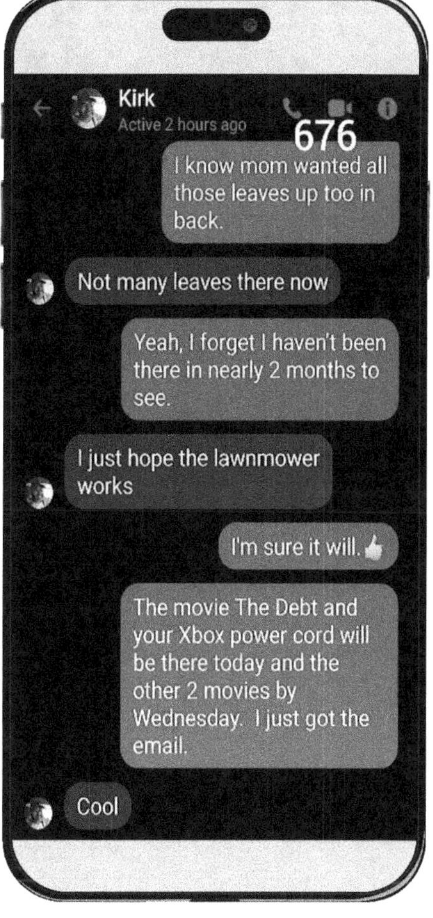

Kirk
Active 2 hours ago
676
I know mom wanted all those leaves up too in back.
Not many leaves there now
Yeah, I forget I haven't been there in nearly 2 months to see.
I just hope the lawnmower works
I'm sure it will.
The movie The Debt and your Xbox power cord will be there today and the other 2 movies by Wednesday. I just got the email.
Cool

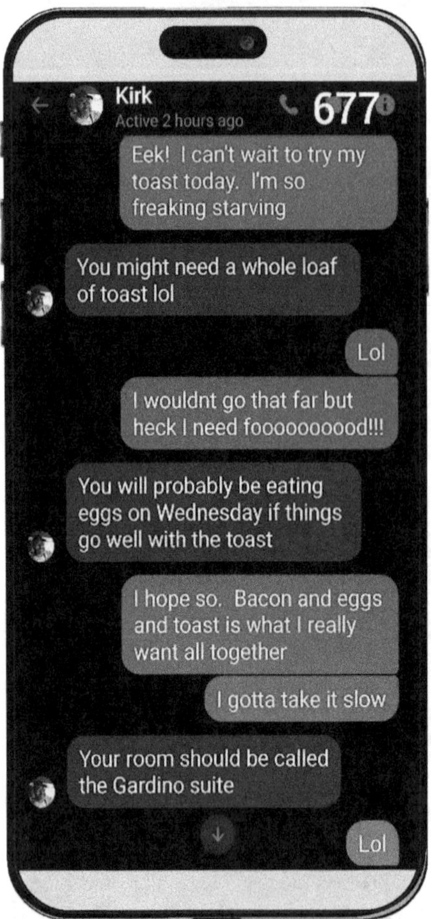

Kirk
Active 2 hours ago
677
Eek! I can't wait to try my toast today. I'm so freaking starving
You might need a whole loaf of toast lol
Lol
I wouldnt go that far but heck I need fooooooooood!!!
You will probably be eating eggs on Wednesday if things go well with the toast
I hope so. Bacon and eggs and toast is what I really want all together
I gotta take it slow
Your room should be called the Gardino suite
Lol

Kirk
Active 2 hours ago
678
Totally
Im going to watch some youtube now
Ok sweetie. Me too. Try and rest later if you can. I love you.
Love you too
MAR 29, 2021 AT 7:21 AM
You awake
Yep
Just had my very first food. A Graham cracker
Need a favor. Can you pay a toll for me on the DriveERT like you did before

11:42
679
Kirk
Active 2 hours ago
Its not letting me pay with my debit card
Sure. Let me see if I can remember. I know I got an email after I did it last time.
Take a screenshot.
Screenshot of what
The bill. Theres a bill like last time, right?

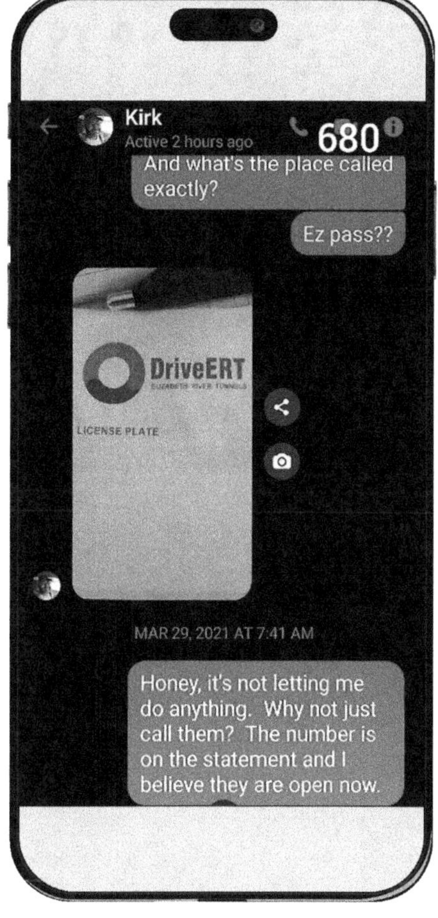

Kirk
Active 2 hours ago
680
And what's the place called exactly?
Ez pass??
DriveERT
ELIZABETH RIVER TUNNELS
LICENSE PLATE
MAR 29, 2021 AT 7:41 AM
Honey, it's not letting me do anything. Why not just call them? The number is on the statement and I believe they are open now.

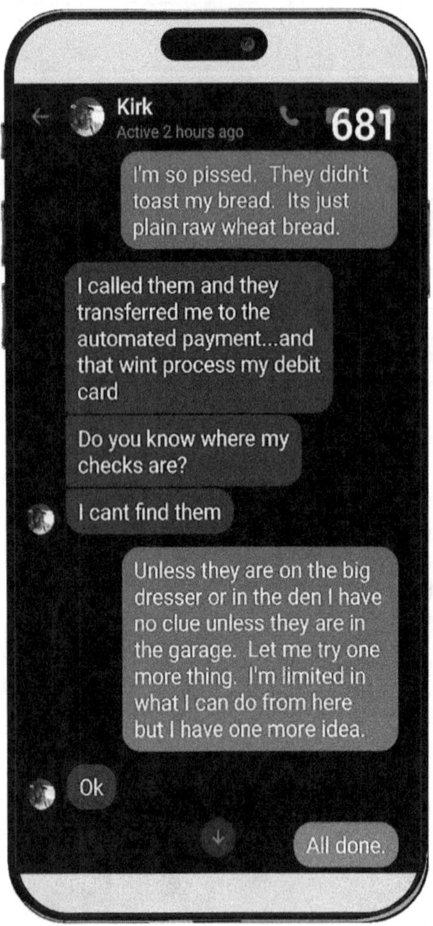

Kirk
Active 2 hours ago
681
I'm so pissed. They didn't toast my bread. Its just plain raw wheat bread.
I called them and they transferred me to the automated payment...and that wint process my debit card
Do you know where my checks are?
I cant find them
Unless they are on the big dresser or in the den I have no clue unless they are in the garage. Let me try one more thing. I'm limited in what I can do from here but I have one more idea.
Ok
All done.

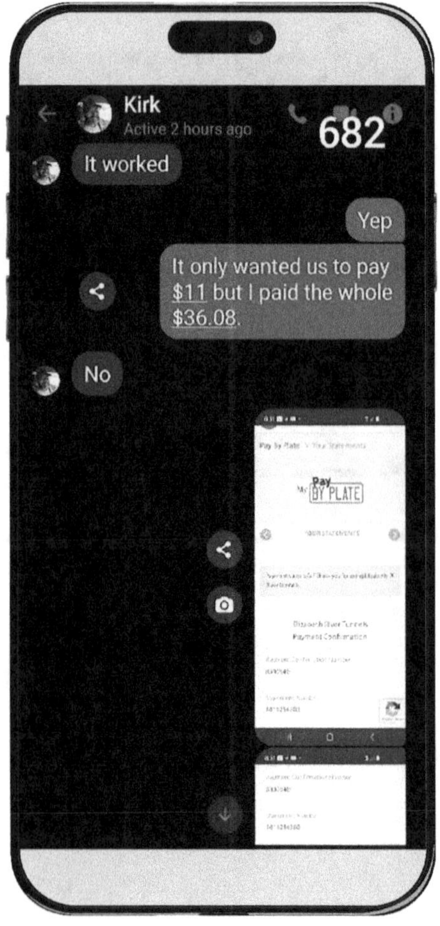

Kirk
Active 2 hours ago
682
It worked
Yep
It only wanted us to pay $11 but I paid the whole $36.08.
No

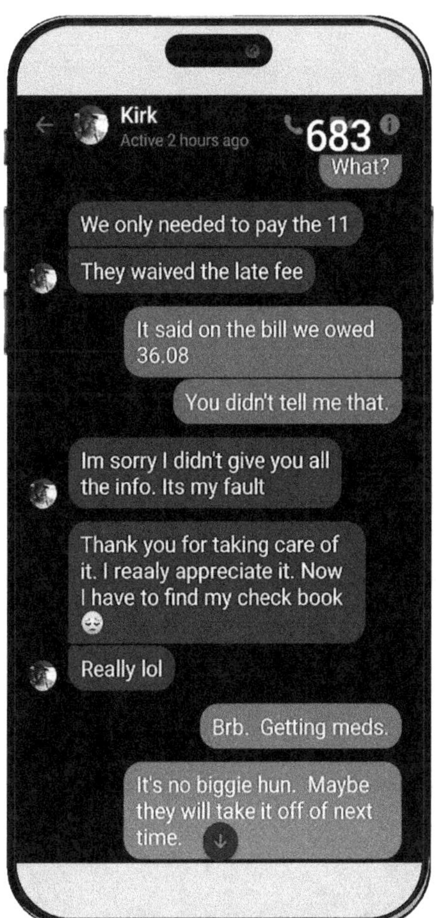
Kirk
Active 2 hours ago
683
What?
We only needed to pay the 11
They waived the late fee
It said on the bill we owed 36.08
You didn't tell me that.
Im sorry I didn't give you all the info. Its my fault
Thank you for taking care of it. I reaaly appreciate it. Now I have to find my check book
Really lol
Brb. Getting meds.
It's no biggie hun. Maybe they will take it off of next time.

Kirk
Active 2 hours ago
684
Im on the phone with godaddy about my email
The visit for tomorrow is a go.
Ok
Thats good
MAR 29, 2021 AT 8:20 PM
Let me know if you got your stuff. It says those 2 were delivered today.
Ill go check ...hold on
Got the power cord and the debt movie

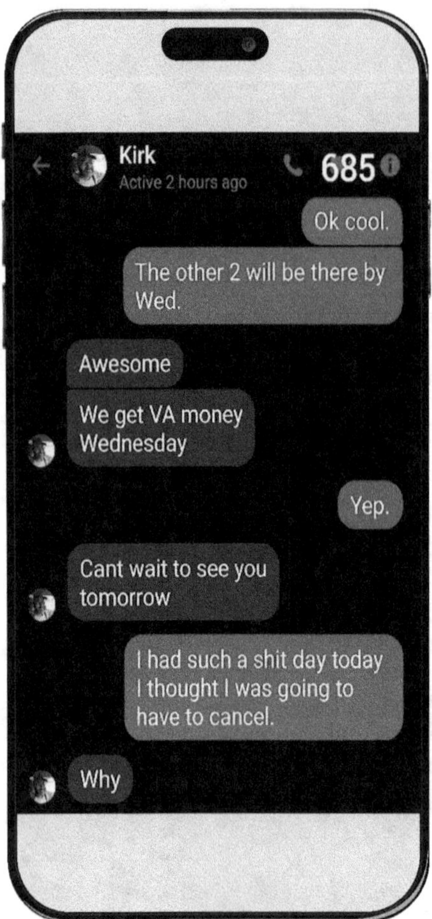

Kirk
Active 2 hours ago
685
Ok cool.
The other 2 will be there by Wed.
Awesome
We get VA money Wednesday
Yep.
Cant wait to see you tomorrow
I had such a shit day today I thought I was going to have to cancel.
Why

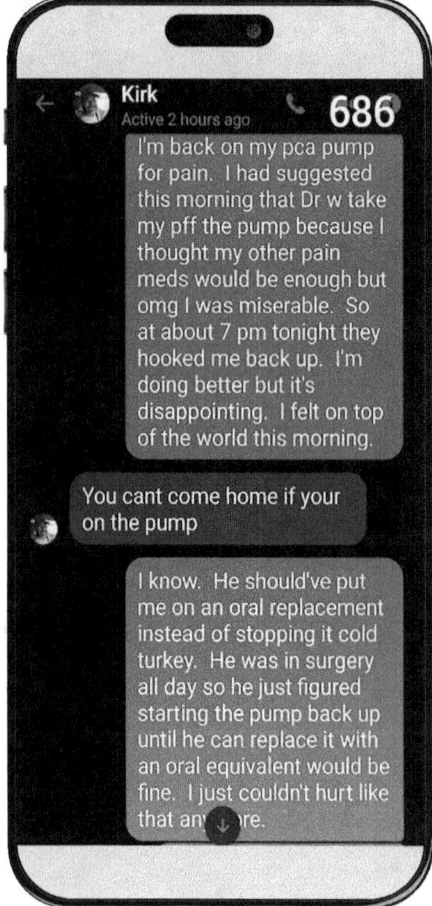

Kirk
Active 2 hours ago
686
I'm back on my pca pump for pain. I had suggested this morning that Dr w take my pff the pump because I thought my other pain meds would be enough but omg I was miserable. So at about 7 pm tonight they hooked me back up. I'm doing better but it's disappointing. I felt on top of the world this morning.
You cant come home if your on the pump
I know. He should've put me on an oral replacement instead of stopping it cold turkey. He was in surgery all day so he just figured starting the pump back up until he can replace it with an oral equivalent would be fine. I just couldn't hurt like that anymore.

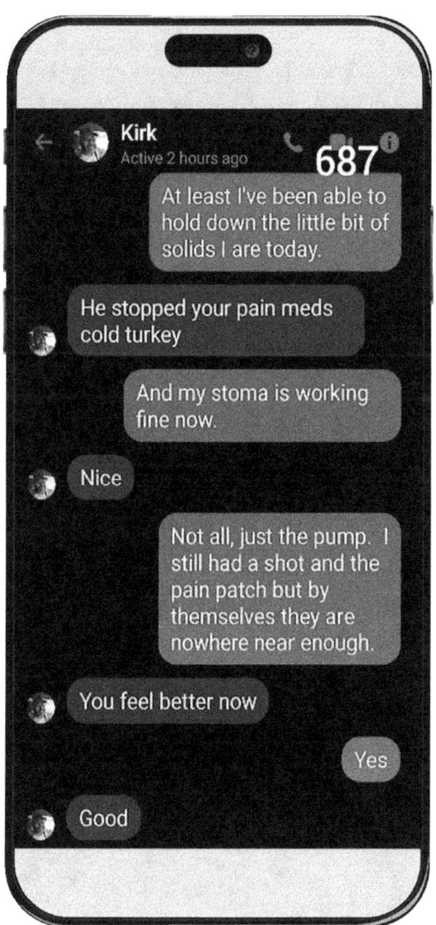

Kirk
Active 2 hours ago
687
At least I've been able to hold down the little bit of solids I are today.
He stopped your pain meds cold turkey
And my stoma is working fine now.
Nice
Not all, just the pump. I still had a shot and the pain patch but by themselves they are nowhere near enough.
You feel better now
Yes
Good

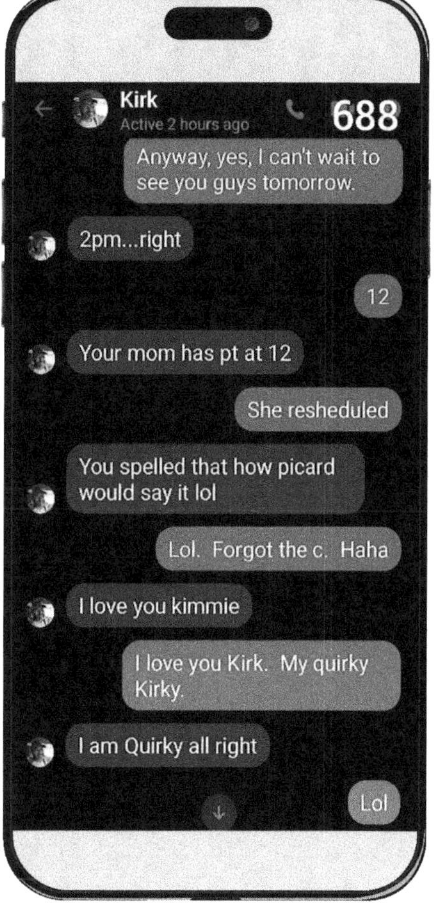

Kirk
Active 2 hours ago
688
Anyway, yes, I can't wait to see you guys tomorrow.
2pm...right
12
Your mom has pt at 12
She resheduled
You spelled that how picard would say it lol
Lol. Forgot the c. Haha
I love you kimmie
I love you Kirk. My quirky Kirky.
I am Quirky all right
Lol

Kirk
Active 2 hours ago
689
I hope I sleep better tonight
Me too. Did you ever fall asleep?
A little
Good
Not much
Oh. Bad.
Then I hope you can sleep tonight. Is it cooler?
Yes
Good, that'll help.
Yep
You going to bed now?
Gettin there

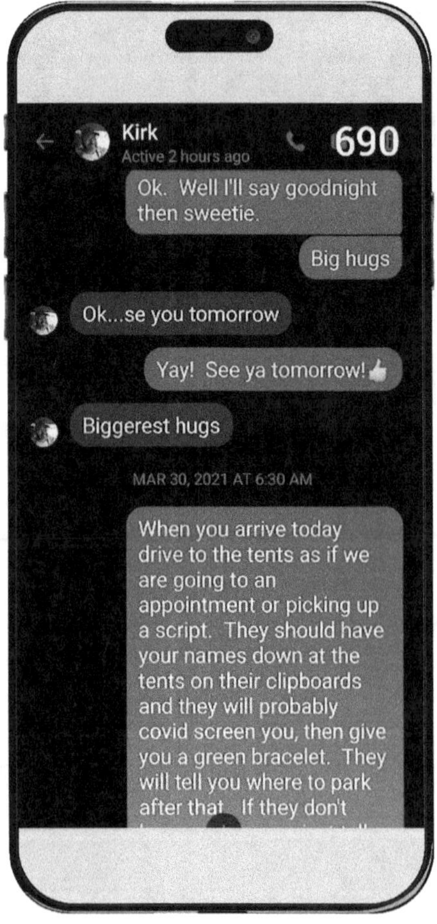
Kirk
Active 2 hours ago
690
Ok. Well I'll say goodnight then sweetie.
Big hugs
Ok...se you tomorrow
Yay! See ya tomorrow!
Biggerest hugs
MAR 30, 2021 AT 6:30 AM
When you arrive today drive to the tents as if we are going to an appointment or picking up a script. They should have your names down at the tents on their clipboards and they will probably covid screen you, then give you a green bracelet. They will tell you where to park after that. If they don't

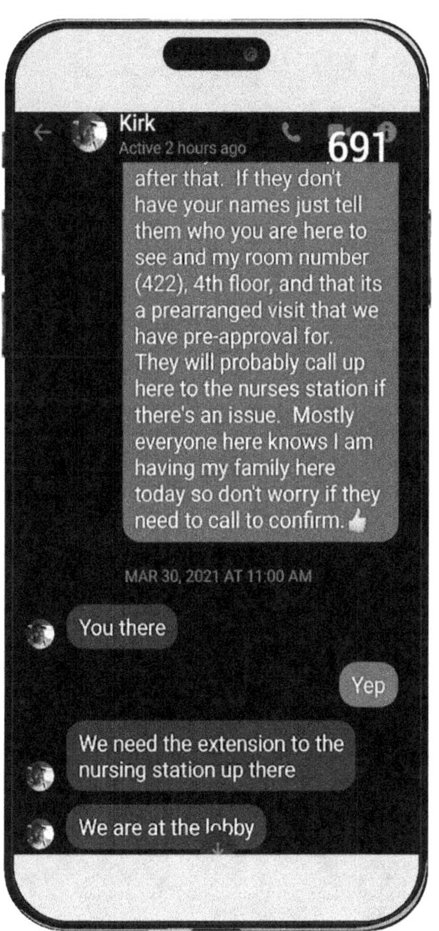

Kirk
Active 2 hours ago
691
after that. If they don't have your names just tell them who you are here to see and my room number (422), 4th floor, and that its a prearranged visit that we have pre-approval for. They will probably call up here to the nurses station if there's an issue. Mostly everyone here knows I am having my family here today so don't worry if they need to call to confirm.
MAR 30, 2021 AT 11:00 AM
You there
Yep
We need the extension to the nursing station up there
We are at the lobby

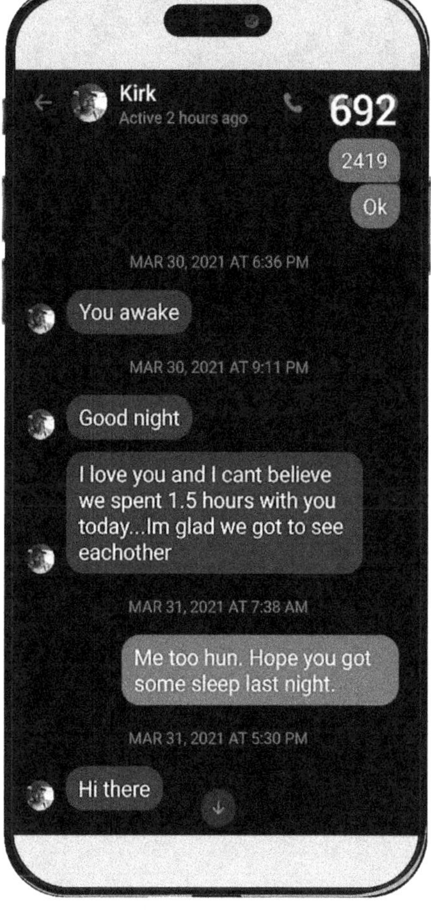

Kirk
Active 2 hours ago
692
2419
Ok
MAR 30, 2021 AT 6:36 PM
You awake
MAR 30, 2021 AT 9:11 PM
Good night
I love you and I cant believe we spent 1.5 hours with you today...Im glad we got to see eachother
MAR 31, 2021 AT 7:38 AM
Me too hun. Hope you got some sleep last night.
MAR 31, 2021 AT 5:30 PM
Hi there

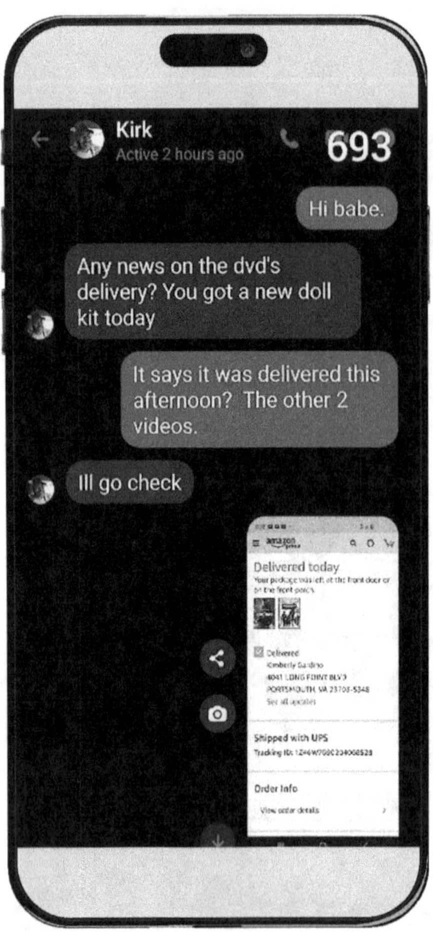
Kirk
Active 2 hours ago
693
Hi babe.
Any news on the dvd's delivery? You got a new doll kit today
It says it was delivered this afternoon? The other 2 videos.
Ill go check
Delivered today
Your package was left at the front door or on the front porch.
Delivered
Kimberly Gardino
4041 LONG POINT BLVD
PORTSMOUTH, VA 23703-5348
See all updates
Shipped with UPS
Tracking ID: 1Z46W790C234068528
Order Info
View order details

Kirk
Active 2 hours ago
694
Have you tried out your Xbox cable yet?
Not yet
Os that doll kit your gift from yourself
I'm not sure. One of my friends was giving me a couple kits to cheer me up so I don't know.
Its from a company. Not a person...or did she buy it and have it sent to you
No, I think it was from her own stash. I had assumed anyway. I'll see when I get home.
Ok

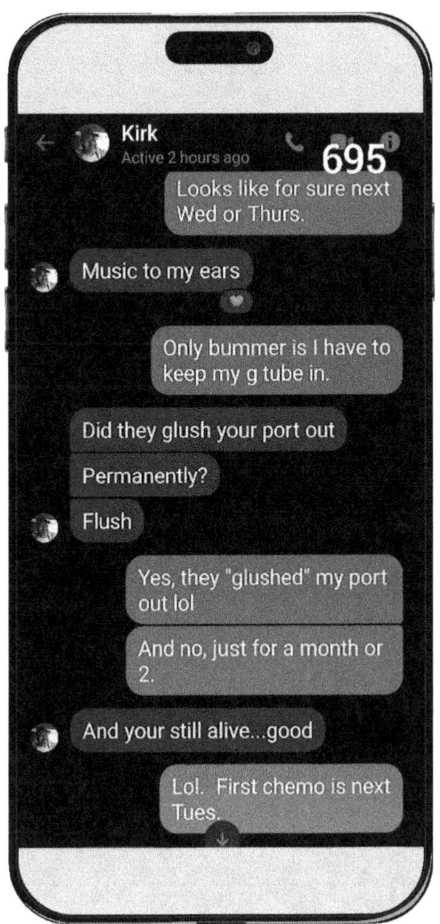

Kirk
Active 2 hours ago
695
Looks like for sure next Wed or Thurs.
Music to my ears
Only bummer is I have to keep my g tube in.
Did they glush your port out
Permanently?
Flush
Yes, they "glushed" my port out lol
And no, just for a month or 2.
And your still alive...good
Lol. First chemo is next Tues.

Kirk
Active 2 hours ago
696
Effing A
Not that I'm looking forward to chemo but I don't think they'd give it to me if I wasn't strong enough.
Your a strong girl...look at everything you've been through

Kirk
Active 2 hours ago
697
The food thing is gonna take a while. I'm getting my last tpn bag right now. Dr w said my appetite might come back after that.
Thank you babe.
Thank you for what sweetheart
For saying I was strong and stuff.
You are sweetheart
You have to be since your with me
Lol. No joke lol
I cut the grass today...frickin sore AF

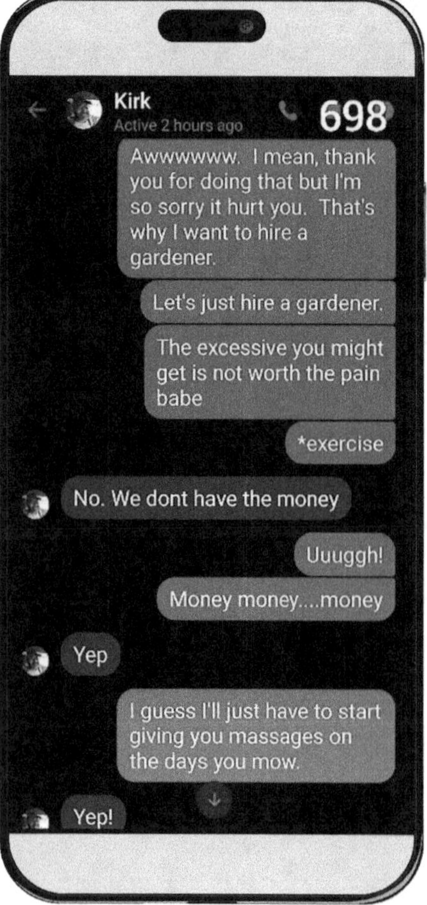
Kirk
Active 2 hours ago
698
Awwwwww. I mean, thank you for doing that but I'm so sorry it hurt you. That's why I want to hire a gardener.
Let's just hire a gardener.
The excessive you might get is not worth the pain babe
*exercise
No. We dont have the money
Uuuggh!
Money money....money
Yep
I guess I'll just have to start giving you massages on the days you mow.
Yep!

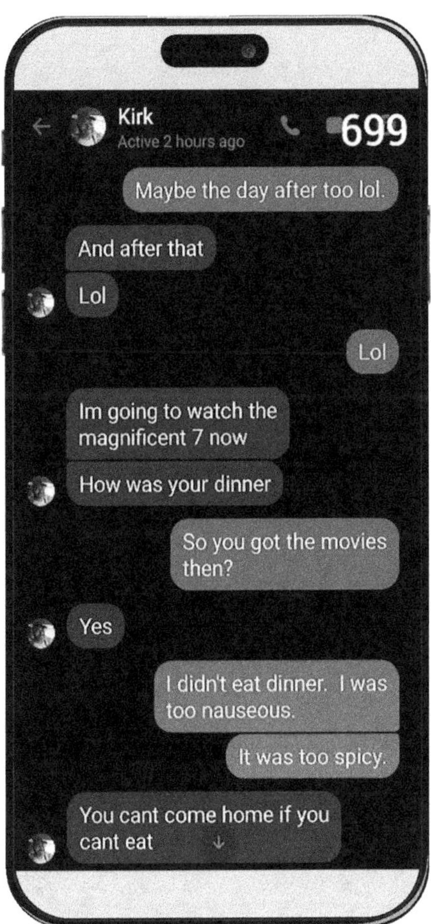
Kirk
Active 2 hours ago
699
Maybe the day after too lol.
And after that
Lol
Lol
Im going to watch the magnificent 7 now
How was your dinner
So you got the movies then?
Yes
I didn't eat dinner. I was too nauseous.
It was too spicy.
You cant come home if you cant eat

Kirk
Active 2 hours ago
700
They need to switch me to a bland diet.
Tell your doc
They need to stop sending me spaghetti and garlic bread.
I did.
This all just happened today.
Ok
If my meals were like the chicken yesterday it'd be ok.
Ok
Well see tomorrow. Enjoy your movie babe.

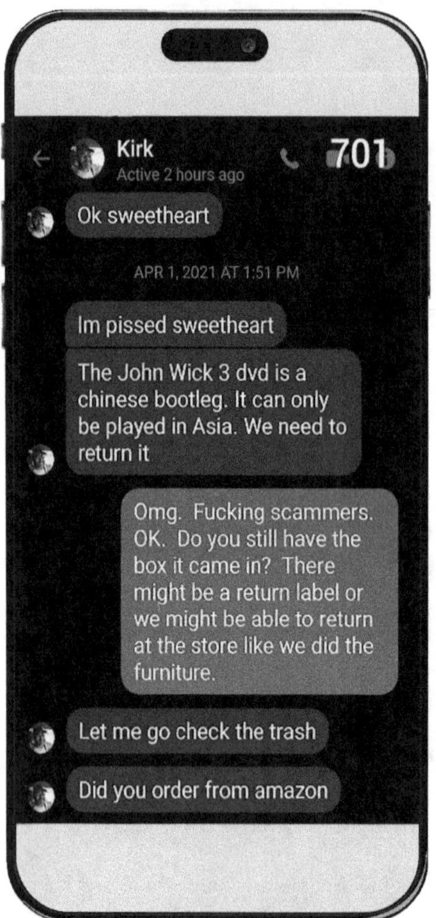

Kirk
Active 2 hours ago
701
Ok sweetheart
APR 1, 2021 AT 1:51 PM
Im pissed sweetheart
The John Wick 3 dvd is a chinese bootleg. It can only be played in Asia. We need to return it
Omg. Fucking scammers. OK. Do you still have the box it came in? There might be a return label or we might be able to return at the store like we did the furniture.
Let me go check the trash
Did you order from amazon

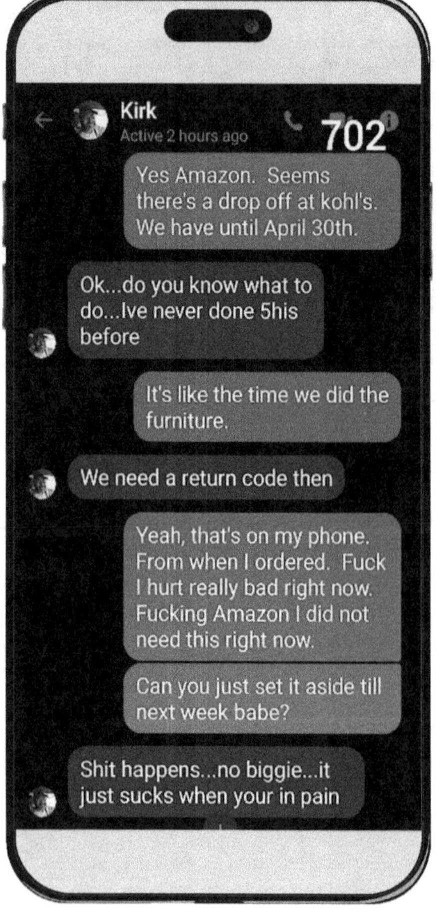

Kirk
Active 2 hours ago
702
Yes Amazon. Seems there's a drop off at kohl's. We have until April 30th.
Ok...do you know what to do...Ive never done 5his before
It's like the time we did the furniture.
We need a return code then
Yeah, that's on my phone. From when I ordered. Fuck I hurt really bad right now. Fucking Amazon I did not need this right now.
Can you just set it aside till next week babe?
Shit happens...no biggie...it just sucks when your in pain

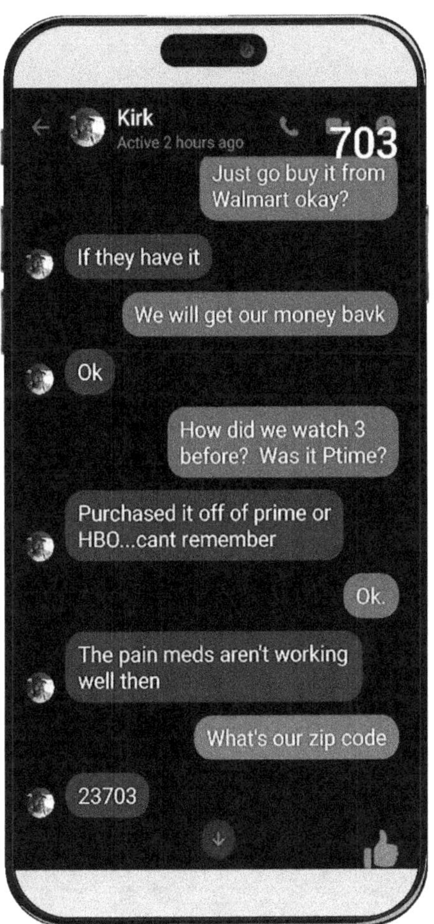

Kirk
Active 2 hours ago
703
Just go buy it from Walmart okay?
If they have it
We will get our money bavk
Ok
How did we watch 3 before? Was it Ptime?
Purchased it off of prime or HBO...cant remember
Ok.
The pain meds aren't working well then
What's our zip code
23703

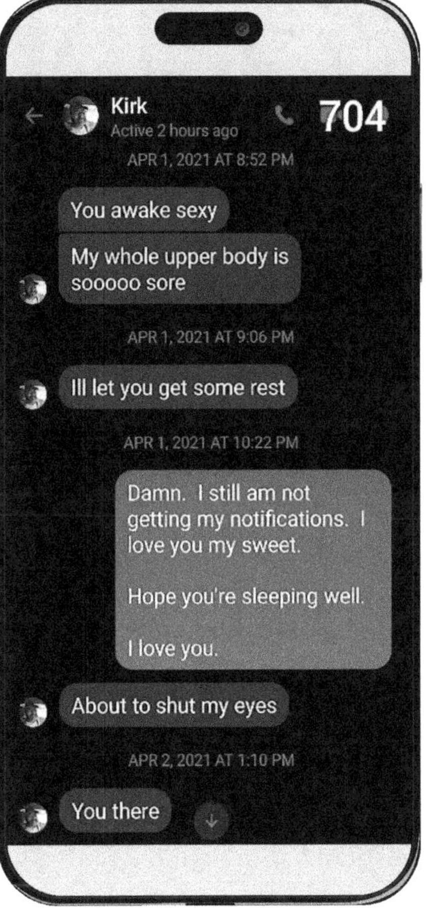

Kirk
Active 2 hours ago
704
APR 1, 2021 AT 8:52 PM
You awake sexy
My whole upper body is sooooo sore
APR 1, 2021 AT 9:06 PM
Ill let you get some rest
APR 1, 2021 AT 10:22 PM
Damn. I still am not getting my notifications. I love you my sweet.
Hope you're sleeping well.
I love you.
About to shut my eyes
APR 2, 2021 AT 1:10 PM
You there

Kirk
Active 2 hours ago
705
Hi.
APR 2, 2021 AT 6:40 PM
Im getting ready to talk to Danil...talk in a couple hours
Ok babe.
I can talk now...Danil is going to church...Good Friday...which is my birthday
I was born on good Friday April 8, 1966
Ohh. I'm like wait, your birthday isn't until the 8th.
My spitshine email is going bye bye. Im going to let the account lapse and not renew it. Tried for 2 hours today to try and get it working and couldnt.

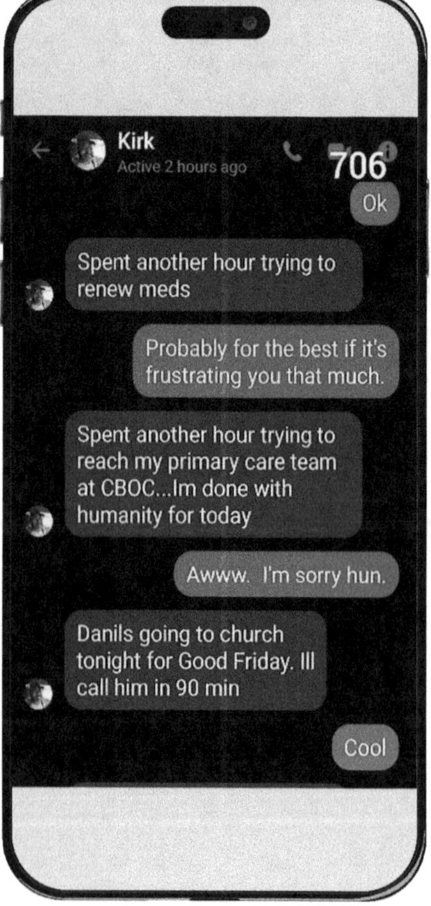
Kirk
Active 2 hours ago
706
Ok
Spent another hour trying to renew meds
Probably for the best if it's frustrating you that much.
Spent another hour trying to reach my primary care team at CBOC...Im done with humanity for today
Awww. I'm sorry hun.
Danils going to church tonight for Good Friday. Ill call him in 90 min
Cool

Kirk
Active 2 hours ago
707
Just started watching a new youtuber who does reaction videos...she cries in her reactions...poor girl lol
Cries from what?
Sad scenes things like that
Oh, she reacts to movies and stuff?
Yep
Her name is Natalie Gold...you should check her out...she is entertaining
Ok. Ive been watching history stuff.
You trying to learn something
Eff you.

Kirk
Active 2 hours ago
708
I know everything. So there.
Lol
Sure you do lol
British history fascinates me.
I know

Kirk
Active 2 hours ago
709
What's he doin?
Looking for something
His bone?
I think someone hacked my mp3 player.
Maybe
What? Hacked???
What happened?
When I was mowing the lawn songs were changing on it without me touching it, then the interface language changed on it..then all the songs got erased on it
Was it in a pocket maybe and was touching the sides

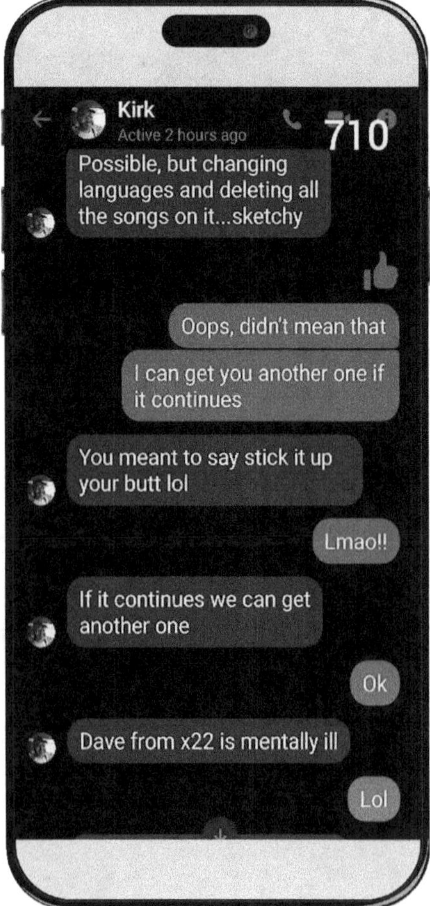

Kirk
Active 2 hours ago
710
Possible, but changing languages and deleting all the songs on it...sketchy
Oops, didn't mean that
I can get you another one if it continues
You meant to say stick it up your butt lol
Lmao!!
If it continues we can get another one
Ok
Dave from x22 is mentally ill
Lol

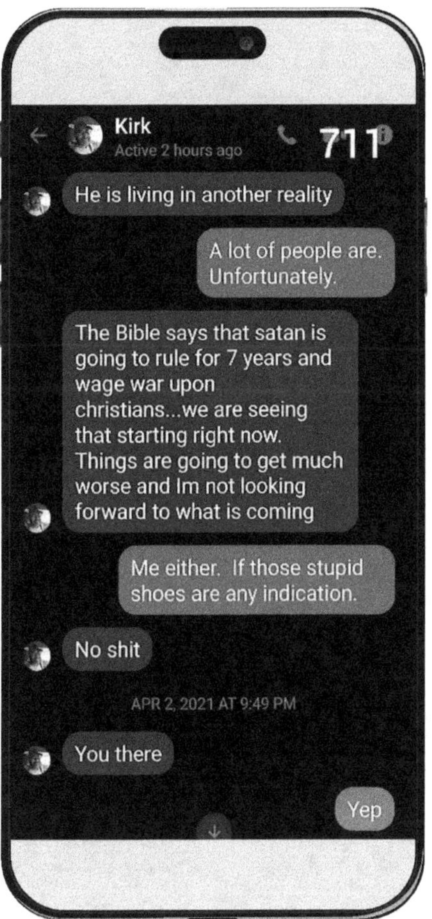

Kirk
Active 2 hours ago
711
He is living in another reality
A lot of people are. Unfortunately.
The Bible says that satan is going to rule for 7 years and wage war upon christians...we are seeing that starting right now. Things are going to get much worse and Im not looking forward to what is coming
Me either. If those stupid shoes are any indication.
No shit
APR 2, 2021 AT 9:49 PM
You there
Yep

Kirk
Active 2 hours ago
712
Where did you go earlier
I'm super nauseous.
Do you want to talk...or do you want to chill by yourself
I think I'm gonna try and sleep.
Ok...BJorn just messaged me
Cool. How is he?
Im just finding out
APR 3, 2021 AT 1:52 PM
Need your computer password
Im going to apply for a job in Norfolk

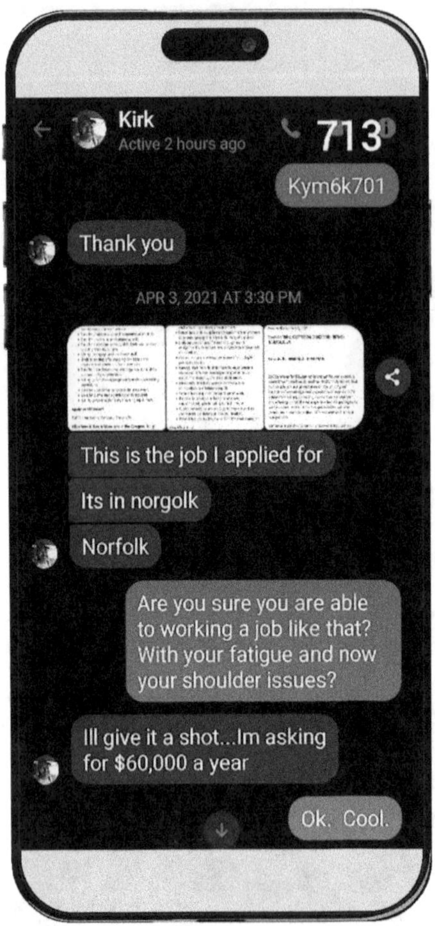

Kirk
Active 2 hours ago
713
Kym6k701
Thank you
APR 3, 2021 AT 3:30 PM
This is the job I applied for
Its in norgolk
Norfolk
Are you sure you are able to working a job like that? With your fatigue and now your shoulder issues?
Ill give it a shot...Im asking for $60,000 a year
Ok. Cool.

Kirk
Active 2 hours ago
715
Yeah
Dr W said my body is just waking up so I need to be patient.
Ok
You get better
I will.. 🤍🤍🤍
hugs and kisses
You might be coming home this week
Wed or Thurs is the plan. I have my last antibiotic on Wed.
Cool

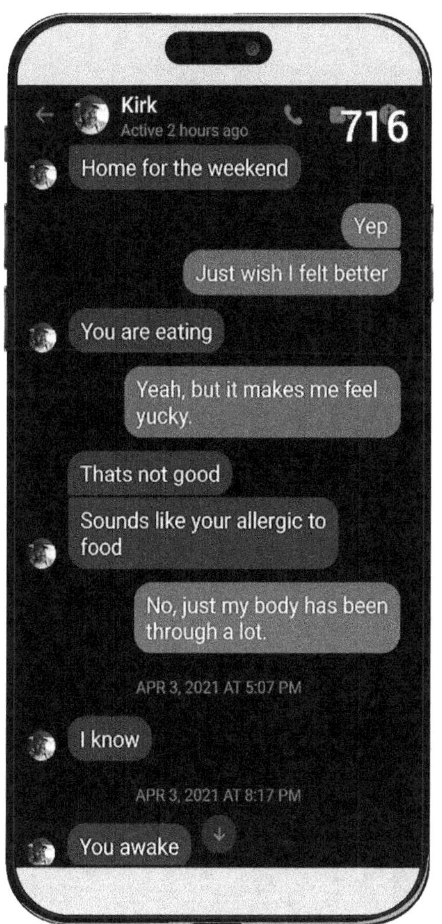

Kirk
Active 2 hours ago
716
Home for the weekend
Yep
Just wish I felt better
You are eating
Yeah, but it makes me feel yucky.
Thats not good
Sounds like your allergic to food
No, just my body has been through a lot.
APR 3, 2021 AT 5:07 PM
I know
APR 3, 2021 AT 8:17 PM
You awake

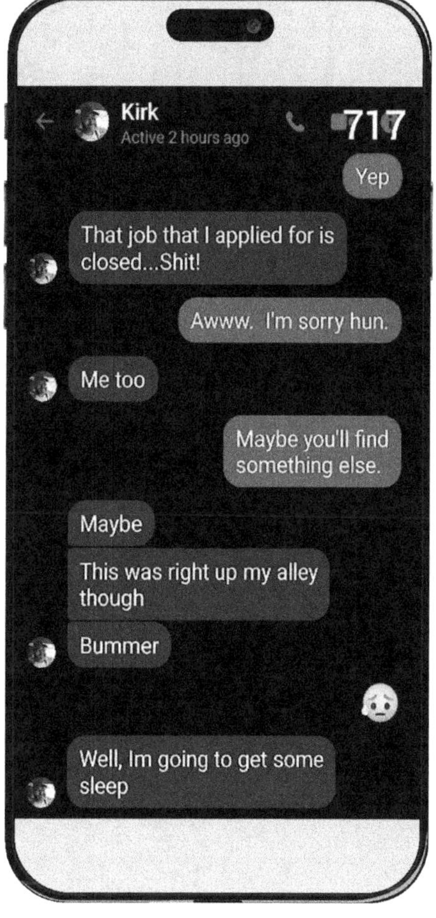

Kirk
Active 2 hours ago
717
Yep
That job that I applied for is closed...Shit!
Awww. I'm sorry hun.
Me too
Maybe you'll find something else.
Maybe
This was right up my alley though
Bummer
Well, Im going to get some sleep

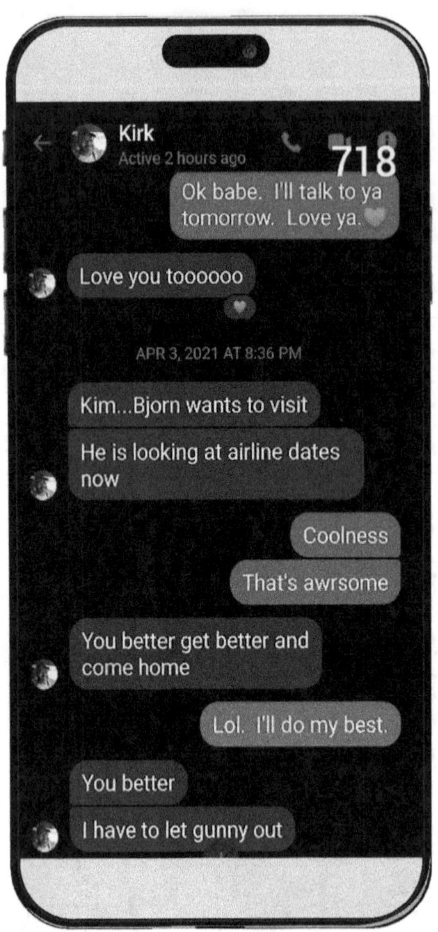

Kirk
Active 2 hours ago
718
Ok babe. I'll talk to ya tomorrow. Love ya.
Love you toooooo
APR 3, 2021 AT 8:36 PM
Kim...Bjorn wants to visit
He is looking at airline dates now
Coolness
That's awrsome
You better get better and come home
Lol. I'll do my best.
You better
I have to let gunny out

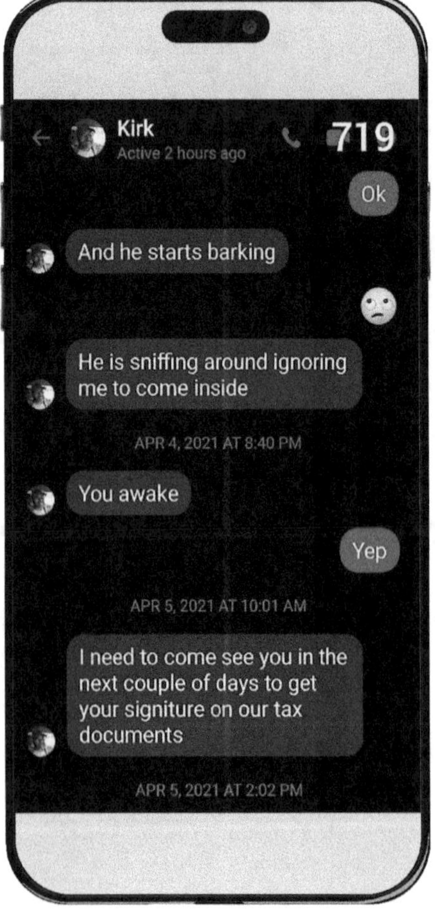

Kirk
Active 2 hours ago
719
Ok
And he starts barking
He is sniffing around ignoring me to come inside
APR 4, 2021 AT 8:40 PM
You awake
Yep
APR 5, 2021 AT 10:01 AM
I need to come see you in the next couple of days to get your signiture on our tax documents
APR 5, 2021 AT 2:02 PM

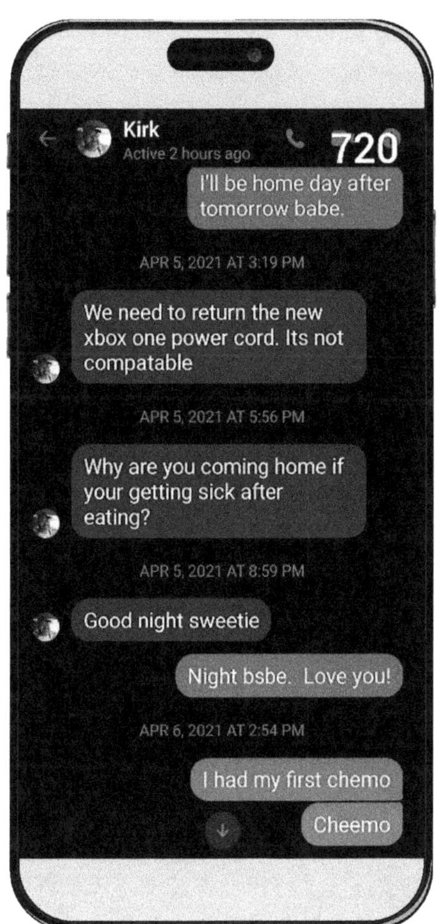
Kirk
Active 2 hours ago
720
I'll be home day after tomorrow babe.
APR 5, 2021 AT 3:19 PM
We need to return the new xbox one power cord. Its not compatable
APR 5, 2021 AT 5:56 PM
Why are you coming home if your getting sick after eating?
APR 5, 2021 AT 8:59 PM
Good night sweetie
Night bsbe. Love you!
APR 6, 2021 AT 2:54 PM
I had my first chemo
Cheemo

Kirk
Active 2 hours ago
721
How was it?
The benadryl is kicking my butt more than the cheemo.
Poor girl
I'll be ok.
I'm coming home tomorrow afternoon.
Awesome
I have this suction thing to help the infection heal faster.
Good. Are you eating
APR 6, 2021 AT 3:09 PM
I ate half a ham sandwich today.

Kirk
Active 2 hours ago
723
Wow!
APR 6, 2021 AT 9:29 PM
Goodnight babe
APR 6, 2021 AT 9:42 PM
Goodnight babeliscious
Im coming to get you tomorrow
Yay!!!!!!!
Im going to have to clean out the truck lol
Lol.
I hope you will be able to sleep upstairs

Kirk
Active 2 hours ago
724
Me too. I don't know of course but I'm gonna try. Maybe the first day or so downstairs but I'm for sure gonna try for our bed.
My doc is sending me tramadol for pain
Excellent!!!
I'm so glad. I hope it helps you like it helps mom.
I get about 4 to 5 hours of broken sleep a night
Awww, sweetie. And you need so much more than that. You are a 10 hour a night man.
Thats what she said
Lmao!!!!

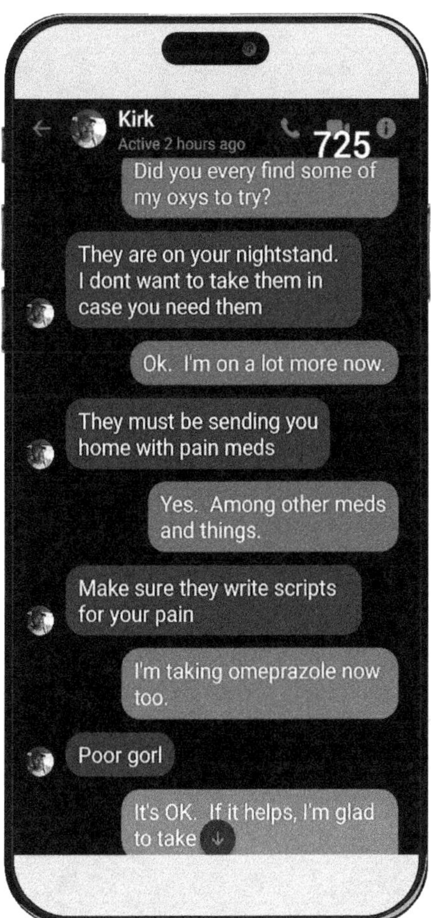

Kirk
Active 2 hours ago
725
Did you every find some of my oxys to try?
They are on your nightstand. I dont want to take them in case you need them
Ok. I'm on a lot more now.
They must be sending you home with pain meds
Yes. Among other meds and things.
Make sure they write scripts for your pain
I'm taking omeprazole now too.
Poor gorl
It's OK. If it helps, I'm glad to take

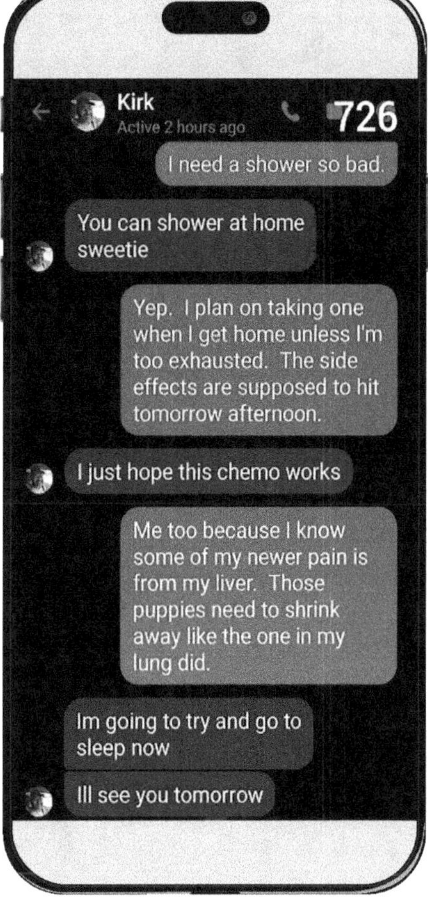

Kirk
Active 2 hours ago
726
I need a shower so bad.
You can shower at home sweetie
Yep. I plan on taking one when I get home unless I'm too exhausted. The side effects are supposed to hit tomorrow afternoon.
I just hope this chemo works
Me too because I know some of my newer pain is from my liver. Those puppies need to shrink away like the one in my lung did.
Im going to try and go to sleep now
Ill see you tomorrow

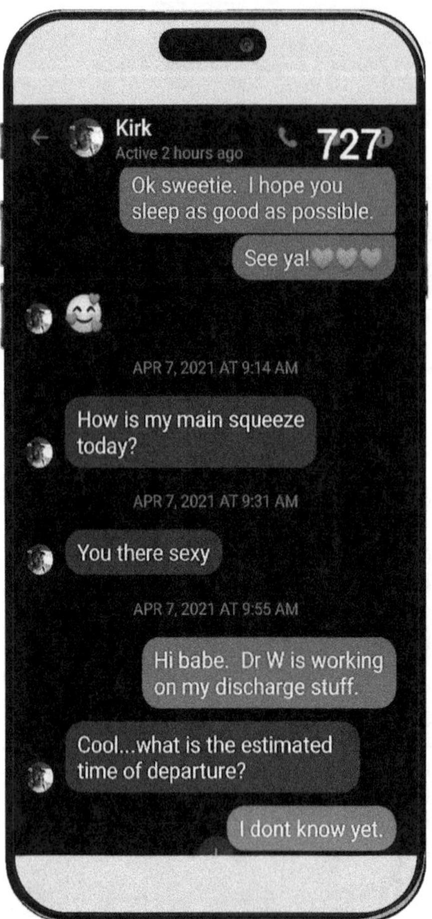

Kirk
Active 2 hours ago
727
Ok sweetie. I hope you sleep as good as possible.
See ya!
APR 7, 2021 AT 9:14 AM
How is my main squeeze today?
APR 7, 2021 AT 9:31 AM
You there sexy
APR 7, 2021 AT 9:55 AM
Hi babe. Dr W is working on my discharge stuff.
Cool...what is the estimated time of departure?
I dont know yet.

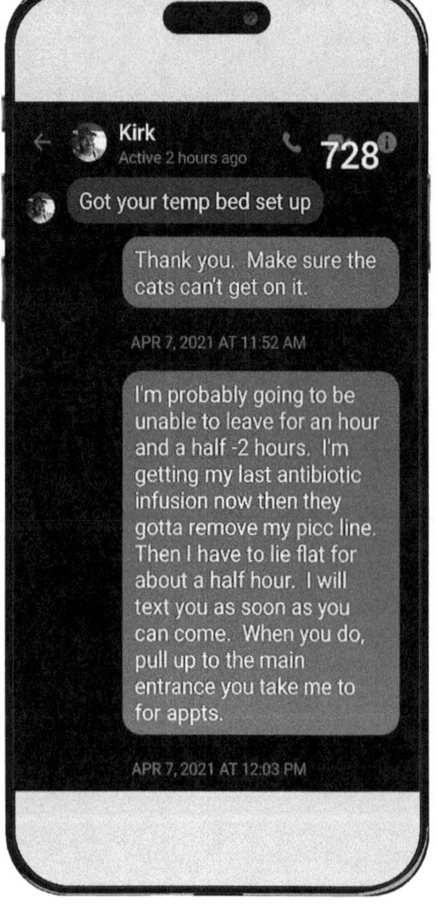

Kirk
Active 2 hours ago
728
Got your temp bed set up
Thank you. Make sure the cats can't get on it.
APR 7, 2021 AT 11:52 AM
I'm probably going to be unable to leave for an hour and a half -2 hours. I'm getting my last antibiotic infusion now then they gotta remove my picc line. Then I have to lie flat for about a half hour. I will text you as soon as you can come. When you do, pull up to the main entrance you take me to for appts.
APR 7, 2021 AT 12:03 PM

Kirk
Active 2 hours ago
729
Oh, mom wants to come too so you'll probably be driving her car.
Just finished talking with my dad for about an hour
Ok cool. Good talk?
Yep
Glad to hear it.
APR 7, 2021 AT 12:56 PM
Just had my picc line removed gotta stay Stull for 1/2 hour
For ahead and come.   Text me when you get here.
Come on forehead?
Go ahead

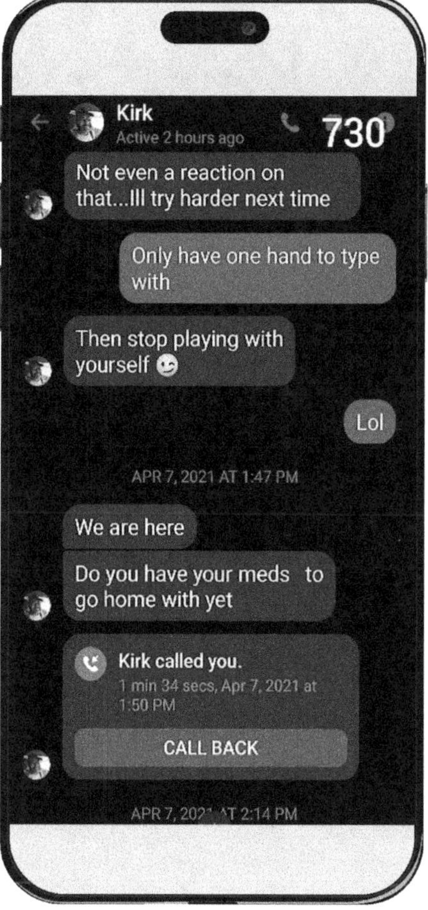
Kirk
Active 2 hours ago
730
Not even a reaction on that...Ill try harder next time
Only have one hand to type with
Then stop playing with yourself
Lol
APR 7, 2021 AT 1:47 PM
We are here
Do you have your meds   to go home with yet
Kirk called you.
1 min 34 secs, Apr 7, 2021 at 1:50 PM
CALL BACK
APR 7, 2021 AT 2:14 PM

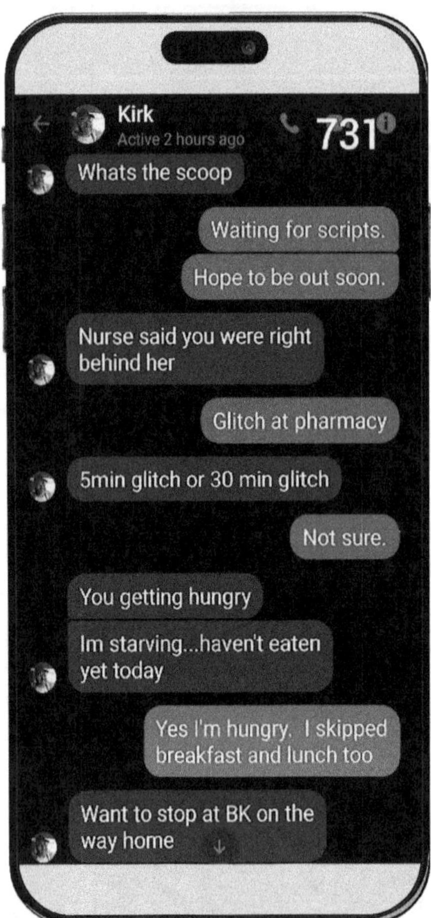
Kirk
Active 2 hours ago
731
Whats the scoop
Waiting for scripts.
Hope to be out soon.
Nurse said you were right behind her
Glitch at pharmacy
5min glitch or 30 min glitch
Not sure.
You getting hungry
Im starving...haven't eaten yet today
Yes I'm hungry. I skipped breakfast and lunch too
Want to stop at BK on the way home

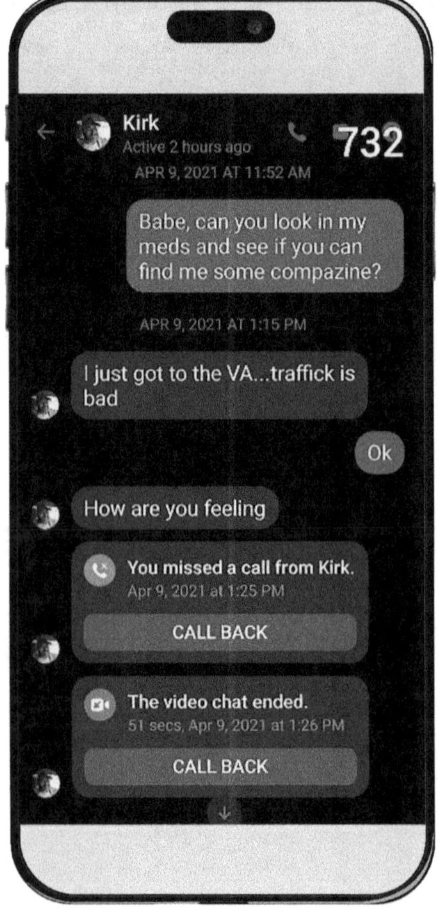
Kirk
Active 2 hours ago
732
APR 9, 2021 AT 11:52 AM
Babe, can you look in my meds and see if you can find me some compazine?
APR 9, 2021 AT 1:15 PM
I just got to the VA...traffick is bad
Ok
How are you feeling
You missed a call from Kirk.
Apr 9, 2021 at 1:25 PM
CALL BACK
The video chat ended.
51 secs, Apr 9, 2021 at 1:26 PM
CALL BACK

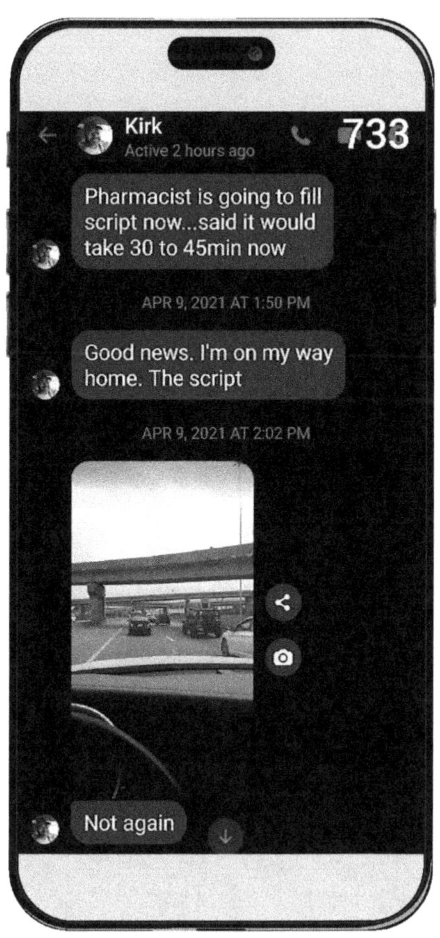
Kirk
Active 2 hours ago
733
Pharmacist is going to fill script now...said it would take 30 to 45min now
APR 9, 2021 AT 1:50 PM
Good news. I'm on my way home. The script
APR 9, 2021 AT 2:02 PM
Not again

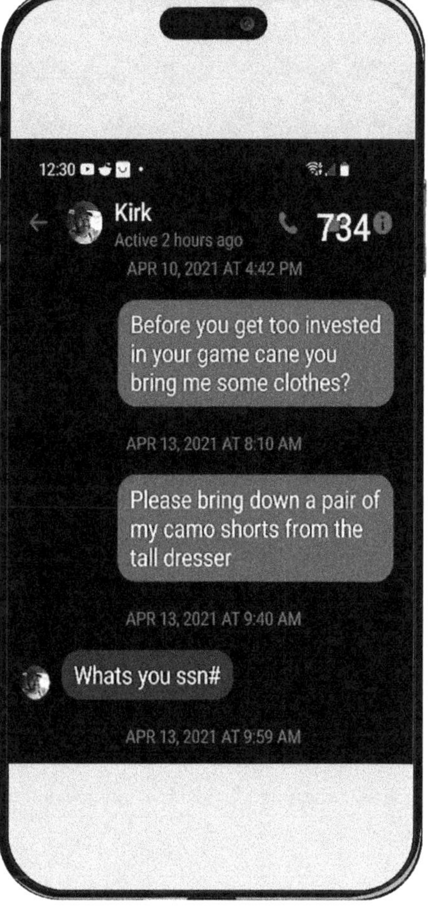
12:30
Kirk
Active 2 hours ago
734
APR 10, 2021 AT 4:42 PM
Before you get too invested in your game cane you bring me some clothes?
APR 13, 2021 AT 8:10 AM
Please bring down a pair of my camo shorts from the tall dresser
APR 13, 2021 AT 9:40 AM
Whats you ssn#
APR 13, 2021 AT 9:59 AM

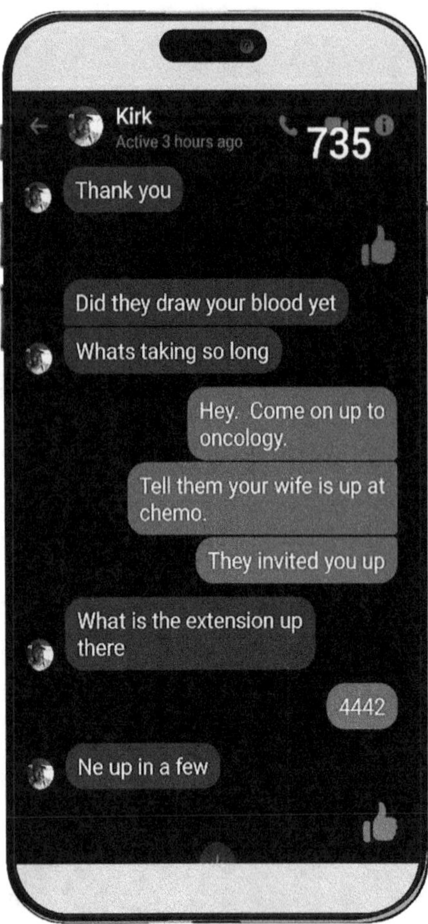

Kirk
Active 3 hours ago
735
Thank you
Did they draw your blood yet
Whats taking so long
Hey. Come on up to oncology.
Tell them your wife is up at chemo.
They invited you up
What is the extension up there
4442
Ne up in a few

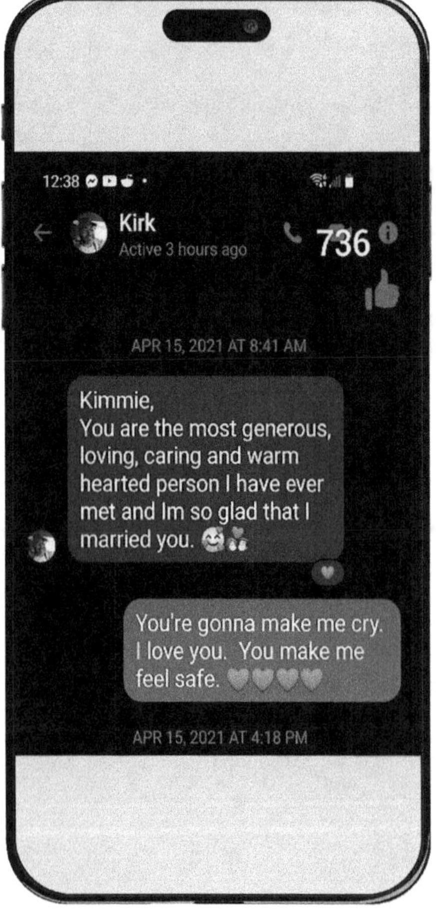

12:38
Kirk
Active 3 hours ago
736
APR 15, 2021 AT 8:41 AM
Kimmie,
You are the most generous, loving, caring and warm hearted person I have ever met and Im so glad that I married you.
You're gonna make me cry. I love you. You make me feel safe.
APR 15, 2021 AT 4:18 PM

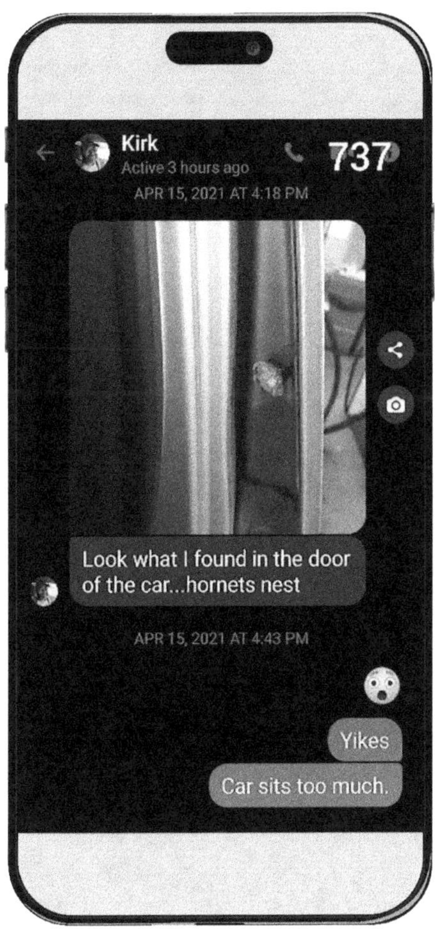
Kirk
Active 3 hours ago
737
APR 15, 2021 AT 4:18 PM
Look what I found in the door of the car...hornets nest
APR 15, 2021 AT 4:43 PM
Yikes
Car sits too much.

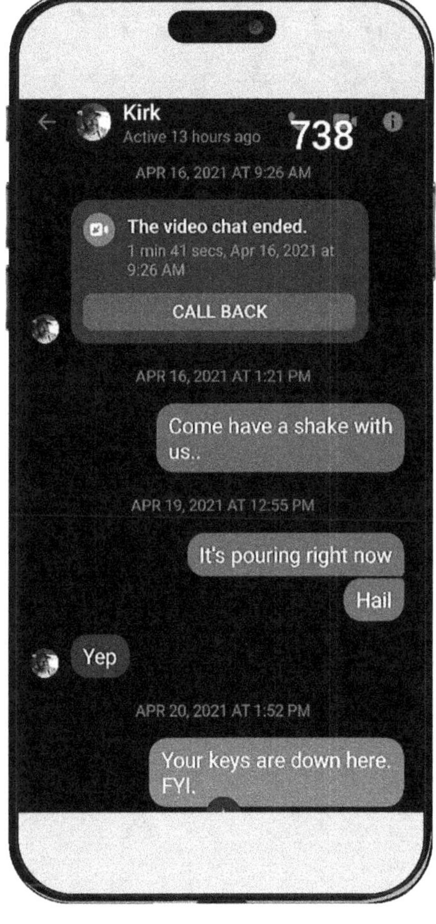
Kirk
Active 13 hours ago
738
APR 16, 2021 AT 9:26 AM
The video chat ended.
1 min 41 secs, Apr 16, 2021 at 9:26 AM
CALL BACK
APR 16, 2021 AT 1:21 PM
Come have a shake with us..
APR 19, 2021 AT 12:55 PM
It's pouring right now
Hail
Yep
APR 20, 2021 AT 1:52 PM
Your keys are down here. FYI.

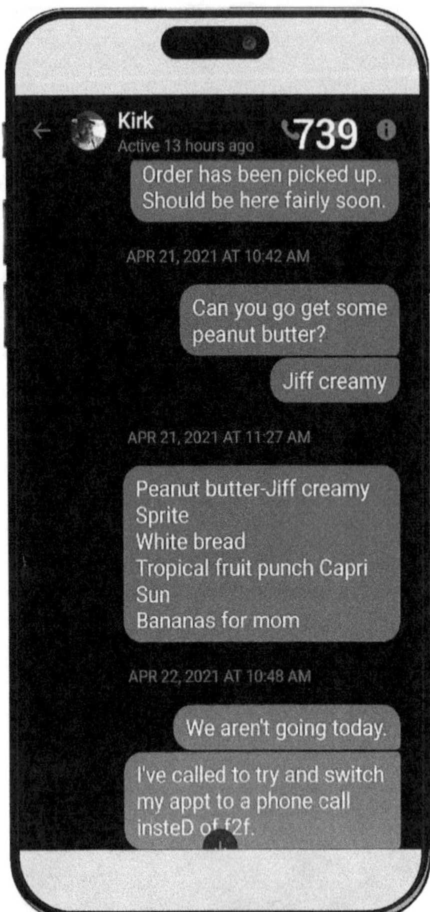

Kirk
Active 13 hours ago
739
Order has been picked up. Should be here fairly soon.
APR 21, 2021 AT 10:42 AM
Can you go get some peanut butter?
Jiff creamy
APR 21, 2021 AT 11:27 AM
Peanut butter-Jiff creamy
Sprite
White bread
Tropical fruit punch Capri Sun
Bananas for mom
APR 22, 2021 AT 10:48 AM
We aren't going today.
I've called to try and switch my appt to a phone call insteD of f2f.

Kirk
Active 13 hours ago
740
I'm too warn out from my shower.
APR 25, 2021 AT 7:00 PM
Can you make me a little ramen?
Nvmd
APR 26, 2021 AT 9:28 AM
Good morning...do you need anything
A pbnj in a little while. I am Still waiting for my nurse
Good morning babe.
She is late
Yeah.

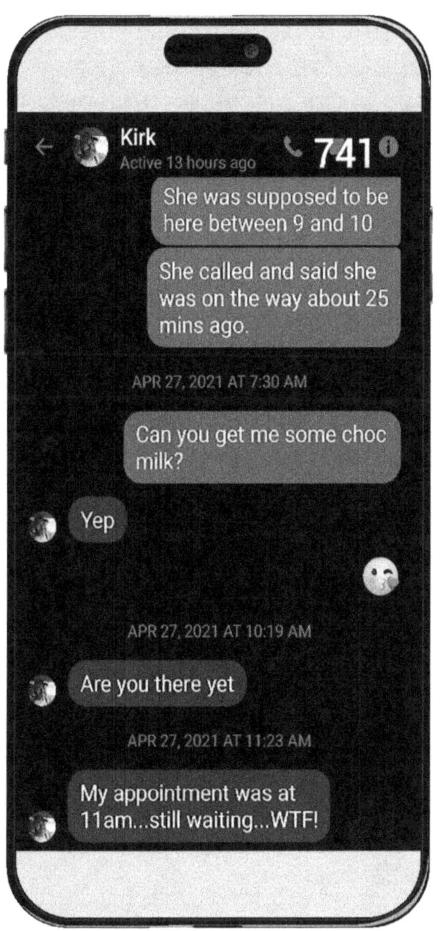

Kirk
Active 13 hours ago
741
She was supposed to be here between 9 and 10
She called and said she was on the way about 25 mins ago.
APR 27, 2021 AT 7:30 AM
Can you get me some choc milk?
Yep
APR 27, 2021 AT 10:19 AM
Are you there yet
APR 27, 2021 AT 11:23 AM
My appointment was at 11am...still waiting...WTF!

Kirk
Active 13 hours ago
742
APR 27, 2021 AT 3:48 PM
Omg
Did she ever csll?
*call
Sorry, didn't mean to call
APR 27, 2021 AT 4:40 PM
How are things going...you coming home soon?
On our way home now. Be there in ess than 10 probably
APR 28, 2021 AT 6:04 PM
Is the vacuum cleaner up there?
APR 28, 2021 AT 8:21 PM
Yes

At this point, Kim has been in and out of the hospital after her initial discharge from her surgery in late March. The messages that are shown here, are messages we traded while she was in the hospital.

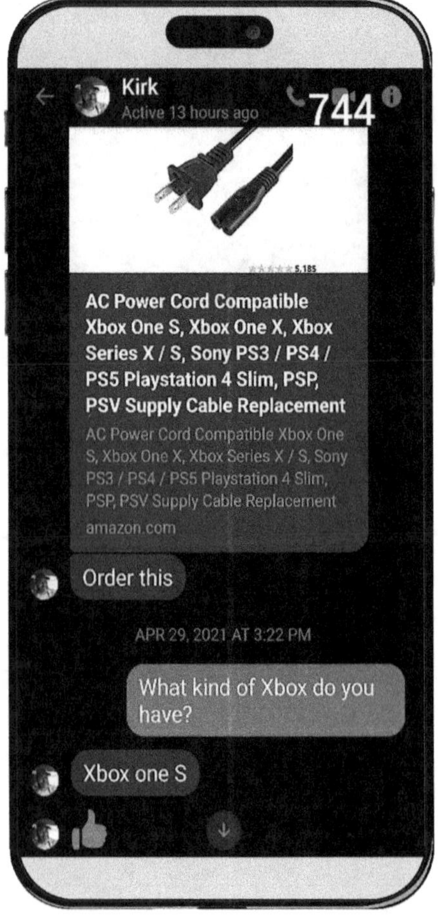

Kirk
745
APR 29, 2021 AT 5:08 PM
Your potatoes is ready
Potato
Ok
MAY 1, 2021 AT 11:34 AM
How are things going
You missed a video chat with Kirk.
May 1, 2021 at 11:36 AM
CALL BACK
I'm getting fluids
Have they started yet
Yes

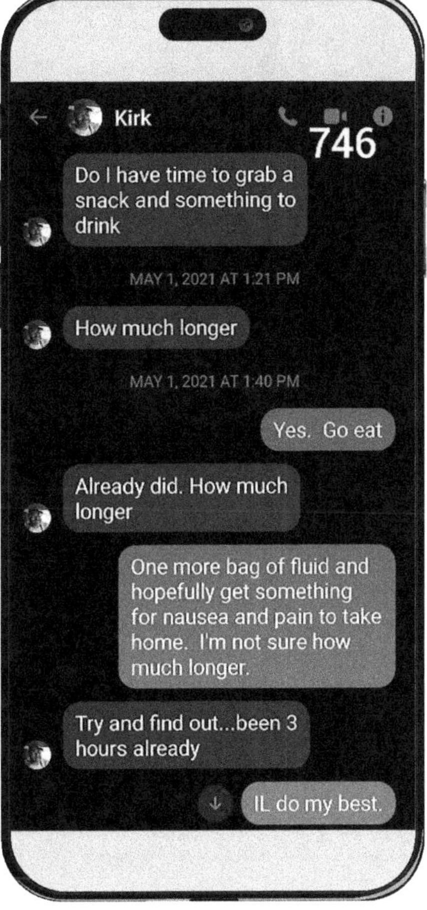

Kirk
746
Do I have time to grab a snack and something to drink
MAY 1, 2021 AT 1:21 PM
How much longer
MAY 1, 2021 AT 1:40 PM
Yes. Go eat
Already did. How much longer
One more bag of fluid and hopefully get something for nausea and pain to take home. I'm not sure how much longer.
Try and find out...been 3 hours already
IL do my best.

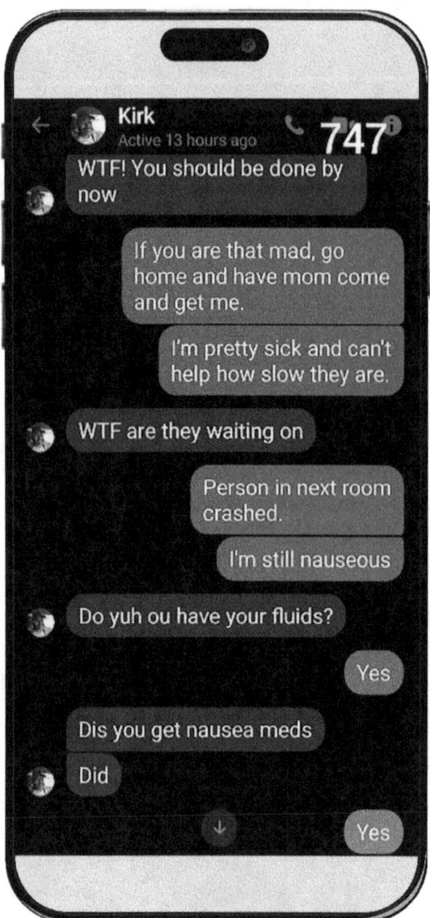

Kirk
Active 13 hours ago
747
WTF! You should be done by now
If you are that mad, go home and have mom come and get me.
I'm pretty sick and can't help how slow they are.
WTF are they waiting on
Person in next room crashed.
I'm still nauseous
Do yuh ou have your fluids?
Yes
Dis you get nausea meds
Did
Yes

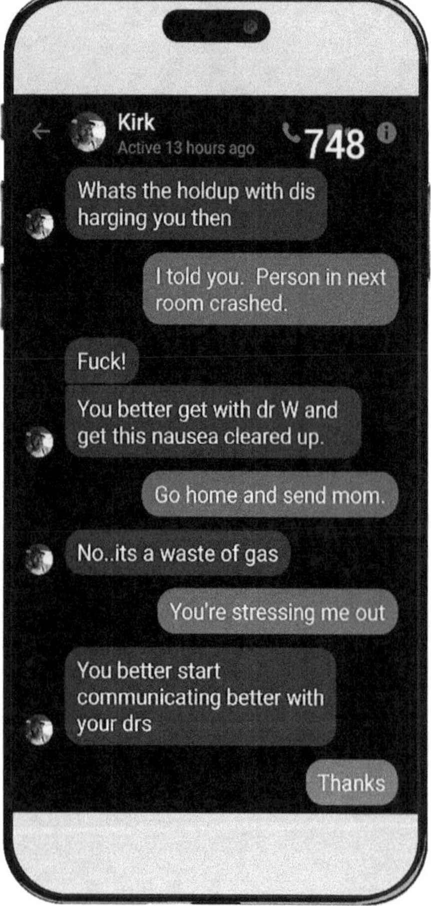

Kirk
Active 13 hours ago
748
Whats the holdup with dis harging you then
I told you. Person in next room crashed.
Fuck!
You better get with dr W and get this nausea cleared up.
Go home and send mom.
No..its a waste of gas
You're stressing me out
You better start communicating better with your drs
Thanks

Kirk
Active 13 hours ago
749
I just told the nurse you are antsy to leave. He went to speak to dr.
Ok. They are keeping me the night for observation. My hr is still to high to safely send me home. Go home.
You were so sweet earlier, I wish you wouldn't get so mad at me. It wrecks me.
MAY 1, 2021 AT 8:50 PM
You ok?
Just checking in on you
Im off to bed now...Good night
I love you

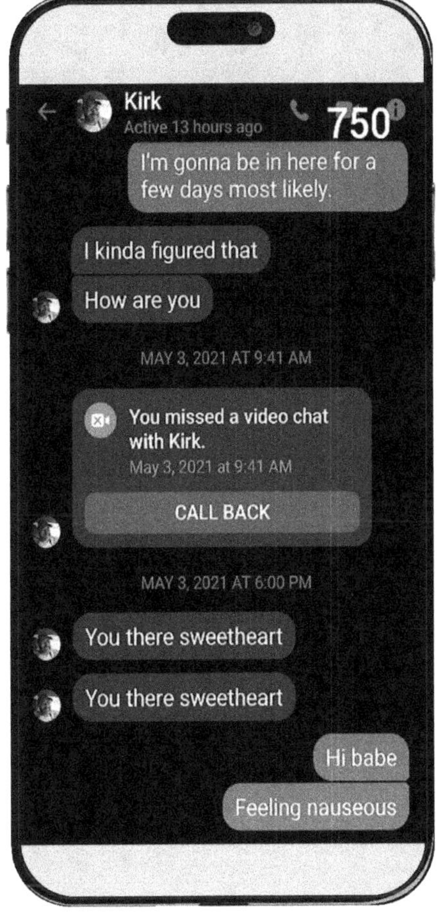
Kirk
Active 13 hours ago
750
I'm gonna be in here for a few days most likely.
I kinda figured that
How are you
MAY 3, 2021 AT 9:41 AM
You missed a video chat with Kirk.
May 3, 2021 at 9:41 AM
CALL BACK
MAY 3, 2021 AT 6:00 PM
You there sweetheart
You there sweetheart
Hi babe
Feeling nauseous

Kirk
Active 13 hours ago
751
We are going to try and come see you tomorrow
Im taking the car in for a safety inspection tomorrow morning
Have you made arrangements to see me?
The head nurse isn't here now.
No...who do we need to talk to?
Your mom tells me that your on 3 nausea medications and your still having issues
The head nurse. She's called the nurse manager and the one who arranged it last time is named

Kirk
Active 13 hours ago
752
it last time is named Brittney. We need to go through her. She won't be in till tomorrow morning.
Ok.
They won't just let you in without arrangements
Your mom is bringing you some stuff
Yeah. I'm going commando right now lol
Getting some air huh?
Lol. You could say that. My bag leaked.
Peew
How are you feeling

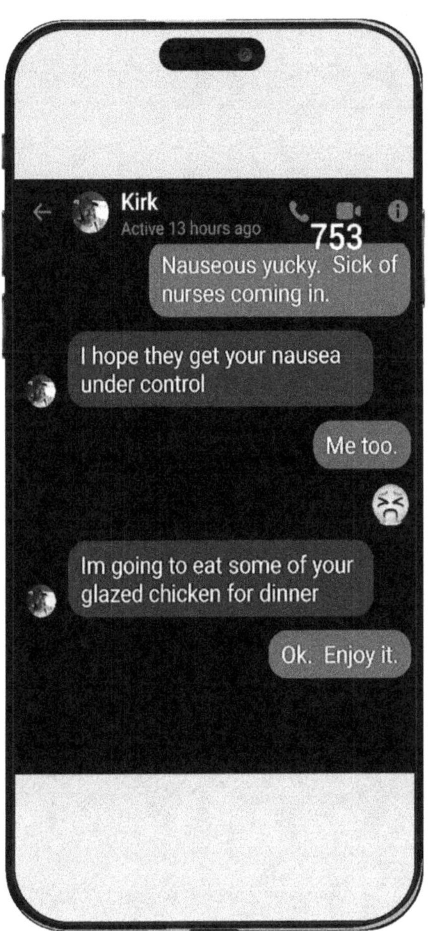

Kirk
Active 13 hours ago
753
Nauseous yucky. Sick of nurses coming in.
I hope they get your nausea under control
Me too.
Im going to eat some of your glazed chicken for dinner
Ok. Enjoy it.

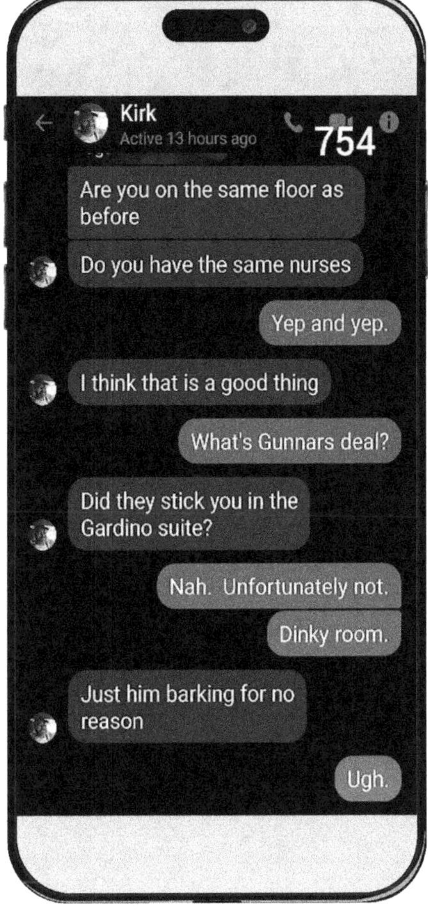

Kirk
Active 13 hours ago
754
Are you on the same floor as before
Do you have the same nurses
Yep and yep.
I think that is a good thing
What's Gunnars deal?
Did they stick you in the Gardino suite?
Nah. Unfortunately not.
Dinky room.
Just him barking for no reason
Ugh.

Kirk
Active 13 hours ago
755
I fed some geese that were in the front yard today
I thought he was giving you attitude.
Cool.
Wish you were home. I miss you
I miss you too. I wish I was home also.<
I bought John Wick3 today from Walmart
MAY 3, 2021 AT 8:46 PM
Good.
MAY 3, 2021 AT 8:57 PM
Good night love
Nighty night!

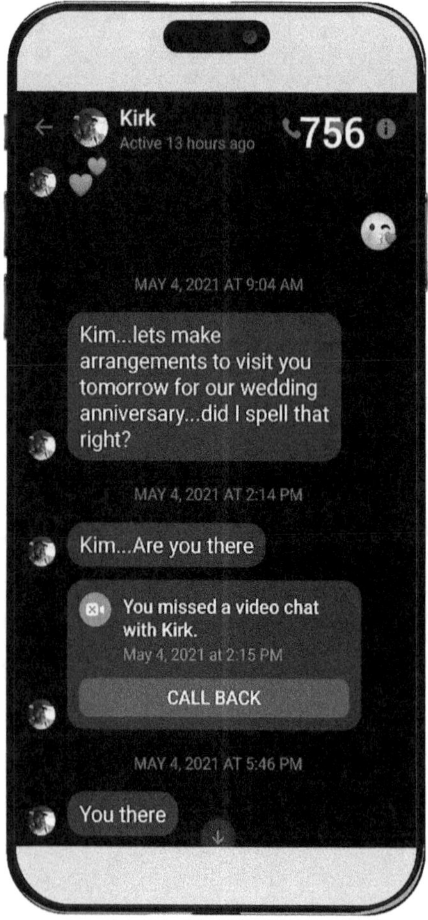

Kirk
Active 13 hours ago
756
MAY 4, 2021 AT 9:04 AM
Kim...lets make arrangements to visit you tomorrow for our wedding anniversary...did I spell that right?
MAY 4, 2021 AT 2:14 PM
Kim...Are you there
You missed a video chat with Kirk.
May 4, 2021 at 2:15 PM
CALL BACK
MAY 4, 2021 AT 5:46 PM
You there

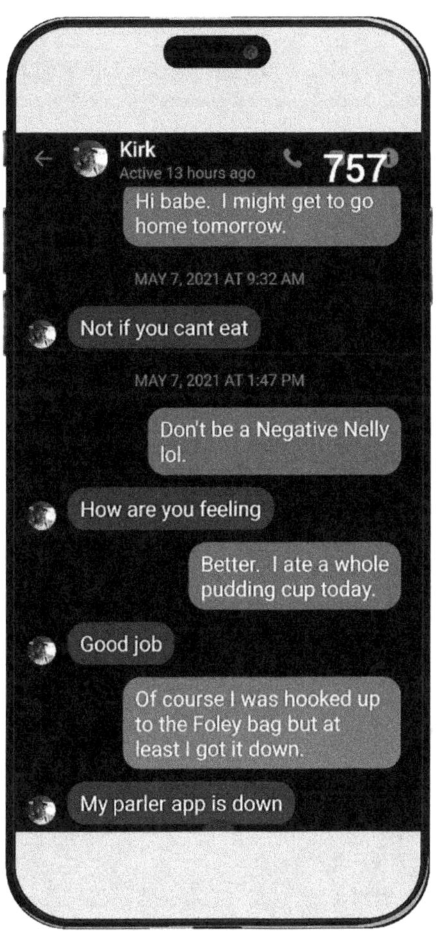
Kirk
Active 13 hours ago
757
Hi babe. I might get to go home tomorrow.
MAY 7, 2021 AT 9:32 AM
Not if you cant eat
MAY 7, 2021 AT 1:47 PM
Don't be a Negative Nelly lol.
How are you feeling
Better. I ate a whole pudding cup today.
Good job
Of course I was hooked up to the Foley bag but at least I got it down.
My parler app is down

Kirk
Active 13 hours ago
758
I wanna burger.
Lol
Just met with the chaplain.
MAY 7, 2021 AT 3:06 PM
Cool
MAY 7, 2021 AT 9:17 PM
Goodnight babe.
MAY 8, 2021 AT 11:05 AM
Hey sexy
MAY 8, 2021 AT 11:55 AM
Hi babe. I dont think I get to come home today after all.
I haven't even seen a doctor yet.

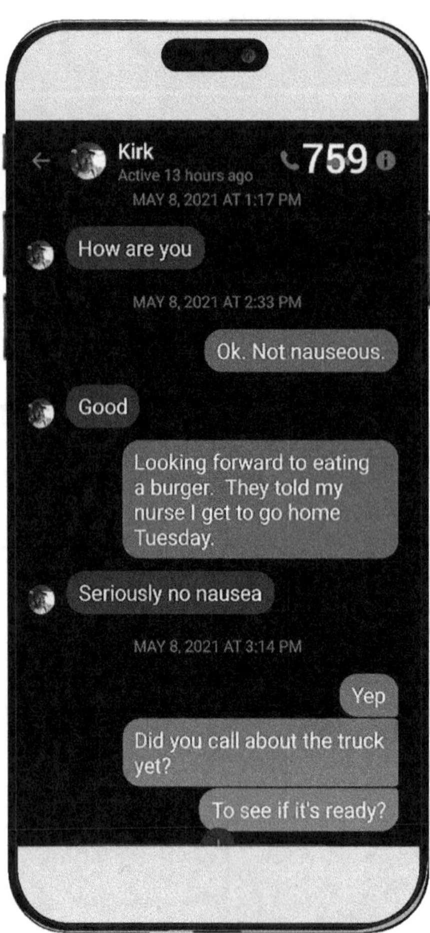

Kirk
Active 13 hours ago
MAY 8, 2021 AT 1:17 PM
How are you
MAY 8, 2021 AT 2:33 PM
Ok. Not nauseous.
Good
Looking forward to eating a burger. They told my nurse I get to go home Tuesday.
Seriously no nausea
MAY 8, 2021 AT 3:14 PM
Yep
Did you call about the truck yet?
To see if it's ready?

Kirk
I called and left a message about 5 min ago
Ok
How did you know about the truck?
Mom was wondering
She's bummed about having to sit with her car all day monday.
That sucks
Yeah

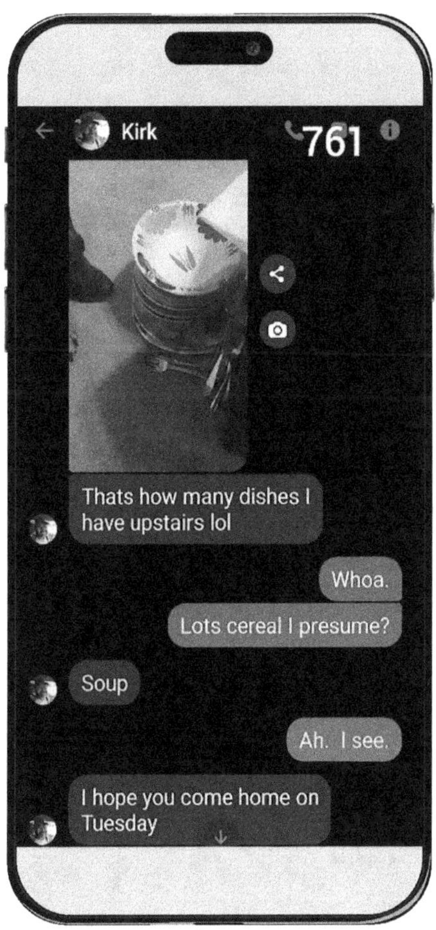

Kirk
761
Thats how many dishes I have upstairs lol
Whoa.
Lots cereal I presume?
Soup
Ah. I see.
I hope you come home on Tuesday

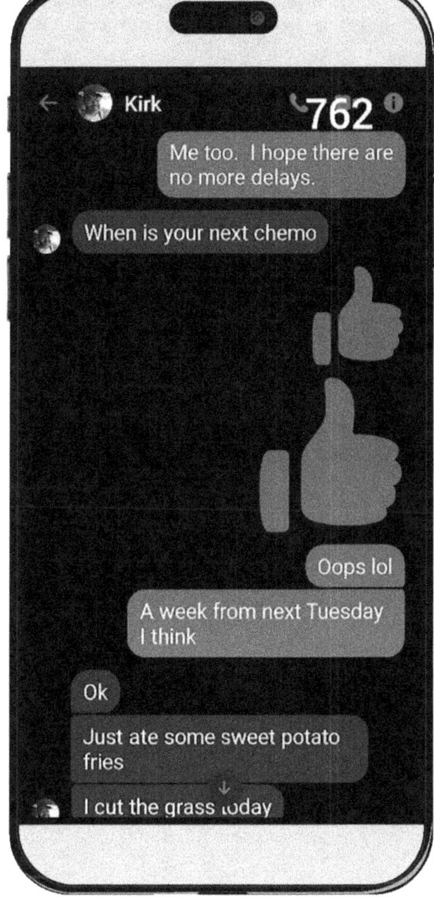

Kirk
762
Me too. I hope there are no more delays.
When is your next chemo
Oops lol
A week from next Tuesday I think
Ok
Just ate some sweet potato fries
I cut the grass today

Kirk
763
Mom told me that too. I know you love those.
Thank you.
She tells you alot lol
Lol. No secrets, she and I. Lol
I guess not
I wonder how sweet potato fries would taste with Carne Asada.
Better stick to real fries lol
What is Carne Asada
A delicious Mexican dish made with steak, cheese, fries, tomatoes, guacamole, sour cream, etc...

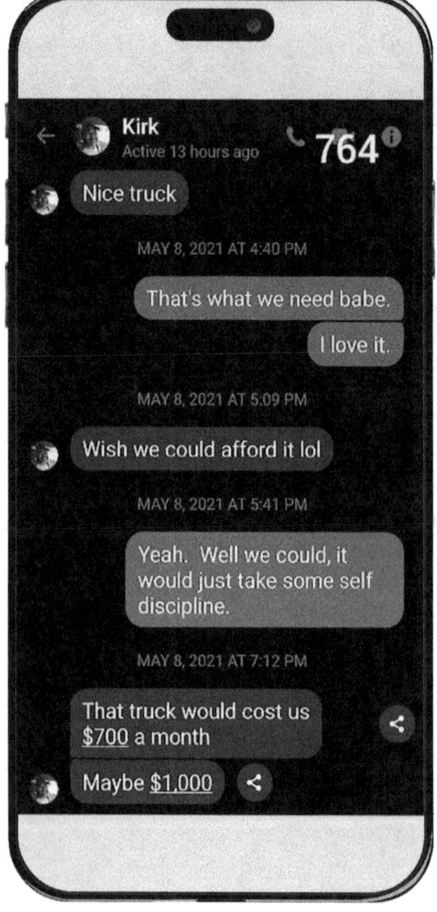
Kirk
Active 13 hours ago
764
Nice truck
MAY 8, 2021 AT 4:40 PM
That's what we need babe.
I love it.
MAY 8, 2021 AT 5:09 PM
Wish we could afford it lol
MAY 8, 2021 AT 5:41 PM
Yeah. Well we could, it would just take some self discipline.
MAY 8, 2021 AT 7:12 PM
That truck would cost us $700 a month
Maybe $1,000

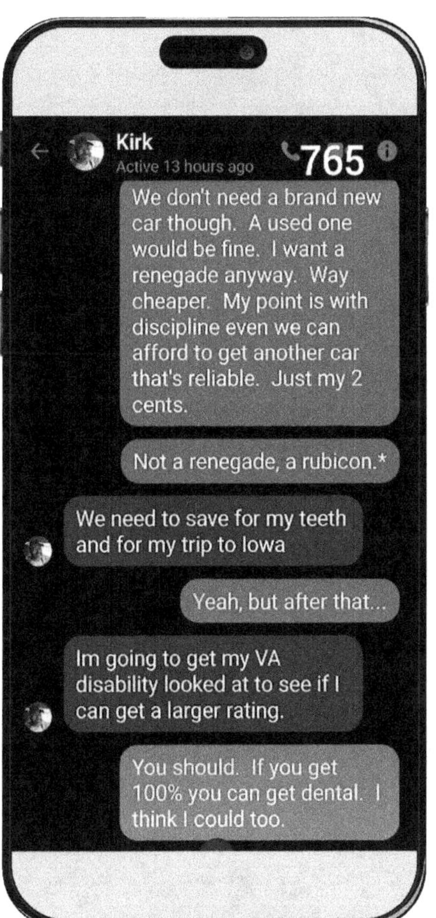
Kirk
Active 13 hours ago
765
We don't need a brand new car though. A used one would be fine. I want a renegade anyway. Way cheaper. My point is with discipline even we can afford to get another car that's reliable. Just my 2 cents.
Not a renegade, a rubicon.*
We need to save for my teeth and for my trip to Iowa
Yeah, but after that...
Im going to get my VA disability looked at to see if I can get a larger rating.
You should. If you get 100% you can get dental. I think I could too.

Kirk
Active 13 hours ago
766
My depression has gotten worse since 20 years ago
And commisary and px privilages I think
Definitely worse in just the time we've been married. Off and on.
Yep. Base priveges
That would be nice
Yes it would. Save us a small fortune in food.
Yep
I only played 1 hr of my tank game this week. That was yrsterday with Danil
Wow
Out of practice?

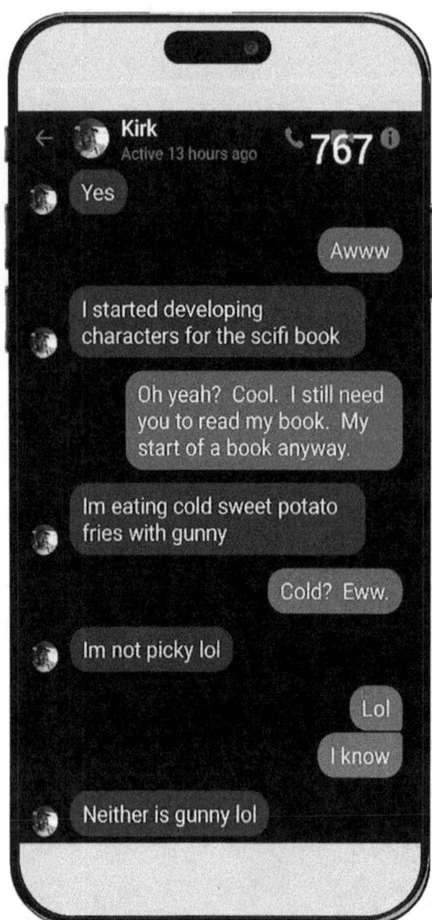

Kirk
Active 13 hours ago
767
Yes
Awww
I started developing characters for the scifi book
Oh yeah? Cool. I still need you to read my book. My start of a book anyway.
Im eating cold sweet potato fries with gunny
Cold? Eww.
Im not picky lol
Lol
I know
Neither is gunny lol

Kirk
Active 13 hours ago
768
You should bring me a burger tomorrow.
We are visiting Monday
I'm hungry
You made arrangements?
Yes
Cool.
If we waited for you to make them we would necer see you
Never
Ha ha
Im going to get you a dvd player for downstairs so you can watch amazon and youtube on the big tv

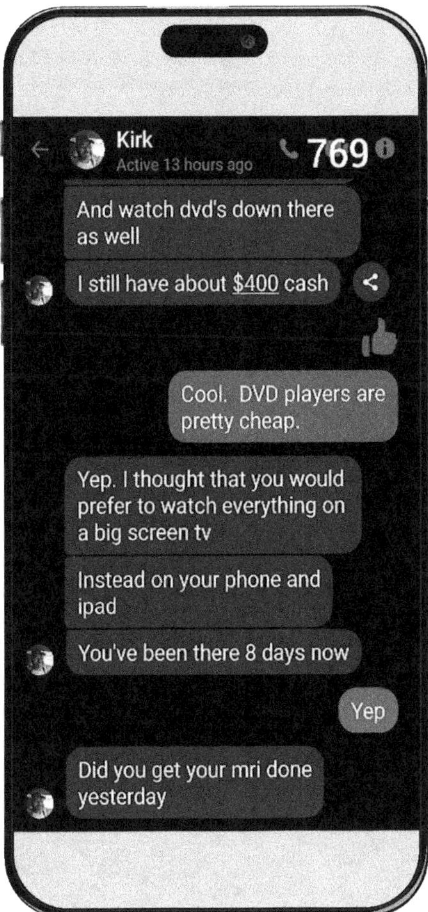

Around this time, Kim kind of resolved herself that she was not going to make it. She started to apologize for asking me to do things and had the attitude that she didn't want to be a burden to anyone.
I got this feeling based off of the tone of her voice, her being overly apologetic, submissive and agreeable.

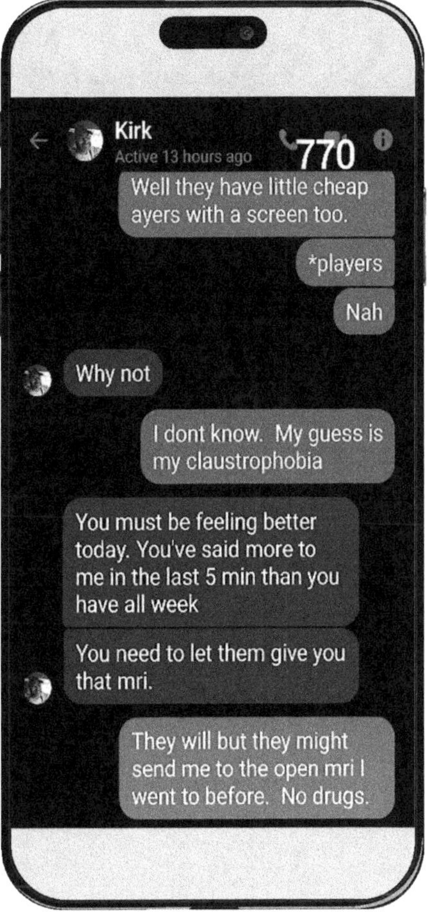

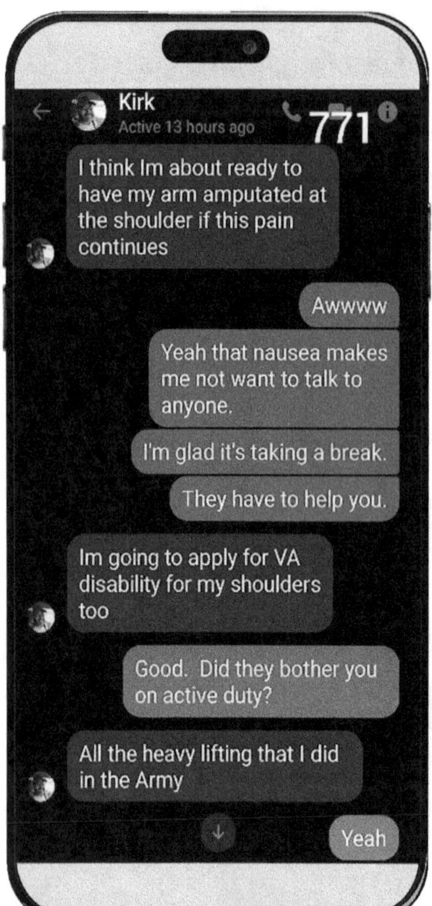
Kirk
Active 13 hours ago
771
I think Im about ready to have my arm amputated at the shoulder if this pain continues
Awwww
Yeah that nausea makes me not want to talk to anyone.
I'm glad it's taking a break.
They have to help you.
Im going to apply for VA disability for my shoulders too
Good. Did they bother you on active duty?
All the heavy lifting that I did in the Army
Yeah

Kirk
Active 13 hours ago
772
No...but what I did could of taken years to show up...like arthritis
True
Wear and tear
Yep
And I was a small dude at 140lbs...I was lifting 70% of my body hundreds of times a day when out in the field
Yeah, I remember you told me how heavy those rounds were.
100lbs
And the other stuff you lift

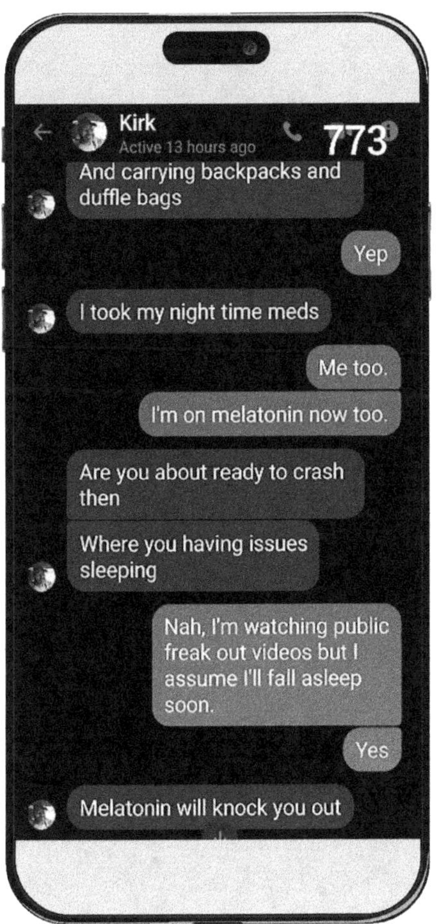

Kirk
Active 13 hours ago
773
And carrying backpacks and duffle bags
Yep
I took my night time meds
Me too.
I'm on melatonin now too.
Are you about ready to crash then
Where you having issues sleeping
Nah, I'm watching public freak out videos but I assume I'll fall asleep soon.
Yes
Melatonin will knock you out

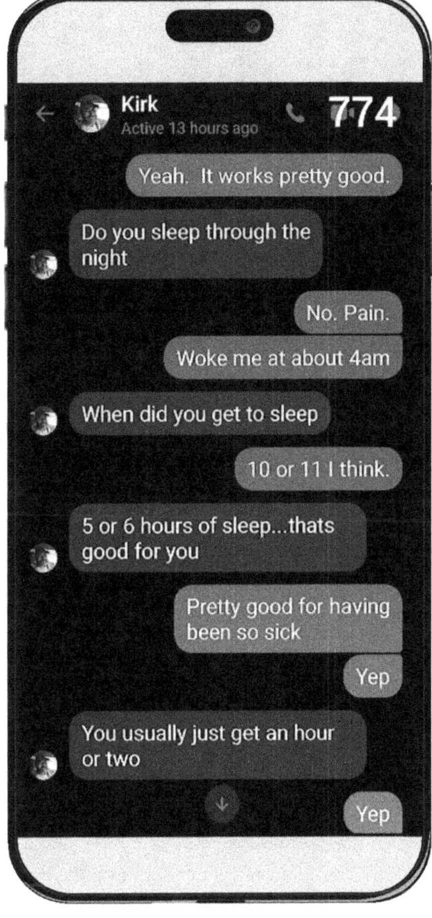

Kirk
Active 13 hours ago
774
Yeah. It works pretty good.
Do you sleep through the night
No. Pain.
Woke me at about 4am
When did you get to sleep
10 or 11 I think.
5 or 6 hours of sleep...thats good for you
Pretty good for having been so sick
Yep
You usually just get an hour or two
Yep

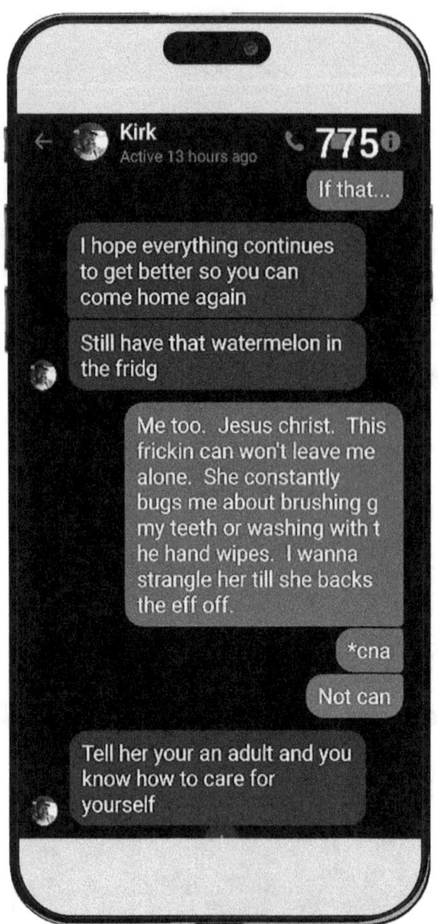

Kirk
Active 13 hours ago
775
If that...
I hope everything continues to get better so you can come home again
Still have that watermelon in the fridg
Me too. Jesus christ. This frickin can won't leave me alone. She constantly bugs me about brushing g my teeth or washing with t he hand wipes. I wanna strangle her till she backs the eff off.
*cna
Not can
Tell her your an adult and you know how to care for yourself

Kirk
Active 13 hours ago
776
Yeah, it's like she's talking to a 5 year old.
I know this would drive you nuts too.
I would have told her not to mention that to me anymore
Lol
I wish you were here then you could tell her for me.
Lol
I would to
I know lol
She's the same one that botched because I wouldn't let her rub me down, the creeper.
*bitched

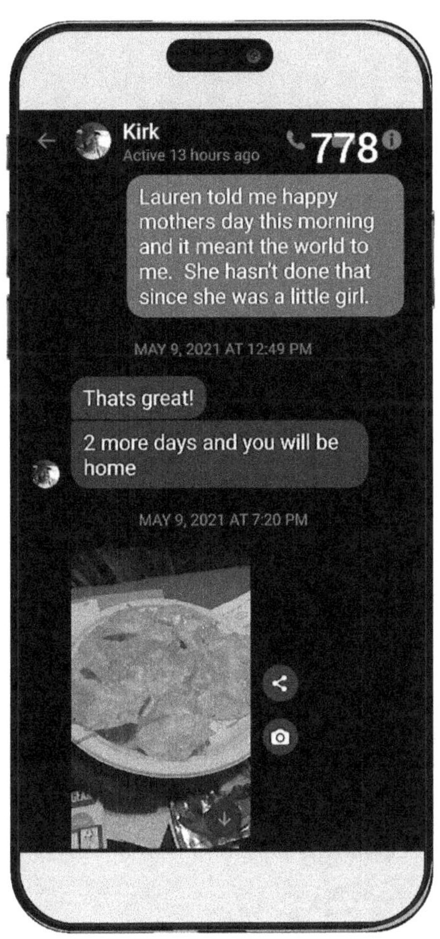

Kirk
Active 13 hours ago
778
Lauren told me happy mothers day this morning and it meant the world to me. She hasn't done that since she was a little girl.
MAY 9, 2021 AT 12:49 PM
Thats great!
2 more days and you will be home
MAY 9, 2021 AT 7:20 PM

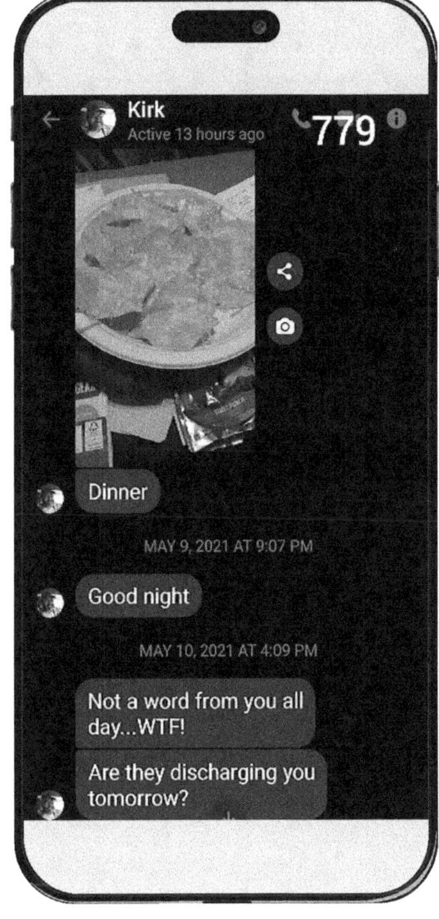

Kirk
Active 13 hours ago
779
Dinner
MAY 9, 2021 AT 9:07 PM
Good night
MAY 10, 2021 AT 4:09 PM
Not a word from you all day...WTF!
Are they discharging you tomorrow?

Kirk
Active 13 hours ago
780
You missed a video chat with Kirk.
May 10, 2021 at 6:27 PM
CALL BACK
I look terrible honey.
Text only
So...your my wife...I can see you in any condition
Please
I haven't showered in forever.
Or even brushed my hair
I havent in 3 weeks
Yeah, but you don't have long hair

Kirk
Active 13 hours ago
781
I have long pubic hair lol
Lol
Lmao
Too funny
You used to manscape that stuff lol
Haven't done that on awhile
Me either and I wish I'd shaved it all off. I keep getting tape stuck on my public hair. Ouch!!
I screwed up. I bought you a dvd player for you to use so you can get on youtube and amazon prime...I got one without wifi only cable...I

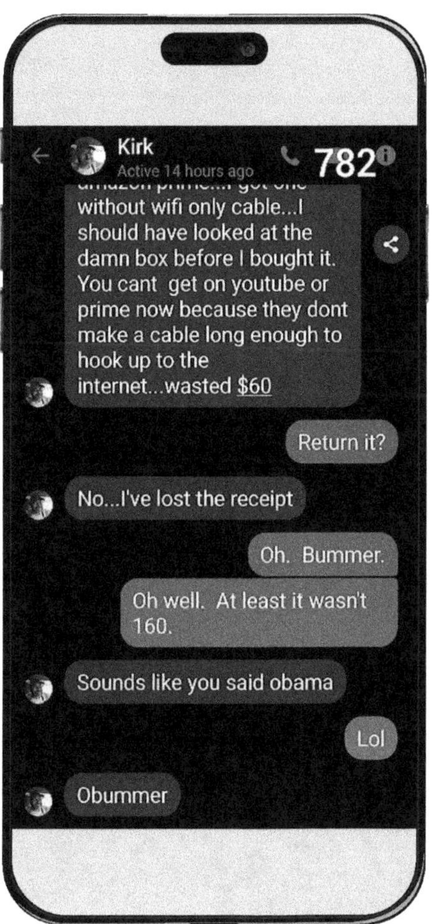
Kirk
Active 14 hours ago
782
without wifi only cable...I should have looked at the damn box before I bought it. You cant get on youtube or prime now because they dont make a cable long enough to hook up to the internet...wasted $60
Return it?
No...I've lost the receipt
Oh. Bummer.
Oh well. At least it wasn't 160.
Sounds like you said obama
Lol
Obummer

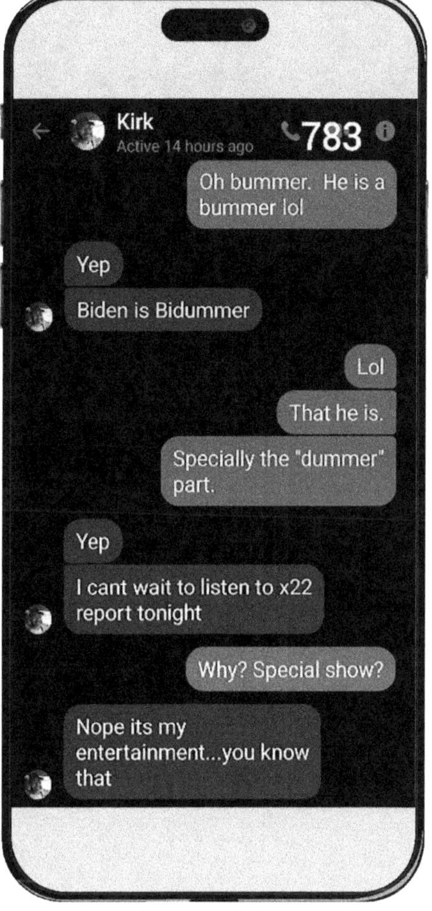
Kirk
Active 14 hours ago
783
Oh bummer. He is a bummer lol
Yep
Biden is Bidummer
Lol
That he is.
Specially the "dummer" part.
Yep
I cant wait to listen to x22 report tonight
Why? Special show?
Nope its my entertainment...you know that

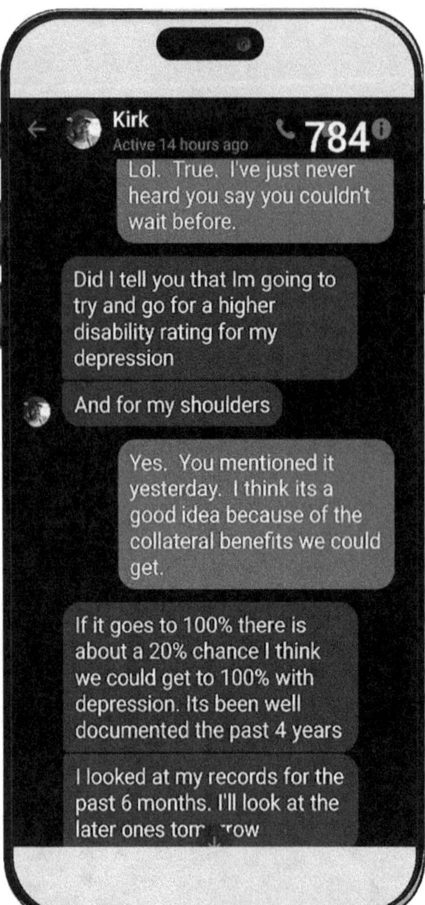
Kirk
Active 14 hours ago
784
Lol. True. I've just never heard you say you couldn't wait before.
Did I tell you that Im going to try and go for a higher disability rating for my depression
And for my shoulders
Yes. You mentioned it yesterday. I think its a good idea because of the collateral benefits we could get.
If it goes to 100% there is about a 20% chance I think we could get to 100% with depression. Its been well documented the past 4 years
I looked at my records for the past 6 months. I'll look at the later ones tomorrow

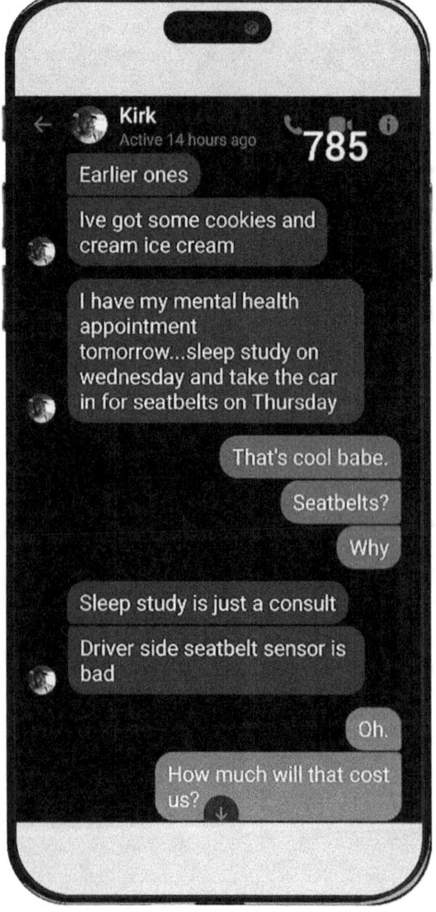
Kirk
Active 14 hours ago
785
Earlier ones
Ive got some cookies and cream ice cream
I have my mental health appointment tomorrow...sleep study on wednesday and take the car in for seatbelts on Thursday
That's cool babe.
Seatbelts?
Why
Sleep study is just a consult
Driver side seatbelt sensor is bad
Oh.
How much will that cost us?

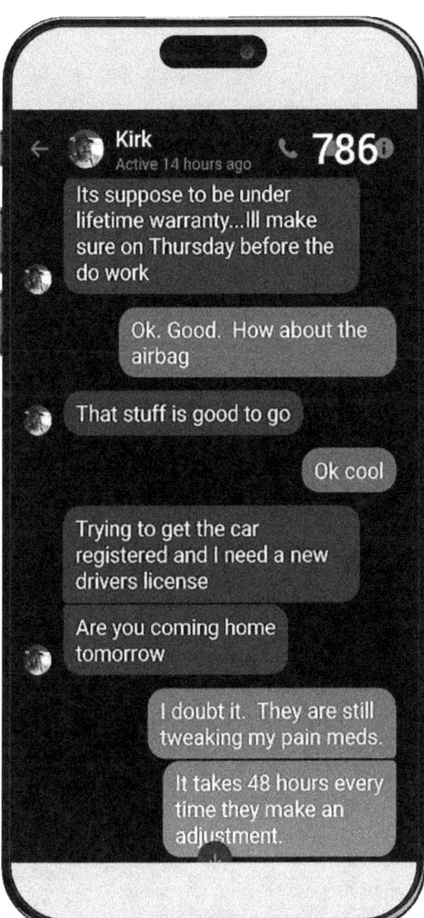
Kirk
Active 14 hours ago
786
Its suppose to be under lifetime warranty...Ill make sure on Thursday before the do work
Ok. Good. How about the airbag
That stuff is good to go
Ok cool
Trying to get the car registered and I need a new drivers license
Are you coming home tomorrow
I doubt it. They are still tweaking my pain meds.
It takes 48 hours every time they make an adjustment.

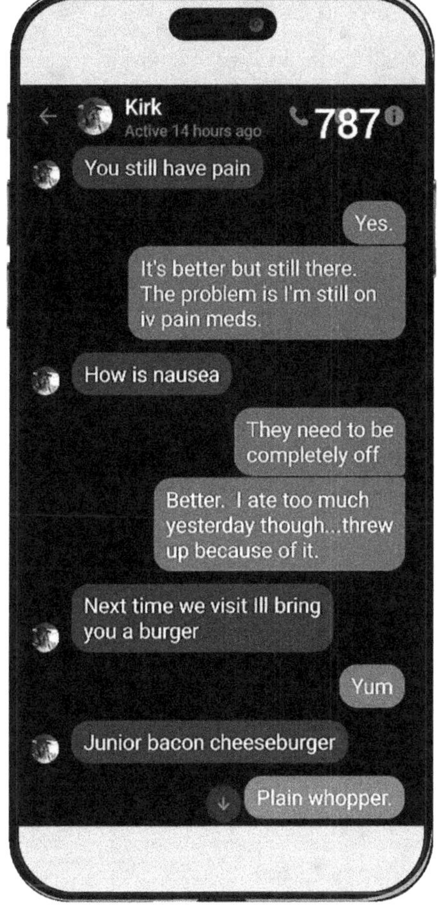
Kirk
Active 14 hours ago
787
You still have pain
Yes.
It's better but still there. The problem is I'm still on iv pain meds.
How is nausea
They need to be completely off
Better. I ate too much yesterday though...threw up because of it.
Next time we visit Ill bring you a burger
Yum
Junior bacon cheeseburger
Plain whopper.

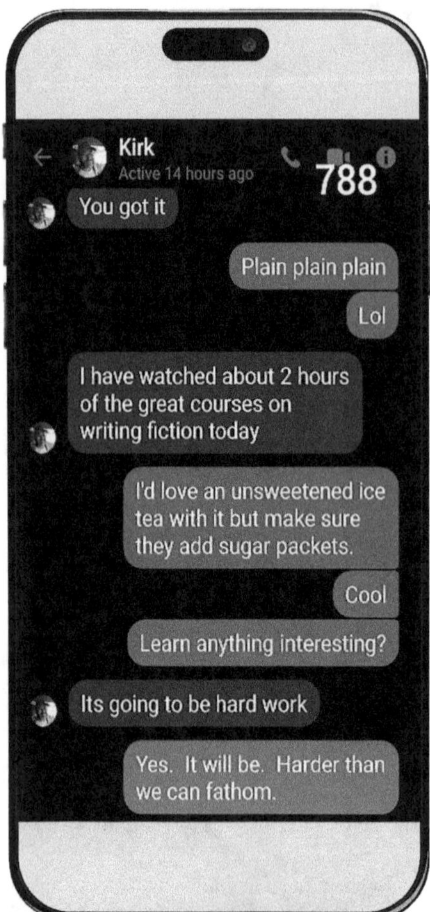
Kirk
Active 14 hours ago
788
You got it
Plain plain plain
Lol
I have watched about 2 hours of the great courses on writing fiction today
I'd love an unsweetened ice tea with it but make sure they add sugar packets.
Cool
Learn anything interesting?
Its going to be hard work
Yes. It will be. Harder than we can fathom.

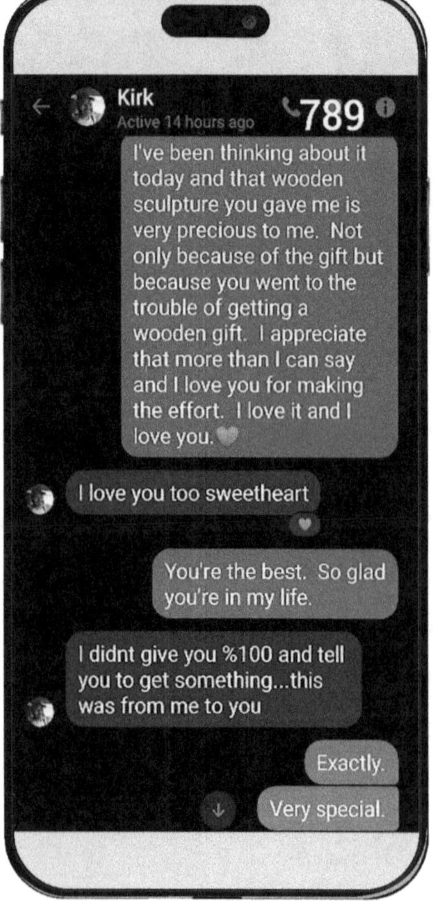
Kirk
Active 14 hours ago
789
I've been thinking about it today and that wooden sculpture you gave me is very precious to me. Not only because of the gift but because you went to the trouble of getting a wooden gift. I appreciate that more than I can say and I love you for making the effort. I love it and I love you.
I love you too sweetheart
You're the best. So glad you're in my life.
I didnt give you %100 and tell you to get something...this was from me to you
Exactly.
Very special.

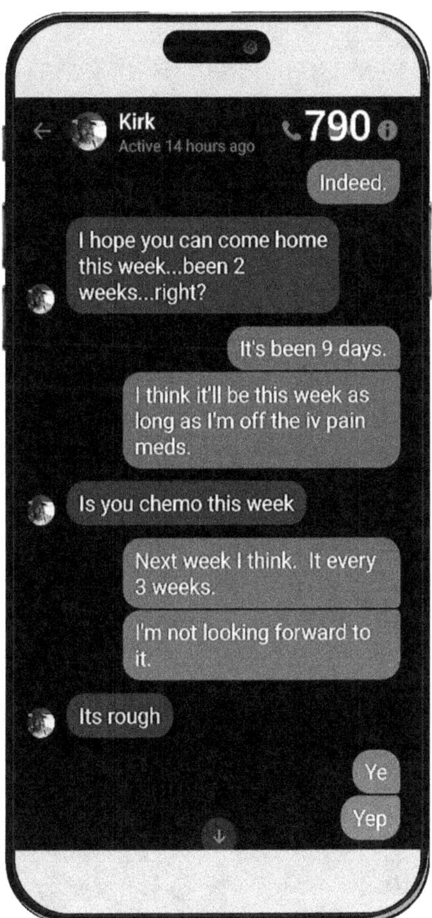
Kirk
Active 14 hours ago
790
Indeed.
I hope you can come home this week...been 2 weeks...right?
It's been 9 days.
I think it'll be this week as long as I'm off the iv pain meds.
Is you chemo this week
Next week I think. It every 3 weeks.
I'm not looking forward to it.
Its rough
Ye
Yep

Kirk
Active 14 hours ago
791
But now you have a large tv to watch movies on
Or watch any of the great courses
Have you talked with your mom at all today
I think I talked to her briefly earlier to tell her I won't be coming home tomorrow.
Time to let gunnar out
Ok babe. After you do that can I have a heated blanket?
Lol. I'm half asleep. That's for the nurse lmao

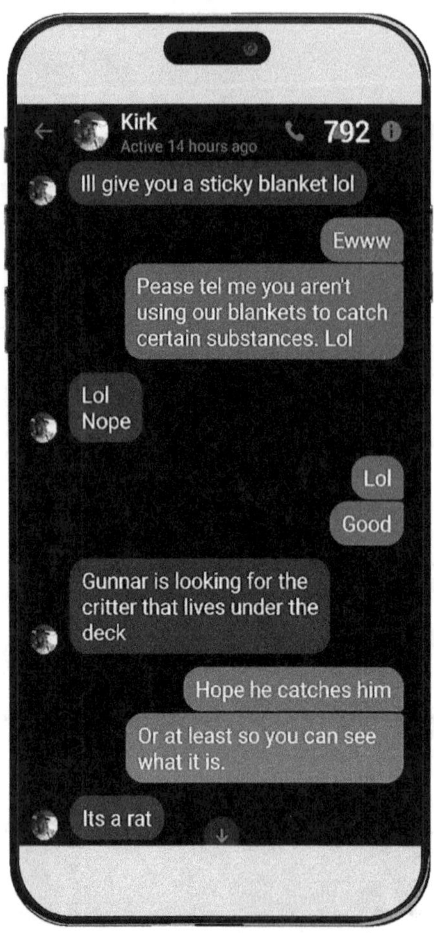

Kirk
Active 14 hours ago
792
Ill give you a sticky blanket lol
Ewww
Pease tel me you aren't using our blankets to catch certain substances. Lol
Lol
Nope
Lol
Good
Gunnar is looking for the critter that lives under the deck
Hope he catches him
Or at least so you can see what it is.
Its a rat

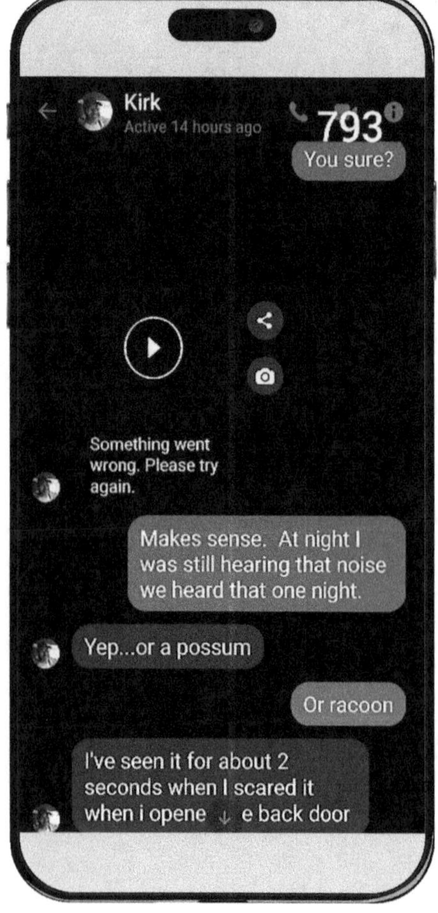

Kirk
Active 14 hours ago
793
You sure?
Something went wrong. Please try again.
Makes sense. At night I was still hearing that noise we heard that one night.
Yep...or a possum
Or racoon
I've seen it for about 2 seconds when I scared it when i opene e back door

Kirk
Active 14 hours ago
794
Probably a rat
Not a racoon
Oh yeah?
I remember when we had a bag of trash on the orch in Iowa and I found an opossum digging in it and I grabbed him by the tail. Very rat like.
Those this ate the fuck out of the pumkins we left out
Yep
Im back upstairs
Taking meds now
Ok babe. They will be bringing mine soon.
I miss you

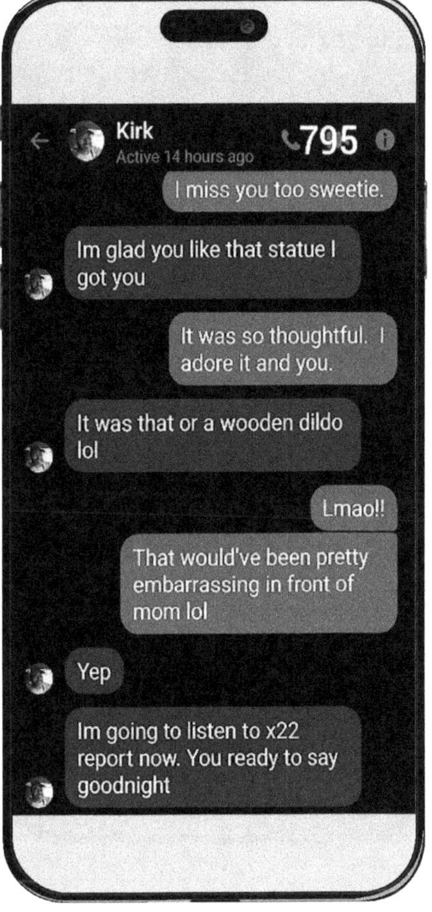

Kirk
Active 14 hours ago
795
I miss you too sweetie.
Im glad you like that statue I got you
It was so thoughtful. I adore it and you.
It was that or a wooden dildo lol
Lmao!!
That would've been pretty embarrassing in front of mom lol
Yep
Im going to listen to x22 report now. You ready to say goodnight

This is about the time that I was going to Hardees every morning to buy her biscuits and gravy. Every morning I would go at 6am when she was home and buy her, her biscuits and gravy. She would be so happy get them, but it would break my heart to see that she would only eat one or two bites and within 15 minutes she would be vomiting. Her nausea was a big problem for her. She would vomit between three to six times a day every time she tried to eat. Our daily ritual would be me getting her breakfast. Then helping her to the bathroom and then emptying and washing out her bed pan full of bile and other fluids. I would then fill her insulated cup with ice water. Then I would go upstairs and watch tv and check in on Kim every ninety minutes to make sure she was doing well. Of course, she would text me if she needed something before like a bathroom trip, refill her drink cup or make her something to eat. At the end of the day, I would go and spend an hour with her before I went to bed to make sure that she went to the bathroom and was all set up for the night.

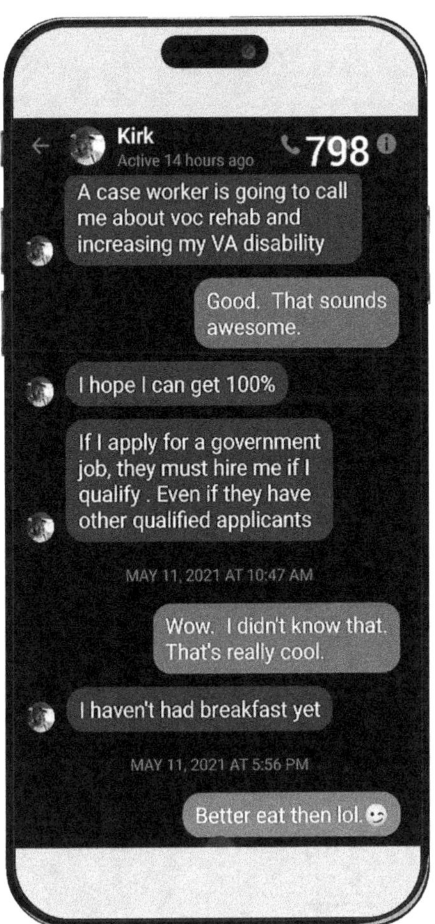

Kirk
Active 14 hours ago
798
A case worker is going to call me about voc rehab and increasing my VA disability
Good. That sounds awesome.
I hope I can get 100%
If I apply for a government job, they must hire me if I qualify . Even if they have other qualified applicants
MAY 11, 2021 AT 10:47 AM
Wow. I didn't know that. That's really cool.
I haven't had breakfast yet
MAY 11, 2021 AT 5:56 PM
Better eat then lol.

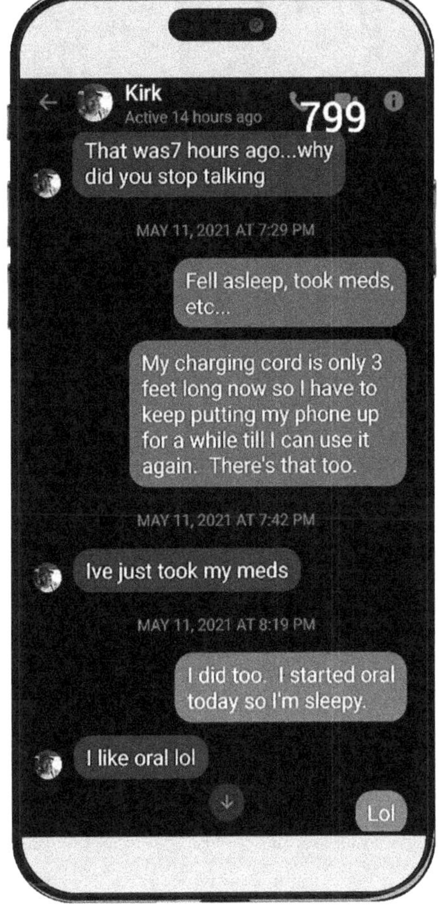

Kirk
Active 14 hours ago
799
That was7 hours ago...why did you stop talking
MAY 11, 2021 AT 7:29 PM
Fell asleep, took meds, etc...
My charging cord is only 3 feet long now so I have to keep putting my phone up for a while till I can use it again. There's that too.
MAY 11, 2021 AT 7:42 PM
Ive just took my meds
MAY 11, 2021 AT 8:19 PM
I did too. I started oral today so I'm sleepy.
I like oral lol
Lol

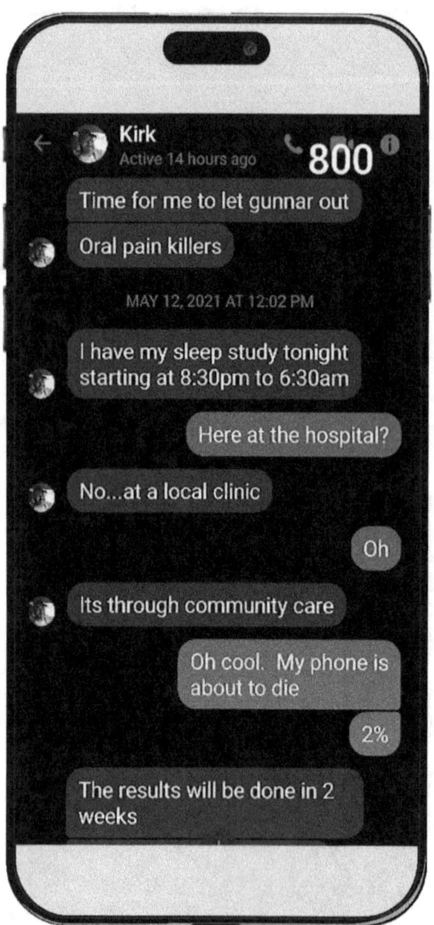

Kirk
Active 14 hours ago
800
Time for me to let gunnar out
Oral pain killers
MAY 12, 2021 AT 12:02 PM
I have my sleep study tonight starting at 8:30pm to 6:30am
Here at the hospital?
No...at a local clinic
Oh
Its through community care
Oh cool. My phone is about to die
2%
The results will be done in 2 weeks

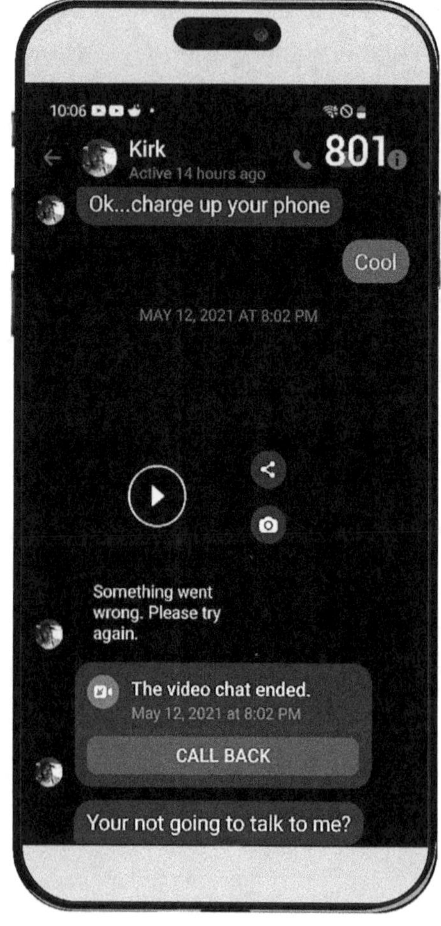

10:06
Kirk
Active 14 hours ago
801
Ok...charge up your phone
Cool
MAY 12, 2021 AT 8:02 PM
Something went wrong. Please try again.
The video chat ended.
May 12, 2021 at 8:02 PM
CALL BACK
Your not going to talk to me?

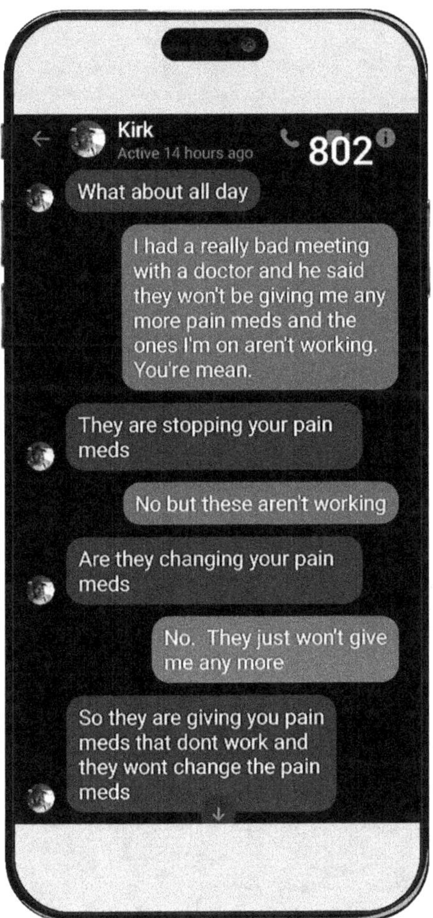

Kirk
Active 14 hours ago
802
What about all day
I had a really bad meeting with a doctor and he said they won't be giving me any more pain meds and the ones I'm on aren't working. You're mean.
They are stopping your pain meds
No but these aren't working
Are they changing your pain meds
No. They just won't give me any more
So they are giving you pain meds that dont work and they wont change the pain meds

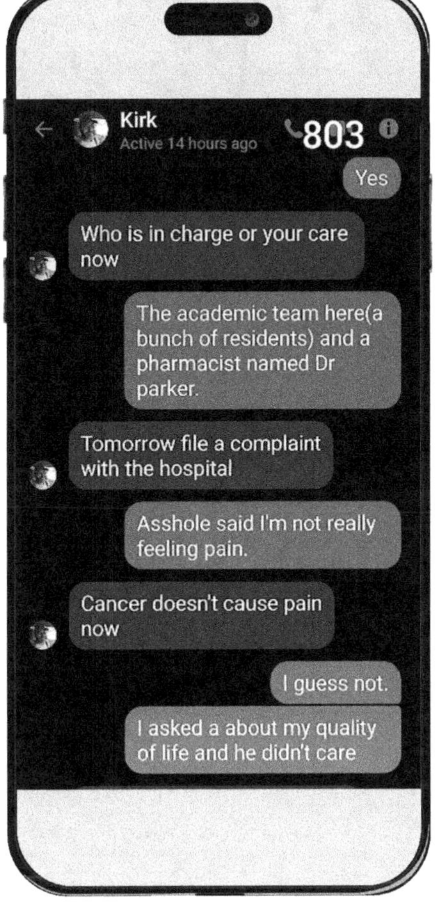

Kirk
Active 14 hours ago
803
Yes
Who is in charge or your care now
The academic team here(a bunch of residents) and a pharmacist named Dr parker.
Tomorrow file a complaint with the hospital
Asshole said I'm not really feeling pain.
Cancer doesn't cause pain now
I guess not.
I asked a about my quality of life and he didn't care

Kirk
Active 14 hours ago
804
Im going to go to the hospital and raise some hell tomorrow or Friday. I have a car Appointment 8am tomorrow
Ok
You're still near you know.
*nean
Mean
Im sorry...just wanted to talk to you.
Ill.be going to the hospital with your mom to file a complaint on your treatment and you should be under the care of an oncologist...not a pharmacist and some residents.
Yeah

Kirk
Active 14 hours ago
805
I might be in jail tomorrow night.
Bo. Dibt di anything stupid
I wont, but Im not go to leave on my own until your taken care of.
Leave where?
The hospital
Oh ok
These fucking beds are hard
That sucks
Im ready to go to sleep but haven't been hooked up yet...this sucks.

Kirk
Active 14 hours ago
806
Are they coming soon?
I hope so
I have to go get an xray now.
So stupid
MAY 12, 2021 AT 9:16 PM
Im going to sleep now...good night
Night
MAY 13, 2021 AT 11:38 AM
I'm coming home tomorrow.
In a cab
In a cab?
Why?

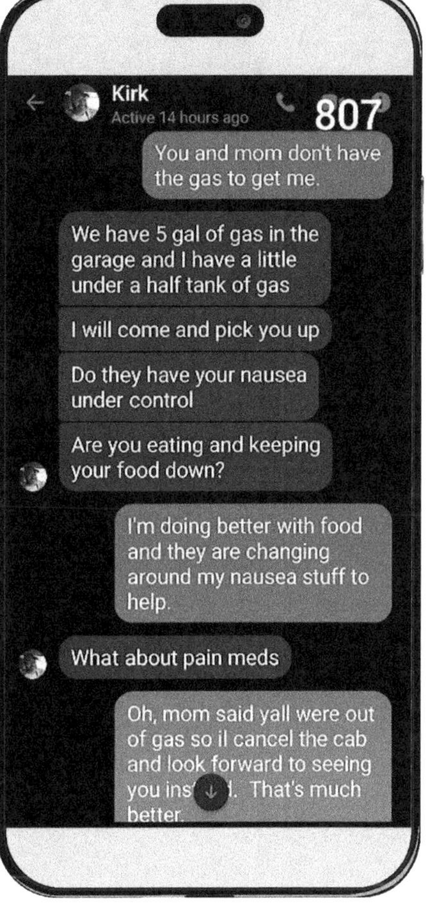
Kirk
Active 14 hours ago
807
You and mom don't have the gas to get me.
We have 5 gal of gas in the garage and I have a little under a half tank of gas
I will come and pick you up
Do they have your nausea under control
Are you eating and keeping your food down?
I'm doing better with food and they are changing around my nausea stuff to help.
What about pain meds
Oh, mom said yall were out of gas so il cancel the cab and look forward to seeing you instead. That's much better.

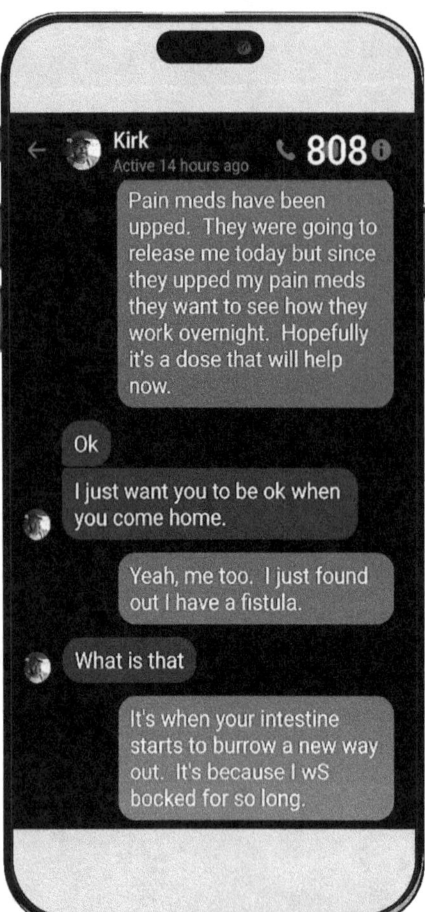

Kirk
Active 14 hours ago
808
Pain meds have been upped. They were going to release me today but since they upped my pain meds they want to see how they work overnight. Hopefully it's a dose that will help now.
Ok
I just want you to be ok when you come home.
Yeah, me too. I just found out I have a fistula.
What is that
It's when your intestine starts to burrow a new way out. It's because I wS bocked for so long.

Kirk
Active 14 hours ago
809
So I guess the stoma wasn't working good enough for your intestines lol
Lol
Oh, how was the sleep study?
How'd you sleep?
I left about 12:30am...the bed was hard and I couldn't get comfortable to sleep
Oh wow.
Bummer
I might have to use your mattress topper for the next one
Did they reschedule?
Not yet

Kirk
Active 14 hours ago
810
Hope they do soon.
I will have to call them
Ok.
I hope your feeling better
A bit. I just wanna go home.
I want you home
MAY 13, 2021 AT 12:13 PM
Text me tomorrow when you find out what time you will be discharged
MAY 13, 2021 AT 2:10 PM
Ok babe. I sure will.

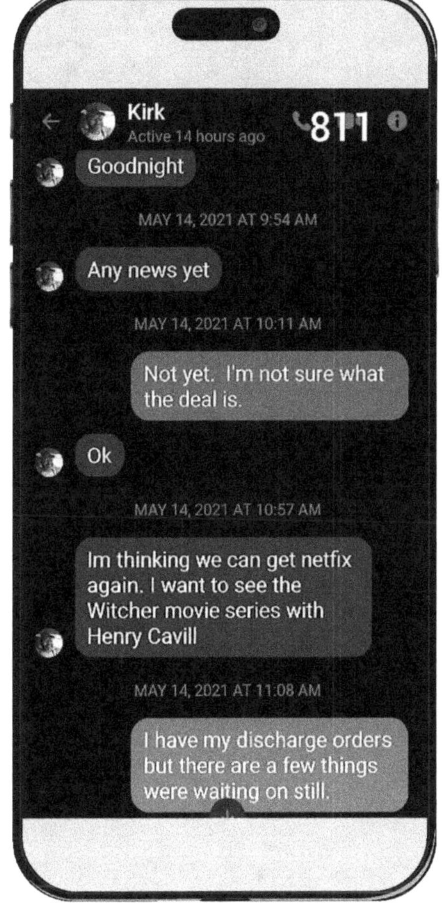

Kirk
Active 14 hours ago
811
Goodnight
MAY 14, 2021 AT 9:54 AM
Any news yet
MAY 14, 2021 AT 10:11 AM
Not yet. I'm not sure what the deal is.
Ok
MAY 14, 2021 AT 10:57 AM
Im thinking we can get netfix again. I want to see the Witcher movie series with Henry Cavill
MAY 14, 2021 AT 11:08 AM
I have my discharge orders but there are a few things were waiting on still.

Kirk
Active 14 hours ago
812
Getting ready to go. Yay.
MAY 14, 2021 AT 12:16 PM
Im 5 min out
The video chat ended.
May 14, 2021 at 12:20 PM
CALL BACK
Im here
Where are you
MAY 15, 2021 AT 9:48 AM
Help mo. With groceries
Pleaze
MAY 19, 2021 AT 6:34 AM
Can you get me breakfast?

Kirk
Active 14 hours ago
813
Love you
MAY 20, 2021 AT 7:56 AM
Just got here
MAY 20, 2021 AT 9:02 AM
Can you bring home a
pizza for lunch or dinner,
whenever you get home
today?
Extra pineapple.
MAY 20, 2021 AT 10:54 AM
On my way home
MAY 20, 2021 AT 12:06 PM
The video chat ended.
2 mins 9 secs, May 20, 2021 at
12:06 PM
CALL BACK

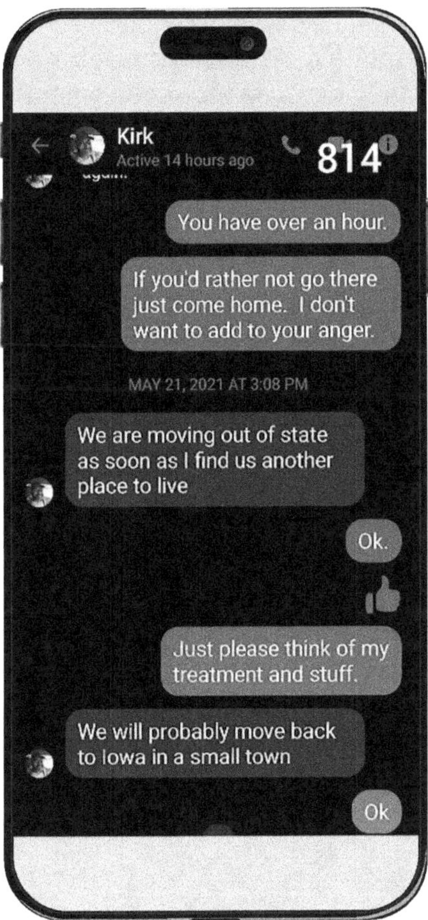

When I went through all the things I hate about Virginia. All was correct except when I said I hated the people. I should have stated Kim's doctors. Kim has suffered so much at the hands of a bureaucracy that paid more attention to the letter of rules than helping Kim beat cancer and help her with her pain.

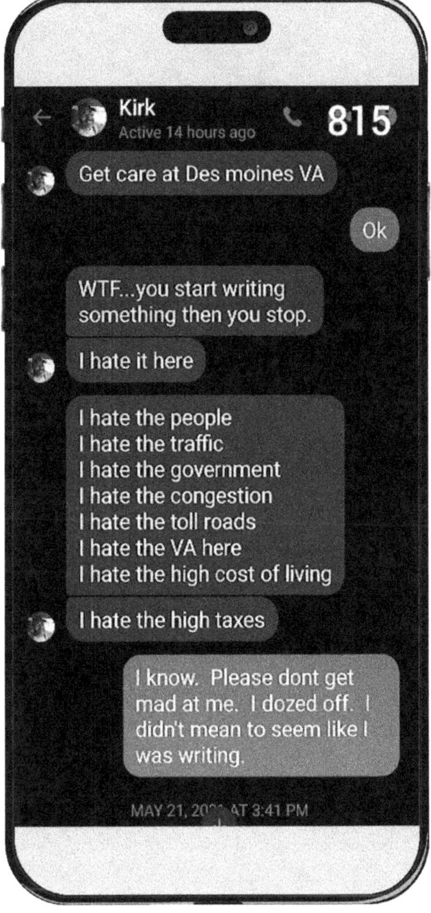

When Kim was talking to palliative care, it was just for show because that department was closed due to covid. So palliative care services were closed to her.

Kirk
Active 14 hours ago
Still no script
816
MAY 21, 2021 AT 3:52 PM
Coming back home
MAY 21, 2021 AT 4:36 PM
They told me it was signed for and ready to get.
Well have to go back on monday.
Goddammit.
MAY 24, 2021 AT 9:39 AM
Mom says we need a trip to the store to get milk and soda. She said she would go if you dont want to.
MAY 26, 2021 AT 8:41 PM
I made it home safe sweetheart

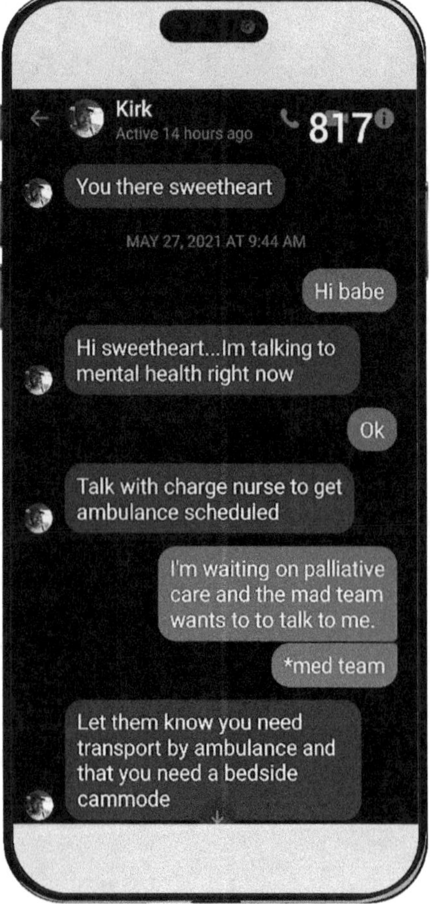
Kirk
Active 14 hours ago
817
You there sweetheart
MAY 27, 2021 AT 9:44 AM
Hi babe
Hi sweetheart...Im talking to mental health right now
Ok
Talk with charge nurse to get ambulance scheduled
I'm waiting on palliative care and the mad team wants to to talk to me.
*med team
Let them know you need transport by ambulance and that you need a bedside cammode

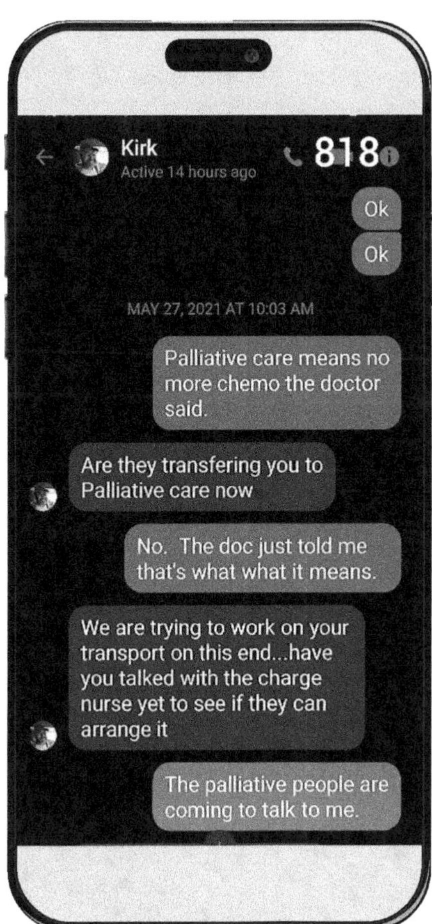
Kirk
Active 14 hours ago
818
Ok
Ok
MAY 27, 2021 AT 10:03 AM
Palliative care means no more chemo the doctor said.
Are they transfering you to Palliative care now
No. The doc just told me that's what what it means.
We are trying to work on your transport on this end...have you talked with the charge nurse yet to see if they can arrange it
The palliative people are coming to talk to me.

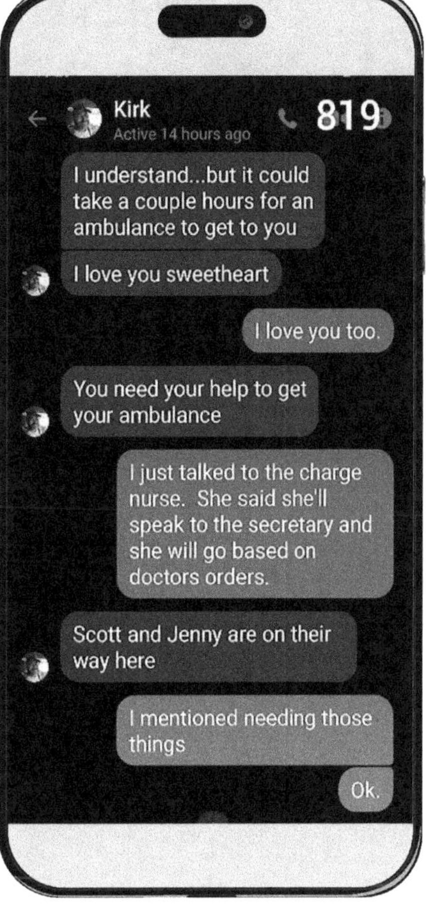
Kirk
Active 14 hours ago
819
I understand...but it could take a couple hours for an ambulance to get to you
I love you sweetheart
I love you too.
You need your help to get your ambulance
I just talked to the charge nurse. She said she'll speak to the secretary and she will go based on doctors orders.
Scott and Jenny are on their way here
I mentioned needing those things
Ok.

Kirk
Active 14 hours ago
820
Your mom is on her way to give you meds.
Thank you
It'll be good to see them.
I missed you last night. I kept looking at your bed expecting to see you
Awwwww
I wake up throughout the night when your here and check on you
Aww
We are trying to get Arslan to prescribe fluids and TPM for home

Kirk
Active 14 hours ago
821
I feel like if I stop chemo I'm giving up. This fucking sucks that I can't talk to you and mom in person right now.
I need your input in person.
Dont agree to anything until we are together and can discuss it
Ok
And I mean you, me and your mom
Yes.
All 3.
Yes!
3 musketeers
Lol

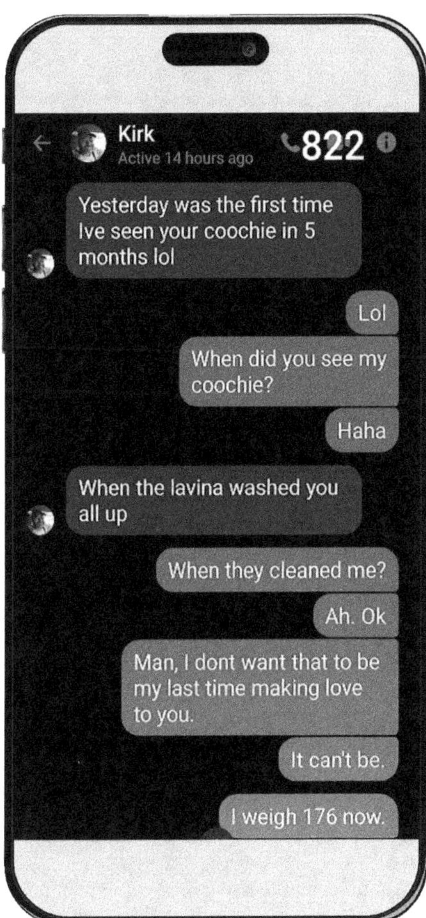
Kirk
Active 14 hours ago
822
Yesterday was the first time Ive seen your coochie in 5 months lol
Lol
When did you see my coochie?
Haha
When the lavina washed you all up
When they cleaned me?
Ah. Ok
Man, I dont want that to be my last time making love to you.
It can't be.
I weigh 176 now.

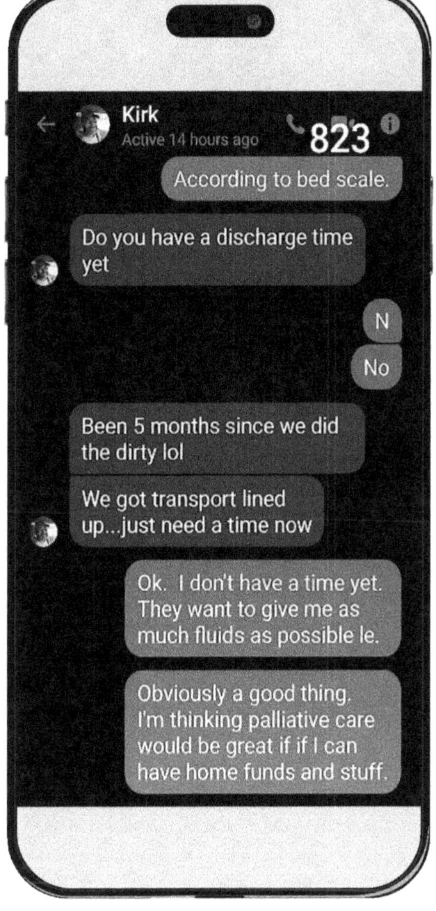
Kirk
Active 14 hours ago
823
According to bed scale.
Do you have a discharge time yet
N
No
Been 5 months since we did the dirty lol
We got transport lined up...just need a time now
Ok. I don't have a time yet. They want to give me as much fluids as possible le.
Obviously a good thing. I'm thinking palliative care would be great if if I can have home funds and stuff.

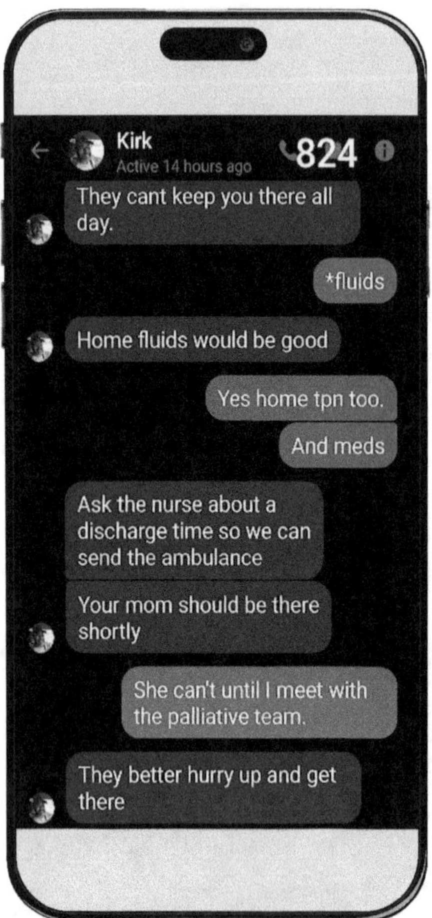

Kirk
Active 14 hours ago
824
They cant keep you there all day.
*fluids
Home fluids would be good
Yes home tpn too.
And meds
Ask the nurse about a discharge time so we can send the ambulance
Your mom should be there shortly
She can't until I meet with the palliative team.
They better hurry up and get there

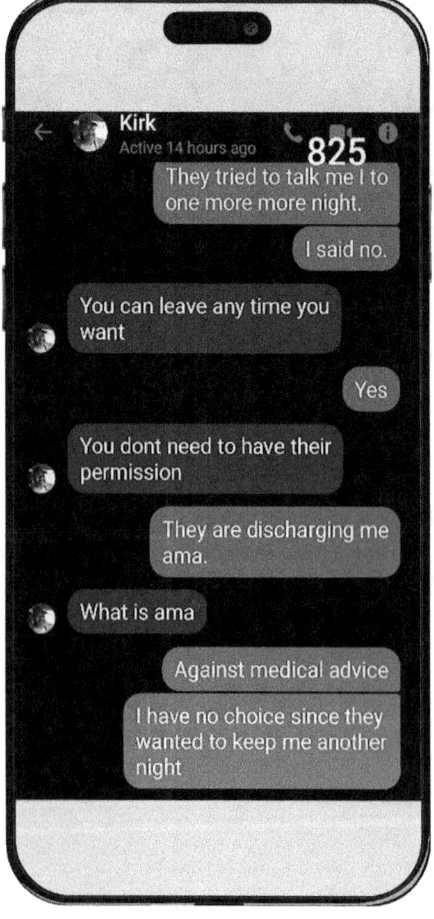

Kirk
Active 14 hours ago
825
They tried to talk me I to one more more night.
I said no.
You can leave any time you want
Yes
You dont need to have their permission
They are discharging me ama.
What is ama
Against medical advice
I have no choice since they wanted to keep me another night

It is around this time that Kim gave me and her mom a big scare. When I was helping Kim back from the bathroom to her bed, she collapsed and fell to the floor. The strength in her legs vanished and she couldn't walk anymore. We had to call the fire department and have them lift Kim from off the floor and set her in bed. Kim got a good-sized bruise on her knees from falling. After this me and her mom started pushing for a wheel chair and a bedside commode.

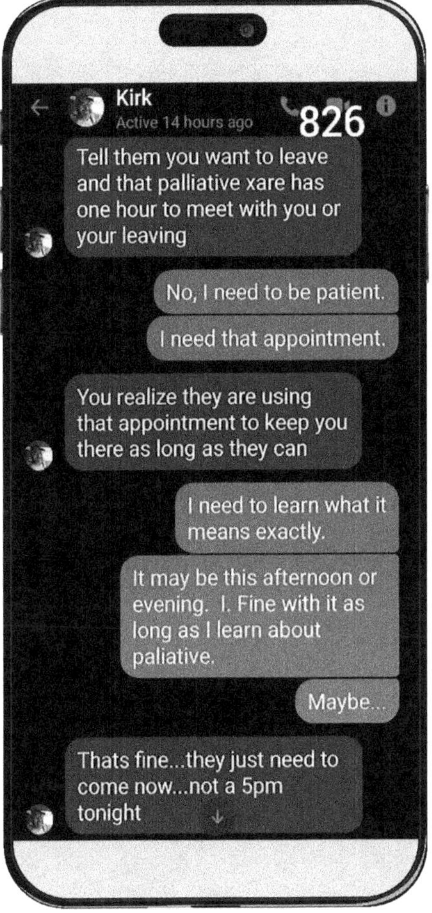

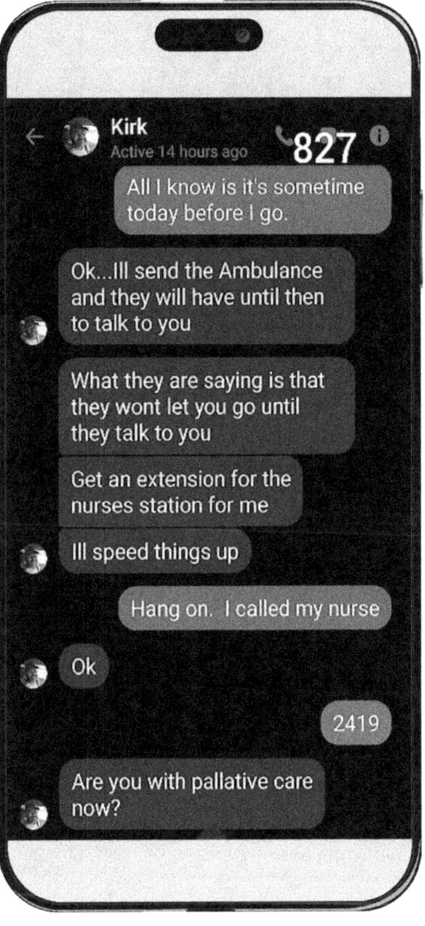

Kirk
Active 14 hours ago
828
You there
MAY 27, 2021 AT 1:03 PM
Hi. Waiting for my ride.
Mon just left. Glad she was here.
Are you in your room or downstairs
In my room
They'll get me on the stretcher.
I cant wait till you get home
I scheduled your puck up to try and avoid afternoon traffic
Pick up

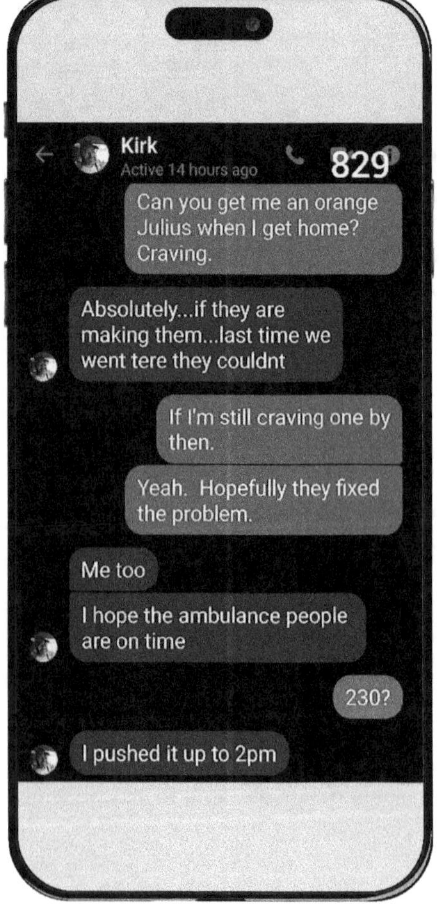

Kirk
Active 14 hours ago
829
Can you get me an orange Julius when I get home? Craving.
Absolutely...if they are making them...last time we went tere they couldnt
If I'm still craving one by then.
Yeah. Hopefully they fixed the problem.
Me too
I hope the ambulance people are on time
230?
I pushed it up to 2pm

Kirk
Active 14 hours ago
830
Ok. Dr. Aransas trying to order my bedside commode and wheelchair before I leave.
Arslan
We have been working nonstop to try and get you what you need
I know.
Thank you babe
I love you
More than you can imagine
I love you and appreciate you

Kirk
Active 14 hours ago
831
You hungry at all
Yeah. For plain burgers. Lol
Or steak dinner.
Ill get you one when I go for your julius
Ok.
If I'm still hungry by then.
Maybe grab a burger for me to
That'd be good.
Actually Im hungry now lol
Lol
Tami says hi

Kirk
Active 14 hours ago
832
I talk with dr. Arslan tomorrow
At 10:30
Mom told me.
I just talked to a doc that is adding another med that works I guess like a cannibinoid that helps with nausea.
Now they are giving you weed lol
Cool
Hopefully the nurse gets it u to me before the ambulance people get here.
Lol.

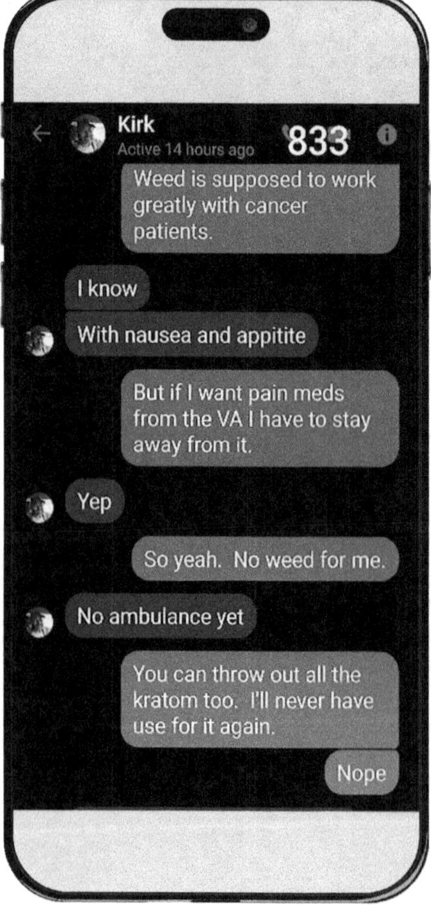
Kirk
Active 14 hours ago
833
Weed is supposed to work greatly with cancer patients.
I know
With nausea and appitite
But if I want pain meds from the VA I have to stay away from it.
Yep
So yeah. No weed for me.
No ambulance yet
You can throw out all the kratom too. I'll never have use for it again.
Nope

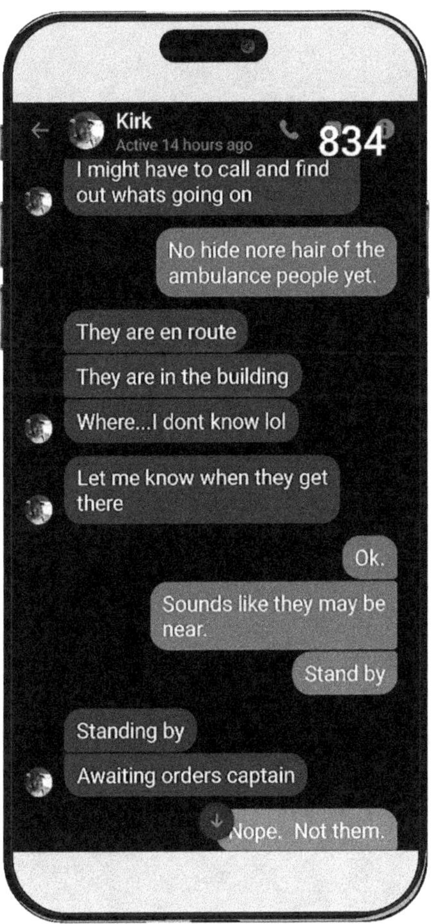

Kirk
Active 14 hours ago
834
I might have to call and find out whats going on
No hide nore hair of the ambulance people yet.
They are en route
They are in the building
Where...I dont know lol
Let me know when they get there
Ok.
Sounds like they may be near.
Stand by
Standing by
Awaiting orders captain
Nope. Not them.

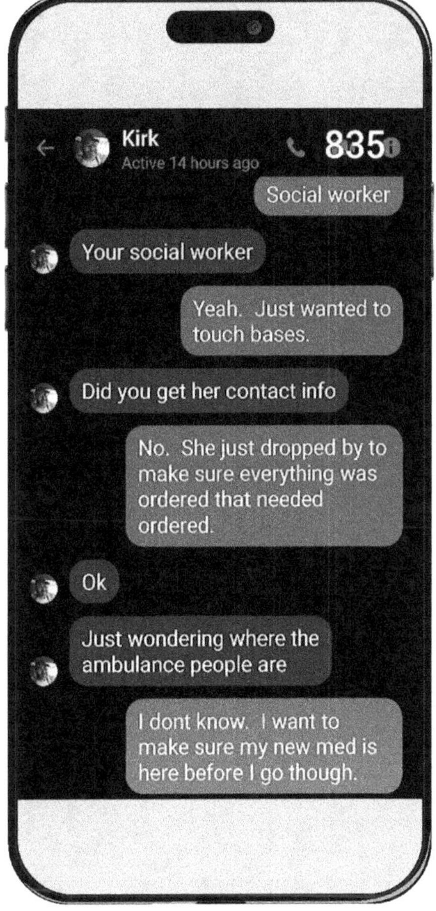

Kirk
Active 14 hours ago
835
Social worker
Your social worker
Yeah. Just wanted to touch bases.
Did you get her contact info
No. She just dropped by to make sure everything was ordered that needed ordered.
Ok
Just wondering where the ambulance people are
I dont know. I want to make sure my new med is here before I go though.

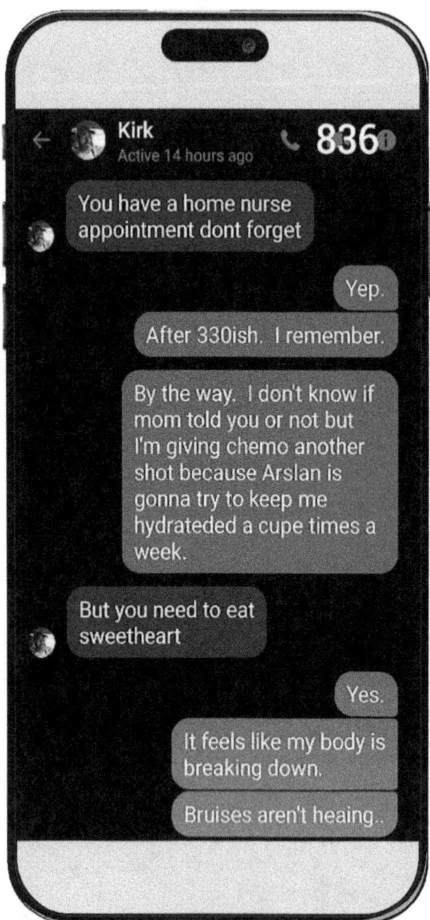

Kirk
Active 14 hours ago
836
You have a home nurse appointment dont forget
Yep.
After 330ish. I remember.
By the way. I don't know if mom told you or not but I'm giving chemo another shot because Arslan is gonna try to keep me hydrateded a cupe times a week.
But you need to eat sweetheart
Yes.
It feels like my body is breaking down.
Bruises aren't heaing..

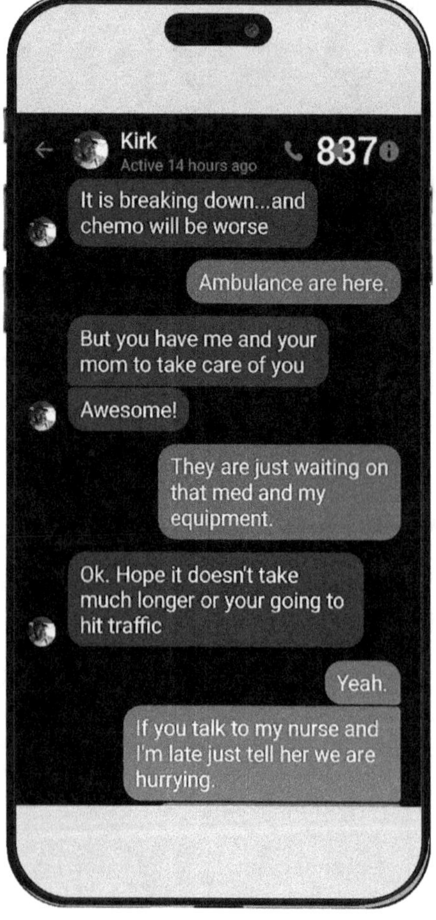

Kirk
Active 14 hours ago
837
It is breaking down...and chemo will be worse
Ambulance are here.
But you have me and your mom to take care of you
Awesome!
They are just waiting on that med and my equipment.
Ok. Hope it doesn't take much longer or your going to hit traffic
Yeah.
If you talk to my nurse and I'm late just tell her we are hurrying.

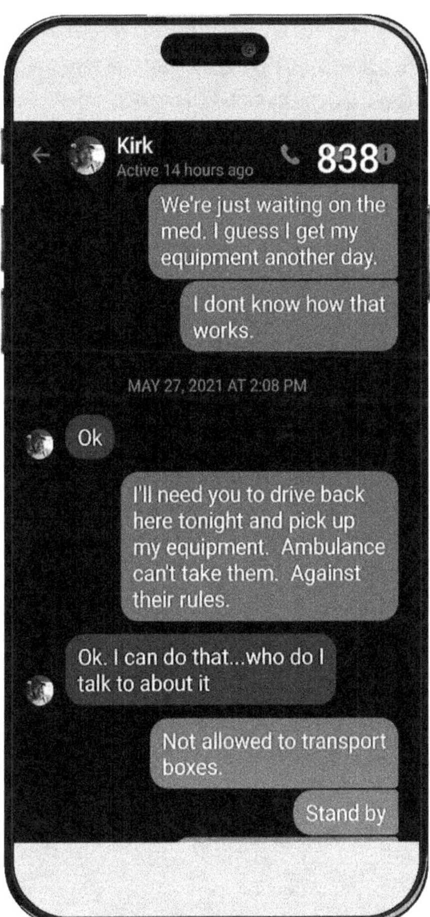

Kirk
Active 14 hours ago
838
We're just waiting on the med. I guess I get my equipment another day.
I dont know how that works.
MAY 27, 2021 AT 2:08 PM
Ok
I'll need you to drive back here tonight and pick up my equipment. Ambulance can't take them. Against their rules.
Ok. I can do that...who do I talk to about it
Not allowed to transport boxes.
Stand by

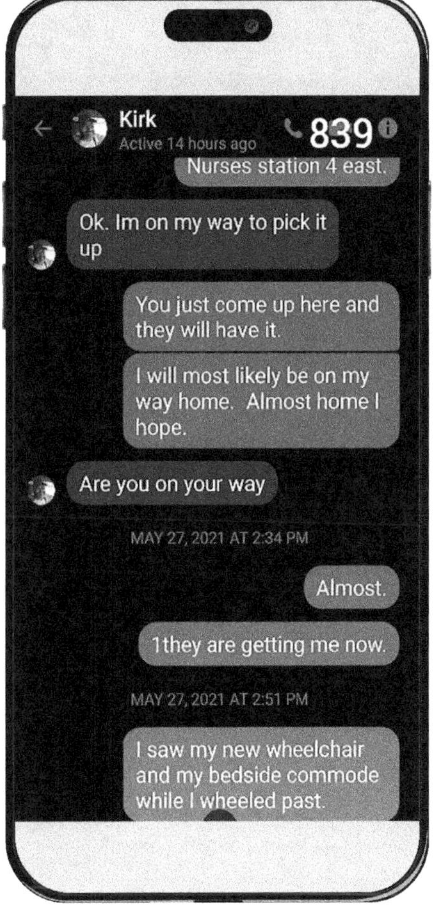

Kirk
Active 14 hours ago
839
Nurses station 4 east.
Ok. Im on my way to pick it up
You just come up here and they will have it.
I will most likely be on my way home. Almost home I hope.
Are you on your way
MAY 27, 2021 AT 2:34 PM
Almost.
1they are getting me now.
MAY 27, 2021 AT 2:51 PM
I saw my new wheelchair and my bedside commode while I wheeled past.

On this day, all of Kim's family showed up at the house. Her two daughters Lauren and Elizabeth, sister Jennifer, father, step sister, brother and his wife and daughter. They stayed in town for two days and Kim had finally got to see her two daughters after not seeing then for two decades.

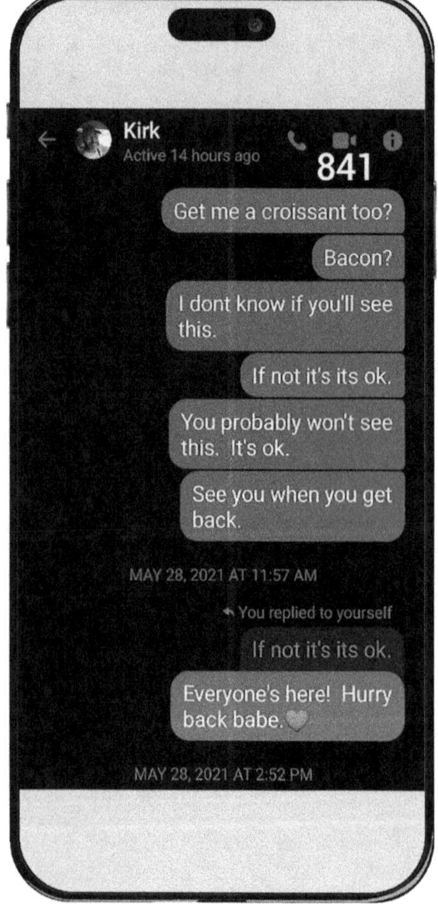

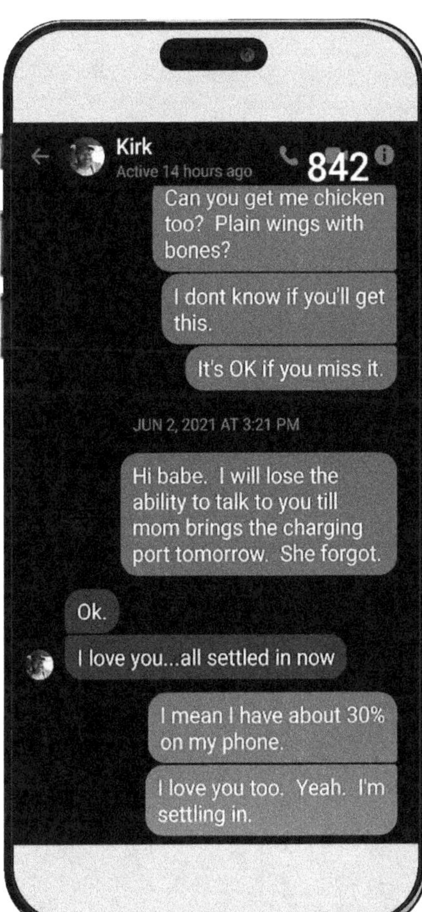

Kirk
Active 14 hours ago
842
Can you get me chicken too? Plain wings with bones?
I dont know if you'll get this.
It's OK if you miss it.
JUN 2, 2021 AT 3:21 PM
Hi babe. I will lose the ability to talk to you till mom brings the charging port tomorrow. She forgot.
Ok.
I love you...all settled in now
I mean I have about 30% on my phone.
I love you too. Yeah. I'm settling in.

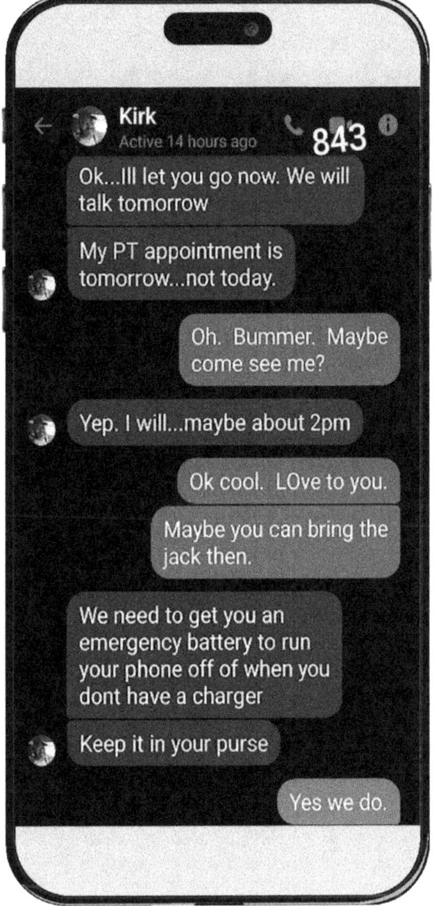

Kirk
Active 14 hours ago
843
Ok...Ill let you go now. We will talk tomorrow
My PT appointment is tomorrow...not today.
Oh. Bummer. Maybe come see me?
Yep. I will...maybe about 2pm
Ok cool. LOve to you.
Maybe you can bring the jack then.
We need to get you an emergency battery to run your phone off of when you dont have a charger
Keep it in your purse
Yes we do.

Kirk
Active 14 hours ago
844
I have an old one that doesn't work well anymore.
Then we need to toss it and get a new one
Yep
Has the doctor been in to see you yet
Not yet.
Just lots of nurses.
I guess its been frantic
How was the bus ride
Good. I felt nauseous through most of it though.

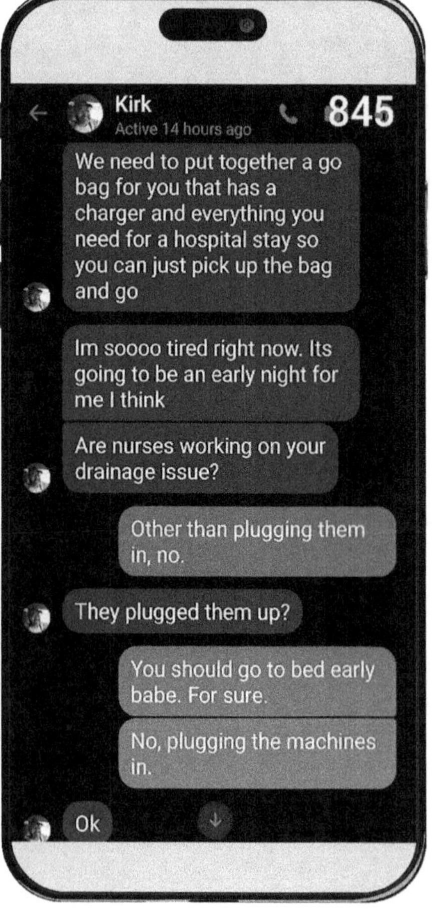

Kirk
Active 14 hours ago
845
We need to put together a go bag for you that has a charger and everything you need for a hospital stay so you can just pick up the bag and go
Im soooo tired right now. Its going to be an early night for me I think
Are nurses working on your drainage issue?
Other than plugging them in, no.
They plugged them up?
You should go to bed early babe. For sure.
No, plugging the machines in.
Ok

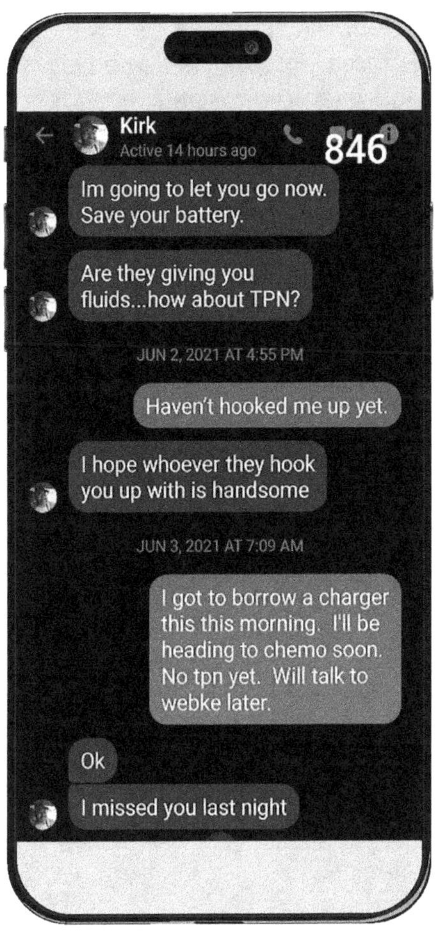
Kirk
Active 14 hours ago
846
Im going to let you go now. Save your battery.
Are they giving you fluids...how about TPN?
JUN 2, 2021 AT 4:55 PM
Haven't hooked me up yet.
I hope whoever they hook you up with is handsome
JUN 3, 2021 AT 7:09 AM
I got to borrow a charger this this morning. I'll be heading to chemo soon. No tpn yet. Will talk to webke later.
Ok
I missed you last night

Kirk
Active 14 hours ago
847
Im at the hospital
JUN 3, 2021 AT 3:46 PM
Hi mommy
mean Kirk. Lol
This is hubby
Yeah, I figured that. Out. Lo
Too late
I came to say hi and you were in xray
No, at chemo but danm.
How are you feeling
You must be really tired

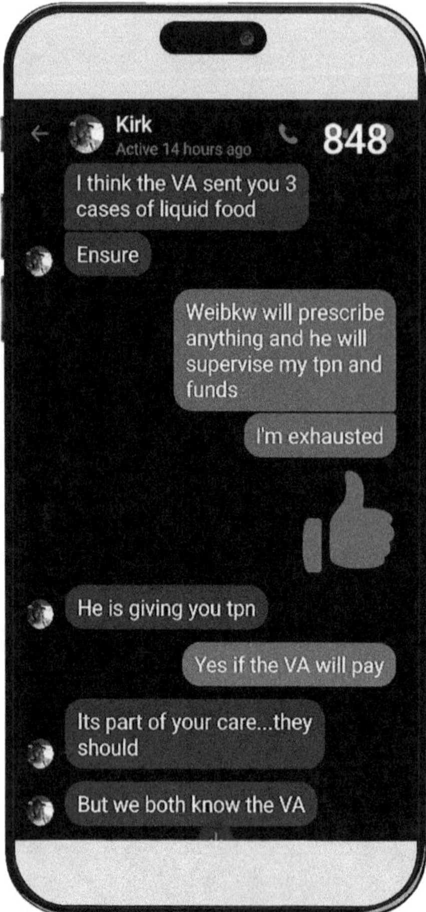

It is about this time that Kim entered hospice care and we had a legitimate pharmacy in our home of food, bandages, tubes, nausea meds and pain killers. Kim told us that she didn't want to die in the hospital alone. She wanted to be at home with her family.

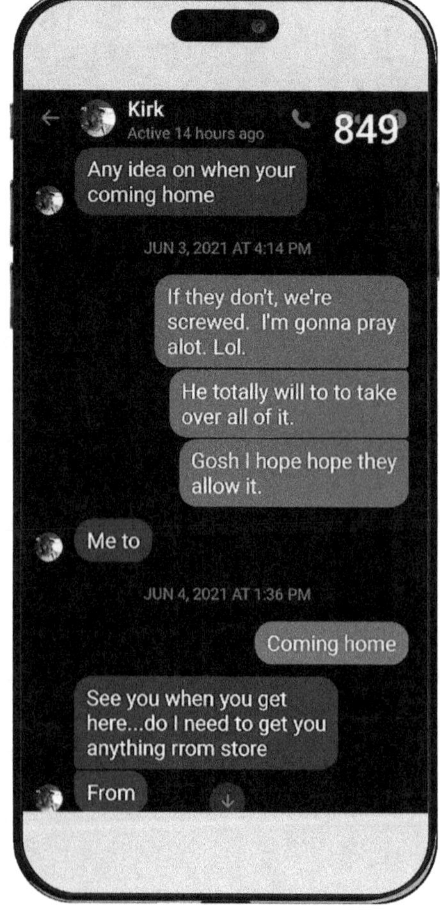

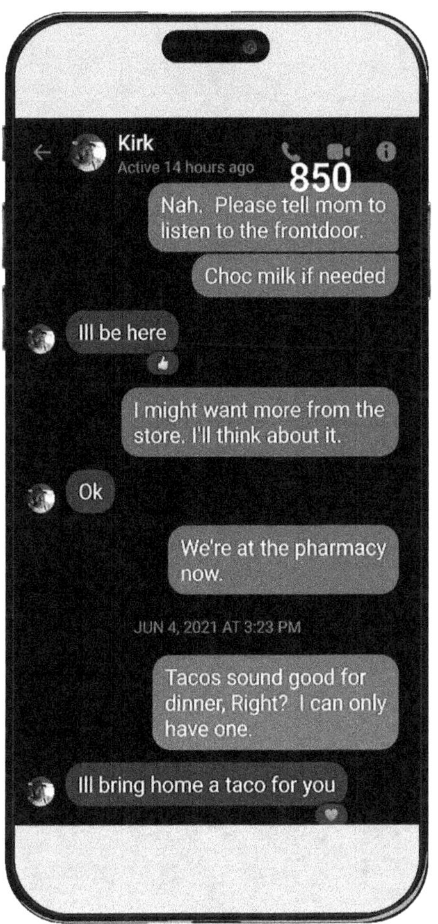
Kirk
Active 14 hours ago
850
Nah. Please tell mom to listen to the frontdoor.
Choc milk if needed
Ill be here
I might want more from the store. I'll think about it.
Ok
We're at the pharmacy now.
JUN 4, 2021 AT 3:23 PM
Tacos sound good for dinner, Right? I can only have one.
Ill bring home a taco for you

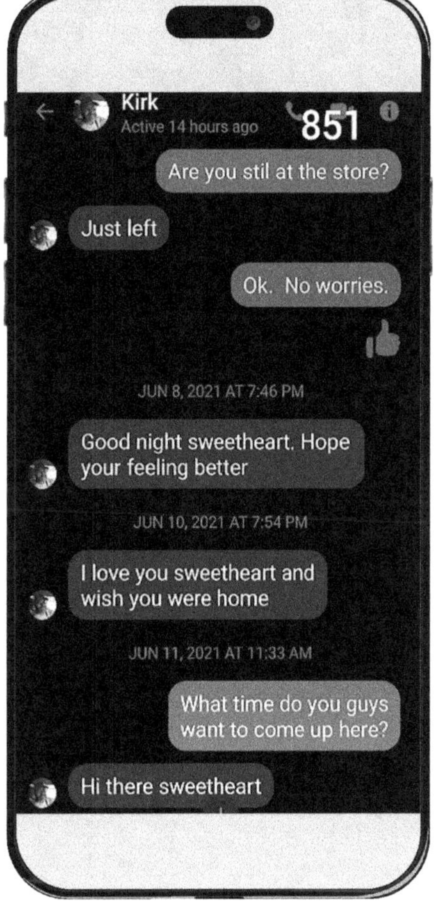
Kirk
Active 14 hours ago
851
Are you stil at the store?
Just left
Ok. No worries.
JUN 8, 2021 AT 7:46 PM
Good night sweetheart. Hope your feeling better
JUN 10, 2021 AT 7:54 PM
I love you sweetheart and wish you were home
JUN 11, 2021 AT 11:33 AM
What time do you guys want to come up here?
Hi there sweetheart

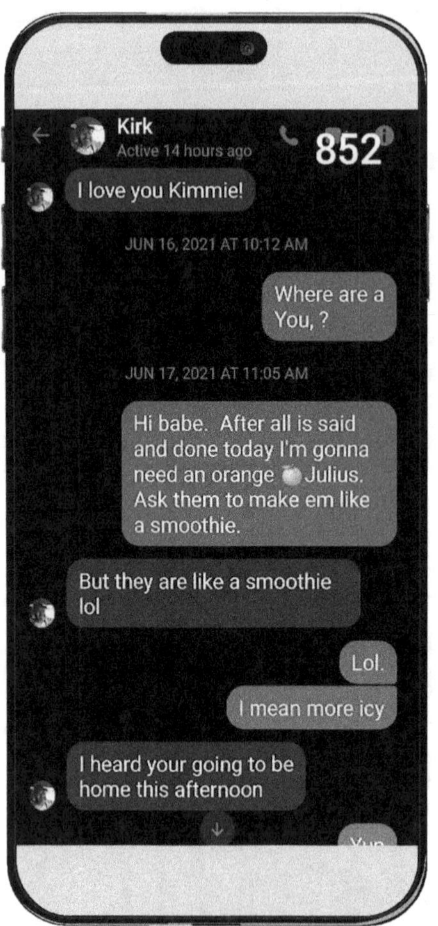

Kirk
Active 14 hours ago
852
I love you Kimmie!
JUN 16, 2021 AT 10:12 AM
Where are a You, ?
JUN 17, 2021 AT 11:05 AM
Hi babe. After all is said and done today I'm gonna need an orange Julius. Ask them to make em like a smoothie.
But they are like a smoothie lol
Lol.
I mean more icy
I heard your going to be home this afternoon

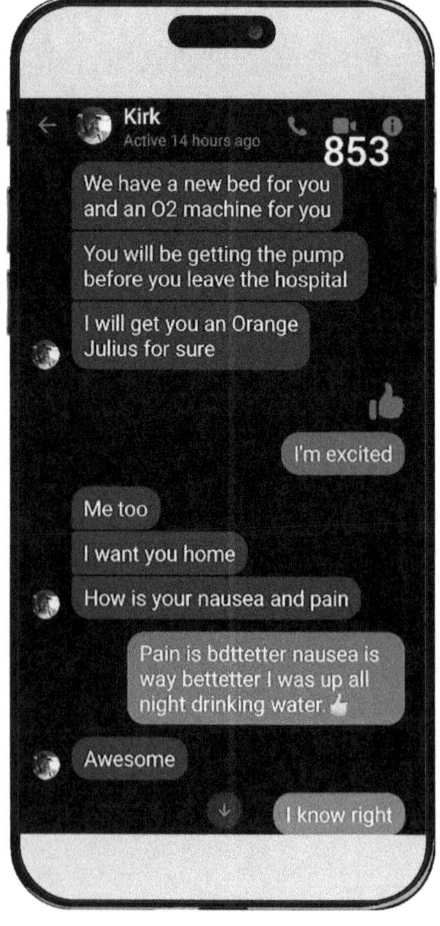

Kirk
Active 14 hours ago
853
We have a new bed for you and an O2 machine for you
You will be getting the pump before you leave the hospital
I will get you an Orange Julius for sure
I'm excited
Me too
I want you home
How is your nausea and pain
Pain is bdttetter nausea is way bettter I was up all night drinking water.
Awesome
I know right

The night that Kim's nausea went away, I had a friend of mine who has a Christian ministry pray for Kim's healing. She prayed for her total recovery. Although Kim was not healed from her cancer, Kim's nausea was gone and she wasn't vomiting five or six times a day. The name of my Friend is Jaclyn Fain. I really appreciate her prayer in which God made Kim's final weeks nausea free.

2013

In 2013, me and Kim first started talking when I was going through my divorce with my second wife. It started out with me complimenting her on her shot grouping for her arrows on her target. She was a pretty good shot and I was truly impressed. Then we began to talk about our pasts and where we went to school and who our friends were. I found out the she was in Tall Flags at Redondo Union High School (RUHS) and was a captain of the Junior Varsity Tall Flags Squad her junior year. She knew my girlfriend Timi O'Donnell, who was in Tall Flags as well.

I also found out that she was in the Air force from January 1989 to September 1994 as an Airframe Specialist and left the Air force with a medical discharge. She constantly told me that she wanted to retire from the Air Force and she loved what she did.

We talked for about five months and then I deleted my Facebook profile and we lost contact.

2015

I believe that this is the year I opened up a new Facebook account and in late 2015 me and Kim reconnected and it was her who sent me a friend request to begin our conversations again.

I started seeing pictures of babies pop up on my timeline from Kim and I started thinking, "how many kids does she have?" When I asked her this, she said that those were not real babies. They were dolls that I make. She said that she was a reborn artist. I then told her that I couldn't tell the difference and that she was an excellent artist.

We talked about her time in the Air Force. She said that she wished she had waited a little longer to have children and should have focused on her career. But she also stated that she does not regret having her two daughters Elizabeth and Lauren (not sure about the spelling). She also told me that she was very angry with her father and step monster (referring to her step mother) who used Kim's illness to trick her into giving up her two daughters. This led to Kim not being able to see her daughters until 5 months before her death. She also mentioned that when she got sick in the Airforce that her command thought that she was faking it. She even got disciplined for malingering. This went on for a couple years and it was Kim's mother Chris, who said she needed to get checked for Crohn's disease. After a positive diagnosis for Crohn's disease, she was then discharged with aa Honorable discharge.

She was very proud of her service and her work on the SR 71.

In December 2015, our conversations became flirtatious and there was definite chemistry there. She appreciated my dirty sense of humor and we continued talking into the next year.

2016

2016 started where 2015 left off. Kim and I would talk just about every night from forty-five minutes to three hours. Our talks would last dependent on how much work I had after my Post Office job for my business. Between January and April, I was always bringing up the positives of Ankeny Iowa. How it was the fastest growing city in the US for the third year in a row and how everything is just a ten-minute drive to get whatever you needed. I was bragging on how we had a Walmart, Target, Best Buy, Hobby Lobby, Kohls, Menards, Home Depot and a Sam's Club. Then there are also the six grocery stores in town that are just a five-minute drive from anywhere in Ankeny.

During this time, I was also talking up my positives to impress her. I had a full-time job with the United States Postal Service (USPS). I had full health and dental which she could be added. I owned my own home; my own business and my car was paid for. I was totally trying to impress her about myself and the quality of life I could give her.

I was doing this because over the past several months Learning about her hobbies of archery, hiking and reborning fascinated me. How an artist can take a blank vinyl doll and turn it into a lifelike baby where you had to do a doubletake to determine it was just a doll. She was patient, detailed and methodical in here approach to make the perfect baby for clients. Kim also knew a lot about archery. When we met, she had three bows. She would go out in the yard at her mother's house to the makeshift range she had set up in Grants pass Oregon on a daily basis weather permitting and practice. She would post her groupings on Facebook and was shocked at how good she was for a fifty-yard distance. Out of ten shots, six would be in the bullseye while the other four were just out of the circle. I would commonly respond with a "Not bad, not bad at all."

Things took a turn for the good in April when She went and got her colonoscopy. On that day, I sent her some flowers that were delivered to her house and were waiting for her when she returned from the doctor's appointment. That is also the day when I asked her to marry me. She obviously said yes after months of telling her how great I was and how Iowa was. But this is also the most tragic day in our lives because during her colonoscopy, the doctor tattooed a spot to watch instead of taking a biopsy and having it tested.

After I asked her to marry me, I immediately started making plans to visiting her in Frants pass so that we can get married. Kim had told me that she had been married before and been in several relationships but that didn't bother me. I did put in for some leave between May 1st through May 8th roughly. These dates are estimates because we got married on May 5th and I spent about nine days there. After my itinerary was set, I told her to tell her mom. She kept on putting off that conversation with her mom and finally told me that she told her a few days before my flight left.

The day came when I was to fly to Grants Pass and I was very excited. I took my dog Cricket to be boarded while I was gone and left to the Airport about 2pm. I boarded my flight about 4pm and ended up in Medford Oregon about 10:30pm. It was actually very funny when I got there. I got off the plane, and walked into the lobby for baggage claim. Kim didn't recognize me (probably I was in a nice suit which I was going to wear for our wedding), so I walked around and stood about fifty feet behind her and just watched her and her mom watch people coming through the exit. After about ten minutes, I called her and told her to look behind her as I was walking up to here. She gave me a hug and introduced me to her mom Chris and we left to go to the car.

On the way back to Grants Pass we spent the forty minutes barely talking to each other. Actually, the atmosphere was kind of tense for some reason. I later learned that Kim had a bad history of picking men and that they were abusive. I'm sure it was tense because Chris was seriously doubting Kim's decision to have me there with them for the next week. I think that was the Friday before Cinco De Mayo. When we got back to Grants Pass Kim and I got our own private room with a newly remodeled bathroom away from the main house but linked by an eight hundred square foot deck. We finally went to bed about 1am and had great sex until about 2am.

We woke up about 8am on Saturday and enjoyed a leisurely day just talking, eating and of course having sex. We also started to plan our wedding. Kim ended up contacting a travelling Pastor who does nothing but conduct wedding ceremonies. I didn't know that it was a thing lol. Kim had a knack for finding things on the internet. She definitely had a gift. We then scheduled a date to get married for May 5th.

Sundy came around and again me and Kim were having sex. It was a day that me and Kim would never forget. I gave her twenty- three orgasms in ninety minutes. Kim then remarked that this gives a new meaning to 23andme lol. We both busted out laughing and kind of snuggled in bed. Around 2pm, me and Kim were in the main house talking with Chris. During our conversation, I said that me and Kim would like to be married here in house. Chris looked at me with a look of disbelief. What I found out at that moment was that Kim told her mom that I was coming to visit, not coming to marry. As you can understand, Chris was surprised and stated that she wished that she would have been notified of this. I turned to Kim and said "I thought you told her last week?"

The Confident Kim I had talked to for the past six months was a façade. She revealed to me that she was non-confrontive and meek. I guess she was a little embarrassed about her past dating choices and her mother might have said something about us getting married after she had to rescue her from her last boyfriend Joe in Wisconsin.

The rest of the week was preparing for the wedding and on Thursday Mays 5th at 11:30am, Me and Kim were married. Celebrating with us were Chris her mom, Forest her uncle, Cheryl her aunt, Cheryl's significant other. After the fifteen-minute ceremony and fifteen minutes of paperwork. We all went to a local restaurant and ate lunch. Oh! I almost forgot. On Sunday, May 1st, I took Kim to McDonalds and had breakfast. I got her a fountain drink for her meal and from that point on, every time we got in the car, Kim wanted a fountain drink. Even if it was just a five-minute drive.

After I got a full tour of the property, I noticed that Chris's patio off of her bedroom was overgrown. I talked with Kim and we decided to clean up her patio so she could go out there during the Spring and Summer to enjoy the weather along with a good book. Since I didn't have any work shoes, Kim let me borrow a pair of her own. Me and Kim spent about $800 in patio Knick knacks and cushions along with two twelve-hour days of elbow grease to make it a nice open place for Chris. Those two days taught me a lot about Kim. She was a slow worker lol. But she was determined, thorough and overall, a hard worker. She was right by my side enduring the hot weather and bees. I got stung once and hurt like a mother fucker lol.

On that Sunday it was time for me to go. I left in the morning and was home in Ankeny Iowa by 3pm.

After arriving home, me and Kim continued to text and talk on the phone about when she would be able come to Iowa. She said she wanted another 23andme experience. I told her it would be two to three months before I would be able to save money for her come. About mid- way through May, Kim told me that her mother was going to pay for her to go to Iowa. I was completely blown away and June 3rd would be the day that she arrived. We already missed each other and Thank Chris for the help. What was really a Blessing, is that Chris told us not to worry about paying her back. I can see where Kim got her generosity and kindness from. Kim was a very selfless person and I admired her for that.

Well, Fast forward to June 3rd. There was no rest for the weary. I had put in a full day at the USPS, then went to pick up Kim at the airport around six pm. From the airport we went straight to a job I had to do for my Business. I had to strip and wax a vinyl composite floor for a dental clinic that makes their own dentures. It was about 1500 square feet and we didn't get out of there until 5am Saturday morning after starting at 8pm Friday night. Kim again was right by my side helping me even after she was travelling all day (we all know how stressful and tiring that can be) and helped me all night. She was of great help to me and was along with me, proud of the end result of the floor. Kim was always up to help me when I needed and extra hand.

What I'm about to go into next is what will lead to my betrayal of Kim. Early on, I realized that Kim was not a good housekeeper. When I visited Oregon, I guess she really did put her best foot forward. Throughout the rest of 2016, I continually commented on how the dirty the house was and I needed her to keep it clean so I can actually relax after I put in a six-teen or twenty- hour day. I got really angry that I would be out working so hard to come home to a wife that was laying on the couch watching Star Trek Reruns while the house was a mess. A few times I blew up and yelled at her. I wouldn't say yelling at her, just yelling because I was angry. I never belittled her or called her names. This was a big no-no for Kim. She took it personally and told me that she didn't like it when I yelled. But unfortunately, that was the only time when she would clean up the house is when I had reached my boiling point and blew up.

Another thing that irritated me was that Kim never cooked a homecooked meal for us. We would always order take out and I was getting angry over how much money we were spending. Towards the end of 2016 she did start cooking more.

2017

I'm going to start off by saying 2017 was the worst year in our marriage. For the first eighteen months of our marriage, I had one foot out the door. Her failure to keep the house clean and cook pissed me off to no end. When she decided to work, she was the hardest and most dedicated worker one could have who paid attention to detail.

When she worked with me, I know that the work would get done and get done right. Just as I took great pride in the work, I gave my clients; she took great pride in doing a great job for me. Because of this, I could not understand how she could put in great effort in helping me with my business when I needed her and how our house looked like a hoarders lived there.

Kim would always help me every Tuesday and Saturday nights from 6 to 11pm. She would clean all eight bathrooms for me in a fifty-six thousand square foot church with about twenty rooms, two kitchens, pre-teen youth center, teen youth center and a fifteen thousand square foot gymnasium to clean. Kim would always complain that the women were hell of lot nastier than the men were. She would tell me of how urine and feces would be on the walls and floor in the women's stalls. She handled all that mess for me and I truly appreciated her for that.

I would always stop by at the convenience store Casey's and get us some fountain drinks and order us a large pizza to eat before we got started at the church. I can tell you one day she wanted Jume to buy her some Reese's peanut butter cups when I went in to Casey's and I told her no because we were getting drinks and pizza. She didn't argue or beg, but two days later, we get several packages from Amazon and I begin to open a them. I get to about the fifth package and what do I see...six king size Reese's peanut butter cups. After seeing these and remembered what happened two days prior, I began to crack a smile and chuckle. I then went to Kim's art studio that I built for her and showed her the box. She looked at them and said "you can have them; I don't want them anymore." I then said, "Did you really want them this bad?" She just giggled while attempting to say "well" and went back to working on her dolls. I could only laugh at how cute she looked sitting there in her baseball cap with her hair in a pony tail pulled through the back of her cap.

June 2017

June 2017 is the beginning of a nightmare. On June 10, 2017, I was accused of stealing from the USPS. On June 11th, I quit the USPS because I didn't want to work for an employer who would make up lies about me. They falsified statements by taking a statement from person A and assigning it to person B because person A was fired before trial. The USPS decided to prosecute and I was found not guilty. I was unable to get unemployment and thirty days later I lost the contract with the church. Because I quit the USPS and the church canceling cost us seven thousand dollars a month in income.

For Kim's Birthday in July, I had rented an entire restaurant for just the two of us for two hours. We had steak with garlic potatoes with steamed veggies. After everything that was going on in our lives, I wanted to make her feel special and loved. This is about the time I started to get depressed. I worked my business part time because I could barely get out of bed most days. I was sleeping eighteen to twenty hours a day and it was because of Kim that I didn't starve to death. During these economic and dark times, I couldn't pay child support. We applied for financial help for our mortgage through Polk County VA and got aid. However, the mortgage company would not accept the vouchers. The vouchers needed to be sent back to the Polk County VA after the Lender filled them out. When the Polk County VA received the return vouchers, they would issue a check to the lender. Since the lender didn't follow through on their end, we feel behind in our mortgage payment. Not only did we fall behind on mortgage payments but I fell behind on my $750 monthly child support obligation

In August I was arrested pertaining to the allegations from the USPS. Apparently, I missed a court date on July 29th, that I was never informed of. I was arrested in Cedar Rapids Iowa and had to post $300 bond. On the two-hour drive home, I talked with Kim and she jokingly called me a hardened criminal.

In September, our finances got so bad that we decided to declare bankruptcy. Kim also resorted to selling off her prized jointed doll collection. She loved those dolls but willingly sold those dolls to help us financially. She was also working on her vinyl reborn dolls to sell.

During this time, Kim was getting well known in the reborn world for her beautiful work and she was getting lots of offers to do prototypes for sculptors. How this works, a sculptor will contact an artist to paint, add hair and eyes, clothing and take pictures. The artist can then sell these prototypes for money. The artist will then send pictures of the finished dolls to the sculptor who can then use these pictures for marketing. Kim worked long hours to produce dolls to help with our finances. On top of her working she was taking care of me and was beginning to cook more homecooked meals to save money.

In December, I went to do a job in Dubuque Iowa. I had a female friend in Dubuque and asked her if I could stay with her. That was a big mistake because I ended up sleeping with her. I felt bad afterward, but decided not to tell Kim about it.

To recap 2017

1)   *I quit my USPS job*

2)   *I was falsely accused of stealing*

3)   *I lost my private healthcare and dental*

4)   *I lost most of my business clients due to my depression*

5)   *Got behind on my mortgage payments*

6)   *Got behind on my child support*

7)   *Had to repay $3,000 to the USPS for leave*

8)   *Fell into a state of deep depression*

9)   *I cheated on Kim*

10)   *Denied unemployment benefits*

All these setbacks fueled my depression and lack of energy and continued to sleep up to twenty hours a day. I showered and brushed my teeth maybe once every three weeks. Kim continued to care for me and care for me.

2018

In January, our bankruptcy was final. We Didn't include our house because we wanted to keep it. That would be a big mistake on our part and would pop up again in March.

In the first half of January, I came down with the rhinovirus and had to go to the emergency room. While I was there getting fluids, Kim took a selfie of us in my room and posted it on Facebook. Within a few days, the woman I had cheated with seen the picture and contacted Kim. Kim confronted me and we talked it over but I didn't apologize.

About this time, I started looking into panning for gold. This became a hobby of me and Kim and I began to research gold claims. I found a twenty-acre gold claim in Northern California and with Kim's counsel, we bought the claim for $300 a month payment for three years.

As Kim started to cook more, I found it strange that she would never eat leftovers lol. She would cook enough for four and five people and I would have leftovers for four or five days. She would always cook herself fresh meals for herself and I would have more left overs. I'm not complaining about it, I just chalked it up to one of Kimmy's quirks.

When Kim was not working on one of her dolls, she was online reading all the drama going on in the reborn community in her Facebook groups. There always was something going on in these groups exposing scammers, sculptors angry about Chinese copying their sculpts and selling them dirt cheap. China is very good about stealing the property of someone else's work, copying it and selling a knock off. There would also be people trying to get free dolls from artist, telling them that their child died a few weeks after birth and would ask if they could make a doll for them free of charge to help them recovery from their loss. When she would argue with someone or try and prove her point, she would let me read what she was about to post so that I can see if she was offending someone. Kim, cared very much about what people thought of her. I told her that the only person whose opinion she should consider is mine and what I thought about her. In the reborn world, just one wrong word would send the woke mafia after you.

Kim's reborn work was the standard. She set the bar high for quality and customer service. When she took pictures of her work, she would take *hundreds of pictures and choose maybe ten or fifteen to show on her doll listing.*

What bothered me about Kim's reborn business is that she had about $30,000 in inventory like dolls, paint, clay, fabrics, glass eyes, mohair, ovens and sculpting tools. Just like how the house was very messy, her art studio was very messy and I specifically built her studio so that she could organize everything. I also was trying to impress upon her the necessity to keep inventory of what she had and what items she actually used per doll so that she adequately set a starting price for her doll listings. Kim would put in about minimum of one hundred hours of work on a doll over a week or two.

Kim was so good that she would paint veins on her dolls that looked like real veins inside a baby's skin. She was so good that you couldn't tell the difference between a real baby and her dolls. That is why in 2018 that she did about twelve prototypes that made her about $8,000. That year I believe she brought in about $12,000 for working eight months. I think she spent every penny of that buying more inventory because we were getting at least five packages a day from China and from amazon. Well, we were actually getting that many packages a day starting in early 2017.

At this time, I still had one foot out the door in our marriage. I believe in 2017 I had told her to pack her shit up and go back to Oregon. I even left the house for 4 days waiting for her to leave. But I came home and told her not to go.

But In August of 2018, me and Kim decided that we were all in on our marriage and wanted things to work. So, I decided to plan a trip to Northern California to our gold claim and we would spend a week panning for gold. Right away, she began to plan. She put together identical backpacks with panning equipment. She bought us water sandals or slippers that can be worn in water. She put together a first aid kit to include sutures and a tourniquet. While She was doing all the research about camping gear, I sold a riding steam cleaner that I purchased for $18,000,   sold it for $5,000 and purchased an RV with it. Then Kim went really wild and decided to fully equip our RV.

I got bummed out within five minutes after buying the RV. I cut a corner too short and I hit a car cutting a groove down the last five feet of the trailer on the passenger side. That was really embarrassing. After I got it home around the 5th of September, I started to go over it to make sure everything worked. About three days before we left, I hooked up the water and pressurized the system only to find out that the water pipes under the shower were broken. I had to take apart the shower, replace the pipes and reassemble the shower.

During this time, Kim was stocking the trailer with everything that we needed to include new curtains that she purchased lol. Kim was a great planner, took great care and thought into what she was doing for our trip. At this time, my father showed up to house sit for us and watch our dogs.

Before we left, we had a day to relax and we watched some movies as she ate a whole carton of Cherry Garcia. That was her favorite ice cream.

After a day of relaxing, Me and Kim went to bed early. We wanted to get an early start on our drive to Callahan California. Our gold claim was a thirty-minute drive West of Callahan. We left on September 10th and that began our three-day trip of what we would call our honeymoon since we never took one after we got married.

Kim said that having the same music interests was important in our relationship. She said this during one of our arguments and I was angry about the dirty house. I then told her that having the same music interests is not important as I laughed off her comment. After being on the road for three days, I can assure you that having the same musical interest is important lol. Kim and I both loved music from the seventies and eighties. She like groups such as Depeche Mode, Tove Lo, Eagles, Ac/Dc, Thompson Twins and Gerry Rafferty from classic rock to new wave and we shared many good times listening to forty-year-old music. As we drove, the highways of Iowa, Nebraska, Wyoming, Utah, Nevada and California, we really got a chance to talk to each-other. It's as if we got to know each-other and fell in love with her and her beautiful blues eyes all over again.

As we pulled into the Shadow Creek Entrance which is an abandoned campsite that borders our gold claim. What I noticed first about this place is that it had mature pine trees climbing up over one hundred feet and realized that the solar panels that I had brought will not work. The campsite looked as if it wasn't so abandoned because the ground was not overgrown with bushes or shrubs. There was a clear road that formed a circle allowing to access the dozen or so camp sites that are covered in years of accumulating pine needles. There were patches of open spaces through the trees in which you can see the blue sky.

 I parked the trailer and we began to turn the area into our home away from home. Kim brought out the folding table and chairs while I levelled and tended to the trailer. It was about 2pm and the weather was perfect. It took Kim about thirty minutes before she had the trailer and camp site in perfect order. I on the other hand was having an issue with the electricity. I couldn't use the solar panels and the generator that worked perfectly before we left refused to start. So, I got online and ordered the part that was not working which will take seven to ten days to get here which means no electricity unless we kept it hooked up to the truck while it was running. However, we did have a fridge since that ran off of propane.

Kim and I finished up setting up the site and I walked up behind her, placed my hands on her hips, turned her around and gave her a kiss. I then Said, "We are here." She then said that it's so beautiful here and that she was very happy. We then spent the next two hours outside eating MRE's and enjoying our surroundings. As the sun began to set, we went inside, started up the computer and popped in a movie. We ended up watching a couple of movies before going to sleep. To be honest, we did a little bit more than watching a couple of movies before bed. Who could blame us in this romantic and secluded place.

After waking up, I had to use the bathroom. Since the electricity was not working, the toilet wasn't working so I to go dig a hole lol. However, Kim on the other-hand, refused to go to the bathroom outside and that would pose a big problem for me later. I made a joke to her about her being in the Airforce. I mentioned that if she was in the Army, going to the bathroom outside wouldn't be a problem. I then said the she needed to abandon her Airforce sensibilities lol.

After we ate breakfast and got dressed, we gathered our panning backpacks and loaded then with our lunches and drinks. She also said in her best English accent "Don't forget second breakfast" referring to the Hobbits in Lord of the Rings as she winked at me. I could only laugh under my breath as we walked away to the gold claim.

The gold claim was about one hundred yards from the campsite and down a ravine which Kim needed help to navigate. The claim had a *slow flowing through it that varied in depth from six inches to five feet. It had trees along the side of the river and had river lilies in some places. The water was crystal clear and had a temp around fifty degrees. The trees and the mountains formed a Vee in which the river flowed. There were large boulders and fallen trees about sitting on beds of sand and gravel. The mountains and trees blocked out direct sunlight except for when the sun was at its highest point at noon.*

Kim was wearing shorts, T-shirt, boots and socks and her iconic sun cap with her pony tail pulled through the back of it. Kim and I took off our boots and socks and began to pan for gold. Keep in mind we had no clue what we were doing other than from what we learned from YouTube videos. At lunch time, I went back to the campsite and got the tow chain that was in the back of the truck. I then tied it around a tree and let it lay along the slope of the ravine so Kim can go up and down the ravine on her own. Because there were bears in the area, I did carry a firearm with me at the river.

It got so hot at the river, I stripped to my underwear. Kim said that she wasn't expecting Tarzan to make an appearance. For the rest of the trip, she called me Tarzan. At about 5pm we headed up to the camp for dinner and this would be our schedule for the rest of the week. After we had dinner and the darkness surrounded the trailer, Kim would stare out into the darkness. I asked her if she was looking for Bigfoot and she let out a fifteen second belly laugh and said, how did you know? I said serious. I was just joking. We then faced each-other, kissed and went to sleep.

This was our routine for the next ten days until we ran out of money. We were hoping to find some gold in which we could sell and finance our honeymoon. Unfortunately, this didn't pan out. So, we packed everything up and drove three hours to Kim's mothers house in Grants pass Oregon. We went there to ask Chris if we can park the RV at her house so we didn't have to tow it back to Iowa. It cost us $800 in gas going from Iowa to California towing the trailer. We had $300 left in our bank account and could no way tow the trailer back to Iowa. I then asked my dad for some money and he sent us $300. So, we had just enough money to make it back to Iowa without any hotel stays. We then spent the next three days visiting with Chris and she agreed to let us park our RV there. Kim was very close to her mom and enjoyed the three days they spent together.

On the day we left, we left about 8am and I told Kim I was going to keep on driving until I could drive no more. She kinda gave me a side-eye and booted up google maps so we can start our journey home. This trip to our Northern California gold mine was a success. Kim forgave me for me cheating on her and I realized that Kim was everything I wanted in a woman. I then told her that I would always be by her side.

It took us about three hours driving East for us to reach the border with Nevada. We stopped at a gas station, filled up our tank because the next gas station was about seventy miles away, bought some bigfoot sighting window stickers and filled up our cooler with ice, drinks and snacks just in case we broke down in the middle of the Nevada Desert. I also filled up our five- gallon gas can just in case. The Northern Nevada desert is empty and completely devoid of people. At one point, we drove thirty minutes without seeing another car or homestead. As we came upon the border of Nevada and Utah, we saw a giant casino on the Nevada side and actually wondered how much money they made a year since they had a monopoly on the main highway.

As we entered Utah there is this long stretch of flat highway with white sand. Kim and I were going back and forth on this wondering if that was sand or if it was salt. But along this highway, there were many forms of art along the side of the road. People had formed names in the sand by arranging stones on the ground. They had made dragons in the sand by halfway burying tires to form humps. There were other forms of creativity that we saw and Kim and I both realized the creativity of people. We also saw miles of salt fields that were being mined as we approached Salt Lake City.

Coming into Salt Lake City was a great change of scenery from the emptiness we had been use to for the past three hours. It was at this time I told Kim to turn off the GPS. After about fifteen minutes I hadn't seen any signs for Highway 80 and told Kim that I think we were going the wrong way. I then jokingly told Kim that she should have never turned off the GPS like I told her not to. We both had a good laugh, I turned the car around and from that point on, the GPS was up and running. That set us back about forty minutes. We then stopped to get gas before leaving Salt Lake City. It has been about thirteen hours since we left Grants pass and I was feeling good so we continued on driving East on Highway 80.

Before we left Iowa, Kim had ordered a Bluetooth device that would plug into the cigarette lighter and allow us to play music from a cell phone or mp3 player. This was a life saver and Kim we listened to eighties music without interruption or interference for our entire trip. Kim was a great planner who took the time to tend to every detail and make sure we had our creature comforts every step of the way. She was the most genuine, loving and caring person and for the past month, she has won me over and is slowly changing my life.

We hit the Wyoming border about 10pm and I felt good and we were still driving on. About 2am I brought up the idea of writing romance novels to make a little extra money. We then started imagining plots to stories and what they would entail. It's really unfortunate that I can't remember everything that was said because we were having a great time with it. Then I said that I could never use my real name as the author because all the lonely housewives would be falling in love with me through my stories. We then started to come up with a pseudonym for me. This is where the belly laughs came out as we mentioned a dozen names, Kim almost pissed her pants lol. This went on for about forty-five minutes of coming up with names and heart felt laughs. We finally agreed on one name...Dick Daily. Kim said she had never laughed so hard in her life. After about six hours of driving through Wyoming, we came to somewhat familiar landscape. Nebraska!

It was now about 4am hitting the Western border of Nebraska. We had been on the road for twenty hours now and things were going smoothly. Kim being the great copilot she was, was keeping me alert, fed and high on caffeine. I couldn't believe that my Honda Ridgeline was holding up very well. Driving On average of seventy miles an hour for twenty hours is no easy feat. Based on our time entering Nebraska, I knew that we would miss rush hour traffic in Omaha which was perfect timing. When we hit Omaha, I started to get a little drowsy and decided to take an hour nap before entering Iowa.

We Entered Iowa at about 11am and made it safely home to Ankeny about 2pm. This means we drove from Grants Pass Oregon to Ankeny Iowa in thirty hours. Not only did we do it in thirty hours, we did it as a couple getting to truly know each-other. I realized that Kim was willing to go as far as was needed in our relationship and never give up. I don't know too many people let alone women who would sit in the co-pilot seat and stay awake for thirty hours with me while I drove. Not only stay awake, but to actively engage me in conversation. Just thinking about this brings both joy and sadness. Joy of the adventure we went on and sadness of the memory of her passing.

We finally got back to Iowa around the 25th of September and our two dogs Cricket and Squeak missed us very much. Cricket is a Jack Russell Terrier and Squeak is a Chihuahua mix. Kim use to call Chihuahua's cha hoo ah hoo ah's. I bought Squeak for Kim in 2016 and I had Cricket before me and Kim got married. We had just returned from a relationship changing trip and everything was great. Little did we know that in three months, our lives would change forever.

Cricket and Squeak were best buddies, but Squeak was a bad influence on Cricket. Squeak showed Cricket how to climb our four-foot chain link fence and due to the city's building codes, we couldn't do anything to the fence to make it harder for the dogs to climb it. The dogs would climb the fence if we let them stay outside without supervision for longer than ten minutes. One day in mid-October about 7pm we got a knock on the door and I saw two Ankeny police officers standing there. They asked me if I had two dogs and I said yes. I then called for Cricket and Squeak as I stood there in my underwear and T-shirt. Kim came down to the side door where I was standing and I told her that the police were looking for Cricket and Squeak. The police stated that they have found our dogs and that they were in that car and that they had been hit by a car and were killed. After hearing this my heart sank and felt disappointment in that we couldn't keep them in the yard and sadness at the loss of two friendly and loving dogs. The officers then handed me a box with the remains of Cricket and Squeak. Since we didn't have the money to dispose of the remains, I then put the box in our shipping container since it was twenty degrees outside and it would remain so for the next four months preserving their remains until we had the extra money for their cremation.

After I came in from outside, me and Kim sat down and remembered all the good times we had with the two. Kim began to reminisce about Squeak and they day we picked her up. We had to drive two hours to Osceola Iowa and paid $100. Squeak was about three pounds at twelve weeks old and curled up in Kim's lap for the two-hour drive back *home. Kim fell in love with Squeak at first sight and over the two years, Squeak would snuggle with Kim as she rooted the hair on her dolls while she listened to Star Trek reruns.*

After seeing my sorrow at the loss of Cricket, Kim began a covert plan to replace search for another dog for me. In the second week of December, Kim told me that we were having a one of her friends come by with her husband watch a movie that night. I then said that we need to clean up the house before they came over and she agreed. We had about two hours to organize everything and Kim was playing the part well hiding her true motives lol. When her "friend" came over, they had a one of the biggest dogs I had ever seen and began to pet him. Kim then stated that these were not her friends and that these people were the owners of the dog who she found on Facebook Marketplace who were giving their dog away to a good home. I turned to look at Kim and she gave me a smile and a wink. She then said that he was for me since I loved dogs so much. He has given me so much love and companionship since Kim's passing and he reminds me every day of Kim's love for me.

Christmas came a week later and Kim made me my favorite meal of Steak with sautéed mushrooms and onions, baked potato and steamed broccoli. For dessert, we had pumpkin pie with whipped cream. Kim made herself a steak but preferred rice instead of baked potato. To drink we shared a bottle of sweet red wine from Tassel Ridge winery.

Right after Christmas, Kim began to spend more and more time in the bathroom. I'm talking two, three and sometimes four hours. She said that she couldn't fully empty and we tried many different kinds of laxatives but nothing worked.

2019

Around the second week of January, Kim started to have abdominal pain and we took her into the Emergency room. We found out that night that her white blood cell count was at 21,000. She was then admitted to the hospital. After she got her room, I kissed her goodnight and told her that I would be back in the morning with her phone charger, a doodling book, all her sanitary and hygiene items. Kim was telling her doctors and nurses that she thinks this is a resurgence of Crohn's disease all the while she was being pumped up with Antibiotics and fluids. I spent every night next to her giving her my support. Kim and I talked for hours every-night and we became closer. Kim was sure that these issues were due to her Crohn's. She was released six days later.

After she got home, she was still not going pooping. She would sit in the bathroom for hours and nothing. A week after she came home, we had to take her back to the Emergency Room at the VA where she was admitted again, but was scheduled to do a colonoscopy three days after she was admitted for the second time. Kim was in good spirits and still insisted this was her Crohn's.

The day of her colonoscopy was quick. The procedure took less than five minutes because the camera couldn't get more than twelve inches into her colon because it was swelled shut. The doctor doing the procedure said he had seen a spot that was tattooed on the swollen area. This really pissed me and Kim off, because the doctor who did her colonoscopy in 2016 said there was nothing to worry about, but finding out now that was not true. The Doctor that did the recent colonoscopy did take a biopsy and we had to wait two days for the results to come back. This is when cancer was staring to come up and Kim and I were so nervous and afraid. We started talking about what if's? What will we do? What kind of treatment will she have to endure? I reassured her that if it's cancer, she will beat it.

We got the biopsy back and it came back positive for cancer. Kim was quiet for about twenty seconds. I broke the silence asking the doctor what is the course of action now? Since Kim was unable to go to the bathroom (for the past four weeks), she was being scheduled for a resection of her colon and she would also be going through Ostomy surgery to install a stoma the next day. During this surgery, they would also be looking at the extent of the cancer. We got this information at 10am and we had to be back at the hospital at 6am for surgery.

After getting home, me and Kim just laid in bed and watched some movies. We really didn't talk much throughout the day and evening, then just went to sleep. We woke up at 4am and I reassured her that everything was going to be fine as we drove to the hospital.

After arriving at the hospital, we got her checked in and they whisked her off prep for surgery and I was left to worry and pray for her for the next six to eight hours. I was thinking that the cancer they would remove the cancerous portion of her colon and that Kim might have to go through some chemo and that would be the end of it as a worst-case scenario. Never had I expected what I heard from the doctor when he came out to tell me after the surgery that Kim had Stage 4 cancer and that it had spread throughout her abdominal wall. During the next week in the hospital, I visited Kim every day for a couple of hours. She confided in me that she was very afraid her stage 4 diagnosis and that I would leave her. I reassured her that we will fight this together. She had stood by me when I was broke, depressed and had cheated on her and there was no way in hell I was going to abandon her in her hour of need.

While she was in the hospital for observation after the surgery, Kim was setting up appointments with an oncologist to start her first round of chemo that would start in six weeks. She was also getting training on how to replace her coloscopy bags for her stoma and how to reorder her supplies through the VA. Although Kim was worried and afraid, she appeared to be handling everything well. Maybe it was because she really didn't have much time to think about her cancer with all the preparations, she had to make concerning her chemo. I spent the night a few times with her at the hospital and went walking with her every night through the halls which was mandatory per doctors' orders.

Kim was eating and she was producing output into her coloscopy bag. This was necessary before she could be discharged. Since she had successfully replaced her own coloscopy bag, was eating and producing output, she was able to leave the hospital when her week was up.

On the way home, I stopped by Chik-fil-A to treat her after having to suffer through all the hospital food she had to endure for the past week. She must have been really hungry because she had finished her sandwich before reaching the halfway point to our house lol. Over the next six weeks I was fully prepared to care for her but she wasn't having *that. She wanted to start working on her dolls and insisted on caring for me and cooking dinner every night. I told her that it was not necessary and she should relax. She then said that working on her dolls was relaxing and that her husband would not go to bed without first eating a home cooked meal for dinner and she tilted her head forward just a bit giving the effect as if she was looking up at me and winked.*

In March of 2019, we got some bad news that our house would be foreclosed on and that we had six months to vacate the property. We knew that this day was coming because the bank would never go through the process of collecting the money through the Polk County VA via vouchers. Kim also started her first round of chemo and I would go with her and keep her company for the two or three hours it took to administer the drugs. Sometimes they added fluids if she was dehydrated. I would always buy her a fountain drink on the way to her appointments. She loved to drink Dr. Pepper.

Since we had to move out of our home By September, we started making plans and we ended up getting a gift from God when Kim's mother offered to let us come live with her and we would pay $300 in rent and help her with home repairs. She knew we needed help and I think she wanted to help with Kim's recovery as well.

Kim's first round of chemo lasted four weeks but wasn't that hard on her. She was tired, but she continued to work on her dolls and was in good spirits. Once Kim started work on a doll, she would lose all sense of time. I would on occasion throughout the day I would ask her if she wanted anything to eat or drink and usually said no. But on occasion she would ask for a PB&J sandwich or something simple like that. She really didn't snack very often when she worked on her dolls. She became very focused and dedicated to finish whatever doll she was working on. In the last six months of us living in Iowa, Kim was able to finish about eight prototypes from three or four different sculptors on top of the three dolls she completed from her own stock. At about $800 per doll on average, Kim was the bread winner when you include her Social Security and VA benefits. I just had my VA disability. I couldn't believe the physical and mental strength that she was showing during this time.

Before we left Iowa, Kim would go through her second round of chemo and Kim seemed unphased by its side effects. She was either suffering in silence or she truly wasn't bothered by the side effects.

The last month we were in Iowa which was in September 2019. We had to start her transfer of care to white city Oregon and start to sell off everything we owned. Kim's mother told us that she would pay for our expenses to move and we thanked her very much. We ended up making about $7,000 from the sale of all of our possessions and left Iowa on September 28th.

We arrived in Oregon on August 2nd 2019 and Kim's mother Chris accepted us with open arms. Kim talked with her mother while I unloaded the truck. Over the next few days, we settled in and got in our routines. Kim and I would do our own thing and then spend about an hour with her mom in the late afternoon. Kim would be on the phone talking to the VA to get her third round of chemo started. I on the other hand started to look for places to pan for gold lol. It took a month for our things to be shipped from Iowa to Oregon (that was a real pain in the ass). We ended up missing twenty-five boxes that they lost. Roughly twenty percent of what we shipped. Fucking retards. I think that they went through our stuff while it sat in their warehouse for a month.

When we unloaded all of our things, Kim set up shop in her old studio that she had while living with her mother before she moved to Iowa. I still can't fathom how I still can't fathom how Kim would always make dinner for me regardless of what she was doing or how tired she was. After not cooking at all at the beginning of our marriage to cooking every night that consisted of pot roast, thick juicy steaks and perfectly salt and peppered pork chops. She ended up being one of the best cooks I have ever known. One good thing is that we enjoyed the same kind of food, meat and potatoes (she liked rice). She would always give my dinner or any meal by saying "here honey" with a subtle smile on her face.

For the next several months, we settled into a routine of waking up, having breakfast together and then her going down to her studio to work on her dolls. I on the other hand would work on the property clearing brush, cutting the grass and making home repairs. I would work about three to four hours a day, four days a week and managed to accumulate two very large burn piles on this secluded five-acre plot of land in Josephine County Oregon. It had a main house with three bedrooms, one bathroom, living room, kitchen with a dining room and a pantry with a laundry room. It also had a 600 square foot deck that connected to another building that Kim and I were staying in which had one bedroom, bathroom and a pantry at the main level. There was covered walkway that connected the main house and the building Kim and I were staying in. Directly below us was another bedroom which Kim used as her studio and it had a half bathroom.

It also had another 800 square foot house with a living room, kitchen, bathroom and two storage rooms under the house. This is the house that Kim's uncle lived in before he was sent to hospice care. If I remember correctly, he had liver cancer. He was in Hospice care by the time Kim and I moved to Oregon in September.

One thing that I learned about her uncle Forrest is that he and I were both in the Army, both stationed at the same military post in Germany (Fliegerhorst) and lived in the same building. He was posted there 20 years before me and we had a great time, sharing stories about Germany and military life.

Kim was close to her uncle because all three of them lived on the same property together for several years engaging in conversation and going out to eat. In late December 2019, Forrest went downhill and we were told that he would have just a few more days to live. Just a few days before New Years eve about 11:50pm, The landline began to ring. Kim and I looked at each other and we both knew where that call was coming from and what it was about. I immediately told Kim to go check on her mom. She then got up, opened the door and enter the pitch-black night to cross over to the main house. She spent a little over an hour comforting her mother before she returned. I asked her how her mother was doing and she said that she is upset, but has been preparing for this for a while now.

Chris was a nurse and has been around death many times. When I saw her the next day, she was handling the loss of her brother very well. She was appreciative that the VA was handling most or the arrangements and all she had to do is sign documents. As I got to know Chris, I understood where Kim got her good nature, loving and generous heart. Chris also had a dry sense of humor that I came to love about her. For Christmas me and Kim decided to not get each other presents and decided to buy Chris a new set of tires for her car to show our appreciation for letting us stay with her in our time of need.

2020

In January or February, Kim started Chemo again. This was a pain in the ass because that was the start of all this covid 19 bullshit. I could no longer go inside and sit with her. But I did still buy her a fountain drink for her to take inside with her which made her happy. I usually just dropped her off at the doctor's office and she would message me twenty minutes before she was finished and I would go and pick her up.

Three to four times a week, me and Kim would go and pan for gold at the Hog Creek boat ramp off of the Rogue River. Before we went to the river, we would always go to the Lil pantry which is a convenience store in Oregon. We would buy chicken on a stick which are breaded chicken strips on a stick with various sauces on them. We always got the BBQ ones along with a large fountain drink and sometimes some donuts or chips. Kim wouldn't pane for gold with me, but she would watch and take pictures when she wasn't following the drama on her Facebook doll groups. We would bring Gunnar along with us and Kim would help carry everything down to the river which was about two hundred yards. She would always wear her khaki shorts, boots, T-shirt and hoodie, along with her ball cap with her pony tail through that back of it. On occasion, me and Kim would take a dip in the river, but didn't go in more than knee deep at this location because the river was fast flowing.

Going back to 2019, I was sitting on the couch with Kim and I got a song in my head. I could remember the basic tune of it and only one line of the chorus that I heard way back in 1982. I told Kim the line that I remembered and fifteen minutes later she asked me to listen to a song. She began to play it and I was shocked. She found the song. It was "Take her where the boys are" by eye protection. That woman could find anything online. That was here superpower. She then without me knowing bought me a record player and a vinyl record of that song as a gift. I still have both of those to this day.

When Kim and I were alone together, we didn't need to be in constant conversation. Some days we would be in the same room and not say a word to each other for hours. She would be for instance rooting a doll while I was watching a movie. We just enjoyed being with each other. Either one of us would break the silence by asking if they wanted something from the kitchen if either one of us was getting something to eat or getting up to go to the bathroom. Kim and I were both what I would call independent introverts. We didn't need constant affirmation from each other because we both new that we loved each other.

Kim also had the habit of staying awake while I was out working. Let's say I had to work until two or three O'clock in the morning. Kim would stay awake working on her dolls until I got home. I would engage her in some brief text messaging to let her know that I was alright and when she could expect me home. I told her many times that she doesn't need to stay awake and that she should get some sleep when I'm out working. One time I told her that, she turned to look at me, gave me a big hug and said that she can't sleep when I'm gone and that she worries about me. She then pulled away a little and her face was about a foot away from mine and I could see tears starting to form in her eyes.

Jumping back to 2020 and Kim's chemo. She again handled the treatment very well. Other than being a little tired for a day after her treatment she was doing well. She was doing so well we were positive she was going to beat this cancer and we were planning a life together in what we were going to do five and even ten years out. Kim wanted to open a factory that made vinyl dolls so that sculptors didn't have to send their prototypes to China where the Chinese would copy their designs and sell knock offs of the original designs. I really wanted to help her achieve this because I had the business and organizational sense to help her get to her dream. She, herself, had done some sculpting, but never sent in her designs to get any prototypes done. She was a very talented artist and to this day her peers miss her.

After Kim finished her third round of chemo, she felt good and she looked good as well. Her eyes were bright, blue and full of life. Her hair was thin, but looked healthy. She had lots of energy and things were looking very good for her and us. Then in June or July, Kim had a PET scan done (I think that is what it was) and it came back that there were no signs of cancer. We celebrated and I told her that she would beat it.

It was about this time that Chris wanted to sell her house in Oregon and move to Virginia. Her motive was to try and rebuild the relationship between Kim and her daughters. So, she put her house on the market and it sold within a week and closing was set for September first. That gave us about five weeks to sell any unwanted items and pack up everything for the move. Kim and I organized a garage sale that made about $1,500 which Chris said that we could keep even though eighty percent of the things sold belonged to her and Forrest.

Chris then paid to have three pods delivered and I was tasked with loading them up. About the twentieth of August, the pods were picked up and me and Kim were sleeping on the floor and Chris was sleeping on an air mattress.

On August 25th, me and Kim left for Virginia about five days before closing because we were going to spend 3 or four days in Iowa so that I could see my son who I haven't seen in a year. The plan was that we would meet in Virginia at our new house that Chris bought about the same time the first week in September.

The next 4 weeks was a nightmare. Apparently, the home buyers for Chris's house were not preapproved and hadn't applied for the loan until two weeks before closing. This means that Kim and I had to live out of a hotel from the first week of September to the first week of October until the house in Oregon closed so that the house in Portsmouth Virginia closed to end our hotel living arrangement. This was a living hell for Chris because she was paying for me and Kim's living arrangements in the hotel.

While we were in the hotel for our September stay, Kim was trying to establish her care through the Hampton VA. Our average day was watching tv, surfing the internet and talking. But in late September, Kim started having troubles eating and started having pain in her lower back. All the while Kim was trying to get her oncology appointment but she was running into government Bureaucracy. I forgot to mention that when Kim was selecting our hotel, she found one with a large refrigerator for a hotel. It was actually about half the size of a regular fridge. She always took the time to figure out the little details to make our lives easier.

We finally moved into the new house and we had the pods delivered and I spent three days unloading everything into the house. Chris arrived about a week later. The day Chris arrived; I helped Chris unload her car. After about ten minutes, I was bringing in something and I saw Kim crying. I asked her what was wrong and she said that her mother was ignoring her. I knew that was not true because Chris had spent all day on the road and just wanted to get everything unloaded and to relax. I then went to Chis and told her what Kim said and she made a bee line to Kim and told her that was not true. I then continued to unload the car and left then to have a mother and daughter moment.

Over the next two weeks we all were working on putting the house together and unpacking. Chris did something unexpected and bought me and Kim a new queen size mattress and box springs. Kim installed a privacy sticky sheet for the spare downstairs bathroom window. Kim was full of energy but was still having issues eating and pain in her lower back. She continued to cook for me and made me those delicious Steaks and sauteed onions and mushrooms and pork chops. She continued to show me love and we were happy that she was cancer free.

Her pain in her lower back was getting worse through the first half of November and I finally convinced Kim to go to the emergency room. On November 24th, 2020, we found out that Kim had a growth in her abdomen about the size of a baseball. This completely floored me and Kim and deep down inside we both knew what it was. Since she was cancer free in June or July, we knew that the cancer came back and was very aggressive.

At this point, my memory gets a little fuzzy. At this point, it took about one month to get her an oncology appointment to get the ball rolling on her treatment. Kim and I were dumbfounded by the inept treatment she was getting by the Hampton VA. Her first oncologist didn't even review her medical records before Kim's first appointment. Her oncologist didn't even know what stage her cancer was and was nonchalant about Kim's treatment. It's sad to say this, but it really pissed me off that the VA hires so many foreign doctors who couldn't care less about American veterans and the sacrifices they have made for their country. They treated Kim as an emotionless number as if she was non-human. A project they were working on that they didn't care of the final outcome. If it wasn't for Kim, my anger would have taken over and I would have ended up in jail on death row.

When Christmas came around, we were blessed by Kim's sister Jennifer. She sent us Christmas dinner that was enough for at least ten people. It had Turkey and all the fixin's. we ate for a whole week on the food she had delivered to us. I don't remember what company she used, but the food was great and made our last Christmas together full of good memories. Kim would go downstairs every evening to warm me up a plate of leftovers. Since Kim didn't eat leftovers and Chris was a vegetarian, I ended up eating most of the Christmas food.

From the stress and emotions starting in September, our sex life took a hit. Kim and I usually had sex two to three times a week, but since her recurrence of cancer it dwindled to once or twice a month and I usually let her initiate it because I didn't want her to feel obligated to have sex with me if she wasn't feeling good. Kim is the kind of woman who would have had sex with me even if she was hurting or not feeling well. She loved me so much; she would have allowed herself to suffer to give me the physical love I desired. That woman was the epitome of unconditional and selfless love. Just thinking about Kim and all the love she had is bringing tears to my eyes because she didn't deserve the terrible treatment she was getting from the VA.

2021

In January, Kim was finally prescribed some pain killers which was the only advancement in her treatment she got. The VA has been dragging its feet with her treatment as if they were waiting for her to just die so they didn't have to treat her at all. January, was also the last time that Kim and I were intimate. Kim was expressing her concerns with her treatment and we had several arguments that she was not being forceful enough with her doctors and I that she had to push the treatment she needed because I couldn't be with her for her appointments due to covid restrictions. This is also the time where we complained to the person in charge of patient care at the Hampton VA. He apologized for the way Kim was being treated and soon after, Kim got an appointment with the surgical team.

In February, Kim met with the surgeon Dr. Wiebke and Kim's care was transferred to him. Kim and I had a tradition of watching a movie together every night and talk about it. Me and Kim learned a lot about each other by talking about these movies. What we would do in a particular circumstance or would we ever engage in a particular activity. Kim knew about my fear of heights and understood that if I jumped off a building to kill myself, she would know immediately it was murder lol. I get dizzy off of the third rung of a ladder and can't get within twenty feet of a high-rise building office window or a cliffs edge. I become paralyzed from fear. Kim was also afraid of heights but not to the extant I was.

Kim was also admitted to the hospital the first week of February and soon after her admission, she had her surgery and had a mass the size of a cantaloupe and had both her ovaries removed. Doctor Wiebke noticed in the surgery that there were spots on her liver and were biopsied. Kim then spent the next six weeks in the hospital and Chris and I visited her about every two weeks and she looked better and better which each visit. Her skin and hair looked healthy. Her eyes were bright and clear and her countenance was happy and cheerful. Her lengthy stay was due to the fact that they couldn't get her pain under control. They couldn't get her oral pain meds right and had to constantly put her back on IV pain meds. This really pissed me off because they really didn't want to up her opiate based medication and this confounded me and Kim because she was suffering from stage four cancer and that she might not live long enough to get addicted to the pain meds. The least that they can do is make her pain free.

While still in the hospital, she started her chemo treatments, she had been in the same room for so long that we called it the Gardino suite which me and Kim joked about on several occasions. I remember the day she had her port flushed out for her chemo. There were concerns about this procedure but I don't remember what they were. I'm sure there are some medical professionals who would know about the hazards of flushing a port after about eight months of no use.

Me and Chris would visit Kim about every two weeks while she was recovering which is about all the hospital would allow due to covid restrictions.

I don't remember when she came home after her long stay in the Gardino suite at the Hampton VA, but when she did come home, she came home to a twin bed she had ordered online that was set up in the living room downstairs so that she didn't have to go up and down the stairs with her legs being so weak and could barely support her weight.

Kim settled into a routine of watching her shows on her iPad. She loved watching the Bachelor and the bachelorette and knew everything about the drama of both shows and from which seasons. Kim loved pop culture and had to explain to me about was trending on the internet, YouTube and the drama on here reborn groups. She would also watch "My 600lb Life" which she was binge watching lol. I once caught her watching a stolen valor video which is about people pretend to be military veterans. She despised these people who did this and she went on a couple of rants about people who did this. During this time, YouTube and Amazon Prime were Kim's best friends. Plus, the channel where the bachelor and bachelorette were streaming.

Through March, April and May, I would go to Hardee's two to three times a week at 6am to get her Biscuits and gravy. She loved them so much but would only eat half of a biscuit usually and gave the rest to Gunnar. She really didn't eat very much during this time but was constantly asking me to refresh her ice water which I gladly did. About every hour I would add ice to her insulated container. I would be upstairs watching YouTube as well and kept a close eye on my phone in case Kim needed me and sent me a text message that she needed help. But I would go down and check on her about every two hours.

At this time, Kim would stay awake most of the day and night and would sleep in forty-five-to-ninety-minute naps at various times of the day or night. I remember walking through the laundry room to the kitchen and would glance over at Kim laying in her bed with her back propped up by four or five pillow to raise her head and I would see her beautiful blue eyes focusing on what she was watching on her iPad and I would wonder what was she thinking about? When I would pass by her field of vision going to the kitchen, she would occasionally look up at me and give me that special wink of hers. That wink meant so many things. It could mean acknowledgment, a flirtation or invitation and sometimes a Fuck around and find out hint to it.

One day in April I was walking to the kitchen and I looked over at her and stopped dead in my tracks. At that moment, I felt a wave of guilt come over me for cheating on her. Up until this point, about three years I had never apologized to her for me cheating. I stood there, then slowly began to walk the ten feet to her bed. As I said her name, she looked up at me and gave me a worried look. That surprised me because I was wondering if she was reading the look on my face or if my face was clearly representing regret and the shame, I was feeling at the moment which made her worry. As she looked up at me, we locked eyes and I acknowledged that I had never apologized to her for cheating and that I was sorry what I had done and asked her to forgive me. After I said this, we held each-others gaze for about three seconds. I then said I was sorry as I turned and walked back upstairs. Kim never said word for that thirty second encounter and the subject never came up again.

From February to June, her family visited her several times to boost her mood. These visits made her very happy. The one who was able to visit her the most was her daughter Liz. Liz was there visiting just two days before Kim's passing. It was a difficult visit because Kim at this point was sleeping most of the time and wasn't able to interact much.

Sometime in May, Kim's attitude changed. She became apologetic in her attitude when she asked for things. It was as if she was giving up and didn't want to become a burden to anyone. It was right after she started her second round of chemo and had to stop it because it was too hard on her. Around June 1st she entered hospice care.

The first couple of weeks in hospice, Kim was alert and awake most days. She slept off and on for about twelve hours a day. Our daily routine was me giving her Pedialyte through her g-tube which is a tube that inserted directly into her stomach in which she can get nourishment or to drain her tummy. This was inserted when she had her surgery in February. At this time, Kim had given up on eating. She ended up not eating for the last month of her life. These days were spent with me laying next to her in a twin bed she had purchased in March while she laid in her hospital bed that hospice care provided for her. These days also consisted of us cleaning her around her leaking ostomy bag and around the wound that appeared when her fistula broke through her lower abdomen just below her belly button. This wound continued to drain 24/7. This wound was covered with a clear plastic bandage that was hooked up to a pump that would pump out the liquid into a container which would have to be emptied every four to six hours.

We would also watch movies and YouTube videos together as I held her hand. The hospice nurses came about four times a week to look after her wounds because the plastic bandages covering the wounds and tubing kept leaking for some reason and Kim was constantly having to hold a towel around her hip and lower abdomen to absorb the blackish fluid seeping from her wounds.

Kim had a catheter inserted so that she didn't have to get up to pee because at this point, she was too week to even sit up on her own. Kim's mental capabilities in the second week of June deteriorated to the point she couldn't remember her password to her banking app which proved to be an unforeseen problem in which we should have gotten a power of attorney for months ago. When she passed away, we couldn't even close her bank account. It's a shame that the hospice nurses took better care of her than the doctors at the VA did.

Kim became more week in the third week of June 2021. It appeared that her digestive system was failing because she was getting dehydrated so easily even after we were giving her two liters of Pedialyte a day. But I have to a that some of the Pedialyte was exiting through her g-tube. Her urine was a dark yellow and we had to empty her collection bag about every thirty-six hours. She began to sleep about eighteen hours a day and was not very interactive during this time

Since Kim was having issues with pain, Hospice gave us a pump to administer pain medicine every 15 minutes in the second week of June. I don't remember what the pain killer was that was being administered.

So, Kim was being kept pain free for the last three weeks of her life. My guess is that the pain meds also made her so drowsy that she could barely interact with people.

On June 25, 2021, me and Chris raised holy hell over Kim's hydration. When Kim was admitted to hospice care, we were told that she would get IV fluids. After two weeks of no IV fluids, we put up a big fight and demanded that she get the fluids. After about eight hours of arguing with the hospice doctor, we were able to get her fluids. The reason that they didn't want to give her fluids is due to swelling of the body which could lead to death due to Kim's condition. I believe the term is called hypervolemia but I'm not sure about that.

After Kim received the fluids, she was alert and interacted with her environment. She was looking forward to watching "Tomorrow War" on Amazon Prime on Friday, July 3rd. Starting Monday, June 28th, we started watching one of Kim's favorite movies every day which she enjoyed. On Wednesday, they positive effect the fluids had on Kim started to disappear. On that day we watched Guardians of the Galaxy which is her favorite movie. Unfortunately, she slept through half of it but I'm sure that she could still hear the movie even though her eyes were shut.

On Thursday, July 3rd, this is where Kim started to deteriorate very quickly. Her Daughter Lizzy came by to visit her and spent a little over an hour with her. Kim was in and out of consciousness and tried very hard to interact with her daughter and I believe that at this point, Kim was not able to speak. But I am sure that Lizzy understood that Kim loved her and was very happy that she visited. I'm glad she did because Kim would pass away two days later. I could tell in her eyes that she alert, but her body betrayed her by remaining motionless. It took great effort for her just lift her hand. Every time Kim tried to speak, she would just grunt as she tried to say anything. This is when me and Chris had to remain by her side to push the button on her pump to administer her pain meds every fifteen minutes. The Hospice nurse came about five o'clock to check Kim's vitals. It is at this point the nurse said that "Kim was transitioning" which is polite speak for Kim did not have much time.

Friday came and the release of Tomorrow War was here but Kim was unable to watch it. She had been asleep since five o'clock the previous day. Unfortunately, that would be the last time Kim would have her eyes open. She never opened her eyes again. Ever since her death, I watch the Tomorrow War every July 3rd to remind me of Kim.

Saturday, July 3, 2021, it was a long night and both me and Chris were exhausted. It was seven O'clock in the morning and it was my turn to watch Kim while Chris went to take a nap. The sun was out and it was a beautiful Summer day in Virginia. I just sat there looking at Kim knowing that she didn't have long to live. She was fighting for each breath she took with apnea occurring every third or fourth breath as she gasped for air. At 9:10am, Kim let out a guttural sound resembling the word "Momma." Before I could call Chris, she was standing on the right side of Kim's bed holding her right hand. I would guess that within ten minutes Kim's sister Jen called and Chris was monitoring Kim's pulse as she spoke to her daughter. Kim's breathing became eradic and at times she wouldn't breathe for ten seconds then gasp for air. On July 3, 2021, at 9:40am, while Chris and I each held one of Kim's hands, Kim took her last breath. I turned to look at Chris and Chris said that she was gone as she was checking her pulse. I stood up and leaned over her to kiss her on her forehead to say goodbye as Chris told Jen that her sister had passed away. Chris and I were heart broken but neither of us showed any emotion. Chris continued to talk to Jen for a few more minutes as I began to make calls to hospice to let them know that Kim had passed away.

Within forty-five minutes, the hospice nurse showed up and began to remove all the tubes and pumps that were connected to Kim's body. After the nurse disconnected everything, she pulled Kim's blanket up to her chin covering her entire body. At this point, I was emotionally numb and in shock. The only peace I had was knowing that Kim was no longer suffering. I believe that Chris was experiencing a greater loss than me because Kim was her child but her emotions were somewhat reserved. I can only assume that Chris had already mourned the loss of her daughter buy crying countless times in the previous months. I also had the suspicion that she was trying to be strong to help me with my grief.

An hour after the nurse left, the funeral home arrived to pick up Kim. As I watched them prepare Kim for transport, they tilted tiled Kim's stiff body up to detangle her from the bedding and move her to the gurney. Seeing Kim's body in a state of rigor mortis, I finally realized that this was it, the end of the road and Kim was really gone.

Over the next month, I had little time to mourn because I had to find a new place to live and I had to handle Kim's estate. With the help of Sarah Mellman, I was able to liquidate all of Kim's reborn supplies which allowed me to have the money to move back to Iowa to be closer to my son and to help me with dental work that still needed to done. I would like to point out that Sarah Mellman offered her assistance without asking for any compensation. She did this out of the kindness of her heart and she was an ANGEL sent by God to help me.

As I reflect on Kim two and a half years after her passing, I realize that she had a profound impact on my life. Kim's work of showing me unconditional love made me reflect on my attitude and belief that someone needed to do something for me, for me to love them in return. That way of thinking led me to cheat on Kim. Because she didn't keep the house clean that I had the right to cheat. Because she rarely cooked that I had the right to cheat. After we had forgiven each other in 2018, Kim worked had at cooking more meals and she became a DAMN GOOD COOK. I don't think I will ever have a steak as tasty as the steaks Kim prepared for me.

After 2018, we became a loving couple who had lost just about all our material possessions and began living with her mother. We became closer through our hardships and Kim became a woman that I truly loved. When it came to love, Kim was my teacher. When it came to living each day to its fullest, I was her teacher. I brought her out of her shell. I showed her that she had someone in her corner that would fight for her and protect her. I'm sadden that we only had about six months of pure marital bliss before we got the news of her cancer diagnosis. We did live life carefree after that, but her fight with cancer was always looming in the background that we rarely talked about other than discussing chemo appointments.

Our favorite thing to do was going to the river and pan for gold. Kim enjoyed being by the river, sitting in her chair, drinking her fountain drink and watch some YouTube videos on her phone while I panned for gold. Kim liked being there with me because I liked doing it. She just wanted to be with me and a part of my life. She got really happy when I would show here the shiny gold flakes I had found and would take delight in the pride of my achievement. Kim would have been happy if we lived in a ten thousand square foot home or be homeless living in a car. Kim just wanted to be with me.